Praise for Ellie Quigley's Books

"I picked up a copy of *JavaScript by Example* over the weekend and wanted to thank you for putting out a book that makes JavaScript easy to understand. I've been a developer for several years now and JS has always been the "monster under the bed," so to speak. Your book has answered a lot of questions I've had about the inner workings of JS but was afraid to ask. Now all I need is a book that covers Ajax and Coldfusion. Thanks again for putting together an outstanding book."

—Chris Gomez, Web services manager,
Zunch Worldwide, Inc.

"I have been reading your *UNIX® Shells by Example* book, and I must say, it is brilliant. Most other books do not cover all the shells, and when you have to constantly work in an organization that uses tcsh, bash, and korn, it can become very difficult. However, your book has been indispensable to me in learning the various shells and the differences between them...so I thought I'd email you, just to let you know what a great job you have done!"

—Farogh-Ahmed Usmani, B.Sc. (Honors), M.Sc., DIC,
project consultant (Billing Solutions), Comverse

"I have been learning Perl for about two months now; I have a little shell scripting experience but that is it. I first started with *Learning Perl* by O'Reilly. Good book but lacking on the examples. I then went to *Programming Perl* by Larry Wall, a great book for intermediate to advanced, didn't help me much beginning Perl. I then picked up *Perl by Example, Third Edition*—this book is a superb, well-written programming book. I have read many computer books and this definitely ranks in the top two, in my opinion. The examples are excellent. The author shows you the code, the output of each line, and then explains each line in every example."

—Dan Patterson, software engineer,
GuideWorks, LLC

"Ellie Quigley has written an outstanding introduction to Perl, which I used to learn the language from scratch. All one has to do is work through her examples, putz around with them, and before long, you're relatively proficient at using the language. Even though I've graduated to using *Programming Perl* by Wall et al., I still find Quigley's book a most useful reference."

—Casey Machula, support systems analyst,
Northern Arizona University, College of Health and Human Services

"When I look at my bookshelf, I see eleven books on Perl programming. *Perl by Example, Third Edition,* isn't on the shelf; it sits on my desk, where I use it almost daily. When I bought my copy I had not programmed in several years and my programming was mostly in COBOL so I was a rank beginner at Perl. I had at that time purchased several popular books on Perl but nothing that really put it together for me. I am still no pro, but my book has many dog-eared pages and each one is a lesson I have learned and will certainly remember.

"I still think it is the best Perl book on the market for anyone from a beginner to a seasoned programmer using Perl almost daily."

—Bill Maples, network design tools and automations analyst,
Fidelity National Information Services

"We are rewriting our intro to OS scripting course and selected your text for the course. It's an exceptional book. The last time we considered it was a few years ago (second edition). The debugging and system administrator chapters at the end nailed it for us."

—Jim Leone, Ph.D., professor and chair, Information Technology,
Rochester Institute of Technology

"Quigley's book acknowledges a major usage of PHP. To write some kind of front end user interface program that hooks to a back end MySQL database. Both are free and open source, and the combination has proved popular. Especially where the front end involves making an HTML web page with embedded PHP commands.

"Not every example involves both PHP and MySQL. Though all examples have PHP. Many demonstrate how to use PHP inside an HTML file. Like writing user-defined functions, or nesting functions. Or making or using function libraries. The functions are a key idea in PHP, that take you beyond the elementary syntax. Functions also let you gainfully use code by other PHP programmers. Important if you are part of a coding group that has to divide up the programming effort in some manner."

—Dr. Wes Boudville, CTO,
Metaswarm Inc.

Perl by Example

Fourth Edition

Perl by Example

Fourth Edition

Ellie Quigley

PRENTICE
HALL

Upper Saddle River, NJ • Boston • Indianapolis • San Francisco
New York • Toronto • Montreal • London • Munich • Paris • Madrid
Cape Town • Sydney • Tokyo • Singapore • Mexico City

The publisher offers excellent discounts on this book when ordered in quantity for bulk purchases or special sales, which may include electronic versions and/or custom covers and content particular to your business, training goals, marketing focus, and branding interests. For more information, please contact:

U.S. Corporate and Government Sales
(800) 382-3419
corpsales@pearsontechgroup.com

For sales outside the United States please contact:

International Sales
international@pearsoned.com

Visit us on the Web: www.prenhallprofessional.com

Library of Congress Cataloging-in-Publication Data

Quigley, Ellie.
Perl by example / Ellie Quigley. — 4th ed.
p. cm.
Includes index.
ISBN 978-0-13-238182-6 (pbk. : alk. paper) 1. Perl (Computer program language) I. Title.
QA76.73.P22Q53 2007
005.13'3—dc22

2007029600

ISBN-13: 978-0-13-238182-6
ISBN-10: 0-13-238182-6

Text printed in the United States on recycled paper at Courier in Stoughton, Massachusetts.
First printing, October 2007

Editor-in-Chief
Mark L. Taub

Managing Editor
John Fuller

Full-Service Production Manager
Julie B. Nahil

Production Editor
Dmitri Korzh,
Techne Group

Copy Editor
Techne Group

Indexer
Larry Sweazy

Proofreader
Evelyn Pyle

Publishing Coordinator
Noreen Regina

Cover Designer
Alan Clements

Composition
Techne Group

Contents

Preface

You may wonder, why a new edition of *Perl by Example*? Perl 5 hasn't really changed that much; in fact, it's changed very little at all since the third edition of this book was published. And since Perl 6 hasn't been officially released, why not wait? Well, consider this. Let's say you bought a new Whirlpool washing machine six years ago. It's running perfectly. But since then, the mounds of laundry washed by that machine have come and gone. Now you're sporting a new trendy fashion, you have designer sheets and towels, and the detergent brand you use is hypoallergenic, nontoxic, and biodegradable, not available when you bought the washer. Even though Perl 5 has changed very little, the computer world has. It is always in a flux of new innovations, technologies, applications, and fads, and programs are being written to accommodate those changes. Whether analyzing data from the GenBank sequence database, writing applications for an iPhone, creating a personal blog on "myspace," or adjusting to the changes in a new Vista version of Windows, some computer program is involved, and very possibly it is a Perl program. Whatever the case, we like to keep up with the times. This new edition of *Perl by Example* was written for just that purpose.

As we speak, I am teaching Perl at the UCSC[1] extension in Sunnyvale, California, to a group of professionals coming from all around the Silicon Valley. I always ask at the beginning of a class, "So why do you want to learn Perl?" The responses vary from, "Our company has an auction site on the Web and I'm the webmaster. I need to use Perl and Apache to process our order information and send it to Oracle," or "I work in a genetics research group at Stanford and have to sift through and analyze masses of data, and I heard that if I learn Perl, I won't have to depend on programmers to do this," or "I'm a UNIX/Linux system administrator and our company has decided that all admin scripts should be converted to Perl," or "I just got laid off and heard that it's an absolute must to have Perl on my resume." And I am always amazed at the variety of people who show up: engineers, scientists, geneticists, meteorologists, managers, salespeople, programmers, techies, hardware guys, students, stockbrokers, administrators of all kinds,

1. University of California, Santa Cruz.

librarians, authors, bankers, artists—you name it. Perl does not exclude anyone. Perl is for everyone and it runs on everything.

No matter who you are, I think you'll agree that a picture is worth a thousand words, and so is a good example. *Perl by Example* is organized to teach you Perl from scratch with examples of complete, succinct programs. Each line of a script example is numbered, and important lines are highlighted in bold. The output of the program is then displayed with line numbers corresponding to the script line numbers. Following the output is a separate explanation for each of the numbered lines. The examples are small and to the point for the topic at hand. Since the backbone of this book was used as a student guide to a Perl course, the topics are modularized. Each chapter builds on the previous one with a minimum of forward referencing and a logical progression from one topic to the next. There are exercises at the end of the chapters. You will find all of the examples on the CD at the back of the book. They have been thoroughly tested on a number of major platforms.

Perl by Example is not just a beginner's guide but a complete guide to Perl. It covers many aspects of what Perl can do, from regular expression handling, to formatting reports, to interprocess communication. It will teach you about Perl and, in the process, a lot about UNIX and Windows. Since Perl was originally written on and for UNIX systems, some UNIX knowledge will greatly accelerate your learning curve, but it is not assumed that you are by any means a guru. Anyone reading, writing, or just maintaining Perl programs can greatly profit from this text.

Perl has a rich variety of functions for handling strings, arrays, the system interface, networking, and more. In order to understand how these functions work, background information concerning the hows, whys, and what-fors is provided before demonstrating functional sample programs. This eliminates constinually wading through manual pages and other books to understand what is going on, what the arguments mean, and what the function actually does.

The appendices contain a complete list of functions and definitions, command-line switches, special variables, popular modules, and the Perl debugger; a bioinformatics tutorial to introduce *BioPerl*, and a tutorial covering *mod_perl*, the fast way to create server side Perl scripts that replace the need for the Common Gateway Interface.

I have been teaching for the past thirty years and am committed to understanding how people learn. Having taught Perl now for more than 14 years, all over the world, I find that many new Perlers get frustrated when trying to teach themselves how to program. Most people seem to learn best from succinct little examples and practice. So I wrote a book to help myself learn and to help my students, and now to help you. As Perl has grown, so have my books. This latest, fourth, edition includes a new chapter on Perl and DBI with MySQL, a revised chapter on Perl objects, and new examples and explanations for the rest of the chapters to keep things current and interesting. The appendix material has been revised to include BioPerl and *mod_perl*. In this book, you will not only learn Perl, but also save yourself a great deal of time. At least that's what my students and readers have told me. You be the judge.

Acknowledgments

I'd like to acknowledge the following people for their contributions to the fourth edition.

Thanks to Dmitri Korzh and Techne Group for their skill in editing, formatting, and indexing that turned my attempts at using FrameMaker from a rough chunk of raw text into a real professional, polished book.

I'd like to acknowledge Oleg Orel, a brilliant student from NetApp, who wrote the initial program to illustrate "closures" in the chapter on objects, and who helped me with the problems I was having downloading modules from CPAN.

Thank you, Mark Taub, the editor-in-chief to be praised for being very cool in every step of the process from the signing of the contract to the final book that you have now in your hand. Mark has a way of making such an arduous task seem possible; he soft talks impossible deadlines, keeps up a steady pressure, and doesn't get crazy over missed deadlines, quietly achieving his goal and always with a subtle sense of humor. Thank you, Mark, for being the driving force behind this new edition!

Of course, none of this would have been possible without the contributions of the Perl pioneers—Larry Wall, Randal Schwartz, and Tom Christiansen. Their books are must reading and include *Learning Perl* by Randal Schwartz and *Programming Perl* by Larry Wall, Tom Christiansen, and Jon Orwant.

And last, but certainly not least, a huge thanks to all the students, worldwide, who have done all the real troubleshooting and kept the subject alive.

chapter 1

The Practical Extraction and Report Language

1.1 What Is Perl?

"Laziness, impatience, and hubris. Great Perl programmers embrace those virtues."

—Larry Wall

Perl is an all-purpose, open source (free software) interpreted language maintained and enhanced by a core development team called the Perl Porters. It is used primarily as a scripting language and runs on a number of platforms. Although inititally designed for the UNIX operating system, Perl is renowned for its portability and now comes bundled with most operating systems, including RedHat Linux, Solaris, FreeBSD, Macintosh, and more. Due to its versatility, Perl is often referred to as the Swiss Army knife of programming languages.

Larry Wall wrote the Perl language to manage log files and reports scattered over the network. According to Wikipedia.org, "Perl was originially named "Pearl" after the "Parable of the Pearl" from the "Gospel of Matthew." The parable is brief: A merchant is seeking pearls. He finds one that is so valuable and beautiful that he is willing to sell everything he has to purchase it. And in the end he is even wealthier than he was before. However you interpret this, it has very positive implications.

Before its official release in 1987 the "a" in "Pearl" was dropped and the language has since been called "Perl," later dubbed the Practical Extraction and Report Language, and by some, it is referred to as the Pathologically Eclectic Rubbish Lister. Perl is really much more than a practical reporting language or eclectic rubbish lister as you'll soon see. Perl makes programming easy, flexible, and fast. Those who use it, love it. And those who use it range from experienced programmers to novices with little computer background at all. The number of users continues to grow at a phenomenal rate.[1]

1. Perl is spelled "Perl" when referring to the language, and "perl" when referring to the interpreter.

Perl's heritage is UNIX. Perl scripts are functionally similar to UNIX *awk*, *sed*, shell scripts, and *C* programs. Shell scripts consist primarily of UNIX commands; Perl scripts do not. Whereas *sed* and *awk* are used to edit and report on files, Perl does not require a file in order to function. Whereas C has none of the pattern matching and wildcard metacharacters of the shells, *sed,* and *awk*, Perl has an extended set of characters. Perl was originally written to manipulate text in files, extract data from files, and write reports, but through continued development, it can manipulate processes, perform networking tasks, process Web pages, talk to databases, and analyze scientific data. Perl is truly the Swiss Army knife of programming languages; there is a tool for everyone.

The examples in this book were created on systems running Solaris, Linux, Macintosh UNIX, and Win32.

Perl is often associated with a camel symbol, a trademark of O'Reilly Media, which published the first book on Perl, called *Programming Perl* by Larry Wall and Randal Schwartz, referred to as "the Camel Book."

1.2 What Is an Interpreted Language?

To write Perl programs, you need two things: a text editor and a Perl interpreter, which you can download very quickly from any number of Web sites, including *perl.org*, *cpan.org*, and *activestate.com*. Unlike with compiled languages, such as C++ and Java, you do not need to first compile your program into machine-readable code before it can be executed. The Perl interpreter does it all; it handles the compilation, interpretation, and execution of your program. Advantages of using an interpreted language like Perl is that it runs on almost every platform, is relatively easy to learn, and is very fast and flexible.

Languages such as Python, Java, and Perl are interpreted languages that use an intermediate representation, which combines both compilation and interpretation. It compiles the user's code into an internal condensed format called bytecode, or threaded code, which is then executed by the interpreter. When you run Perl programs, you need to be aware of two phases: the compilation phase and then the run phase, where you will see the program results. If you have syntax errors, such as a misspelled keyword or missing quote, the compiler will send an error. If you pass the compiler phase, you could have other problems when the program starts running. If you pass both of these phases, you will probably start working on formatting to make the output look nicer or improving the program to make it more efficient, etc.

The interpreter also provides a number of command-line switches (options) to control its behavior. There are switches to check syntax, send warnings, loop through files, execute statements, turn on the debugger, etc. You will learn about these options throughout the following chapters.

1.3 Who Uses Perl?

Because Perl has built-in functions for easy manipulation of processes and files, and because Perl is portable (i.e., it can run on a number of different platforms), it is especially popular with system administrators, who often oversee one or more systems of different types. The phenomenal growth of the World Wide Web greatly increased interest in Perl, which was the most popular language for writing CGI scripts to generate dynamic Web pages. Even today, with the advent of other languages, such as Perl and ASP.net, focused on processing Web pages, Perl continues increased popularity with system and database administrators, scientists, geneticists, and anyone who has a need to collect data from files and manipulate it.

Anyone can use Perl, but it is easier to learn if you are already experienced in writing UNIX shell scripts, Perl, or languages derived from C, such as C++ and *Java*. For these people, the migration to Perl will be relatively easy. For those who have little programming experience, the learning curve might be a little steeper, but after learning Perl, there may be no reason to ever use anything else.

If you are familiar with UNIX utilities such as *awk*, *grep*, *sed*, and *tr*, you know that they don't share the same syntax; the options and arguments are handled differently, and the rules change from one utility to the other. If you are a shell programmer, you usually go through the grueling task of learning a variety of utilities, shell metacharacters, regular expression metacharacters, quotes, and more quotes, etc. Also, shell programs are limited and slow. To perform more complex mathematical tasks and to handle interprocess communication and binary data, for example, you may have to turn to a higher-level language, such as C, C++, or *Java*. If you know C, you also know that searching for patterns in files and interfacing with the operating system to process files and execute commands are not always easy tasks.

Perl integrates the best features of shell programming, C, and the UNIX utilities *awk*, *grep*, *sed*, and *tr*. Because it is fast and not limited to chunks of data of a particular size, many system administrators and database administrators have switched from the traditional shell scripting to Perl. C++ and *Java* programmers can enjoy the object-oriented features added in Perl 5, including the ability to create reusable, extensible modules. Now Perl can be generated in other languages, and other languages can be embedded in Perl. There is something for everyone who uses Perl, and for every task "there's more than one way to do it" (*http://www.oreilly.com/catalog/opensources/book/larry.html*).

You don't have to know everything about Perl to start writing scripts. You don't even have to be a programmer. This book will help you get a good jump-start, and you will quickly see some of its many capabilities and advantages. Then you can decide how far you want to go with Perl. If nothing else, Perl is fun!

1.3.1 Which Perl?

Perl has been through a number of revisions. There are two major versions of Perl: Perl 4 and Perl 5. The last version of Perl 4 was Perl 4, patchlevel 36 (Perl 4.036), released in 1992, making it ancient. Perl 5.000 (ancient), introduced in fall 1994, was a complete rewrite of the Perl source code that optimized the language and introduced objects and many other features. Despite these changes, Perl 5 remains highly compatible with the previous releases. (Examples in this book have been tested using both versions, and where there are differences, they are noted.) As of this writing, the current version of Perl is 5.8.8. Perl 6 is the next generation of another Perl redesign and does not have an official release date. It will have new features, but the basic language you learn here will be essentially the same.

1.3.2 What Is Perl 6?

> "Perl 5 was my rewrite of Perl. I want Perl 6 to be the community's rewrite of Perl and of the community."
>
> —Larry Wall, State of the Onion speech, TPC4

Perl 6 is essentially Perl 5 with many new features. The basic language syntax, features, and purpose will be the same. If you know Perl, you will still know Perl. If you learn Perl from this book, you will be prepared to jump into Perl 6 when it is released. Perl 6 has been described as learning Australian English if you speak American English, rather than trying to switch from English to Chinese.

To get information about everything happening with Perl 6, go to: *http://www.perl.com/pub/a/2006/01/12/what_is_perl_6.html?page=2*

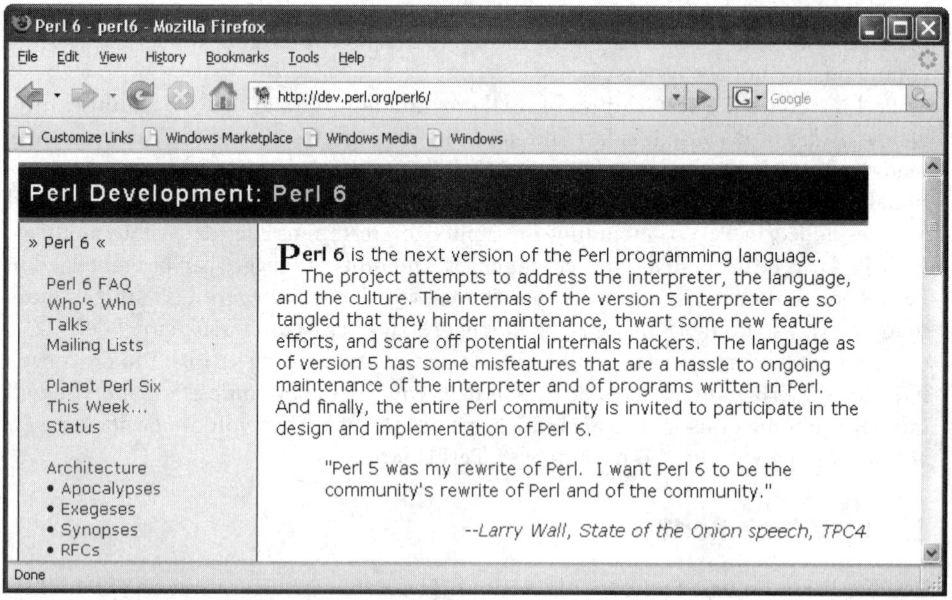

Figure 1.1 Perl 6 development Web page.

And for a sketch of Larry Wall and history of Perl, go to:
http://www.softpanorama.org/People/Wall/index.shtml#Perl_history

1.4 Where to Get Perl

Perl is available from a number of sources. The primary source for Perl distribution is CPAN, the Comprehensive Perl Archive Network (*www.cpan.org*).

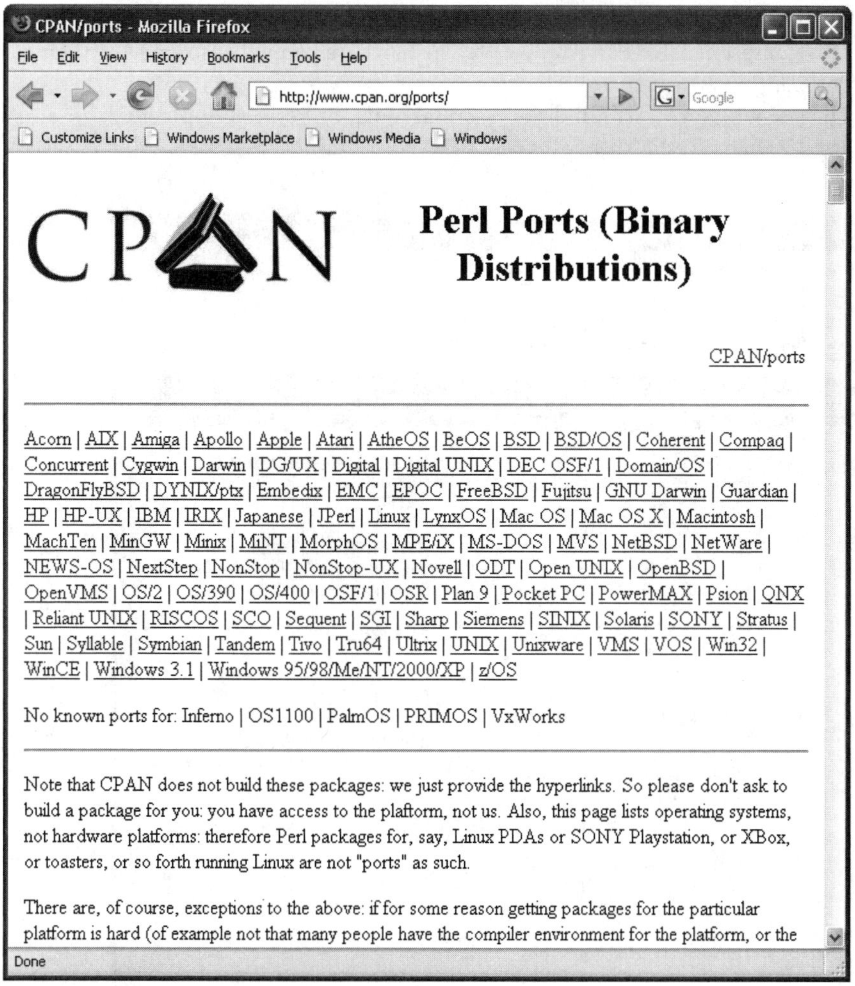

Figure 1.2 CPAN ports for binary distribution.

Go to *http://www.cpan.org/ports/* to find out more about what's available for your platform. If you want to install Perl quickly and easily, ActivePerl is a complete, self-installing distribution of Perl based on the standard Perl sources for Windows, Mac OS X, Linux, Solaris, AIX, and HP-UX. It is distributed online at the ActiveState site (*www.activestate.com*). The complete ActivePerl package contains the binary of the core Perl distribution and complete online documentation.

Here are some significant Web sites to help you find more information about Perl:

- The official Perl home page, run by O'Reilly Media, Inc.: *www.perl.com*
- The Perl Directory, run by the Perl Foundation, with the aim of being "the central directory of all things Perl": *www.perl.org*
- The Comprehensive Perl Archive Network, where you will also find "All Things Perl": *http://www.cpan.org/*
- The site where you will find the essential tools for Perl development: *http://www.activestate.com/*

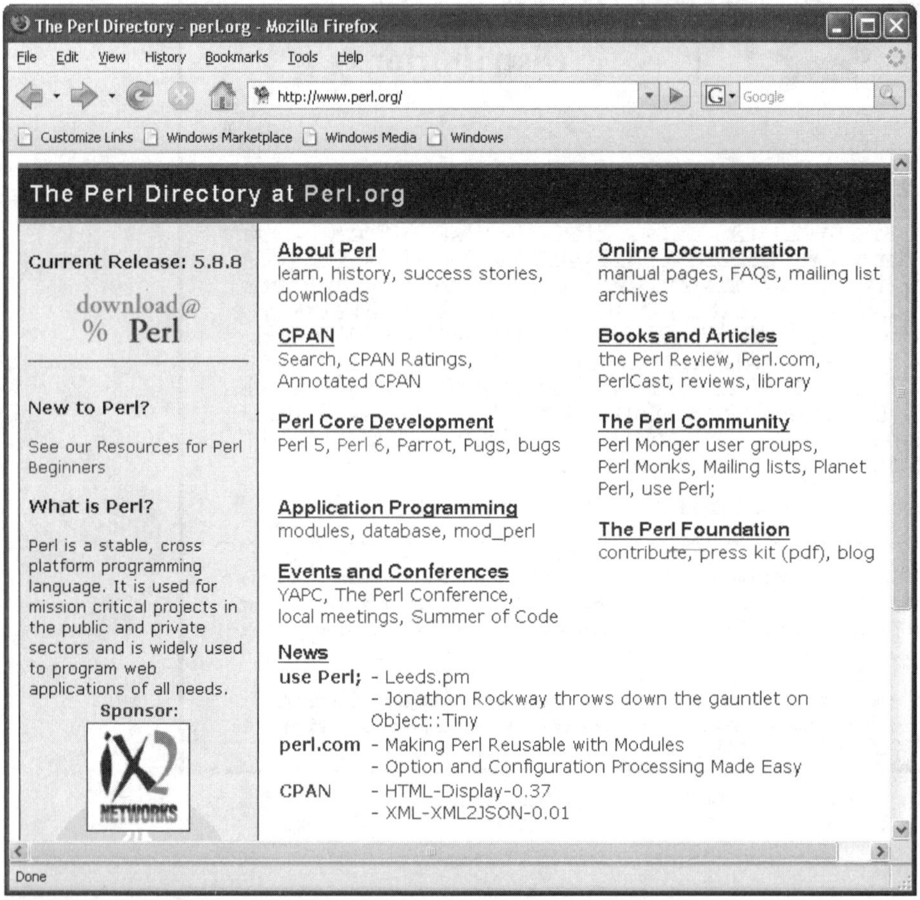

Figure 1.3 The Perl directory with links to resources.

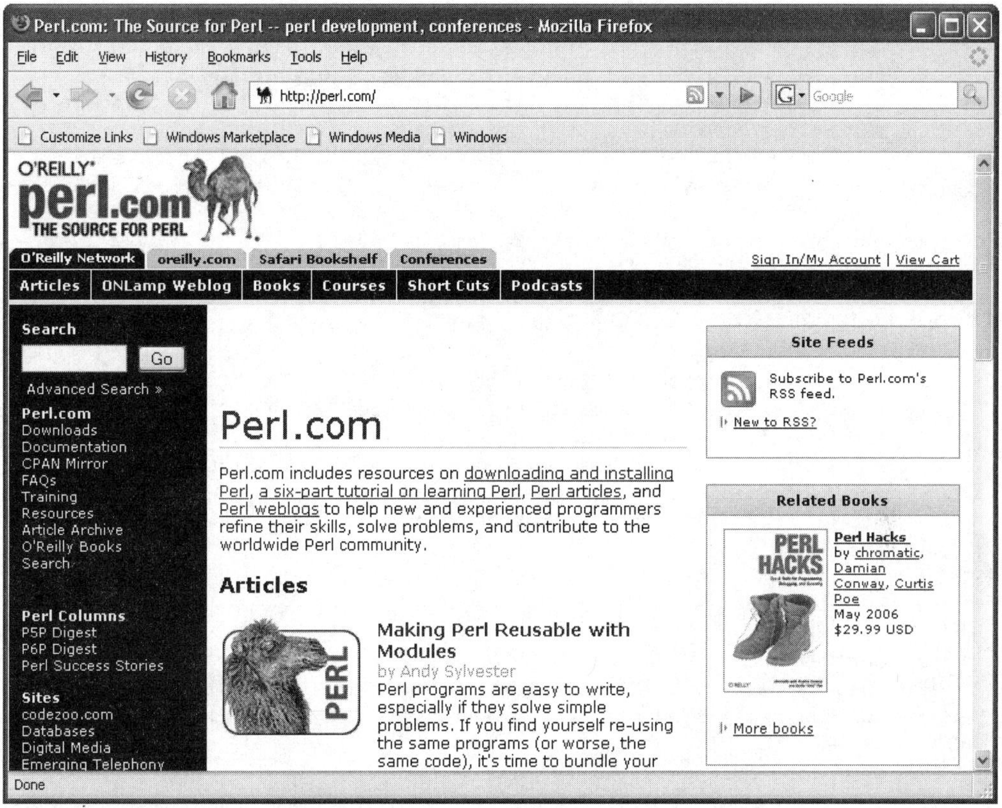

Figure 1.4 The official Perl home page (run by O'Reilly Media).

1.4.1 What Version Do I Have?

To obtain your Perl version, date this binary version was built, patches, and some copyright information, type the following line shown in Example 1.1 (the dollar sign is the shell prompt):

EXAMPLE 1.1

```
$ perl -v
1   This is perl, v5.8.8 built for MSWin32-x86-multi-thread
    (with 50 registered patches, see perl -V for more detail)

2   Copyright 1987-2006, Larry Wall

3   Binary build 820 [274739] provided by ActiveState
    http://www.ActiveState.com
    Built Jan 23 2007 15:57:46
```

EXAMPLE 1.1 (CONTINUED)

```
4   Perl may be copied only under the terms of either the Artistic
    License or the GNU General Public License, which may be found in
    the Perl 5 source kit.
       Complete documentation for Perl, including FAQ lists, should be
    found on this system using "man perl" or "perldoc perl".  If you
    have access to the Internet, point your browser at
    http://www.perl.org/, the Perl Home Page.

    This is perl, v5.8.8 built for MSWin32-x86-multi-thread
    (with 1 registered patch, see perl -V for more detail)

5   Perl may be copied only under the terms of either the Artistic
    License or the GNU General Public License, which may be found in
    the Perl 5.0 source kit.
      Complete documentation for Perl, including FAQ lists, should be
    found on this system using man perl or perldoc perl. If you have
    access to the Internet, point your browser to www.perl.com/, the
    Perl home page.

    ------------------------------------------------------------

6   perl -v
    This is perl, v5.8.3 built for sun4-solaris-thread-multi
    (with 8 registered patches, see perl -V for more detail)

    Copyright 1987-2003, Larry Wall

    Binary build 809 provided by ActiveState Corp.
    http://www.ActiveState.com
    ActiveState is a division of Sophos.
    Built Feb  3 2004 00:32:12

    Perl may be copied only under the terms of either the Artistic
    License or the GNU General Public License, which may be found in
    the Perl 5 source kit.

    Complete documentation for Perl, including FAQ lists, should be
    found on this system using `man perl' or `perldoc perl'.  If you
    have access to the Internet, point your browser at
    http://www.perl.com/, the Perl Home Page.
```

EXPLANATION

1 This version of Perl is 5.8.8 from ActiveState for Windows.
2 Larry Wall, the author of Perl, owns the copyright.
3 This build was obtained from ActiveState.
5 Perl may be copied under the terms specified by the Artistic License or GNU. Perl is distributed under GNU, the Free Software Foundation, meaning that Perl is free.
6 This version of Perl is 5.8.3 for Solaris (UNIX).

1.5 What Is CPAN?

CPAN, the "gateway to all things Perl," stands for the Comprehensive Perl Archive Network, a Web site that houses all the free Perl material you will ever need, including documentation, FAQs, modules and scripts, binary distributions and source code, and announcements. CPAN is mirrored all over the world, and you can find the nearest mirror at

www.perl.com/CPAN
www.cpan.org

CPAN is the place you will go to if you want to find modules to help you with your work. The CPAN search engine will let you find modules under a large number of categories. Modules are discussed in Chapter 12, "Modularize It, Package It, and Send It to the Library!"

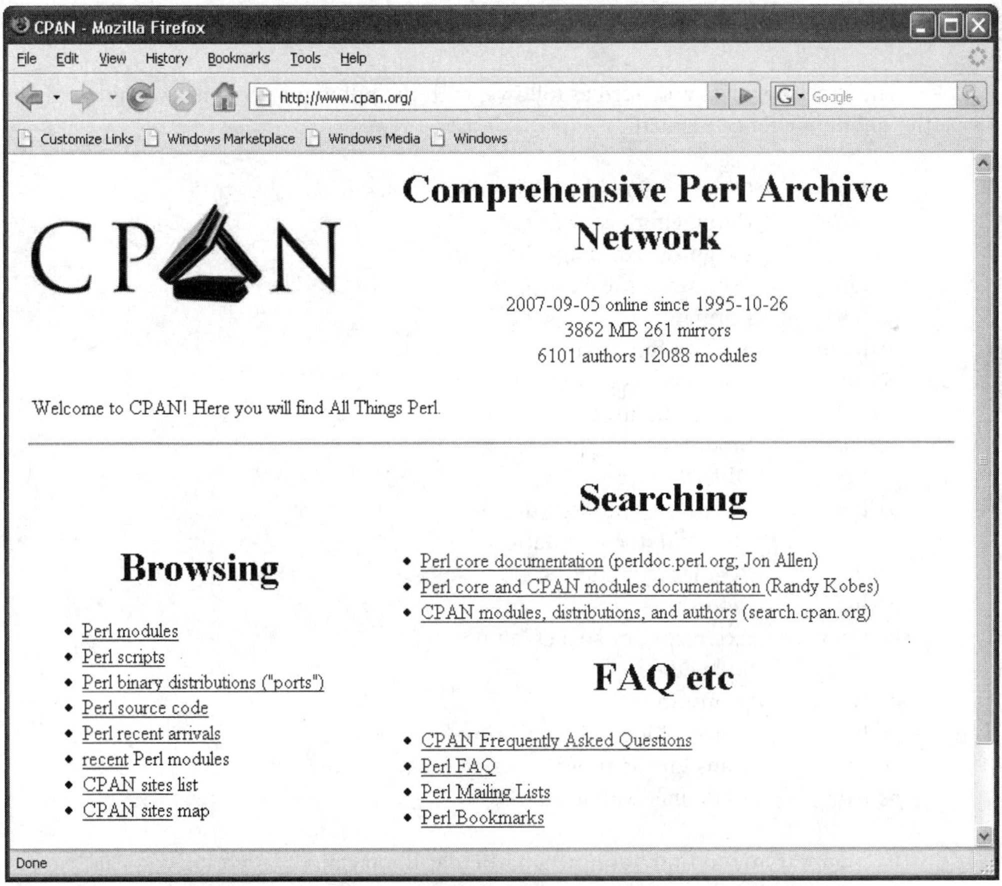

Figure 1.5 A comprehensive index of Perl modules.

1.6 Perl Documentation

1.6.1 Perl Man Pages

The standard Perl distribution comes with complete online documentation called *man* pages, which provide help for all the standard utilities. (The name derives from the UNIX *man* [manual] pages.) Perl has divided its *man* pages into categories. If you type the following at your command-line prompt:

```
man perl
```

you will get a list of all the sections by category. So, if you want help on how to use Perl's regular expresssions, you would type

```
man perlre
```

and if you want help on subroutines, you would type

```
man perlsub
```

The Perl categories are listed as follows, with the following sections available only in the online reference manual:

perlbot	Object-oriented tricks and examples
perldebug	Debugging
perldiag	Diagnostic messages
perldsc	Data structures: intro
perlform	Formats
perlfunc	Built-in functions
perlipc	Interprocess communication
perllol	Data structures: lists of lists
perlmod	Modules
perlobj	Objects
perlop	Operators and precedence
perlpod	Plain old documentation
perlre	Regular expressions
perlref	References
perlsock	Extension for socket support
perlstyle	Style guide
perlsub	Subroutines
perltie	Objects hidden behind simple variables
perltrap	Traps for the unwary
perlvar	Predefined variables

If you are trying to find out how a particular library module works, you can use the *perldoc* command to get the documentation. For example, if you want to know about the *CGI.pm* module, type at the command line

```
perldoc CGI
```

and the documentation for the *CGI.pm* module will be displayed. If you type

```
perldoc English
```

the documentation for the *English.pm* module will be displayed.

To get documentation on a specific Perl function, type *perldoc -f* and the name of the function. For example, to find out about the *localtime* function, you would execute the following command at your command-line prompt. (You may have to set your UNIX/DOS path to execute this program directly.)

```
perldoc -f localtime
localtime EXPR
localtime
          Converts a time as returned by the time function to a 9-element
          list with the time analyzed for the local time zone. Typically
          used as follows:
             #   0    1    2     3     4    5     6     7     8
              ($sec,$min,$hour,$mday,$mon,$year,$wday,$yday,$isdst) =
                                                        localtime(time);
<continues>
```

1.6.2 HTML Documentation

ActivePerl provides execllent documentation (from ActiveState.com) when you download Perl from its site. As shown in Figure 1.6, there are links to everything you need to know about Perl.

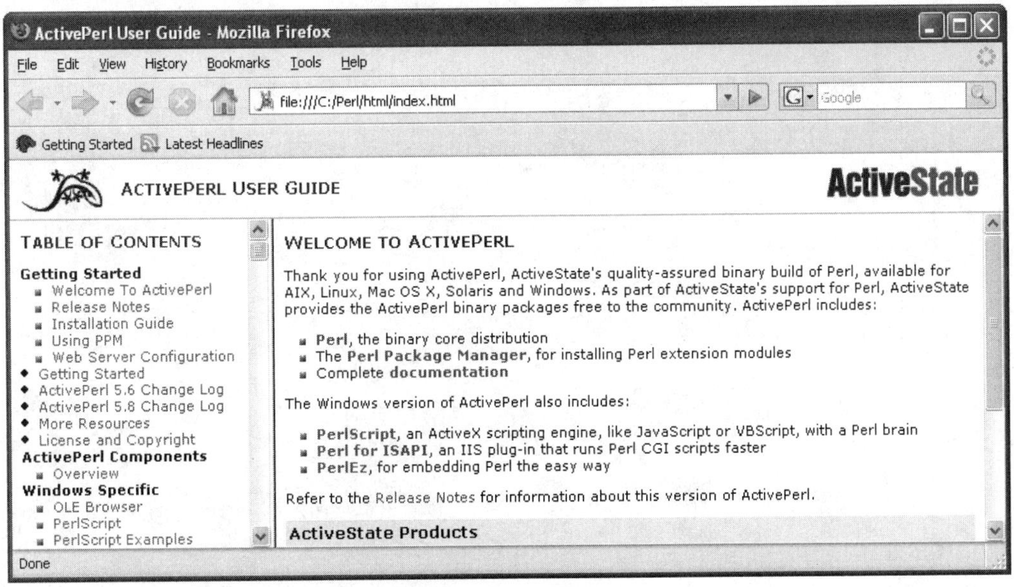

Figure 1.6 HTML Perl documentation from ActiveState.

1.7 What You Should Know

1. Who wrote Perl?
2. What does Perl stand for?
3. What is the meaning of "open source"?
4. What is the current release?
5. What is Perl used for?
6. What is an interpreter?
7. Where can you get Perl?
8. What is ActivePerl?
9. What is CPAN?
10. Where do you get documentation?
11. How would you find documentation for a specific Perl function?

1.8 What's Next?

In the next chapter, you will learn how to create basic Perl scripts and execute them. You will learn what goes in a Perl script, about Perl syntax, statements, and comments. You will learn how to check for syntax errors and how to execute Perl at the command-line with a number of Perl options.

chapter

2

Perl Quick Start

2.1 Quick Start, Quick Reference

2.1.1 A Note to Programmers

If you have had previous programming experience in another language, such as Visual Basic, C/C++, Java, ASP, or PHP, and you are familiar with basic concepts, such as variables, loops, conditional statements, and functions, Table 2.1 will give you a quick overview of the constructs and syntax of the Perl language.

At the end of each section, you will be given the chapter number that describes the particular construct and a short, fully functional Perl example designed to illustrate how that constuct is used.

2.1.2 A Note to Non-Programmers

If you are not familiar with programming, skip this chapter and go to Chapter 5. You may want to refer to this chapter later for a quick reference.

2.1.3 Perl Syntax and Constructs

Table 2.1 Perl Syntax and Constructs

The Script File

A Perl script is created in a text editor. Normally, there is no special extension required in the filename, unless specified by the application running the script; e.g., if running under Apache as a *cgi* program, the filename may be required to have a *.pl* or *.cgi* extension.

Free Form

Perl is a free-form language. Statements must be terminated with a semicolon but can be anywhere on the line and span multiple lines.

Comments

Perl comments are preceded by a # sign. They are ignored by the interpreter. They can be anywhere on the line and span only one line.

EXAMPLE

```
print "Hello, world";   # This is a comment
    #  And this is a comment
```

Printing Output

The *print and printf* functions are built-in functions used to display output.
The *print* function arguments consist of a comma-separated list of strings and/or numbers.
The *printf* function is similar to the C *printf()* function and is used for formatting output.
Parentheses are not required around the argument list.
(See Chapter 3.)

```
print value, value, value;
printf ( string format [, mixed args [, mixed ...]] );
```

EXAMPLE

```
print "Hello, world\n";
print "Hello,", " world\n";
print ("It's such a perfect day!\n");   # Parens optional;.
print "The the date and time are: ", localtime, "\n";
printf "Hello, world\n";
printf("Meet %s%:Age 5d%:Salary \$10.2f\n", "John", 40, 55000);
```

(See Chapter 4.)

Data Types/Variables

Perl supports three basic data types to hold variables: scalars, arrays, and associative arrays (hashes).
Perl variables don't have to be declared before being used.
Variable names start with a "funny character," followed by a letter and any number of alphanumeric characters, including the underscore. The funny character represents the data type and context. The characters following the funny symbol are case sensitive.
If a variable name starts with a letter, it may consist of any number of letters (an underscore counts as a letter) and/or digits. If the variable does not start with a letter, it must consist of only one character.
(See Chapter 5.)

Table 2.1 Perl Syntax and Constructs (continued)

Scalar

A scalar is a variable that holds a single value, a single string, or a number. The name of the scalar is preceded by a "$" sign. Scalar context means that one value is being used.

EXAMPLE

```
$first_name = "Melanie";
$last_name = "Quigley";
$salary = 125000.00;
print $first_name, $last_name, $salary;
```

Array

An array is an ordered list of scalars; i.e., strings and/or numbers. The elements of the array are indexed by integers starting at 0. The name of the array is preceeded by an "@" sign.

```
@names = ( "Jessica", "Michelle", "Linda" );
print "@names";  # Prints the array with elements separated by a space
print "$names[0] and $names[2]";  # Prints "Jessica" and "Linda"
print "$names[-1]\n";  # Prints "Linda"
$names[3]="Nicole";     # Assign a new value as the 4th element
```

Some commonly used built-in functions:

pop	removes last element
push	adds new elements to the end of the array
shift	removes first element
unshift	adds new elements to the beginning of the array
splice	removes or adds elements from some position in the array
sort	sorts the elements of an array

Hash

An associative array, called a hash, is an unordered list of key/value pairs, indexed by strings. The name of the hash is preceded by a "%" symbol. (The % is not evaluated when enclosed in either single or double quotes.)

EXAMPLE

```
%employee =  (
    "Name"      => "Jessica Savage",
    "Phone"     => "(925) 555-1274",
    "Position"  => "CEO"
);

print "$employee{"Name"};   # Print a value
$employee{"SSN"}="999-333-2345";   # Assign a key/value
```

Some commonly used built-in functions:

keys	retrieves all the keys in a hash
values	retrieves all the values in a hash
each	retrieves a key/value pair from a hash
delete	removes a key/value pair

Continues

Table 2.1 Perl Syntax and Constructs (continued)

Predefined Variables	Perl provides a large number of predefined variables. The following is a list of some common predefined variables: $_ The default input and pattern-searching space. $. Current line number for the last filehandle accessed. $@ The Perl syntax error message from the last *eval()* operator. *$!* Yields the current value of the error message, used with *die*. *$0* Contains the name of the program being executed. $$ The process number of the Perl running this script. *$PERL_VERSION* / *$^V* The revision, version, and subversion of the Perl interpreter. *@ARGV* Contains the command-line arguments. *ARGV* A special filehandle that iterates over command-line filenames in *@ARGV*. *@INC* Search path for libarary files. *@_* Within a subroutine the array @_ contains the parameters passed to that subroutine. *%ENV* The hash *%ENV* contains your current environment. *%SIG* The hash *%SIG* contains signal handlers for signals.
Constants (Literals)	A constant value, once set, cannot be modified. An example of a constant is PI or the number of feet in a mile. It doesn't change. Constants are defined with the *constant pragma* as shown here.
Numbers	Perl supports integers (decimal, octal, hexadecimal), floating point numbers, scientific notation, Booleans, and null.

(Constants example:)

EXAMPLE

```
use constant BUFFER_SIZE => 4096;
use constant PI => 4 * atan2 1, 1;
use constant DEBUGGING => 0;
use contstant ISBN => "0-13-028251-0";
PI=6;  # Cannot modify PI; produces an error.
```

(Numbers example:)

EXAMPLE

```
$year = 2006;  # integer
$mode = 0775;  # octal number in base 8
$product_price = 29.95;  # floating point number in base 10
$favorite_color = 0x33CC99;  # integer in base 16 (hexadecimal)
$distance_to_moon=3.844e+5;  # floating point in scientific notation
$bits = 0b10110110;  # binary number
```

Table 2.1 Perl Syntax and Constructs (continued)

Strings and Quotes

A string is a sequence of bytes (characters) enclosed in quotes.
When quoting strings, make sure the quotes are matched; e.g., "string" or 'string'. Scalar and array variables ($x, @name) and backslash sequences (\n, \t, \", etc.) are interpreted within double quotes; a backslash will escape a quotation mark, a single quote can be embedded in a set of double quotes, and a double quote can be embedded in a set of single quotes. A *here document* is a block of text embedded between user-defined tags, the first tag preceded by <<.

The following shows three ways to quote a string:

Single quotes: 'It rains in Spain';
Double quotes: "It rains in Spain";
Here document:

```
print <<END;
    It
    rains in
    Spain
END
```

EXAMPLE

```
$question = 'He asked her if she wouldn\'t mind going to Spain';
        # Single quotes
$answer = 'She said: "No, but it rains in Spain."';   # Single quotes
$line = "\tHe said he wouldn't take her to Spain\n";
$temperature = "78";
print "It is currently $temperature degrees";
        # Prints: "It is currently 78 degrees.". Variables are
        # interpreted when enclosed  in double quotes, but not
        # single quotes
```

Alternative Quotes

Perl provides an alternative form of quoting. The string to be quoted is delimted by a nonalphanumeric character or characters that can be paired, such as ( ), { }, [ ].
The constructs are: **qq, q, qw, qx**

EXAMPLE

```
print qq/Hello\n/;    # same as: print "Hello\n";
print q/He owes $5.00/, \n"; #  same as: print 'He owes $5.00', "\n";
@states=qw( ME MT CA FL );   # same as ("ME", "MT", "CA","FL")
$today = qx(date);  # same as $today = `date`;
```

Continues

Table 2.1 Perl Syntax and Constructs (continued)

Operators

Perl offers many types of operators, but for the most part they are the same as C/C++/Java or PHP operators. Types of operators are (see Chapter 6):

- Assignment: =, +=, -=, *= , %=, ^=, &=, |=, .=
- Numeric equality: = =, !=, <=>
- String equality: eq, ne, cmp
- Relational numeric: > >= < <=
- Relational string: gt, ge, lt, le
- Range: 5 .. 10 # range between 5 and 10, increment by 1
- Logical: &&, and, ||, or, XOR, xor, !
- Autoincrement/decrement: ++ --
- File: -r, -w, -x,-o, -e, -z, -s, -f, -d, -l, etc.
- Bitwise: ~ & | ^ << >>
- String concatenation: .
- String repetition: x
- Arithmetic: * / - + %
- Pattern matching: =~, !~

EXAMPLE

```
print "\nArithmetic Operators\n";
print ((3+2) * (5-3)/2);

print "\nString Operators\n";  # Concatenation
print "\tTommy" . ' ' . "Savage";

print "\nComparison Operators\n";
print 5>=3 , "\n";
print 47==23 , "\n";

print "\nLogical Operators\n";
$a > $b && $b < 100
$answer eq "yes" || $money == 200

print "\nCombined Assignment Operators\n";
$a = 47;
$a += 3;        # short for $a = $a + 3
$a++;           # autoincrement
print $a;  # Prints 51

print "\nPattern Matching Operators\n"
$color = "green";
print if $color =~ /^gr/;     # $color matches a pattern
                              # starting with 'gr'
$answer = "Yes";
print if $answer !~ /[Yy]/;   # $answer matches a pattern
                              # containing 'Y' or 'y'
```

Table 2.1 Perl Syntax and Constructs (continued)

Conditionals

The basic *if* construct evaluates an expression enclosed in parentheses, and if the condition evaluates to true, the block following the expression is executed.
(See Chapter 7.)

if statement

```
if ( expression ){
    statements;
}
```

EXAMPLE

```
if ( $a == $b ){ print "$a is equal to $b"; }
```

if/else statement

The *if/else* block is a two-way decision. If the expression after the *if* condition is true, the block of statements is executed; if false, the *else* block of statements is executed.

```
if ( expression ){
    statements;
else{
    statements;
}
```

EXAMPLE

```
$coin_toss = int (rand(2 )) + 1; # Generate a random
                                 # number between 1 and 2
if( $coin_toss == 1 ) {
    print "You tossed HEAD\n";
}
else {
    print "You tossed TAIL\n";
}
```

if/elsif statement

The *if/elsif/else* offers multiway branch; if the expression following the if is not true, each of the *elsif* expressions is evaluated until one is true; otherwise, the optional *else* statements are executed.

```
if ( expression ){
    statements;
elsif ( expression ){
    statements;
}
elsif (expression){
    statements;
else{
    statements;
}
```

Continues

Table 2.1 Perl Syntax and Constructs (continued)

EXAMPLE

```
#  1 is Monday, 7 Sunday
$day_of_week = int(rand(7)) + 1;
print "Today is: $day_of_week\n";
if ( $day_of_week >=1 && $day_of_week <=4 ) {
    print "Business hours are from 9 am to 9 pm\n";
}
elsif ( $day_of_week == 5) {
    print "Business hours are from 9 am to 6 pm\n";
}
else {
    print "We are closed on weekends\n";
}
```

Conditional Operator

Like C/C++, Perl also offers a shortform of the *if/else* syntax, which uses three operands and two operators (also called the ternary operator). The question mark is followed by a statement that is executed if the condition being tested is true, and the colon is followed by a statement that is executed if the condition is false.

(condition) ? statement_if_true : statement_if_false;

EXAMPLE

```
$coin_toss = int (rand(2 )) + 1; # Generate a random number
                                 # between 1 and 2
print ( $coin_toss == 1 ? "You tossed HEAD\n" : "You tossed TAIL\n" );
```

Loops

A loop is a way to specify a piece of code that repeats many times. Perl supports several types of loops: the *while* loop, *do-while* loop, *for* loop, and *foreach* loop. (See Chapter 7.)

while/until Loop

The while loop:

The *while* is followed by an expression enclosed in parentheses, and a block of statements. As long as the expression tests true, the loop continues to iterate.

while (conditional expression) {
    code block A
}

EXAMPLE

```
$count=0;  # Initial value
while ($count < 10 ){  # Test
    print $n;
    $count++;  # Increment value
}
```

Table 2.1 Perl Syntax and Constructs (continued)

The until loop:

The *until* is followed by an expression enclosed in parentheses, and a block of statements. As long as the expression tests false, the loop continues to iterate.

```
until ( conditional expression ) {
    code block A
}
```

EXAMPLE

```
$count=0;   # Initial value
until ($count == 10 ){   # Test
    print $n;
    $count++;   # Increment value
}
```

do-while Loop

The do-while loop:

The *do-while* loop is similar to the *while* loop except it checks its looping expresssion at the end of the loop block rather than at the beginning, guaranteeing that the loop block is executed at least once.

```
do {
    code block A
} while (expression);
```

EXAMPLE

```
$count=0;   # Initial value
do {
    print "$n ";
    $count++;   # Increment value
    while ($count < 10 );   # Test
}
```

for Loop

The for loop:

The *for* loop has three expressions to evaluate, each separated by a semicolon. The first inititializes a variable and is evaluated only once. The second tests whether the value is true, and if it is true, the block is entered; if not, the loop exits. After the block of statements is executed, control returns to the third expression, which changes the value of the variable being tested. The second expression is tested again, etc.

```
for( initialization; conditional expression; increment/decrement ) {
    block of code
}
```

Continues

Table 2.1 Perl Syntax and Constructs (continued)

EXAMPLE

```
for( $count = 0; $count < 10; $count = $count + 1 ) {
    print "$count\n";
}
```

foreach Loop

The **foreach loop:**
The *foreach* is used only to iterate through a list, one item at a time.

```
foreach $item ( @list ) {
    print $item,"\n";
}
```

EXAMPLE

```
@dessert =  ( "ice cream", "cake", "pudding", "fruit");

foreach $choice (@dessert){
    # Iterates through each element of the array
    echo "Dessert choice is: $choice\n";
}
```

Loop Control

The *last* statement is used to break out of a loop from within the loop block. The *next* statement is used to skip over the remaining statements within the loop block and start back at the top of the loop.

EXAMPLE

```
$n=0;
while( $n < 10 ){
    print $n;
    if ($n == 3){
        last;  # Break out of loop
    }
    $n++;
}
print "Out of the loop.<br>";
```

EXAMPLE

```
for($n=0; $n<10; $n++){
    if ($n == 3){
        next;  # Start at top of loop;
               # skip remaining statements in block
    }
    echo "\$n = $n<br>";
}
print "Out of the loop.<br>";
```

Table 2.1 Perl Syntax and Constructs (continued)

Subroutines/ Functions	A function is a block of code that peforms a task and can be invoked from another part of the program. Data can be passed to the function via arguments. A function may or may not return a value. Any valid Perl code can make up the definition block of a function. Variables outside the function are available inside the function. The *my* function will make the specified variables local. (See Chapter 11.)

```
sub function_name{
      block of code
}
```

EXAMPLE

```
sub greetings() {
   print "Welcome to Perl!<br>";   # Function definition
}
&greetings;   # Function call
greetings(); # Function call
```

EXAMPLE

```
$my_year = 2000;

if ( is_leap_year( $my_year ) ) {    # Call function with an argument
   print "$my_year is a leap year\n";
}
else {
   print "$my_year is not a leap year";
}

sub is_leap_year {    # Function definition

   my $year = shift(@_);   # Shift off the year from
                           # the parameter list, @_
   return ((($year % 4 == 0) && ($year % 100 != 0)) ||
   ($year % 400 == 0)) ? 1 : 0;    # What is returned from the function
}
```

Continues

Table 2.1 Perl Syntax and Constructs (continued)

Files

Perl provides the *open* function to open files, and pipes for reading, writing, and appending. The *open* function takes a user-defined filehandle (normally a few uppercase characters) as its first argument and a string containing the symbol for read/write/append followed by the real path to the system file. (See Chapter 10.)

EXAMPLE

To open a file for reading:

```
open(FH, "<filename");       # Opens "filename" for reading.
                             # The < symbol is optional.
open (DB, "/home/ellie/myfile") or die "Can't open file: $!\n";
```

To open a file for writing:

```
open(FH, ">filename");       # Opens "filename" for writing.
                             # Creates or truncates file.
```

To open a file for appending:

```
open(FH, ">>filename");      # Opens "filename" for appending.
                             # Creates or appends to file.
```

To open a file for reading and writing:

```
open(FH, "+<filename");      # Opens "filename" for read, then write.
open(FH, "+>filename");      # Opens "filename" for write, then read.
```

To close a file:

```
close(FH);
```

To read from a file:

```
while(<FH>){ print; }        # Read one line at a time from file.
@lines = <FH>;               # Slurp all lines into an array.
print "@lines\n";
```

To write to a file:

```
open(FH, ">file") or die "Can't open file: $!\n";

print FH "This line is written to the file just opened.\n";
print FH "And this line is also written to the file just opened.\n";
```

EXAMPLE

To Test File Attributes

```
print "File is readable, writeable, and executable\n" if -r $file and
-w _ and -x _;
            # Is it readble, writeable, and executable?
print "File was last modified ",-M $file, " days ago.\n";
            # When was it last modified?
print "File is a directory.\n " if -d $file;     # Is it a directory?
```

Table 2.1 Perl Syntax and Constructs (continued)

Pipes	Pipes can be used to send the output from system commands as input to Perl and to send Perl's output as input to a system command. To create a pipe, also called a filter, the *open* system call is used. It takes two arguments: a user-defined handle and the operating system command, either preceded or appended with the "|" symbol. If the command is preceded with a "|", the operating system command reads Perl output. If the command is appended with the "|" symbol, Perl reads from the pipe; if the command is prepended with "|", Perl writes to the pipe.
	(See Chapter 10.)
	
	EXAMPLE
	
	Input filter
	`open(F, " ls |") or die;    # Open a pipe to read from`
	`while(<F>){ print ; }    # Prints list of UNIX files`
	
	Output filer
	`open(SORT, "| sort" ) or die;  # Open pipe to write to`
	`print SORT "dogs\ncats\nbirds\n"`
	`    #  Sorts birds, cats, dogs on separate lines.`

Regular Expressions. A regular expression is set of characters enclosed in forward slashes. They are to match patterns in text and to refine searches and substitutions. Perl is best known for its pattern matching. (See Chapter 8.)

Table 2.2 Some Regular Expression Metacharacters

Metacharacter	*What It Represents*
^	Matches at the beginning of a line
$	Matches at the end of a line
a.c	Matches an 'a', any single character, and a 'c'
[abc]	Matches an 'a' or 'b' or 'c'
[^abc]	Matches a character that is not an 'a' or 'b' or 'c'
[0-9]	Matches one digit between '0' and '9'
ab*c	Matches an 'a', followed by zero or more 'b's and a 'c'
ab+c	Matches an 'a', followed by one or more 'b's and a 'c'
ab?c	Matches an 'a', followed by zero or one 'b' and a 'c'
(ab)+c	Matches one or more occurrences of 'ab' followed by a 'c'
(ab) (c)	Captures 'ab' and assigns it to $1, captures 'c' and assigns it to $2.

EXAMPLE

```
$_ = "looking for a needle in a haystack";
print if /needle/;
    If $_contains needle, the string is printed.

$_ = "looking for a needle in a haystack"; # Using regular expression metacharacters
print if  /^[Nn]..dle/;
    # characters and "dle".

$str = "I am feeling blue, blue, blue..."
$str =~ s/blue/upbeat/;  # Substitute first occurrence of "blue" with "upbeat"
print $str;
I am feeling upbeat, blue, blue...

$str="I am feeling BLue, BLUE...";
$str = ~ s/blue/upbeat/ig;  # Ignore case, global substitution
print $str;
I am feeling upbeat, upbeat...

$str = "Peace and War";
$str =~ s/(Peace) and (War)/$2, $1/i;  # $1 gets 'Peace', $2 gets' War'
print $str;
War and Peace.

$str = "He gave me 5 dollars.\n"
s/5/6*7/e; #  Rather than string substitution, evaluate replacement side
print $str;
He gave me 42 dollars."
```

Passing Arguments at the Command Line. The *@ARGV* array is used to hold command-line arguments. If the ARGV filehandle is used, the arguments are treated as files; otherwise, arugments are strings coming in from the command line to be used in a script. (See Chapter 10.)

EXAMPLE

```
$ perlscript filea fileb filec

(In Script)
print "@ARGV\n";  # lists arguments: filea fileb filec
while(<ARGV>){  # filehandle ARGV -- arguments treated as files
   print;  # Print each line of every file listed in @ARGV
}
```

References, Pointers. Perl references are also called pointers. A pointer is a scalar variable that contains the address of another variable. To create a pointer, the backslash operator is used. (See Chapter 13.)

EXAMPLE

```
# Create variables
$age = 25;
@siblings = qw("Nick", "Chet", "Susan","Dolly");
%home = ("owner" => "Bank of America",
         "price" => "negotiable",
         "style" => "Saltbox",
);

# Create pointer
$pointer1 = \$age;   # Create pointer to scalar
$pointer2 = \@siblings;  # Create pointer to array
$pointer3 = \%home; # Create pointer to hash
$pointer4 = [ qw(red yellow blue green) ]; # Create anonymous array
$pointer5 = { "Me" => "Maine", "Mt" => "Montana", "Fl" => "Florida" };
           # Create anonymous hash

# Dereference pointer
print $$pointer1; # Dereference pointer to scalar; prints: 25
print @$pointer2; # Dereference pointer to array;
        # prints: Nick Chet Susan Dolly
print %$pointer3; # Dereference pointer to hash;
        # prints: styleSaltboxpricenegotiableownerBank of America
print $pointer2->[1];    # prints "Chet"
print $pointer3->{"style"}; # prints "Saltbox"
print @{$pointer4}; # prints elements of anonymous array
```

Objects. Perl supports objects, a special type of variable. A Perl class is a package containing a collection of variables and functions, called properties and methods. There is no "class" keyword. The properties (also called attributes) are variables used to describe the object. Methods are special functions that allow you to create and manipulate the object. Objects are created with the *bless* function. (See Chapter 14.)

Creating a Class

EXAMPLE

```
package Pet

sub new{ # Constructor
    my $class = shift;
    my $pet = {
         "Name"   => undef,
         "Owner"  => undef,
         "Type"   => undef,
    };
    bless($pet, $class);
# Returns a pointer to the object

    sub set_pet{      # Accessor methods
         my $self = shift;
         my ($name, $owner, $type)= @_;
         $self->{'Name'} = $name;
         $self->{'Owner'}= $owner;
         $self->{'Type'}= $type;
    }
    sub get_pet{
    my $self = shift;
    while(($key,$value)=each($%self)){
         print "$key: $value\n";
    }
}
```

Instantiating a Class

EXAMPLE

```
$cat = Pet->new();  # alternative form is: $cat = new Pet();
# Create an object with a constructor method
$cat->set_pet("Sneaky", "Mr. Jones", "Siamese");
# Access the object with an instance
$cat->get_pet;
```

Perl also supports method inheritance by placing base classes in the *@ISA* array.

Libraries and Modules. Library files have a *.pl* extenson; modules have a .pm extension. Today, *.pm* files are more commonly used than *.pl* files. (See Chapter 12.)

Path to Libraries

@INC array contains list of path to standard Perl libraries.

To include a File

To load an external file, use either *require* or *use*.

```
require("getopts.pl"); # Loads library file at run time
use CGI;   # Loads CGI.pm module at compile time
```

Diagnostics. To exit a Perl script with the cause of the error, you can use the built-in *die* function or the *exit* function.

EXAMPLE

```
open(FH, "filename") or die "Couldn't open filename: $!\n";
if ($input !~ /^\d+$/){
        print STDERR "Bad input. Integer required.\n";
        exit(1);
}
```

You can also use the Perl pragmas:
use *warnings*; *# Provides warning messages; does not abort program*
use *diagnostics*; *# Provides detailed warnings; does not abort program*
use *strict*; *# Checks for global variable, unquoted words, etc.; aborts program*
use *Carp*; *# Like the* ***die*** *function with more information about program's errors*

2.2 Chapter Summary

This chapter was provided for programmers who need a quick peek at what Perl looks like, its general syntax, and programming constructs. It is an overview. There is a lot more to Perl as you'll see as you read through the following chapters.

Later, after you have programmed for awhile, this chapter can also serve as a little tutorial to refresh your memory without having to search through the index to find what you are looking for.

2.3 What's Next?

In Chapter 3, we will discuss Perl script setup; i.e., how to name a script, execute it, and add comments, statements, and built-in functions. We will also see how to use Perl command-line switches and how to identify certain types of errors.

chapter

3

Perl Scripts

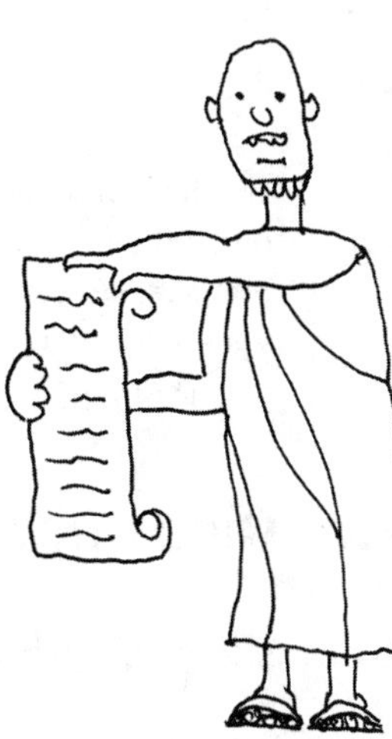

3.1 Script Setup

A Simple Perl Script

EXAMPLE 3.1

```
(The Script)
#!/usr/bin/perl
print "What is your name? ";
chomp($name = <STDIN>);  # Program waits for user input from keyboard
print "Welcome, $name, are you ready to learn Perl now? ";
chomp($response = <STDIN>);
$response=lc($response);  # response is converted to lowercase
if($response eq "yes" or $response eq "y"){
     print "Great! Let's get started learning Perl by example.\n";
}
else{
   print "O.K. Try again later.\n";
}
$now = localtime;  # Use a Perl function to get the date and time
print "$name, you ran this script on $now.\n";

(Output)
What is your name? Ellie
Welcome, Ellie, are you ready to learn Perl now? yes
Great! Let's get started learning Perl by example.
Ellie, you ran this script on Wed Apr  4 21:53:21 2007.
```

Example 3.1 is an example of a Perl script. In no time, you will be able to write a similar script. Perl scripts consist of a list of Perl statements and declarations. Statements are terminated with a semicolon (;). (Since only subroutines and report formats require declarations, they will be discussed when those topics are presented.) Variables can be created anywhere in the script and, if not initialized, automatically get a value of 0 or "null," depending on their context. Notice that the variables in this program start with a $. Values such as numbers, strings of text, or the output of functions can be assigned to variables. Different types of variables are preceded by different "funny symbols," as you'll see in Chapter 4.

Perl executes each statement just once, starting from the first to the last line.

3.2 The Script

3.2.1 Startup

UNIX/Mac OS. If the **first line** of the script contains the *#!* symbols (called the *shbang* line) followed by the full pathname of the file where your version of the Perl executable resides, this tells the kernel what program is interpreting the script. An example of the startup line might be

```
#!/usr/bin/perl
```

It is extremely important that the path to the interpreter is entered correctly after the *shbang* (*#!*). Perl may be installed in different directories on different systems. Most Web servers will look for this line when invoking CGI scripts written in Perl. Any inconsistency will cause a fatal error. To find the path to the Perl interpreter on your system, type at your UNIX prompt[1]:

```
which perl
```

If the *shbang* line is the first line of the script, you can execute the script directly from the command line by its name. If the *shbang* **is not the first line** of the script, the UNIX shell will try to interpret the program as a shell script, and the *shbang* line will be interpreted as a comment line. (See "Executing the Script" on page 36 for more on how to execute Perl programs.)

Mac OS is really just a version of UNIX and comes bundled with Perl 5.8. You open a terminal and use Perl exactly the same way you would use it for Solaris, Linux, *BSD, HP-UX, AIX OSX, etc.

Windows. Win32 platforms don't provide the *shbang* syntax or anything like it.[2] For Windows XP and Windows NT 4.0[3] you can associate a Perl script with extensions such as *.pl* or *.plx* and then run your script directly from the command line. At the command-line prompt or from the system control panel, you can set the *PATHEXT* environment

---

1. Another way to find the interpreter would be: *find / -name '*perl*' -print;*
2. Although Win32 platforms don't ordinarily require the *shbang* line, the Apache Web server does, so you will need the *shbang* line if you are writing CGI scripts that will be executed by Apache.
3. File association does not work on Windows 95 unless the program is started from the Explorer window.

variable to the name of the extension that will be associated with Perl scripts. At the command line, to set the environment variable, type

```
SET PATHEXT=.pl;%PATHEXT%
```

At the control panel, to make the association permanent, do the following:

1. Go to the Start menu.
2. Select Settings or just select Control Panel.
3. Select Control Panel.
4. In the control panel, click on the System icon.
5. Click on Advanced.
6. Click on Environment Variables.
7. Click on New.
8. Type *PATHEXT* in the Variable Name box.
9. In the Variable Value box, type the extension you want, followed by a semicolon and *%PATHEXT%*.
10. OK the setting.

From now on when you create a Perl script, append its name with the extension you have chosen, such as *myscript.pl* or *myscript.plx*. Then the script can be executed directly at the command line by just typing the script name without the extension, e.g., *myscript.pt*. (See “Executing the Script” on page 36 for more on script execution.)

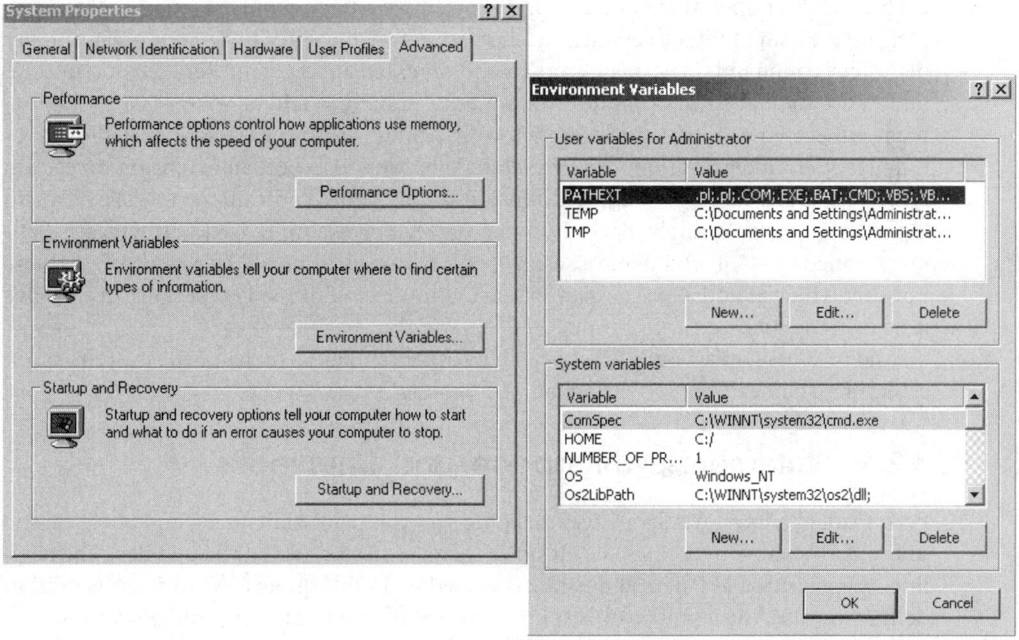

Figure 3.1 Setting the *PATHEXT* environment variable.

3.2.2 Finding a Text Editor

Since you will be using a text editor to write Perl scripts, you can use any of the editors provided by your operating system or download more sophisticated editors specifically designed for Perl, including third-party editors and Integrated Development Environments (IDEs). Table 3.1 lists some of the editors available.

Table 3.1 Types of Editors

BBEdit, JEdit	Macintosh
Wordpad, Notepad, UltraEdit, vim, PerlEdit, JEdit, TextPad	Windows
pico, vi, emacs, PerlEdit, JEdit	Linux/UNIX
Komodo	Linux, Mac OS, Windows
OptiPerl, PerlExpress	Windows
Affus	Mac OS X

3.2.3 Naming Perl Scripts

The only naming convention for a Perl script is that it follow the naming conventions for files on your operating system (upper-/lowercase letters, numbers, etc.). If, for example, you are using Linux, filenames are case sensitive, and since there are a great number of system commands, you may want to add an extension to your Perl script names to make sure the names are unique. You are not required to add an extension to the filename unless you are creating libraries or modules, writing CGI scripts if the server requires a specific extension, or have set up Windows to expect an extension on certain types of files. By adding a unique extension to the name, you can prevent clashes with other programs that might have the same name. For example, UNIX provides a command called "test". If you name a script "test", which version will be executed? If you're not sure, you can add a *.plx* or *.perl* extension to the end of the Perl script name to give it its own identity.

And of course, give your scripts sensible names that indicate the purpose of the script rather than names like "foo", "foobar", or "testing".

3.2.4 Statements, Whitespace, and Linebreaks

Perl is called a free-form language, meaning you can place statements anywhere on the line and even cross over lines. Whitespace refers to spaces, tabs, and newlines. The newline is represented as "\n" and must be enclosed in double quotes. Whitespace is used to delimit words. Any number of blank spaces are allowed between symbols and words. Whitespace enclosed in single or double quotes is preserved; otherwise, it is ignored. The following expressions are the same:

5+4*2 is the same as 5 + 4 * 2;

And both of the following Perl statements are correct even though the output will show that the whitespace is preserved when quoted.

```
print "This is a Perl statement.";

    print "This
                  is
                     also
                        a Perl
                             statement.";
```

Even though you have a lot of freedom when writing Perl scripts, it is better to put statements on their own line and to provide indentation when using blocks of statements (we'll discuss this in Chapter 5). Of course, annotating your program with comments, so that you and others will understand what is going on, is vitally important. See the next section for more on comments.

3.2.5 Comments

You may write a very clever Perl script today and in two weeks have no idea what your script was trying to do. If you pass the script on to someone else, the confusion magnifies. Comments are plain text that allow you to insert documentation in your Perl script with no effect on the execution of the program. They are used to help you and other programmers maintain and debug scripts. Perl comments are preceded by a # mark. They extend across the line, but do not continue onto the next line.

Perl does **not** understand the *C* language comments /* and */ or *C*++ comments //.

EXAMPLE 3.2

```
1   # This is a comment
2   print "hello";   # And this is a comment
```

EXPLANATION

1. Comments, as in UNIX shell, *sed*, and *awk* scripts, are lines preceded with the pound sign (#) and can continue to the end of the line.
2. Comments can be anywhere on the line. Here the comment follows a valid Perl *print* statement.

3.2.6 Perl Statements

Perl executable statements make up most of the Perl script. As in *C*, the statement is an expression, or series of expressions, terminated with a semicolon. Perl statements can be simple or compound, and a variety of operators, modifiers, expressions, and functions make up a statement, as shown in the following example.

```
print "Hello, to you!\n";
$now = localtime();
print "Today is $now.\n";
$result = 5 * 4 / 2;
print "Good-bye.\n";
```

3.2.7 Using Perl Built-in Functions

A big part of any programming language is the set of functions built into the language or packaged in special libraries (see Apendix A.1). Perl comes with many useful functions, independent program code that performs some task. When you call a Perl built-in function, you just type its name, or optionally you can type its name followed by a set of parentheses. All function names must be typed in lowercase. Many functions require arguments, messages that you send to the function. For example, the *print* function won't display anything if you don't pass it an argument, the string of text you want to print on the screen. If the function requires arguments, then place the arguments, separated by commas, right after the function name. The function usually returns something after it has performed its particular task. In the script shown at the beginning of this chapter, we called two built-in Perl functions, *print* and *localtime*. The *print* function took a string as its argument and displayed the string of text on the screen. The *localtime* function, on the other hand, didn't require an argument but returned the current date and time. Both of the following statements are valid ways to call a function with an argument. The argument is "Hello, there.\n"

```
print("Hello, there.\n");
print "Hello, there.\n";
```

3.2.8 Executing the Script

A Perl script can be executed at the command line directly by its name when the *#!* startup line is included in the script file and the script has execute permission (see Example 3.3) or, if using Windows, filename association has been set as discussed in "Startup" on page 32. If the *#!* is **not** the first line of the script, you can execute a script by passing the script as an argument to the Perl interpreter.
Perl will then compile and run your script using its own internal form. If you have syntax errors, Perl will let you know. You can check to see if your script has compiled successfully by using the *-c* switch as follows:

```
$ perl -c scriptname
```

To execute a script at either the UNIX or MS-DOS prompt, type

```
$ perl scriptname
```

3.2.9 Sample Script

The following example illustrates the five parts of a Perl script:

1. The startup line (UNIX)
2. Comments
3. The executable statements in the body of the script
4. Checking Perl syntax
5. The execution of the script (UNIX, Windows)

EXAMPLE 3.3

```
  $ cat first.perl        (UNIX display contents)
1 #!/usr/bin/perl
2 # My first Perl script

3 print "Hello to you and yours!\n";

4 $ perl -c first.perl    # The $ is the shell prompt
  first.perl syntax OK

5 $ chmod +x first.perl   (UNIX)

6 $ first.perl or ./first.perl
7 Hello to you and yours!
```

EXPLANATION

1 The startup line tells the shell where Perl is located.

2 A comment describes information the programmer wants to convey about the script.

3 An executable statement includes the *print* function.

4 The *-c* switch is used to check for syntax errors. Hopefully, everything is "OK."

5 The *chmod* command turns on execute permission.

6 The script is executed (as long as your UNIX path includes the "." directory). If you get "Command not found" (or a similar message), precede the script name with a dot and a forward slash.

7 The string *Hello to you and yours!* is printed on the screen.

EXAMPLE 3.4

```
$ type first.perl       (MS-DOS display contents)
# No startup line; This is a comment.
# My first Perl script
print "Hello to you and yours!\n";
```

EXAMPLE 3.4 (CONTINUED)

```
4   $ perl first.perl   (Both UNIX and Windows)
5   Hello to you and yours!
```

EXPLANATION

1 The startup line with *#!* is absent. It is not necessary when using Windows. If using ActiveState, you create a batch file with a utility called *pl2bat*.

2 This is a descriptive line; a comment explains that the startup line is missing.

3 An executable statement includes the *print* function.

4 At the command line, the Perl program takes the script name as an argument and executes the script. The script's output is printed. You can execute a Perl script this way with any operating system.

3.2.10 What Kinds of Errors to Expect

Expect to make errors and maybe lots of them. You may try many times before you actually get a program to run perfectly. Knowing your error messages is like knowing the quirks of your boss, mate, or even yourself. Some programmers make the same error over and over again. Don't worry. In time, you will learn what most of these messages mean and how to prevent them.

When you execute a Perl script, it takes just one step on your part, but internally the Perl interpreter takes two steps. First, it compiles the entire program into bytecode, an internal representation of the program. After that, Perl's bytecode engine runs the bytecode line by line. If you have compiler errors, such as a missing semicolon at the end of the line, misspelled keyword, or mismatched quotes, you will get what is called a syntax error. These types of errors are picked up by using the *-c* switch and are usually easy to find once you have become acquainted with them.

EXAMPLE 3.5

```
     (The Script)
    print "Hello, world";
1   print "How are you doing?
2   print "Have you found any problems in this script?";

(Output)
Bareword found where operator expected at errors.plx line 3, near
"print "Have"
  (Might be a runaway multi-line "" string starting on line 2)
        (Do you need to predeclare print?)
syntax error at errors.plx line 3, near "print "Have you "
Search pattern not terminated at errors.plx line 3.
```

EXPLANATION

1 This line should have a closing double quote and a terminating semicolon.

2 This Perl statement is correct, but Perl is still looking for the closing quote on the previous line and is confused by the word "print" on this line because this line is still part of the last line. Why? Because the previous line is missing a double quote and was not terminated with a semicolon. Whenever you see the word "runaway" in the error message, it usually means a quote that has "run away"; i.e., missing. If you see "Bareword," it means that a word has no quotes surrounding it.

After the program passes the compile phase (i.e., you don't get any syntax errors or complaints from the compiler), then you may get what are called runtime, or logical, errors. These errors are harder to find and are probably caused by not anticipating problems that might occur when the program starts running. Or it's possible that the program has faulty logic in the way it was designed. Runtime errors may be caused if a file or database you're trying to open doesn't exist, a user enters bad input, you get into an infinite loop, or you try to illegally divide by zero.Whatever the case, these problems, called "bugs," are harder to find. Perl comes with a debugger that is helpful in determining what caused these logical errors by letting you step through your program line by line. (See "Debugger" on page 858.)

3.3 Perl at the Command Line

Although most of your work with Perl will be done in scripts, Perl can also be executed at the command line for simple tasks, such as testing a function, a print statement, or simply testing Perl syntax. Perl has a number of command-line switches, also called command-line options, to control or modify its behavior. The switches discussed next are not a complete list (see Appendix A) but will demonstrate a little about Perl syntax at the command line.

When working at the command line, you will see a shell prompt. The shell is called a "command interpreter." UNIX shells such as *Korn* and *Bourne* display a default $ prompt, and *C* shell displays a % prompt. The UNIX, Linux (*bash* and *tcsh*), Mac OS shells are quite similar in how they parse the command line. By default, if you are using Windows XP or Vista, the MS-DOS shell is called *command.com,* and if you are using Windows NT, the command shell is a console application residing in *cmd.exe*. It too displays a $ prompt.[4] The Win32 shell has its own way of parsing the command line. Since most of your Perl programming will be done in script files, you will seldom need to worry about the shell's interaction, but when a script interfaces with the operating system, problems will occur unless you are aware of what commands you have and how the shell executes them on your behalf.

---

4. It is possible that your command-line prompt has been customized to contain the current directory, history number, drive number, etc.

3.3.1 The *-e* Switch

The *-e* switch allows Perl to **execute** Perl statements at the command line instead of from a script. This is a good way to test simple Perl statements before putting them into a script file.

EXAMPLE 3.6

```
1   $ perl -e 'print "hello dolly\n";'      # UNIX/Linux
    hello dolly
2   $ perl -e "print qq/hello dolly\n/;"    # Windows and UNIX/Linux
    hello dolly
```

EXPLANATION

1. Perl prints the string *hello dolly* to the screen followed by a newline *\n*. The dollar sign ($) is the UNIX shell prompt. The single quotes surrounding the Perl statement protect it from the UNIX shell when it scans and interprets the command line. This will fail to execute on a Windows system.
2. At the MS-DOS prompt, Perl statements must be enclosed in double quotes. The *qq* construct surrounding *hello dolly* is another way Perl represents double quotes. For example, *qq/hello/* is the same as *"hello"*. An error is displayed if you type the following at the MS-DOS prompt:

```
$ perl -e 'print "hello dolly\n";'
Can't find string terminator "" anywhere before EOF at -e line 1.
```

   Note: UNIX systems can use this format as well.

3.3.2 The *-n* Switch

If you need to print the contents of a file or search for a line that contains a particular pattern, the *-n* switch is used to implicitly loop through the file one line at a time. Like *sed* and *awk*, Perl uses powerful pattern-matching techniques for finding patterns in text. Only specified lines from the file are printed when Perl is invoked with the *-n* switch.

Reading from a File. The *-n* switch allows you to loop through a file whose name is provided at the command line. The Perl statements are enclosed in quotes, and the file or files are listed at the end of the command line.

EXAMPLE 3.7

```
(The Text File)
1   $ more emp.first
    Igor Chevsky:6/23/83:W:59870:25:35500:2005.50
    Nancy Conrad:6/18/88:SE:23556:5:15000:2500
    Jon DeLoar:3/28/85:SW:39673:13:22500:12345.75
    Archie Main:7/25/90:SW:39673:21:34500:34500.50
    Betty Bumble:11/3/89:NE:04530:17:18200:1200.75
```

EXAMPLE (CONTINUED) 3.7 (CONTINUED)

```
2  $ perl -ne 'print;' emp.first        # Windows: use double quotes
   Igor Chevsky:6/23/83:W:59870:25:35500:2005.50
   Nancy Conrad:6/18/88:SE:23556:5:15000:2500
   Jon DeLoar:3/28/85:SW:39673:13:22500:12345.75
   Archie Main:7/25/90:SW:39673:21:34500:34500.50
   Betty Bumble:11/3/89:NE:04530:17:18200:1200.75

3  $ perl -ne 'print if /^Igor/;' emp.first
   Igor Chevsky:6/23/83:W:59870:25:35500:2005.50
```

EXPLANATION

1 The text file *emp.first* is printed to the screen. Perl will use this filename as a command-line argument in line 2.

2 Perl prints all the lines in the file *emp.first* by implicitly looping through the file one line at a time. (Windows users should enclose the statement in double quotes instead of single quotes.)

3 Perl uses **regular expression** metacharacters to specify what patterns will be matched. The pattern *Igor* is placed within forward slashes and preceded by a caret (^). The caret is called a "beginning of line anchor." Perl prints only lines beginning with the pattern *Igor*. (Windows users should enclose the statement in double quotes instead of single quotes.)

Reading from a Pipe. Since Perl is just another program, the output of commands can be piped to Perl, and Perl output can be piped to other commands. Perl will use what comes from the pipe as input, rather than a file. The *-n* switch is needed so Perl can read the input coming in from the pipe.

EXAMPLE 3.8

```
(UNIX)
1  $ date | perl -ne 'print "Today is $_";'
2  Today is Mon Mar 12 20:01:58 PDT 2007

(Windows)
3  $ date /T | perl -ne "print qq/Today is $_/;"
4  Today is Tue 04/24/2007
```

EXPLANATION

1 The output of the UNIX *date* command is piped to Perl and stored in the $_ variable. The quoted string *Today is* and the contents of the $_ variable will be printed to the screen followed by a newline.

EXAMPLE 3.8 (CONTINUED)

2 The output illustrates that today's date was stored in the $_ variable.
3 The Windows *date* command takes */T* as an option that produces today's date. That ouput is piped to Perl and stored in the $_ variable. The double quotes are required around the print statement.

Perl can take its input from a file and send its output to a file using standard I/O redirection.

EXAMPLE 3.9

```
1   $ perl -ne 'print;' < emp.first
    Igor Chevsky:6/23/83:W:59870:25:35500:2005.50
    Nancy Conrad:6/18/88:SE:23556:5:15000:2500
    Jon DeLoar:3/28/85:SW:39673:13:22500:12345.75
    Archie Main:7/25/90:SW:39673:21:34500:34500.50
    Betty Bumble:11/3/89:NE:04530:17:18200:1200.75
2   $ perl -ne 'print' emp.first > emp.temp
```

EXPLANATION

1 Perl's input is taken from a file called *emp.first*. The output is sent to the screen. For Windows users, enclose the statement in double quotes instead of single quotes.
2 Perl's input is taken from a file called *emp.first*, and its output is sent to the file *emp.temp*. For Windows users, enclose the statement in double quotes instead of single quotes.

3.3.3 The *-c* Switch

As we demonstrated earlier in this chapter, the *-c* switch is used to check the Perl syntax without actually executing the Perl commands. If the syntax is correct, Perl will tell you so. It is a good idea to always check scripts with the *-c* switch. This is especially important with CGI scripts written in Perl, because error messages that are normally sent to the terminal screen are sent to a log file instead. (See also the *-w* switch in Chapter 4.)

EXAMPLE 3.10

```
1   print "hello';    Search pattern not terminated at  line 1.
  Can't find string terminator '"' anywhere before EOF at test.plx
2   print "hello";
    test.plx syntax OK
```

EXPLANATION

1 The string *hello* starts with a double quote but ends with a single quote. The quotes should be matched; i.e., the first double quote should be matched at the end of the string with another double quote but instead ends with a single quote. With the *-c* switch, Perl will complain if it finds syntax errors while compiling.

2 After correcting the previous problem, Perl lets you know that the syntax is correct.

3.4 What You Should Know

1. How do you set up a script?
2. How are statements terminated?
3. What is whitespace?
4. What is meant by free form?
5. What is a built-in function?
6. What is the #! line in UNIX?
7. How do you make the script executable?
8. Why use comments?
9. How do you execute a Perl script if not using the *shbang* line.
10. What comand-line option lets you check Perl syntax?
11. What is the *-e* switch for?

3.5 What's Next?

If you can't print what your program is supposed to do, it's like trying to read the mind of a person who can't speak. In the next chapter, we discuss Perl functions to print output to the screen (*stdout*) and how to format the output. You will learn how Perl views words, whitespace, literals, backslash sequences, numbers, and strings. You will learn how to use single, double, and backquotes and their alternative form. We will discuss *here documents* and how to use them in CGI scripts. You will also learn how to use warnings and diagnostics to help debug your scripts.

EXERCISE 3
Getting with It Syntactically

1. At the command-line prompt, write a Perl statement that will print

   Hello world!!
   Welcome to Perl programming.

2. Execute another Perl command that will print the contents of the *datebook* file. (The file is found on the accompanying CD.)

3. Execute a Perl command that will display the version of the Perl distribution you are currently using.

4. Copy the program sample in Example 3.1 into your editor, save it, check the syntax, and execute it.

chapter

4

Getting a Handle on Printing

4.1 The Filehandle

By convention, whenever your program starts execution, the parent process (normally a shell program) opens three predefined streams called *stdin*, *stdout*, and *stderr*. All three of these streams are connected to your terminal by default.

stdin is the place where input comes from, the terminal keyboard; *stdout* is where output normally goes, the screen; and *stderr* is where errors from your program are printed, also the screen.

Perl inherits *stdin*, *stdout*, and *stderr* from the shell. Perl does not access these streams directly but gives them names called *filehandles*. Perl accesses the streams via the filehandle. The filehandle for *stdin* is called *STDIN*; the filehandle for *stdout* is called *STDOUT*; and the filehandle for *stderr* is called *STDERR*. Later, we'll see how you can create your own filehandles, but for now we'll stick with the predefined ones.

The *print* and *printf* functions by default send their output to the *STDOUT* filehandle, your screen.

4.2 Words

When printing a list of words to *STDOUT*, it is helpful to understand how Perl views a word. Any unquoted word must start with an alphanumeric character. It can consist of other alphanumeric characters and an underscore. Perl words are case sensitive. If a word is unquoted, it could conflict with words used to identify filehandles, labels, and other reserved words. If you see the error "Bareword," it means that the word has not been surrounded by quotes. If the word has no special meaning to Perl, it will be treated as if surrounded by single quotes.

4.3 The *print* Function

The *print* function prints a string or a list of comma-separated words to the Perl filehandle *STDOUT*. If successful, the *print* function returns 1; if not, it returns 0.

The string literal \n adds a newline to the end of the string. It can be embedded in the string or treated as a separate string. To interpret backslashes, Perl requires that escape sequences like \n be enclosed in double quotes.

EXAMPLE 4.1

```
(The Script)
1   print "Hello", "world", "\n";
2   print "Hello world\n";

(Output)
1   Helloworld
2   Hello world
```

EXPLANATION

1 Each string passed to the *print* function is enclosed in double quotes and separated by a comma. To print whitespace, the whitespace must be enclosed within the quotes. The \n escape sequence must be enclosed in double quotes for it to be interpreted as a newline character.

2 The entire string is enclosed in double quotes and printed to standard output.

EXAMPLE 4.2

```
(The Script)
1   print Hello, world, "\n";

(Output)
1   No comma allowed after filehandle at ./perl.st line 1
```

EXPLANATION

1 If the strings are not quoted, the filehandle *STDOUT* must be specified, or the *print* function will treat the first word it encounters as a filehandle (i.e., the word *Hello* would be treated as a filehandle). The comma is not allowed after a filehandle; it is used only to separate strings that are to be printed.

EXAMPLE 4.3

```
(The Script)
1   print STDOUT Hello, world, "\n";

(Output)
1   Helloworld
```

EXPLANATION

1. The filehandle *STDOUT* must be specified if strings are not quoted. The *\n* must be double quoted if it is to be interpreted. It is not a good practice to use unquoted text in this way. Unquoted words are called "Barewords."
   Note: There is **no** comma after *STDOUT*.

4.3.1 Quotes

Quoting rules affect almost everything you do in Perl, especially when printing a string of words. Strings are normally delimited by a matched pair of either double or single quotes. When a string is enclosed in single quotes, all characters are treated as literals. When a string is enclosed in double quotes, however, **almost** all characters are treated as literals with the exception of those characters that are used for variable substitution and special escape sequences. We will look at the special escape sequences in this chapter and discuss quoting and variables in Chapter 5, "What's in a Name."

Perl uses some characters for special purposes, such as the dollar sign ($) and the (@) sign. If these special characters are to be treated as literal characters, they may be preceded by a backslash (\) or enclosed within single quotes (' '). The backslash is used to quote a single character rather than a string of characters.

EXAMPLE 4.4

```
(The Script)
1  $name="Ellie";
2  print "Hello, $name.\n";# $name and \n evaluated
3  print 'Hello, $name.\n';# String is literal; newline not
                           # interpreted

4  print "I don't care!\n";# \n is interpreted in double quotes
5  print 'I don\'t care!', "\n";# Backslash protects single quote
                                # in string "don\'t"

(Output)
2  Hello, Ellie.
3,4  Hello, $name.\nI don't care!
5 I don't care!
```

It is so common to make mistakes with quoting that we will introduce here the most common error messages you will receive resulting from mismatched quotes and bare words.

Think of quotes as being the "clothes" for Perl strings. If you take them off, you may get a "Bareword" message such as:

Bareword *"there" not allowed while "strict subs" in use at try.pl line 3. Execution of program.pl aborted due to compilation errors.*

Also think of quotes as being mates. A double quote is mated with a matching double quote, and a single quote with a matching single quote. If you don't match the quotes, if one is missing, the missing quote has "run away." Where did the mate go? You may receive an error like this:

(Might be a ***runaway*** *multi-line "" string starting on line 3)*

Breaking the Quoting Rules

EXAMPLE 4.5

```
(The Script)
   #!/usr/bin/perl
   # Program to illustrate printing literals
1  print "Hello, "I can't go there";  # Unmatched quotes
2  print "Good-bye";

(Output)
Bareword found where operator expected at qtest.plx line 2, near
""Hello, "I"
        (Missing operator before I?)
Bareword found where operator expected at qtest.plx line 3, near
"print "Good"
  (Might be a runaway multi-line "" string starting on line 2)
        (Do you need to predeclare print?)
String found where operator expected at qtest.plx line 3, at end of line
        (Missing semicolon on previous line?)
syntax error at qtest.plx line 2, near ""Hello, "I can't "
Can't find string terminator '"' anywhere before EOF at qtest.plx line 3
```

EXPLANATION

1. The string *"Hello* starts with an opening double quote but is missing the ending quote. This cascades into a barrage of troubles. Perl assumes the double quote preceding the word "I" is the mate for the first quote in "Hello." That leaves the rest of the string "I can't go there" exposed as a bare string. The double quote at the end of the line will be mated with the double quote on the next line. Not good.
2. The word "Good_bye" is considered a bareword because Perl can't find an opening quote. The double quote at the end of "there" on line 1 has been matched with the double quote at the beginning of "Good-bye," leaving "Good-bye" exposed and bare, with an unmatched quote at the end of the string. Ugh!

4.3.2 Literals (Constants)

When assigning literal values[1] to variables or printing literals, the literals can be represented numerically as integers in decimal, octal, or hexadecimal or as floats in floating point or scientific notation.

Strings enclosed in double quotes may contain string literals, such as *\n* for the newline character, *\t* for a tab character, or *\e* for an escape character. String literals are alphanumeric (**and only alphanumeric**) characters preceded by a backslash. They may be represented in decimal, octal, or hexadecimal or as control characters.

Perl also supports special literals for representing the current script name, the line number of the current script, and the logical end of the current script.

Since you will be using literals with the *print* and *printf* functions, let's see what these literals look like. (For more on defining constants, see the "*constant*" pragma in Appendix A.)

Numeric Literals. Literal numbers can be represented as positive or negative integers in decimal, octal, or hexadecimal (see Table 4.1). Floats can be represented in floating point notation or scientific notation. Octal numbers contain a leading *0* (zero), hex numbers a leading *0x* (zero and x), and numbers represented in scientific notation contain a trailing *E* followed by a negative or positive number representing the exponent.

Table 4.1 Numeric Literals

Example	*Description*
12345	Integer
0b1101	Binary
0x456fff	Hex
0777	Octal
23.45	Float
.234E–2	Scientific notation

String Literals. Like shell strings, Perl strings are normally delimited by either single or double quotes. Strings containing string literals, also called **escape sequences**, are delimited by **double quotes** for backslash interpretation (see Table 4.2).

---

1. Literals may also be called constants, but the Perl experts prefer the term "literal," so in deference to them, we'll use the term "literal."

Table 4.2 String Literals

Escape Sequences	*Descriptions (ASCII Name)*
\t	Tab
\n	Newline
\r	Carriage return
\f	Form feed
\b	Backspace
\a	Alarm/bell
\e	Escape
\033	Octal character
\xff	Hexadecimal character
\c[	Control character
\l	Next character is converted to lowercase
\u	Next character is converted to uppercase
\L	Next characters are converted to lowercase until *\E* is found
\U	Next characters are converted to uppercase until *\E* is found
\Q	Backslash all following nonalphanumeric characters until *\E* is found
\E	Ends upper- or lowercase conversion started with *\L* or *\U*
\\	Backslash

EXAMPLE 4.6

```
print "This string contains \t\ttwo tabs and a newline.\n" # Double quotes
(Output)
This string containstabs and a newline.

print 'This string contains\t\ttwo tabs and a newline.\n; #Single quotes
(Output)
This string contains\t\ttwo tabs and a newline.\n
```

Special Literals. Perl's special literals *__LINE__* and *__FILE__* are used as separate words and will **not** be interpreted if enclosed in quotes, single or double. They represent the current line number of your script and the name of the script, respectively. These special literals are equivalent to the predefined special macros used in the *C* language.

The *__END__* special literal is used in scripts to represent the logical end of the file. Any trailing text following the *__END__* literal will be ignored, just as if it had been commented. The control sequences for end of input in UNIX is *<Ctrl>-d* (*\004*), and *<Ctrl>-z* (*\032*) in MS-DOS; both are synonyms for *__END__*.

The *__DATA__* special literal is used as a filehandle to allow you to process textual data from within the script instead of from an external file.

EXAMPLE 4.7

```
print "The script is called", __FILE__, "and we are on line number ",
__LINE__,"\n";
(Output)
The script is called ./testing.plx and we are on line number 2
```

Note: There are two underscores on either side of the special literals (see Table 4.3).

Table 4.3 Special Literals

Literal	***Description***
__LINE__	Represents the current line number
__FILE__	Represents the current filename
__END__	Represents the logical end of the script; trailing garbage is ignored
__DATA__	Represents a special filehandle
__PACKAGE__	Represents the current package; default package is *main*

4.3.3 Printing Literals

Now that you know what the literals look like, let's see how they are used with the *print* function.

Printing Numeric Literals

EXAMPLE 4.8

```
(The Script)
    #!/usr/bin/perl
    # Program to illustrate printing literals
1   print "The price is $100.\n";
2   print "The price is \$100.\n";
3   print "The price is \$",100, ".\n";
4   print "The binary number is converted to: ",0b10001,".\n";
5   print "The octal number is converted to: ",0777,".\n";
6   print "The hexadecimal number is converted to: ",0xAbcF,".\n";
7   print "The unformatted number is ", 14.56, ".\n";
8   $now = localtime(); # A Perl function
9   $name = "Ellie"; # A string is assigned to a Perl variable
10  print "Today is $now, $name.";
11  print ‘Today is $now, $name.’;
```

```
(Output)
1   The price is .
2   The price is $100.
3   The price is $100.
4   The binary number is converted to: 17.
5   The octal number is converted to: 511.
6   The hexadecimal number is converted to: 43983.
7   The unformatted number is 14.56.
10  Today is Sat Mar 24 15:46:08 2007, Ellie.
11  Today is $now, $name.
```

EXPLANATION

1 The string *The price is $100* is enclosed in double quotes. The dollar sign is a special Perl character. It is used to reference scalar variables (see Chapter 5, "What's in a Name"), not money. Therefore, since there is no variable called *$100*, nothing prints. Since single quotes protect all characters from interpretation, they would have sufficed here, or the dollar sign could have been preceded with a backslash. But when surrounded by single quotes, the *\n* will be treated as a literal string rather than a newline character.

2 The backslash quotes the dollar sign, so it is treated as a literal.

3 To be treated as a numeric literal, rather than a string, the number *100* is a single word. The dollar sign must be escaped even if it is not followed by a variable name. The *\n* must be enclosed within double quotes if it is to be interpreted as a special string literal.

4 The number is represented as a binary number because of the leading *0b* (zero and b). The decimal value is printed.

EXPLANATION (CONTINUED)

5 The number is represented as an octal value because of the leading *0* (zero). The decimal value is printed.

6 The number is represented as a hexadecimal number because of the leading *0x* (zero and x). The decimal value is printed.

7 The number, represented as *14.56*, is printed as is. The *print* function does not format output.

8 Perl has a large set of functions. You have already learned about the *print* function. The *localtime()* function is another. (The parentheses are optional.) This functions returns the current date and time. We are assigning the result to a Perl variable called *$now*. You will learn all about variables in the next chapter.

9 The variable *$name* is assigned the string "Ellie".

10 When the string is enclosed in double quotes, the *print* function will display the value of the variables *$now* and *$name*.

11 When the string is enclosed in single quotes, the *print* function prints all characters literally.

Printing String Literals

EXAMPLE 4.9

```
(The Script)
   #!/usr/bin/perl
1  print "***\tIn double quotes\t***\n";    # Backslash interpretation
2  print '%%%\t\tIn single quotes\t\t%%%\n'; # All characters are
                                             # printed as literals
3  print "\n";

(Output)
1  ***      In double quotes        ***
2  %%%\t\tIn single quotes\t\t%%%\n
3
```

EXPLANATION

1 When a string is enclosed in double quotes, backslash interpretation is performed. The \t is a string literal and produces a tab; the \n produces a newline.

2 When enclosed within single quotes, the special string literals \t and \n are not interpreted. They will be printed as is.

3 The newline \n must be enclosed in double quotes to be interpreted. A "\n" produces a newline.

EXAMPLE 4.10

```
(The Script)
    #!/usr/bin/perl
1   print "\a\t\tThe \Unumber\E \LIS\E ",0777,".\n";

(Output)
1   (BEEP)          The NUMBER is 511.
```

EXPLANATION

1 The *\a* produces an alarm or beep sound, followed by *\t\t* (two tabs). *\U* causes the string to be printed in uppercase until *\E* is reached or the line terminates. The string *number* is printed in uppercase until the *\E* is reached. The string *is* is to be printed in lowercase, until the *\E* is reached, and the decimal value for octal *0777* is printed, followed by a period and a newline character.

Printing Special Literals

EXAMPLE 4.11

```
(The Script)
    #!/usr/bin/perl
    # Program, named literals.perl, written to test special literals
1   print "We are on line number ", __LINE__, ".\n";
2   print "The name of this file is ",__FILE__,".\n";
3   __END__
    And this stuff is just a bunch of chitter-chatter that is to be
     ignored by Perl.
    The __END__ literal is like Ctrl-d or \004.[a]

(Output)
1   We are on line number 3.
2   The name of this file is literals.perl.
```

a. See the *-x* switch in Appendix A for discarding leading garbage.

EXPLANATION

1 The special literal __LINE__ cannot be enclosed in quotes if it is to be interpreted. It holds the current line number of the Perl script.
2 The name of this script is *literals.perl*. The special literal __FILE__ holds the name of the current Perl script.
3 The special literal __END__ represents the logical end of the script. It tells Perl to ignore any characters that follow it.

EXAMPLE 4.12

```
(The Script)
    #!/usr/bin/perl
    # Program, named literals.perl2,
    # written to test special literal __DATA__
1   print <DATA>;
2   __DATA__
    This line will be printed.
    And so will this one.

(Output)
This line will be printed.
And so will this one.
```

EXPLANATION

1. The *print* function will display whatever text is found under the special literal *__DATA__*. Because the special literal *__DATA__* is enclosed in angle brackets, it is treated as a filehandle opened for reading. The *print* function will display lines as they are read by *<DATA>*.
2. This is the data that is used by the *<DATA>* filehandle. (You could use *__END__* instead of *__DATA__* to get the same results.)

4.3.4 The *warnings* Pragma and the *-w* Switch

The *-w* switch is used to warn you about the possibility of using future reserved words and a number of other problems that may cause problems in the program. (Often, these warnings are rather cryptic and hard to understand if you are new to programming.) Larry Wall says in the Perl 5 *man* pages, "Whenever you get mysterious behavior, try the *-w* switch! Whenever you don't get mysterious behavior, try the *-w* switch anyway."

You can use the *-w* switch either as a command-line option to Perl, as

```
perl -w <scriptname>
```

or after the *shbang* line in the Perl script, such as

```
#!/usr/bin/perl -w
```

A pragma is a special Perl module that hints to the compiler about how a block of statements should be compiled. You can use this type of module to help control the way your program behaves. Starting with Perl version 5.6.0, *warnings.pm* was added to the standard Perl library; similar to the *-w* switch, it is a pragma that allows you to control the types of warnings printed.

In your programs, add the following line under the *#!* line or, if not using the *#!* line, at the top of the script:

```
use warnings;
```

This enables all possible warnings. To turn off warnings, simply add as a line in your script

```
no warnings;
```

This disables all possible warnings for the rest of the script.

EXAMPLE 4.13

```
    (The Script)
        #!/usr/bin/perl
        # Scriptname: warnme
    1   print STDOUT Ellie, what\'s up?;

(Output) (At the Command Line)
$ perl -w warnme
  Unquoted string "what" may clash with future reserved word at warnme line 3.
  Backslash found where operator expected at warnme line 3, near "what\"
  Syntax error at warnme line 3, near "what\"
  Can't find string terminator "'" anywhere before EOF at warnme line 3.
```

EXPLANATION

1. Among many other messages, the *-w* switch (see Appendix A) prints warnings about ambiguous identifiers, such as variables that have been used only once, improper conversion of strings and numbers, etc. Since the string *Ellie* is not quoted, Perl could mistake it for a reserved word or an undefined filehandle. The rest of the error message results from having an unmatched quote in the string.

EXAMPLE 4.14

```
    (The Script)
        #!/usr/bin/perl
        # Scriptname: warnme
    1   use warnings;
    2   print STDOUT Ellie, what\'s up?;

(Output)
Unquoted string "what" may clash with future reserved word at warnme line 3.
Backslash found where operator expected at warnme line 3, near "what\"
Syntax error at warnme line 3, near "what\"
Can't find string terminator "'" anywhere before EOF at warnme line 3.
```

EXPLANATION

In Perl versions 5.6 and later, the *warnings* pragma is used instead of the *-w* switch. The *use* function allows you to use modules located in the standard Perl library. The *warnings* pragma sends warnings about ambiguous identifiers. Since the string *Ellie* is not quoted, Perl could mistake it for a reserved word or an undefined filehandle. The compiler complains because the string is not terminated with a closing quote.

4.3.5 The *diagnostics* Pragma

This special pragma enhances the warning messages to a more verbose explanation of what went wrong in your program. Like the *warnings* pragma, it affects the compilation phase of your program, but unlike the warnings pragma, it attempts to give you an explanation that doesn't assume you are an experienced programmer.

EXAMPLE 4.15

```
(The Script)
use diagnostics;
print "Hello there';  # Unmatched quote
print "We are on line number ", _ _LINE_ _,"\n";

(The output)
Bareword found where operator expected at test.plx line 3, near "$now
= "Ellie"
  (Might be a runaway multi-line "" string starting on line 2) (#1)
    (S syntax) The Perl lexer knows whether to expect a term or an
operator.
    If it sees what it knows to be a term when it was expecting to see
    an operator, it gives you this warning.  Usually it indicates that
    an operator or delimiter was omitted, such as a semicolon.

        (Missing operator before Ellie?)
String found where operator expected at test.plx line 3, at end of
line (#1)
        (Missing semicolon on previous line?)

syntax error at test.plx line 3, near "$now = "Ellie"
Can't find string terminator '"' anywhere before EOF at test.plx line
3 (#2)
    (F) Probably means you had a syntax error.  Common reasons
include:

        A keyword is misspelled.
        A semicolon is missing.
        A comma is missing.
        An opening or closing parenthesis is missing.
print "hello there';
print "We are on line number ", _ _LINE_ _,"\n";
```

EXPLANATION

In Perl versions 5.6 and later, the *diagnostics* pragma is used instead of the *-w* switch or the *warnings* pragma. This special Perl module sends detailed messages about the problems that occurred in the script. Since the string *Hello there* does not contain matched quotes, the *diagnostics* pragma issues a list of all the potential causes for the failed program. The compiler expects the string to be terminated with another double quote.

4.3.6 The *strict* Pragma and Words

Another pragma we will mention now is the *strict* pragma. If your program disobeys the restrictions placed on it, it won't compile. If there is a chance that you might have used "bare," i.e., unquoted, words[2] as in Example 4.15, the *strict* pragma will catch you and your program will abort. The *strict* pragma can be controlled by giving it various arguments. (See Appendix A for complete list.)

EXAMPLE 4.16

```
(The Script)
    #!/usr/bin/perl
    # Program: stricts.test
    # Script to demonstrate the strict pragma
1   use strict "subs";
2   $name = Ellie;                # Unquoted word Ellie
3   print "Hi $name.\n";


(Output)
$ stricts.test
  Bareword "Ellie" not allowed while "strict subs" in use at
./stricts.test line 5.
  Execution of stricts.test aborted due to compilation errors.
```

EXPLANATION

1 The *use* function allows you to use modules located in the standard Perl library. When the *strict* pragma takes *subs* as an argument, it will catch any barewords found in the program while it is being internally compiled. If a bareword is found, the program will be aborted with an error message.

2. Putting quotes around a word is like putting clothes on the word—take off the quotes, and the word is "bare."

4.4 The *printf* Function

The *printf* function prints a formatted string to the selected filehandle, the default being *STDOUT*. It is like the *printf* function used in the *C* and *awk* languages. The return value is *1* if *printf* is successful and *0* if it fails.

The *printf* function consists of a quoted control string that may include format specifications. The quoted string is followed by a comma and a list of comma-separated arguments, which are simply expressions. The format specifiers are preceded by a % sign. For each % sign and format specifier, there must be a corresponding argument. (See Tables 4.4 and 4.5.)

Placing the quoted string and expressions within parentheses is optional.

EXAMPLE 4.17

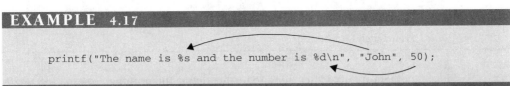

```
printf("The name is %s and the number is %d\n", "John", 50);
```

EXPLANATION

1 The string to be printed is enclosed in double quotes. The first format specifier is *%s*. It has a corresponding argument, *John*, positioned directly to the right of the comma after the closing quote in the control string. The *s* following the percent sign is called a **conversion character**. The *s* means *string* conversion will take place at this spot. In this case *John* will replace the *%s* when the string is printed.

2 The *%d* format specifies that the decimal (integer) value *50* will be printed in its place within the string.

Table 4.4 Format Specifiers

Conversion	***Definition***
%b	Unsigned binary integer
%c	Character
%d, i	Decimal number
%e	Floating point number in scientific notation
%E	Floating point number in scientific notation using capital *E*
%f, %F	Floating point number
%g	Floating point number using either *e* or *f* conversion, whichever takes the least space
%G	Floating point number using either *e* or *f* conversion, whichever takes the least space
%ld, %D	Long decimal number

Continues

Table 4.4 Format Specifiers (continued)

Conversion	Definition
%lu, %U	Long unsigned decimal number
%lo, %O	Long octal number
%p	Pointer (hexadecimal)
%s	String
%u	Unsigned decimal number
%x	Hexadecimal number
%X	Hexadecimal number using capital *X*
%lx	Long hexidecimal number
%%	Print a literal percent sign

Flag modifiers are used after the % to further define the printing; for example, *%-20s* represents a 20-character left-justified field.

Table 4.5 Flag Modifiers

Conversion	Definition
%-	Left-justification modifier
%#	Integers in octal format are displayed with a leading *0*; integers in hexadecimal form are displayed with a leading *0x*
%+	For conversions using *d*, *e*, *f*, and *g*, integers are displayed with a numeric sign, + or -
%0	The displayed value is padded with zeros instead of whitespace
%number	Maximum field width; for example, if number is 6, as in *%6d*, maximum field width is six digits
%.number	Precision of a floating point number; for example, *%.2f* specifies a precision of two digits to the right of the decimal point, and *%8.2* represents a maximum field width of eight, where one of the characters is a decimal point followed by two digits after the decimal point

When an argument is printed, the **field** holds the value that will be printed, and the **width** of the field is the number of characters the field should contain. The width of a field is specified by a percent sign and a number representing the maximum field width, followed by the conversion character; for example, *%20s* is a right-justified 20-character string; *%-25s* is a left-justified 25-character string; and *%10.2f* is a right-justified 10-character floating point number, where the decimal point counts as one of the characters and the precision is two places to the right of the decimal point. If the argument exceeds the maximum field width, *printf* will **not** truncate the number, but your formatting may not look nice. If the number to the right of the decimal point is truncated, it will be rounded up; for example, if the formatting instruction is *%.2f*, the corresponding argument, *56.555555*, would be printed as *56.6*.

EXAMPLE 4.18

```
(The Script)
    #!/usr/bin/perl
1   printf "Hello to you and yours %s!\n","Sam McGoo!";
2   printf("%-15s%-20s\n", "Jack", "Sprat");
3   printf "The number in decimal is %d\n", 45;
4   printf "The formatted number is |%10d|\n", 100;
5   printf "The number printed with leading zeros is |%010d|\n", 5;

6   printf "Left-justified the number is |%-10d|\n", 100;
7   printf "The number in octal is %o\n",15;
8   printf "The number in hexadecimal is %x\n", 15;
9   printf "The formatted floating point number is |%8.2f|\n",
       14.3456;
10  printf "The floating point number is |%8f|\n", 15;
11  printf  "The character is %c\n", 65;

(Output)
1   Hello to you and yours Sam McGoo!
2   Jack                Sprat
3   The number in decimal is 45
4   The formatted number is |       100|
5   The number printed with leading zeros is |0000000005|.
6   Left-justified the number is |100       |
7   The number in octal is 17
8   The number in hexadecimal is f
9   The formatted floating point number is |   14.35|
10  The floating point number is |15.000000|
11  The character is A
```

EXPLANATION

1. The quoted string contains the *%s* format conversion specifier. The string *Sam Magoo* is converted to a string and replaces the *%s* in the printed output.
2. The string *Jack* has a field width of 15 characters and is left-justified. The string *Sprat* has a field width of 20 characters and is also left-justified. Parentheses are optional.
3. The number *45* is printed in decimal format.
4. The number *100* has a field width of 10 and is right-justified.

EXPLANATION (CONTINUED)

5 The number *5* has a field width of 10, is right-justified, and is preceded by leading zeros rather than whitespace. If the modifier *0* is placed before the number representing the field width, the number printed will be padded with leading zeros if it takes up less space than it needs.
6 The number *100* has a field width of 10 and is left-justified.
7 The number *15* is printed in octal.
8 The number *15* is printed in hexadecimal.
9 The number *14.3456* is given a field width of eight characters. One of them is the decimal point; the fractional part is given a precision of two decimal places. The number is then rounded up.
10 The number *15* is given a field width of eight characters, right-justified. The default precision is six decimal places to the right of the decimal point.
11 The number *65* is converted to the ASCII character *A* and printed.

4.4.1 The *sprintf* Function

The *sprintf* function is just like the *printf* function, except it allows you to assign the formatted string to a variable. *sprintf* and *printf* use the same conversion tables (Tables 4.4 and 4.5). Variables are discussed in Chapter 5, "What's in a Name."

EXAMPLE 4.19

```
(The Script)
1   $string = sprintf("The name is: %10s\nThe number is: %8.2f\n",
                      "Ellie", 33);
2   print "$string";

(Output)
2   The name is:       Ellie
    The number is:     33.00
```

EXPLANATION

1 The *sprintf* function follows the same rules as *printf* for conversion of characters, strings, and numbers. The only real difference is that *sprintf* allows you to store the formatted output in a variable. In this example, the formatted output is stored in the scalar variable *$string*. The *\n* inserted in the string causes the remaining portion of the string to be printed on the next line. Scalar variables are discussed in Chapter 5, "What's in a Name." Parentheses are optional.
2 The value of the variable is printed showing the formatted output produced by *sprintf*.

4.4.2 Printing without Quotes—The *here document*

The Perl *here document* is derived from the UNIX shell *here document*. It allows you to quote a whole block of text enclosed between words called user-defined terminators. From the first terminator to the last terminator, the text is quoted, or you could say "from *here* to *here*" the text is quoted. The *here document* is a line-oriented form of quoting, requiring the << operator followed by an initial terminating word and a semicolon. There can be no spaces after the << unless the terminator itself is quoted. If the terminating word is not quoted or double quoted, variable expansion is performed. If the terminating word is singly quoted, variable expansion is not performed. Each line of text is inserted between the first and last terminating word. The final terminating word must be on a line by itself, with no surrounding whitespace.

Perl, unlike the shell, does not perform command substitution (backquotes) in the text of a *here document*. Perl, on the other hand, does allow you to execute commands in the *here document* if the terminator is enclosed in backquotes. (Not a good idea.)

Here documents are used extensively in CGI scripts for enclosing large chunks of HTML tags for printing.

EXAMPLE 4.20

```
(The Script)
1   $price=1000;     # A variable is assigned a value.
2   print <<EOF;
3   The consumer commented, "As I look over my budget, I'd say
4   the price of $price is right. I'll give you \$500 to start."\n
5   EOF

6   print <<'FINIS';
    The consumer commented, "As I look over my budget, I'd say
7   the price of $price is too much.\n I'll settle for $500."
8   FINIS

9   print << x 4;
    Here's to a new day.
    Cheers!
10
    print "\nLet's execute some commands.\n";
    # If terminator is in backquotes, will execute OS commands
11  print <<`END`;
    echo Today is
    date
    END

(Output)
3   The consumer commented, "As I look over my budget, I'd say
    the price of 1000 is right. I'll give you $500 to start."
```

EXAMPLE 4.20 (CONTINUED)

```
6   The consumer commented, "As I look over my budget, I'd say
    the price of $price is too much. \n I'll settle for $500."
9   Here's to a new day.
    Cheers!
    Here's to a new day.
    Cheers!
    Here's to a new day.
    Cheers!
    Here's to a new day.
    Cheers!
11  Let's execute some commands.
    Today is
    Fri Oct 27 12:48:36 PDT 2007
```

EXPLANATION

1 A scalar variable, *$price*, is assigned the value *1000*.

2 Start of *here document*. *EOF* is the terminator. The block is treated as if in double quotes. If there is any space preceding the terminator, then enclose the terminator in double quotes, such as *"EOF"*.

3 All text in the body of the *here document* is quoted as though the whole block of text were surrounded by double quotes.

4 The dollar sign has a special meaning when enclosed in double quotes. Since the text in this *here document* is treated as if in double quotes, the variable has special meaning here as well. The $ is used to indicate that a scalar variable is being used. The value of the variable will be interpreted. If a backslash precedes the dollar sign, it will be treated as a literal. If special backslash sequences are used, such as *\n*, they will be interpreted.

5 End of *here document* marked by matching terminator, *EOF.* There can be no space surrounding the terminator.

6 By surrounding the terminator, *FINIS*, with single quotes, the text that follows will be treated literally, turning off the meaning of any special characters, such as the dollar sign or backslash sequences.

7 Text is treated as if in single quotes.

8 Closing terminator marks the end of the *here document*.

9 The value *x 4* says that the text within the *here document* will be printed four times. The *x* operator is called the *repetition operator*. There must be a **blank line** at the end of the block of text, so that the *here document* is terminated.

10 The blank line is required here to end the *here document*.

11 The terminator is enclosed in backquotes. The shell will execute the commands between *`END`* and *END*. This example includes UNIX commands. If you are using another operating system, such as Windows or Mac OS, the commands must be compatible with that operating system.

***Here Documents* and CGI.** The following program is called a CGI (Common Gateway Interface) program, a simple Perl program executed by a Web server rather than by the shell. It is just like any other Perl script with two exceptions:

1. There is a line called the MIME line (e.g., *Content-type: text/html*) that describes what kind of content will be sent back to the browser.
2. The document consists of text embedded with HTML tags, the language used by browsers to render text in different colors, fonts faces, types, etc. Many CGI programmers take advantage of the *here document* to avoid using the *print* function for every line of the program.

CGI programs are stored in a special directory called *cgi-bin,* which is normally found under the Web server's root directory. See Chapter 16, "CGI and Perl: The Hyper Dynamic Duo," for a complete discussion of CGI.

To execute the following script, you will start up your Web browser and type in the Location box: *http://servername/cgi-bin/scriptname.*[3] See Figure 4.1.

EXAMPLE 4.21

```
   #!/bin/perl
   # The HTML tags are embedded in the here document to avoid using
   # multiple print statements
1  print <<EOF;      # here document in a CGI script
2  Content-type: text/html
3
4  <HTML><HEAD><TITLE>Town Crier</TITLE></HEAD>
   <H1><CENTER>Hear ye, hear ye, Sir Richard cometh!!</CENTER></H1>
   </HTML>
5  EOF
```

EXPLANATION

1 The *here document* starts here. The terminating word is *EOF.* The *print* function will receive everything from *EOF* to *EOF.*

2 This line tells the browser that the type of content that is being sent is text mixed with HTML tags. This line **must** be followed by a blank line.

4 The body of the document consists of text and HTML tags.

5 The word *EOF* marks the end of the *here document.*

---

3. You must supply the correct server name for your system and the correct filename. Some CGI files must have a *.cgi* or *.pl* extension.

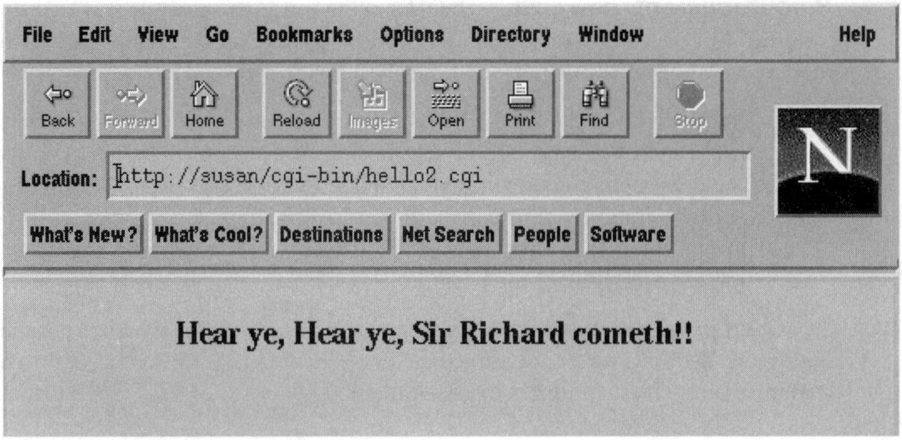

Figure 4.1 The Web browser in Example 4.21.

4.5 What You Should Know

1. How do you define *stdin*, *stdout*, and *stderr*?
2. What is meant by the term "filehandle"?
3. How do you represent a number in octal? Hexadecimal? Binary?
4. What is the main difference between the *print* and *printf* functions?
5. How do double and single quotes differ in the way they treat a string?
6. What are "literals"?
7. What is the use of _ _END_ _?
8. What are backslash sequences?
9. What is the purpose of the *sprintf* function?
10. What is a pragma?
11. How can you check to make sure your syntax is ok?
12. What is a *here document*? How is it useful in CGI programs?

4.6 What's Next?

In the next chapter, you will learn about Perl variables and the meaning of the "funny symbols." You will be able to create and access scalars, arrays, and hashes understand context and namespaces. You will also learn how to get input from a user and why we need to "chomp." A number of array and hash functions will be introduced.

EXERCISE 4
A String of Perls

1. Use the *print* function to output the following string:

   "Ouch," cried Mrs. O'Neil, "You musn't do that Mr. O'Neil!"

2. Use the *printf* function to print the number $34.6666666 as $34.67.

3. Write a Perl script called *literals.plx* that will print the following:

```
$ perl literals
Today is Mon Mar 12 12:58:04 PDT 2007  (Use localtime())
The name of this PERL SCRIPT is literals.
Hello. The number we will examine is 125.5.
The NUMBER in decimal is 125.
The following number is taking up 20 spaces and is right justified.
|                    125|
                The number in hex is 7d
                The number in octal is 175
The number in scientific notation is 1.255000e+02
The unformatted number is 125.500000
The formatted number is 125.50
My boss just said, "Can't you loan me $12.50 for my lunch?"
I flatly said, "No way!"
Good-bye (Makes a beep sound)
```

   Note: The words PERL SCRIPT and NUMBER are capitalized by using string literal escape sequences.

   What command-line option would you use to check the syntax of your script?

4. Add to your literals script a *here document* to print:

   Life is good with Perl.
   I have just completed my second exercise!

5. How would you turn on warnings in the script? How would you turn on diagnostics?

chapter

5

What's in a Name

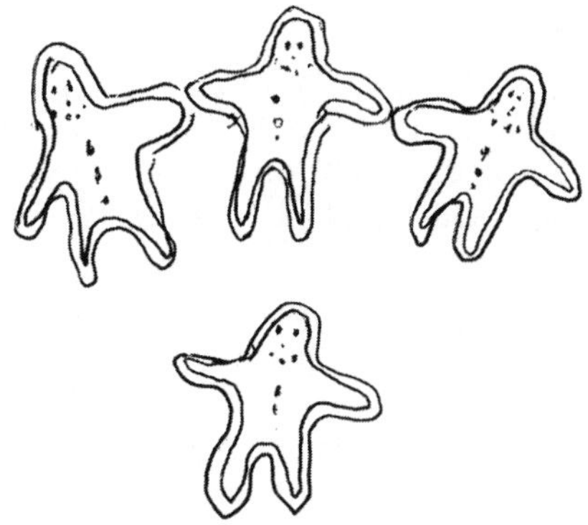

5.1 About Perl Variables

Before starting this chapter, a note to you, the reader. Each line of code in an example is numbered. The output and explanations are also numbered to match the number in the code. These numbers are provided to help you understand important lines of each program. When copying examples into your text editor, don't include these numbers, or you will generate many unwanted errors! With that said, let's proceed.

5.1.1 Types

Variables are fundamental to all programming languages. They are data items whose values may change throughout the run of the program, whereas literals or constants remain fixed. They can be placed anywhere in the program and do not have to be declared as in other higher languages, where you must specify the data type that will be stored there. You can assign strings, numbers, or a combination of these to Perl variables. For example, you may store a number in a variable and then later change your mind and store a string there. Perl doesn't care.

Perl variables are of three types: scalar, array, and associative array (more commonly called hashes). A scalar variable contains a single value (e.g., one string or one number), an array variable contains an ordered list of values indexed by a positive number, and a hash contains an unordered set of key/value pairs indexed by a string (the key) that is associated with a corresponding value. (See "Scalars, Arrays, and Hashes" on page 77.)

5.1.2 Scope and the Package

The scope of a variable determines where it is visible in the program. In Perl scripts, the variable is visible to the entire script (i.e., global in scope) and can be changed anywhere within the script.

The Perl sample programs you have seen in the previous chapters are compiled internally into what is called a **package**, which provides a **namespace** for variables. Almost all variables are **global** within that package. A global variable is known to the whole package and, if changed anywhere within the package, the change will permanently affect the variable. The default package is called *main*, similar to the *main()* function in the *C* language. Such variables in *C* would be classified as **static**. At this point, you don't have to worry about naming the *main* package or the way in which it is handled during the compilation process. The only purpose in mentioning packages now is to let you know that the scope of variables in the *main* package, your script, is global. Later, when we talk about the *our*, *local*, and *my* functions in packages, you will see that it is possible to change the scope and namespace of a variable.

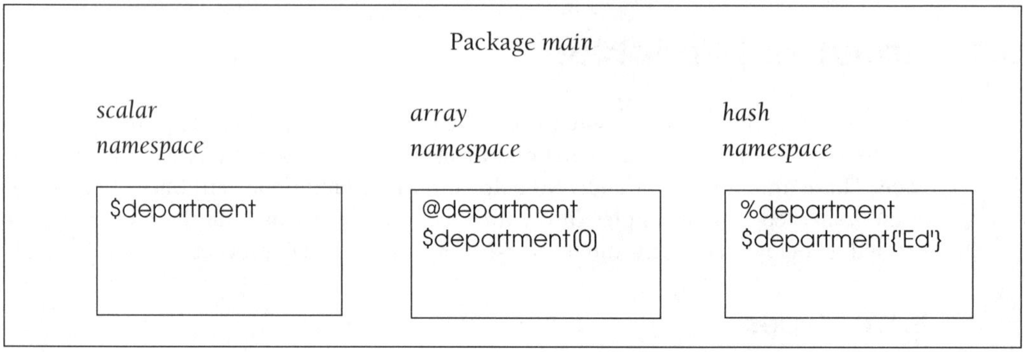

Figure 5.1 Namespaces for scalars, lists, and hashes in package *main*.

5.1.3 Naming Conventions

Unlike *C* or *Java*, Perl variables don't have to be declared before being used. They spring to life just by the mere mention of them. Variables have their own namespace in Perl. They are identified by the "funny characters" that precede them. Scalar variables are preceded by a $ sign, array variables are preceded by an @ sign, and hash variables are preceded by a % sign. Since the "funny characters" indicate what type of variable you are using, you can use the same name for a scalar, array, or hash and not worry about a naming conflict. For example, *$name*, *@name*, and *%name* are all different variables; the first is a scalar, the second is an array, and the last is a hash.[1]

Since reserved words and filehandles are not preceded by a special character, variable names will not conflict with reserved words or filehandles. Variables are **case sensitive**. The variables named *$Num*, *$num*, and *$NUM* are all different.

If a variable starts with a letter, it may consist of any number of letters (an underscore counts as a letter) and/or digits. If the variable does not start with a letter, it must consist of

1. Using the same name is allowed but not recommended; it makes reading too confusing.

only one character. Perl has a set of special variables (e.g., $_, $^, $., *$1*, $2, etc.) that fall into this category. (See "Special Variables" on page 845 in Appendix A.) In special cases, variables may also be preceded with a single quote but only when packages are used.

An unitialized variable will get a value of zero or null, depending on whether its context is numeric or string.

5.1.4 Assignment Statements

The assignment operator, the equal sign (=), is used to assign the value on its right-hand side to a variable on its left-hand side. Any value that can be "assigned to" represents a named region of storage and is called an *lvalue*.[2] Perl reports an error if the operand on the left-hand side of the assignment operator does not represent an *lvalue*.

When assigning a value or values to a variable, if the variable on the left-hand side of the equal sign is a scalar, Perl evaluates the expression on the right-hand side in a scalar context. If the variable on the left of the equal sign is an array, then Perl evaluates the expression on the right in an array context. (See "Scalars, Arrays, and Hashes" on page 77.)

A simple statement is an expression terminated with a semicolon.

FORMAT

```
variable=expression;
```

EXAMPLE 5.1

```
(The Script)
    # Scalar, array, and hash assignment
    $salary=50000;                          # Scalar assignment
    @months=('Mar', 'Apr', 'May');          # Array assignment
    %states= (                              # Hash assignment
       'CA' => 'California',
       'ME' => 'Maine',
       'MT' => 'Montana',
       'NM' => 'New Mexico',
           );
    print "$salary\n";
    print "@months\n";
    print "$months[0], $months[1], $months[2]\n";
    print "$states{'CA'}, $states{'NM'}\n";
    print $x + 3, "\n";                     # $x just came to life!
    print "***$name***\n";                  # $name is born!
```

2. The value on the left-hand side of the equal sign is called an *lvalue*, and the value on the right-hand side an *rvalue*.

EXAMPLE 5.1 (CONTINUED)

```
(Output)
4   50000
5   Mar Apr May
6   Mar, Apr, May
7   California, New Mexico
8   3
9   ******
```

EXPLANATION

1 The scalar variable *$salary* is assigned the numeric literal *50000*.
2 The array *@months* is assigned the comma-separated list, *Mar, Apr, May*. The list is enclosed in parentheses and each list item is quoted.
3 The hash, *%states*, is assigned a list consisting of a set of strings separated by either a digraph symbol (=>) or a comma.[a] The string on the left is called the *key*.[b] The string to the right is called the *value*. The *key* is associated with its *value*.
4 The value of the scalar, *$salary*, is printed, followed by a newline.
5 The *@months* array is printed. The double quotes preserve spaces between each element.
6 The individual elements of the array, *@months*, are scalars and are thus preceded by a dollar sign ($). The array index starts at zero.
7 The *key* elements of the hash, *%states*, are enclosed in curly braces ({}). The associated *value* is printed. Each *value* is a single value, a scalar. The *value* is preceded by a dollar sign ($).
8 The scalar variable, *$x*, is referenced for the first time. Because the number *three* is added to *$x*, the context is numeric. *$x* has an initial value of *zero*.
9 The scalar variable, *$name*, is referenced for the first time. The context is string and the initial value is null.

a. The comma can be used in both Perl 4 and Perl 5. The => symbol was introduced in Perl 5.

b. The => operator, unlike the comma, causes the key to be quoted, but if the key consists of more than one word or begins with a number, then it must be quoted.

5.1.5 Quoting Rules

Since quoting affects the way in which variables are interpreted, this is a good time to review Perl's quoting rules. Perl quoting rules are similar to shell quoting rules. This may not be good news to shell programmers, who find using quotes frustrating, to say the least. It is often difficult to determine which quotes to use, where to use them, and how to find the culprit if they are misused; in other words, it's a real debugging nightmare.[3] For those of you who fall into this category, Perl offers an alternative method of quoting.[4]

3. Barry Rosenberg, in his book *KornShell Programming Tutorial*, has a chapter titled "The Quotes From Hell."

4. Larry Wall, creator of Perl, calls his alternative quoting method "syntactic sugar."

Perl has three types of quotes and all three types have a different function. They are **single quotes**, **double quotes**, and **backquotes**.

The backslash (\) behaves like a set of single quotes but can be used only to quote a single character.

A pair of single or double quotes may delimit a string of characters. Quotes will either allow the interpretation of special characters or protect special characters from interpretation, depending on the kind of quotes you use.

Single quotes are the "democratic" quotes. All characters enclosed within them are treated equally; in other words, there are no special characters. But the double quotes discriminate. They treat some of the characters in the string as special characters. The special characters include the $ sign, the @ symbol, and escape sequences such as *t* and *n*.

When backquotes surround an operating system command, the command will be executed by the shell. This is called **command substitution**. The output of the command will either be printed as part of a *print* statement or assigned to a variable. If you are using Windows, Linux, or UNIX, the commands enclosed within backquotes must be supported by the particular operating system and will vary from system to system.

No matter what kind of quotes you are using, they **must** be matched. Because the quotes mark the beginning and end of a string, Perl will complain about a *"Might be a multiline runaway string"* or *"Execution of quotes aborted..."* or *"Can't find string terminator anywhere before EOF..."* and fail to compile if you forget one of the quotes.

Double Quotes. Double quotes must be matched unless embedded within single quotes or preceded by a backslash.

When a string is enclosed in double quotes, scalar variables (preceded with a $) and arrays (preceded by the @ symbol) are interpolated (i.e., the value of the variable replaces the variable name in the string). Hashes (preceded by the % sign) are **not** interpolated within the string enclosed in double quotes.

Strings that contain string literals (e.g., *t*, *n*) must be enclosed in double quotes for backslash interpretation.

A single quote may be enclosed in double quotes, as in *"I don't care!"*

EXAMPLE 5.2

```
(The Script)
    # Double quotes
    $num=5;
    print "The number is $num.\n";
    print "I need \$5.00.\n";
    print "\t\tI can't help you.\n";

(Output)
    The number is 5.
    I need $5.00.
            I can't help you.
```

EXPLANATION

1. The scalar variable *$num* is assigned the value 5.
2. The string is enclosed in double quotes. The value of the scalar variable is printed. The string literal, *\n*, is interpreted.
3. The dollar sign ($) is printed as a literal dollar sign when preceded by a backslash; in other words, variable substitution is ignored.
4. The special literals *\t* and *\n* are interpreted when enclosed within double quotes.

Single Quotes. If a string is enclosed in single quotes, it is printed literally (what you see is what you get).

If a single quote is needed within a string, then it can be embedded within double quotes or backslashed. If double quotes are to be treated literally, they can be embedded within single quotes.

EXAMPLE 5.3

```
(The Script)
    # Single quotes
1   print 'I need $100.00.', "\n";
2   print 'The string literal, \t, is used to represent a tab.', "\n";
3   print 'She cried, "Help me!"', "\n";

(Output)
1   I need $100.00.
2   The string literal, \t, is used to represent a tab.
3   She cried, "Help me!"
```

EXPLANATION

1. The dollar sign is interpreted literally. In double quotes, it would be interpreted as a scalar. The *\n* is in double quotes in order for backslash interpretation to occur.
2. The string literal, *\t*, is not interpreted to be a tab but is printed literally.
3. The double quotes are protected when enclosed in single quotes (i.e., they are printed literally).

Backquotes. UNIX/Windows[5] commands placed within backquotes are executed by the shell, and the output is returned to the Perl program. The output is usually assigned to a variable or made part of a *print* string. When the output of a command is assigned to a variable, the context is scalar (i.e., a single value is assigned).[6] For command substitution

---

5. If using other operating systems, such as DOS or Mac OS 9.1 and below, the OS commands available for your system will differ.
6. If output of a command is assigned to an array, the first line of output becomes the first element of the array, the second line of output becomes the next element of the array, and so on.

to take place, the backquotes cannot be enclosed in either double or single quotes. (Make note, UNIX shell programmers, backquotes cannot be enclosed in double quotes as in shell programs.)

EXAMPLE 5.4

```
(The Script for Unix/Linux)
   # Backquotes and command substitution
1  print "The date is ", `date`;        # Windows users: `date /T`
2  print "The date is `date`", ".\n"; # Backquotes treated literally
3  $directory=`pwd`;                    # Windows users: `cd`
4  print "\nThe current directory is $directory.";

(Output)
1  The date is Mon Jun 25 17:27:49 PDT 2007.
2  The date is `date`.
4  The current directory is /home/jody/ellie/perl.
```

EXPLANATION

1 The UNIX *date* command will be executed by the shell, and the output will be returned to Perl's *print* string. The output of the *date* command includes the newline character. For Windows users, the command is *'date /T'*.

2 Command substitution will not take place when the backquotes are enclosed in single or double quotes.

3 The scalar variable *$dir*, including the newline, is assigned the output of the UNIX *pwd* command (i.e., the present working directory). For Windows users, the command is *'cd'*.

4 The value of the scalar, *$dir*, is printed to the screen.

Perl's Alternative Quotes. Perl provides an alternative form of quoting—the *q*, *qq*, *qx*, and *qw* constructs.

- The *q* represents single quotes.
- The *qq* represents double quotes.
- The *qx* represents backquotes.
- The *qw* represents a quoted list of words. (See "Array Slices" on page 84.)

Table 5.1 Alternative Quoting Constructs

Quoting Construct	***What It Represents***
`q/Hello/`	`'Hello'`
`qq/Hello/`	`"Hello"`
`qx/date/`	`` `date` ``
`@list=qw/red yellow blue/;`	`@list=( 'red', 'yellow', 'blue');`

The string to be quoted is enclosed in **forward slashes**, but alternative delimiters can be used for all four of the *q* constructs. You can use a nonalphanumeric character for the delimeter, such as a # sign, ! point, or paired characters, such as parentheses, square brackets, etc. A single character or paired characters can be used:

q/Hello/
q#Hello#
q{Hello}
q[Hello]
q(Hello)

EXAMPLE 5.5

```
(The Script)
    # Using alternative quotes
1   print 'She cried, "I can\'t help you!"',"\n";     # Clumsy
2   print qq/She cried, "I can't help you!" \n/;      # qq for double
                                                      # quotes
3   print qq(I need $5.00\n);  # Really need single quotes
                               # for a literal dollar sign to print
4   print q/I need $5.00\n/;   # What about backslash interpretation?
    print qq(I need \$5.00\n); # Can escape the dollar sign
5   print qq/\n/, q/I need $5.00/,"\n";
6   print q!I need $5.00!,"\n";
7   print "The present working directory is ", 'pwd';
8   print qq/Today is /, qx/date/;
9   print "The hour is ", qx{date +%H};

(Output)
1   She cried, "I can't help you!"
2   She cried, "I can't help you!"
3   I need .00
4   I need $5.00\nI need $5.00

5   I need $5.00
6   I need $5.00
7   The present working directory is /home/jody/ellie/perl
8   Today is Mon Jun 25 17:29:34 PDT 2007
9   The hour is 17
```

EXPLANATION

1 The string is enclosed in single quotes. This allows the conversational quotes to be printed as literals. The single quote in *can\'t* is quoted with a backslash so that it will also be printed literally. If it were not quoted, it would be matched with the first single quote. The ending single quote would then have no mate, and, alas, the program would either tell you that you have a runaway quote or search for its mate until it reached the end of file unexpectedly.

EXPLANATION (CONTINUED)

2 The *qq* construct replaces double quotes. Now parentheses delimit the string.
3 Because the *qq* is used, the dollar sign ($) in *$5.00* is interpreted as a scalar variable with a null value. The *.00* is printed. (This is not the way to handle your money!)
4 The single *q* replaces single quotes. The *$5* is treated as a literal. Unfortunately, so is the *\n* because backslash interpretation does not take place within single quotes. Without a newline, the next line is run together with line 4. In the next line, if the dollar sign is preceded by a backslash, the backslash "escapes" the special meaning of the $. Now the string will print correctly.
5 The *\n* is double quoted with the *qq* construct, the string *I need $5.00* is single quoted with the *q* construct, and old-fashioned double quotes are used for the second *\n*.
6 An alternative delimiter, the exclamation point (*!*), is used with the *q* construct (instead of the forward slash) to delimit the string.
7 The string *The present working directory is* enclosed in double quotes; the UNIX command *pwd* is enclosed in backquotes for command substitution.
8 The *qq* construct quotes *Today is*; the *qx* construct replaces the backquotes used for command substitution.
9 Alternative delimiters, the curly braces, are used with the *qx* construct (instead of the forward slash). The output of the UNIX *date* command is printed.

5.2 Scalars, Arrays, and Hashes

Now that we have discussed the basics of Perl variables (types, visibility, funny characters, etc.), we can look at them in more detail and without (or, should I say, with less) confusion about the quoting mechanism and how quoting affects variable interpretation.

5.2.1 Scalar Variables

Scalar variables hold a single number or string and are preceded by a dollar sign ($). Perl scalars need a preceding dollar sign whenever the variable is referenced, even when the scalar is being assigned a value. If you are familiar with shell programs, using the dollar sign when making assignments may seem a little strange at first.

Assignment. When making an assignment, the value on the right-hand side of the equal sign is evaluated as a single value (i.e., its context is scalar). A quoted string, then, is considered a single value even if it contains a number of words.

EXAMPLE 5.6

```
1   $number = 150;
2   $name = "Jody Savage";
3   $today = localtime();
```

EXPLANATION

1. The numeric literal, *150*, is assigned to the scalar variable *$number*.
2. The string literal *Jody Savage* is assigned to the scalar *$name* as a single string.
3. The output of Perl's *localtime* function will be assigned as a string to *$today*.

Curly Braces. If a scalar variable is surrounded by curly braces (*{}*), the scalar is shielded from any characters that may be appended to the variable.

EXAMPLE 5.7

```
(The Script)
1   $var="net";
2   print "${var}work\n";

(Output)
2   network
```

EXPLANATION

1. The value *net* is assigned to the scalar variable *$var*.
2. The curly braces surrounding the variable insulate it from the string *work* that has been appended to it. Without the curly braces, nothing would be printed, because a variable called *$varwork* has not been defined. You could also concatenate the two strings with the dot operator; e.g.,

```
print $var . "work";
```

EXAMPLE 5.8

```
(The Script)
    # Initializing scalars and printing their values
1   $num = 5;
2   $friend = "John Smith";
3   $money = 125.75;
4   $now = localtime();          # localtime() is a Perl function
5   $month="Jan";
6   print "$num\n";
7   print "$friend\n";
8   print "I need \$$money.\n";     # Protecting our money
9   print qq/$friend gave me \$$money.\n/;
10  print qq/The time is $now\n/;
11  print "The month is ${month}uary.\n";    # Curly braces shield
                                             # the variable
12 print "The month is $month" . "uary.\n"; # Concatenate
```

EXAMPLE 5.8 (CONTINUED)

```
(Output)
6   5
7   John Smith
8   I need $125.75.
9   John Smith gave me $125.75.
10  The time is Sat Jan 24 16:12:49 2007.
11  The month is January.
12  The month is January.
```

EXPLANATION

1. The scalar *$num* is assigned the numeric literal, *5*.
2. The scalar *$friend* is assigned the string literal, *John Smith.*
3. The scalar *$money* is assigned the numeric floating point literal, *125.75*.
4. The scalar *$now* is assigned the output of Perl's *localtime()* function.
5. The scalar *$month* is assigned *Jan*.
6. The value of the scalar *$num* is printed.
7. The value of the scalar *$friend* is printed.
8. The quoted string is printed. The backslash allows the first dollar sign ($) to be printed literally; the value of *$money* is interpolated within double quotes, and its value printed.
9. The Perl *qq* construct replaces double quotes. The string to be quoted is enclosed in forward slashes. The value of the scalar *$friend* is interpolated; a literal dollar sign precedes the value of the scalar interpolated variable, *$money.*
10. The quoted string is printed. The *$now* variable is interpolated.
11. Curly braces can be used to shield the variable from characters that are appended to it. *January* will be printed.
12. You can also join two strings together with the dot operator (see Chapter 6), called concatenation.

The *defined* Function. If a scalar has neither a valid string nor a valid numeric value, it is undefined. The *defined* function allows you to check for the validity of a variable's value. It returns 1 if the variable has a value and null if it does not. The function is also used to check the validity of arrays, subroutines, and null strings.

EXAMPLE 5.9

```
$name="Tommy";
print "OK \n" if defined $name;
```

The *undef* Function. This function *undefines* an already defined variable. It releases whatever memory that was allocated for the variable. The function returns the undefined value. This function also releases storage associated with arrays and subroutines.

EXAMPLE 5.10

```
undef $name;
```

The *$_* Scalar Variable. The $_ is a ubiquitous little character. Although it is very useful in Perl scripts, it is often not seen. It is used as the default pattern space for searches and to hold the current line. Once a value is assigned to $_, functions such as *chomp*, *split*, and *print* will use $_ as an argument. You will learn more about functions and their arguments later, but for now, consider the following example:

EXAMPLE 5.11

```
1   $_ = "Donald Duck";
2   print;    # The value of $_ is printed
    Donald Duck
```

EXPLANATION

1. The $_ scalar variable is assigned the string "*Donald Duck*".
2. The *print* function has been given nothing to print, so it will print $_, the default if no other string is given.

5.2.2 Arrays

When you have a collection of similar data elements, it is easier to use an array than to create a separate variable for each of the elements. The array name allows you to associate a single variable name with a list of data elements. Each of the elements in the list is referenced by its name and a subscript (also called an index).

Perl, unlike C-like languages, doesn't care whether the elements of an array are of the same data type. They can be a mix of numbers and strings. To Perl, an array is a named list containing an ordered set of scalars. The name of the array starts with an @ sign. The subscript follows the array name and is enclosed in square brackets (*[]*). Subscripts are simply integers and start at zero.

Assignment. If the array is initialized, the elements are enclosed in parentheses, and each element is separated by a comma. The list is parenthesized due to the lower precedence of the comma operator over the assignment operator. Elements in an array are simply scalars.

Perl 5 introduced the *qw* construct for creating a list (similar to *qq*, *q*, and *qx*). The items in the list are treated as singly quoted words.

$pal = "John"; # *Scalar holds one value*
@pals = ("John", "Sam", "Nicky", "Jake"); # *Array holds a list of values*

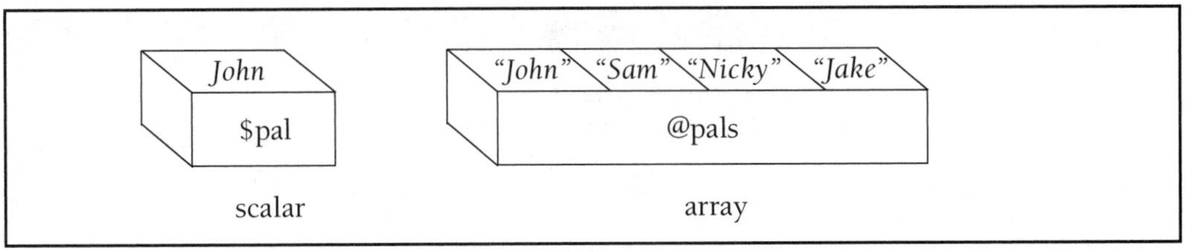

Figure 5.2 A scalar and an array.

EXAMPLE 5.12

```
1   @name=("Guy", "Tom", "Dan",  "Roy");
2   @list=(2..10);
3   @grades=(100, 90, 65, 96, 40, 75);
4   @items=($a, $b, $c);
5   @empty=();
6   $size=@items;
7   @mammals = qw/dogs cats cows/;
8   @fruit = qw(apples pears peaches);
```

EXPLANATION

1. The array *@name* is initialized with a list of four string literals.
2. The array *@list* is assigned numbers ranging from 2 through *10*. (See Example 5.14.)
3. The array *@grades* is initialized with a list of six numeric literals.
4. The array *@items* is initialized with the values of three scalar variables.
5. The array *@empty* is assigned a null list.
6. The array *@items* is assigned to the scalar variable *$size*. The value of the scalar is the number of elements in the array (in this example, 3).
7. The *qw* (quote word) construct is followed by a delimiter of your choice. Each word in the list is treated as a singly quoted word. The list is terminated with a closing delimiter. This example could be written:

   ```
   @mammals = ( 'cats', 'dogs', 'cows' );
   ```

8. The *qw* construct accepts paired characters *( )*, *{ }*,< >, and *[ ]*, as optional delimeters.

Special Scalars and Array Assignment. The special scalar variable *$#arrayname* returns the number of the last subscript in the array. Since the array subscripts start at zero, this value is one less than the array size. The *$#arrayname* variable can also be used to shorten or truncate the size of the array.

The *$[* variable is the current array base subscript, zero. Its value can be changed so that the subscript starts at 1 instead of 0, but changing this value is discouraged by Larry Wall.

EXAMPLE 5.13

```
1   @grades = (90,89,78,100,87);
    print "The original array is: @grades\n";
2   print "The number of the last index is $#grades\n";

3   $#grades=3;
    print "The array is truncated to 4 elements: @grades\n";

4   @grades=();
    print "The array is completely truncated: @grades\n";

(Output)
  The original array is: 90 89 78 100 87
  The number of the last index is 4
  The array is truncated to 4 elements: 90 89 78 100
  The array is completely truncated:
```

EXPLANATION

1. The array *@grades* is assigned a list of five numbers.
2. The $# construct gets the subscript (index) value of the last element in the array.
3. The last subscript in the array has been shortened to 3.
4. Using an empty list causes the array to be completely truncated to an empty list.

The Range Operator and Array Assignment. The .. operator, called the **range** operator, when used in an array context, returns an array of values starting from the left value to the right value, counting by ones.

EXAMPLE 5.14

```
1   @digits=(0 .. 10);
2   @letters=( 'A' .. 'Z' );
3   @alpha=( 'A' .. 'Z', 'a' .. 'z' );
4   @n=( -5 .. 20 );
```

EXPLANATION

1. The array *@digits* is assigned a list of numbers, *0* through *10*.
2. The array *@letters* is assigned a list of capital letters, *A* through *Z*.
3. The array *@alpha* is assigned a list of uppercase and lowercase letters.
4. The array *@n* is assigned a list of numbers, *–5* through *20*.

Accessing Elements. To reference the individual elements in an array, each element is considered a scalar (preceded by a dollar sign), and the subscripts start at zero. The subscripts are positive whole numbers. For example, in the array *@names*, the first element in the array is *$name[0]*, the next element is *$name[1]*, and so forth.

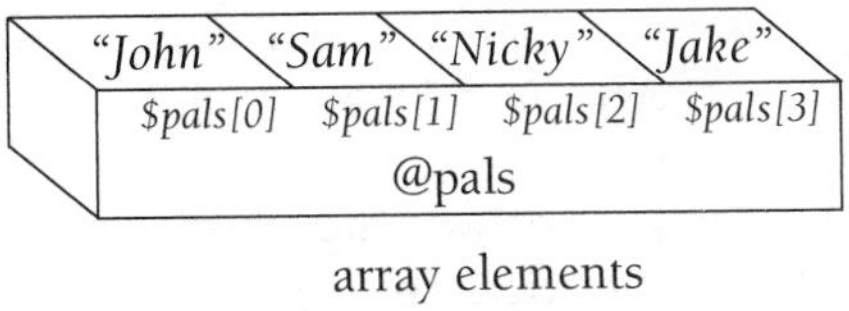

Figure 5.3 Array elements.

EXAMPLE 5.15

```
(The Script)
    # Populating an array and printing its values
1   @names=('John', 'Joe', 'Jake');      # @names=qw/John Joe Jake/;
2   print @names, "\n";  # prints without the separator
3   print "Hi $names[0], $names[1], and $names[2]!\n";
4   $number=@names;         # The scalar is assigned the number
                            # of elements in the array
5   print "There are $number elements in the \@names array.\n";
6   print "The last element of the array is $names[$number - 1].\n";
7   print "The last element of the array is $names[$#names].\n";
                            # Remember, the array index starts at zero!!
8   @fruit = qw(apples pears peaches plums);
9   print "The first element of the \@fruit array  is $fruit[0];
        the second element is $fruit[1].\n";
10  print "Starting at the end of the array; @fruit[-1, -3]\n";

(Output)
2   JohnJoeJake
3   Hi John, Joe, and Jake!
5   There are 3 elements in the @names array.
6   The last element of the array is Jake.
7   The last element of the array is Jake.
9   The first element of the @fruit array is apples; the second
element is pears.
10  Starting at the end of the array: plums pears
```

EXPLANATION

1. The *@names* array is initialized with three strings: *John*, *Joe*, and *Jake*.
2. The entire array is printed to *STDOUT*. The space between the elements is not printed.
3. Each element of the array is printed, starting with subscript number zero.
4. The scalar variable *$number* is assigned the array *@names*. The value assigned is the number of elements in the array *@names*.
5. The number of elements in the array *@names* is printed.

EXPLANATION (CONTINUED)

6 The last element of the array is printed. Since subscripts start at zero, the number of elements in the array decremented by one evaluates to the number of the last subscript.

7 The last element of the array is printed. The *$#names* value evaluates to the number of the last subscript in the array. This value used as a subscript will retrieve the last element in the *@names* array.

8 The *qw* construct allows you to create an array of singly quoted words without enclosing the words in quotes or separating the words with commas. The delimiter is any pair of nonalphanumeric characters. (See "Perl's Alternative Quotes" on page 75.)

9 The first two elements of the *@fruit* array are printed.

10 With a negative offset as a subscript, the elements of the array are selected from the end of the array. The last element (*$fruit[-1]*) is *plums*, and the third element from the end (*$fruit[-3]*) is *pears*. Note that when both index values are within the same set of brackets, as in *@fruit[-1,-3]*, the reference is to a list, not a scalar; that is why the @ symbol precedes the name of the array, rather than the $.

Array Slices. When the elements of one array are assigned the values from another array, the resulting array is called an **array slice**.

If the array on the right-hand side of the assignment operator is larger than the array on the left-hand side, the unused values are discarded. If it is smaller, the values assigned are undefined. As indicated in the following example, the array indices in the slice do not have to be consecutively numbered; each element is assigned the corresponding value from the array on the right-hand side of the assignment operator.

EXAMPLE 5.16

```
(The Script)
     # Array slices
1    @names=('Tom', 'Dick', 'Harry', 'Pete' );
2    @pal=@names[1,2,3];   # slice -- @names[1..3] also O.K.
3    print "@pal\n\n";

4    ($friend[0], $friend[1], $friend[2])=@names;     # Array slice
5    print "@friend\n";

(Output)
3    Dick Harry Pete

5    Tom Dick Harry
```

EXPLANATION

1. The array *@names* is assigned the elements *'Tom'*, *'Dick'*, *'Harry'*, and *'Pete'*.
2. The array *@pal* is assigned the elements *1*, *2*, and *3* of the *@names* array. The elements of the *@names* array are sliced out and stored in the *@pal* array.
3. The *@friend* array is created by taking a slice from the *@names* array; i.e., elements *0*, *1*, and 2.

EXAMPLE 5.17

```
(The Script)
    # Array slices
    @colors=('red','green','yellow','orange');
    ($c[0], $c[1],$c[3], $c[5])=@colors;  # The slice
    print "**********\n";
    print @colors,"\n";  # Prints entire array, but does
                         # not separate elements quoted
    print "@colors,\n";  # Prints the entire array with
                         # elements separated
    print "**********\n";
    print $c[0],"\n";    # red
    print $c[1],"\n";    # green
    print $c[2],"\n";    # undefined
    print $c[3],"\n";    # yellow
    print $c[4],"\n";    # undefined
    print $c[5],"\n";    # orange
    print "**********\n" ;
    print "The size of the \@c array is ", $#c + 1,".\n";

(Output)
    **********
    redgreenyelloworange
    red  green yellow orange
    **********
    red
    green

    yellow

    orange
    **********
    The size of the @c array is 6.
```

EXPLANATION

1. The array *@colors* is assigned the elements *'red'*, *'green'*, *'yellow'*, and *'orange'*.
2. An array slice is created, consisting of four scalars, *$c[0]*, *$c[1]*, *$c[3]*, and *$c[5]*. Note: The subscripts in the array slice are not numbered sequentially.
3. A row of stars is printed, just for clarity.
4. The elements are not separated when printed.
5. When the array is enclosed in double quotes, the whitespace between elements is preserved.
6. Another row of stars is printed.
7. The first element of the array slice, *red*, is printed.
8. The second element of the array slice, *green*, is printed.
9. The third element of the array slice is undefined. Its value is null because it was not assigned a value.
10. The fourth element of the array slice, *yellow*, is printed.
11. The fifth element of the array slice is undefined.
12. The sixth element of the array slice, *orange*, is printed.
13. Another row of stars is printed.
14. Even though some of the elements of the *@c* array are undefined, the size of the array indicates that the elements exist.

Multidimensional Arrays—Lists of Lists. Multidimensional arrays are sometimes called **tables**, or **matrices**. They consist of rows and columns and can be represented with multiple subscripts. In a two-dimensional array, the first subscript represents the row, and the second subscript represents the column.

In Perl, each row in a two-dimensional array is enclosed in square brackets. The row is an unnamed list. An unnamed list is called an **anonymous** array and contains its own elements. The arrow operator, also called an **infix** operator, can be used to get the individual elements of an array. There is an implied –> between adjacent brackets. (Anonymous variables will be discussed in detail in Chapter 13, "Does This Job Require a Reference?")

EXAMPLE 5.18

```
(The Script)
    # A two-dimensional array consisting of 4 rows and 3 columns
    @matrix=( [ 3 , 4, 10 ],     # Each row is an unnamed list
              [ 2,  7, 12 ],
              [ 0,  3,  4 ],
              [ 6,  5,  9 ],
            ) ;
    print "@matrix\n";
    print "Row 0, column 0 is $matrix[0][0].\n";
                       # can also be written - $matrix[0]->[0]
```

EXAMPLE 5.18 (CONTINUED)

```
4   print "Row 1, column  0 is $matrix[1][0].\n";
                      # can also be written - $matrix[1]->[0]
5   for($i=0; $i < 4; $i++){
6       for($x=0; $x < 3; $x++){
7           print "$matrix[$i][$x] ";
        }
        print "\n";
    }

(Output)
2   ARRAY(0xbf838) ARRAY(0xc7768) ARRAY(0xc77a4) ARRAY(0xc77e0)
3   Row 0, column 0 is 3.
4   Row 1, column 0 is 2.
7   3 4 10
    2 7 12
    0 3 4
    6 5 9
```

EXPLANATION

1. The array *@matrix* is assigned four unnamed, or anonymous, arrays. Each of the arrays has three values.
2. The addresses of the four anonymous arrays are printed. To access the individual elements of an anonymous array, double subscripts or the arrow operator must be used.
3. The first element of the first anonymous array in the *@matrix* array is printed. The -> is called the **arrow**, or **infix**, operator. It is used to dereference array and hash references. *$matrix[0][0]* or *$matrix[0]->[0]* is the first element of the first row, where subscripts start at zero.
4. The second row, first element of the *@matrix*, is printed. *$matrix[1]->[0]* is another way to say *$matrix[1][0]*.
5. The outer *for* loop will iterate through each of the rows, starting at row zero. After the first iteration of the loop, the second *for* loop is entered.
6. The inner *for* loop iterates faster than the outer loop. Each element of a row is printed, and then control returns to the outer *for* loop.
7. Print each element in the matrix. The first index represents the row, and the second index represents the column.

5.2.3 Hashes

An associative array, more commonly called a **hash**, consists of one or more pairs of scalars—strings, numbers, or Booleans. The first set of scalars is associated with the second set of scalars. The first string in the pair of strings is called the **key**, and the second string is called the **value**. Whereas arrays are ordered lists with numeric indices starting at 0, hashes are unordered lists with string indices randomly distributed. (When you print out the hash, don't expect to see the output ordered just as you typed it!)

Hashes, then, are defined as an unordered list of key/value pairs, similar to a table where the keys are on the left-hand side and the values associated with those keys are on the right-hand side. The name of the hash is preceded by the %.

```
% pet = ( "Name"  => "Sneaky",
          "Type"  => "Cat",
          "Owner" => "Carol",
          "Color" => "yellow",
        );
```

keys	values
“Name”	“Sneaky
“Type”	“Cat”
“Owner”	“Carol”
“Color”	“yellow”

Hash Table

Assignment. A hash must be defined before the elements can be referenced. Since a hash consists of pairs of values, indexed by the first element of each pair, if one of the elements in a pair is missing within the array definition, the association of the keys and their respective values will be affected. When assigning keys and values, make sure you have a key associated with its corresponding value. When indexing a hash, curly braces are used instead of square brackets.

EXAMPLE 5.19

```
1   %seasons=("Sp" => "Spring",
              "Su" => "Summer",
              "F"  => "Fall",
              "W"  => "Winter",
             );
2   %days=("Mon" => "Monday",
           "Tue" => "Tuesday",
           "Wed" => undef,
          );
3   $days{"Wed"}="Wednesday";
4   $days{5}="Friday";
```

EXPLANATION

1 The hash *%seasons* is assigned keys and values. Each key and value is separated by the digraph operator, =>. The string *Sp* is the key with a corresponding value of *Spring*; the string *Su* is the key for its corresponding value *Summer*, etc. It is not necessary to quote the key if it is a single word.

EXPLANATION (CONTINUED)

2 The hash *%days* is assigned keys and values. The third key, *Wed*, is assigned *undef*. The *undef* function evaluates to a null string.

3 Individual elements of a hash are scalars. The key *Wed* is assigned the string value *Wednesday*. The index is enclosed in curly braces.

4 The key *5* is assigned the string value *Friday*. Note: the keys do not have any consecutive numbering order, and the pairs can consist of numbers and/or strings.

Accessing Elements. When accessing the values of a hash, the subscript consists of the key enclosed in curly braces. Perl provides a set of functions to list the keys, values, and each of the elements of the hash. (See "Array Functions" on page 100.)

Due to the internal hashing techniques used to store the keys, Perl does not guarantee the order in which an entire hash is printed.

EXAMPLE 5.20

```
(The Script)
    # Assigning keys and values to a hash
1   %department = (
2                      "Eng" => "Engineering",
                       "M"   => "Math",
                       "S"   => "Science",
                       "CS"  => "Computer Science",
                       "Ed"  => "Education",
3                    );
4   $department = $department{'M'}; # Either single or double quotes
                                    # ok for the keys
5   $school = $department{'Ed'};
6   print "I work in the $department section\n" ;
7   print "Funds in the $school department are being cut.\n";
8   print qq/I'm currently enrolled in a $department{'CS'} course.\n/;
9   print qq/The department hash looks like this:\n/;
10  print %department, "\n";   # The printout is not in the expected
                               # order due to internal hashing

(Output)
6   I work in the Math section
7   Funds in the Education department are being cut.
8   I'm currently enrolled in a Computer Science course.
9   The department hash looks like this:
10  SScienceCSComputer ScienceEdEducationMMathEngEngineering
```

EXPLANATION

1 The hash is called *%department*. It is assigned keys and values.

2 The first **key** is the string *Eng*, and the **value** associated with it is *Engineering*.

3 The closing parenthesis and semicolon end the assignment.

EXPLANATION (CONTINUED)

4 The scalar *$department* is assigned *Math*, the value associated with the *M* key.
5 The scalar *$school* is assigned *Education*, the value associated with the *Ed* key.
6 The quoted string is printed; the scalar *$department* is interpolated.
7 The quoted string is printed; the scalar *$school* is interpolated.
8 The quoted string and the value associated with the *CS* key are printed.
9 The quoted string is printed.
10 The entire hash is printed, with keys and values packed together and not in the expected order.

Hash Slices. A hash slice is a list of hash keys whose corresponding values are assigned to another list of keys. The list consists of the hash name preceded by the @ symbol. The list of hash keys is enclosed in curly braces.

EXAMPLE 5.21

```
(The Script)
    # Hash slices
1   %officer= ("NAME"=> "Tom Savage",
               "SSN" => "510-22-3456",
               "DOB" => "05/19/66"
              );

2   @info=qw(Marine Captain 50000);
3   @officer{'BRANCH', 'TITLE', 'SALARY'}=@info;
    # This is a hash slice
4   @sliceinfo=@officer{'NAME','BRANCH','TITLE'};
    # This is also a hash slice
5   print "The new values from the hash slice are: @sliceinfo\n\n";
    print "The hash now looks like this:\n";
6   foreach $key ('NAME', 'SSN', 'DOB', 'BRANCH', 'TITLE', 'SALARY'){
7       printf "Key: %-10sValue: %-15s\n", $key, $officer{$key};
    }

(Output)
5   The new values from the hash slice are: Tom Savage Marine Captain

    The hash now looks like this:
7   Key: NAMEValue: Tom Savage
    Key: SSNValue: 510-22-3456
    Key: DOBValue: 05/19/66
    Key: BRANCHValue: Marine
    Key: TITLEValue: Captain
    Key: SALARYValue: 50000
```

EXPLANATION

1 The hash *%officer* is assigned keys and values.
2 The array *@info* is assigned three values.
3 This is an example of a hash slice. The hash *officer* is assigned an array (*@info*) of values *Marine*, *Captain*, and *50000* to the corresponding keys, *BRANCH*, *TITLE*, *SALARY*. The name of the hash is prepended with an @ symbol because it is a list of keys that will receive its corresponding values from another list, *@info*.
4 The hash slice is used in the assignment to create an array called *@sliceinfo*. The array will consist of the hash values associated with keys *NAME*, *BRANCH*, and *TITLE*.
5 The values created by the hash slice are printed.
6 The *foreach* loop is used to iterate through the list of keys.
7 The keys and their corresponding values are printed. On line 3, the new key/value pairs were created by the slice.

5.2.4 Complex Data Structures

By combining arrays and hashes, you can make more complex data structures, such as arrays of hashes, hashes with nested hashes, arrays of arrays, etc. To create these structures, you should have an understanding of how Perl pointers are used. A few examples will be provided here as part of this topic, but a complete discussion of how to build complicated data structures is deferred until Chapter 13.

Hashes of Hashes. A hash can contain another hash. It is like a record that contains records. The nested hash has no name. It is an anonymous hash and can be dereferenced with the arrow operator. Each of the keys in the named hash contains a value, which is itself another hash. This anonymous hash consists of its own key/value pairs.

EXAMPLE 5.22

```
(The Script)
    # Nested hashes
                                                values
                     keys         key      value      key      value
1   %students=( "Math"    => { "Joe"  => 100,    "Joan" => 95 },
                "Science" => { "Bill" => 85,     "Dan"  => 76 }
           );
2   print "On the math test Joan got ";
3   print qq/$students{Math}->{Joan}.\n/;
4   print "On the science test Bill got ";
5   print qq/$students{Science}->{Bill}.\n/;

(Output)
3   On the math test Joan got 95.
5   On the science test Bill got 85.
```

EXPLANATION

1 The hash *%students* consists of two keys, *Math* and *Science*. The values associated with those keys are enclosed in curly braces. The value contains a set of nested keys and values. The value for the *Math* key contains two nested keys, *Joe* and *Joan*, with their respective values, *100* and *95*. The value for the *Science* key contains two nested keys, *Bill* and *Dan*, with their respective values, *85* and *76*. The nested keys and values are in an unnamed, or anonymous, hash.

3 The arrow (infix) operator, –>, allows you to access the anonymous nested hash value of the *%students* hash.

EXAMPLE 5.23

```
(The Script)
    # Anonymous arrays as keys in a hash
1   %grades=("Math"    => [ 90, 100, 94 ],
             "Science" => [ 77, 87, 86 ],
             "English" => [ 65, 76, 99, 100 ],
            );
2   print %grades, "\n";
3   print "The third math grade is: $grades{Math}->[2]\n";
4   print "All of the science grades are: @{$grades{Science}}\n";

(Output)
2   EnglishARRAY(0x8a65128)ScienceARRAY(0x8a650b0)MathARRAY(0x8a6f134)
3   The third math grade is: 94
4   All of the science grades are: 77 87 86
```

EXPLANATION

1 The hash *%grades* is assigned keys and values. The values are an unnamed list of numbers. Perl knows that this is an anonymous list because it is enclosed in square brackets. The anonymous arrays are stored at a memory location that can be accessed by using the arrow notation.

2 The values of each key are printed as hexadecimal addresses preceded by the data type *ARRAY* stored at that location.

3 The third element of the first list is retrieved by placing an arrow after the hash key, *Math*, that points to the index of the anonymous array. Since indices start at zero, *$grades{Math}–>[2]* references the third element of the array.

4 To access the entire list of *Science* grades, the key/value pair is enclosed in curly braces and prepended with an @ symbol.

Array of Hashes. An array can contain nested hashes. It's like an array of records. Each of the elements of the array is an anonymous hash with a set of keys and corresponding values.

EXAMPLE 5.24

```
(The Script)
    # An array of hashes
1   @stores=( { "Boss" =>"Ari Goldberg",
                "Employees" => 24,
                "Registers" => 10,
                "Sales" => 15000.00,
              },
2             { "Boss" =>"Ben Chien",
                "Employees" => 12,
                "Registers" => 5,
                "Sales" => 3500.00,
              },
    );
3   print "The number of elements in the array: ",
4       $#stores + 1, "\n";    # The number of the last subscript + 1

5   for($i=0; $i< $#stores + 1; $i++){
6       print $stores[$i]->{"Boss"},"\n";    # Access an array element
        print $stores[$i]->{"Employees"},"\n";
        print $stores[$i]->{"Registers"},"\n";
        print $stores[$i]->{"Sales"},"\n";
        print "-" x 20 ,"\n";
    }

(Output)
3   The number of elements in the array: 2
6   Ari Goldberg
    24
    10
    15000
    --------------------
    Ben Chien
    12
    5
    3500
    --------------------
```

EXPLANATION

1 The array *@stores* contains two anonymous hashes, one for *Ari Goldberg*'s store and one for *Ben Chien*'s store. Each of the elements of the array is a hash.

2 This is the second element of the *@stores* array. It is a hash.

4 *$#stores* evaluates to the number of the last subscript in the *@stores* array. Since subscripts start at *0*, by adding *1* we get the number of elements in the array, which is 2.

6 To access a value in one of the elements of the array, first the number of the index is specified and then the key into the hash. The arrow operator is not required here, but it makes the program a little more readable.

5.3 Reading from *STDIN*

The three filehandles *STDIN*, *STDOUT*, and *STDERR*, as you may recall, are names given to three predefined streams, *stdin*, *stdout*, and *stderr*. By default, these filehandles are associated with your terminal. When printing output to the terminal screen, *STDOUT* is used. When printing errors, *STDERR* is used. When assigning user input to a variable, *STDIN* is used.

The Perl <> input operator encloses the *STDIN* filehandle so that the next line of standard input can be read from the terminal keyboard and assigned to a variable. Unlike the shell and *C* operations for reading input, Perl retains the newline on the end of the string when reading a line from standard input. If you don't want the newline, then you have to explicitly remove it, or "chomp" it off (see "The *chop* and *chomp* Functions" on page page 95).

5.3.1 Assigning Input to a Scalar Variable

When reading input from the filehandle *STDIN*, if the context is scalar, one line of input is read, including the newline, and assigned to a scalar variable as a single string.

EXAMPLE 5.25

```
(The Script)
    # Getting a line of input from the keyboard.
1   print "What is your name?  ";
2   $name = <STDIN>;
3   print "What is your father's name? ";
4   $paname=<>;
5   print "Hello respected one, $paname";

(Output)
1   What is your name? Isabel
3   What is your father's name? Nick
5   Hello respected one, Nick
```

EXPLANATION

1. The string *What is your name?* is sent to *STDOUT*, which is the screen by default.
2. The input operator <> (called the diamond operator) surrounding *STDIN* reads one line of input and assigns that line and its trailing newline to the scalar variable *$name*. When input is assigned to a scalar, characters are read until the user presses the Enter key.
3. The string is printed to *STDOUT*.
4. If the input operator is empty, the next line of input is read from *STDIN*, and the behavior is identical to line 2, except input is assigned to *$paname*.

5.3.2 The *chop* and *chomp* Functions

The *chop* function removes the last character in a scalar variable and the last character of each word in an array. Its return value is the character it chopped. *Chop* is used primarily to remove the newline from the line of input coming into your program, whether it is *STDIN*, a file, or the result of command substitution. When you first start learning Perl, the trailing newline can be a real pain!

The *chomp* function was introduced in Perl 5 to remove the last character in a scalar variable and the last character of each word in an array **only if** that character is the newline (or, to be more precise, the character that represents the input line separator, initially defined as a newline and stored in the $/ variable). It returns the number of characters it chomped. Using *chomp* instead of *chop* protects you from inadvertently removing some character other than the newline.

EXAMPLE 5.26

```
(The Script)
   # Getting rid of the trailing newline. Use chomp instead of chop.
   print "Hello there, and what is your name? ";
   $name = <STDIN>;
   print "$name is a very high class name.\n";
   chop($name);    # Removes the last character no matter what it is.
   print "$name is a very high class name.\n\n";
   chop($name);
   print "$name has been chopped a little too much.\n";
   print "What is your age?  ";
   chomp($age=<STDIN>); # Removes the last character if
                        # it is the newline.
   chomp($age);         # The last character is not removed
                        # unless a newline.
   print "For $age, you look so young!\n";

(Output)
1  Hello there, and what is your name? Joe Smith
3  Joe Smith
   is a very high class name.
5  Joe Smith is a very high class name.

7  Joe Smit has been chopped a little too much.

8  What is your age? 25
11 For 25, you look so young!
```

EXPLANATION

1 The quoted string is printed to the screen, *STDOUT*, by default.
2 The scalar variable is assigned a single line of text typed in by the user. The <> operator is used for read operations. In this case, it reads from *STDIN*, which is your keyboard, until the carriage return is pressed. The newline is included in the text that is assigned to the variable *$name*.
3 The value of *$name* is printed. Note that the newline breaks the line after *Joe Smith*, the user's input.
4 The *chop* function removes the last character of the string assigned to *$name*. The character that was chopped is returned.
5 The string is printed again after the *chop* operation. The last character was removed (in this case, the newline).
6 This time *chop* will remove the last character in *Joe Smith's* name; i.e., the *h* in *Smith*.
7 The quoted string is printed to *STDOUT*, indicating that the last character was removed.
9 The user input is first assigned to the variable *$age*. The trailing newline is chomped. The character whose value is stored in the special variable, $/, is removed. This value is by default the newline character. The number of characters chomped is returned. Because of the low precedence of the equal (=) operator, parentheses ensure that the assignment occurs before the *chomp* function chomps.
10 The second *chomp* will have no effect. The newline has already been removed, and *chomp* removes only the newline. It's safer than using *chop*.
11 The chomped variable string is printed.

5.3.3 The *read* Function

The *read* function[7] allows you to read a number of bytes into a variable from a specified filehandle. If reading from standard input, the filehandle is *STDIN*. The *read* function returns the number of bytes that were read.

FORMAT

```
number_of_bytes = read(FILEHANDLE,buffer,how_many_bytes);
```

EXAMPLE 5.27

```
(The Script)
    # Reading input in a requested number of bytes
1   print "Describe your favorite food in 10 bytes or less.\n";
    print "If you type less than 10 characters, press Ctrl-d on a line
          by itself.\n";
```

7. The *read* function is similar to the *fread* function in the C language.

EXAMPLE 5.27 (CONTINUED)

```
2   $number=read(STDIN, $favorite, 10);
3   print "You just typed: $favorite\n";
4   print "The number of bytes read was $number.\n";

(Output)
1   Describe your favorite food in 10 bytes or less.
    If you type less than 10 characters, press Ctrl-d on a line by
    itself.
    apple pie and ice cream          <-user input
3   You just typed: apple pie
4   The number of bytes read was 10.
```

EXPLANATION

1. The user is asked for input. If he types less than 10 characters, he should press <Ctrl>-d to exit.
2. The *read* function takes three arguments: the first argument is *STDIN*, the place from where the input is coming; the second argument is the scalar *$favorite*, where the input will be stored; and the third argument is the number of characters (bytes) that will be read.
3. The 10 characters read in are printed. The rest of the characters were discarded.
4. The number of characters (bytes) actually read was stored in *$number* and is printed.

5.3.4 The *getc* Function

The *getc* function gets a single character from the keyboard or from a file. At EOF, *getc* returns a null string.

FORMAT

```
getc(FILEHANDLE)
getc FILEHANDLE
getc
```

EXAMPLE 5.28

```
(The Script)
    # Getting only one character of input
    print "Answer y or n    ";
1   $answer=getc;        # Gets one character from stdin
2   $restofit=<>;        # What remains in the input buffer is
                         # assigned to $restofit
3   print "$answer\n";
4   print "The characters left in the input buffer were:
            $restofit\n";
```

EXAMPLE 5.28 (CONTINUED)

```
(Output)
1   Answer  y or n yessirreebob <ENTER>
3   y
4   The characters left in the input buffer were: essirreebob
```

EXPLANATION

1. Only one character is read from the input buffer by *getc* and stored in the scalar *$answer*.
2. The characters remaining in the input buffer are stored in *$restofit*. This clears the input buffer. Now, if you ask for input later in the program, you will not be picking up those characters that were left hanging around in the buffer.
3. The character that was read in by *getc* is printed.
4. The characters stored in *$restofit* are displayed.

5.3.5 Assigning Input to an Array

When reading input from the filehandle *STDIN*, if the context is an array, then each line is read with its newline and is treated as a single list item, and the read is continued until you press <Ctrl>-d (in UNIX) or <Ctrl>-z (in Windows) for end of file (EOF). Normally, you will not assign input to an array, because it could eat up a large amount of memory, or because the user of your program may not realize that he should press <Ctrl>-d or <Ctrl>-z to stop reading input.

EXAMPLE 5.29

```
(The Script)
    # Assigning input to an array
1   print "Tell me everything about yourself.\n ";
2   @all = <STDIN>;
3   print "@all";
4   print "The number of elements in the array are: ",
           $#all + 1, ".\n";
5   print "The first element of the array is: $all[0]";

(Output)
1   Tell me everything about yourself.
2   OK. Let's see I was born before computers.
    I grew up in the 50s.
    I was in the hippie generation.
    I'm starting to get bored with talking about myself.
    <Ctrl>-d
```

EXAMPLE 5.29

```
3   OK. Let's see I was born before computers.
    I grew up in the 50s.
    I was in the hippie generation.
    I'm starting to get bored with talking about myself.
4   The number of elements in the array are: 4.
5   The first element of the array is:
    OK. Let's see I was born before computers.
```

EXPLANATION

1. The string *Tell me everything about yourself.* is printed to *STDOUT.*
2. The input operator <> surrounding *STDIN* reads input lines until <Ctrl>-d, EOF, is reached. (For Windows users, use <Ctrl>-z instead of <Ctrl>-d.) Each line and its trailing newline are stored as a list element of the array *@all.*
3. The user input is printed to the screen after the user presses <Ctrl>-d or <Ctrl>-z.
4. The *$#* construct lets you get the last subscript or index value in the array. By adding *1* to *$#all*, the size of the array is obtained; i.e., the number of lines that were read.
5. *$all[0]* is the first element of the array that evaluates to the first line of input from the user. Each line read is an element of the array.

5.3.6 Assigning Input to a Hash

EXAMPLE 5.30

```
(The Script)
    # Assign input to a hash
1   $course_number=101;
2   print "What is the name of course 101?";
3   chomp($course{$course_number} = <STDIN>);
4   print %course, "\n";

(Output)
2   What is the name of course 101? Linux Administration
4   101Linux Administration
```

EXPLANATION

1. The scalar variable *$course_number* is assigned the value *101.*
2. The string *What is the name of course 101?* is printed to *STDOUT.*
3. The name of the hash is *%course.* We are assigning a value to one of the hash elements. The key is *$course_number* enclosed in curly braces. The *chomp* function will remove the newline from the value assigned by the user.
4. The new array is printed. It has one key and one value.

5.4 Array Functions

Arrays can grow and shrink. The Perl array functions allow you to insert or delete elements of the array from the front, middle, or end of the list.

5.4.1 The *chop* and *chomp* Functions (with Lists)

The *chop* function chops off the last character of a string and returns the chopped character, usually for removing the newline after input is assigned to a scalar variable. If a list is chopped, *chop* will remove the last letter of each string in the list.

The *chomp* function removes the last character of each element in a list if it ends with a newline and returns the number of newlines it removed.

FORMAT

```
chop(LIST)
chomp(LIST)
```

EXAMPLE 5.31

```
(In the Script)
    # Chopping and chomping a list
1   @line=("red", "green", "orange");
2   chop(@line);      # Chops the last character off each
                      # string in the list
3   print "@line";
4   @line=( "red", "green", "orange");
5   chomp(@line);     # Chomps the newline off each string in the list
6   print "@line";

(Output)
3   re gree orang
6   red green orange
```

EXPLANATION

1. The array *@line* is assigned list elements.
2. The array is chopped. The *chop* function chops the last character from each element of the array.
3. The chopped array is printed.
4. The array *@line* is assigned elements.
5. The *chomp* function will chop off the newline character from each word in the array. This is a safer function than *chop*.
6. Since there were no newlines on the end of the words in the array, it was not chomped.

5.4.2 The *exists* Function

The *exists* function returns **true** if an array index (or hash key) has been defined, and **false** if it has not.

FORMAT

```
exists $ARRAY[index];
```

EXAMPLE 5.32

```
    #!/usr/bin/perl
1   @names = qw(Tom Raul Steve Jon);
2   print "Hello $names[1]\n", if exists $names[1];
3   print "Out of range!\n", if not exists $names[5];

(Output)
2   Hello Raul
3   Out of range!
```

EXPLANATION

1 An array of names is assigned to *@names*.
2 If the index *1* is defined, the *exists* function returns true and the string is printed.
3 If the index *5* does not exist (and in this example it doesn't), then the string *Out of range!* is printed.

5.4.3 The *delete* Function

The *delete* function allows you to remove a value from an element of an array but not the element itself. The value deleted is simply undefined.

EXAMPLE 5.33

```
(The Script)
# Removing an array element
1 @colors=("red","green","blue","yellow");
2  print "@colors\n";
3 delete $colors[1];  # green is removed
4 print "@colors\n";
5 print $colors[1],"\n";
6 $size=@colors;       # value is now undefined
7 print "The size of the array is $size.\n";

(Output)
2 red green blue yellow
4 red  blue yellow

7 The size of the array is 4.
```

5.4.4 The *grep* Function

The *grep* function evaluates the expression (*EXPR*) for each element of the array (*LIST*). The return value is another array consisting of those elements for which the expression evaluated as true. As a scalar value, the return value is the number of times the expression was true (i.e., the number of times the pattern was found).

FORMAT

```
grep(EXPR,LIST)
```

EXAMPLE 5.34

```
(The Script)
    # Searching for patterns in a list
1   @list = (tomatoes, tomorrow, potatoes, phantom, Tommy);
2   $count = grep( /tom/i, @list);
    @items= grep( /tom/i, @list);
    print "Found items: @items\nNumber found: $count\n";

(Output)
4   Found items: tomatoes tomorrow phantom Tommy
    Number found: 4
```

EXPLANATION

1. The array *@list* is assigned list elements.
2. The *grep* function searches for the regular expression *tom*. The *i* turns off case sensitivity. When the return value is assigned to a scalar, the result is the number of times the regular expression was matched.
3. *grep* again searches for the regular expression *tom*. The *i* turns off case sensitivity. When the return value is assigned to an array, the result is a list of the matched items.

5.4.5 The *join* Function

The *join* function joins the elements of an array into a single string and separates each element of the array with a given delimiter—the opposite of *split* (see "The *split* Function" on page 110). It can be used after the *split* function has broken a string into array elements. The expression *DELIMITER* is the value of the delimiter that will separate the array elements. The *LIST* consists of the array elements.

FORMAT

```
join(DELIMITER, LIST)
```

EXAMPLE 5.35

```
(The Script)
    # Joining each elements of a list with colons
1   $name="Joe Blow";
    $birth="11/12/86";
    $address="10 Main St.";
2   print join(":", $name, $birth, $address ), "\n";

(Output)
2   Joe Blow:11/12/86:10 Main St.
```

EXPLANATION

1 A string is assigned to a scalar.
2 The *join* function joins the three scalars, using a colon delimiter, and the new string is printed.

EXAMPLE 5.36

```
(The Script)
    # Joining each element of a list with a newline
1   @names=('Dan','Dee','Scotty','Liz','Tom');
2   @names=join("\n", sort(@names));
3   print @names,"\n";

(Output)
3   Dan
    Dee
    Liz
    Scotty
    Tom
```

EXPLANATION

1 The array *@names* is assigned a list.
2 The *join* function will *join* each word in the list with a newline (*\n*) after the list has been sorted alphabetically.
3 The sorted list is printed with each element of the array on a line of its own.

5.4.6 The *map* Function

The *map* function maps each of the values in an array to an expression or block, returning another array with the results of the mapping. This is easier to demonstrate in an example than to describe in words.

FORMAT

```
map EXPR, LIST;
map {BLOCK} LIST;
```

EXAMPLE 5.37

```
(The Script)
    # Mapping a list to an expression
1   @list=(0x53,0x77,0x65,0x64,0x65,0x6e,012);
2   @words = map chr, @list;
3   print @words;
4   @n = (2, 4, 6, 8);
5   @n = map $_ * 2 + 6, @n;
6   print "@n\n";

(Output)
3   Sweden
6   10 14 18 22
```

EXPLANATION

1. The array *@list* consists of six hexadecimal numbers and one octal number.
2. The *map* function maps each item in *@list* to its corresponding *chr* (character) value and returns a new list.
3. The new list is printed. Each numeric value was converted with the *chr* function to a character corresponding to its ASCII value.
4. The array *@n* consists of a list of integers.
5. The *map* function evaluates the expression for each element in the *@n* array and returns the new list to *@n*, resulting from the evaluation.
6. The results of the mapping are printed.

EXAMPLE 5.38

```
(The Script)
    # Map using a block
    open(FH, "datebook.master") or die;
    @lines=<FH>;
    @fields = map { split(":") } @lines;
    foreach $field (@fields){
        print $field,"\n";
    }
```

EXAMPLE 5.38 (CONTINUED)

```
(Output)
5   Sir Lancelot
    837-835-8257
    474 Camelot Boulevard, Bath, WY 28356
    5/13/69
    24500

    Tommy Savage
    408-724-0140
    1222 Oxbow Court, Sunnyvale, CA 94087
    5/19/66
    34200

    Yukio Takeshida
    387-827-1095
    13 Uno Lane, Asheville, NC 23556
    7/1/29
    57000

    Vinh Tranh
    438-910-7449
    8235 Maple Street, Wilmington, VT 29085
    9/23/63
    68900
```

EXPLANATION

1. The *datebook.master* file is opened for reading from the *FH* filehandle. Each line consists of colon-separated fields terminated by a newline.
2. The contents of the file are read and assigned to *@lines*. Each line of the file is an element of the array.
3. The *map* function uses the block format. The *split* function splits up the array at colons, resulting in a list where each field becomes an element of the array.
4. The *foreach* loop iterates through the array, assigning each element, in turn, to *$field*.
5. The display demonstrates the results of the mapping. Before mapping, the line was: *Sir Lancelot:837-835-8257:474 Camelot Boulevard, Bath, WY 28356:5/13/69:24500*

5.4.7 The *pack* and *unpack* Functions

The *pack* and *unpack* functions have a number of uses. These functions are used to pack a list into a binary structure and then expand the packed values back into a list. When working with files, you can use these functions to create uuencoded files, relational databases, and binary files.

The *pack* function converts a list into a scalar value that may be stored in machine memory. The *TEMPLATE* is used to specify the type of character and how many characters will be formatted. For example, the string *c4*, or *cccc*, packs a list into 4 unsigned characters, and *a14* packs a list into a 14-byte ASCII string, null padded. The *unpack* function converts a binary formatted string into a list, and puts a string back into Perl format.

Table 5.2 The Template *pack* and *unpack*—Types and Values

Template	*Description*
a	An ASCII string (null padded)
A	An ASCII string (space padded)
b	A bit string (low-to-high order, like *vec*)
B	A bit string (high-to-low order)
c	A signed *char* value
C	An unsigned *char* value
d	A double-precision float in the native format
f	A single-precision float in the native format
h	A hexadecimal string (low nybble first, to high)
H	A hexadecimal string (high nybble first)
i	A signed integer
I	An unsigned integer
l	A signed long value
L	An unsigned long value
n	A short in "network" (big-endian) order
N	A long in "network" (big-endian) order
p	A pointer to a null-terminated string
P	A pointer to a structure (fixed-length string)
q	A signed 64-bit value
Q	An unsigned 64-bit value
s	A signed short value (16-bit)
S	An unsigned short value (16-bit)
u	A uuencoded string

Table 5.2 The Template *pack* and *unpack*—Types and Values (continued)

Template	*Description*
v	A short in "VAX" (little-endian) order
V	A long in "VAX" (little-endian) order
w	A BER compressed unsigned integer in base 128, high bit first
x	A null byte
X	Back up a byte
@	Null fill to absolute position

5.4.8 The *pop* Function

The *pop* function pops off the last element of an array and returns it. The array size is subsequently decreased by 1.

FORMAT

```
pop(ARRAY)
pop ARRAY
```

EXAMPLE 5.39

```
(In Script)
   # Removing an element from the end of a list
1  @names=("Bob", "Dan", "Tom", "Guy");
2  print "@names\n";
3  $got = pop(@names);    # Pops off last element of the array
4  print "$got\n";
5  print "@names\n";

(Output)
2  Bob Dan Tom Guy
4  Guy
5  Bob Dan Tom
```

EXPLANATION

1. The *@name* array is assigned list elements.
2. The array is printed.
3. The *pop* function removes the last element of the array and returns the popped item.
4. The *$got* scalar contains the popped item, *Guy*.
5. The new array is printed.

5.4.9 The *push* Function

The *push* function pushes values onto the end of an array, thereby increasing the length of the array.

FORMAT

```
push(ARRAY, LIST)
```

EXAMPLE 5.40

```
(In Script)
   # Adding elements to the end of a list
1  @names=("Bob", "Dan", "Tom", "Guy");
2  push(@names, "Jim", "Joseph", "Archie");
3  print "@names \n";

(Output)
2  Bob Dan Tom Guy Jim Joseph Archie
```

EXPLANATION

1. The array *@names* is assigned list values.
2. The *push* function pushes three more elements onto the end of the array.
3. The new array has three more elements appended to it.

5.4.10 The *shift* Function

The *shift* function shifts off and returns the first element of an array, decreasing the size of the array by one element. If *ARRAY* is omitted, then the *ARGV* array is shifted, and, if in a subroutine, the @_ array is shifted.

FORMAT

```
shift(ARRAY)
shift ARRAY
shift
```

EXAMPLE 5.41

```
(In Script)
   # Removing elements from front of a list
1  @names=("Bob", "Dan", "Tom", "Guy");
2  $ret  = shift @names;
3  print "@names\n";
4  print "The item shifted is $ret.\n";
```

EXAMPLE 5.41 (CONTINUED)

```
(Output)
3   Dan Tom Guy
4   The item shifted is Bob.
```

EXPLANATION

1 The array *@names* is assigned list values.
2 The *shift* function removes the first element of the array and returns that element to the scalar *$ret*, which is *Bob*.
3 The new array has been shortened by one element.

5.4.11 The *splice* Function

The *splice* function removes and replaces elements in an array. The *OFFSET* is the starting position where elements are to be removed. The *LENGTH* is the number of items from the *OFFSET* position to be removed. The *LIST* consists of new elements that are to replace the old ones.

FORMAT

```
splice(ARRAY, OFFSET, LENGTH, LIST)
splice(ARRAY, OFFSET, LENGTH)
splice(ARRAY, OFFSET)
```

EXAMPLE 5.42

```
(The Script)
    # Splicing out elements of a list
1   @colors=("red", "green", "purple", "blue", "brown");
2   print "The original array is @colors\n";
3   @discarded = splice(@colors, 2, 2);
4   print "The elements removed after the splice are: @discarded.\n";
5   print "The spliced array is now @colors.\n";

(Output)
2   The original array is red green purple blue brown
4   The elements removed after the splice are: purple blue.
5   The spliced array is now red green brown.
```

EXPLANATION

1 An array of five colors is created.
2 The original array is printed.
3 The *splice* function will delete elements starting at offset 2 (offset is initially 0), remove the two elements, *purple* and *blue*, and return the removed elements to another array, named *@discarded*.

EXPLANATION

4 The splice removed elements *purple* and *blue* and returned them to *@discarded*, starting at element *$colors[2]*, with a length of two elements.

5 The array *@colors* has been spliced. *purple* and *blue* were removed.

EXAMPLE 5.43

```
(The Script)
    # Splicing and replacing elements of a list
1   @colors=("red", "green", "purple", "blue", "brown");
2   print "The original array is @colors\n";
3   @lostcolors=splice(@colors, 2, 3, "yellow", "orange");
4   print "The removed items are @lostcolors\n";
5   print "The spliced array is now @colors\n";

(Output)
2   The original array is red green purple blue brown
4   The removed items are purple blue brown
5   The spliced array is now red green yellow orange
```

EXPLANATION

1 An array of five colors is created.

2 The original array is printed.

3 The *splice* function will delete elements starting at offset 2 (offset is initially 0) and remove the next three elements. The removed elements (*purple*, *blue*, and *brown*) are stored in *@lostcolors*. The colors *yellow* and *orange* will replace the ones that were removed.

4 The values that were removed are stored in *@lostcolors* and printed.

5 The new array, after the splice, is printed.

5.4.12 The *split* Function

The *split* function splits up a string (*EXPR*) by some delimiter (whitespace by default) and returns an array. The first argument is the delimiter, and the second is the string to be split. The Perl *split* function can be used to create fields when processing files, just as you would with *awk*. If a string is not supplied as the expression, the $_ string is split.

The *DELIMITER* statement matches the delimiters that are used to separate the fields. If *DELIMITER* is omitted, the delimiter defaults to whitespace (spaces, tabs, or newlines). If the *DELIMITER* doesn't match a delimiter, *split* returns the original string. You can specify more than one delimiter, using the regular expression metacharacter *[ ]*. For example, *[+\t:]* represents zero or more spaces or a tab or a colon.

LIMIT specifies the number of fields that can be split. If there are more than *LIMIT* fields, the remaining fields will all be part of the last one. If the *LIMIT* is omitted, the *split* function has its own *LIMIT*, which is one more than the number of fields in *EXPR*. (See the *-a* switch for autosplit mode, in Appendix A.)

FORMAT

```
split("DELIMITER",EXPR,LIMIT)
split(/DELIMITER/,EXPR,LIMIT)
split(/DELIMITER/,EXPR)
split("DELIMITER",EXPR)
split(/DELIMITER/)
split
```

EXAMPLE 5.44

```
(The Script)
    # Splitting a scalar on whitespace and creating a list
1   $line="a b c d e";
2   @letter=split(' ',$line);
3   print "The first letter is $letter[0]\n";
4   print "The second letter is $letter[1]\n";

(Output)
3   The first letter is a
4   The second letter is b
```

EXPLANATION

1. The scalar variable *$line* is assigned the string *a b c d e*.
2. The value in *$line* (scalar) is a single string of letters. The *split* function will split the string, using whitespace as a delimiter. The *@letter* array will be assigned the individual elements *a*, *b*, *c*, *d*, and *e*. Using single quotes as the delimiter is **not** the same as using the regular expression / /. The ' ' resembles *awk* in splitting lines on whitespace. Leading whitespace is ignored. The regular expression / / includes leading whitespace, creating as many null initial fields as there are whitespaces.
3. The first element of the *@letter* array is printed.
4. The second element of the *@letter* array is printed.

EXAMPLE 5.45

```
(The Script)
    # Splitting up $_
1   while(<DATA>){
2       @line=split(":");        # or split (":", $_);
3       print "$line[0]\n";
    }
```

EXAMPLE 5.45 (CONTINUED)

```
__DATA__
Betty Boop:245-836-8357:635 Cutesy Lane, Hollywood, CA 91464:6/23/23:14500
Igor Chevsky:385-375-8395:3567 Populus Place, Caldwell, NJ 23875:6/18/68:23400
Norma Corder:397-857-2735:74 Pine Street, Dearborn, MI 23874:3/28/45:245700
Jennifer Cowan:548-834-2348:583 Laurel Ave., Kingsville, TX 83745:10/1/35:58900
Fred Fardbarkle:674-843-1385:20 Park Lane, Duluth, MN 23850:4/12/23:78900

     (Output)
     Betty Boop
     Igor Chevsky
     Norma Corder
     Jennifer Cowan
     Fred Fardbarkle
```

EXPLANATION

1. The $_ variable holds each line of the file *DATA* filehandle; the data being processed is below the *__DATA__* line. Each line is assigned to $_. $_ is also the default line for *split*.
2. The *split* function splits the line, ($_), using the : as a delimiter and returns the line to the array, *@line*.
3. The first element of the *@line* array, *line[0]*, is printed.

EXAMPLE 5.46

```
     (The Script)
         # Splitting up $_ and creating an unnamed list
         while(<DATA>){
     1       ($name,$phone,$address,$bd,$sal)=split(":");
     2       print "$name\t $phone\n" ;
         }

__DATA__
Betty Boop:245-836-8357:635 Cutesy Lane, Hollywood, CA 91464:6/23/23:14500
Igor Chevsky:385-375-8395:3567 Populus Place, Caldwell, NJ 23875:6/18/68:23400
Norma Corder:397-857-2735:74 Pine Street, Dearborn, MI 23874:3/28/45:245700
Jennifer Cowan:548-834-2348:583 Laurel Ave., Kingsville, TX 83745:10/1/35:58900
Fred Fardbarkle:674-843-1385:20 Park Lane, Duluth, MN 23850:4/12/23:78900

     (Output)
     2   Betty Boop 245-836-8357
         Igor Chevsky 385-375-8395
         Norma Corder 397-857-2735
         Jennifer Cowan 548-834-2348
         Fred Fardbarkle 674-843-1385
```

EXPLANATION

1. Perl loops through the *DATA* filehandle one line at a time. Each line of the file is stored in the $_ variable. The *split* function splits each line, using the colon as a delimiter.
2. The array consists of five scalars, *$name*, *$phone*, *$address*, *$bd*, and *$sal*. The values of *$name* and *$phone* are printed.

EXAMPLE 5.47

```
(The Script)
   # Many ways to split a scalar to create a list
1  $string= "Joe Blow:11/12/86:10 Main St.:Boston, MA:02530";
2  @line=split(":", $string);     # The string delimiter is a colon
3  print @line,"\n";
4  print "The guy's name is $line[0].\n";
5  print "The birthday is $line[1].\n\n";

6  @str=split(":", $string, 2);
7  print $str[0],"\n";  # The first element of the array
8  print $str[1],"\n";  # The rest of the array because limit is 2
9  print $str[2],"\n";  # Nothing is printed

10 @str=split(":", $string);  # Limit not stated will be one more
                              # than total number of fields
11 print $str[0],"\n";
12 print $str[1],"\n";
13 print $str[2],"\n";
14 print $str[3],"\n";
15 print $str[4],"\n";
16 print $str[5],"\n";

17 ( $name, $birth, $address )=split(":", $string);
             # Limit is implicitly 4, one more than
             # the number of fields specified
18 print $name , "\n";
19 print $birth,"\n";
20 print $address,"\n";

(Output)
3  Joe Blow11/12/8610 Main St.Boston, MA02530
4  The guy's name is Joe Blow.
5  The birthday is 11/12/86.

7  Joe Blow
8  11/12/86:10 Main St.:Boston, MA:02530
9
```

EXAMPLE 5.47 (CONTINUED)

```
11  Joe Blow
12  11/12/86
13  10 Main St.
14  Boston, MA
15  02530
16
18  Joe Blow
19  11/12/86
20  10 Main St.
```

EXPLANATION

1. The scalar *$string* is split at each colon.
2. The delimiter is a colon. The limit is 2.
3. *LIMIT*, if not stated, will be one more than total number of fields.
4. *LIMIT* is implicitly 4, one more than the number of fields specified.

5.4.13 The *sort* Function

The *sort* function sorts and returns a sorted array. If *SUBROUTINE* is omitted, the sort is in string comparison order; i.e., the array is sorted alphabetically. If *SUBROUTINE* is specified, the first argument to *sort* is the name of the subroutine, followed by a list of values to be sorted. If the string "cmp" operator is used, the values in the list will be sorted alphabetically (ASCII sort), and if the <=> operator (called the "space ship" operator) is used, the values will be sorted numerically. The subroutine returns an integer less than, equal to, or greater than 0. The values are passed to the subroutine by reference and are received by the special Perl variables *$a* and *$b*, not the normal @_ array.(See subroutines in Chapter 11 for further discussion.) Do not try to modify *$a* or *$b*, as they represent the values that are being sorted.

If you want Perl to sort your data according to a particular locale, your program should include the *use locale* pragma. For a complete discusion on the steps needed to do this, see: *http://search.cpan.org/~nwclark/perl-5.8.8/pod/perllocale.pod*

FORMAT

```
sort(SUBROUTINE LIST)
sort(LIST)
sort SUBROUTINE LIST
sort LIST
```

EXAMPLE 5.48

```
(The Script)
# Simple alphabetic sort
1 @list=("dog","cat", "bird","snake" );
  print "Original list: @list\n";
2 @sorted = sort(@list);
3  print "Ascii sort: @sorted\n";

 # Reversed alphabetic sort
4  @sorted = reverse(sort(@list));
   print "Reversed Ascii sort: @sorted\n";

(Output)
Original list: dog cat bird snake
Ascii sort: bird cat dog snake
Reversed Ascii sort: snake dog cat bird
```

EXPLANATION

1. The *@list* array will contain a list of items to be sorted.
2. The *sort* function performs a string (ASCII) sort on the items. The sorted values must be assigned to another list or the same list. The *sort* function doesn't change the orginial list.
3. The sorted string is printed.
4. This list is sorted alphabetically and then reversed.

ASCII and Numeric Sort Using Subroutine

EXAMPLE 5.49

```
(The Script)
1 @list=("dog","cat", "bird","snake" );
  print "Original list: @list\n";
   # ASCII sort using a subroutine
2  sub asc_sort{
3          $a cmp $b;  # Sort ascending order
   }
4  @sorted_list=sort asc_sort(@list);
   print "Ascii sort: @sorted_list\n";

   # Numeric sort using subroutine
5  sub numeric_sort {
       $a <=> $b ;
   }  # $a and $b are compared numerically

6  @number_sort=sort numeric_sort 10, 0, 5, 9.5, 10, 1000;
        print "Numeric sort: @number_sort.\n";
```

EXAMPLE 5.49 (CONTINUED)

```
(Output)
Original list: dog cat bird snake
Ascii sort: bird cat dog snake
Numeric sort: 0 5 9.5 10 10 1000.
```

EXPLANATION

1 The *@list* array will contain a list of items to be sorted.
2 The subroutine *asc_sort()* is sent a list of strings to be sorted.
3 The special variables *$a* and *$b* compare the items to be sorted in ascending order. If *$a* and *$b* are reversed (e.g., *$b cmp $a*), then the sort is done in descending order. The "cmp" operator is used when comparing strings.
4 The *sort* function sends a list to the *asc_sort()*, user-defined subroutine, where the sorting is done. The sorted list will be returned and stored in *@sorted_list*.
5 This is a user-defined subroutine, called *numeric_sort()*. The special variables *$a* and *$b* compare the items to be sorted numerically, in ascending order. If *$a* and *$b* are reversed (e.g., *$b <=> $a*), then the sort is done in numeric descending order. The "<=>" operator is used when comparing numbers.
6 The *sort* function sends a list of number to the *numeric_sort()* function and gets back a list of sorted numbers, stored in the *@number_sort* array.

Using an Inline Function to Sort a Numeric List

EXAMPLE 5.50

```
(The Script)
    # Sorting numbers with an unamed subroutine
1   @sorted_numbers= sort {$a <=> $b} (3,4,1,2);
2   print "The sorted numbers are: @sorted_numbers", ".\n";

(Output)
2   The sorted numbers are: 1 2 3 4.
```

EXPLANATION

1 The *sort* function is given an unnamed subroutine, also called an inline function, to sort a list of numbers passed as arguments. The <=> operator is used with variables *$a* and *$b* to compare the numbers. The sorted numeric list is returned and stored in the array *@sorted_numbers*.
2 The sorted list is printed.

5.4.14 The *reverse* Function

The *reverse* function reverses the elements in an array, so that if the values appeared in descending order, now they are in ascending order, and so on.

FORMAT

```
reverse(LIST)
reverse LIST
```

EXAMPLE 5.51

```
(In Script)
   # Reversing the elements of an array
1  @names=("Bob", "Dan", "Tom", "Guy");
2  print "@names \n";
3  @reversed=reverse(@names),"\n";
4  print "@reversed\n";

(Output)
2  Bob Dan Tom Guy
4  Guy Tom Dan Bob
```

EXPLANATION

1. The array *@names* is assigned list values.
2. The original array is printed.
3. The *reverse* function reverses the elements in the list and returns the reversed list. It does not change the original array; i.e., the array *@names* is not changed. The reversed items are stored in *@reversed*.
4. The reversed array is printed.

5.4.15 The *unshift* Function

The *unshift* function prepends *LIST* to the front of the array.

FORMAT

```
unshift(ARRAY, LIST)
```

EXAMPLE 5.52

```
(In Script)
   # Putting new elements at the front of a list
1  @names=("Jody", "Bert", "Tom") ;
2  unshift(@names, "Liz", "Daniel");
3  print "@names\n";

(Output)
3  Liz Daniel Jody Bert Tom
```

EXPLANATION

1. The array *@names* is assigned three values, *Jody, Bert,* and *Tom.*
2. The *unshift* function will prepend *Liz* and *Daniel* to the array.
3. The *@names* array is printed.

5.5 Hash (Associative Array) Functions

5.5.1 The *keys* Function

The *keys* function returns, in random order, an array whose elements are the keys of a hash (see "The *values* Function" and "The *each* Function").

FORMAT

```
keys(ASSOC_ARRAY)
keys ASSOC_ARRAY
```

EXAMPLE 5.53

```
(In Script)
    # The keys function returns the keys of a hash
1   %weekday= (
                '1'=>'Monday',
                '2'=>'Tuesday',
                '3'=>'Wednesday',
                '4'=>'Thursday',
                '5'=>'Friday',
                '6'=>'Saturday',
                '7'=>'Sunday',
               );
2   foreach $key ( keys(%weekday) ){print "$key ";}
    print "\n";
3   foreach $key ( sort keys(%weekday) ){print "$key ";}
    print "\n";

(Output)
2   7 1 2 3 4 5 6
3   1 2 3 4 5 6 7
```

EXPLANATION

1 The hash *%weekday* is assigned keys and values.
2 For each value in *%weekday*, call the *keys* function to get the key. Assign the key value to the scalar *$key* and print it in random order.
3 Now the keys are sorted and printed.

5.5.2 The *values* Function

The *values* function returns, in random order, an array consisting of all the values of a hash.

FORMAT

```
values(ASSOC_ARRAY)
values ASSOC_ARRAY
```

EXAMPLE 5.54

```
(In Script)
    # The values function returns the values in a hash
1   %weekday= (
                '1'=>'Monday',
                '2'=>'Tuesday',
                '3'=>'Wednesday',
                '4'=>'Thursday',
                '5'=>'Friday',
                '6'=>'Saturday',
                '7'=>'Sunday',
               );
2   foreach $value ( values(%weekday)){print "$value";}
    print "\n";

(Output)
2   Monday Tuesday Wednesday Thursday Friday Saturday Sunday
```

EXPLANATION

1. The hash *%weekday* is assigned keys and values.
2. For each value in *%weekday,* call the *values* function to get the value associated with each key. Assign that value to the scalar *$value*, and print it to *STDOUT.*

5.5.3 The *each* Function

The *each* function returns, in random order, a two-element array whose elements are the *key* and the corresponding *value* of a hash.

FORMAT

```
each(ASSOC_ARRAY)
```

EXAMPLE 5.55

```
(In Script)
#! /usr/bin/perl
# The each function retrieves both keys and values from a hash
1  %weekday=(
                'Mon' => 'Monday',
                'Tue' => 'Tuesday',
                'Wed' => 'Wednesday',
                'Thu' => 'Thursday',
                'Fri' => 'Friday',
                'Sat' => 'Saturday',
                'Sun' => 'Sunday',
              );
2  while(($key,$value)=each(%weekday)){
3      print "$key = $value\n";
   }

(Output)
3  Sat = Saturday
   Fri = Friday
   Sun = Sunday
   Thu = Thursday
   Wed = Wednesday
   Tue = Tuesday
   Mon = Monday
```

EXPLANATION

1. The hash *%weekday* is assigned keys and values.
2. The *each* function returns each key and its associated *value* of the *%weekday* hash. They are assigned to the scalars *$key* and *$value*, respectively.
3. The keys and values are printed but in an unordered way.

5.5.4 Sorting a Hash

When sorting a hash, you can sort the keys alphabetically very easily by using the built-in *sort()* command, as we did with arrays in the preceding section. But you may want to sort the keys numerically or sort the hash by its values. To do this requires a little more work. You can define a subroutine to compare the keys or values. (See subroutines in Chapter 11). The subroutine will be called by the built-in *sort()* function. It will be sent a list of keys or values to be compared. The comparison is either an ASCII (alphabetic) or a numeric comparison, depending upon the operator used. The "cmp" operator is used for comparing strings, and the "<=>" operator is used for comparing numbers. The reserved global scalars *$a*, and *$b* are used in the subroutine to hold the values as they are being compared. The names of these scalars cannot be changed.

Sort Hash by Keys in Ascending Order. To perform an Ascii or alphabetic sort on the keys in a hash is relatively easy. The *sort()* function is given a list of keys and returns them sorted in ascending order. A *foreach* loop is used to loop through the hash one key at a time. See Example 5.56.

EXAMPLE 5.56

```
(In Script)
1   %wins = (
         "Portland Panthers"    => 10,
         "Sunnyvale Sluggers"   => 12,
         "Chico Wildcats"       => 5,
         "Stevensville Tigers"  => 6,
         "Lewiston Blazers"     => 11,
         "Danville Terriors"    => 8,
    );
    print "\n\tSort Teams in Ascending Order:\n\n";
2   foreach $key( sort(keys %wins)) {
3        printf "\t% -20s%5d\n", $key, $wins{$key};
    }
(Output)
Sort Teams in Ascending  Order:

         Chico Wildcats          5
         Danville Terriors       8
         Lewiston Blazers       11
         Portland Panthers      10
         Stevensville Tigers     6
         Sunnyvale Sluggers     12
```

EXPLANATION

1. A hash called *%wins* is assigned key/value pairs.
2. The *foreach* loop will be used to iterate through each of the elements in the hash. The *foreach* receives an alphabetically sorted list as output from the *sort()* function. The *sort()* function gets its list from the built-in *keys* function, which returns a list of all the keys in a hash.
3. The *printf()* function formats and prints the keys and sorted values.

Sort Hash by Keys in Reverse Order. To sort a hash by keys alphabetically and in descending order, just add the built-in *reverse()* function to the previous example. The *foreach* loop is used to get each key from the hash, one at a time, after the reversed sort.

EXAMPLE 5.57

```
1  %wins = (
        "Portland Panthers"    => 10,
        "Sunnyvale Sluggers"   => 12,
        "Chico Wildcats"       => 5,
        "Stevensville Tigers"  => 6,
        "Lewiston Blazers"     => 11,
        "Danville Terriors"    => 8,
   );
   print "\n\tSort Teams in Descending/Reverse Order:\n\n";
2  foreach $key (reverse sort(keys %wins)) {
3     printf "\t% -20s%5d\n", $key, $wins{$key};
   }
```

```
(Output)
Sort Teams in Descending/Reverse Order:

        Sunnyvale Sluggers      12
        Stevensville Tigers      6
        Portland Panthers       10
        Lewiston Blazers        11
        Danville Terriors        8
        Chico Wildcats           5
```

EXPLANATION

1. A hash called *%wins* is assigned key/value pairs.
2. The *foreach* loop will be used to iterate through each of the elements in the hash. The *reverse()* function takes the alphabetically sorted list returned from the *sort()* function and reverses it. This reversed list is used by the *foreach* function to extract each key and value from the hash *%wins*.
3. The *printf()* function formats and prints the keys and sorted values.

Sort Hash by Keys Numerically. A user-defined subroutine is used to sort a hash by keys numerically. In the subroutine, Perl's special *$a* and *$b* variables are used to hold the value being compared with the appropriate operator. For numeric comparison, the <=> operator is used, and for string comparison, the "cmp" operator is used. The *sort()* function will send a list of keys to the user-defined subroutine. The sorted list is returned.

EXAMPLE 5.58

```
1  sub desc_sort_subject {
2       $b <=> $a;              # Numeric sort descending
   }
3  sub asc_sort_subject{
4       $a <=> $b;              # Numeric sort ascending
   }
```

EXAMPLE 5.58 (CONTINUED)

```
5    %courses = (
        "101" => "Intro to Computer Science",
        "221" => "Linguistics",
        "300" => "Astronomy",
        "102" => "Perl",
        "103" => "PHP",
        "200" => "Language arts",
     );
     print "\n\tCourses in Ascending Numeric Order:\n";
6    foreach $key (sort asc_sort_subject(keys(%courses))) {
7       printf "\t%-5d%s\n", $key, $courses{"$key"};
     }
     print "\n\tCourses in Descending Numeric Order:\n";
     foreach $key (sort desc_sort_subject(keys(%courses))) {
        printf "\t%-5d%s\n", $key, $courses{"$key"};
     }
(Output)
   Courses in Ascending Numeric Order:
        101  Intro to Computer Science
        102  Perl
        103  PHP
        200  Language arts
        221  Linguistics
        300  Astronomy

   Courses in Descending Numeric Order:
        300  Astronomy
        221  Linguistics
        200  Language arts
        103  PHP
        102  Perl
        101  Intro to Computer Science
```

EXPLANATION

1. This is a user-defined subroutine called *desc_sort_subject()*. When its name is given to the *sort()* function, this function will be used to compare the keys passed to it. It will sort the keys numerically.
2. The special Perl variables *$a* and *$b* are used to compare the values of the keys from the hash called *$courses*. The <=> operator is a numeric comparison operator that will compare each of the keys to be sorted as numbers. In the previous examples, we sorted the keys alphabetically. Since *$b* precedes *$a*, the sort is descending.
3. This is also a user-defined subroutine called *asc_sort_subject()*. This function is identical to the previous function on line 1, except it will sort the keys of the hash in ascending numeric order rather than descending.
4. In this function, the special variables *$a* and *$b* have been reversed, causing the sort after the comparison to be in ascending order.

EXPLANATION (CONTINUED)

5 The hash called *%courses* is defined with key/value pairs.

6 The *foreach* loop will be used to iterate through each of the elements in the hash. It receives its list from the output of the *sort()* command.

7 The *printf()* function formats and prints the keys and sorted values.

Numerically Sort a Hash by Values in Ascending Order. To sort a hash by its values, a user-defined function is also defined. The values of the hash are compared by the special variables *$a* and *$b*. If *$a* is on the left-hand side of the comparison operator, the sort is in ascending order, and if *$b* is on the left-hand side, then the sort is in descending order. The <=> operator compares its operands numerically.

EXAMPLE 5.59

```
(In Script)
sub asc_sort_wins {
      $wins{$a} <=> $wins{$b};
}


  %wins = (
      "Portland Panthers"    => 10,
      "Sunnyvale Sluggers"   => 12,
      "Chico Wildcats"       => 5,
      "Stevensville Tigers"  => 6,
      "Lewiston Blazers"     => 11,
      "Danville Terriors"    => 8,
  );
  print "\n\tWins in Ascending Numeric Order:\n\n";
  foreach $key (sort asc_sort_wins(keys(%wins))) {
      printf "\t% -20s%5d\n", $key, $wins{$key};
  }

(Output)

Wins in Ascending Numeric Order:

        Chico Wildcats          5
        Stevensville Tigers     6
        Danville Terriors       8
        Portland Panthers      10
        Lewiston Blazers       11
        Sunnyvale Sluggers     12
```

EXPLANATION

1 This is a user-defined subroutine called *asc_sort_wins()*. When its name is given to the *sort()* function, this function will be used to compare the hash values passed to it. It will sort the values by value, numerically.
2 The special Perl variables *$a* and *$b* are used to compare the values of the hash called *$wins*. The <=> operator is a numeric comparison operator that will compare each of the values to be sorted. To compare strings, the "cmp" operator is used.
3 The hash called *%wins* is assigned key/value pairs.
4 The *foreach* loop iterates through each of the elements in the hash. It receives its list from the output of the *sort()* command.
5 The *printf()* function formats and prints the keys and sorted values.

Numerically Sort a Hash by Values in Descending Order. To sort a hash numerically and in descending order by its values, a user-defined function is defined as in the previous example. However, this time the *$b* variable is on the left-hand side of the <=> numeric operator, and the *$a* variable is on the right-hand side. This causes the *sort()* function to sort in descending order.

EXAMPLE 5.60

```
    (In Script)
   # Sorting a Hash by Value in Descending Order

1  sub desc_sort_wins {
2       $wins{$b} <=> $wins{$a};   # Reverse $a and $b
   }

3  %wins = (
        "Portland Panthers"     => 10,
        "Sunnyvale Sluggers"    => 12,
        "Chico Wildcats"        => 5,
        "Stevensville Tigers"   => 6,
        "Lewiston Blazers"      => 11,
        "Danville Terriors"     => 8,
    );
    print "\n\tWins in Descending Numeric Order:\n\n";
4   foreach $key (sort desc_sort_wins(keys(%wins))) {
5       printf "\t% -20s%5d\n", $key, $wins{$key};
    }
```

EXAMPLE 5.60 (CONTINUED)

```
(Output)

Wins in Descending Numeric Order:

          Sunnyvale Sluggers        12
          Lewiston Blazers          11
          Portland Panthers         10
          Danville Terriors          8
          Stevensville Tigers        6
          Chico Wildcats             5
```

EXPLANATION

1 This is a user-defined subroutine called *desc_sort_wins()*. When its name is given to the *sort()* function, this function will be used to compare the hash values passed to it. It will sort the values by value, numerically but in descending order.

2 The special Perl variables *$a* and *$b* are used to compare the values of the hash called *$wins*. The position of *$a* and *$b* determines whether the sort is in ascending or descending order. If *$a* is on the left-hand side of the <=> operator, the sort is a numeric ascending sort; if *$b* is on the left-hand side of the <=> operator, the sort is descending. To compare strings, the "cmp" operator is used.

3 The hash called *%wins* is assigned key/value pairs.

4 The *foreach* loop will be used to iterate through each of the elements in the hash. It receives its list from the output of the *sort()* command.

5 The *printf()* function formats and prints the keys and sorted values.

5.5.5 The *delete* Function

The *delete* function deletes a value from a hash. The deleted value is returned if successful.[8]

FORMAT

```
delete $ASSOC_ARRAY{KEY}
```

EXAMPLE 5.61

```
(In Script)
    #!/usr/bin/perl
1   %employees=(
                 "Nightwatchman" => "Joe Blow",
                 "Janitor" => "Teddy Plunger",
                 "Clerk" => "Sally Olivetti",
                );
```

8. If a value in an *%ENV* hash is deleted, the environment is changed. (See "The *%ENV* Hash" on page 129.)

EXAMPLE 5.61 (CONTINUED)

```
2   $layoff=delete $employees{"Janitor"};
    print "We had to let $layoff go.\n";
    print "Our remaining staff includes: ";
    print "\n";
    while(($key, $value)=each(%employees)){
        print "$key: $value\n";
    }

(Output)
We had to let Teddy Plunger go.
Our remaining staff includes:
Nightwatchman: Joe Blow
Clerk: Sally Olivetti
```

EXPLANATION

1 A hash is defined with three key/value pairs.
2 The *delete* function deletes an element from the specified hash by specifying the key. *Janitor* is the key. Both key and value are removed.
3 The hash value associated with the key *Janitor* is removed and returned. The value *Teddy Plunger* is returned and assigned to the scalar *$layoff*.

5.5.6 The *exists* Function

The *exists* function returns true if a hash key (or array index) has been defined, and false if not.

FORMAT

```
exists $ASSOC_ARRAY{KEY}
```

EXAMPLE 5.62

```
    #!/usr/bin/perl
1   %employees=( "Nightwatchman" => "Joe Blow",
                 "Janitor" => "Teddy Plunger",
                 "Clerk" => "Sally Olivetti",
               );

2   print "The Nightwatchman exists.\n" if exists
          $employees{"Nightwatchman"};
3   print "The Clerk exists.\n" if exists $employees{"Clerk"};
4   print "The Boss does not exist.\n" if not exists
$employees{"Boss"};

(Output)
2   The Nightwatchman exists.
3   The Clerk exists.
4   The Boss does not exist.
```

EXPLANATION

1. A hash is defined with three key/value pairs.
2. If a key *"Nightwatchman"* has been defined, the *exists* function returns true.
3. If a key *"Clerk"* has been defined, the exists function returns true.
4. If the key *"Clerk"* does **not** exist, the return value of the *exists* function is reversed.

5.6 More Hashes

5.6.1 Loading a Hash from a File

EXAMPLE 5.63

```
(The Database)
    1 Steve Blenheim
    2 Betty Boop
    3 Igor Chevsky
    4 Norma Cord
    5 Jon DeLoach
    6 Karen Evich

(The Script)
    #!/usr/bin/perl
    # Loading a Hash from a file.
    open(NAMES,"emp.names") || die "Can't open emp.names: $!\n";
    while(<NAMES>){
        ( $num, $name )= split(' ', $_, 2);
        $realid{$num} = $name;
    }
    close NAMES;

    while(1){
        print "Please choose a number from the list of names? ";
        chomp($num=<STDIN>);
        last unless $num;
        print $realid{$num},"\n";
    }

(Output)
    Please choose a number from the list of names? 1
    Steve Blenheim
    Number for which name? 4
    Norma Cord
    Number for which name? 5
    Jon DeLoach
    Number for which name? 2
    Betty Boop
```

EXAMPLE 5.63 (CONTINUED)

```
Number for which name? 6
Karen Evich
Number for which name? 8
Number for which name? 3
Igor Chevsky
Number for which name?
<Ctrl>-d or <Ctrl>-z (Exit the program)
```

EXPLANATION

1 A file called *emp.names* is opened for reading via the *NAMES* filehandle.
2 A line at a time is read from the file via the *while* loop.
3 The line just read in, $_, is split into two fields with whitespace (spaces, tabs, and newline) as the delimiter. After splitting up the $_ line, the *split* function returns a list, *$num* and *$name* (consisting of both the first and last names).
4 A hash called *%realid* is created on the fly with *$num* as the key and *$name* as the value associated with that key. Each time through the loop, a new key/value pair is added to *%realid*.
5 The filehandle is closed.
6 The *while* loop is reentered.
7 The user is asked for a number to be associated with a name.
8 The number is read from standard input (the keyboard) as the user types it and is assigned to *$num* and *chomp*ed.
9 The loop exits if *$num* does not have a value.
10 The "name" value, *$name*, associated with the "number" key, *$num*, from the *%realid* hash is printed.

5.6.2 Special Hashes

The *%ENV* Hash. The *%ENV* hash contains the environment variables handed to Perl from the parent process; e.g., a shell or a Web server. The key is the name of the environment variable, and the value is what was assigned to it. If you change the value of *%ENV*, you will alter the environment for your Perl script and any processes spawned from it but not the parent process. Environment variables play a significant roll in CGI Perl scripts, discussed in Chapter 16.

EXAMPLE 5.64

```
(In Script)
#!/usr/bin/perl
foreach $key (keys(%ENV)){
    print "$key\n";
}
print "\nYour login name $ENV{'LOGNAME'}\n";
$pwd=$ENV{'PWD'};
print "\n", $pwd, "\n";
```

EXAMPLE 5.64 (CONTINUED)

```
(Output)
2   OPENWINHOME
    MANPATH
    FONTPATH
    LOGNAME
    USER
    TERMCAP
    TERM
    SHELL
    PWD
    HOME
    PATH
    WINDOW_PARENT
    WMGR_ENV_PLACEHOLDER

3   Your login name is ellie

5   /home/jody/home
```

EXPLANATION

1. Iterate through the *foreach* loop to get the keys of the *%ENV* hash.
2. Print the key value.
3. Print the value of the key *LOGNAME*.
4. Assign the value of the key *PWD* to *$pwd*.
5. Print the value of *$pwd*.

The *%SIG* Hash. The *%SIG* hash allows you to set signal handlers for signals. If, for example, you press <Ctrl>-C when your program is running, that is a signal, identified by the name *SIGINT*. (See UNIX manual pages for a complete list of signals.) The default action of *SIGINT* is to interrupt your process. The signal handler is a subroutine that is automatically called when a signal is sent to the process. Normally, the handler is used to perform a clean-up operation or to check some flag value before the script aborts. (All signal handlers are assumed to be set in the main package.)

The *%SIG* array contains values only for signals set within the Perl script.

EXAMPLE 5.65

```
(In Script)
    #!/usr/bin/perl
1   sub handler{
2       local($sig) = @_;  # First argument is signal name
        print "Caught SIG$sig -- shutting down\n";
        exit(0);
    }
```

EXAMPLE 5.65 (CONTINUED)

```
4   $SIG{'INT'} = 'handler';   # Catch <Ctrl>-c
    print "Here I am!\n";
5   sleep(10);
6   $SIG{'INT'}='DEFAULT';
7   $SIG{'INT'}='IGNORE';
      < Program continues here >
```

EXPLANATION

1. *handler* is the name of the subroutine. The subroutine is defined.
2. *$sig* is a local variable and will be assigned the signal name.
3. When the *SIGINT* signal arrives, this message will appear, and the script will exit.
4. The value assigned to the key *INT* is the name of the subroutine, *handler*. When the signal arrives, the handler is called.
5. The *sleep* function gives you 10 seconds to press <Ctrl>-c to see what happens.
6. The default action is restored. The default action is to abort the process if the user presses <Ctrl>-c.
7. If you assign the value "IGNORE" to the $SIG hash, then <Ctrl>-c will be completely ignored and the program will continue.

The *%INC* Hash. The *%INC* hash contains the entries for each filename that has been included via the *do* or *require* functions. The **key** is the filename; the **value** is the location of the actual file found.

5.6.3 Context

In summary, the way Perl evaluates variables—the "funny" characters—depends on how the variables are being used; they are evaluated by context, either scalar or list.

If the value on the left-hand side of an assignment statement is a scalar, the expression on the right-hand side is evaluated in a scalar context; whereas if the value on the left-hand side is an array, the right-hand side is evaluated in a list context.

See "Reading from *STDIN*" on page 94 for a good review of how context is handled. You'll see examples throughout the rest of this book where context plays a major role.

EXAMPLE 5.66

```
(The perldoc function describes how reverse works)
1  $ perldoc -f reverse
    reverse LIST
              In list context, returns a list value consisting of the
elements of LIST in the opposite order. In scalar context,
concatenates the elements of LIST and returns a string value with all
characters in the opposite order.
    .....
```

EXAMPLE 5.66 (CONTINUED)

```
     (The Perl Script)
      @list = (90,89,78,100,87);
      $str="Hello, world";
      print "Original array: @list\n";4
      print "Original string: $str\n";5
2     @revlist = reverse(@list);
3     $revstr = reverse($str);
4     print "Reversed array is: @revlist\n";
5     print "Reversed string is: $revstr\n";

6    $newstring = reverse(@list);  print "List reversed, context
string: $newstring\n";
(Output)
Original array: 90 89 78 100 87
Original string: Hello, world
Reversed array is: 87 100 78 89 90
Reversed string is: dlrow ,olleH
List reversed, context string: 78001879809
```

EXPLANATION

1 Context is demonstrated in the documentation for Perl's built-in *reverse* function.
2 The reverse function reverses the elements of an array and returns the reversed elements to another array. Context is array.
3 This time, the *reverse* function reverses the characters in a string. It returns the reverse string as a scalar. Context is scalar.
4 The elements of the reversed array are displayed.
5 The reversed string is displayed.
6 Here the *reverse* function reverses the array again, but the returned value will be assigned to a string. The context being scalar, the function will reverse the array elements and convert the list into a string of characters.

5.7 What You Should Know

1. About data types.
2. If you don't give a variable a value, what will Perl assign to it?
3. What are "funny symbols"?
4. What data types are interpreted within double quotes?
5. How many numbers or strings can you store in a scalar variable?
6. What is the nickname for "associative array"?

7. In a hash, can you have more than one key with the same name? More than one value with the same name?
8. What is a list?
9. How do you find the size of an array?
10. Why are elements of an array or hash are preceded by a $?
11. What is the difference between *chop* and *chomp?*
12. How do you read just 25 bytes keyboard input into a variable?
13. What is the difference between *splice* and *slice*?
14. How do you sort a numeric array? Hash by value?
15. What function extracts both keys and values from a hash?
16. Can you have more than one key with the same name?
17. What is the *%SIG* hash used for?
18. What are environment variables?
19. What is meant by the term scope?

5.8 What's Next?

In the next chapter, we discuss the Perl operators. We will cover the different types of assignment operators, comparison and logical operators, arithmetic and bitwise operators, how Perl sees strings and numbers, how to create a range of numbers, how to generate random numbers, and some special string functions.

EXERCISE 5
The Funny Characters

1. Write a script called *foods.plx* that will ask the user for his five favorite foods. The foods will be stored as a string in a scalar, each food separated by a comma.
   a. Split the scalar and create an array.
   b. Print the array.
   c. Print the first and last elements of the array.
   d. Print the number of elements in the array.
   e. Create an array slice from three elements of the *food* array and print the values.

2. Given the array *@names=qw(Nick Susan Chet Dolly Bill)*, write a statement that would
   a. Replace *Susan* and *Chet* with *Ellie*, *Beatrice*, and *Charles*.
   b. Remove *Bill* from the array.
   c. Add *Lewis* and *Izzy* to the end of the array.
   d. Remove *Nick* from the beginning of the array.
   e. Reverse the array.
   f. Add *Archie* to the beginning of the array.
   g. Sort the array.
   h. Remove *Chet* and *Dolly* and replace them with *Christian* and *Daniel*.

3. Write a script called *elective* that will contain a hash.
   a. The keys will be code numbers—*2CPR2B*, *1UNX1B*, *3SH414*, *4PL400*.
   b. The values will be course names—*C Language, Intro to UNIX*, *Shell Programming, Perl Programming.*
   c. Sort the hash by values and print it.
   d. Ask the user to type the code number for the course he plans to take this semester and print a line resembling the following:

      You will be taking Shell Programming this semester.

4. Modify your *elective* script to produce output resembling that appearing below. The user will be asked to enter registration information and to select an EDP number from a menu. The course name will be printed. It doesn't matter if the user types in the EDP number with upper- or lowercase letters. A message will confirm the user's address and thank him for enrolling.

   Output should resemble the following:
   REGISTRATION INFORMATION FOR SPRING QUARTER
   Today's date is Wed Apr 19 17:40:19 PDT 2007
   Please enter the following information:
   Your full name: Fred Z. Stachelin

What is your Social Security Number (xxx–xx–xxxx): 004–34–1234
Your address:
Street: 1424 Hobart St.
City, State, Zip: Chico, CA 95926

"EDP" NUMBERS AND ELECTIVES:

2CPR2B | C Programming

1UNX1B | Intro to UNIX

4PL400 | Perl Programming

3SH414 | Shell Programming

What is the EDP number of the course you wish to take? 4pl400
The course you will be taking is "Perl Programming."

Registration confirmation will be sent to your address at
1424 HOBART ST.
CHICO, CA 95926

Thank you, Fred, for enrolling.

5. Write a script called *findem* that will
   a. Assign the contents of the *datebook* file to an array. (File is on the CD.)
   b. Ask the user for the name of a person to find. Use the built-in *grep* function to find the elements of the array that contain the person and number of times that person is found in the array. The search will ignore case.
   c. Use the *split* function to get the current phone number.
   d. Use the *splice* function to replace the current phone number with the new phone number, or use any of the other built-in array functions to produce output that resembles the following:

   Who are you searching for? Karen
   What is the new phone number for Karen? 530-222-1255
   Karen's phone number is currently 284-758-2857.

   Here is the line showing the new phone number:
   Karen Evich:530-222-1255:23 Edgecliff Place, Lincoln, NB 92086:7/25/53:85100

   Karen was found in the array three times.

6. Write a script called *tellme* that will print out the names, phones, and salaries of all the people in the *datebook* file. To execute, type at the command line

   tellme datebook

   Output should resemble the following:

   Salary: 14500
   Name: Betty Boop
   Phone: 245–836–8357

chapter

6

Where's the Operator?

6.1 About Perl Operators

In the real world, there are operators who operate switchboards, computers, bulldozers, tanks, etc. In Perl, operators operate on numbers and strings or a combination of them. Operators are symbols, such as +, -, =, >, <, that produce a result based on some rules. An **operator** manipulates data objects called **operands**; e.g., 5 and 4 are operands in the expression 5 + 4. Operators and operands are found in expressions. An expression combines a group of values to make a new value, *n* = 5 + 4. And when you terminate an expression with a semicolon, you have a complete statement; e.g., *n* = 5 + 4.

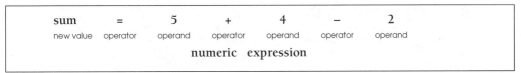

sum	=	5	+	4	–	2
new value	operator	operand	operator	operand	operator	operand
			numeric expression			

Figure 6.1 Evaluating an Expression.

In the numeric **expression**, 5 + 4 – 2, three numbers are combined. The **operators** are the + and – signs. The **operands** for the + sign are 5 and 4. After that part of the expression is evaluated to 9, the expression becomes 9 – 2. After evaluating the complete expression, the result is 7. Since the plus sign and minus operators each manipulate two operands, they are called binary operators. If there is only one operand, the operator is called a unary operator, and if there are three operands, it is called a ternary operator. We'll see examples of these operators later in the chapter.

Most of the Perl operators are borrowed from the *C* language, although Perl has some additional operators of its own.[1]

1. The operators can be symbols or words. Perl 5 functions can be used as operators if the parentheses are omitted.

6.2 Mixing Data Types

If you have operands of mixed types (i.e., numbers and strings), Perl will make the appropriate conversion by testing whether the operator expects a number or a string for an operand. This is called overloading the operator.

If the operator is a numeric operator, such as an arithmetic operator, and the operand(s) is a string, Perl will convert the string to a decimal floating point value. Undefined values will become zero. If there is leading whitespace or trailing non-numeric characters, they will be ignored, and if a string cannot be converted to a number, it will be converted to zero.

```
$string1 = "5 dogs ";
$string2 = 4;
$number = $string1 + $string2;  # Numeric context
print "Number is $number.\n";   # Result is  9
```

Likewise, if Perl encounters a string operator and the operand(s) is numeric, Perl will treat the number as a string. The concatenation operator, for example, expects to join two strings together.

```
$number1 = 55;
$number2 = "22";
$string = $number1 . $number2;  # Context is string
print "String is string.\n"     # Result is "5522"
```

Table 6.1 How Strings Are Converted to Numbers

String	***→ Converts to →***	***Number***
"123 go!"		*123*
"hi therev		*0*
"4e3"		*4000*
*"-6**3xyz"*		*–6*
" .456!!"		*0.456*
"x.1234"		*0*
"0xf"		*0*

EXAMPLE 6.1

```
(The Script)
1  $x = "      12hello!!" + "4abc\n";
# Perl will remove leading whitespace and trailing non-numeric
# characters
2  print "$x";
3  print "\n";

4  $y = ZAP . 5.5;
5  print "$y\n";

(Output)
2  16
5  ZAP5.5
```

EXPLANATION

1 The plus sign (+) is a numeric operator. The strings "   *12hello!!*" and "*4abc\n*" are converted to numbers (leading whitespace and trailing non-numeric characters are removed) and addition is performed. The result is stored in the scalar *$x*.
2 The scalar *$x* is printed.
3 Since the *\n* was stripped from the string *4\n* in order to convert it to a number, another *\n* is needed to get the newline in the printout.
4 The period (.), when surrounded by whitespace, is a string operator. It concatenates two strings. The number *5.5* is converted to a string and concatenated to the string *ZAP*.
5 The value of the scalar *$y* is printed.

6.3 Precedence and Associativity

When an expression contains a number of operators and operands, and the result of the operation is potentially ambiguous, the order of precedence and associativity tells you how the compiler evaluates such an expression. **Precedence** refers to the way in which the operator binds to its operand. The multiplication operator binds more tightly to its operands than the addition operator, so it is of higher precedence, whereas the assignment operators are low in precedence and thus bind loosely to their operands.[2] Parentheses are of the highest precedence and are used to control the way an expression is evaluated. When parentheses are nested, the expression contained within the innermost set of parentheses is evaluated first.

Associativity refers to the order in which an operator evaluates its operands: left to right, in no specified order, or right to left.

---

2. An easy rule to remember precedence: Please Excuse My Dear Aunt Sally, which stands for Parentheses, Exponentiation, Multiplication, Division, Addition, and Subtraction.

In the following example, how is the expression evaluated? Is addition, multiplication, or division done first? And in what order—right to left or left to right?

EXAMPLE 6.2

```
(The Script)
1   $x = 5 + 4  * 12 / 4;
2   print "The result is  $x\n";

(Output)
2   The result is 17
```

EXPLANATION

1 The order of associativity is from left to right. Multiplication and division are of a higher precedence than addition and subtraction, and addition and subtraction are of higher precedence than assignment. To illustrate this, we'll use parentheses to group the operands as they are handled by the compiler. In fact, if you want to force precedence, use the parentheses around the expression to group the operands in the way you want them evaluated.

```
$x = (5 + ( ( 4 * 12 ) / 4));
```

2 The expression is evaluated and the result is printed to *STDOUT*.

Table 6.2 summarizes the rules of precedence and associativity for the Perl operators. The operators on the same line are of equal precedence. The rows are in order of highest to lowest precedence.

Table 6.2 Precedence and Associativity

Operator	*Description*	*Associativity*
() [] {}	Function call, array subscripts	Left to right
->	Dereferencing operator	Left to right
++ --	Autoincrement, autodecrement	None
**	Exponentiation	Right to left
! ~ \ + -	Logical *not*, bitwise *not*, backslash, unary plus, unary minus	Right to left
=~ !~	Match and not match	Left to right
* / % x	Multiply, divide, modulus, string repetition	Left to right
+ - .	Add, subtract, string concatenation	Left to right

Table 6.2 Precedence and Associativity (continued)

<table>
<tr><th>Operator</th><th>Description</th><th>Associativity</th></tr>
<tr><td><< >></td><td>Bitwise left shift, right shift</td><td>Left to right</td></tr>
<tr><td>-r -w -x -o etc.</td><td>Named unary operators; e.g., file test operators</td><td>None</td></tr>
<tr><td>< <= > >= lt le gt ge</td><td>Numeric and string tests; e.g., less than, greater than, etc.</td><td>None</td></tr>
<tr><td>== != <=> eq ne cmp</td><td>Numeric and string tests; e.g., equal to, not equal to, etc.</td><td>None</td></tr>
<tr><td>&</td><td>Bitwise and</td><td>Left to right</td></tr>
<tr><td>| ^</td><td>Bitwise or, exclusive or (xor)</td><td>Left to right</td></tr>
<tr><td>&&</td><td>Logical and</td><td>Left to right</td></tr>
<tr><td>||</td><td>Logical or</td><td>Left to right</td></tr>
<tr><td>..</td><td>Range operator</td><td>None</td></tr>
<tr><td>? :</td><td>Ternary, conditional</td><td>Right to left</td></tr>
<tr><td>= += -= *= /= %=</td><td>Assignment</td><td>Right to left</td></tr>
<tr><td>, =></td><td>Evaluate left operand, discard it, and evaluate right operand</td><td>Left to right</td></tr>
<tr><td>not</td><td>Synonym for ! with lower precedence</td><td>Right</td></tr>
<tr><td>and</td><td>Synonym for &&</td><td>Left to right</td></tr>
<tr><td>or xor</td><td>Synonym for ||, ^</td><td>Left to right</td></tr>
</table>

6.3.1 Assignment Operators

The = sign is an assignment operator. The value on the right-hand side of the equal sign is assigned to the variable on the left-hand side. Table 6.3 illustrates assignment and shortcut assignment statements borrowed from the *C* language.

Table 6.3 Assignment Operators

Operator	Example	Meaning
=	*$var = 5;*	Assign 5 to *$var*
+=	*$var += 3;*	Add 3 to *$var* and assign result to *$var*
−=	*$var -= 2;*	Subtract 2 from *$var* and assign result to *$var*

Continues

Table 6.3 Assignment Operators (continued)

Operator	*Example*	*Meaning*
.=	*$str.=“ing”;*	Concatenate *ing* to *$str* and assign result to *$str*
*=	*$var *= 4;*	Multiply *$var* by 4 and assign result to *$var*
/=	*$var /= 2;*	Divide *$var* by 2 and assign result to *$var*
**=	*$var **= 2;*	Square *$var* and assign result to $var
%=	*$var %= 2;*	Divide *$var* by 2 and assign remainder to *$var*
x=	*$str x= 20;*	Repeat value of *$str* 20 times and assign result to *$str*
<<=	*$var <<= 1;*	Left-shift bits in *$var* one position and assign result to *$var*
>>=	*$var>>= 2;*	Right-shift bits in *$var* two positions and assign result to *$var*
&=	*$var &= 1;*	One is bitwise-*AND*ed to *$var* and the result is assigned to *$var*
|=	*$var |= 2;*	Two is bitwise-*OR*ed to *$var* and the result is assigned to *$var*
^=	*$var ^= 2;*	Two is bitwise-exclusive *OR*ed to *$var* and the result is assigned to *$var*

EXAMPLE 6.3

```
(The Script)
    #!/usr/bin/perl
1   $name="Dan";
    $line="*";
    $var=0;          # Assign 0 to var

2   $var += 3;       # Add 3 to $var; same as $var=$var+3
    print  "\$var += 3 is $var \n";

3   $var -= 1;       # Subtract 1 from $var
    print "\$var -= 1 is $var\n";

4   $var **= 2;           # Square $var
    print "\$var squared is $var\n";

5   $var %= 3;            # Modulus
    print "The remainder of \$var/3 is $var\n";

6   $name .= "ielle";  # Concatenate string "Dan" and "ielle"
    print "$name is the girl's version of Dan.\n";
```

EXAMPLE 6.3 (CONTINUED)

```
7   $line x= 10;          # Repetition; print 10 stars
    print "$line\n";

8   printf "\$var is %.2f\n", $var=4.2 + 4.69;

(Output)
2   $var += 3 is 3
3   $var -=1 is 2
4   $var squared is 4
5   The remainder of $var/3 is 1
6   Danielle is the girl's version of Dan.
7   **********
8   $var is 8.89
```

EXPLANATION

1. Values on the right-hand side of the equal sign are assigned to scalar variables on the left-hand side of the equal sign.
2. The shortcut assignment operator, +=, adds 3 to the scalar *$var*. This is equivalent to *$var = $var + 3;*
3. The shortcut assignment operator, –=, subtracts 1 from the scalar *$var*. This is equivalent to *$var = $var – 1;*
4. The shortcut assignment operator, **, squares the scalar *$var*. This is equivalent to *$var = $var ** 2;*
5. The shortcut assignment modulus operator, %, yields the integer amount that remains after the scalar *$var* is divided by 3. The operator is called the modulus operator, or remainder operator. The expression *$var% = 3* is equivalent to *$var = $var % 3*; .
6. The shortcut assignment operator, . , concatenates the string "*ielle*" to the string value of the scalar, *$name*. This is equivalent to *$name = $name . "ielle"*.
7. The repetition operator takes two operands. The operand on the right is the number of times the string operand on the left is repeated. The value of the scalar *$line*, an asterisk (*), is repeated 10 times.
8. The *printf* function is used to format and print the result of the addition of two floating point numbers.

6.3.2 Relational Operators

Relational operators are used to compare operands. The result of the comparison is either **true** or **false**.[3] Perl has two classes of relational operators: one set that compares

3. As in other languages, Perl doesn't support a Boolean data type where "true" and "false" are keywords that evaluate to either 1 or 0. However, any nonzero number can be used in an expression to represent true, and ! 1 is used to represent false; e.g., while(1) or if ! 1....

numbers and another that compares strings. Normally, these operators are used to test a condition when using if/else, *while loops,* etc., as follows:

```
if ( $x > $b ){ print "$x is greater.\n"; }
```

We will discuss conditionals in Chapter 7.

The expression (5 > 4 > 2) will produce a syntax error because there is no associativity. (See Table 6.2.)

Numeric. Table 6.4 contains a list of numeric relational operators.

Table 6.4 Relational Operators and Numeric Values

Operator	*Example*	*Meaning*
>	*$x* > *$y*	*$x* is greater than *$y*
>=	*$x* >= *$y*	*$x* is greater than or equal to *$y*
<	*$x* < *$y*	*$x* is less than *$y*
<=	*$x* <= *$y*	*$x* is less than or equal to *$y*

EXAMPLE 6.4

```
(The Script)
    $x = 5;
    $y = 4;
1   $result = $x > $y;
2   print "$result\n";

3   $result = $x < $y;
4   print $result;

(Output)
2   1
4   0
```

EXPLANATION

1. If *$x* is greater than *$y*, the value *1* (true) is returned and stored in *$result*; otherwise, *0* (false) is returned.
2. Since the expression was true, the value of *$result*, *1*, is printed to *STDOUT.*
3. If *$x* is less than *$y*, the value *1* (true) is returned and stored in *$result;* otherwise, *0* (false) is returned.
4. Since the expression was false, the value of *$result*, *0*, is printed to *STDOUT.*

String. The string relational operators evaluate their operands (strings) by comparing the ASCII value of each character in the first string with the corresponding character in the second string. The comparison includes trailing whitespace.

If the first string contains a character that is of a higher or lower ASCII value than the corresponding character in the second string, the value *1* is returned; otherwise, *0* is returned.

Table 6.5 contains a list of relational string operators.

Table 6.5 Relational Operators and String Values

Operator	Example	Meaning
gt	*$str1 gt $str2*	*$str1* is greater than *$str2*
ge	*$str1 ge $str2*	*$str1* is greater than or equal to *$str2*
lt	*$str1 lt $str2*	*$str1* is less than *$str2*
le	*$str1 le $str2*	*$str1* is less than or equal to *$str2*

EXAMPLE 6.5

```
(The Script)
1   $fruit1 = "pear";
2   $fruit2 = "peaR";
3   $result = $fruit1 gt $fruit2;
4   print "$result\n";

5   $result = $fruit1 lt $fruit2;
6   print "$result\n";

(Output)
4   1
6   0
```

EXPLANATION

1. The scalar *$fruit1* is assigned the string value *pear*.
2. The scalar *$fruit2* is assigned the string value *peaR*.
3. When lexographically comparing each of the characters in *$fruit1* and *$fruit2*, all of the characters are equal until the *r* and *R* are compared. The ASCII value of the lowercase *r* is 114, and the ASCII value of the uppercase *R* is 82. Since 114 is greater than 82, the result of evaluating the strings is *1* (true); i.e., *pear* is greater than *peaR*.
4. Since the expression was true, the value of *$result*, *1*, is printed to *STDOUT*.
5. This is the reverse of #3. The ASCII value of uppercase *R* (82) is less than the value of the lowercase *r* (114). The result of evaluating the two strings is *0* (false); i.e., *pear* is less than *peaR*.
6. Since the expression was false, the value of *$result*, *0*, is printed to *STDOUT*.

6.3.3 Equality Operators

The equality operators evaluate numeric operands and string operands. (See Tables 6.6 and 6.7.) Be sure if you are testing equality that you use the string operators for strings and the numeric operators for numbers! If, for example, you have the expression:

```
"5 cats" == "5 dogs"
```

the expression will evaluate to true. Why? Because Perl sees a numeric operator, ==. The == operator expects its operands to be numbers, not strings. Perl will then convert the "5 cats" to a number 5 and the string "5 dogs" to the number 5, resulting in 5 == 5, which evaluates to true. (In the conversion, Perl starts on the left-hand side of the string and looks for a number; if there is a number, Perl keeps it. As soon as a non-number is found, the conversion stops.)

Numeric. The numeric equality operators evaluate their operands (numbers) by comparing their numeric values. If the operands are equal, *1* (true) is returned; if the operands are not equal, *0* (false) is returned.

The numeric comparison operator evaluates its operands, returning a *–1* if the first operand is less than the second operand, *0* if the numbers are equal, or *1* if the first operand is greater than the second.

Table 6.6 Equality Operators and Numeric Values

Operator	***Example***	***Meaning***
==	*$num1* == *$num2*	*$num1* is equal to *$num2*
!=	*$num1* != *$num2*	*$num1* is not equal to *$num2*
<=>	*$num1* <=> *$num2*	*$num1* is compared to *$num2* with a signed return; *1* if *$num1* is greater than *$num2*, *0* if *$num1* is equal to *$num2*, and *–1* if *$num1* is less than *$num2*

EXAMPLE 6.6

```
(The Script)
    $x = 5;
    $y = 4;
1   $result = $x == $y;
2   print "$result\n";

3   $result = $x != $y;
4   print "$result\n";
```

EXAMPLE 6.6 (CONTINUED)

```
5  $result = $x <=> $y;
6  print "$result\n";

7  $result = $y <=> $x;
8  print "$result\n";

(Output)
2  0
4  1
6  1
8  -1
```

EXPLANATION

1 If *$x* is equal to *$y*, the value *1* (true) is returned and stored in *$result*; otherwise, *0* (false) is returned.
2 Since the expression was not true, the value of *$result*, *0*, is printed to *STDOUT*.
3 If *$x* is not equal to *$y*, the value *1* (true) is returned and stored in *$result*; otherwise, *0* (false) is returned.
4 Since the expression was true, the value of *$result*, *1*, is printed to *STDOUT*.
5 The scalars, *$x* and *$y*, are compared. If *$x* is greater than *$y*, *1* is returned; if *$x* is equal to *$y*, *0* is returned; if *$x* is less than *$y*, a signed *–1* is returned.
6 Since *$x* is greater than *$y*, the value of *$result*, *1*, is printed to *STDOUT*.
7 The scalars *$x* and *$y* are compared. If *$y* is greater than *$x*, *1* is returned; if *$x* is equal to *$y*, *0* is returned; if *$y* is less than *$x*, a signed *–1* is returned.
8 Since *$x* is less than *$y*, the value of *$result*, *–1*, is printed to *STDOUT*.

String. The string equality operators evaluate their operands (strings) by comparing the ASCII value of each character in the first string with the corresponding character in the second string. The comparison includes trailing whitespace.

If the first string contains a character that is of a higher ASCII value than the corresponding character in the second string, the value *1* is returned; if the strings are equal, *0* is returned; if the first string character has a lesser ASCII value than the corresponding character in the second string, *–1* is returned. (See Table 6.7.)

Table 6.7 Equality Operators and String Values

Operator	***Example***	***Meaning***
eq	*$str1 eq $str2*	*$str1* is equal to *$str2*
ne	*$str1 ne $str2*	*$str1* is not equal to *$str2*
cmp	*$str1 cmp $str2*	*$str1* is compared to *$str2*, with a signed return

EXAMPLE 6.7

```
(The Script)
1   $str1 = "A";
    $str2 = "C";
    $result = $str1 eq $str2;
    print "$result\n";

2   $result = $str1 ne $str2;
    print "$result\n";

3   $result = $str1 cmp $str2;
    print "$result\n";

4   $result = $str2 cmp $str1;
    print "$result\n";

5   $str1 = "C";        # Now both strings are equal
6   $result = $str1 cmp $str2;
    print "$result\n";

(Output)
1  0
2  1
3  -1
4  1
6  0
```

EXPLANATION

1 The scalar *$str1* is assigned the value *A*, and scalar *$str2* is assigned the value *C*. If *$str1* is **equal** to *$str2*, the value *1* (true) is returned, assigned to *$result*, and printed.

2 If *$str1* is **not equal** to *$str2*, the value *1* (true) is returned, assigned to *$result*, and printed.

3 If *$str1* is compared with *$str2* (i.e., an ASCII comparison is made on each character), and all characters are the same, the value *0* is returned and assigned to *$result*. If *$str1* is greater than *$str2*, the value *1* is returned, and if *$str1* is less than *$str2, –1* is returned. In this example, *$str1* is less than *$str2*. The value of *$result* is printed.

4 In this example, we reverse the order of comparison. Since *$str2* is greater than *$str1*, the result is *1*. The value of *$result* is printed.

5 *$str1* is assigned *C*. It has the same value as *$str2*.

6 Now *$str1* and *$str2* are equal. Since all of the characters are the same, the value *0* is returned and assigned to *$result*. The value of *$result* is printed.

EXAMPLE 6.8

```
(The Script)
     # Don't use == when you should use eq!
1    $x = "yes";
     $y = "no";
     print "\nIs yes equal to no? If so, say 1; if not say 'null'.\n";
2    print "The result is: ",$x == $y,"\n";      # Should be $x eq $y

(Output)
1    Is yes equal to no? If so, say 1; if not say 'null'.
2    The result is: 1
```

EXPLANATION

1 The scalars *$x* and *$y* are assigned string values *yes* and *no*, respectively.

2 The numeric equality operator, ==, is being used incorrectly to test the equality of two strings. The strings are converted to numbers. Since the characters are nonnumeric, the result is to convert each string to *0* (zero). *0* is equal to *0*, resulting in *1* (true). The string equality operator *eq* should have been used in this test.

6.3.4 Logical Operators (Short-Circuit Operators)

The short-circuit operators evaluate their operands, from left to right, testing the truth or falsity of each operand in turn. There is no further evaluation once a true or false condition is satisfied. Unlike C, the short-circuit operators do not return *0* (false) or *1* (true) but rather the **value** of the last operand evaluated. These operators are most often used in conditional statements. (See Chapter 7, "If Only, Unconditionally, Forever.")

If the expression on the left-hand side of the *&&* evaluates to *0*, the expression is false and *0* is returned. If the expression on the left-hand side of the operator evaluates to true (nonzero), the right-hand side is evaluated and its value is returned.

The logical operators can also be represented as *and*, *or*, or *not*, but the precedence for them is **lower**. See Table 6.2 on page 140. If the expression on the left-hand side of the || operator is evaluated as true (nonzero), the value of the expression is returned. If the value on the left-hand side of the || is false, the value of the expression on the right-hand side of the operator is evaluated, and its value is returned.

A list of logical operators can be found in Table 6.8.

Table 6.8 Logical Operators (Short-Circuit Operators)

Operator	*Alternative Form*	*Example*	*Meaning*
&&	*and*	*$x && $y*	If *$x* is true, evaluate *$y* and return *$y*
		*$x **and** $y*	If *$x* is false, evaluate *$x* and return *$x*

Continues

Table 6.8 Logical Operators (Short-Circuit Operators) (continued)

Operator	*Alternative Form*	*Example*	*Meaning*
||	*or*	$x || $y	If $x is true, evaluate $x and return $x
		$x **or** $y	If $x is false, evaluate $y and return $y
	xor	$x **xor** $y	True if $x **or** $y is true, but not both
!	*not*	! $x	Not $x; true if $x is not true
		not $x	

EXAMPLE 6.9

```
(The Script)
   #!/usr/bin/perl
   # Short-circuit operators
1  $num1=50;
2  $num2=100;
3  $num3=0;

4  print $num1 && $num3, "\n";    # result is 0
5  print $num3 && $num1, "\n";    # result is 0
6  print $num1 && $num2, "\n";    # result is 100
7  print $num2 && $num1, "\n\n";  # result is 50

8  print $num1 || $num3, "\n";    # result is 50
9  print $num3 || $num1, "\n";    # result is 50
10 print $num1 || $num2, "\n";    # result is 50
11 print $num2 || $num1, "\n";    # result is 100

(Output)
4  0
5  0
6  100
7  50
8  50
9  50
10 50
11 100
```

EXPLANATION

1 The scalar *$num1* is assigned the value *50*.
2 The scalar *$num2* is assigned the value *100*.
3 The scalar *$num3* is assigned the value *0*.
4 Since the expression to the left of the *&&* operator, *$num1*, is nonzero (true), the expression to the right of the *&&*, *$num3*, is returned.

EXPLANATION (CONTINUED)

5 Since the expression to the left of the *&&* operator, *$num3*, is zero (false), the expression *$num3* is returned.

6 Since the expression to the left of the *&&* operator, *$num1*, is true (true), the expression on the right-hand side of the *&&* operator, *$num2*, is returned.

7 Since the expression to the left of the *&&* operator, *$num2*, is true (true), the expression on the right-hand side of the *&&* operator, *$num1*, is returned.

8 Since the expression to the left of the || operator, *$num1*, is nonzero (true), the expression *$num1* is returned.

9 Since the expression to the left of the || operator, *$num3*, is zero (false), the expression to the right of the || operator, *$num1*, is returned.

10 Since the expression to the left of the || operator, *$num1*, is nonzero (true), the expression *$num1* is returned.

11 Since the expression to the left of the || operator, *$num2*, is nonzero (true), the expression *$num2* is returned.

6.3.5 Logical Word Operators

These logical operators are of lower precedence than the short-circuit operators but basically work the same way and make the program easier to read and also short-circuit. In addition to the short-circuit operators, the *xor* (exclusive *or*) operator has been added to the logical word operators.

EXAMPLE 6.10

```
    # Examples using the word operators
1   $num1=50;
    $num2=100;
    $num3=0;
    print "\nOutput using the word operators.\n\n";
2   print "\n$num1 and $num2: ",($num1 and $num2);, "\n";
3   print "\n$num1 or $num3: ", ($num1 or $num3), "\n";
4   print "\n$num1 xor $num3: ",($num1 xor $num3), "\n";
5   print "\nnot $num3: ", not $num3;
    print "\n";

(Output)
    Output using the word operators.

2   50 and 100: 100

3   50 or 0: 50

4   50 xor  0: 1

5   not 0: 1
```

EXPLANATION

1. Initial values are assigned to *$num1*, *$num2*, and *$num3*.
2. The *and* operator evaluates its operands. *$num1* and *$num2* are both true, resulting in the value of the last expression evaluated, *100*. Since *100* is a nonzero value, the expression is true.
3. The *or* operator evaluates its operands. *$num1* is true. The word operators also short-circuit, so that if the first expression is true, there is no need to continue evaulating. The result returned is *50*, which is true.
4. The exclusive *xor* operator evaluates both its operands. It does not short-circuit. If one of the operands is *true*, then the expression is true and *1* is returned; if both sides are either true or false, the result is false.
5. The logical *not* operator evaluates the operand to the right; if it is true, false is returned if false, true is returned.

EXAMPLE 6.11

```
   (The Script)
   # Precedence with word operators and short-circuit operators
   $x=5;
   $y=6;
   $z=0;
1  $result=$x && $y && $z;       # Precedence of = lower than &&
   print "Result: $result\n";

2  $result2 = $x and $y and $z;  # Precedence of = higher than and
   print "Result: $result2\n";

3  $result3 = ( $x and $y and $z );
   print "Result: $result3\n";

(Output)
1  Result: 0
2  Result: 5
3  Result: 0
```

EXPLANATION

1. The logical short-circuit operators evaluate each of the expressions and return the value of the last expression evaluated. The value *0* is assigned to *$result*. Since *&&* is higher in precedence than the equal sign, the logical operators evaluated their expressions first.
2. The word operators are used here, but they are lower in precedence than the equal sign. The first expression to the right of the equal sign is assigned to *$result2*.
3. By adding parentheses to the expression on the right-hand side of the equal sign, that expression is evaluated first and the result assigned to *$result3*.

6.3.6 Arithmetic Operators

Perl's arithmetic operators are listed in Table 6.9.

Table 6.9 Arithmetic Operators

Operator	*Example*	*Meaning*
+	$x + $y	Addition
–	$x – $y	Subtraction
*	$x * $y	Multiplication
/	$x / $y	Division
%	$x % $y	Modulus
**	$x ** $y	Exponentiation

EXAMPLE 6.12

```
(The Script)
1   printf "%d\n", 4 * 5 / 2;
2   printf "%d\n", 5 ** 3;
3   printf "%d\n", 5 + 4 - 2 * 10;
4   printf "%d\n", (5 + 4 - 2 ) * 10;
5   printf "%d\n", 11 % 2;

(Output)
1   10
2   125
3   -11
4   70
5   1
```

EXPLANATION

1 The *printf* function formats the result of arithmetic expression in decimal. Multiplication and division are performed. Operators are of the same precedence, left to right associativity. Same as: *(4 * 5) / 2*.
2 The *printf* function formats the result of arithmetic expression in decimal. The exponentiation operator cubes its operand, *5*, same as 5^3.
3 The *printf* function formats the result of arithmetic expression in decimal. Since the multiplication operator is of higher precedence than the addition and subtraction operators, multiplication is performed first, left to right associativity. Same as: *5 + 4 – (2 * 10)*.

EXPLANATION (CONTINUED)

4 The *printf* function formats the result of arithmetic expression in decimal. Since the parentheses are of highest precedence, the expression enclosed in parentheses is calculated first.

5 The *printf* function formats the result of arithmetic expression in decimal. The modulus operator produces the remainder after performing division on its operands. (See "The *printf* Function" on page 59.)

6.3.7 Autoincrement and Autodecrement Operators

The autoincrement operator and autodecrement operators are taken straight from the C language (see Table 6.10). The autoincrement operator adds 1 to the value of a variable, and the autodecrement operator subtracts 1 from the value of a variable. When used with a single variable, these operators are just a shortcut for the traditional method of adding and subtracting 1. However, if used in an assignment statement or if combined with other operators, the end result depends on the placement of the operator. (See Table 6.11.)

Table 6.10 Autoincrement and Autodecrement Operators

Example	Description	Equivalence
++$x	Preincrement	$x = $x + 1
$x++	Postincrement	$x = $x + 1
--$x	Predecrement	$x = $x – 1
$x--	Postdecrement	$x = $x – 1

Table 6.11 Autoincrement and Autodecrement Operators and Assignment

Example	Description	Equivalence	Result
If $y is 0 and $x is 0: $y = $x++;	Assign the value of $x to $y, then increment $x	$y = $x; $x = $x + 1;	$y is 0 $x is 1
If $y is 0 and $x is 0: $y = ++$x;	Increment $x, then assign $x to $y	$x = $x + 1; $y = $x;	$x is 1 $y is 1
If $y is 0 and $x is 0: $y = $x--;	Assign the value of $x to $y, then decrement $x	$y = $x; $x = $x – 1;	$y is 0 $x is –1
If $y is 0 and $x is 0: $y = --$x;	Decrement $x, then assign $x to $y	$x = $x – 1; $y = $x;	$x is –1 $y is –1

EXAMPLE 6.13

```
(The Script)
   #!/usr/bin/perl
1  $x=5; $y=0;
2  $y=++$x;     # Add 1 to $x first; then assign to $y
3  print "Pre-increment:\n";
4  print "y is $y\n";
5  print "x is $x\n";
6  print  "-----------------------\n";
7  $x=5;
8  $y=0;
9  print "Post-increment:\n";
10 $y=$x++;     # Assign value in $x to $y; then add 1 to $x
11 print "y is $y\n";
12 print "x is $x\n";

(Output)
3  Pre-increment:
4  y is 6
5  x is 6
   -----------------------
9  Post-increment
11 y is 5
12 x is 6
```

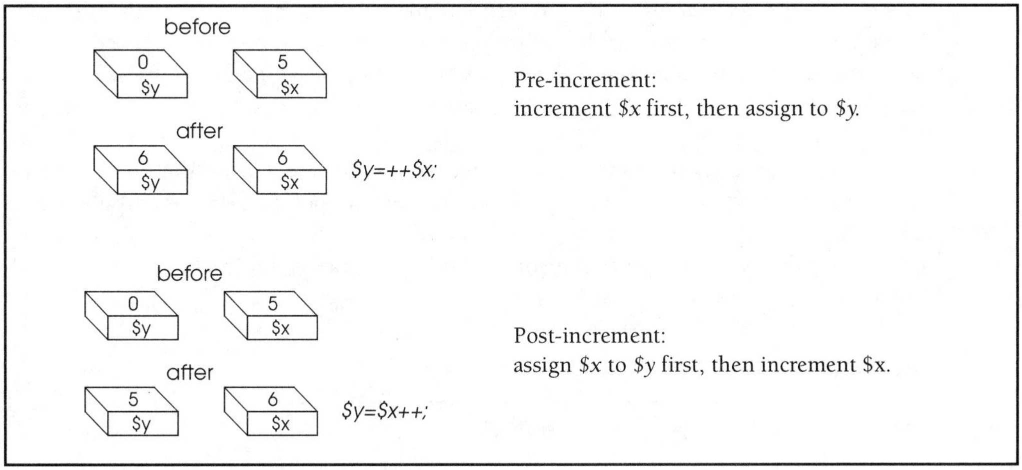

Figure 6.2 Pre- and post-increment operators.

6.3.8 Bitwise Logical Operators

A Little Bit about Bits. People represent numbers in decimal, or base 10, a numbering system based on 10 values starting from 0 to 9; e.g., $100,00 and 1955. The HTML color codes are represented in hexadecimal, base 16, values ranging from 0 to 15; e.g., #00FFFF is cyan and #FF00FF is fuschia. Computers store everything in binary, or base 2. A binary numbering system represents numbers in two values, 0 or 1. Each of the individual 1s and 0s are called bits. All the data you use is stored in your computer using bits. A byte is made up of 8 bits, a word is 2 bytes, or 16 bits, and finally, two words together are called a double word, or dword, which is a 32-bit value. The reason a computer uses only 0s and 1s for everything is because a binary digit is represented by the presence of an electric current. If the level of electricity reaches a certain level, the digit is 1. Otherwise, the digit is a 0. Using just two numbers makes building hardware less difficult and cheaper than if electrical levels were represented by a bigger combination of bits, like base 10 (decimal) or base 16 (hexadecimal). Hence, computers store everything in binary.

Bitwise Operators. Most processors today are built to operate on 32-bit numbers. For example, the term Win32 is derived from the fact that an integer on a Win32 compiler defaults to 32 bits. Bitwise operators allow you to turn specific bits within an integer on or off. For example, if you are setting a read-only flag on a file, you need only two values, on or off, represented as 1 or 0. And if both the left- and right-hand parameters are strings, the bitwise operator will operate on the characters within the string.

Bitwise operators treat their operands as a set of 32 bits (0s and 1s), rather than as decimal, hexadecimal, or octal numbers. For example, the decimal number 9 has a binary representation of 1001. Although bitwise operators perform their operations on bits rather than expressions, they return standard Perl numerical values as shown in Example 6.13. If you are working with graphics, games, encryption, registers, setting switches, etc., or any operation that requires "twiddling bits," then the bitwise operators may become useful. Generally speaking, those types of operations are more fitting for higher-level languages like C or Java.

When you're ready to manipulate integer values at the bit level, the bitwise logical operators are used. The bitwise operators are binary operators and manipulate their operands in terms of the internal binary representation of those operands. A bit-by-bit comparison is made on each of the corresponding operands, producing its result as the binary value (see Tables 6.12 and 6.13).

Table 6.12 Bitwise Logical Operators

Operator	*Example*	*Meaning*
&	*$x* & *$y*	Bitwise *and*
|	*$x* \| *$y*	Bitwise *or*
^	*$x* ^ *$y*	Bitwise exclusive *or*

Table 6.12 Bitwise Logical Operators (continued)

Operator	*Example*	*Meaning*
<<	*$x << 1*	Bitwise left shift, integer multiply by two
>>	*$x >> 1*	Bitwise right shift, integer divide by two

Table 6.13 Resulting Values of Bitwise Operators

$x	$y	$x & $y	$x | $y	$x ^ $y
0	0	0	0	0
0	1	0	1	1
1	0	0	1	1
1	1	1	1	0

EXAMPLE 6.14

```
(The Script)
1  print 5 & 4,"\n";         # 101 & 100
2  print 5 & 0,"\n";         # 101 & 000
3  print 4 & 0,"\n";         # 100 & 000
4  print 0 & 4,"\n";         # 000 & 100
5  print "=" x 10,"\n";      # print 10 equal signs
6  print 1 | 4,"\n";         # 001 & 100
7  print 5 | 0,"\n";         # 101 | 000
8  print 4 | 0,"\n";         # 100 | 000
9  print 0 | 4,"\n";         # 000 | 100
   print "=" x 10,"\n";      # print 10 equal signs
10 print 5 ^ 4,"\n";         # 101 ^ 100
11 print 5 ^ 0,"\n";         # 101 ^ 000
12 print 4 ^ 0,"\n";         # 100 ^ 000
13 print 0 ^ 4,"\n";         # 000 ^ 100

(Output)
1  4
2  0
3  0
4  0
5  ==========
6  5
7  5
8  4
```

EXAMPLE 6.14 (CONTINUED)

```
9   4
    ==========
10  1
11  5
12  4
13  4
```

EXPLANATION

1 *5* bitwise *and*ed to *4* results in *000* binary, *4* decimal.
2 *5* bitwise *and*ed to *0* results in *000* binary, *0* decimal.
3 *4* bitwise *and*ed to *0* results in *000* binary, *0* decimal.
4 *0* bitwise *and*ed to *4* results in *000* binary, *0* decimal.
5 The *x* operator tells the *print* function to print 10 equal signs.
6 *1* bitwise *or*ed to *4* results in *101* binary, *5* decimal.
7 *5* bitwise *or*ed to *0* results in *101* binary, *5* decimal.
8 *4* bitwise *or*ed to *0* results in *100* binary, *4* decimal.
9 *0* bitwise *or*ed to *4* results in *100* binary, *4* decimal.
10 *5* bitwise exclusively *or*ed to *4* results in *001* binary, *1* decimal.
11 *5* bitwise exclusively *or*ed to *0* results in *101* binary, *5* decimal.
12 *4* bitwise exclusively *or*ed to *0* results in *100* binary, *4* decimal.
13 *0* bitwise exclusively *or*ed to *4* results in *100* binary, *4* decimal.

EXAMPLE 6.15

```
(The Script)
    #!/usr/bin/perl
    # Convert a number to binary
1   while (1) {
2      $mask = 0x80000000;        # 32-bit machine
3      printf("Enter an unsigned integer: ");
4      chomp($num=<STDIN>);
5      printf("Binary of %x hex is: ", $num);
6      for ($j = 0; $j < 32; $j++) {
7         $bit = ($mask & $num) ? 1 : 0;
8         printf("%d", $bit);
9         if ($j == 15)){
10           printf("--");
          }
11     $mask /=2;                 # $mask >>= 1;  not portable
       }
       printf("\n");
    }
```

EXAMPLE 6.15 (CONTINUED)

```
(Output)
Enter an unsigned integer: 1
Binary of 1 hex is: 0000000000000000--0000000000000001
Enter an unsigned integer: 5
Binary of 5 hex is: 0000000000000000--0000000000000101
Enter an unsigned integer: 10
Binary of a hex is: 0000000000000000--0000000000001010
Enter an unsigned integer: 12
Binary of c hex is: 0000000000000000--0000000000001100
Enter an unsigned integer: 15
Binary of f hex is: 0000000000000000--0000000000001111
Enter an unsigned integer: 200
Binary of c8 hex is: 0000000000000000--0000000011001000
```

EXPLANATION

1 This little program introduces some constructs that have not yet been discussed. It is presented here as an example of using bitwise operations to perform a real task (in this case, to convert a number to binary and print it). The first line starts a loop that will continue until the user presses <Ctrl>-c (UNIX) or <Ctrl>-z (Windows).
2 The scalar is set to the hexadecimal value representing 32 zeros. This program works on a machine with a 32-bit word.
3 The user is asked to type in an integer.
4 The number is assigned and the newline is *chomp*ed.
5 The *printf* will print the value of the number in hexadecimal notation.
6 The *for* loop will iterate 32 times, once for each bit.
7 The value of *$mask* is bitwise *and*ed to *$num*. If the result is *1*, *1* will be assigned to *$bit*; otherwise, *0* is assigned. (See "Conditional Operators.")
8 The value of *$bit* is printed.
9 If the value of *$j* is *15* (the loop has iterated 16 times), a double underscore is printed.
11 The value of *$mask* is divided by 2. This has the same effect as shifting the bits to the right once but will not try to shift the sign bit if one exists.

6.3.9 Conditional Operators

The conditional operator is another taken from the *C* language. It requires three operands and thus it is often called a **ternary** operator. It is used as a shortcut for the *if/else* construct.

FORMAT

```
conditional expression ? expression : expression
```

EXAMPLE 6.16

```
$x ? $y : $z
```

EXPLANATION

If *$x* is true, *$y* becomes the value of the expression. If *$x* is false, *$z* becomes the value of the expression.

EXAMPLE 6.17

```
(The Script)
     print "What is your age? ";
2    chomp($age=<STDIN>);

3    $price=($age > 60 ) ? 0 : 5.55;
4    printf "You will pay \$%.2f.\n", $price;

(Output)
1    What is your age? 44
4    You will pay $5.55.

(Output)
1    What is your age? 77
4    You will pay $0.00.
```

EXPLANATION

1. The string *What is your age?* is printed to *STDOUT.*
2. The input is read from the terminal and stored in the scalar *$age*. The newline is *chomped*.
3. The scalar *$price* is assigned the result of the conditional operator. If the age is greater than *60*, the price is assigned the value to the right of the question mark (*?*). Otherwise, the value after the colon (*:*) is assigned to the scalar *$price*.
4. The *printf* function prints the formatted string to *STDOUT.*

EXAMPLE 6.18

```
(The Script)
1    print "What was your grade? ";
2    $grade = <STDIN>;
3    print $grade > 60 ? "Passed.\n" : "Failed.\n";

(Output)
1    What was your grade? 76
3    Passed.
```

EXAMPLE 6.18 (CONTINUED)

```
(Output)
1   What was your grade? 34
3   Failed.
```

EXPLANATION

1 The user is asked for input.
2 The input is assigned to the scalar *$grade*.
3 The *print* function takes as its argument the result of the conditional expression. If the grade is greater than *60*, *Passed.* is printed; otherwise, *Failed.* is printed.

6.3.10 Range Operator

The range operator is used in both scalar and array context. In a scalar context, the value returned is a Boolean, *1* or *0*. In an array context, it returns a list of items starting on the left side of the operator and counting by ones until the value on the right-hand side is reached.

EXAMPLE 6.19

```
1   print 0 .. 10,"\n";
    0 1 2 3 4 5 6 7 8 9 10

2   @alpha=('A' .. 'Z');
print "@alpha";'
    A B C D E F G H I J K L M N O P Q R S T U V W X Y Z

3   @a=('a'..'z', 'A'..'Z');
print "@a\n";'
    a b c d e f g h i j k l m n o p q r s t u v w x y z A B C D E F G H
I J K L M N O P Q R S T U V W X Y Z

4   @n=( -5 .. 20 );
print "@n\n";'
    -5 -4 -3 -2 -1 0 1 2 3 4 5 6 7 8 9 10 11 12 13 14 15 16 17 18 19 20
```

EXPLANATION

1 Print the numbers *0* to *10*.
2 Create an array called *@alpha* and store all uppercase letters in the array in the range from *A* to *Z*. The context is array. Print the array.
3 Create an array called *@alpha* and store all lowercase letters in one list and all uppercase letters in another list. Print the array.
4 Create an array called *@n* and store all numbers in the range between *–5* and *20*. Print the array.

6.3.11 Special String Operators and Functions

A number of operations can be performed on strings. For example, the concatenation operator joins two strings together, and the string repetition operator concatenates as many copies of its operand as specified.

Perl also supports some special functions for manipulating strings (see Table 6.14). The *substr* function returns a substring found within an original string, starting at a byte offset in the original string and ending with the number of character positions to the right of that offset. The *index* function returns the byte offset of the first character of a substring found within the original string. The *length* function returns the number of characters in a given expression.

Table 6.14 String Operations

Example	***Meaning***
$str1 . $str2	Concatenate strings *$str1* and *$str2*
$str1 x $num	Repeat *$str1*, *$num* times
substr($str1, $offset, $len)	Substring of *$str1* at *$offset* for *$len* bytes
index($str1, $str2)	Byte offset of string *$str2* in string *$str1*
length(EXPR)	Returns the length in characters of expression, *EXPR*
rindex($str, $substr, POSITION)	Returns the position of the last occurrence of *$substr* in *$str*. If *POSITION* is specified, start looking there. If *POSITION* is not specified, start at the end of the string.
chr(NUMBER)	Returns the character represented by that *NUMBER* in the ASCII character set. For example, *chr(65)* is the letter *A*.
lc($str)	Returns a lowercase string
uc($str)	Returns an uppercase string

EXAMPLE 6.20

```
(The Script)
    #!/usr/bin/perl
    $x="pop";
    $y="corn";
    $z="*";
    print $z x 10, "\n";          # Print 10 stars
    print $x . $y, "\n";          # Concatenate "pop" and "corn"
    print $z x 10, "\n";          # Print 10 stars
```

EXAMPLE 6.20 (CONTINUED)

```
7   print (($x . $y ."  ") x 5 );   # Concatenate "pop" and "corn"
                                    # and print 5 times
8   print "\n";
9   print uc($x . $y), "!\n";       # Convert string to uppercase

(Output)
4   **********
5   popcorn
6   **********
7   popcorn popcorn popcorn popcorn popcorn
9   POPCORN!
```

EXPLANATION

1 The scalar *$x* is assigned *pop*.
2 The scalar *$y* is assigned *corn*.
3 The scalar *$z* is assigned *.
4 The string * is concatenated 10 times and printed to *STDOUT*.
5 The value of *$x*, string *pop*, and the value of *$y*, string *corn*, are concatenated and printed to *STDOUT*.
6 The value of *$x*, string *, is concatenated 10 times and printed to *STDOUT*.
7 The strings *pop* and *corn* are concatenated five times and printed to *STDOUT*.
8 Print a newline to *STDOUT*.
9 The *uc* function converts and returns the string in uppercase. The *lc* function will convert a string to lowercase.

EXAMPLE 6.21

```
(The Script)
$line="Happy New Year";
print substr($line, 6, 3),"\n";        # Offset starts at zero
print index($line, "Year"),"\n";
print substr($line, index($line, "Year")),"\n";
substr($line, 0, 0)="Fred, ";
print $line,"\n";
substr($line, 0, 1)="Ethel";
print $line,"\n";
substr($line, -1, 1)="r to you!";
print $line,"\n";
$string="I'll eat a tomato tomorrow.\n";
print rindex($string, tom), "\n";
```

EXAMPLE 6.21 (CONTINUED)

```
(Output)
2  New
3  10
4  Year
6  Fred, Happy New Year
8  Ethelred, Happy New Year
9  Ethelred, Happy New Year to you!
12 18
```

EXPLANATION

1 The scalar *$line* is assigned *Happy New Year.*
2 The substring *New* of the original string *Happy New Year* is printed to *STDOUT.* The offset starts at byte 0. The beginning of the substring is position *6*, the *N*, and the end of the substring is three characters to the right of *N*. The substring *New* is returned.
3 The *index* function returns the first position in the string where the substring is found. The substring *Year* starts at position 10. Remember, the byte offset starts at 0.
4 The *substr* and *index* functions are used together. The *index* function returns the starting position of the substring *Year.* The *substr* function uses the return value from the *index* function as the starting position for the *substring.* The *substring* returned is *Year.*
5 The substring *Fred* is inserted at starting position, byte *0*, and over length *0* of the scalar *$line*; i.e., at the beginning of the string.
6 The new value of *$line* is printed to *STDOUT.*
7 The substring *Ethel* is inserted at starting position, byte *0*, and over length *1* of the scalar *$line.*
8 The new value of *$line, Ethelred, Happy New Year* is printed to *STDOUT.*
9 The substring, *r to you!* is appended to the scalar *$line* starting at the end (*–1*) of the substring, over one character.
10 The new value of *$line, Ethelred, Happy New Year to you!* is printed to *STDOUT.*
11 The *$string* scalar is assigned.
12 The *rindex* function finds the index of the **rightmost** substring, *tom*, and returns the index position where it found the substring. That position, *18*, is the number of characters starting at the zero-ith position from the beginning of the string to the substring *tom* in *tomorrow.*

6.3.12 Arithmetic Functions

In addition to arithmetic operators, Perl provides a number of built-in functions to evaluate arithmetic expressions. (See Table 6.15.)

There are also a number of less-used general utility functions provided by CPAN in a module called *List::Util*, including *first(), max(), maxstr(), min(), minstr(), reduce(), shuffle()*, and *sum*. See: *http://perldoc.perl.org/List/Util.html#DESCRIPTION.*

Table 6.15 Built-in Perl Arithmetic Functions

atan2(Y,X)	Returns the arctangent of Y/X in the range –PI to PI.
cos(EXPR) cos EXPR	Returns the cosine of EXPR (expressed in radians). If EXPR is omitted, takes cosine of $_.
exp(EXPR) exp EXPR	Returns e to the power of EXPR. If EXPR is omitted, gives exp($_).
int(EXPR) int EXPR	Returns the integer portion of EXPR. If EXPR is omitted, uses $_.
log(EXPR) log EXPR	Returns logarithm (base e) of EXPR. If EXPR is omitted, returns log of $_.
rand(EXPR) rand EXPR rand	Returns a random fractional number between 0 and the value of EXPR. (EXPR should be positive.) If EXPR is omitted, returns a value between 0 and 1. See also srand().
sin(EXPR) sin EXPR	Returns the sine of EXPR (expressed in radians). If EXPR is omitted, returns sine of $_.
sqrt(EXPR) sqrt EXPR	Return the square root of EXPR. If EXPR is omitted, returns square root of $_.
srand(EXPR) srand EXPR	Sets the random number seed for the rand operator. If EXPR is omitted, does srand(time).

Generating Random Numbers. When looking for a good description of random number generation on the Web, one of the related categories is *Games>Gambling>Lotteries>Ticket Generators*. Games and lotteries depend on the use of random number generation and so do more sophisticated programs, such as cryptographic protocols that use unpredictable encrypted keys to ensure security when passing information back and forth on the Web.

Random numbers produced by programs are called **pseudorandom** numbers. As described in an article by Ian Goldberg and David Wagner concerning Web security, truly random numbers can be found only in nature, such as the rate of decay of a radioactive element. Apart from using external sources, computers must generate these numbers themselves, but since computers are deterministic, these numbers will not be truly random.[4] Perl programs that need to generate pseudorandom numbers can use the built-in *rand* function described next.

4. Goldberg, I., and Wagner, D., "Randomness and the Netscape Browser. How Secure is the World Wide Web?" *Dr. Dobb's Journal*, *http://www.ddj.com/articles/1996/9601h/9601h.html*.

The *rand/srand* Functions

The *rand* function returns a pseudorandom fractional number between 0 and 1. If *EXPR* has a positive value, *rand* returns a fractional number between 0 and *EXPR*. The *srand* function sets the random number seed for the *rand* function but is no longer required if you are using a version of Perl greater than 5.004. A seed is a random number itself that is fed to the random number generator as the starting number from which new random numbers are produced. The *rand* function is given a seed and, using a complex algorithm, produces random numbers within some range. If the same seed is fed to the *rand* function, the same series of numbers will be produced. A different seed will produce a different series of random numbers. The default seed value used to be the time of day, but now a more unpredictable number is selected for you by Perl.

FORMAT

```
rand(EXPR)
rand EXPR
rand

srand(EXPR)
srand EXPR
```

EXAMPLE 6.22

```
(The Script)
   #!/usr/bin/perl
1  $num=10;
2  srand(time|$$);  # Seed rand with the time or'ed to
                    # the pid of this process
3  while($num){     # srand not necessary in versions 5.004 and above
4     $lotto = int(rand(10)) + 1;
                    # Returns a random number between 1 and 10
5     print "The random number is $lotto\n";
      sleep 3;
      $num--;
   }

(Output)
5  The random number is 5
   The random number is 5
   The random number is 7
   The random number is 8
   The random number is 1
   The random number is 5
   The random number is 4
   The random number is 4
   The random number is 4
   The random number is 6
```

EXPLANATION

1 The value of *$num* will be used in the *while* loop on line 7, which will iterate 10 times.
2 The *srand* function sets the seed for the *rand* function to a unique starting point, the return value of the built-in *time* function bitwise *or*ed to the process identification number of this Perl program ($$).
3 The *while* loop will iterate 10 times.
4 The *rand* function will return an integer value between 1 and 10, inclusive. The value will be assigned to *$lotto*.
5 The value of the random number is printed.

EXAMPLE 6.23

```
(The Script)
     #!/usr/bin/perl
1    $x=5 ;    # Starting point in a range of numbers
2    $y=15;    # Ending point

     # Formula to produce random numbers between 5 and 15 inclusive
     # $random = int(rand($y - $x + 1)) + $x;
     # $random = int(rand(15 - 5 + 1)) + 5

3    while(1){
4       print int(rand($y - $x + 1)) + $x , "\n";
5       sleep 1;
     }

(Output)
15
14
5
10
11
6
12
6
7
10
6
8
6
15
11
```

EXPLANATION

1 The scalar *$x* is assigned the starting value in the range of numbers produced by the *rand* function.
2 The scalar *$y* is assigned the ending value of the range of numbers produced by the *rand* function.
3 An infinite *while* loop is started. To exit, the user must type <Ctrl>-d (UNIX) or <Ctrl>-z (Windows).
4 The *rand* function is given a formula that will produce random integer values in the range 1 to 15, inclusive.
5 The *sleep* function causes the program to pause for 1 second.

6.4 What You Should Know

1. What is meant by the term *operand*?
2. How does Perl treat the expression *"5cats" + 21*?
3. How does Perl treat the expresson *23 . 43*?
4. What is an autoincrement operator?
5. What is a pseudorandom number?
6. What is the difference between "eq" and "=="?
7. Are "and" and "&&" the same?
8. What is a ternary operator?
9. How does Perl use relational operators to compare strings?
10. What is the difference between "and" and "or"?
11. Are && and "and" the same?
12. Where is the equal sign in the precedence table?
13. Does the equal sign associate right to left or left to right?
14. What Perl string function lets you extract a piece of a string?
15. What function converts a string to uppercase?
16. What operator allows you to repeat a string?
17. What operator allows you to concatenate strings together?

6.5 What's Next?

In the next chapter, we discuss the Perl control structures, how to test whether a condition is true or false with *if* and *unless* constructs, how to block statements, how to use loops to repeat a statement(s), and how to break out of loops, use labels, and nest loops.

EXERCISE 6
Operator, Operator

1. Print the average of three floating point numbers with a precision of two decimal places.

2. What are two other ways you could write
   $x = $x + 1;

3. Write the following expression using a shortcut:
   $y = $y + 5;

4. Calculate the volume of a room that is 12.5 ft. long , 9.8 ft. wide and 10.5 ft. high.

5. Square the number 15 and print the result.

6. What would the following program print?
   ```
   $a = 15;
   $b = 4;
   $c = 25.0;
   $d = 3.0;
   printf ("4 + c / 4 * d = %f\n", 4 + $c / 4 * $d);
   printf ("a / d * a + c = %.2f\n", $a / $d * $a + $c);
   printf ("%d\n", $result = $c / 5 – 2);
   printf ("%d = %d + %f\n", $result = $b + $c, $b, $c);
   printf ("%d\n", $result == $d);
   ```

7. Given the values of *$a=10*, *$b=3*, *$c=7*, and *$d=20*, print the value of *$result*:
   a. *$result = ($a >= $b) && ($c < $d);*
      print "$result\n";
   b. *$result = ($a >= $b) and ($c < $d);*
      print "$result\n";
   c. *$result = ($a < $b) || ($c <= $d);*
      print "$result\n";
   d. *$result=($a < $b) or ($c <= $d);*
      print "$result\n";
   e. *$result = $a % $b;*

7. Write a program called *convert* that converts a Fahrenheit temperature to Celsius using the following formula.
   C = (F – 32) / 1.8

8. Create an array of five sayings:

"An apple a day keeps the doctor away"
"Procrastination is the thief of time"
"The early bird catches the worm"
"Handsome is as handsome does"
"Too many cooks spoil the broth"

Each time you run your script, a random saying will be printed. Hint: the index of the array will hold a random number.

9. The following formula is used to calculate the fixed monthly payment required to fully amortize a loan over a term of months at a monthly interest rate. Write a Perl expression to represent the following formula where: P = principal amount borrowed, r = periodic interest rate (annual interest rate divided by 12), n = total number of payments (for a 30-year loan with monthly payments, n = 30 years × 12 months = 360), and A = periodic payment.

$$P = A \cdot \frac{1 - \frac{1}{(1+r)^n}}{r}$$

chapter

7

If Only, Unconditionally, Forever

7.1 Control Structures, Blocks, and Compound Statements

People plan their lives by making decisions, and so do programs. Figure 7.1 is a flow chart. A flow chart is defined as a pictorial representaion of how to plan the stages of a program. It helps you to visualize what decisions need to be made to accomplish a task. According to computer science books, a good language allows you to control the flow of your program in three ways:

- Execute a sequence of statements.
- Based on the results of a test, branch to an alternative sequence of statements.
- Repeat a sequence of statements until some condition is met.

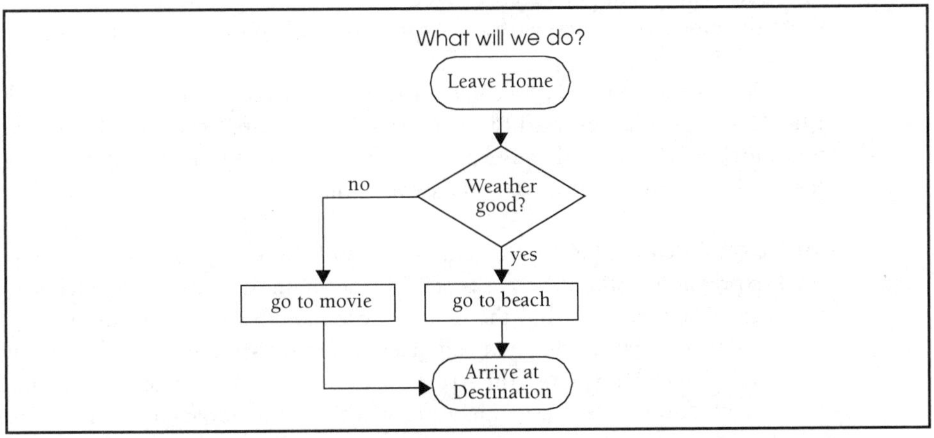

Figure 7.1 A flow chart.

So far, we have seen script examples that are linear in structure; that is, simple statements that are executed in sequence, one after the other. Control structures, such as branching and looping statements, allow the flow of the program's control to change depending on some conditional expression.

The decision-making constructs (*if, if/else, if/elsif/else, unless*, etc.) contain a control expression that determines whether a block of statements will be executed.

The looping constructs (*while, until, for, foreach*) allow the program to repetitively execute a statement block until some condition is satisfied.

A compound statement, or block, consists of a group of statements surrounded by curly braces. The block is syntactically equivalent to a single statement and usually follows an *if, else, while,* or *for* construct. But unlike C, where curly braces are not always required, Perl requires them even with one statement when that statement comes after the *if, else, while,* etc. The conditional modifiers, discussed in Chapter 8, "Regular Expressions—Pattern Matching," can be used when a condition is evaluated within a **single** statement.

7.1.1 Decision Making—Conditional Constructs

_if_ and _unless_ Statements. The *if* and *unless* constructs are followed by an expression surrounded by parentheses and followed by a block of one more statements. The block is always enclosed in curly braces.

An *if* statement is a conditional statement. It allows you to test an expression and, based on the results of the test, make a decision. The expression is enclosed in parentheses, and Perl evaluates the expression in a string context. If the string is non-null, the expression is *true*; if it is null, the expression is *false*. If the expression is a numeric value, it will be converted to a string and tested. If the expression is evaluated to be *true* (non-null), the next statement block is executed; if the condition is *false* (null), Perl will ignore the block associated with the expression and go on to the next executable statement within the script.

The *unless* statement is constructed exactly the same as the *if* statement; the results of the test are simply reversed. If the expression is evaluated to be *false*, the next statement block is executed; if the expression is evaluated to be *true*, Perl will ignore the block of statements controlled by the expression.

The _if_ Construct. The *if* statement consists of the keyword *if*, followed by a conditional expression, followed by a block of one or more statements enclosed in curly braces. Each statement within the block is terminated with a semicolon (;). The block of statements collectively is often called a **compound statement**. Make sure when you are testing strings that you use the string operators shown in Table 6.7 and that if testing numbers, you use the numeric operators also shown in Table 6.6. Perl converts strings and numbers to conform to what the operator expects, so be careful. A test such as "yes" == "no" is incorrect. It should be "yes" eq "no".

FORMAT

```
if (Expression) {Block}
if (Expression) {Block} else {Block}
if (Expression) {Block} elsif (Expression)
   {Block}... else {Block}
```

EXAMPLE 7.1

```
(The Script)
1   print "How old are you? ";
2   chomp($age = <STDIN>);
3   if ($age >= 21 ){  # If true, enter the block
4           print "Let's party!\n";
    }
5   print "You said you were $age.\n";

(Output)
1   How old are you? 32
4   Let's party!
5     You said you were 32.

------------Run the program again ------------
(Output)
1  How old are you? 10
5  You said you were 10.
```

EXPLANATION

1. The user is asked for his age.
2. The scalar *$age* is assigned a value.
3. The scalar *$age* is tested. If its value is greater than or equal to 21 (i.e., the expression evalutaes to true), then the block is entered and line 4 is executed.
4. If the user is older than 21, this line is printed. The curly braces enclosing the block after the *if* are not optional. They are required!
5. Program control continues here whether or not the if block was executed.

The *if/else* Construct. Another form of the *if* statement is the *if/else* construct. This construct allows for a two-way decision. If the first conditional expression following the *if* keyword is true, the block of statements following the *if* are executed. Otherwise, if the conditional expression following the *if* keyword is false, control branches to the *else*, and the block of statements following the *else* are executed. The *else* statement is never an independent statement. It must follow an *if* statement. When the *if* statements are nested within other *if* statements, the *else* statement is associated with the closest previous *if* statement.

FORMAT

```
if (Expression)
      {Block}
else
      {Block}
```

EXAMPLE 7.2

```
(The Script)
1   print "What version of the operating system are you using? ";
2   chomp($os=<STDIN>);
3   if ($os > 2.2) {print "Most of the bugs have been worked
                            out!\n";}
4   else {print "Expect some problems.\n";}

(Output)
1   What version of the operating system are you using?  2.4
3   Most of the bugs have been worked out!

(Output)
1   What version of the operating system are you using?  2.0
4   Expect some problems.
```

EXPLANATION

1. The user is asked for input.
2. The newline is removed.
3. If the value of *$os* is greater than 2.2, the block enclosed in curly braces is executed. If not, program control goes to the *else* on line 4.
4. If *$os* is not greater than 2.2, this block is executed.

The *if/elsif/else* Construct. Yet another form of the *if* statement is the *if/else/elsif* construct. This construct provides a multiway decision structure. If the first conditional expression following the *if* keyword is true, the block of statements following the *if* is executed. Otherwise, the first *elsif* statement is tested. If the conditional expression following the first *elsif* is false, the next *elsif* is tested, etc. If all of the conditional expressions following the *elsif*s are false, the block after the *else* is executed; this is the default action.

FORMAT

```
if (Expression1)
      {Block}
elsif (Expression2)
      {Block}
elsif (Expression3)
      {Block}
else
      {Block}
```

EXAMPLE 7.3

```
(The Script)
1   $hour=(localtime)[2];
2   if ($hour >= 0 && $hour < 12){print "Good-morning!\n";}
3   elsif ($hour == 12){print "Lunch time.\n";}
4   elsif ($hour > 12 && $hour < 17) {print "Siesta time.\n";}
5   else {print "Goodnight. Sweet dreams.\n";}

(Output)
4   Siesta time
```

EXPLANATION

1. The scalar *$hour* is set to the current hour. The *localtime* built-in function returns the hour, the third element of the array of time values.
2. The *if* statement tests whether the value of *$hour* is greater than or equal to *0* and less than *12*. The result of the evaluation is true, so the block following the control expression is executed (i.e., the *print* statement is executed).
3. If the first *if* test is false, this expression is tested. If the value of *$hour* is equal to *12*, the *print* statement is executed.
4. If the previous *elsif* test failed, and this *elsif* expression evaluates to true, the *print* statement will be executed.
5. If none of the above statements is true, the *else* statement, the default action, is executed.

The *unless* Construct. The *unless* statement is similar to the *if* statement, except that the control expression after the *unless* is tested for the reverse condition; that is, if the conditional expression following the *unless* is false, the statement block is executed.

The *unless/else* and *unless/elsif* behave in the same way as the *if/else* and *if /elsif* statements with the same reversed test as previously stated.

FORMAT

```
unless (Expression) {Block}
unless (Expression) {Block} else {Block}
unless (Expression) {Block} elsif (Expression)
   {Block}... else {Block}
```

EXAMPLE 7.4

```
(The Script)
1   print "How old are you? ";
2   chomp($age = <STDIN>);
3   unless ($age <= 21 ){   # If false, enter the block
4           print "Let's party!\n";
    }
5   print "You said you were $age.\n";
```

EXAMPLE 7.4 (CONTINUED)

```
(Output)
1  How old are you? 32
4  Let's party!
5  You said you were 32.

------------Run the program again ------------

(Output)
1  How old are you? 10
5  You said you were 10.
```

EXPLANATION

1. This example is exactly like Example 7.1 except the logic in the condition is reversed. We will test for false rather than true. The user is asked for his age.
2. The scalar *$age* is assigned a value.
3. The scalar *$age* is tested. Unless its value is less than or equal to 21 (i.e., the expression evaluates to false), then the block is entered and line 4 is executed.
4. If the user is not 21 or older, this line is printed. The curly braces enclosing the block after the *if* are not optional. They are required!
5. Program control continues here whether or not the *if* block was executed.

EXAMPLE 7.5

```
(The Script)
   #!/bin/perl
   # Scriptname: excluder
1  while(<>){
2      ($name, $phone)=split(/:/);
3      unless($name eq "barbara"){
          $record="$name\t$phone";
4         print "$record";
       }
   }
5  print "\n$name has moved from this district.\n";

(Output)
$ excluder names
igor chevsky     408-123-4533
paco gutierrez   510-453-2776
ephram hardy     916-235-4455
james ikeda      415-449-0066
barbara kerz     207-398-6755
jose santiago    408-876-5899
tommy savage     408-876-1725
lizzy stachelin  415-555-1234

barbara has moved from this district.
```

EXPLANATION

1 The *while* loop is entered. It will read one line at a time from whatever filename is given as a command-line argument to this script. The argument file is called *names*.
2 Each line is split by a colon delimiter. The first field is assigned to *$name* and the second field to *$phone*.
3 The *unless* statement is executed. It reads: unless *$name* evaluates to *barbara*, enter the block; in other words, anyone except *barbara* is okay.
4 All names and phones are printed with the exception of *barbara*.
5 When the loop exits, this line is printed.

7.2 Repetition with Loops

Sometimes, you may want to repeat a statement or group of statements until some condition is met; for example, continue to ask the user a question until he gives the correct response, or you may want to create a timer that counts down from 10 to 0, or you may want to modify each item in a list, until you reach the end of the list. This is where loops come in. They are used to execute a segment of code repeatedly. Perl's basic looping constructs are:

while
until
for
foreach

Each loop is followed by a block of statements enclosed in curly braces.

7.2.1 The *while* Loop

The *while* statement executes the block as long as the control expression after the *while* is true. An expression is *true* if it evaluates to *nonzero* (non-null); *while(1)* is always true and loops forever. An expression is *false* if it evaluates to *zero* (null); *while(0)* is false and never loops.

Often, the *while* statement is used to loop through a file. (See "Reading from the Filehandle" on page 288.)

FORMAT

```
while (Expression) {Block}
```

EXAMPLE 7.6

```
(The Script)
     #!/usr/bin/perl
1    $num=0;                  # Initialize $num
2    while ($num < 10){       # Test expression
     # Loop quits when expression is false or 0

3        print "$num ";
4        $num++;    # Update the loop variable $num; increment $num
5        }
6    print "\nOut of the loop.\n";

(Output)
3    0 1 2 3 4 5 6 7 8 9
6    Out of the loop.
```

EXPLANATION

1 The scalar *$num* is initialized. The initialization takes place before entering the loop.

2 The test expression is evaluated. If the result is true, the block of statements in curly braces is executed.

4 The scalar *$num* is incremented. If not, the test expression would always yield a true value, and the loop would never end.

EXAMPLE 7.7

```
(The Script)
    #!/usr/bin/perl
    $count=1;          # Initialize variables
    $beers=10;
    $remain=$beers;
    $where="on the shelf";
    while ($count <= $beers) {
        if ($remain == 1){print "$remain bottle of beer $where ." ;}
        else {print "$remain bottles of beer $where $where .";}
        print " Take one down and pass it all around.\n";
        print "Now ", $beers - $count , " bottles of beer $where!\n";

        $count++;
        $remain--;
        if ($count > 10){print "Party's over. \n";}
    }
    print "\n";
```

EXAMPLE 7.7 (CONTINUED)

```
(Output)
10 bottles on the shelf on the shelf. Take one down and pass it all around.
Now 9 bottles of beer on the shelf!
9 bottles on the shelf on the shelf. Take one down and pass it all around.
Now 8 bottles of beer on the shelf!
8 bottles on the shelf on the shelf. Take one down and pass it all around.
Now 7 bottles of beer on the shelf!
7 bottles on the shelf on the shelf. Take one down and pass it all around.
Now 6 bottles of beer on the shelf!
6 bottles on the shelf on the shelf. Take one down and pass it all around.
Now 5 bottles of beer on the shelf!
5 bottles on the shelf on the shelf. Take one down and pass it all around.
Now 4 bottles of beer on the shelf!
4 bottles on the shelf on the shelf. Take one down and pass it all around.
Now 3 bottles of beer on the shelf!
3 bottles on the shelf on the shelf. Take one down and pass it all around.
Now 2 bottles of beer on the shelf!
2 bottles on the shelf on the shelf. Take one down and pass it all around.
Now 1 bottle of beer on the shelf!
1 bottle of beer on the shelf on the shelf. Take one down and pass it all around.
Now 0 bottles of beer on the shelf!
Party's over.
```

EXPLANATION

1 The scalars *$count, $beers, $remain*, and *$where* are initialized.
2 The *while* loop is entered; the control expression is tested and evaluated.
3 The scalar *$count* is incremented.
4 The scalar *$remain* is decremented.
5 When the value of *$count* is greater than *10*, this line is printed.

7.2.2 The *until* Loop

The *until* statement executes the block as long as the control expression after the *until* is false, or zero. When the expression evaluates to true (nonzero), the loop exits.

FORMAT

```
until (Expression) {Block}
```

EXAMPLE 7.8

```
(The Script)
   #!/usr/bin/perl
1  $num=0;        # initialize
2  until ($num == 10){
       # Test expression; loop quits when expression is true or 1
3     print "$num ";
4     $num++;    # Update the loop variable $num; increment $num
5  }
6  print "\nOut of the loop.\n";

(Output)
3  0 1 2 3 4 5 6 7 8 9
6  Out of the loop.
```

EXPLANATION

1. The scalar *$num* is initialized. The initialization takes place before entering the loop.
2. The test expression is evaluated. If the result is false, the block of statements in curly braces is executed. When *$num* is equal to *10*, the loop exits.
4. The scalar *$num* is incremented. If not, the test expression would always yield a false value, and the loop would never end.

EXAMPLE 7.9

```
(The Script)
   #!/usr/bin/perl
1  print "Are you o.k.? ";
2  chomp($answer=<STDIN>);
3  until ($answer eq "yes"){
4     sleep(1);
5     print "Are you o.k. yet? ";
6     chomp($answer=<STDIN>);
7  }
8  print "Glad to hear it!\n";

(Output)
1  Are you o.k.? n
1  Are you o.k. yet? nope
1  Are you o.k. yet? yup
1  Are you o.k. yet? yes
8  Glad to hear it!
```

EXPLANATION

1. The user is asked an initial question.
2. The user's response is taken from standard input and stored in the scalar *$answer*. The newline is *chomped*.
3. The *until* loop checks the expression enclosed in parentheses, and if the value of *$answer* is not exactly equal to the string *yes*, the block following the expression will be entered. When *$answer* evaluates to *yes*, the loop exits and control begins at line 8.
4. If the value of *$answer* is not equal to *yes*, this line will be executed; in other words, the program will pause for one minute (*sleep 1*). This gives the user time before being asked the question again.
5. The user is asked again if he is okay.
6. The user's response is read again from *STDIN* and stored in *$answer*. This line is very important. If the value of *$answer* never changes, the loop will go on forever.
7. The closing curly brace marks the end of the block connected to the *until* loop. Control will returned to line 3 and the expression will be tested again. If the value of *$answer* is *yes*, control will go to line 8; otherwise, the statements in the block will be reexecuted.
8. When the loop exits, this line is executed; in other words, when the value of *$answer* is equal to *yes*.

The *do/while* and *do/until* Loops. The *do/while* or *do/until* loops evaluate the conditional expression for true and false just as in the *while* and *until* loop statements. However, the expression is not evaluated until after the block is executed at least once.

FORMAT

```
do {Block} while (Expression);
do {Block} until (Expression);
```

EXAMPLE 7.10

```
(The Script)
   #!/usr/bin/perl
   $x = 1;
   do {
       print "$x ";
       $x++;
   } while ($x <= 10);
   print "\n";

   $y = 1;
   do {
       print "$y " ;
       $y++;
   } until ($y > 10);
```

EXAMPLE 7.10 (CONTINUED)

```
(Output)
3   1 2 3 4 5 6 7 8 9 10
8   1 2 3 4 5 6 7 8 9 10
```

EXPLANATION

1 The scalar *$x* is assigned the value *1*.
2 The *do/while* loop statement starts.
3 The block of statements is executed.
4 The scalar *$x* is incremented once.
5 The conditional expression following the *while* is evaluated. If true, the block of statements is executed again, and so on.
6 The scalar *$y* is assigned the value *1*.
7 The *do/until* loop statement starts.
8 The block of statements is executed.
9 The scalar *$y* is incremented once.
10 The conditional expression following the *until* is evaluated. If false, the block of statements is executed again, and so on.

7.2.3 The *for* Loop

The *for* statement is like the *for* loop in C. The *for* keyword is followed by three expressions separated by semicolons and enclosed within parentheses. Any or all of the expressions can be omitted, but the two semicolons cannot.[1] The first expression is used to set the initial value of variables, the second expression is used to test whether the loop should continue or stop, and the third expression updates the loop variables.

FORMAT

```
for (Expression1;Expression2;Expression3) {Block}
```

The above format is equivalent to the following *while* statement:

```
Expression1;
while (Expression2)
     {Block; Expression3};
```

1. The infinite loop can be written as: *for(;;)*

EXAMPLE 7.11

```
(The Script)
    #!/usr/bin/perl
1   for ($i=0; $i<10; $i++){    # Initialize, test, and increment $i
2       print "$i ";
    }
3   print "\nOut of the loop.\n";

(Output)
2   0 1 2 3 4 5 6 7 8 9
3   Out of the loop.
```

EXPLANATION

1 The *for* loop contains three expressions. In the first expression, the scalar *$i* is assigned the value *0*. This statement is executed just once. The second expression tests whether *$i* is less than *10*, and if so, the block statements are executed (i.e., the value of *$i* is printed). The last expression increments the value of *$i* by 1. The second expression is again tested, and the block is executed, *$i* is incremented, and so on, until the test evaluates to false.

2 The value of *$i* is printed.

EXAMPLE 7.12

```
(The Script)
    #!/usr/bin/perl
    # Initialization, test, and increment, decrement of
    # counters is done in one step.
1   for ($count=1, $beers=10, $remain=$beers, $where="on the shelf";
        $count <= $beers; $count++, $remain--)
        {
2   if ($remain == 1){
        print "$remain bottle of beer $where $where " ;
    }
    else {
        print "$remain bottles of beer $where $where.";
        }
        print " Take one down and pass it all around.\n";
        print "Now ", $beers - $count , " bottles of beer $where!\n";
3       if ($count == 10 ){print "Party's over.\n";}
    }
```

EXAMPLE 7.12 (CONTINUED)

```
(Output)
10 bottles of beer on the shelf  on the shelf. Take one down and pass it all around.
Now 9 bottles of beer on the shelf!
9 bottles of beer on the shelf on the shelf. Take one down and pass it all around.
Now 8 bottles of beer on the shelf!
8 bottles of beer on the shelf on the shelf. Take one down and pass it all around.
Now 7 bottles of beer on the shelf!

  < continues >

2 bottles of beer on the shelf on the shelf. Take one down and pass it all around.
Now 1 bottle of beer on the shelf!
1 bottle of beer on the shelf on the shelf. Take one down and pass it all around.
Now 0 bottles of beer on the shelf!
Party's over.
```

EXPLANATION

1 The initialization of all scalars is done in the first expression of the *for* loop. Each initialization is separated by a comma, and the expression is terminated with a semicolon. The first expression is executed only once, when the loop starts. The second expression is the test. If it evaluates to true, the statements in the block are executed. After the last statement in the block is executed, the third expression is evaluated. The control is then passed to the second expression in the *for* loop, and so on.

2 The block is executed if the second expression in the *for* loop is evaluated as true.

3 This statement will be tested and, if the condition is true, the statement will be executed and control will go to the third expression within the *for* loop, incrementing *$count* for the last time.

7.2.4 The *foreach* Loop

If you are familiar with C shell programming, the Perl *foreach* loop is similar in appearance and behavior to the C shell *foreach* loop, but appearances can be deceiving and there are some obvious differences between the two constructs. So, read on.

The *foreach* loop iterates over each element in the parenthesized list, an array, assigning each element of the array to a scalar variable, one after the other, until the end of the list.

The *VARIABLE* is local to the *foreach* block. It will regain its former value when the loop is exited. Any changes made when assigning values to *VARIABLE* will, in turn, affect the individual elements of the array. If *VARIABLE* is not present, the $_ special scalar variable is implicitly used.

FORMAT

```
foreach VARIABLE (ARRAY)
{BLOCK}
```

EXAMPLE 7.13

```
(The Script)
    #!/usr/bin/perl
1   foreach $pal ('Tom', 'Dick', 'Harry', 'Pete') {
2       print "Hi $pal!\n";
    }

(Output)
2   Hi Tom!
    Hi Dick!
    Hi Harry!
    Hi Pete!
```

EXPLANATION

1. The *foreach* is followed by the scalar *$pal* and a list of names. *$pal* points to each name in the list, starting with *Tom*. You can think of *$pal* as an alias, or reference, for each item in the list. Each time the loop is entered, *$pal* goes to the next item in the list and gets that value. So, for example, after *Tom*, *Dick* is fetched, and then *Harry*, and so on until all list items have been used, at which time the loop exits.
2. Each time through the loop, the value referenced by *$pal* is printed. (See Figure 7.2.)

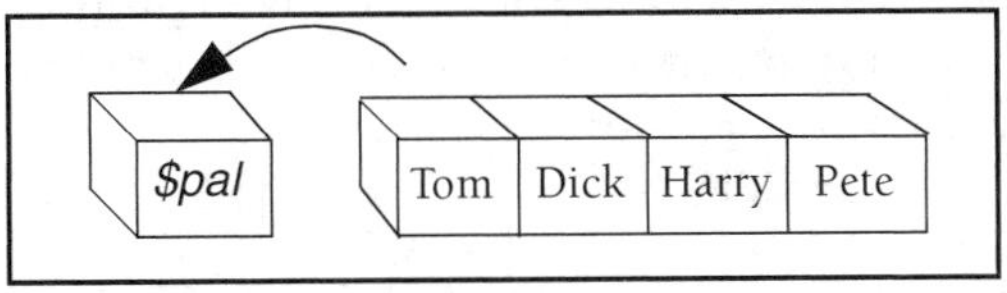

Figure 7.2 The *foreach* loop.

EXAMPLE 7.14

```
(The Script)
foreach $hour (1 .. 24){   # The range operator is used here
  if ($hour > 0 && $hour < 12) {print "Good-morning.\n";}
  elsif ($hour == 12) {print "Happy Lunch.\n";}
  elsif ($hour > 12 && $hour < 17) {print "Good afternoon.\n";}
  else {print "Good-night.\n";}
}
```

EXAMPLE 7.14 (CONTINUED)

```
(Output)
2   Good-morning.
    Good-morning.
    Good-morning.
    Good-morning.
    Good-morning.
    Good-morning.
    Good-morning.
    Good-morning.
    Good-morning.
    Good-morning.
    Good-morning.
3   Happy Lunch.
4   Good afternoon.
    Good afternoon.
    Good afternoon.
    Good afternoon.
5   Good-night.
    Good-night.
    Good-night.
    Good-night.
    Good-night.
    Good-night.
    Good-night.
    Good-night.
```

EXPLANATION

1 The list *(1 .. 24)* is a range of list items starting with *1* and ending with *24*. Each of those values is referenced in turn by the scalar *$hour*. The block is executed, and the next item in the list is assigned to *$hour*, and so on.

2 The scalar *$hour* is tested, and if the value is greater than *0* and less than *12*, the *print* statement is executed.

3 If the previous *elsif* statement is false, this statement is tested. If the scalar *$hour* is equal to *12*, the *print* statement is executed.

4 If the previous *elsif* statement is false, this statement is tested. If the scalar *$hour* is greater than *12* and less than *17*, the *print* statement is executed.

5 If all of the previous statements are false, the *else*, or default statement, is executed.

EXAMPLE 7.15

```
(The Script)
    #!/usr/bin/perl
1   $str="hello";
2   @numbers = (1, 3, 5, 7, 9);
3   print "The scalar \$str is initially $str.\n";
4   print "The array \@numbers is initially @numbers.\n";
```

EXAMPLE 7.15 (CONTINUED)

```
5   foreach $str (@numbers ){
6       $str+=5;
7       print "$str\n";
8   }
9   print "Out of the loop--\$str is $str.\n";
10  print "Out of the loop--The array \@numbers is now @numbers.\n";

(Output)
3   The scalar $str is initially hello.
4   The array @numbers is initially 1 3 5 7 9.
7   6
    8
    10
    12
    14
9   Out of the loop--$str is hello.
10  Out of the loop--The array @numbers is now 6 8 10 12 14.
```

EXPLANATION

1. The scalar *$str* is assigned the string *hello*.
2. The array *@numbers* is assigned the list of numbers: 1, 3, 5, 7, and 9.
3. The *print* function prints the initial value of *$str* to *STDOUT*.
4. The *print* function prints the initial value of *@numbers* to *STDOUT*.
5. The *foreach* statement assigns, in turn, each element in the list to *$str*. The variable *$str* is local to the loop and references each item in the list so that whatever is done to *$str* will affect the array *@numbers*. When the loop exits, it will regain its former value.
6. Each time through the loop, the value referenced by *$str* is incremented by 5.
7. The *print* function prints the new value of *$str* to *STDOUT*.
8. After exiting the loop, the original value of *$str* is printed to *STDOUT*.
9. After exiting the loop, the new and modified values of the *@number* array are printed to *STDOUT*.

EXAMPLE 7.16

```
(The Script)
    #!/usr/bin/perl
1   @colors=(red, green, blue, brown);
2   foreach (@colors) {
3       print "$_ ";
4       $_="YUCKY";
    }
5   print "\n@colors\n";

(Output)
3   red green blue brown
5   YUCKY  YUCKY  YUCKY  YUCKY
```

EXPLANATION

1 The array *@colors* is initialized.
2 The *foreach* loop is not followed by an explicit variable, but it does have a list. Since the variable is missing, the $_ special scalar is used implicitly.
3 $_ is really a reference to the item in the list that is currently being evaluated. As each item of the list *@colors* is referenced by the $_ variable, the value is printed to *STDOUT*.
4 The $_ variable is assigned the string *YUCKY*. Each original element in the array *@colors* will be replaced permanently by the value *YUCKY*, in turn.
5 The *@color* array has really been changed. The $_ variable is null, its value before entering the loop.

7.2.5 Loop Control

To interrupt the normal flow of control within a loop, Perl provides labels and simple control statements. These statements are used for controlling a loop when some condition is reached; that is, the control is transferred directly to either the bottom or the top of the loop, skipping any statements that follow the control statement condition.

Labels. Labels are optional but can be used to control the flow of a loop. By themselves, labels do nothing. They are used with the loop control modifiers, listed next. A block by itself, whether or not it has a label, is equivalent to a loop that executes only **once**. If labels are capitalized, they will not be confused with reserved words.

FORMAT

```
LABEL: while (Expression){Block}
LABEL: while (Expression) {Block} continue{Block}
LABEL: for (Expression; Expression; Expression)
    {BLOCK}
LABEL: foreach Variable (Array){Block}
LABEL: {Block} continue {Block}
```

To control the flow of loops, the following simple statements may be used within the block:

```
next
next LABEL
last
last LABEL
redo
redo LABEL
goto LABEL
```

The *next* statement restarts the next iteration of the loop, skipping over the rest of the statements in the loop and reevaluating the loop expression, like a C, *awk*, or shell *continue* statement. Since a block is a loop that iterates once, *next* can be used (with a *continue* block, if provided) to exit the block early.

The *last* statement leaves or breaks out of a loop and is like the *break* statement in C, *awk*, and shell. Since a block is a loop that iterates once, *last* can be used to break out of a block.

The *redo* statement restarts the block without evaluating the loop expression again.

The *continue block* is executed just before the conditional expression is about to be evaluated again.

The *goto* statement, although frowned upon by most programmers, is allowed in Perl programs. It takes a label as its argument and jumps to the label when the *goto* statement is executed. The label can be anywhere in your script but does not work when it appears inside a *do* statement or within a subroutine.

A Labeled Block without a Loop. A block is like a loop that executes once. A block can be labeled.

The *redo* statement causes control to start at the top of the innermost or labeled block without reevaluating the loop expression if there is one (similar to a *goto*).

EXAMPLE 7.17

```
(The Script)
      #!//usr/bin/perl
      # Program that uses a label without a loop and the redo statement
1     ATTEMPT: {
2     print "Are you a great person? ";
          chomp($answer = <STDIN>);
3         unless ($answer eq "yes"){redo ATTEMPT ;}
      }

(Output)
2     Are you a great person? Nope
2     Are you a great person? Sometimes
2     Are you a great person? yes
```

EXPLANATION

1. The label is user defined. It precedes a block. It is as though you had named the block *ATTEMPT.*
2. The user is asked for input.
3. The *redo* statement restarts the block, similar to a *goto* statement, unless the *$answer* evaluates to *yes.*

EXAMPLE 7.18

```
(The Script)
    #!/usr/bin/perl
1   while(1){    # start an infinite loop

2       print "What was your grade? ";
        $grade = <STDIN>;

3       if ($grade < 0 || $grade > 100) {
            print "Illegal choice\n";
4           next; }   # start control at the beginning of
                      # the innermost loop
5       if  ($grade  > 89 && $grade < 101) {print "A\n";}
        elsif ($grade > 79 && $grade < 90) {print "B\n";}
        elsif ($grade > 69 && $grade < 80) {print "C\n";}
        elsif ($grade > 59 && $grade < 70) {print "D\n";}
        else {print "You Failed."};
6       print "Do you want to enter another grade? (y/n) ";
        chomp($choice = <STDIN>);
7       if ($choice ne "y"){last ;}  # break out of the innermost
                                     # loop if the condition is true
    }

(Output)
2   What was your grade? 94
    A
6   Do you want to enter another grade (y/n)?  y
2   What was your grade? 66
    D
6   Do you want to enter another grade (y/n)?  n
```

EXPLANATION

1 Start an infinite loop.
2 Ask for user input.
3 Logical test. If the value of *$grade* is less than *0* or greater than *100*.
4 If the test yields *false*, control starts again at the beginning of the *while* loop.
5 Test each of the *if* conditional statements.
6 Ask for user input.
7 Break out of the innermost loop if the conditional tests true.

EXAMPLE 7.19

```
(The Script)
1   ATTEMPT:{
2       print "What is the course number? ";
        chomp($number = <STDIN>);
        print "What is the course name? ";
        chomp($course = <STDIN>);

3       $department{$number} = $course;

        print "\nReady to quit? ";
        chomp($answer = <STDIN>);
        $answer=lc($answer);  # Convert to lowercase
4       if ($answer eq  "yes" or $answer eq "y") {last;}
5       redo ATTEMPT;
    }
6   print "Program continues here.\n";

(Output)
2   What is the course number? 101
    What is the course name?  CIS342
3   Ready to quit? n
2   What is the course number? 201
    What is the course name? BIO211
3   Ready to quit? n
2   What is the course number? 301
    What is the course name? ENG120
3   Ready to quit? yes
6   Program continues here.
```

EXPLANATION

1. The label *ATTEMPT* prepends the block. A block without a looping construct is like a loop that executes only once.
2. The script gets user input in order to fill an associative array. Both the key and value are provided by the user.
3. The hash *%department* is assigned a value.
4. If the user is ready to quit, the *last* statement sends the control out of the block.
5. The *redo* statement returns control to the top of the labeled block. Each of the statements is executed again.
6. After exiting the block (line 4), the program continues here.

Nested Loops and Labels. A loop within a loop is a **nested loop**. The outside loop is initialized and tested, the inside loop then iterates completely through all of its cycles, and the outside loop starts again where it left off. The inside loop moves faster than the outside loop. Loops can be nested as deeply as you wish, but there are times when it is necessary to terminate the loop when some condition is met. Normally, if you use loop-control statements, such as *next* and *last*, the control is directed to the innermost loop. There are times when it might be necessary to switch control to some outer loop. This is accomplished by using labels.

By prefixing a loop with a label, you can control the flow of the program with *last*, *next*, and *redo* statements. Labeling a loop is like giving the loop its own name.

EXAMPLE 7.20

```
(A Demo Script)
1   OUT: while(1){
2       < Program continues here >
3       MID: while(1){
4           if (<expression is true>) {last OUT;}
            < Program continues here >
5           INNER: while(1){
6               if (<expression is true>) {next OUT;}
                <Program continues here>
            }
        }
    }
7   print "Out of all loops.\n";
```

EXPLANATION

1. The *OUT* label is used to control this infinite *while* loop, if necessary. The label is followed by a colon and the loop statement.
2. The program code continues here.
3. The *MID* label is used to control this inner *while* loop, if necessary.
4. If the expression being evaluated is true, the *last* loop-control statement is executed, breaking from this loop, labeled *OUT*, all the way out to line 7.
5. The innermost *while* loop is labeled *INNER*.
6. This time, the *next* statement with the *OUT* label causes loop control to branch back to line 1.
7. This statement is outside all of the loops and is where the *last* statement branches, if given the *OUT* label.

EXAMPLE 7.21

```
(The Script)
for ($rows=5; $rows>=1; $rows--){
    for ($columns=1; $columns<=$rows; $columns++){
        printf "*";
    }
    print "\n";
}
```

EXAMPLE 7.21 (CONTINUED)

```
(Output)
3   *****
    ****
    ***
    **
    *
```

EXPLANATION

1 The first expression in the outside loop initializes the scalar *$rows* to *5*. The variable is tested. Since it is greater than or equal to *1*, the inner loop starts.
2 The first expression in the inner loop initializes the scalar *$columns* to *1*. The scalar *$columns* is tested. The inner loop will iterate through all of its cycles. When the inner loop has completed, the outer loop will pick up where it left off; that is, *$rows* will be decremented, then tested, and if true, the block will be executed again, and so on.
3 This statement belongs to the inner *for* loop and will be executed for each iteration of the loop.
4 This curly brace closes the inner *for* loop.
5 The *print* statement is executed for each iteration of the outer *for* loop.
6 This curly brace closes the outer *for* loop.

When a label is omitted, the loop-control statements, *next, last*, and *redo* reference the innermost loop. When branching out of a nested loop to an outer loop, labels may precede the loop statement.

EXAMPLE 7.22

```
(The Script)
    # This script prints the average salary of employees
    # earning over $50,000 annually
    # There are 5 employees. If the salary falls below $50,000
    # it is not included in the tally

1   EMPLOYEE: for ($emp=1,$number=0; $emp <= 5; $emp++){
2       do { print "What is the monthly rate for employee #$emp? ";
            print "(Type q to quit) ";
3           chomp($monthly=<STDIN>);
4           last EMPLOYEE if $monthly eq 'q';
5           next EMPLOYEE if (($year=$monthly * 12.00) <= 50000);
6           $number++;
7           $total_sal += $year;
            next EMPLOYEE;
8       } while($monthly ne 'q');
    }
```

EXAMPLE 7.22 (CONTINUED)

```
9   unless($number == 0){
10     $average = $total_sal/$number;
11     print "There were $number employees who earned over \$50,000
            annually.\n";
       printf "Their average annual salary is \$%.2f.\n", $average;
       }
    else{
       print "None of the employees made over \$50,000\n";
    }

(Output)
2   What is the monthly rate for employee #1? (Type q to quit) 4000
2   What is the monthly rate for employee #2? (Type q to quit) 5500
2   What is the monthly rate for employee #3? (Type q to quit) 6000
2   What is the monthly rate for employee #4? (Type q to quit) 3400
2   What is the monthly rate for employee #5? (Type q to quit) 4500
11  There were 3 employees who earned over $50,000 annually.
    Their average annual salary is $64000.00.
```

EXPLANATION

1. The label *EMPLOYEE* precedes the outer loop. This loop keeps track of five employees.
2. The *do/while* loop is entered.
3. The script gets user input for the monthly salary.
4. If the user types *q*, the *last* control statement is executed and branching goes to the bottom of the outer loop, labeled *EMPLOYEE*.
5. The *next* control statement transfers execution to the top of the outer *for* loop labeled *EMPLOYEE*, if the condition is true.
6. The scalar *$number* is incremented.
7. The value of the scalar *$total_sal* is calculated.
8. The *next* control statement transfers execution to the top of the outermost *for* loop, labeled *EMPLOYEE*.
9. Unless the value of *$number* equals *0*, in the case that no one earned over $50,000, the block is entered.
10. The average annual salary is calculated.
11. The results are displayed.

The *continue* Block. The *continue* block with a *while* loop preserves the correct semantics as a *for* loop, even when the *next* statement is used.

EXAMPLE 7.23

```
(The Script)
    #! /usr/bin/perl#
    # Example using the continue block
    for ($i=1; $i<=10; $i++) {       # $i is incremented only once
        if ($i==5){
            print "\$i == $i\n";
            next;
        }
        print "$i ";
    }

    print "\n"; print '=' x 35; print "\n";
# ------------------------------------------------------------

    $i=1;
    while ($i <= 10){
        if ($i==5){
            print "\$i == $i\n";
            $i++;     # $i must be incremented here or an
                      # infinite loop will start
            next;
        }
        print "$i ";
        $i++;           # $i is incremented again
    }

    print "\n"; print '=' x 35; print "\n";
    # ------------------------------------------------------------
    # The continue block allows the while loop to act like a for loop
    $i=1;
    while ($i <= 10) {
        if ($i == 5) {
            print "\$i == $i\n";
            next;
        }
        print "$i ";
    }continue {$i++; }     # $i is incremented only once

(Output)
1 2 3 4 $i == 5
6 7 8 9 10
===================================
1 2 3 4 $i == 5
6 7 8 9 10
===================================
1 2 3 4 $i == 5
6 7 8 9 10
```

EXPLANATION

1 The *for* loop is entered and will loop 10 times.
2 If the value of *$i* is 5, the block is entered and . . .
3 . . . the value of *$i* is printed.
4 The *next* statement returns control back to the *for* loop. When control is returned to the *for* loop, the third expression is always evaluated before the second expression is tested. **Before** the second expression is tested, *$i* is incremented.
5 Each time through the loop, the value of *$i* is printed unless *$i* equals 5.
6 *$i* is initialized to 5.
7 The body of the *while* loop is entered if the expression tested is true.
8 If *$i* is equal to 5, the value of *$i* is displayed.
9 *$i* is incremented by 1. If the *$i* is not incremented here, it will never be incremented and the program will go into an infinite loop.
10 The *next* statement causes control to start again at the top of the *while* loop, where the expression after *while* is evaluated.
11 The current value of *$i* is displayed.
12 After *$i* is incremented, control will go back to the top of the *while* loop and the expression will be tested again.
13 While *$i* is less than or equal to *10*, enter the loop body.
14 If *$i* is equal to 5, the block is entered.
15 The current value of *$i* is displayed.
16 The *next* statement normally causes control to go back to the top of the *while* loop, but because there is a *continue* block at the end of the loop, control will go into the *continue* block first and then back to the top of the *while* loop where the expression will be tested.
17 The value of *$i* is displayed.
18 The *continue* block is executed at the end of the *while* loop block, before the *next* statement returns control to the top of the loop or, if *next* is not executed, after the last statement in the loop block.

7.2.6 The *switch* Statement

A *switch* statement is another type of control statement similar to *if/elsif/else* but evaluates an expression by matching the expression to a set of case labels. When a match is found, program control is transferred to that block where the expression matched the label value. The following example demonstrates the way a *switch* statement is designed in the C language, PHP, etc.

```
switch (expression) {
   case value1 :
      /* statements */
      break;
```

```
    case value2 :
        /* statements */
        break;
    case value3 :
        /* statements */
        break;
    default:
        /* statements */
        break;
}
```

Although the *switch/case* mechanism is a common control structure provided by most modern programming languages, it is **not** available in Perl 5. (It will be in Perl 6.) You can achieve the same goal in Perl with the traditional *if/elsif/else* constructs or by creating labeled blocks as shown next. Since a block (labeled or not) is equivalent to a loop that executes once, and loop control statements, such as *last*, *next*, and *redo*, can be used within this block, you can create a "phoney" *switch* statement by adding a *do* block, which will execute a sequence of commands within the block. See Example 7.24.

EXAMPLE 7.24

```
(The Script)
    #! /usr/bin/perl
    $hour=0;
    while($hour < 24) {
      SWITCH: {         # SWITCH is just a user-defined label
          $hour < 12                   && do {  print "Good-morning!\n";
                                                 last SWITCH;};

          $hour == 12                  && do {  print "Lunch!\n";
                                                 last SWITCH;};

          $hour > 12 && $hour <= 17    && do {  print "Siesta time!\n";
                                                 last SWITCH;};

          $hour > 17                   && do {  print "Good night.\n";
                                                 last SWITCH;};
      } # End of block labeled SWITCH

      $hour++;
    } # End of loop block
```

EXAMPLE 7.24 (CONTINUED)

```
(Output)
Good-morning!
Good-morning!
Good-morning!

<Output continues>

Good-morning!
Good-morning!
Good-morning!
Lunch!
Siesta time!
Siesta time!
Siesta time!
Siesta time!
Siesta time!
Good night.
Good night.
Good night.
Good night.
Good night.
```

EXPLANATION

1 The *$hour* scalar is assigned an initial value of *0* before entering the loop.
2 The *while* loop expression is evaluated.
3 The label *SWITCH* labels the block. It is simply a label, nothing more.
4 After entering the block, the expression is evaluated. The expression reads *if $hour is less than 12...*, the expression on the right of the *&&* is evaluated. This is a *do* block. Each of the statements within this block is executed in sequence. The value of the last statement evaluated is returned.
5 The *last* statement causes control to branch to the end of this block labeled *SWITCH* to line 8.
6 This statement is evaluated if the expression in the previous statement evaluates to false. The expression reads *if $hour is equal to 12...*
7 This statement is evaluated if the expression in the previous statement evaluates to false. The expression reads *if $hour is greater than 12 and also less than or equal to 17...*
8 If this statement is true, the *do* block is executed. The expression reads *if $hour is greater than 17...*
9 The *$hour* scalar is incremented once each time after going through the loop.

The *Switch.pm* Module. If you still want a *switch* statement, the *Switch.pm* module can be found at: *http://search.cpan.org/~rgarcia/Switch-2.13/Switch.pm*. See Example 7.25.

EXAMPLE 7.25

```
(The Script)
1 use Switch; # Loads a Perl module

2 print "What is your favorite color? ";
  chomp($color=<STDIN>);
3 switch("$color"){
4  case "red"   { print "Red hot mama!\n"; }
   case "blue" { print "I got a feeling called the blues.\n"; }
   case "green" { print "How green my valley\n";}
   case "yellow" { print "In my yellow submarine";}
5  else          { print "$color is not in our list.\n";}
 }
6   print "Execution continues here....\n";

(Output)
2 What is your favorite color? blue
  I got a feeling called the blues.
6 Execution continues here....
--------------------------------------
2 What is your favorite color? pink
  pink is not in our list.
6 Execution continues here....
```

EXPLANATION

1 This line loads the *Switch.pm* module into your program's memory from the standard Perl library.

2 The user is asked to input his favorite color, which is stored in a scalar, *$color*.

3 The *switch* statement evaluates the value of *$color* and tests it against the strings provided in the case statements below. The keyword "case" replaces *elsif* in the *if/elsif* construct.

4 If the color matched is "red," then the block after case "red" is executed, and control goes to line 6. If not "red," then the next case, "blue," is tested, etc.

5 If none of the cases matches what is in the *switch* expression, the *else* block is executed.

7.3 What You Should Know

1. What are control structures?
2. What are blocks?
3. Are curly braces optional after the *if* or *else* constructs?
4. What is the purpose of the *else* block?
5. What construct allows for multiple choices?
6. How does a *while* loop differ from a *do/while*? From an *until*?
7. How do you break out of a loop before you reach the end of the enclosing block?
8. What is a *redo* statement? How does it differ from the *next* statement?
9. Why would you use *next* rather than *redo* to control a loop?
10. What is an infinite loop?
11. How does a *foreach* loop work?
12. Does Perl support a *switch* statement? What is *Switch.pm*?
13. What is a *continue* block used for?

7.4 What's Next?

In the next chapter, you will learn about pattern matching with regular expressions, one of the best and most important features of the language. You will learn about expression modifiers and how to find patterns in text strings. If you are familiar with the UNIX *grep* or the vi editor, you will see how Perl enhances and simplifies the power of pattern matching with its matching and substitution operators and large selection of regular expression metacharacters.

EXERCISE 7
What Are Your Conditions?

1. Physicists tell us that the lowest possible temperature is absolute zero. Absolute zero is –459.69 degrees Fahrenheit.
   a. Accept inputs from the user: a beginning temperature, an ending temperature, and an increment value (all Fahrenheit).
   b. Check for bad input: a temperature less than absolute zero and an ending temperature less than a beginning temperature. The program will send a message to *STDERR* if either condition is detected.
   c. Print a header showing: "*Fahrenheit   Celcius*". Print all the values from the beginning to the ending temperatures. Use a looping mechanism. The conversion formula is: C = (F – 32) / 1.8

2. Ask the user for a list of grades, separated by whitespace. The grades will be stored in a string called *$input*.
   a. Split the string *$input* and create an array.
   b. Use the *foreach* loop to get the total sum of all the grades.
   c. Print the average.

3. Write a script that will print 10 random number cards from a deck.
   a. The script will build a deck of 52 cards by using nested *foreach* loops.
   b. The outer loop will iterate through a list consisting of cards for each suit: *clubs, diamonds, hearts, spades.* The inner loop will iterate through a list for each type of card within the suit: *ace, 1 through 10, jack, queen,* and *king.* A card of each suit will be assigned to an array
   c. The *rand()* function will be used to get a random card from the pack. There should be no duplicates in the 10 cards selected from the deck.

chapter

8

Regular Expressions—Pattern Matching

8.1 What Is a Regular Expression?

If you are familiar with UNIX utilities, such as *vi, sed, grep*, and *awk*, you have met face-to-face with the infamous regular expressions and metacharacters used in delimiting search patterns. Well, with Perl, they're back!

What is a regular expression, anyway? A **regular expression** is really just a sequence, or pattern, of characters that is matched against a string of text when performing searches and replacements. A simple regular expression consists of a character or set of characters that matches itself. The regular expression is normally delimited by forward slashes.[1] The special scalar $_ is the default search space where Perl does its pattern matching. $_ is like a shadow. Sometimes you see it; sometimes you don't. Don't worry; all this will become clear as you read through this chapter.

EXAMPLE 8.1

```
1   /abc/
2   ?abc?
```

EXPLANATION

1 The pattern *abc* is enclosed in forward slashes. If searching for this pattern, for example, in a string or text file, any string that contained the pattern *abc* would be matched.
2 The pattern *abc* is enclosed in question marks. If searching for this pattern, only the first occurrence of the string is matched. (See the *reset* function in Appendix A.)

1. Actually, any character can be used as a delimiter. See Table 8.1 on page 210 and Example 8.12 on page 211.

8.2 Expression Modifiers and Simple Statements

A **simple statement** is an expression terminated with a semicolon. Perl supports a set of modifiers that allow you to further evaluate an expression based on some condition. A simple statement may contain an expression **ending** with a single modifier. The modifier and its expression are always terminated with a semicolon. When evaluating regular expressions, the modifiers may be simpler to use than the full-blown conditional constructs (discussed in Chapter 7, "If Only, Unconditionally, Forever").

The modifiers are

if
unless
while
until
foreach

8.2.1 Conditional Modifiers

The *if* Modifier. The *if* modifier is used to control a simple statement consisting of two expressions. If *Expression1* is true, *Expression2* is executed.

FORMAT

```
Expression2 if Expression1;
```

EXAMPLE 8.2

```
(In Script)
1   $x = 5;
2   print $x  if $x == 5;

(Output)
5
```

EXPLANATION

1 $x is assigned 5. The value of $x is printed only if $x is equal to 5.
2 The *if* modifier must be placed at the end of a statement and, in this example, controls the *print* function. If the expression $x == 5 is true, then the value of $x is printed.
It could be written *if ($x == 5) {print $x;}*.

EXAMPLE 8.3

```
(In Script)
1   $_ = "xabcy\n";
2   print if /abc/;     # Could be written: print $_ if $_ =~ /abc/;

(Output)
xabcy
```

EXPLANATION

1. The $_ scalar variable is assigned the string *xabcy.*
2. When the *if* modifier is followed directly by a regular expression, Perl assumes that the line being matched is $_, the default placeholder for pattern matching. The value of $_, *xabcy,* is printed if the regular expression *abc* is matched anywhere in the string.[a] The expression could have been written as *if $_ =~ /abc/.* (The =~ match operator will be discussed at the end of this chapter.)

a. $_ is the default output for the *print* function.

EXAMPLE 8.4

```
(In Script)
1   $_ = "I lost my gloves in the clover.";
2   print "Found love in gloves!\n" if /love/;
                         # Long form: if $_ =~ /love

(Output)
Found love in gloves!
```

EXPLANATION

1. The $_ is assigned the string *I lost my gloves in the clover.*
2. The regular expression *love* is matched in the $_ variable, and the string *Found love in gloves!* is printed; otherwise, nothing will be printed. The regular expression *love* is found in both *gloves* and *clover.* The search starts at the left-hand side of the string, so that matching *love* in *gloves* will produce the true condition before *clover* is reached. If $_ (or, for that matter, any other scalar) is used explicitly after the *if* modifier, then the =~ pattern matching operator is necessary when evaluating the regular expression.

8.2.2 The *DATA* Filehandle

In the following examples, the special filehandle called *DATA* is used as an expression in a *while* loop. This allows us to directly get the data from the same script that is testing it, rather than reading input from a separate text file. (You will learn all about filehandles in Chapter 10, "Getting a Handle on Files.") The data itself is located after the _ _DATA_ _[2] special literal at the bottom of each of the example scripts. The _ _DATA_ _ literal marks the logical end of the script and opens the *DATA* filehandle for reading. Each time a line of input is read from <*DATA*>, it is assigned by default to the special $_ scalar. Although $_ is implied, you could also use it explicitly, or even some other scalar. The format used is shown in the following examples.

FORMAT

```
while(<DATA>){
    Do something with the data here
}
__DATA__
    The actual data is stored here
```

Or you could use the $_ explicitly as follows:

```
while($_=<DATA>){
    Do something with the data here
}
__DATA__
    The actual data is stored here
```

Or use another variable instead of $_ as follows:

```
while($inputline=<DATA>){
    Do something with the data here
}
__DATA__
    The actual data is stored here
```

EXAMPLE 8.5

```
(The Script)
   while(<DATA>){
       print if /Norma/;      # Print the line if it matches Norma
   }
   __DATA__
   Steve Blenheim
   Betty Boop
   Igor Chevsky
   Norma Cord
   Jon DeLoach
   Karen Evich
```

2. Instead of _ _DATA_ _, you can use _ _END_ _, but _ _END_ _ opens the *DATA* filehandle in the *main* package and _ _DATA_ _ in any package.

EXAMPLE 8.5 (CONTINUED)

```
(Output)
Norma Cord
```

EXPLANATION

1 The special *DATA* filehandle gets its input from the text after the __DATA__ token. When the *while* loop is entered, a line of input is stored in the $_ scalar variable. The first line stored in $_ is *Steve Blenheim*. The next time around the loop, *Betty Boop* is stored in $_, and this continues until all of the lines following the __DATA__ token are read and processed.

2 Only the lines containing the regular expression *Norma* are printed. $_ is the default for pattern matching; it could also have been written as *print $_ if $_ =~ /Norma/;*.

3 The *DATA* filehandle gets its data from the lines that follow the __DATA__ token.

EXAMPLE 8.6

```
(The Script)
1   while(<DATA>){
2       if /Norma/ print;     # Wrong!
    }

3   __DATA__
    Steve Blenheim
    Betty Boop
    Igor Chevsky
    Norma Cord
    Jon DeLoach
    Karen Evich

(Output)
Execution of script aborted due to compilation errors.
```

EXPLANATION

1 The special *DATA* filehandle gets its input from the text after the __DATA__ token. The *while* loop iterates through each line of text. Each line of input is assigned to $_, the default scalar used to hold a line of input and to test pattern matches.

2 The modifier must be at the end of the expression, or a syntax error results. This statement should be *print if /Norma/* or *if(/Norma/) {print;}*. (Similar to the *grep* command for UNIX.)

The *unless* Modifier. The *unless* modifier is used to control a simple statement consisting of two expressions. If *Expression1* is false, *Expression2* is executed. Like the *if* modifier, *unless* is placed at the end of the statement.

FORMAT

```
Expression2 unless Expression1;
```

EXAMPLE 8.7

```
(The Script)
$x=5;
print $x unless $x == 6;

(Output)
5
```

EXPLANATION

The *unless* modifier controls the *print* statement. If the expression *$x* == 6 is false, then the value of *$x* is printed.

EXAMPLE 8.8

```
(The Script)
1   while(<DATA>){
2       print unless /Norma/;  # Print line if it doesn't match Norma
    }

3   __DATA__
    Steve Blenheim
    Betty Boop
    Igor Chevsky
    Norma Cord
    Jon DeLoach
    Karen Evich

(Output)
Steve Blenheim
Betty Boop
Igor Chevsky
Jon DeLoach
Karen Evich
```

EXPLANATION

1. The special *DATA* filehandle gets its input from the text after the *_ _DATA_ _* token. The *while* loop is entered and the first line below the *_ _DATA_ _* token is read in and assigned to $_, and so on.
2. All lines that don't contain the pattern *Norma* are matched and printed. (Similar to the *grep -v* command for UNIX.)
3. The *DATA* filehandle gets its data from the lines that follow the *_ _DATA_ _* token.

8.2.3 Looping Modifiers

The *while* Modifier. The *while* modifier repeatedly executes the second expression as long as the first expression is true.

FORMAT

```
Expression2 while Expression1;
```

EXAMPLE 8.9

```
(The Script)
$x=1;
print $x++,"\n" while $x != 5;

(Output)
1
2
3
4
```

EXPLANATION

Perl prints the value of *$x* while *$x* is not *5*.

The *until* Modifier. The *until* modifier repeatedly executes the second expression as long as the first expression is false.

FORMAT

```
Expression2 until Expression1;
```

EXAMPLE 8.10

```
(The Script)
1   $x=1;
2   print $x++,"\n" until $x == 5;

(Output)
1
2
3
4
```

EXPLANATION

1. *$x* is assigned an initial value of *1*.
2. Perl prints the value of *$x* until *$x* is equal to *5*. The variable *$x* is set to 1 and then incremented. Be careful that you don't get yourself into an infinite loop.

The *foreach* Modifier. The *foreach* modifier evaluates once for each element in its list, with $_ aliased to each element of the list, in turn.

EXAMPLE 8.11

```
(The Script)
1   @alpha=(a .. z, "\n");
2   print foreach @alpha;

(Output)
abcdefghijklmnopqrstuvwxyz
```

EXPLANATION

1 A list of lowercase letters is assigned to array *@alpha*.
2 Each item in the list is aliased to $_ and printed, one at a time, until there are no more items in the list.

8.3 Regular Expression Operators

The regular expression operators are used for matching patterns in searches and for replacements in substitution operations. The *m* operator is used for matching patterns, and the *s* operator is used when substituting one pattern for another.

8.3.1 The *m* Operator and Matching

The *m* operator is used for matching patterns. The *m* operator is optional if the delimiters enclosing the regular expression are forward slashes (the forward slash is the default) but required if you change the delimiter. You may want to change the delimiter if the regular expression itself contains forward slashes (e.g., when searching for birthdays, such as *3/15/93*, or pathnames, such as */usr/var/adm*).

FORMAT

```
/Regular Expression/        default delimiter
m#Regular Expression#       optional delimiters
m{regular expression}       pair of delimiters
```

Table 8.1 Matching Modifiers

Modifier	***Meaning***
i	Turn off case sensitivity.
m	Treat a string as multiple lines.

Table 8.1 Matching Modifiers (continued)

Modifier	**Meaning**
o	Compile pattern only once. Used to optimize the search.
s	Treat string as a single line when a newline is embedded.
x	Permit comments in a regular expression and ignore whitespace.
g	Match globally; i.e., find all occurrences. Return a list if used with an array context, or true or false if a scalar context.

EXAMPLE 8.12

```
1   m/Good morning/
2   /Good evening/
3   /\/usr\/var\/adm/
4   m#/usr/var/adm#
5   m(Good evening)
6   m'$name'
```

EXPLANATION

1 The *m* operator is not needed in this example, since forward slashes delimit the regular expression.

2 The forward slash is the delimiter; therefore, the *m* operator is optional.

3 Each of the forward slashes in the search path is quoted with a backslash so it will not be confused with the forward slash used for the pattern delimiter—a messy approach.

4 The *m* operator is required because the pound sign (#) is used as an alternative to the forward slash. The pound sign delimiter clarifies and simplifies the previous example.

5 If the opening delimiter is a parenthesis, square bracket, angle bracket, or brace, then the closing delimiter must be the corresponding closing character, such as *m(expression)*, *m[expression]*, *m<expression>*, or *m{expression}*.

6 If the delimiter is a single quote, then variable interpolation is turned off; in other words, *$name* is treated as a literal.

EXAMPLE 8.13

```
(The Script)
    while(<DATA>){
        print if /Betty/;      # Print the line if it matches Betty
    }
```

EXAMPLE 8.13 (CONTINUED)

```
3   __DATA__
    Steve Blenheim
    Betty Boop
    Igor Chevsky
    Norma Cord
    Jon DeLoach
    Karen Evich

(Output)
Betty Boop
```

EXPLANATION

1. The special *DATA* filehandle gets its input from the text after the __DATA__ token. The *while* loop is entered and the first line after the __DATA__ token is read in and assigned to $_.
2. All lines that match the pattern *Betty* are matched and printed.
3. The *DATA* filehandle gets its data from the lines that follow the __DATA__ token.

EXAMPLE 8.14

```
(The Script)
1   while(<DATA>){
2       print unless /Evich/;    # Print line unless it matches Evich
    }
3   __DATA__
    Steve Blenheim
    Betty Boop
    Igor Chevsky
    Norma Cord
    Jon DeLoach
    Karen Evich

(Output)
Steve Blenheim
Betty Boop
Igor Chevsky
Norma Cord
Jon DeLoach
```

EXPLANATION

1. The special *DATA* filehandle gets its input from the text after the __DATA__ token. The *while* loop is entered and the first line from under the __DATA__ token is read in and assigned to $_.
2. All lines that don't match the pattern *Evich* are printed.
3. The *DATA* filehandle gets its data from the lines that follow the __DATA__ token.

EXAMPLE 8.15

```
(The Script)
1   while(<DATA>){
2       print if m#Jon#       # Print the line if it matches Jon
    }
3   __DATA__
    Steve Blenheim
    Betty Boop
    Igor Chevsky
    Norma Cord
    Jon DeLoach
    Karen Evich

(Output)
Jon DeLoach
```

EXPLANATION

1. The special *DATA* filehandle gets its input from the text after the *__DATA__* token. The *while* loop is entered and the first line following the *__DATA__* token is read in and assigned to $_.
2. The *m* (match) operator is necessary because the delimiter has been changed from the default forward slash to a pound sign (#). The line is printed if it matches *Jon*.
3. The *DATA* filehandle gets its data from the lines that follow the *__DATA__* token.

EXAMPLE 8.16

```
(The Script)
1   while(<DATA>){
2       print if m(Karen E);    # Print the line if it matches Karen E
    }
3   $name="Jon";
4   $_=qq/$name is a good sport.\n/;
5   print if m'$name';
6   print if m"$name";

7   __DATA__
    Steve Blenheim
    Betty Boop
    Igor Chevsky
    Norma Cord
    Jon DeLoach
    Karen Evich

(Output)
2   Karen Evich
5   <No output>
6   Jon is a good sport.
```

EXPLANATION

1. The special *DATA* filehandle gets its input from the text after the _ _*DATA*_ _ token. The *while* loop is entered and the first line below the _ _*DATA*_ _ token is read in and assigned to $_.
2. The *m* (match) operator is necessary because the delimiter has been changed from the default forward slash to a set of opening and closing parentheses. Other pairs that could be used are square brackets, curly braces, angle brackets, and single quotes. If single quotes are used, and the regular expression contains variables, the variables will not be interpolated. The line is printed if it matches *Karen E.*
3. The scalar *$name* is assigned *Jon*.
4. $_ is assigned a string including the scalar *$name.*
5. When the matching delimiter is a set of single quotes, variables in the regular expression are not interpolated. The literal value *$name* is not found in $_; therefore, nothing is printed.
6. If double quotes enclose the expression, the variable *$name* will be interpolated. The string assigned to $_ is printed if it contains *Jon*.
7. The *DATA* filehandle gets its data from the lines that follow the _ _*DATA*_ _ token.

The *g* Modifier—Global Match. The g modifier is used to cause a global match; in other words, all occurrences of a pattern in the line are matched. Without the g, only the first occurrence of a pattern is matched. The *m* operator will return a list of the patterns matched.

FORMAT

```
m/search pattern/g
```

EXAMPLE 8.17

```
(The Script)
    #!/usr/bin/perl
1   $_ = "I lost my gloves in the clover, Love.";
2   @list=/love/g;
3   print "@list.\n";

(Output)
3   love love.
```

EXPLANATION

1. The $_ scalar variable is assigned a string of text.
2. If the search is done with the g modifier, in an array context, each match is stored in the *@list* array. The regular expression *love* was found in the string twice, once in *gloves* and once in *clover. Love* is not matched, since the *L* is uppercase.
3. The list of matched items is printed.

The *i* Modifier—Case Insensitivity. Perl is sensitive to whether characters are upper- or lowercase when performing matches. If you want to turn off case sensitivity, an *i* (insensitive) is appended to the last delimiter of the match operator.

FORMAT

```
m/search pattern/i
```

EXAMPLE 8.18

```
1   $_ = "I lost my gloves in the clover, Love.";
2   @list=/love/gi;
3   print "@list.\n";

(Output)
3   love love Love.
```

EXPLANATION

1. The $_ scalar variable is assigned the string.
2. This time the *i* modifier is used to turn off the case sensitivity. Both *love* and *Love* will be matched and assigned to the array *@list*.
3. The pattern was found three times. The list is printed.

Special Scalars for Saving Patterns. The *$&* special scalar is assigned the string that was matched in the last successful search. *&`* saves what was found preceding the pattern that was matched, and *&'* saves what was found after the pattern that was matched.

EXAMPLE 8.19

```
1   $_="San Francisco to Hong Kong\n";

2   /Francisco/;         # Save 'Francisco' in $& if it is found
3   print $&,"\n";

4   /to/;
5   print $`,"\n";       # Save what comes before the string 'to'

6   /to\s/;              # \s represents a space
7   print $', "\n";      # Save what comes after the string 'to'

(Output)
3   Francisco
5   San Francisco
7   Hong Kong
```

EXPLANATION

1 The $_ scalar is assigned a string.
2 The search pattern contains the regular expression *Francisco*. Perl searches for this pattern in the $_ variable. If found, the pattern *Francisco* will be saved in another special scalar, $&.
3 The search pattern *Francisco* was successfully matched, saved in $&, and printed.
4 The search pattern contains the regular expression *to*. Perl searches for this pattern in the $_ variable. If the pattern *to* is matched, the string to the **left** of this pattern, *San Francisco*, is saved in the $` scalar (note the backquote).
5 The value of $` is printed.
6 The search pattern contains the regular expression *to\s* (*to* followed by a space; \s represents a space). Perl searches for this pattern in the $_ variable. If the pattern *to\s* is matched, the string to the **right** of this pattern, *Hong Kong*, is saved in the $' scalar (note the straight quote).
7 The value of &' is printed.

The *x* Modifier—The Expressive Modifier. The *x* modifier allows you to place comments within the regular expression and add whitespace characters (spaces, tabs, newlines) for clarity without having those characters interpreted as part of the regular expression; in other words, you can *express* your intentions within the regular expression.

EXAMPLE 8.20

```
1  $_="San Francisco to Hong Kong\n";
2  /Francisco  # Searching for Francisco
   /x;
3  print "Comments and spaces were removed and \$& is $&\n";

(Output)
3  Comments and spaces were removed and $& is Francisco
```

EXPLANATION

1 The $_ scalar is assigned a string.
2 The search pattern consists of *Francisco* followed by a space, comment, and another space. The *x* modifier allows the additional whitespace and comments to be inserted in the pattern space without being interpreted as part of the search pattern.
3 The printed text illustrates that the search was unaffected by the extra spaces and comments. $& holds the value of what was matched as a result of the search.

8.3.2 The *s* Operator and Substitution

The *s* operator is used for substitutions. The substitution operator replaces the first regular expression pattern with the second. The delimiter can also be changed. The *g* modifier placed after the last delimiter stands for **global change** on a line. The return value from the s operator is the number of substitutions that were made. Without it, only the first occurrence of the pattern is affected by the substitution.

The special built-in variable $& gets the value of whatever was found in the search string.

FORMAT

```
s/old/new/;
s/old/new/i;
s/old/new/g;
s+old+new+g;
s(old)/new/;    s[old]{new};
s/old/expression to be evaluated/e;
s/old/new/ige;
s/old/new/x;
```

EXAMPLE 8.21

```
s/Igor/Boris/;
s/Igor/Boris/g;
s/norma/Jane/i;
s!Jon!Susan!;
s{Jon} <Susan>;
s/$sal/$sal * 1.1/e
s/dec/"Dec" . "ember"       # Replace "dec" or "Dec" with "December"
 /eigx;
```

Table 8.2 Substitution Modifiers

Modifier	Meaning
e	Evaluate the replacement side as an expression.
i	Turn off case sensitivity.
m	Treat a string as multiple lines.[a]
o	Compile pattern only once. Used to optimize the search.
s	Treat string as single line when newline is embedded.
x	Allow whitespace and comments within the regular expression.
g	Replace globally; i.e., find all occurrences.

a. The *m*, *s*, and *x* options are defined only for Perl 5.

EXAMPLE 8.22

```
(The Script)
1   while(<DATA>){
2      s/Norma/Jane/;      # Substitute Norma with Jane
3      print;
    }
4   _ _DATA_ _
    Steve Blenheim
    Betty Boop
    Igor Chevsky
    Norma Cord
    Jon DeLoach
    Karen Evich

(Output)
Steve Blenheim
Betty Boop
Igor Chevsky
Jane Cord
Jon DeLoach
Karen Evich
```

EXPLANATION

1. The special *DATA* filehandle gets its input from the text after the *_ _DATA_ _* token. The *while* loop is entered and the first line after the *_ _DATA_ _* token is read in and assigned to $_.
2. In lines where $_ contains the regular expression *Norma*, the substitution operator, s, will replace *Norma* with *Jane* for the first occurrence of *Norma* on each line. (Similar to vi and *sed* commands for UNIX.)
3. Each line will be printed, whether or not the substitution occurred.
4. The *DATA* filehandle gets its data from the lines that follow the *_ _DATA_ _* token.

EXAMPLE 8.23

```
(The Script)
1   while($_= <DATA>){
2      print if s/Igor/Ivan/;      # Substitute Igor with Ivan
    }
3   _ _DATA_ _
    Steve Blenheim
    Betty Boop
    Igor Chevsky
    Norma Cord
    Jon DeLoach
    Karen Evich
```

EXAMPLE 8.23 (CONTINUED)

```
(Output)
Ivan Chevsky
```

EXPLANATION

1. The special *DATA* filehandle gets its input from the text after the *__DATA__* token. The *while* loop is entered and the first line following the *__DATA__* token is read in and assigned to $_.
2. In lines where $_ contains the regular expression *Igor*, the substitution operator, *s*, will replace *Igor* with *Ivan* for the first occurrence of *Igor* on each line. Only if the substitution is successful will the line be printed.
3. The *DATA* filehandle gets its data from the lines that follow the *__DATA__* token.

Changing the Substitution Delimiters. Normally, the forward slash delimiter encloses both the search pattern and the replacement string. Any nonalphanumeric character following the s operator can be used in place of the slash. For example, if a # follows the s operator, it must be used as the delimiter for the replacement pattern. If pairs of parentheses, curly braces, square brackets, or angle brackets are used to delimit the search pattern, any other type of delimiter may be used for the replacement pattern, such as *s(John) /Joe/;*

EXAMPLE 8.24

```
(The Script)
while(<DATA>){
    s#Igor#Boris#;          # Substitute Igor with Boris
    print;
}
__DATA__
Steve Blenheim
Betty Boop
Igor Chevsky
Norma Cord
Jon DeLoach
Karen Evich

(Output)
Steve Blenheim
Betty Boop
Boris Chevsky
Norma Cord
Jon DeLoach
Karen Evich
```

EXPLANATION

1 The special *DATA* filehandle gets its input from the text after the *_ _DATA_ _* token. The *while* loop is entered and the first line after the *_ _DATA_ _* token is read in and assigned to $_.

2 The delimiter following the s operator has been changed to a pound sign (#). This is fine as long as all three delimiters are pound signs. The regular expression *Igor* is replaced with *Boris*.

3 The *DATA* filehandle gets its data from the lines that follow the *_ _DATA_ _* token.

EXAMPLE 8.25

```
(The Script)
1   while(<DATA>){
2       s(Blenheim){Dobbins};      # Substitute Blenheim with Dobbins
3       print;
    }
4   __DATA__
    Steve Blenheim
    Betty Boop
    Igor Chevsky
    Norma Cord
    Jon DeLoach
    Karen Evich

(Output)
Steve Dobbins
Betty Boop
Igor Chevsky
Norma Cord
Jon DeLoach
Karen Evich
```

EXPLANATION

1 The special *DATA* filehandle gets its input from the text after the *_ _DATA_ _* token. The *while* loop is entered and the first line following the *_ _DATA_ _* token is read in and assigned to $_.

2 The search pattern *Blenheim* is delimited with parentheses and the replacement pattern, *Dobbins*, is delimited with forward slashes.

3 The substitution is shown in the output when it is printed. *Blenheim* is replaced with *Dobbins*.

4 The *DATA* filehandle gets its data from the lines that follow the *_ _DATA_ _* token.

The *g* Modifier—Global Substitution. The g modifier is used to cause a global substitution; that is, all occurrences of a pattern are replaced on the line. Without the g, only the first occurrence of a pattern on each line is changed.

FORMAT

```
s/search pattern/replacement string/g;
```

EXAMPLE 8.26

```
(The Script)
# Without the g option
    (The Script)
1   while(<DATA>){
2       print if s/Tom/Christian/;  # First occurrence of Tom on each
                                    # line is replaced with Christian
    }
3   __DATA__
    Tom Dave Dan Tom
    Betty Tom Henry Tom
    Igor Norma Tom Tom

(Output)
Christian Dave Dan Tom
Betty Christian Henry Tom
Igor Norma Christian Tom
```

EXPLANATION

1. The special *DATA* filehandle gets its input from the text after the *__DATA__* token. The *while* loop is entered and the first line following the *__DATA__* token is read in and assigned to $_.
2. The **first** occurrence of *Tom* will be replaced with *Christian* for each line that is read.
3. The *DATA* filehandle gets its data from the lines that follow the *__DATA__* token.

EXAMPLE 8.27

```
(The Script)
# With the g option
1   while(<DATA>){
2       print if s/Tom/Christian/g; # All occurrences of Tom on each
                                    # line are replaced with Christian
    }
3   __DATA__
    Tom Dave Dan Tom
    Betty Tom Henry Tom
    Igor Norma Tom Tom

(Output)
Christian Dave Dan Christian
Betty Christian Dick Christian
Igor Norma Christian Christian
```

EXPLANATION

1 The special *DATA* filehandle gets its input from the text after the *__DATA__* token. The *while* loop is entered and the first line after the *__DATA__* token is read in and assigned to $_.

2 With the *g* option, the substitution is global. Every occurrence of *Tom* will be replaced with *Christian* for each line that is read.

3 The *DATA* filehandle gets its data from the lines that follow the *__DATA__* token.

The *i* Modifier—Case Insensitivity. Perl is sensitive to upper- or lowercase characters when performing matches. If you want to turn off case sensitivity, an *i* (insensitive) is appended to the last delimiter of the match or substitution operator.

FORMAT

```
s/search pattern/replacement string/i;
```

EXAMPLE 8.28

```
(The Script)
     # Matching with the i option
1    while(<DATA>){
2        print if /norma cord/i;     # Turn off case sensitivity
     }
3    __DATA__
     Steve Blenheim
     Betty Boop
     Igor Chevsky
     Norma Cord
     Jon DeLoach
     Karen Evich

(Output)
Norma Cord
```

EXPLANATION

1 The special *DATA* filehandle gets its input from the text after the *__DATA__* token. The *while* loop is entered and the first line following the *__DATA__* token is read in and assigned to $_.

2 Without the *i* option, the regular expression */norma cord/* would not be matched, because all the letters are not lowercase in the lines that are read as input. The *i* option turns off case sensitivity.

3 The *DATA* filehandle gets its data from the lines that follow the *__DATA__* token.

EXAMPLE 8.29

```
(The Script)
1   while(<DATA>){
2       print if s/igor/Daniel/i;     # Substitute igor with Daniel
    }

3   __DATA__
    Steve Blenheim
    Betty Boop
    Igor Chevsky
    Norma Cord
    Jon DeLoach
    Karen Evich

(Output)
Daniel Chevsky
```

EXPLANATION

1. The special *DATA* filehandle gets its input from the text after the *__DATA__* token. The *while* loop is entered and the first line after the *__DATA__* token is read in and assigned to $_. Each time the loop is entered, the next line following *__DATA__* is assigned to $_ until all the lines have been processed.
2. The regular expression in the substitution is also caseinsensitive, owing to the *i* option. If *igor* or *Igor* (or any combination of upper- and lowercase) is matched, it will be replaced with *Daniel*.
3. The *DATA* filehandle gets its data from the lines that follow the *__DATA__* token.

The *e* Modifier—Evaluating an Expression. On the replacement side of a substitution operation, it is possible to evaluate an expression or a function. The search side is replaced with the result of the evaluation.

FORMAT

```
s/search pattern/replacement string/e;
```

EXAMPLE 8.30

```
(The Script)
    # The e and g modifiers
1   while(<DATA>){
2       s/6/6 * 7.3/eg;          # Substitute 6 with product of 6 * 7.3

3       print;
    }
```

EXAMPLE 8.30 (CONTINUED)

```
__DATA__
Steve Blenheim    5
Betty Boop        4
Igor Chevsky      6
Norma Cord        1
Jon DeLoach       3
Karen Evich       66
```

```
(Output)
Steve Blenheim      5
Betty Boop          4
Igor Chevsky        43.8
Norma Cord          1
Jon DeLoach         3
Karen Evich         43.843.8
```

EXPLANATION

1 The special *DATA* filehandle gets its input from the text after the *__DATA__* token. The *while* loop is entered and the first line following the *__DATA__* token is read in and assigned to $_. Each time the loop is entered, the next line after *__DATA__* is assigned to $_ until all the lines have been processed.

2 If the $_ scalar contains the number 6, the replacement side of the substitution is evaluated. In other words, the *6* is multiplied by *7.3* (*e* modifier); the product of the multiplication (*43.8*) replaces the number *6* each time the number *6* is found (g modifier).

3 Each line is printed. The last line contained two occurrences of 6, causing each 6 to be replaced with *43.8*.

EXAMPLE 8.31

```
(The Script)
     # The e modifier
1    $_=5;
2    s/5/6 * 4 - 22/e;
3    print "The result is: $_\n";

4    $_=1055;
5    s/5/3*2/eg;
6    print "The result is: $_\n";

(Output)
3    The result is: 2
6    The result is: 1066
```

EXPLANATION

1 The $_ scalar is assigned 5.
2 The s operator searches for the regular expression *5* in $_. The *e* modifier evaluates the replacement string as a numeric expression and replaces it with the result of the arithmetic operation, *6* 4 – 22*, which results in 2.
3 The result of the evaluation is printed.
4 The $_ variable is assigned *1055*.
5 The s operator searches for the regular expression *5* in $_. The *e* modifier evaluates the replacement string as a numeric expression and replaces it with the product of *3*2*; i.e., every time *5* is found, it is replaced with *6*. Since the substitution is global, all occurrences of *5* are replaced with *6*.
6 The result of the evaluation is printed.

EXAMPLE 8.32

```
(The Script)
1   $_ = "knock at heaven's door.\n";
2   s/knock/"knock, " x  2  . "knocking"/ei;
3   print "He's $_;

(Output)
He's knock, knock, knocking at heaven's door.
```

EXPLANATION

1 The $_ variable is the string *knock at heaven's door.\n*;
2 The *s* operator searches for the regular expression *knock* in $_. The *e* modifier evaluates the replacement string as a string expression and replaces it with *knock x 2* (repeated twice) and concatenates (the dot operator) with the string *knocking*, ignoring case.
3 The resulting string is printed.

EXAMPLE 8.33

```
(The Script)
    # Saving in the $& special scalar
1   $_=5000;
2   s/$_/$& * 2/e;
3   print "The new value is $_\.n";

4   $_="knock at heaven's door.\n";
5   s/knock/"$&," x 2 . "$&ing"/ei;
6   print "He's $_";
```

EXAMPLE 8.33 (CONTINUED)

```
(Output)
3   The new value is 10000.
6   He's knock,knock,knocking at heaven's door.
```

EXPLANATION

1 The $_ scalar is assigned *5000*.
2 The search string, *5000*, is stored in the *$&* variable. In the replacement side the expression is evaluated; in other words, the value of *$&* is multiplied by 2. The new value is substituted for the original value. $_ is assigned the new value.
3 The resulting value is printed.
4 The $_ scalar is assigned the string *knock at heaven's door.\n*.
5 If the search string (*knock*) is found, it is stored in the *$&* variable. In the replacement side, the expression is evaluated. So, the value of *$&* (*knock*) is replicated twice and concatenated with *$&ing* (*knocking*). The new value is substituted for the original value. $_ is assigned the new value and printed.

8.3.3 Pattern Binding Operators

The **pattern binding** operators are used to bind a matched pattern, substitution, or translation (see *tr* in Appendix A) to another scalar expression. In the previous examples, pattern searches were done implicitly (or explicitly) on the $_ variable, the default pattern space. That is, each line was stored in the $_ variable when looping through a file. In the previous example, the $_ was assigned a value and used as the search string for the substitution. But what if you store a value in some variable other than $_?

Instead of

```
$_ = 5000;
```

you would write

```
$salary = 5000;
```

Then if a match or substitution is performed on *$salary* instead of

`print if /5/;` or `s/5/6;`

you would write

`print if $salary =~ /5/;` or `$salary =~ s/5/6/;`

So, if you have a string that is not stored in the $_ variable and need to perform matches or substitutions on that string, the pattern binding operators =~ or *!~* are used. They are also used with the *tr* function for string translations.

The pattern matching operators are listed in Table 8.3.

FORMAT

```
Variable =~ /Expression/
Variable !~ /Expression/
Variable =~ s/old/new/
```

Table 8.3 Pattern Matching Operators

Example	***Meaning***
$name =~ /John/	True if *$name* contains pattern. Returns 1 for *true*, null for *false*.
$name !~ /John/	True if *$name* does not contain pattern.
$name =~ s/John/Sam/	Replace first occurrence of *John* with *Sam*.
$name =~ s/John/Sam/g	Replace all occurrences of *John* with *Sam*.
$name =~ tr/a–z/A–Z/	Translate all lowercase letters to uppercase.
$name =~ /$pal/	A variable can be used in the search string.

EXAMPLE 8.34

```
(The Script)
    # Using the $_ scalar explicitly
    while($_=<DATA>){
        print $_ if  $_ =~ /Igor/;   # $_ holds the current input line
    #   print if /Igor/;
    }
    __DATA__
    Steve Blenheim
    Betty Boop
    Igor Chevsky
    Norma Cord
    Jon DeLoach
    Karen Evich

(Output)
Igor Chevsky
```

EXPLANATION

1. The special *DATA* filehandle gets its input from the text after the *__DATA__* token. The *while* loop is entered and the first line following the *__DATA__* token is read in and assigned to $_. Each time the loop is entered, the next line after *__DATA__* is assigned to $_ until all the lines have been processed.
2. If the regular expression */Igor/* is matched in the $_ variable, the *print* function will print the value of $_. The =~ is necessary here only if the $_ scalar is explicitly used as an operand.
3. If the =~ pattern matching operator is omitted, the default is to match on $_, and if the *print* function is given no arguments, the value of $_ is also printed.

EXAMPLE 8.35

```
(The Script)
    #!/usr/bin/perl
1   $name="Tommy Tuttle";
2   print "Hello Tommy\n"  if $name =~ /Tom/;
                                        # Prints Hello Tommy,if true
3   print "$name\n" if  $name !~ /Tom/;  # Prints nothing if false

4   $name =~ s/T/M/;                   # Substitute first T with an M
5   print "$name.\n";

6   $name="Tommy Tuttle";
7   print "$name\n" if $name =~ s/T/M/g;  # Substitute every T with M
8   print "What is Tommy's last name? ";
9   print "You got it!\n" if <STDIN> =~ /Tuttle/;

(Output)
2   Hello Tommy
5   Mommy Tuttle.
7   Mommy Muttle
8   What is Tommy's last name? Tuttle
9   You got it!
```

EXPLANATION

1. The scalar *$name* is assigned *Tommy Tuttle*.
2. The string *$name* is printed if *$name* contains the pattern *Tom*. The return value from a successful match is *1*.
3. The string *$name* is not printed if *$name* does **not** contain the pattern *Tom*. The return value from an unsuccessful match is null.
4. The first occurrence of the letter *T* in *$name* is replaced with the letter *M*.
5. *$name* is printed, reflecting the substitution.
6. *$name* is assigned *Tommy Tuttle*.

EXPLANATION (CONTINUED)

7 All occurrences of the letter *T* in *$name* are replaced with the letter *M*. The g at the end of the substitution expression causes a global replacement across the line.

8 User input is requested.

9 The user input (*<STDIN>*) is matched against the regular expression *Tuttle*, and if there is a match, the *print* statement is executed.

EXAMPLE 8.36

```
(The Script)
1   $salary=50000;
2   $salary =~ s/$salary/$& * 1.1/e;
3   print "\$& is $&\n";
4   print "The salary is now \$$salary.\n";

(Output)
3   $& is 50000
4   The salary is now $55000.
```

EXPLANATION

1 The scalar *$salary* is assigned *50000*.

2 The substitution is performed on *$salary*. The replacement side evaluates the expression. The special variable *$&* holds the value found on the search side. To change the value in *$salary* after the substitution, the pattern matching operator =~ is used. This binds the result of the substitution to the scalar *$salary*.

3 The *$&* scalar holds the value of what was found on the search side of the substitution.

4 The scalar *$salary* has been increased by *10%*.

EXAMPLE 8.37

```
(The Script)
    # Using split and pattern matching
1   while(<DATA>){
2       @line = split(":", $_);
3       print $line[0],"\n"  if $line[1] =~ /408-/
                                # Using the pattern matching operator
    }
4   __DATA__
    Steve Blenheim:415-444-6677:12 Main St.
    Betty Boop:303-223-1234:234 Ethan Ln.
    Igor Chevsky:408-567-4444:3456 Mary Way
    Norma Cord:555-234-5764:18880 Fiftieth St.
    Jon DeLoach:201-444-6556:54 Penny Ln.
    Karen Evich:306-333-7654:123 4th Ave.
```

EXAMPLE 8.37 (CONTINUED)

```
(Output)
Igor Chevsky
```

EXPLANATION

1. The special *DATA* filehandle gets its input from the text after the *__DATA__* token. The *while* loop is entered and the first line following the *__DATA__* token is read in and assigned to *$_*. Each time the loop is entered, the next line from *__DATA__* is assigned to *$_* until all the lines have been processed.
2. Each line from the file will be split at the colons and the value returned stored in an array, *@line*.
3. The pattern */408–/* is matched against the array element *$line[1]*. If that pattern is matched in *$line[1]*, the value of *$line[0]* is printed. Prints *Igor*'s name, *$line[0]*, because his phone, *$line[1]*, matches the *408* area code.
4. The text following *__DATA__* is used as input by the special *DATA* filehandle.

EXAMPLE 8.38

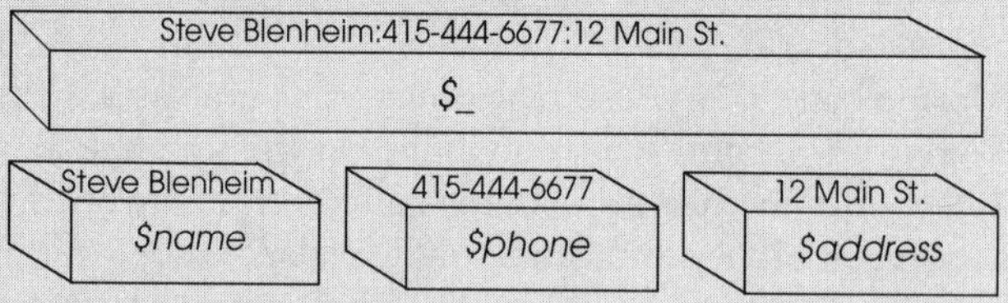


```
(The Script)
    # Using split, an anonymous list, and pattern matching
1   while(<DATA>){
2       ($name, $phone, $address) = split(":", $_);
3           print $name  if $phone =~ /408-/    # Using the pattern
                                                # matching operator
    }

4   __DATA__
    Steve Blenheim:415-444-6677:12 Main St.
    Betty Boop:303-223-1234:234 Ethan Ln.
    Igor Chevsky:408-567-4444:3456 Mary Way
    Norma Cord:555-234-5764:18880 Fiftieth St.
    Jon DeLoach:201-444-6556:54 Penny Ln.
    Karen Evich:306-333-7654:123 4th Ave.

(Output)
Igor Chevsky
```

EXPLANATION

1 The special *DATA* filehandle gets its input from the text after the _ _*DATA*_ _ token. The *while* loop is entered and the first line after the _ _*DATA*_ _ token is read in and assigned to $_. Each time the loop is entered, the next line following _ _*DATA*_ _ is assigned to $_ until all the lines have been processed.

2 Each line from the file will be split at the colons and the value returned stored in an anonymous list consisting of three scalars: *$name*, *$phone*, and *$address*. Using the anonymous list makes the program easier to read and manipulate than in the previous example where an array was used. With the array, you have to make sure you get the right index number to represent the various fields, whereas the named scalars are straightforward.

3 The pattern */408-/* is matched against the *$phone* variable. If that pattern is matched in *$phone*, the value of *$name* is printed. *Igor*'s name is printed because his phone matches the *408* area code.

4 The text following _ _*DATA*_ _ is used as input by the special *DATA* filehandle.

EXAMPLE 8.39

```
(The Script)
1   while($inputline=<DATA>){
2       ($name, $phone, $address) = split(":", $inputline);
3       print $name if $phone =~ /^408-/;  # Using the pattern
                                           # matching operator
4       print $inputline if $name =~ /^Karen/;
5       print if /^Norma/;
    }

6   _ _DATA_ _
    Steve Blenheim:415-444-6677:12 Main St.
    Betty Boop:303-223-1234:234 Ethan Ln.
    Igor Chevsky:408-567-4444:3456 Mary Way
    Norma Cord:555-234-5764:18880 Fiftieth St.
    Jon DeLoach:201-444-6556:54 Penny Ln.
    Karen Evich:306-333-7654:123 4th Ave.

(Output)
3   Igor Chevsky
4   Karen Evich:306-333-7654:123 4th Ave.
5   < No output >
```

EXPLANATION

1 The special *DATA* filehandle gets its input from the text after the *__DATA__* token. The *while* loop is entered and the first line after the *__DATA__* token is read in and assigned to a user-defined variable, *$inputline*, rather than *$_*. Each time the loop is entered, the next line from *__DATA__* is assigned to *$inputline* until all the lines have been processed.

2 Each line from the file, stored in *$inputfile*, will be split at the colons and the value returned stored in an anonymous list consisting of three scalars: *$name*, *$phone*, and *$address*.

3 The pattern */408-/* is matched against the *$phone* variable. If that pattern is matched in *$phone*, the value of *$name* is printed. Prints *Igor's* name because his phone matches the *408* area code.

4 Each line is stored in *$inputline*, one after the other, until the end of the file is reached. The value of *$inputline* is displayed if it begins with the regular expression *Karen*.

5 Since the default line holder, $_, is no longer being used, nothing is assigned to it, and nothing is matched against it or displayed. The lines are now being stored and matched in the user-defined variable *$inputline*.

6 The text following *__DATA__* is used as input by the special *DATA* filehandle.

8.4 What You Should Know

1. What is meant by a regular expression?
2. How are the *if* and *unless* modifiers used?
3. How do you change the forward slash delimiter used in the search pattern to something else?
4. What does the s operator do?
5. What is meant by a global search?
6. When do you need the pattern binding operators, =~ and !~?
7. What is the default pattern space holder?
8. What is the __DATA__ filehandle used for?
9. What do the *ieg* modifiers mean?

8.5 What's Next?

In the next chapter, you will harness the power of pattern matching by learning Perl's plethora of regular expression metacharacters. You will learn how to anchor patterns, how to search for alternating patterns, whitespace characters, sets of characters, repeating patterns, etc. You will learn about greedy metacharacters and how to control them. You will learn about capturing and grouping patterns, to look ahead and behind. By the time you have completed this chapter, you should be able to search for data by regular expressions based on a specific criterion in order to validate the data and to modify the text that was found.

EXERCISE 8
A Match Made in Heaven

```
(sample.file found on CD)
Tommy Savage:408-724-0140:1222 Oxbow Court, Sunnyvale,CA 94087:5/19/66:34200
Lesle Kerstin:408-456-1234:4 Harvard Square, Boston, MA 02133:4/22/62:52600
JonDeLoach:408-253-3122:123 Park St., San Jose, CA 94086:7/25/53:85100
Ephram Hardy:293-259-5395:235 Carlton Lane, Joliet, IL 73858:8/12/20:56700
Betty Boop:245-836-8357:635 Cutesy Lane, Hollywood, CA 91464:6/23/23:14500
William Kopf:846-836-2837:6937 Ware Road, Milton, PA 93756:9/21/46:43500
Norma Corder:397-857-2735:74 Pine Street, Dearborn, MI 23874:3/28/45:245700
James Ikeda:834-938-8376:23445 Aster Ave., Allentown, NJ 83745:12/1/38:45000
Lori Gortz:327-832-5728:3465 Mirlo Street, Peabody, MA 34756:10/2/65:35200
Barbara Kerz:385-573-8326:832 Ponce Drive, Gary, IN 83756:12/15/46:268500
```

1. Print all lines containing the pattern *Street*.
2. Print lines where the first name matches a *B* or *b*.
3. Print last names that match *Ker*.
4. Print phone numbers in the *408* area code.
5. Print Lori Gortz's name and address.
6. Print Ephram's name in capital letters.
7. Print lines that do not contain a *4*.
8. Change William's name to Siegfried.
9. Print Tommy Savage's birthday.
10. Print the names of those making over $40,000.
11. Print the names and birthdays of those people born in June.
12. Print the zip code for Massachusetts.

chapter

9

Getting Control—Regular Expression Metacharacters

9.1 Regular Expression Metacharacters

Regular expression metacharacters are characters that do not represent themselves. They are endowed with special powers to allow you to control the search pattern in some way (e.g., find the pattern only at the beginning of line or at the end of the line or only if it starts with an upper- or lowercase letter). Metacharacters lose their special meaning if preceded with a backslash (\). For example, the dot metacharacter represents any single character but when preceded with a backslash is just a dot or period.

If you see a backslash preceding a metacharacter, the backslash turns off the meaning of the metacharacter, but if you see a backslash preceding an alphanumeric character in a regular expression, then the backslash means something else. Perl provides a simpler form of some of the metachacters, called **metasymbols**, to represent characters. For example, *[0–9]* represents numbers in the range between 0 and 9, and *\d* represents the same thing. *[0–9]* uses the bracket metacharacter; *\d* is a metasymbol.

EXAMPLE 9.1

```
/^a...c/
```

EXPLANATION

This regular expression contains metacharacters. (See Table 9.1.) The first one is a caret (^). The caret metacharacter matches for a string only if it is at the beginning of the line. The period (.) is used to match for any single character, including whitespace. This expression contains three periods, representing any three characters. To find a literal period or any other character that does not represent itself, the character must be preceded by a backslash to prevent interpretation.

In Example 9.1, the regular expression reads: Search at the beginning of the line for an *a*, followed by any three single characters, followed by a *c*. It will match, for example: *abbbc, a123c, a   c,* or *aAx3c* only if those patterns were found at the beginning of the line.

Table 9.1 Metacharacters

Metacharacter	What It Matches
Character Class: Single Characters and Digits	
.	Matches any character except a newline
[a–z0–9]	Matches any single character in set
[^a–z0–9]	Matches any single character **not** in set
\d	Matches one digit
\D	Matches a nondigit, same as *[^0–9]*
\w	Matches an alphanumeric (word) character
\W	Matches a nonalphanumeric (nonword) character
Character Class: Whitespace Characters	
\s	Matches a whitespace character, such as spaces, tabs, and newlines
\S	Matches nonwhitespace character
\n	Matches a newline
\r	Matches a return
\t	Matches a tab
\f	Matches a form feed
\b	Matches a backspace
\0	Matches a null character
Character Class: Anchored Characters	
\b	Matches a word boundary (when not inside [ ])
\B	Matches a nonword boundary
^	Matches to beginning of line
$	Matches to end of line
\A	Matches the beginning of the string only
\Z	Matches the end of the string or line
\z	Matches the end of string only
\G	Matches where previous *m//g* left off

Table 9.1 Metacharacters *(continued)*

Metacharacter	***What It Matches***
Character Class: Repeated Characters	
x?	Matches 0 or 1 *x*
x*	Matches 0 or more occurrences of *x*
x+	Matches 1 or more occurrences of *x*
(xyz)+	Matches 1 or more patterns of *xyz*
x{m,n}	Matches at least *m* occurrences of *x* and no more than *n* occurrences of *x*
Character Class: Alternative Characters	
was|were|will	Matches one of *was, were,* or *will*
Character Class: Remembered Characters	
(string)	Used for backreferencing (see Examples 9.38 and 9.39)
\1 or $1	Matches first set of parentheses[a]
\2 or $2	Matches second set of parentheses
\3 or $3	Matches third set of parentheses
Character Class: Miscellaneous Characters	
\12	Matches that octal value, up to \377
\x811	Matches that hex value
\cX	Matches that control character; e.g., *\cC* is *<Ctrl>-C* and *\cV* is *<Ctrl>-V*
\e	Matches the ASCII ESC character, not backslash
\E	Marks the end of changing case with *\U*, *\L*, or *\Q*
\l	Lowercase the next character only
\L	Lowercase characters until the end of the string or until *\E*
\N	Matches that named character; e.g., *\N{greek:Beta}*
\p{PROPERTY}	Matches any character with the named property; e.g., *\p{IsAlpha}/*
\P{PROPERTY}	Matches any character without the named property

a. *\1* and *$1* are called backreferences. They differ in that the *\1* backreference is valid within a pattern, whereas the *$1* notation is valid within the enclosing block or until another successful search.

Table 9.1 Metacharacters *(continued)*

Metacharacter	What It Matches
\Q	Quote metacharacters until \E
\u	Titlecase next character only
\U	Uppercase until \E
\x{NUMBER}	Matches Unicode NUMBER given in hexadecimal
\X	Matches Unicode "combining character sequence" string
\[	Matches that metacharacter
\\	Matches a backslash

9.1.1 Metacharacters for Single Characters

If you are searching for a particular character within a regular expression, you can use the **dot** metacharacter to represent a single character or a **character class** that matches one character from a set of characters. In addition to the dot and character class, Perl has added some backslashed symbols (called **metasymbols**) to represent single characters. (See Table 9.2.)

Table 9.2 Metacharacters for Single Characters

Metacharacter	What It Matches
.	Matches any character except a newline
[a–z0–9_]	Matches any single character in set
[^a–z0–9_]	Matches any single character **not** in set
\d	Matches a single digit
\D	Matches a single nondigit; same as *[^0–9]*
\w	Matches a single alphanumeric (word) character; same as *[a–z0–9_]*
\W	Matches a single nonalphanumeric (nonword) character; same as *[^a–z0–9_]*

The Dot Metacharacter. The dot (.) metacharacter matches any single character with the exception of the newline character. For example, the regular expression */a.b/* is matched if the string contains an *a*, followed by any one single character (except the *\n*), followed by *b*, whereas the expression */.../* matches any string containing at least three characters.

EXAMPLE 9.2

```
(The Script)
    # The dot metacharacter
1   while(<DATA>){
2      print "Found Norma!\n" if /N..ma/;
    }
    __DATA__
    Steve Blenheim 101
    Betty Boop 201
    Igor Chevsky 301
    Norma Cord 401
    Jonathan DeLoach 501
    Karen Evich 601

(Output)
Found Norma!
```

EXPLANATION

1 The special *DATA* filehandle gets its input from the text after the *__DATA__* token. The *while* loop is entered and the first line following the *__DATA__* token is read in and assigned to $_. Each time the loop is entered, the next line below *__DATA__* is assigned to $_ until all the lines have been processed.

2 The string *Found Norma!\n* is printed only if the pattern found in $_ contains an uppercase *N*, followed by any two single characters, followed by an *m* and an *a*. It would find *Norma*, *No man*, *Normandy*, etc.

The *s* Modifier—The Dot Metacharacter and the Newline. Normally, the dot metacharacter does not match the newline character, *\n*, because it matches only the characters within a string up until the newline is reached. The *s* modifier treats the line with embedded newlines as a single line, rather than a group of multiple lines, and allows the dot metacharacter to treat the newline character the same as any other character it might match. The *s* modifier can be used with both the *m* (match) and the *s* (substitution) operators.

EXAMPLE 9.3

```
(The Script)
    # The s modifier and the newline
1   $_="Sing a song of sixpence\nA pocket full of rye.\n";
2   print $& if /pence./s;
3   print $& if /rye\../s;
4   print if s/sixpence.A/twopence, a/s;

(Output)
2   pence
3   rye.
4   Sing a song of twopence, a pocket full of rye.
```

EXPLANATION

1. The $_ scalar is assigned; it contains two newlines.
2. The regular expression, */pence./*, contains a dot metacharacter. The dot metacharacter does not match a newline character unless the *s* modifier is used. The *$&* special scalar holds the value the pattern found in the last successful search; i.e., *pence\n*.
3. The regular expression */rye\../* contains a literal period (the backslash makes the period literal), followed by the dot metacharacter that will match on the newline, thanks to the *s* modifier. The *$&* special scalar holds the value the pattern found in the last successful search; i.e., *rye.\n*.
4. The *s* modifier allows the dot to match on the newline character, *\n*, found in the search string. The newline will be replaced with a space.

The Character Class. A character class represents **one** character from a set of characters. For example, *[abc]* matches an *a*, *b*, **or** *c*, and *[a–z]* matches one character from a set of characters in the range from *a* to *z*, and *[0–9]* matches one character in the range of digits between *0* and *9*. If the character class contains a leading caret (^), then the class represents any one character **not** in the set; for example, *[^a–zA–Z]* matches a single character **not** in the range from *a* to *z* or *A* to *Z*, and *[^0–9]* matches a single character not in the range between *0* and *9*.[1] To represent a number between 10 and 13, use *1[0–3]*, not *[10–13]*.

Perl provides additional symbols, **metasymbols**, to represent a character class. The symbols *\d* and *\D* represent a single digit and a single non-digit, respectively; they are the same as *[0–9]* and *[^0–9]*. Similarly, *\w* and *\W* represent a single word character and a single non-word character, respectively; they are the same as *[A–Za–z_0–9]* and *[^A–Za–z_0–9]*.

EXAMPLE 9.4

```
(From a Script)
while(<DATA>){
    print if /[A-Z][a-z]eve/;
}
__DATA__
Steve Blenheim 101
Betty Boop 201
Igor Chevsky 301
Norma Cord 401
Jonathan DeLoach 501
Karen Evich 601

(Output)
Steve Blenheim 101
```

1. Don't confuse the caret inside square brackets with the caret used as a beginning of line anchor. See Table 9.7 on page 258.

EXPLANATION

1 The special *DATA* filehandle gets its input from the text after the _ _DATA_ _ token. The *while* loop is entered and the first line following the _ _DATA_ _ token is read in and assigned to $_. Each time the loop is entered, the next line after _ _DATA_ _ is assigned to $_ until all the lines have been processed.

2 The line $_ is printed only if $_contains a pattern matching one uppercase letter *[A–Z]*, followed by one lowercase letter *[a–z]*, and followed by *eve*.

EXAMPLE 9.5

```
(The Script)
    # The bracketed character class
1   while(<DATA>){
2       print if /[A-Za-z0-9_]/;
    }
    _ _DATA_ _
    Steve Blenheim 101
    Betty Boop 201
    Igor Chevsky 301
    Norma Cord 401
    Jonathan DeLoach 501
    Karen Evich 601

(Output)
Steve Blenheim 101
Betty Boop 201
Igor Chevsky 301
Norma Cord 401
Jonathan DeLoach 501
Karen Evich 601
```

EXPLANATION

1 The special *DATA* filehandle gets its input from the text after the _ _DATA_ _ token. The *while* loop is entered and the first line after the _ _DATA_ _ token is read in and assigned to $_. Each time the loop is entered, the next line from _ _DATA_ _ is assigned to $_ until all the lines have been processed.

2 The line $_ is printed only if it contains a pattern matching one alphanumeric word character, represented by the character class, *[A–Za–z0–9_]*. All lines are printed.

EXAMPLE 9.6

```
(The Script)
    # The bracket metacharacters and negation
1   while(<DATA>){
2       print if / [^123]0/
    }
    _ _DATA_ _
    Steve Blenheim 101
    Betty Boop 201
    Igor Chevsky 301
    Norma Cord 401
    Jonathan DeLoach 501
    Karen Evich 601

(Output)
Norma Cord 401
Jonathan DeLoach 501
Karen Evich 601
```

EXPLANATION

1 The special *DATA* filehandle gets its input from the text after the *_ _DATA_ _* token. The *while* loop is entered and the first line after the *_ _DATA_ _* token is read in and assigned to $_. Each time the loop is entered, the next line from *_ _DATA_ _* is assigned to $_ until all the lines have been processed.

2 The line $_ is printed only if $_ contains a pattern matching one space, followed by one number **not** in the range between *1* and *3* (not *1*, *2*, or *3*), followed by *0*.

EXAMPLE 9.7

```
(The Script)
    # The metasymbol, \d
1   while(<DATA>){
2       print if /6\d\d/
    }
    _ _DATA_ _
    Steve Blenheim 101
    Betty Boop 201
    Igor Chevsky 301
    Norma Cord 401
    Jonathan DeLoach 501
    Karen Evich 601
```

EXAMPLE 9.7 (CONTINUED)

```
(Output)
Karen Evich 601
```

EXPLANATION

1 The special *DATA* filehandle gets its input from the text after the *__DATA__* token. The *while* loop is entered and the first line after the *__DATA__* token is read in and assigned to $_. Each time the loop is entered, the next line from *__DATA__* is assigned to $_ until all the lines have been processed.

2 The line $_ is printed only if it contains a pattern matching the number 6, followed by two single digits. The metasymbol *\d* represents the character class *[0–9]*.

EXAMPLE 9.8

```
(The Script)
    # Metacharacters and metasymbols
1   while(<DATA>){
2       print if /[ABC]\D/
    }
    __DATA__
    Steve Blenheim 101
    Betty Boop 201
    Igor Chevsky 301
    Norma Cord 401
    Jonathan DeLoach 501
    Karen Evich 601

(Output)
Steve Blenheim 101
Betty Boop 201
Igor Chevsky 301
Norma Cord 401
```

EXPLANATION

1 The special *DATA* filehandle gets its input from the text after the *__DATA__* token. The *while* loop is entered and the first line after the *__DATA__* token is read in and assigned to $_. Each time the loop is entered, the next line from *__DATA__* is assigned to $_ until all the lines have been processed.

2 The line $_ is printed only if $_ contains a pattern matching an uppercase *A*, *B*, or *C [ABC]*, followed by one single **non**digit, *\D*. The metasymbol *\D* represents the character class *[^0–9]*; that is, a number **not** in the range between *0* and *9*.

EXAMPLE 9.9

```
(The Script)
    # The word metasymbols
1   while(<DATA>){
2       print if / \w\w\w\w \d/
    }
    __DATA__
    Steve Blenheim 101
    Betty Boop 201
    Igor Chevsky 301
    Norma Cord 401
    Jonathan DeLoach 501
    Karen Evich 601

(Output)
Betty Boop 201
Norma Cord 401
```

EXPLANATION

1 The special *DATA* filehandle gets its input from the text after the *__DATA__* token. The *while* loop is entered and the first line after the *__DATA__* token is read in and assigned to $_. Each time the loop is entered, the next line from *__DATA__* is assigned to $_ until all the lines have been processed.

2 The line $_ is printed only if it matches a pattern containing a space, followed by four alphanumeric word characters, *\w*, followed by a space and a digit, *\d*. The metasymbol *\w* represents the character class *[A–Za–z0–9_]*.

EXAMPLE 9.10

```
(The Script)
    # The word metasymbols
    while(<DATA>){
        print if /\W\w\w\w\w\W/
    }
    __DATA__
    Steve Blenheim 101
    Betty Boop 201
    Igor Chevsky 301
    Norma Cord 401
    Jonathan DeLoach 501
    Karen Evich 601
```

EXAMPLE 9.10 (CONTINUED)

```
(Output)
Betty Boop 201
Norma Cord 401
```

EXPLANATION

1 The special *DATA* filehandle gets its input from the text after the *__DATA__* token. The *while* loop is entered and the first line after the *__DATA__* token is read in and assigned to $_. Each time the loop is entered, the next line from *__DATA__* is assigned to $_ until all the lines have been processed.

2 The line $_ is printed only if $_ matches a pattern containing a non-alphanumeric word character, followed by four alphanumeric word characters, *\w*, followed by another nonalphanumeric word character, *\W*. The metasymbol *\W* represents the character class *[^A–Za–z0–9_]*. Both *Boop* and *Cord* are four word characters surrounded by whitespace (nonalphanumeric characters).

The POSIX Character Class. Perl 5.6 introduced the POSIX character classes. POSIX (the Portable Operating System Interface[2]) is an industry standard used to ensure that programs are portable across operating systems. In order to be portable, POSIX recognizes that different countries or locales may vary in the way characters are encoded, the symbols used to represent currency, and how times and dates are represented. To handle different types of characters, POSIX added the bracketed character class of characters shown in Table 9.3 to regular expressions.

The class *[:alnum:]* is another way of saying *A–Za–z0–9*. To use this class, it must be enclosed in another set of brackets for it to be recognized as a regular expression. For example, *A–Za–z0–9*, by itself, is not a regular expression character class, but *[A–Za–z0–9]* is. Likewise, *[:alnum:]* should be written *[[:alnum:]]*. The difference between using the first form, *[A–Za–z0–9]*, and the bracketed form, *[[:alnum:]]*, is that the first form is dependent on ASCII character encoding, whereas the second form allows characters from other languages to be represented in the class.

To negate one of the characters in the POSIX character class, the syntax is:

```
[^[:space:]] - all non-whitespace characters
```

2. POSIX is a registered trademark of the IEEE. See: *h.ttp://www.opengroup.org/austin/papers/backgrounder.html.*

Table 9.3 The Bracketed Character Class

Bracket Class	***Meaning***
[:alnum:]	Alphanumeric characters
[:alpha:]	Alphabetic characters
[:ascii]:	Any character with ordinal value between *0* and *127*
[:cntrl:]	Control characters
[:digit:]	Numeric characters, *0* to *9*, or *\d*
[:graph:]	Nonblank characters (not spaces, control characters, etc.) other than alphanumeric or punctuation characters
[:lower:]	Lowercase letters
[:print:]	Like *[:graph:]* but includes the space character
[:punct:]	Punctuation characters
[:space:]	All whitespace characters (newlines, spaces, tabs); same as *\s*
[:upper:]	Uppercase letters
[:word:]	Any alphanumeric or underline characters[a]
[:xdigit:]	Allows digits in a hexadecimal number (*0–9a–fA–F*)

a. This is a Perl extension, same as *\w*.

EXAMPLE 9.11

```
(In Script)
    # The POSIX character classes
    require 5.6.0;
    while(<DATA>){
        print if /[[:upper:]][[:alpha:]]+ [[:upper:]][[:lower:]]+/;
    }
    __DATA__
    Steve Blenheim
    Betty Boop
    Igor Chevsky
    Norma Cord
    Jon DeLoach
    Betty Boop
    Karen Evich
```

EXAMPLE 9.11 (CONTINUED)

```
(Output)
Steve Blenheim
Betty Boop
Igor Chevsky
Norma Cord
Jon DeLoach
Betty Boop
Karen Evich
```

EXPLANATION

1 Perl version 5.6.0 (and above) is needed to use the POSIX character class.

2 The special *DATA* filehandle gets its input from the text after the *__DATA__* token. The *while* loop is entered and the first line after the *__DATA__* token is read in and assigned to $_. Each time the loop is entered, the next line following *__DATA__* is assigned to $_ until all the lines have been processed.

3 The regular expression contains POSIX character classes. The line is printed if $_ contains one uppercase letter, *[[:upper:]]*, followed by one or more (+) alphabetic characters, *[[:alpha:]]*, followed by an uppercase letter and one or more lowercase letters, *[[:lower:]]*. (The + is a regular expression metacharacter representing one or more of the previous characters and is discussed in "Metacharacters to Repeat Pattern Matches" on page 250.)

9.1.2 Whitespace Metacharacters

A whitespace character represents a space, tab, return, newline, or formfeed. The whitespace character can be represented literally, by pressing a Tab key or the spacebar or the Enter key.

Table 9.4 Whitespace Metacharacters

Metacharacter	What It Matches
\s	Matches whitespace character, spaces, tabs, and newlines
\S	Matches nonwhitespace character
\n	Matches a newline, the end-of-line character (012 UNIX, 015 Mac OS)
\r	Matches a return
\t	Matches a tab
\f	Matches a form feed

EXAMPLE 9.12

```
(The Script)
    # The \s metasymbol and whitespace
1   while(<DATA>){
2       print if s/\s/*/g;     # Substitute all spaces with stars
    }
    __DATA__
    Steve Blenheim 101
    Betty Boop 201
    Igor Chevsky 301
    Norma Cord 401
    Jonathan DeLoach 501
    Karen Evich 601

(Output)
Steve*Blenheim*101*Betty*Boop*201*Igor*Chevsky*301*Norma*
*Cord*401*Jonathan*DeLoach*501*Karen*Evich*601
```

EXPLANATION

1 The special *DATA* filehandle gets its input from the text after the *__DATA__* token. The *while* loop is entered and the first line after the *__DATA__* token is read in and assigned to $_. Each time the loop is entered, the next line following *__DATA__* is assigned to $_ until all the lines have been processed.

2 The line $_ is printed if it matches a pattern containing a whitespace character (space, tab, newline) \s. All whitespace characters are replaced with a *.

EXAMPLE 9.13

```
(The Script)
    # The \S metasymbol and nonwhitespace
    while(<DATA>){
        print if s/\S/*/g;
    }
    __DATA__
    Steve Blenheim 101
    Betty Boop 201
    Igor Chevsky 301
    Norma Cord 401
    Jonathan DeLoach 501
    Karen Evich 601
```

EXAMPLE 9.13 (CONTINUED)

```
(Output)
***** ********* ***
***** **** ***
**** ******* ***
***** **** ***
******** ******* ***
***** ****** ***
```

EXPLANATION

1 The special *DATA* filehandle gets its input from the text after the _ _*DATA*_ _ token. The *while* loop is entered and the first line after the _ _*DATA*_ _ token is read in and assigned to $_. Each time the loop is entered, the next line following _ _*DATA*_ _ is assigned to $_ until all the lines have been processed.

2 The line $_ is printed if $_ matches a pattern containing a nonwhitespace character (**not** a space, tab, or newline), \S. This time, all nonwhitespace characters are replaced with a *. When a metasymbol is capitalized, it negates the meaning of the lowercase version of the metasymbol; \d is a digit; \D is a nondigit.

EXAMPLE 9.14

```
(The Script)
   # Escape sequences, \n and \t
1  while(<DATA>){
2     print if s/\n/\t/;
   }
   __DATA__
   Steve Blenheim 101
   Betty Boop 201
   Igor Chevsky 301
   Norma Cord 401
   Jonathan DeLoach 501
   Karen Evich 601

(Output)
Steve Blenheim 101    Betty Boop 201    Igor Chevsky 301
Norma Cord 401    Jon DeLoach 501    Karen Evich 601
```

EXPLANATION

1 The special *DATA* filehandle gets its input from the text after the _ _*DATA*_ _ token. The *while* loop is entered and the first line after the _ _*DATA*_ _ token is read in and assigned to $_. Each time the loop is entered, the next line following _ _*DATA*_ _ is assigned to $_ until all the lines have been processed.

2 The regular expression contains the \n escape sequence, representing a single newline character. The expression reads: Replace each newline with a tab (\t).

9.1.3 Metacharacters to Repeat Pattern Matches

In the previous examples, the metacharacter matched on a single character. What if you want to match on more than one character? For example, let's say you are looking for all lines containing names, and the first letter must be in uppercase—which can be represented as *[A–Z]*—but the following letters are lowercase, and the number of letters varies in each name. *[a–z]* matches on a single lowercase letter. How can you match on one or more lowercase letters? Or zero or more lowercase letters? To do this, you can use what are called **quantifiers**. To match on one or more lowercase letters, the regular expression can be written */[a–z]+/* where the + sign means "one or more of the previous characters," in this case, one or more lowercase letters. Perl provides a number of quantifiers, as shown in Table 9.5.

Table 9.5 The Greedy Metacharacters

Metacharacter	***What It Matches***
x?	Matches 0 or 1 occurrences of *x*
(xyz)?	Matches 0 or 1 occurrences of pattern *xyz*
x*	Matches 0 or more occurrences of *x*
(xyz)*	Matches 0 or more occurrences of pattern *xyz*
x+	Matches 1 or more occurrences of *x*
(xyz)+	Matches 1 or more occurrences of pattern *xyz*
x{m,n}	Matches at least *m* occurrences of *x* and no more than *n* occurrences of *x*

The Greed Factor. Normally, quantifiers are greedy; in other words, they match on the largest possible set of characters starting at the left-hand side of the string and searching to the right, look for the last possible character that would satisfy the condition. For example, given the following string:

```
$_="ab1234567834455544437AB"
```

and the regular expression

```
s/ab[0-9]*/X/;
```

the search side would match

```
ab12345678344555 4437
```

All of this will be replaced with an *X*. After the substitution, $_ would be

```
XAB
```

The asterisk (*) is a greedy metacharacter. It matches for zero or more of the preceding character. In other words, it attaches itself to the character preceding it. In the preceding example, the asterisk attaches itself to the character class *[0–9]*. The matching starts on the left, searching for *ab* followed by zero or more numbers in the range between *0* and *9*. The matching continues until the last number is found; in this example, the number *7*. The pattern *ab* and all of the numbers in the range between *0* and *9* are replaced with a single *X*.

Greediness can be turned off so that instead of matching on the greatest number of characters, the match is made on the least number of characters found. This is done by appending a question mark after the greedy metacharacter. See Example 9.15.

EXAMPLE 9.15

```
(The Script)
     # The zero or one quantifier
1    while(<DATA>){
2        print if / [0-9]\.?/;
     }
     __DATA__
     Steve Blenheim 1.10
     Betty Boop .5
     Igor Chevsky 555.100
     Norma Cord 4.01
     Jonathan DeLoach .501
     Karen Evich 601

(Output)
Steve Blenheim 1.10
Igor Chevsky 555.100
Norma Cord 4.01
Karen Evich 601
```

EXPLANATION

1. The special *DATA* filehandle gets its input from the text after the *__DATA__* token. The *while* loop is entered and the first line after the *__DATA__* token is read in and assigned to $_. Each time the loop is entered, the next line following *__DATA__* is assigned to $_ until all the lines have been processed.
2. The regular expression contains the ? metacharacter, representing zero or one of the preceding characters. The expression reads: Find a space, followed by a number between *0* and *9*, followed by either one literal period or no period at all.

EXAMPLE 9.16

```
(The Script)
     # The zero or more quantifier
1    while(<DATA>){
2       print if /\sB[a-z]*/;
     }
     _ _DATA_ _
     Steve Blenheim 1.10
     Betty Boop .5
     Igor Chevsky 555.100
     Norma Cord 4.01
     Jonathan DeLoach .501
     Karen Evich 601

(Output)
Steve Blenheim 1.10
Betty Boop .5
```

EXPLANATION

1 The special *DATA* filehandle gets its input from the text after the *_ _DATA_ _* token. The *while* loop is entered and the first line after the *_ _DATA_ _* token is read in and assigned to $_. Each time the loop is entered, the next line following *_ _DATA_ _* is assigned to $_ until all the lines have been processed.

2 The regular expression contains the * metacharacter, representing zero or more of the preceding character. The expression reads: Find a space, *\s*, followed by a *B* and zero or more lowercase letters *[a–z]**.

EXAMPLE 9.17

```
(The Script)
     # The dot metacharacter and the zero or more quantifier
1     while(<DATA>){
2       print if s/[A-Z].*y/Tom/;
     }
     _ _DATA_ _
     Steve Blenheim 101
     Betty Boop 201
     Igor Chevsky 301
     Norma Cord 401
     Jonathan DeLoach 501
     Karen Evich 601

(Output)
Tom Boop 201
Tom 301
```

EXPLANATION

1 The special *DATA* filehandle gets its input from the text after the _ _*DATA*_ _ token. The *while* loop is entered and the first line after the _ _*DATA*_ _ token is read in and assigned to $_. Each time the loop is entered, the next line following _ _*DATA*_ _ is assigned to $_ until all the lines have been processed.

2 The regular expression contains .*, where the * represents zero or more of the previous character. In this example, the previous character is the dot metacharacter, which represents any character at all. This expression reads: Find an uppercase letter, *[A–Z]*, followed by zero or more of any character, .*, followed by the letter *y*. If there is more than one *y* on the line, the search will include all characters up until the **last** *y*. Both *Betty* and *Igor Chevsky* are matched. Note that the space in *Igor Chevsky* is included as one of the characters matched by the dot metacharacter.

EXAMPLE 9.18

```
(The Script)
    # The one or more quantifier
1   while(<DATA>){
2       print if /5+/;
    }
    __DATA__
    Steve Blenheim 1.10
    Betty Boop .5
    Igor Chevsky 555.100
    Norma Cord 4.01
    Jonathan DeLoach .501
    Karen Evich 601

(Output)
Betty Boop .5
Igor Chevsky 555.100
Jonathan DeLoach .501
```

EXPLANATION

1 The special *DATA* filehandle gets its input from the text after the _ _*DATA*_ _ token. The *while* loop is entered and the first line after the _ _*DATA*_ _ token is read in and assigned to $_. Each time the loop is entered, the next line following _ _*DATA*_ _ is assigned to $_ until all the lines have been processed.

2 The regular expression contains the + metacharacter, representing one or more of the preceding characters. The expression reads: Find one or more repeating occurrence of the number 5.

EXAMPLE 9.19

```
(The Script)
   # The one or more quantifier
1  while(<DATA>){
2     print if s/\w+/X/g;
   }
   __DATA__
   Steve Blenheim 101
   Betty Boop 201
   Igor Chevsky 301
   Norma Cord 401
   Jonathan DeLoach 501
   Karen Evich 601

(Output)
X X X
X X X
X X X
X X X
X X X
X X X
```

EXPLANATION

1. The special *DATA* filehandle gets its input from the text after the *__DATA__* token. The *while* loop is entered and the first line after the *__DATA__* token is read in and assigned to $_. Each time the loop is entered the next line following *__DATA__* is assigned to $_ until all the lines have been processed.
2. The regular expression contains *\w* followed by a + metacharacter, representing one or more alphanumeric word characters. For example, the first set of alphanumeric word characters is *Steve,* and *Steve* is replaced by an *X*. Since the substitution is global, the next set of alphanumeric characters, *Blenheim*, is replaced by an *X*. Lastly, the alphanumeric characters, *101*, are replaced by an *X*.

EXAMPLE 9.20

```
(The Script)
   # Repeating patterns
1  while(<DATA>){
2     print if /5{1,3}/;
   }
   __DATA__
   Steve Blenheim 1.10
   Betty Boop .5
   Igor Chevsky 555.100
   Norma Cord 4.01
   Jonathan DeLoach .501
   Karen Evich 601
```

EXAMPLE 9.20 (CONTINUED)

```
(Output)
Betty Boop .5
Igor Chevsky 555.100
Jonathan DeLoach .501
```

EXPLANATION

1 The special *DATA* filehandle gets its input from the text after the __DATA__ token. The *while* loop is entered and the first line after the __DATA__ token is read in and assigned to $_. Each time the loop is entered, the next line following __DATA__ is assigned to $_ until all the lines have been processed.

2 The regular expression contains the curly brace ({}) metacharacters, representing the number of times the preceding expression will be repeated. The expression reads: Find at least one occurrence of the pattern 5 and as many as three in a row.

EXAMPLE 9.21

```
(The Script)
   # Repeating patterns
1  while(<DATA>){
2     print if /5{3}/;
   }
   __DATA__
   Steve Blenheim 1.10
   Betty Boop .5
   Igor Chevsky 555.100
   Norma Cord 4.01
   Jonathan DeLoach .501
   Karen Evich 601

(Output)
Igor Chevsky 555.100
```

EXPLANATION

1 The special *DATA* filehandle gets its input from the text after the __DATA__ token. The *while* loop is entered and the first line after the __DATA__ token is read in and assigned to $_. Each time the loop is entered, the next line following __DATA__ is assigned to $_ until all the lines have been processed.

2 The expression reads: Find three consecutive occurrences of the pattern 5. This does not mean that the string must contain exactly three, and no more, of the number 5. It just means that there must be **at least** three consecutive occurrences of the number 5. If the string contained 5555555, the match would still be successful. To find exactly three occurrences of the number 5, the pattern would have to be anchored in some way, either by using the ^ and $ anchors or by placing some other character before and after the three occurrences of the number 5; for example, */^5{3}$/* or */ 5{3}898/* or */95{3}\.56/*.

EXAMPLE 9.22

```
(The Script)
     # Repeating patterns
1    while(<DATA>){
2       print if /5{1,}/;
     }
     _ _DATA_ _
     Steve Blenheim 1.10
     Betty Boop .5
     Igor Chevsky 555.100
     Norma Cord 4.01
     Jonathan DeLoach .501
     Karen Evich 601

(Output)
Betty Boop .5
Igor Chevsky 555.100
Jonathan DeLoach .501
```

EXPLANATION

1. The special *DATA* filehandle gets its input from the text after the *_ _DATA_ _* token. The *while* loop is entered and the first line after the *_ _DATA_ _* token is read in and assigned to $_. Each time the loop is entered, the next line following *_ _DATA_ _* is assigned to $_ until all the lines have been processed.
2. The expression reads: Find at least one or more repeating occurrences of 5.

Metacharacters that Turn off Greediness. By placing a question mark after a greedy quantifier, the greed is turned off, and the search ends after the first match rather than the last one.

EXAMPLE 9.23

```
(The Script)
    # Greedy and not greedy
1   $_="abcdefghijklmnopqrstuvwxyz";
2   s/[a-z]+/XXX/;
3   print $_, "\n";

4   $_="abcdefghijklmnopqrstuvwxyz";
5   s/[a-z]+?/XXX/;
6   print $_, "\n";

(Output)
3   XXX
6   XXXbcdefghijklmnopqrstuvwxyz
```

EXPLANATION

1 The scalar $_ is assigned a string of lowercase letters.

2 The regular expression reads: Search for one or more lowercase letters, and replace them with *XXX*. The + metacharacter is greedy. It takes as many characters as match the expression; i.e., it starts on the left-hand side of the string, grabbing as many lowercase letters as it can find until the end of the string.

3 The value of $_ is printed after the substitution.

4 The scalar $_ is assigned a string of lowercase letters.

5 The regular expression reads: Search for one or more lowercase letters, and, after finding the first one, stop searching and replace it with *XXX*. The ? affixed to the + turns off the greediness of the metacharacter. The minimal number of characters is searched for.

6 The value of $_ is printed after the substitution.

Table 9.6 Turning Off Greediness

Metacharacter	*What It Matches*
x??	Matches 0 or 1 occurrences of *x*
(xyz)??	Matches 0 or 1 occurrences of pattern *xyz*
x*?	Matches 0 or more occurrences of *x*
(xyz)*?	Matches 0 or more occurrences of pattern *xyz*
x+?	Matches 1 or more occurrences of *x*
(xyz)+?	Matches 1 or more occurrences of pattern *xyz*
x{m,n}?	Matches at least *m* occurrences of *x* and no more than *n* occurrences of *x*
x{m}?	Matches at least *m* occurrences of *x*
x{m,}?	Matches at least *m* times

EXAMPLE 9.24

```
(The Script)
    # A greedy quantifier
1   $string="I got a cup of sugar and two cups of flour
            from the cupboard.";

2   $string =~ s/cup.*/tablespoon/;
3   print "$string\n";
```

EXAMPLE 9.24 (CONTINUED)

```
   # Turning off greed
4  $string="I got a cup of sugar and two cups of flour
         from the cupboard.";
5  $string =~ s/cup.*?/tablespoon/;
6  print "$string\n";

(Output)
3  I got a tablespoon
6  I got a tablespoon of sugar and two cups of flour from the
cupboard.
```

EXPLANATION

1. The scalar *$string* is assigned a string containing the pattern *cup* three times.
2. The *s* (substitution) operator searches for the pattern *cup* followed by zero or more characters; that is, *cup* and all characters to the end of the line are matched and replaced with the string *tablespoon*. The .* is called a greedy quantifier because it matches for the largest possible pattern.
3. The output shows the result of a greedy substitution.
4. The scalar *$string* is reset.
5. This time the search is not greedy. By appending a question mark to the .*, the smallest pattern that matches *cup*, followed by zero or more characters, is replaced with *tablespoon*.
6. The new string is printed.

Anchoring Metacharacters. Often, it is necessary to anchor a metacharacter so that it matches only if the pattern is found at the beginning or end of a line, word, or string. These metacharacters are based on a position just to the left or to the right of the character that is being matched. Anchors are technically called **zero-width assertions** because they correspond to positions, not actual characters in a string. For example, */^abc/* means: Find *abc* at the beginning of the line, where the ^ represents a position, not an actual character.

Table 9.7 Anchors (Assertions)

Metacharacter	*What It Matches*
^	Matches to beginning of line or beginning of string
$	Matches to end of line or end of a string
\A	Matches the beginning of the string only
\Z	Matches the end of the string or line

Table 9.7 Anchors (Assertions) (continued)

Metacharacter	*What It Matches*
\z	Matches the end of string only
\G	Matches where previous *m//g* left off
\b	Matches a word boundary (when not inside *[ ]*)
\B	Matches a nonword boundary

EXAMPLE 9.25

```
(The Script)
     # Beginning of line anchor
1    while(<DATA>){
2        print if /^[JK]/;
     }
     __DATA__
     Steve Blenheim 1.10
     Betty Boop .5
     Igor Chevsky 555.100
     Norma Cord 4.01
     Jonathan DeLoach .501
     Karen Evich 601

(Output)
Jonathan DeLoach .501
Karen Evich 601.100
```

EXPLANATION

1. The special *DATA* filehandle gets its input from the text after the *__DATA__* token. The *while* loop is entered and the first line after the *__DATA__* token is read in and assigned to $_. Each time the loop is entered, the next line following *__DATA__* is assigned to $_ until all the lines have been processed.
2. The regular expression contains the caret (^) metacharacter, representing the beginning of line anchor only when it is the first character in the pattern. The expression reads: Find a *J* or *K* at the beginning of the line. *\A* would produce the same result as the caret in this example. The expression */^[^JK]/* reads: Search for a non-*J* or non-*K* character at the beginning of the line. Remember that when the caret is within a character class, it negates the character class. It is a beginning of line anchor only when positioned **directly after** the opening delimiter.

EXAMPLE 9.26

```
(The Script)
     # End of line anchor
1    while(<DATA>){
2        print if /10$/;
     }
     __DATA__
     Steve Blenheim 1.10
     Betty Boop .5
     Igor Chevsky 555.10
     Norma Cord 4.01
     Jonathan DeLoach .501
     Karen Evich 601

(Output)
Steve Blenheim 1.10
Igor Chevsky 555.10
```

EXPLANATION

1. The special *DATA* filehandle gets its input from the text after the *__DATA__* token. The *while* loop is entered and the first line after the *__DATA__* token is read in and assigned to $_. Each time the loop is entered, the next line following *__DATA__* is assigned to $_ until all the lines have been processed.
2. The regular expression contains the $ metacharacter, representing the end of line anchor only when the $ is the last character in the pattern. The expression reads: Find a *1* and a *0* followed by a newline.

EXAMPLE 9.27

```
(The Script)
    # Word anchors or boundaries
    while(<DATA>){
        print if /\bJon/;
    }
    __DATA__
    Steve Blenheim 1.10
    Betty Boop .5
    Igor Chevsky 555.100
    Norma Cord 4.01
    Jonathan DeLoach .501
    Karen Evich 601

(Output)
Jonathan DeLoach .501
```

EXPLANATION

1 The special *DATA* filehandle gets its input from the text after the _ _DATA_ _ token. The *while* loop is entered and the first line after the _ _DATA_ _ token is read in and assigned to $_. Each time the loop is entered, the next line following _ _DATA_ _ is assigned to $_ until all the lines have been processed.

2 The regular expression contains the *\b* metacharacter, representing a word boundary. The expression reads: Find a word beginning with the pattern *Jon*.

EXAMPLE 9.28

```
(The Script)
    # Beginning and end of word anchors
1   while(<DATA>){
2       print if /\bJon\b/;
    }
    _ _DATA_ _
    Steve Blenheim 1.10
    Betty Boop .5
    Igor Chevsky 555.100
    Norma Cord 4.01
    Jonathan DeLoach .501
    Karen Evich 601

(Output)
<No output>
```

EXPLANATION

1 The special *DATA* filehandle gets its input from the text after the _ _DATA_ _ token. The *while* loop is entered and the first line after the _ _DATA_ _ token is read in and assigned to $_. Each time the loop is entered, the next line following _ _DATA_ _ is assigned to $_ until all the lines have been processed.

2 The regular expression also contains the *\b* metacharacter, representing a word boundary. The expression reads: Find a word beginning and ending with *Jon*. Nothing is found.

The *m* Modifier. The *m* modifier is used to control the behavior of the $ and ^ anchor metacharacters. A string containing newlines will be treated as multiple lines. If the regular expression is anchored with the ^ metacharacter, and that pattern is found at the beginning of any one of the multiple lines, the match is successful. Likewise, if the regular expression is anchored by the $ metacharacter (or \Z) at the end of any one of the multiple lines, and the pattern is found, it too will return a successful match. The *m* modifier has no effect with \A and \z.

EXAMPLE 9.29

```
(The Script)
    # Anchors and the m modifier
1   $_="Today is history.\nTomorrow will never be here.\n";
2   print if /^Tomorrow/;     # Embedded newline

3   $_="Today is history.\nTomorrow will never be here.\n";
4   print if /\ATomorrow/;    # Embedded newline

5   $_="Today is history.\nTomorrow will never be here.\n";
6   print if /^Tomorrow/m;

7   $_="Today is history.\nTomorrow will never be here.\n";
8   print if /\ATomorrow/m;

9   $_="Today is history.\nTomorrow will never be here.\n";
10  print if /history\.$/m;

(Output)
6   Today is history.
    Tomorrow will never be here.
10  Today is history.
    Tomorrow will never be here.
```

EXPLANATION

1 The $_ scalar is assigned a string with embedded newlines.

2 The ^ metacharacter anchors the search to the beginning of the line. Since the line does not begin with *Tomorrow*, the search fails and nothing is returned.

3 The $_ scalar is assigned a string with embedded newlines.

4 The \A assertion matches only at the beginning of a string, no matter what. Since the string does not begin with *Tomorrow*, the search fails and nothing is returned.

5 The $_ scalar is assigned a string with embedded newlines.

6 The *m* modifier treats the string as multiple lines, each line ending with a newline. In this example, the ^ anchor matches at the beginning of any of these multiple lines. The pattern */^Tomorrow/* is found in the second line.

7 The $_ scalar is assigned a string with embedded newlines.

8 The \A assertion matches only at the beginning of a string, no matter how many newlines are embedded, and the *m* modifier has no effect. Since *Tomorrow* is not found at the beginning of the string, nothing is matched.

9 The $_ scalar is assigned a string with embedded newlines.

10 The $ metacharacter anchors the search to the end of a line. With the *m* modifier, embedded newlines create multiple lines. The pattern */history\.$/* is found at the end of the first line. This will also work with the \Z assertion but not with \z.

Alternation. Alternation allows the regular expression to contain alternative patterns to be matched. For example, the regular expression */John|Karen|Steve/* will match a line containing *John* or *Karen* or *Steve*. If *Karen, John*, or *Steve* are all on different lines, all lines are matched. Each of the alternative expressions is separated by a vertical bar (pipe symbol) and the expressions can consist of any number of characters, unlike the character class that matches for only one character; e.g., */a|b|c/* is the same as *[abc]*, whereas */ab|de/* cannot be represented as *[abde]*. The pattern */ab|de/* is either *ab* or *de*, whereas the class *[abcd]* represents only **one** character in the set, *a*, *b*, *c*, or *d*.

EXAMPLE 9.30

```
(The Script)
    # Alternation: this, that, and the other thing
1   while(<DATA>){
2       print if /Steve|Betty|Jon/;
    }
    _ _DATA_ _
    Steve Blenheim
    Betty Boop
    Igor Chevsky
    Norma Cord
    Jonathan DeLoach
    Karen Evich

(Output)
2   Steve Blenheim
    Betty Boop
    Jonathan DeLoach
```

EXPLANATION

1 The special *DATA* filehandle gets its input from the text after the *_ _DATA_ _* token. The *while* loop is entered and the first line after the *_ _DATA_ _* token is read in and assigned to $_. Each time the loop is entered, the next line following *_ _DATA_ _* is assigned to $_ until all the lines have been processed.

2 The pipe symbol, |, is used in the regular expression to match on a set of alternative patterns. If any of the patterns *Steve*, *Betty*, or *Jon*, are found, the match is successful.

Grouping or Clustering. If the regular expression pattern is enclosed in parentheses, a subpattern is created. Then, for example, instead of the greedy metacharacters matching on zero, one, or more of the previous single character, they can match on the previous subpattern. Alternation can also be controlled if the patterns are enclosed in parentheses. This process of grouping characters together is also called **clustering** by the Perl wizards.

EXAMPLE 9.31

```
(The Script)
    # Clustering or grouping
1   $_=qq/The baby says, "Mama, Mama, I can say Papa!"\n/;
2   print if s/(ma|pa)+/goo/gi;

(Output)
The baby says, "goo, goo, I can say goo!"
```

EXPLANATION

1 The $_ scalar is assigned the doubly quoted string.

2 The regular expression contains a pattern enclosed in parentheses, followed by a + metacharacter. The parentheses group the characters that are to be controlled by the + metacharacter. The expression reads: Find one or more occurrences of the pattern *ma* or *pa* and replace that with *goo*.

EXAMPLE 9.32

```
(The Script)
    # Clustering or grouping
1   while(<DATA>){
2       print if /\s(12){3}$/;   # Print lines matching exactly 3
                                 # consecutive occurrences of 12 at
                                 # the end of the line
    }
    __DATA__
    Steve Blenheim   121212
    Betty Boop       123
    Igor Chevsky     123444123
    Norma Cord       51235
    Jonathan DeLoach123456
    Karen Evich      121212456

(Output)
Steve Blenheim  121212
```

EXPLANATION

1 The special *DATA* filehandle gets its input from the text after the *__DATA__* token. The *while* loop is entered and the first line after the *__DATA__* token is read in and assigned to $_. Each time the loop is entered, the next line following *__DATA__* is assigned to $_ until all the lines have been processed.

2 The pattern *12* is grouped in parentheses. It is controlled by the quantifier *{3}*; i.e., a row of exactly *3* occurrences of *12* at the end of the line ($) will be matched.

EXAMPLE 9.33

```
The Script)
     # Clustering or grouping
1    $_="Tom and Dan Savage and Ellie Main are cousins.\n";
2    print if s/Tom|Ellie Main/Archie/g;

3    $_="Tom and Dan Savage and Ellie Main are cousins.\n";
4    print if s/(Tom|Ellie) Main/Archie/g;

(Output)
2    Archie and Dan Savage and Archie are cousins.
4    Tom and Dan Savage and Archie are cousins.
```

EXPLANATION

1. The $_ scalar is assigned the string.
2. If either the pattern *Tom* or the pattern *Ellie Main* is matched in $_, both patterns will be replaced with *Archie*.
3. The $_ scalar is assigned the string.
4. By enclosing *Tom* and *Ellie* in parentheses, the alternative now becomes either *Tom Main* or *Ellie Main*. Since the pattern *Ellie Main* is the only one matched in $_, *Ellie Main* is replaced with *Archie*.

EXAMPLE 9.34

```
(The Script)
     # Clustering and anchors
1    while(<DATA>){
2        # print if /^Steve|Boop/;
3          print if /^(Steve|Boop)/;
     }
     __DATA__
     Steve Blenheim
     Betty Boop
     Igor Chevsky
     Norma Cord
     Jonathan DeLoach
     Karen Evich

(Output)
Steve Blenheim
```

EXPLANATION

1. The special *DATA* filehandle gets its input from the text after the *__DATA__* token. The *while* loop is entered and the first line after the *__DATA__* token is read in and assigned to $_. Each time the loop is entered, the next line following *__DATA__* is assigned to $_ until all the lines have been processed.
2. This line has been commented. It would print any line that begins with *Steve* and any line containing the pattern *Boop*. The beginning of line anchor, the caret, applies only to the pattern *Steve*.
3. The line will be printed if it begins with either *Steve* or *Boop*. The parentheses group the two patterns so that the beginning of line anchor, the caret, applies to both patterns *Steve* and *Boop*. It could also be written as */(^Steve|^Boop)/*.

Remembering or Capturing. If the regular expression pattern is enclosed in parentheses, a subpattern is created. The subpattern is saved in special numbered scalar variables, starting with *$1*, then *$2*, and so on. These variables can be used later in the program and will persist until another successful pattern match occurs, at which time they will be cleared. Even if the intention was to control the greedy metacharacter or the behavior of alternation as shown in the previous example, the subpatterns are saved as a side effect.[3]

EXAMPLE 9.35

```
(The Script)
    # Remembering subpatterns
1   while(<DATA>){
2       s/([Jj]on)/$1athan/;      # Substitute Jon or jon with
                                  # Jonathan or jonathan
```

```
3       print;
    }
    __DATA__
    Steve Blenheim
    Betty Boop
    Igor Chevsky
    Norma Cord
    Jon DeLoach
    Karen Evich

(Output)
Steve Blenheim
Betty Boop
Igor Chevsky
Norma Cord
Jonathan DeLoach
Karen Evich
```

3. It is possible to prevent a subpattern from being saved.

EXPLANATION

1 The special *DATA* filehandle gets its input from the text after the _ _DATA_ _ token. The *while* loop is entered and the first line after the _ _DATA_ _ token is read in and assigned to $_. Each time the loop is entered, the next line following _ _DATA_ _ is assigned to $_ until all the lines have been processed.

2 The regular expression contains the pattern *Jon* enclosed in parentheses. This pattern is captured and stored in a special scalar, *$1*, so it can be *remembered.* If a second pattern is enclosed in parentheses, it will be stored in $2, and so on. The numbers are represented on the replacement side as *$1*, $2, *$3*, and so on. The expression reads: Find *Jon* or *jon* and replace with either *Jonathan* or *jonathan*, respectively. The special numbered variables are cleared after the next successful search is performed.

EXAMPLE 9.36

```
(The Script)
    # Remembering multiple subpatterns
1   while(<DATA>){
2       print if s/(Steve) (Blenheim)/$2, $1/
```

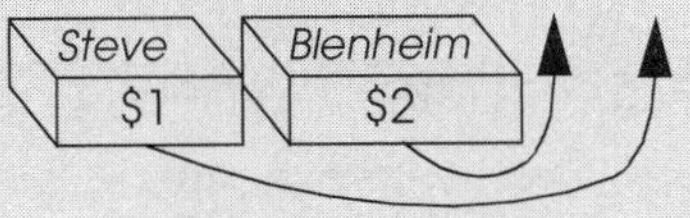


```
    }
    _ _DATA_ _
    Steve Blenheim
    Betty Boop
    Igor Chevsky
    Norma Cord
    Jonathan DeLoach
    Karen Evich

(Output)
Blenheim, Steve
```

EXPLANATION

1 The special *DATA* filehandle gets its input from the text after the _ _DATA_ _ token. The *while* loop is entered and the first line after the _ _DATA_ _ token is read in and assigned to $_. Each time the loop is entered, the next line following _ _DATA_ _ is assigned to $_ until all the lines have been processed.

2 The regular expression contains two patterns enclosed in parentheses. The first pattern is captured and saved in the special scalar *$1*, and the second pattern is captured and saved in the special scalar $2. On the replacement side, since $2 is referenced first, *Blenheim* is printed first, followed by a comma and then by *$1*, which is *Steve* (i.e., the effect is to reverse *Steve* and *Blenheim*).

EXAMPLE 9.37

```
(The Script)
     # Reversing subpatterns
1    while(<DATA>){
2        s/([A-Z][a-z]+)\s([A-Z][a-z]+)/$2, $1/;
                                        # Reverse first and last names
3        print;
     }
     __DATA__
     Steve Blenheim
     Betty Boop
     Igor Chevsky
     Norma Cord
     Jon DeLoach
     Karen Evich

(Output)
Blenheim, Steve
Boop, Betty
Chevsky ,Igor
Cord, Norma
De, JonLoach        # Whoops!
Evich, Karen
```

EXPLANATION

1. This regular expression also contains two patterns enclosed in parentheses. In this example, metacharacters are used in the pattern matching process. The first pattern reads: Find an uppercase letter followed by one or more lowercase letters. A space follows the remembered pattern. The second pattern reads: Find an uppercase letter followed by one or more lowercase letters. The patterns are saved in *$1* and $2, respectively, and then reversed on the replacement side. Note the problem that arises with the last name *DeLoach*. That is because *DeLoach* contains **both** uppercase and lowercase letters after the first uppercase letter in the name. To allow for this case, the pattern should be *s/([A-Z][a-z]+)\s([A-Z][A-Za-z]+)/$2, $1/*.

EXAMPLE 9.38

```
(The Script)
     # Metasymbols and subpatterns
1    while(<DATA>){
2        s/(\w+)\s(\w+)/$2, $1/;     # Reverse first and last names
3        print;
     }
```

EXAMPLE 9.38 (CONTINUED)

```
   __DATA__
   Steve Blenheim
   Betty Boop
   Igor Chevsky
   Norma Cord
   Jon DeLoach
   Betty Boop

(Output)
Blenheim, Steve
Boop, Betty
Chevsky, Igor
Cord, Norma
DeLoach, Jon
Boop, Betty
```

EXPLANATION

1. The special *DATA* filehandle gets its input from the text after the *_ _DATA_ _* token. The *while* loop is entered and the first line after the *_ _DATA_ _* token is read in and assigned to $_. Each time the loop is entered, the next line following *_ _DATA_ _* is assigned to $_ until all the lines have been processed.
2. The regular expression contains two subpatterns enclosed in parentheses. The *\w+* represents one or more word characters. The regular expression consists of two parenthesized subpatterns (called **backreferences**) separated by a space (*\s*). Each subpattern is saved in *$1* and *$2*, respectively. *$1* and *$2* are used in the replacement side of the substitution to reverse the first and last names.

EXAMPLE 9.39

```
(The Script)
    # Backreferencing
1   while(<DATA>){
2       ($first, $last)=/(\w+) (\w+)/;    # Could be: (\S+) (\S+)/
3       print "$last, $first\n";
    }
    __DATA__
    Steve Blenheim
    Betty Boop
    Igor Chevsky
    Norma Cord
    Jon DeLoach
    Betty Boop
```

EXAMPLE 9.39 (CONTINUED)

```
(Output)
Blenheim, Steve
Boop, Betty
Chevsky, Igor
Cord, Norma
DeLoach, Jon
Boop, Betty
```

EXPLANATION

1 The special *DATA* filehandle gets its input from the text after the *__DATA__* token. The *while* loop is entered and the first line after the *__DATA__* token is read in and assigned to $_. Each time the loop is entered, the next line following *__DATA__* is assigned to $_ until all the lines have been processed.

2 The regular expression contains two patterns enclosed in parentheses. The \w+ represents one or more word characters. The regular expression consists of two parenthesized patterns (called backreferences). The return value is an array of all the backreferences. Each word is assigned to *$first* and *$last*, respectively.

3 The values of the variables are printed for each line of the file.

EXAMPLE 9.40

```
(The Script)
    # The greedy quantifier
1   $string="ABCdefghiCxyzwerC YOU!";
2   $string=~s/.*C/HEY/;
3   print "$string", "\n";

(Output)
HEY YOU!
```

EXPLANATION

1 The scalar *$string* is assigned a string containing a number of the pattern *C*.

2 The search side of the substitution, */.*C/*, reads: Find the largest pattern that contains any number of characters ending in *C*. This search is greedy. It will search from left to right until it reaches the last *C*. The string *HEY* will replace what was found in *$string*.

3 The new string is printed showing the result of the substitution.

EXAMPLE 9.41

```
(The Script)
    # Backreferencing and greedy quantifiers
1   $string="ABCdefghiCxyzwerC YOU!";
2   $string=~s/(.*C)(.*)/HEY/; # Substitute the whole string with HEY
3   print $1, "\n";
4   print $2, "\n";
5   print "$string\n";

(Output)
3   ABCdefghiCxyzwerC
4   YOU!
5   HEY
```

EXPLANATION

1. The scalar *$string* is assigned the string.
2. The */*.C/* regular expression is enclosed in parentheses. The pattern found will be stored in the *$1* special variable. Whatever is left will be stored in $2.
3. The largest possible pattern was stored in *$1*. It is printed.
4. The remainder of the string was stored in $2. It is printed.
5. The entire string was replaced with *HEY* after the substitution.

EXAMPLE 9.42

```
(The Script)
    # Backreferencing and greed
1   $fruit="apples pears peaches plums";
2   $fruit =~ /(.*)\s(.*)\s(.*)/;
3   print "$1\n";
4   print "$2\n";
5   print "$3\n";
    print "-" x 30, "\n";
6   $fruit="apples pears peaches plums";
7   $fruit =~ /(.*?)\s(.*?)\s(.*?)\s/;    # Turn off greedy quantifier
8   print "$1\n";
9   print "$2\n";
10  print "$3\n";

(Output)
3   apples pears
4   peaches
5   plums
    ------------------------------
8   apples
9   pears
10  peaches
```

EXPLANATION

1 The scalar *$fruit* is assigned the string.
2 The string is divided into three remembered substrings, each substring enclosed within parentheses. The .* metacharacter sequence reads zero or more of any character. The * always matches for the largest possible pattern. The largest possible pattern would be the whole string. However, there are two whitespaces outside of the parentheses that must also be matched in the string. What is the largest possible pattern that can be saved in *$1* and still leave two spaces in the string? The answer is *apples pears*.
3 The value of *$1* is printed.
4 The first substring was stored in *$1*. *peaches plums* is what remains of the original string. What is the largest possible pattern (.*) that can be matched and still have one whitespace remaining? The answer is *peaches*. *peaches* will be assigned to $2. The value of $2 is printed.
5 The third substring is printed. *plums* is all that is left for $3.
6 The scalar *$fruit* is assigned the string again.
7 This time, a question mark follows the greedy quantifier (*). This means that the pattern saved will be the minimal, rather than the maximal, number of characters found. *apples* will be the minimal numbers of characters stored in *$1*, *pears* the minimal number in $2, and *peaches* the minimal number of characters in $3. The \s is required or the minimal amount of characters would be zero, since the * means zero or more of the preceding character.
8 The value of *$1* is printed.
9 The value of $2 is printed.
10 The value of $3 is printed.

Turning Off Capturing. When the only purpose is to use the parentheses for grouping, and you are not interested in saving the subpatterns in *$1*, *$2*, or *$3*, the special *?:* metacharacter can be used to suppress the capturing of the subpattern.

EXAMPLE 9.43

```
(In Script)
$_="Tom Savage and Dan Savage are brothers.\n";
print if /(?:D[a-z]*|T[a-z]*) Savage/;   # Perl will not capture
                                         # the pattern
print $1,"\n";      # $1 has no value

(Output)
Tom Savage and Dan Savage are brothers.
<Nothing is printed>
```

EXPLANATION

1. The $_ scalar is assigned a string.
2. The ?: turns off capturing when a pattern is enclosed in parentheses. In this example, alternation is used to search for any of two patterns. If the search is successful, the value of $_ is printed, but whichever pattern is found, it will not be captured and assigned to *$1*.
3. Without the ?:, the value of *$1* would be *Tom*, since it is the first pattern found. ?: says "Don't save the pattern when you find it." Nothing is saved and nothing is printed.

Metacharacters that Look Ahead and Behind. Looking ahead and looking behind in a string for a particular pattern gives you further control of a regular expression.

With a positive look ahead, Perl looks forward or ahead in the string for a pattern (*?=pattern*) and if that pattern is found, will continue pattern matching on the regular expression. A negative look ahead looks ahead to see if the pattern (*?!pattern*) is **not** there, and if it is not, finishes pattern matching.

With a positive look behind, Perl looks backward in the string for a pattern (*?<=pattern*) and if that pattern is found, will then continue pattern matching on the regular expression. A negative look behind looks behind in the string to see if a pattern (*?<!pattern*) is not there, and if it is not, finishes the matching.

Table 9.8 Look Around Assertions

Metacharacter	***What It Matches***
/PATTERN(?=pattern)/	Positive look ahead
/PATTERN(?!pattern)/	Negative look ahead
(?<=pattern)/PATTERN/	Positive look behind
(?<!pattern)/PATTERN/	Negative look behind

EXAMPLE 9.44

```
(The Script)
   # A positive look ahead
1  $string="I love chocolate cake and chocolate ice cream.";
2  $string =~ s/chocolate(?= ice)/vanilla/;
3  print "$string\n";

4  $string="Tomorrow night Tom Savage and Tommy Johnson will leave
           for vacation.";
5  $string =~ s/Tom(?=my)/Jere/g;
6  print "$string\n";
```

EXAMPLE 9.44 (CONTINUED)

```
(Output)
3   I love chocolate cake and vanilla ice cream.
6   Tomorrow night Tom Savage and Jeremy Johnson will leave for
vacation.
```

EXPLANATION

1. The scalar *$string* contains *chocolate* twice; the word *cake* follows the first occurrence of *chocolate,* and the word *ice* follows the second occurrence.
2. This is an example of a **positive look ahead**. The pattern *chocolate* is followed by *(?=ice)* meaning, if *chocolate* is found, look ahead (?=) and see if *ice* is the next pattern. If *ice* is found just ahead of *chocolate*, the match is successful and *chocolate* will be replaced with *vanilla.*
3. After the substitution on line 2, the new string is printed.
4. The scalar *$string* is assigned a string of text consisting of three words starting with *Tom.*
5. The pattern is matched if it contains *Tom*, only if *Tom* is followed by *my.* If the positive look ahead is successful, then *Tom* will be replaced with *Jere* in the string.
6. After the substitution on line 5, the new string is printed. *Tommy* has been replaced with *Jeremy.*

EXAMPLE 9.45

```
(The Script)
    # A negative look ahead
    while(<DATA>){
        print if /^\w+\s(?![BC])/;
    }
    __DATA__
    Steve Blenheim
    Betty Boop
    Igor Chevsky
    Norma Cord
    Jon DeLoach
    Karen Evich

(Output)
Jon DeLoach
Karen Evich
```

EXPLANATION

1 The special *DATA* filehandle gets its input from the text after the _ _*DATA*_ _ token. The *while* loop is entered and the first line after the _ _*DATA*_ _ token is read in and assigned to $_. Each time the loop is entered, the next line following _ _*DATA*_ _ is assigned to $_ until all the lines have been processed.

2 The regular expression means: Search at the beginning of the line for one or more word characters (\w+), followed by a space (\s), and look ahead for any character that is **not** a *B* or *C*. This is called a **negative look ahead**.

EXAMPLE 9.46

```
(The Script)
    # A positive look behind
1   $string="I love chocolate cake, chocolate milk,
             and chocolate ice cream.";
2   $string =~ s/(?<= chocolate) milk/ candy bars/;
3   print "$string\n";

4   $string="I love coffee, I love tea, I love the boys
             and the boys love me.";
5   $string =~ s/(?<=the boys) love/ don't like/;
6   print "$string\n";

(Output)
3   I love chocolate cake, chocolate candy bars, and chocolate ice
cream.
6   I love coffee, I love tea, I love the boys and the boys don't like
me.
```

EXPLANATION

1 The scalar *$string* is assigned a string with three different occurrences of *chocolate*.

2 The pattern in parentheses is called a **positive look behind**, meaning that Perl looks **backward** in the string to make sure this pattern occurs. If the pattern *milk* is found, Perl will look back in the string to see if it is preceded by *chocolate* and, if so, *milk* will be replaced with *candy bars*.

3 The string is printed after the substitution.

4 This is another example of a positive look behind. Perl looks backward in the string for the pattern *the boys*, and if the pattern is found, the regular expression *love* will be replaced with *don't like*.

EXAMPLE 9.47

```
(The Script)
    # A negative look behind
1   while(<DATA>){
2       print if /(?<!Betty) B[a-z]*/;
    }
    _ _DATA_ _
    Steve Blenheim
    Betty Boop
    Igor Chevsky
    Norma Cord
    Jon DeLoach
    Karen Evich

(Output)
Steve Blenheim
```

EXPLANATION

1 The special *DATA* filehandle gets its input from the text after the *_ _DATA_ _* token. The *while* loop is entered and the first line after the *_ _DATA_ _* token is read in and assigned to $_. Each time the loop is entered, the next line following *_ _DATA_ _* is assigned to $_ until all the lines have been processed.

2 The pattern in parentheses is called a **negative look behind**, meaning that Perl looks **backward** in the string to make sure this pattern does not occur. Any line that contains the letter *B*, followed by zero or more lowercase letters, *[a–z]**, will be printed, as long as the pattern behind it is **not** *Betty*.

9.1.4 The *tr* or *y* Function

The *tr* function[4] translates characters, in a one-on-one correspondence, from the characters in the search string to the characters in the replacement string. *tr* returns the number of characters it replaced. The *tr* function does not interpret regular expression metacharacters but allows a dash to represent a range of characters. The letter *y* can be used in place of *tr*. This strangeness comes from UNIX, where the *sed* utility has a *y* command to translate characters, similar to the UNIX *tr*. This illustrates the role UNIX has played in the development of Perl.

The *d* option deletes the search string.

The *c* option complements the search string.

The *s* option is called the squeeze option. Multiple occurrences of characters found in the search string are replaced by a single occurrence of that character (e.g., you may want to replace multiple tabs with single tabs). See Table 9.9 for a list of modifiers.

4. The Perl *tr* function is derived from the UNIX *tr* command.

FORMAT

```
tr/search/replacement/
tr/search/replacement/d
tr/search/replacement/c
tr/search/replacement/s
y/search/replacement/      (same as tr; uses same modifiers)
```

Table 9.9 *tr* Modifiers

Modifier	***Meaning***
d	Delete characters
c	Complement the search list
s	Squeeze out multiple characters to single character

EXAMPLE 9.48

```
(The Input Data)
    Steve Blenheim 101
    Betty Boop 201
    Igor Chevsky 301
    Norma Cord 401
    Jon DeLoach 501
    Karen Evich 601

(Lines from a Script)
1   tr/a-z/A-Z/;print;

(Output)
STEVE BLENHEIM  101
BETTY BOOP  201
IGOR CHEVSKY  301
NORMA CORD  401
JON DELOACH  501
KAREN EVICH  601

2   tr/0-9/:/; print;

(Output)
Steve Blenheim :::
Betty Boop :::
Igor Chevsky :::
Norma Cord :::
Jon DeLoach :::
Karen Evich :::
```

EXAMPLE 9.48 (CONTINUED)

```
3   tr/A-Z/a-c/;print;

(Output)
cteve blenheim 101
betty boop 201
cgor chevsky 301
corma cord 401
con cecoach 501
caren cvich 601

4   tr/  /#/; print;

(Output)
Steve#Blenheim#101
Betty#Boop#201
Igor#Chevsky#301
Norma#Cord#401
Jon#DeLoach#501
Karen#Evich#601

5   y/A-Z/a-z/;print;

(Output)
steve blenheim 101
betty boop 201
igor chevsky 301
norma cord 401
jon deloach 501
karen evich 601
```

EXPLANATION

1. The *tr* function makes a one-on-one correspondence between each character in the search string with each character in the replacement string. Each lowercase letter will be translated to its corresponding uppercase letter.
2. Each number will be translated to a colon.
3. The translation is messy here. Since the search side represents more characters than the replacement side, all letters from *D* to *Z* will be replaced with a *c*.
4. Each space will be replaced with pound signs (#).
5. The *y* is a synonym for *tr*. Each uppercase letter is translated to its corresponding lowercase letter.

The *tr* Delete Option. The *d* (delete) option removes all characters in the search string not found in the replacement string.

EXAMPLE 9.49

```
1   tr/ //; print;

(Output)
1 Steve Blenheim
2 Betty Boop
3 Igor Chevsky
4 Norma Cord
5 Jon DeLoach
6 Karen Evich

2   tr/ //d;print;

(Output)
1SteveBlenheim
2BettyBoop
3IgorChevsky
4NormaCord
5JonDeLoach
6KarenEvich
```

EXPLANATION

1. In this example, the translation does not take place as it would if you were using *sed* or *vi*.
2. The *d* option is required to delete each space when using the *tr* function.

The *tr* Complement Option. The *c* (complement) option complements the search string; that is, it translates each character not listed in this string to its corresponding character in the replacement string.

EXAMPLE 9.50

```
1   tr/0-9/*/; print;

(Output)
* Steve Blenheim
* Betty Boop
* Igor Chevsky
* Norma Cord
* Jon DeLoach
* Karen Evich
```

EXAMPLE 9.50 (CONTINUED)

```
2   tr/0-9/*/c; print;

(Output)
1****************2************3**************4************5****
*********6*************
```

EXPLANATION

1. Without the *c* option, *tr* translates each number to an asterisk (*).
2. With the *c* option, *tr* translates each character that is **not** a number to an asterisk (*); this includes the newline character.

The *tr* Squeeze Option. The *s* (squeeze) option translates all characters that are repeated to a single character and can be used to get rid of excess characters, such as excess whitespace or delimiters, sqeezing these characters down to just one.

EXAMPLE 9.51

```
(The Text File)
1   while (<DATA>){
        tr/:/:/s;
        print;
    {
    __DATA__
    1:::Steve Blenheim
    2::Betty Boop
    3:Igor Chevsky
    4:Norma Cord
    5:::::Jon DeLoach
    6:::Karen Evich

(Output)
1:Steve Blenheim
2:Betty Boop
3:Igor Chevsky
4:Norma Cord
5:Jon DeLoach
6:Karen Evich
```

EXPLANATION

1. The "squeeze" option causes the multiple colons to be translated (squeezed) to single colons.

9.2 Unicode

For every character, Unicode specifies a unique identification number that remains consistent across applications, languages, and platforms.

With the advent of the Internet, it became obvious that the ASCII coding for characters was insufficient if the whole world were to be included in transferring data from one Web site to another without corrupting the data. The ASCII sequence of characters consists of only 256 (one-byte) characters and could hardly accommodate languages like Chinese and Japanese, where a given symbol is drawn from a set of thousands of characters.

The Unicode standard is an effort to solve the problem by creating new characters sets, called UTF8 and UTF16, where characters are not limited to one byte. UTF8, for example, allows two bytes that can hold up to 65,536 characters, and each character has a unique number. To remove ambiguity, any given 16-bit value would always represent the same character, thereby allowing for consistent sorting, searching, displaying, and editing of text. According to the Unicode Consortium,[5] Unicode has the capacity to encode over one million characters, which is sufficient to encompass all the world's written languages. Further, all symbols are treated equally, so that all characters can be accessed without the need for escape sequences or control codes.

9.2.1 Perl and Unicode

The largest change in Perl 5.6 was to provide UTF8 Unicode support. By default, Perl represents strings internally in Unicode, and all the relevant built-in functions (*length*, *reverse*, *sort*, *tr*) now work on a character-by-character basis instead of on a byte-by-byte basis. Two new Perl pragmas are used to turn Unicode settings on and off. The *utf8* pragma turns on the Unicode settings and loads the required character tables, while the *bytes* pragma refers to the old byte meanings, reading one byte at a time.

When *utf8* is turned on, you can specify string literals in Unicode using the *\x{N}* notation, where *N* is a hexadecimal character code such as *\x{395}*.

Unicode also provides support for regular expressions and matching characters based on Unicode properties, some of which are defined by the Unicode standard and some by Perl. The Perl properties are composites of the standard properties; in other words, you can now match any uppercase character in any language with *\p{IsUpper}*. For more information, go to *http://www.perl.com/pub/a/2000/04/whatsnew.html*.

Table 9.10 is a list of Perl's composite character classes. If the *p* in *\p* is capitalized, the meaning is a negation; so, for example, *\p{IsASCII}* represents an ASCII character, whereas \P*{IsASCII}* represents a non-ASCII character.

---

5. The Unicode Consortium is a nonprofit organization founded to develop, extend, and promote use of the Unicode standard. For more information on Unicode and the Unicode Consortium, go to *http://www.unicode.org/unicode/standard/whatisunicode.html*.

Table 9.10 *utf8* Composite Character Classes

utf8 Property	*Meaning*
\p{IsASCII}	ASCII character
\p{Cntrl}	Control character
\p{IsDigit}	A digit between *0* and *9*
\p{IsGraph}	Alphanumeric or punctuation character
\p{IsLower}	Lowercase letter
\p{IsPrint}	Alphanumeric, punctuation character, or space
\p{IsPunct}	Any punctuation character
\p{IsSpace}	Whitespace character
\p{IsUpper}	Uppercase letter
\p{IsWord}	Alphanumeric word character or underscore
\p{IsXDigit}	Any hexadecimal digit

EXAMPLE 9.52

```
1   use utf8;
2   $chr=11;
3   print "$chr is a digit.\n"if $chr =~ /\p{IsDigit}/;
4   $chr = "junk";
5   print "$chr is not a digit.\n"if $chr =~ /\P{IsDigit}/;
6   print "$chr is not a control character.\n"if $chr =
        ~ /\P{IsCntrl}/;

(Output)
3   11 is a digit.
5   junk is not a digit.
6   junk is not a control character.
```

EXPLANATION

1. The *utf8* pragma is used to turn on the Unicode settings.
2. Scalar *$chr* is assigned a number.
3. The Perl Unicode property *IsDigit* is used to check for a number between *0* and *9*, the same as using *[0–9]*.
4. Scalar *$chr* is assigned the string *junk*.
5. The \p is now \P, causing the escape sequence to mean **not** a digit, the same as using *[^0–9]*. Since *junk* is not a digit, the condition is true.
6. The opposite of *junk* is not a control character.

9.3 What You Should Know

1. What are metacharacters used for?
2. What is a character class?
3. What is meant by a "greedy" metacharacter?
4. What is an anchoring metacharacter?
5. How do you search for a literal period?
6. What is capturing? Can you turn it off?
7. What is grouping?
8. How does a character class differ from alternation?
9. How do you search for one or more digits?
10. How do you search for zero or one digit?
11. What is a metasymbol?
12. What is the purpose of the "squeeze" option when used with *tr*?
13. What is *utf8*?

9.4 What's Next?

In the next chapter, we discuss how Perl deals with files, how to open them, read from them, write to them, append to them, and close them. You will learn how "die" works. You will learn how to seek to a position within a file, how to rewind back to the top, how to mark a spot for the next read operation. You will learn how to perform file tests to see if a file is readable, writeable, executable, etc. We will also discuss pipes, how Perl sends output to a pipe, and how Perl reads from a pipe. You will learn how to pass arguments to a Perl script at the command line and all the variations of *ARGV.*

EXERCISE 9
And the Search Goes On...

```
(Sample file found on CD)
Tommy Savage:408-724-0140:1222 Oxbow Court, Sunnyvale,CA
94087:5/19/66:34200
Lesle Kerstin:408-456-1234:4 Harvard Square, Boston, MA
02133:4/22/62:52600
JonDeLoach:408-253-3122:123 Park St., San Jose, CA 94086:7/25/53:85100
Ephram Hardy:293-259-5395:235 Carlton Lane, Joliet, IL
73858:8/12/20:56700
etty Boop:245-836-8357:635 Cutesy Lane, Hollywood, CA
91464:6/23/23:14500
Wilhelm Kopf:846-836-2837:6937 Ware Road, Milton, PA
93756:9/21/46:43500
Norma Corder:397-857-2735:74 Pine Street, Dearborn, MI
23874:3/28/45:245700
James Ikeda:834-938-8376:23445 Aster Ave., Allentown, NJ
83745:12/1/38:45000
Lori Gortz:327-832-5728:3465 Mirlo Street, Peabody, MA
34756:10/2/65:35200
Barbara Kerz:385-573-8326:832 Ponce Drive, Gary, IN
83756:12/15/46:268500
```

1. Print the city and state where Norma lives.
2. Give everyone a $250.00 raise.
3. Calculate Lori's age.
4. Print lines 2 through 6. (The $. variable holds the current line number.)
5. Print names and phone numbers of those in the 408 area code.
6. Print names and salaries in lines 3, 4, and 5.
7. Print a row of stars after line 3.
8. Change *CA* to *California*.
9. Print the file with a row of stars after the last line.
10. Print the names of the people born in March.
11. Print all lines that don't contain *Karen*.
12. Print lines that end in exactly five consecutive digits.
13. Print the file with the first and last names reversed.

chapter

10

Getting a Handle on Files

10.1 The User-Defined Filehandle

If you are processing text, you will regularly be opening, closing, reading from, and writing to files. In Perl, we use filehandles to get access to system files.

A **filehandle** is a name for a file, device, pipe, or socket. In Chapter 4, "Getting a Handle on Printing," we discussed the three default filehandles, *STDIN*, *STDOUT*, and *STDERR*. Perl allows you to create your own filehandles for input and output operations on files, devices, pipes, or sockets. A filehandle allows you to associate the filehandle name with a system file[1] and to use that filehandle to access the file.

10.1.1 Opening Files—The *open* Function

The *open* function lets you name a filehandle and the file you want to attach to that handle. The file can be opened for reading, writing, or appending (or both reading and writing), and the file can be opened to pipe data to or from a process. The *open* function returns a nonzero result if successful and an undefined value if it fails. Like scalars, arrays, and labels, filehandles have their own namespace. So that they will not be confused with reserved words, it is recommended that filehandle names be written in all uppercase letters. (See the *open* function in Appendix A.)

When opening text files on Win32 platforms, the *\r\n* (characters for return and newline) are translated into *\n* when text files are read from disk, and the *^Z* character is read as an end-of-file marker (EOF). The following functions for opening files should work fine with text files but will cause a problem with binary files. (See "Win32 Binary Files" on page 292.)

1. A system file would be a UNIX, Win32, Macintosh file, etc., stored on the system's disk.

10.1.2 Open for Reading

The following examples illustrate how to open files for reading. Even though the examples represent UNIX files, they will work the same way on Windows, Mac OS, etc.

FORMAT

```
1    open(FILEHANDLE, "FILENAME");
2    open(FILEHANDLE, "<FILENAME");
2    open(FILEHANDLE);
3    open FILEHANDLE;
```

EXAMPLE 10.1

```
1    open(MYHANDLE, "myfile");
2    open (FH, "</etc/passwd");
3    open (MYHANDLE);
```

EXPLANATION

1 The *open* function will create the filehandle *MYHANDLE* and attach it to the system file *myfile*. The file will be opened for reading. Since a full pathname is not specified for *myfile*, it must be in the current working directory, and you must have read permission to open it for reading.

2 The *open* function will create the filehandle *FH* and attach it to the system file */etc/passwd*. The file will be opened for reading, but this time the < symbol is used to indicate the operation. The < symbol is not necessary but may help clarify that this is a *read* operation. The full pathname is specified for *passwd*.

3 If *FILENAME* is omitted, the name of the filehandle is the same name as a scalar variable previously defined. The scalar variable has been assigned the name of the real file. In the example, the filename could have been defined as

```
$MYHANDLE="myfile";
open(MYHANDLE);
```

The *open* function will create the filehandle *MYHANDLE* and attach it to the value of the variable, *$MYHANDLE*. The effect will be the same as the first example. The parentheses are optional.

Closing the Filehandle. The *close* function closes the file, pipe, socket, or device attached to *FILEHANDLE*. Once *FILEHANDLE* is opened, it stays open until the script ends or you call the *open* function again. (The next call to *open* closes *FILEHANDLE* before reopening it.) If you don't explicitly close the file, when you reopen it this way, the line counter variable, $., will not be reset. Closing a pipe causes the process to wait until the pipe is complete and reports the status in the *$!* variable (see "The *die* Function" on page 287). It's a good idea to explicitly close files and handles after you are finished using them.

FORMAT

```
close (FILEHANDLE);
close FILEHANDLE;
```

EXAMPLE 10.2

```
1   open(INFILE, "datebook");
    close(INFILE);
```

EXPLANATION

1 The user-defined filehandle *INFILE* will be closed.

The *die* Function. In the following examples, the *die* function is used if a call to the *open* function fails. If Perl cannot open the file, the *die* function is used to exit the Perl script and print a message to *STDERR*, usually the screen.

If you were to go to your shell or MS-DOS prompt and type

```
cat junk  (UNIX)
```

or

```
type junk (DOS)
```

and if *junk* is a nonexistent file, the following system error would appear on your screen:

```
cat: junk: No such file or directory     (UNIX "cat" command)
The system cannot find the file specified.    (Windows "type" command)
```

When using the *die* function, Perl provides a special variable *$!* to hold the value of the system error (see "Error Handling" on page 755) that occurs when you are unable to successfully open a file or execute a system utility. This is very useful for detecting a problem with the filehandle before continuing with the execution of the script. (See use of *Carp.pm* discussed in Example 12.10 on page 384.)

EXAMPLE 10.3

```
(Line from Script)
1   open(MYHANDLE, "/etc/password) || die "Can't open: $!\n";
2   open(MYHANDLE, "/etc/password) or die "Can't open: $!\n";

(Output)
1   Can't open: No such file or directory
```

EXAMPLE 10.3 (CONTINUED)

```
(Line from Script)
3   open(MYHANDLE, "/etc/password") || die "Can't open: ";

(Output)
3   Can't open: No such file or directory at ./handle line 3.
```

EXPLANATION

1. When trying to open the file */etc/password*, the *open* fails (it should be */etc/passwd*). The short-circuit operator causes its right operand to execute if the left operand fails. The *die* operator is executed. The string *Can't open:* is printed, followed by the system error *No such file or directory.* The \n suppresses any further output from the *die* function. All of *die*'s output is sent to *STDERR* after the program exits.
2. For readability, you may want to use the *or* operator instead of ||.
3. This is exactly like the first example, except that the \n has been removed from the string *Can't open:*. Omitting the \n causes the *die* function to append a string to the output, indicating the line number in the script where the system error occurred.

Reading from the Filehandle. In Example 10.4, a file called *datebook* is opened for reading. Each line read is assigned, in turn, to $_, the default scalar that holds what was just read until the end of file is reached.

EXAMPLE 10.4

```
(The Text File: datebook)
    Steve Blenheim
    Betty Boop
    Lori Gortz
    Sir Lancelot
    Norma Cord
    Jon DeLoach
    Karen Evich

--------------------------------------------------------------

(The Script)
    #!/usr/bin/perl
    # Open a file with a filehandle
1   open(FILE, "datebook") || die "Can't open datebook: $!\n";
2   while(<FILE>) {
3       print  if /Sir Lancelot/;
4   }
5   close(FILE);

(Output)
3   Sir Lancelot
```

EXPLANATION

1. The *open* function will create a filehandle called *FILE* (opened for reading) and attach the system file *datebook* to it. If *open* fails because the file *datebook* does not exist, the *die* operator will print to the screen, *Can't open datebook: No such file or directory.*
2. The expression in the *while* loop is the filehandle *FILE*, enclosed in angle brackets. The angle brackets are the operators used for reading input. (They are not part of the filehandle name.) When the loop starts, the first line from the filehandle *FILE* will be stored in the $_ scalar variable. (Remember, the $_ variable holds each line of input from the file.) If it has not reached end of file, the loop will continue to take a line of input from the file, execute statements 3 and 4, and continue until end of file is reached.
3. The default input variable $_ is implicitly used to hold the current line of input read from the filehandle. If the line contains the regular expression *Sir Lancelot*, that line (stored in $_) is printed to *STDOUT*. For each loop iteration, the next line read is stored in $_ and tested.
4. The closing curly brace marks the end of the loop body. When this line is reached, control will go back to the top of the loop (line 2) and the next line of input will be read from file; this process will continue until all the lines have been read.
5. After looping through the file, the file is closed by closing the filehandle.

EXAMPLE 10.5

```
(The Text File: datebook)
    Steve Blenheim
    Betty Boop
    Lori Gortz
    Sir Lancelot
    Norma Cord
    Jon DeLoach
    Karen Evich

----------------------------------------------------------------

(The Script)
    #!/usr/bin/perl
    # Open a file with a filehandle
1   open(FILE, "datebook") || die "Can't open datebook: $!\n";
2   while($line = <FILE>) {
3       print "$line" if  $line =~ /^Lori/;
4   }
5   close(FILE);

(Output)
3   Lori Gortz
```

EXPLANATION

1. The *datebook* file is opened for reading.
2. When the *while* loop is entered, a line is read from the file and stored in the scalar *$line*.
3. The value of the scalar *$line* is printed if it contains the pattern *Lori*, and *Lori* is at the beginning of the line.
4. When the closing brace is reached, control goes back to line 2, and another line is read from the file. The loop ends when the file has no more lines.
5. The file is closed by closing the filehandle.

EXAMPLE 10.6

```
(The Text File: datebook)
    Steve Blenheim
    Betty Boop
    Lori Gortz
    Sir Lancelot
    Norma Cord
    Jon DeLoach
    Karen Evich

------------------------------------------------------------------

(The Script)
    #!/usr/bin/perl
    # Open a file with a filehandle
1   open(FILE, "<datebook") || die "Can't open datebook: $!\n";
2   @lines = <FILE>;
3   print @lines;        # Contents of the entire file are printed
4   print "\nThe datebook file contains ", $#lines + 1,
          " lines of text.\n";
5   close(FILE);

(Output)
The datebook file contains 7 lines of text.
```

EXPLANATION

1. The *datebook* file is opened for reading. (The < read operator is not required.)
2. All of the lines are read from the file, via the filehandle, and assigned to *@lines*, where each line is an element of the array. The newline terminates each element.
3. The array *@lines* is printed.
4. The value of *$#lines* is the number of the last subscript in the array. By adding one to *$#lines*, the number of elements (lines) is printed. A *–1* offset, *$lines[–1]*, will also print the last line.

10.1.3 Open for Writing

To open a file for writing, the file will be created if it does not exist, and if it already exists, it must have write permission. If the file exists, its contents will be overwritten. The filehandle is used to access the system file.

FORMAT

```
1  open(FILEHANDLE, ">FILENAME)";
```

EXAMPLE 10.7

```
1   open(MYOUTPUT, ">temp");
```

EXPLANATION

1 The user-defined filehandle *MYOUTPUT* will be used to send output to the file called *temp*. As with the shell, the redirection symbol directs the output from the default filehandle, *STDOUT*, to the *temp* file.

EXAMPLE 10.8

```
(The Script)
    #!/usr/bin/perl
    # Write to a file with a filehandle. Scriptname: file.handle
1   $file="/home/jody/ellie/perl/newfile";
2   open(HANDOUT, ">$file") || die "Can't open newfile: $!\n";

3   print HANDOUT "hello world.\n";
4   print HANDOUT "hello world again.\n";

(At the Command Line)
5   $ perl file.handle
6   $ cat newfile

(Output)
3   hello world.
4   hello world, again.
```

EXPLANATION

1 The scalar variable *$file* is set to the full pathname of a UNIX file called *newfile*. The scalar will be used to represent the name of the UNIX file to which output will be directed via the filehandle. This example will work the same way with Windows, but if you use the backslash as a directory separator, either enclose the path in single quotes, or use two backslashes; e.g., *C:\\home\\ellie\\testing*.

EXPLANATION (CONTINUED)

2 The user-defined filehandle *HANDOUT* will change the default place to where output normally goes, *STDOUT*, to the file that it represents, *newfile*. The > symbol indicates that *newfile* will be created if it does not exist and opened for writing. If it does exist, it will be opened and any text in it will be **overwritten**, so be careful!

3 The *print* function will send its output to the filehandle, *HANDOUT*, instead of to the screen. The string *hello world.* will be written into *newfile* via the *HANDOUT* filehandle. The file *newfile* will remain open unless it is explicitly closed or the Perl script ends (see "Closing the Filehandle" on page 286).

4 The *print* function will send its output to the filehandle *HANDOUT* instead of to the screen. The string *hello world, again.* will be written into *newfile* via the *HANDOUT* filehandle. The operating system keeps track of where the last write occurred and will send its next line of output to the location immediately following the last byte written to the file.

5 The script is executed. The output is sent to *newfile*.

6 The contents of the file *newfile* are printed.

10.1.4 Win32 Binary Files

Win32 distinguishes between text and binary files. If ^Z is found, the program may abort prematurely or have problems with the newline translation. When reading and writing Win32 binary files, use the *binmode* function to prevent these problems. The *binmode* function arranges for a specified filehandle to be read or written to in either binary (raw) or text mode. If the discipline argument is not specified, the mode is set to "raw." The discipline is one of *:raw, :crlf, :text, :utf8, :latin1*, etc. (UNIX and Mac OS do not need binmode. They delimit lines with a single character and encode that character "\n".)

FORMAT

```
binmode FILEHANDLE
binmode FILEHANDLE, DISCIPLINE
```

EXAMPLE 10.9

```
# This script copies one binary file to another.
# Note its use of binmode to set the mode of the filehandle.

$infile="statsbar.gif";
open( INFILE, "<$infile" );
open( OUTFILE, ">outfile.gif" );

binmode( INFILE );      # Crucial for binary files!

binmode( OUTFILE );
# binmode should be called after open() but before any I/O
# is done on the filehandle.
```

EXAMPLE 10.9 (CONTINUED)

```
6   while ( read( INFILE, $buffer, 1024 ) ) {
7       print OUTFILE $buffer;
    }

8   close( INFILE );
    close( OUTFILE );
```

EXPLANATION

1. The scalar *$infile* is assigned a *.gif* filename.
2. The file *statsbar.gif* is opened for reading and attached to the *INFILE* filehandle.
3. The file *outfile.gif* is opened for writing and assigned to the *OUTFILE* filehandle.
4. The *binmode* function arranges for the input file to be read as binary text.
5. The *binmode* function arranges for the output file to be written as binary text.
6. The *read* function reads 1,024 bytes at a time, storing the input read in the scalar *$buffer.*
7. After the 1,024 bytes are read in, they are sent out to the output file.
8. Both filehandles are closed. The result was that one binary file was copied to another binary file.

10.1.5 Open for Appending

To open a file for appending, the file will be created if it does not exist, and if it already exists, it must have write permission. If the file exists, its contents will be left intact, and the output will be appended to the end of the file. Again, the filehandle is used to access the file rather than accessing it by its real name.

FORMAT

```
1   open(FILEHANDLE, ">> FILENAME");
```

EXAMPLE 10.10

```
1   open(APPEND, ">> temp");
```

EXPLANATION

1. The user-defined filehandle *APPEND* will be used to append output to the file called *temp*. As with the shell, the redirection symbol directs the output from the default, standard out filehandle, *STDOUT*, to the *temp* file.

EXAMPLE 10.11

```
(The Text File)
$ cat newfile
hello world.
hello world, again.

(The Script)
    #!/usr/bin/perl
1   open(HANDLE, ">>newfile") ||
            die print "Can't open newfile: $!\n";
2   print HANDLE "Just appended \"hello world\"
            to the end of newfile.\n";

(Output)
$ cat newfile
hello world.
hello world, again.
Just appended "hello world" to the end of newfile.
```

EXPLANATION

1. The user-defined filehandle *HANDLE* will be used to send and append output to the file called *newfile*. As with the shell, the redirection symbol directs the output from the default filehandle, *STDOUT*, and appends the output to the file *newfile*. If the file cannot be opened because, for example, the write permissions are turned off, the *die* operator will print the error message, *Can't open newfile: Permission denied.*, and the script will exit.
2. The *print* function will send its output to the filehandle, *HANDLE*, instead of to the screen. The string, *Just appended "hello world" to the end of newfile,* will be written to end of *newfile* via the *HANDLE* filehandle.

10.1.6 The *select* Function

The *select* function sets the default **output** to the specified *FILEHANDLE* and returns the previously selected filehandle. All printing will go to the selected handle.

EXAMPLE 10.12

```
(The Script)
    #! /usr/bin/perl
1   open (FILEOUT,">newfile") || die "Can't open newfile: $!\n";
2   select(FILEOUT);        # Select the new filehandle for output
3   open (DB, "<datebook") || die "Can't open datebook: $!\n";
```

EXAMPLE 10.12 (CONTINUED)

```
    while(<DB>) {
4      print ;              # Output goes to FILEOUT, i.e., newfile
    }
5   select(STDOUT);         # Send output back to the screen
    print "Good-bye.\n";    # Output goes to the screen
```

EXPLANATION

1. *newfile* is opened for writing and assigned to the filehandle *FILEOUT*.
2. The *select* function assigns *FILEOUT* as the current default filehandle for output. The return value from the *select* function is the name of the filehandle that was closed (*STDOUT*) in order to select *FILEOUT*, the one that is now opened for writing.
3. The *DB* filehandle is opened for reading.
4. As each line is read into the $_ variable from *DB*, it is then printed to the currently selected filehandle, *FILEOUT*. Notice that you don't have to name the filehandle.
5. By selecting *STDOUT*, the rest of the program's output will go to the screen.

10.1.7 File Locking with *flock*

To prevent two programs from writing to a file at the same time, you can lock the file so you have exclusive access to it and then unlock it when you're finished using it. The *flock* function takes two arguments: a filehandle and a file locking operation. The operations are listed in Table 10.1.[2]

Table 10.1 File Locking Operations

Name	*Operation*	*What It Does*
lock_sh	1	Creates a shared lock
lock_ex	2	Creates an exclusive lock
lock_nb	4	Creates a nonblocking lock
lock_un	8	Unlocks an existing lock

Read permission is required on a file to obtain a shared lock, and write permission is required to obtain an exclusive lock. With operations 1 and 2, normally the caller requesting the file will block (wait) until the file is unlocked. If a nonblocking lock is used on a filehandle, an error is produced immediately if a request is made to get the locked file.[3]

2. File locking may not be implemented on non-UNIX systems.
3. *flock* may not work if the file is being accessed from a networked system.

EXAMPLE 10.13

```
   #!/bin/perl
   # Program that uses file locking -- UNIX
1  $LOCK_EX = 2;
2  $LOCK_UN = 8;

3  print "Adding an entry to the datafile.\n";
   print "Enter the name: ";
   chomp($name=<STDIN>);
   print "Enter the address: ";
   chomp($address=<STDIN>);

4  open(DB, ">>datafile") || die "Can't open: $!\n";

5  flock(DB, $LOCK_EX) || die ;          # Lock the file

6  print DB "$name:$address\n";

7  flock(DB, $LOCK_UN) || die;           # Unlock the file
```

EXPLANATION

1. The scalar is assigned the value of the operation that will be used by the *flock* function to lock the file. This operation is to block (wait) until an exclusive lock can be created.
2. This operation will tell *flock* when to unlock the file so others can write to it.
3. The user is asked for the information to update the file. This information will be appended to the file.
4. The filehandle is opened for appending.
5. The *flock* function puts an exclusive lock on the file.
6. The data is appended to the file.
7. Once the data has been appended, the file is unlocked so others can access it.

10.1.8 The *seek* and *tell* Functions

The *seek* Function. Seek allows you to randomly access a file. The *seek* function is the same as the *fseek* standard I/O function in *C*. Rather than closing the file and then reopening it, the *seek* function allows you to move to some byte (not line) position within the file. The *seek* function returns *1* if successful, *0* otherwise.

FORMAT

```
seek(FILEHANDLE, BYTEOFFSET, FILEPOSITION);
```

The *seek* function sets a position in a file, where the first byte is 0. Positions are

0 = Beginning of the file
1 = Current position in the file
2 = End of the file

The offset is the number of bytes from the file position. A positive offset moves the position forward in the file; a negative offset moves the position backward in the file for position 1 or 2.

The *od* command lets you look at how the characters in a file are stored. This file was created on a Win32 platform; on UNIX systems, the linefeed/newline is one character, *\n*.

```
$ od -c db
0000000000   S   t   e   v   e       B   l   e   n   h   e   i   m  \r  \n
0000000020   B   e   t   t   y       B   o   o   p  \r  \n   L   o   r   i
0000000040   G   o   r   t   z  \r  \n   S   i   r       L   a   n   c
0000000060   e   l   o   t  \r  \n   N   o   r   m   a       C   o   r   d
0000000100  \r  \n   J   o   n       D   e   L   o   a   c   h  \r  \n   K
0000000120   a   r   e   n       E   v   i   c   h  \r  \n
0000000134
```

EXAMPLE 10.14

```
(The Text File: db)
Steve Blenheim
Betty Boop
Lori Gortz
Sir Lancelot
Norma Cord
Jon DeLoach
Karen Evich

---------------------------------------------------------------

(The Script)
    # Example using the seek function
1   open(FH,"db") or die "Can't open: $!\n";
2   while($line=<FH>){          # Loop through the whole file
3       if ($line =~ /Lori/) { print "--$line--\n";}
    }
4   seek(FH,0,0);               # Start at the beginning of the file
5   while(<FH>) {
6       print if /Steve/;
    }

(Output)
3   --Lori Gortz--
6   Steve Blenheim
```

EXPLANATION

1. The *db* file is assigned to the *FH* filehandle and opened for reading.
2. Each line of the file is assigned, in turn, to the scalar *$line* while looping through the file.
3. If *$line* contains *Lori*, the *print* statement is executed.
4. The *seek* function causes the file pointer to be positioned at the top of the file (position 0) and starts reading at byte 0, the first character. If you want to get back to the top of the file without using *seek*, the filehandle must first be explicitly closed with the *close* function.
5. Starting at the top of the file, the loop is entered. The first line is read from the filehandle and assigned to $_, the default line holder.
6. If the pattern *Steve* is found in $_, the line will be printed.

EXAMPLE 10.15

```
(The Text File: db)
Steve Blenheim
Betty Boop
Lori Gortz
Sir Lancelot
Norma Cord
Jon DeLoach
Karen Evich

-----------------------------------------------------------------

(The Script)
1   open(FH, "db") or die "Can't open datebook: $!\n";
2   while(<FH>){
3       last if /Norma/;     # This is the last line that
                             # will be processed
    }
4   seek(FH,0,1) or die;     # Seeking from the current position
5   $line=<FH>;              # This is where the read starts again
6   print "$line";
7   close FH;

(Output)
6   Jon DeLoach
```

EXPLANATION

1. The *db* file is opened for reading via the FH filehandle.
2. The *while* loop is entered. A line from the file is read and assigned to $_.
3. When the line containing the pattern *Norma* is reached, the *last* function causes the loop to be exited.

EXPLANATION (CONTINUED)

4. The *seek* function will reposition the file pointer at the byte position 0 where the next read operation would have been performed in the file, position 1: in other words, the line right after the line that contained *Norma*. The byte position could be either a negative or positive value.
5. A line is read from the *db* file and assigned to the scalar *$line*. The line read is the line that would have been read just after the *last* function caused the loop to exit.
6. The value of *$line* is printed.

EXAMPLE 10.16

```
(The Script)
1   open(FH, "db") or die "Can't open datebook: $!\n";
2   seek(FH,-13,2) or die;
3   while(<FH>){
4       print;
    }

(Output)
4   Karen Evich
```

EXPLANATION

1. The *db* file is opened for reading via the *FH* filehandle.
2. The *seek* function starts at the end of the file (position 2) and backs up 13 bytes. The newline (*\r\n*), although not visible, is represented as the last two bytes in the line (Windows).
3. The *while* loop is entered, and each line, in turn, is read from the filehandle *db*.
4. Each line is printed. By backing up 13 characters from the end of the file, *Karen Evich* is printed. Note the output of the *od -c* command and count back 13 characters from the end of the file.

```
0000000000    S   t   e   v   e       B   l   e   n   h   e   i   m  \r  \n
0000000020    B   e   t   t   y       B   o   o   p  \r  \n   L   o   r   i
0000000040        G   o   r   t   z  \r  \n   S   i   r       L   a   n   c
0000000060    e   l   o   t  \r  \n   N   o   r   m   a       C   o   r   d
0000000100   \r  \n   J   o   n       D   e   L   o   a   c   h  \r  \n   K
0000000120    a   r   e   n       E   v   i   c   h  \r  \n
0000000134
```

The *tell* Function. The *tell* function returns the current byte position in the file and is used with the *seek* function to move to that position in the file. If *FILEHANDLE* is omitted, *tell* returns the position of the file last read.

FORMAT

```
tell(FILEHANDLE);
tell;
```

EXAMPLE 10.17

```
(The Text File: db)
Steve Blenheim
Betty Boop
Lori Gortz
Sir Lancelot
Norma Cord
Jon DeLoach
Karen Evich

-----------------------------------------------------------------

(The Script)
     #!/usr/bin/perl
     # Example using the tell function
1    open(FH,"db") || die "Can't open: $!\n";
2    while ($line=<FH>) {        # Loop through the whole file
         chomp($line);
3        if ($line =~ /^Lori/) {
4            $currentpos=tell;
5            print "The current byte position is $currentpos.\n";
6            print "$line\n\n";
         }
     }
7    seek(FH,$currentpos,0);     # Start at the beginning of the file
8    @lines=(<FH>);
9    print @lines;

(Output)
5    The current byte position is 40.
6    Lori Gortz

9    Sir Lancelot
     Norma Cord
     Jon DeLoach
     Karen Evich
```

EXPLANATION

1. The *db* file is assigned to the *FH* filehandle and opened for reading.
2. Each line of the file is assigned, in turn, to the scalar *$line* while looping through the file.
3. If the scalar *$line* contains the regular expression *Lori*, the *if* block is entered.

EXPLANATION (CONTINUED)

4 The *tell* function is called and returns the current byte position (starting at byte 0) in the file. This represents the position of the first character in the line that was just read in after the line containing *Lori* was processed.
5 The value in bytes is stored in *$currentpos*. It is printed. Byte position 40 represents the position where *Sir Lancelot* starts the line.
6 The line containing the regular expression *Lori* is printed.
7 The *seek* function will position the file pointer for *FH* at the byte offset, *$currentpos*, 40 bytes from the beginning of the file. Without *seek*, the filehandle would have to be closed in order to start reading from the top of the file.
8 The lines starting at offset 40 are read in and stored in the array *@lines*.
9 The array is printed, starting at offset 40.

10.1.9 Open for Reading and Writing

Table 10.2 Reading and Writing Operations

Symbol	Open For
+<	Read first, then write
+>	Write first, then read
+>>	Append first, then read

EXAMPLE 10.18

```
(The Script)
    # Scriptname: countem.pl
    # Open visitor_count for reading first, and then writing
1   open(FH, "+<visitor_count") ||
            die "Can't open visitor_count: $!\n";
2   $count=<FH>;              # Read a number from from the file
3   print "You are visitor number $count.";
4   $count++;
5   seek(FH, 0,0) || die;     # Seek back to the top of the file
6   print FH $count;          # Write the new number to the file
7   close(FH);

(Output)
(First run of countem.pl)
You are visitor number 1.

(Second run of countem.pl)
You are visitor number 2.
```

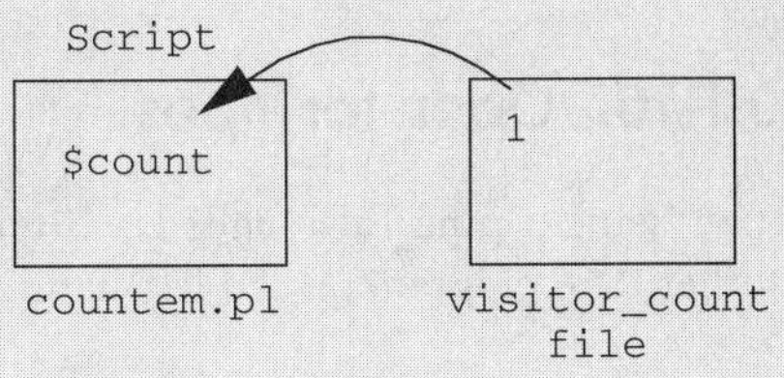

EXPLANATION

1 The file *visitor_count* is opened for reading first, and then writing. If the file does not exist or is not readable, *die* will cause the program to exit with an error message.
2 A line is read from the *visitor_count* file. The first time the script is executed, the number *1* is read in from *visitor_count* file and stored in the scalar *$count*.
3 The value of *$count* is printed.
4 The *$count* scalar is incremented by 1.
5 The *seek* function moves the file pointer to the beginning of the file.
6 The new value of *$count* is written back to the *visitor_count* file. The number that was there is overwritten by the new value of *$count* each time the script is executed.
7 The file is closed.

EXAMPLE 10.19

```
(The Script)
    #!/usr/bin/perl
    # Open for writing first, then reading
    print "\n\n";
1   open(FH, "+>joker") || die;
2   print FH "This line is written to joker.\n";
3   seek(FH,0,0);          # Go to the beginning of the file
4   while(<FH>) {
5       print;             # Reads from joker; the line is in $_
    }

(Output)
5   This line is written to joker.
```

EXPLANATION

1 The filehandle *FH* is opened for writing first. This means that the file *joker* will be created or, if it already exists, it will be truncated. Be careful not to mix up +< and +>.
2 The output is sent to *joker* via the *FH* filehandle.
3 The *seek* function moves the filepointer to the beginning of the file.
4 The *while* loop is entered. A line is read from the file *joker* via the *FH* filehandle and stored in $_.
5 Each line ($_) is printed after it is read until the end of the file is reached.

10.1.10 Open for Pipes

When using a **pipe** (also called a **filter**), a connection is made from one program to another. The program on the left-hand side of a pipe sends its output into a temporary buffer. This program writes into the pipe. On the other side of the pipe is a program that is a reader. It gets its input from the buffer. Here is an example of a typical UNIX pipe:

```
who | wc -l
```

and an MS-DOS pipe:

```
dir /B | more
```

The output of the *who* command is sent to the *wc* command. The *who* command sends its output to the pipe; it writes to the pipe. The *wc* command gets its input from the pipe; it reads from the pipe. (If the *wc* command were not a reader, it would ignore what is in the pipe.) The output is sent to the *STDOUT*, the terminal screen. The number of people logged on is printed. If Perl is on the left-hand side of a pipe, then Perl is the writer and sends output to the buffer; if Perl is on the right-hand side of the pipe, then Perl reads from the buffer. It is important to keep in mind that the process connecting to Perl is an operating system command. If you are running Perl on a UNIX or Linux system, the commands will be different from those on a Windows system, thereby making Perl scripts implementing pipes unportable between systems.

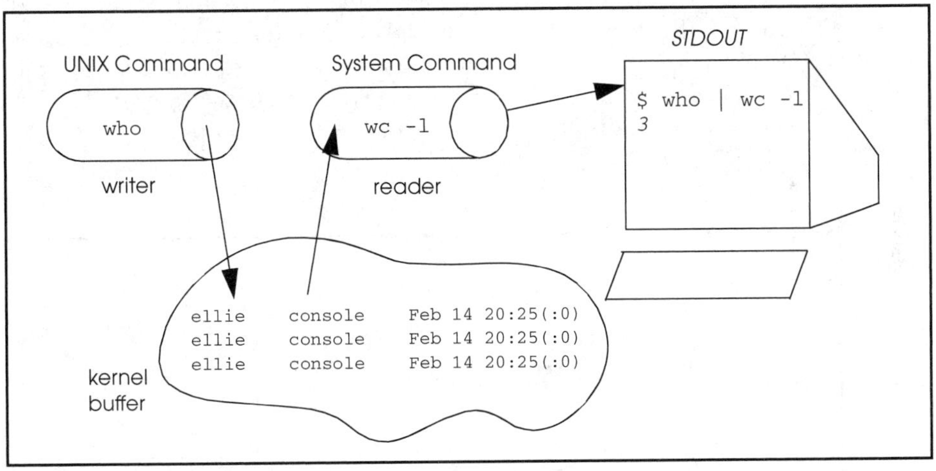

Figure 10.1 UNIX pipe example.

The Output Filter. When creating a filehandle with the *open* function, you can open a filter so that the output is piped to a system command. The command is preceded by a pipe symbol (|) and replaces the filename argument in the previous examples. The output will be piped to the command and sent to *STDOUT*.

FORMAT

```
1   open(FILEHANDLE, |COMMAND);
```

EXAMPLE 10.20

```
(The Script)
    #!/bin/perl
    # Scriptname: outfilter (UNIX)
1   open(MYPIPE, "| wc -w");
2   print MYPIPE "apples pears peaches";
3   close(MYPIPE);

(Output)
3
```

EXPLANATION

1. The user-defined filehandle *MYPIPE* will be used to pipe output from the Perl script to the UNIX command *wc -w*, which counts the number of words in the string.
2. The *print* function sends the string *apples pears peaches* to the output filter filehandle *MYPIPE*; the string is piped to the *wc* command. Since there are three words in the string, the output *3* will be sent to the screen.
3. After you have finished using the filehandle, use the *close* function to close it. This guarantees that the command will complete before the script exits. If you don't close the filehandle, the output may not be flushed properly.

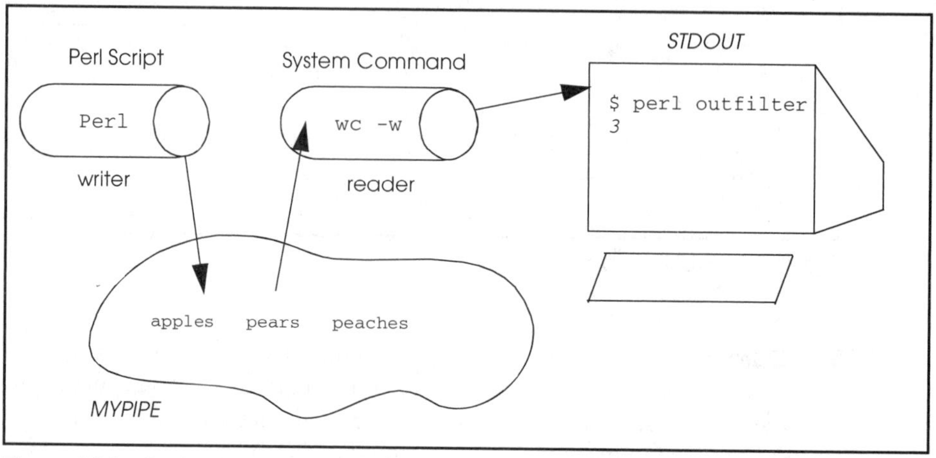

Figure 10.2 Perl output filter.

EXAMPLE 10.21

```
(The Script)
1   open(FOO, "| tr '[a-z]' '[A-Z]'");
2   print FOO "hello there\n";
3   close FOO;    # If you don't close FOO, the output may be delayed

(Output)
2   HELLO THERE
```

EXPLANATION

1. The user-defined filehandle *FOO* will be used to send output from your Perl script to the UNIX command *tr*, which will translate lowercase letters to uppercase.
2. The *print* function sends the string *hello there* to the output filter filehandle *FOO*; that is, the string is piped to the *tr* command. The string, after being filtered, will be sent to the screen with all the characters translated to uppercase.

EXAMPLE 10.22

```
(The Text File)
$ cat emp.names
1 Steve Blenheim
2 Betty Boop
3 Igor Chevsky
4 Norma Cord
5 Jon DeLoach
6 Karen Evich

(The Script)
    #!/usr/bin/perl
    open(FOO, "| sort  +1| tr '[a-z]' '[A-Z]'"); # Open output filter
    open(DB, "emp.names");         # Open DB for reading
    while(<DB>){ print FOO ; }
    close FOO;

(Output)
2   BETTY BOOP
3   IGOR CHEVSKY
5   JON DELOACH
6   KAREN EVICH
4   NORMA CORD
1   STEVE BLENHEIM
```

EXPLANATION

1 The user-defined filehandle *FOO* will be used to pipe output to the UNIX command *sort*, and the output of *sort* will be piped to the *tr* command. The *sort +1* command sorts on the second field, where fields are words separated by whitespace. The UNIX *tr* command translates lowercase letters into uppercase letters.

2 The *open* function creates the filehandle *DB* and attaches it to the UNIX file *emp.names*.

3 The expression in the *while* loop contains the filehandle *DB*, enclosed in angle brackets, indicating a read operation. The loop will read the first line from the *emp.names* file and store it in the $_ scalar variable. The input line will be sent through the output filter, *FOO*, and printed to the screen. The loop will iterate until end of file is reached. Note that when the file is sorted by the second field, the numbers in the first column are no longer sorted.

4 The *close* function closes the filehandle *FOO*.

Sending the Output of a Filter to a File. In the previous example, what if you had wanted to send the output of the filter to a file intead of to *STDOUT*? You can't send output to a filter and a filehandle at the same time, but you can redirect *STDOUT* to a filehandle. Since, later in the program, you may want *STDOUT* to be redirected back to the screen, you can first save it or simply reopen *STDOUT* to the terminal device by typing

```
open(STDOUT, ">/dev/tty");
```

EXAMPLE 10.23

```
#!/usr/bin/perl
# Program to redirect STDOUT from filter to a UNIX file
$| = 1;              # Flush buffers
$tmpfile = "temp";
open(DB, "data") || die qq/Can't open "data": $!\n/;
                                        # Open DB for reading
open(SAVED, ">&STDOUT") || die "$!\n";  # Save stdout
open(STDOUT, ">$tmpfile" ) || die "Can't open: $!\n";
open(SORT, "| sort +1") || die;         # Open output filter
while(<DB>){
    print SORT;   # Output is first sorted and then sent to temp.
}
close SORT;
open(STDOUT, ">&SAVED") || die "Can't open";
print "Here we are printing to the screen again.\n";
                    # This output will go to the screen
rename("temp","data");
```

EXPLANATION

1 The $| variable guarantees an automatic flush of the output buffer after each *print* statement is executed. (See *autoflush* module in Appendix A.)
2 The scalar *$tmpfile* is assigned *temp* to be used later as an output file.
3 The UNIX *data* file is opened for reading and attached to the *DB* filehandle.
4 *STDOUT* is being copied and saved in another filehandle called *SAVED*. Behind the scenes, the file descriptors are being manipulated.
5 The *temp* file is being opened for writing and is assigned to the file descriptor normally reserved for *STDOUT*, the screen. The file descriptor for *STDOUT* has been closed and reopened for *temp*.
6 The output filter will be assigned to *SORT*. Perl's output will be sent to the UNIX *sort* utility.
7 The *DB* filehandle is opened for reading.
8 The output filehandle will be sent to the *temp* file after being sorted.
9 Close the loop.
10 Close the output filter.
11 Open the standard output filehandle so that output is redirected back to the screen.
12 This line prints to the screen because *STDOUT* has been reassigned there.
13 The *temp* file is renamed *data*, overwriting what was in *data* with the contents of *temp*.

Input Filter. When creating a filehandle with the *open* function, you can also open a filter so that input is piped **into** Perl. The command ends with a pipe symbol.

FORMAT

```
open(FILEHANDLE, COMMAND|);
```

EXAMPLE 10.24

```
#!/bin/perl
# Scriptname: infilter
open(INPIPE, "date |");      # Windows (2000/NT) use:  date /T
$today = <INPIPE> ";
print $today;
close(INPIPE);

(Output)
Sun Feb 18 14:12:44 PST 2007
```

EXPLANATION

1. The user-defined filehandle *INPIPE* will be used to pipe the output from the filter as input to Perl. The output of a UNIX *date* command will be used as input by your Perl script via the *INPIPE* filehandle. Windows 2000/NT users: use *date /T*.
2. The scalar *$today* will receive its input from the *INPIPE* filehandle; in other words, Perl reads from *INPIPE*.
3. The value of the UNIX *date* command was assigned to *$today* and is displayed.
4. After you have finished using the filehandle, use the *close* function to close it. This guarantees that the command will complete before the script exits. If you don't close the filehandle, the output may not be flushed properly.

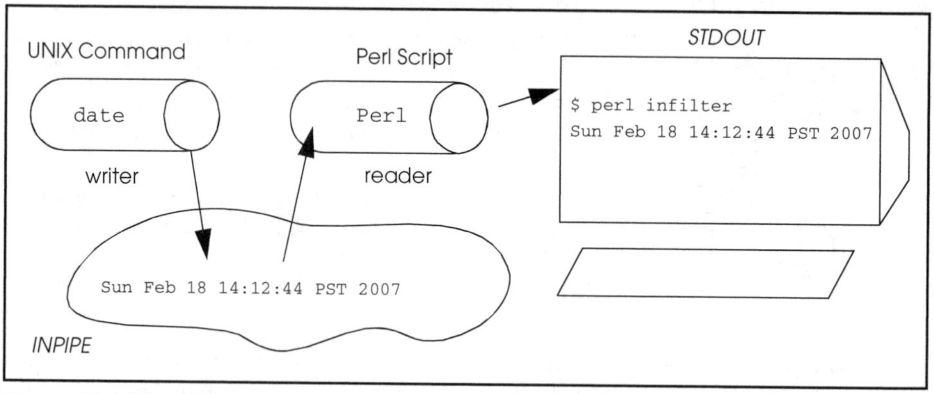

Figure 10.3 Perl input filter.

EXAMPLE 10.25

```
(The Script)
1   open(FINDIT, "find . -name 'perl*' -print |") ||
            die "Couldn't execute find!\n";
2   while( $filename = <FINDIT> ){
3       print $filename;
    }

(Output)
3   ./perl2
    ./perl3
    ./perl.man
    ./perl4
    ./perl5
    ./perl6
    ./perl7
    ./perlsub
    ./perl.arg
```

EXPLANATION

1. The output of the UNIX *find* command will be piped to the input filehandle *FINDIT*. When enclosed in angle brackets, the standard input will come from *FINDIT* instead of *STDIN*. If the open fails, the *die* operator will print *Couldn't execute find!* and exit the script.
2. The output from the UNIX *find* command has been piped into the filehandle *FINDIT*. For each iteration of the *while* loop, one line from the *FINDIT* filehandle will be assigned to the scalar variable *$filename*.
3. The *print* function prints the value of the variable *$filename* to the screen.

EXAMPLE 10.26

```
(The Script)
    # Opening an input filter on a Win32 platform
1   open(LISTDIR, 'dir "C:\perl" |') || die;
2   @filelist = <LISTDIR>;
3   foreach  $file ( @filelist ){
        print $file;
    }

(Output)
 Volume in drive C is 010599
 Volume Serial Number is 2237-130A

 Directory of C:\perl

03/31/1999  10:34p       <DIR>          .
03/31/1999  10:34p       <DIR>          ..
03/31/1999  10:37p               30,366 DeIsL1.isu
03/31/1999  10:34p       <DIR>          bin
03/31/1999  10:34p       <DIR>          lib
03/31/1999  10:35p       <DIR>          html
03/31/1999  10:35p       <DIR>          eg
03/31/1999  10:35p       <DIR>          site
               1 File(s)         30,366 bytes
               7 Dir(s)     488,873,984 bytes free
```

EXPLANATION

1. The output of the Windows *dir* command will be piped to the input filehandle *LISTDIR*. When enclosed in angle brackets, the standard input will come from *dir* instead of *STDIN*. If the open fails, the *die* operator will print an error and exit the script.
2. The output from the Windows *dir* command has been piped into the filehandle *LISTDIR*. The input is read from the filehandle and assigned to the array *@filelist*. Each element of the array represents one line of input.
3. The *foreach* loop iterates through the array, printing one line at a time until the end of the array.

10.2 Passing Arguments

10.2.1 The *ARGV* Array

How does Perl pass command-line arguments to a Perl script? If you are coming from a *C*, *awk*, or *C* shell background, at first glance you might think, "Oh, I already know this!" Beware! There are some subtle differences. So again, read on.

Perl does store arguments in a special array called *ARGV*. The subscript starts at zero and, unlike *C* and *awk*, *ARGV[0]* does **not** represent the name of the program; it represents the name of the first word after the script name. Like the shell languages, the *$0* special variable is used to hold the name of the Perl script. Unlike the *C* shell, the *$#ARGV* variable contains the number of the last subscript in the array, **not** the number of elements in the array. The number of arguments is *$#ARGV + 1*. *$#ARGV* initially has a value of *–1*.

When *ARGV*, the filehandle, is enclosed in angle brackets, *<ARGV>*, the command-line argument is treated as a filename. The filename is assigned to *ARGV* and the *@ARGV* array is shifted immediately to the left by one, thereby shortening the *@ARGV* array.

The value that is shifted off the *@ARGV* array is assigned to *$ARGV*. *$ARGV* contains the name of the currently selected filehandle.

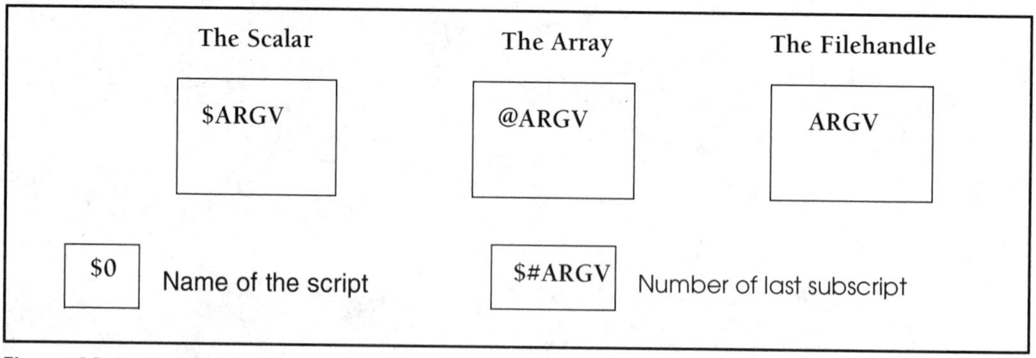

Figure 10.4 The many faces of *ARGV*.

EXAMPLE 10.27

```
(The Script)
   #!/usr/bin/perl
   die "$0 requires an argument.\n" if $#ARGV < 0;
                                  # Must have at least one argument
      print "@ARGV\n";            # Print all arguments
      print "$ARGV[0]\n";         # Print first argument
      print "$ARGV[1]\n";         # Print second argument
      print "There are ", $#ARGV + 1," arguments.\n";
                                   # $#ARGV is the last subscript
      print "$ARGV[$#ARGV] is the last one.\n";  # Print last arg
```

EXAMPLE 10.27 (CONTINUED)

```
(Output)
    $ perl.arg
2   perl.arg requires an argument.

    $ perl.arg f1 f2 f3 f4 f5
2   f1 f2 f3 f4 f5
3   f1
4   f2
5   There are 5 arguments.
6   f5 is the last one.
```

EXPLANATION

1. If there are no command-line arguments, the *die* function is executed and the script is terminated. The *$0* special variable holds the name of the Perl script, *perl.arg*.
2. The contents of the *@ARGV* array are printed.
3. The first argument, not the script name, is printed.
4. The second argument is printed.
5. The *$#ARGV* variable contains the number value of the last subscript. Since the subscript starts at zero, *$#ARGV + 1* is the total number of arguments, not counting the script name.
6. Since *$#ARGV* contains the value of the last subscript, *$ARGV[$#ARGV]* is the value of the last element of the *@ARGV* array.

10.2.2 *ARGV* and the Null Filehandle

When used in loop expressions and enclosed in the input angle brackets (<>), each element of the *ARGV* array is treated as a **special filehandle**. Perl shifts through the array, storing each element of the array in a variable *$ARGV.* A set of empty angle brackets is called the **null filehandle**, and Perl implicitly uses each element of the *ARGV* array as a filehandle. When using the input operators <>, either with or without the keyword *ARGV,* Perl shifts through its arguments one at a time, allowing you to process each argument in turn. Once the *ARGV* filehandle has been opened, the arguments are shifted off one at a time, so if they are to be used later, they must be saved in another array.

EXAMPLE 10.28

```
(The Text Files)
$ cat f1
Hello there. Nice day.
$ cat f2
Are you sure about that?
```

EXAMPLE 10.28 (CONTINUED)

```
$ cat f3
This is it.
This is the end.

(The  Script)
1   while( <ARGV> ) {print ;}
2   print "The value of \$ARGV[0] is $ARGV[0].\n";

(Output)
$ argv.test f1 f2 f3
Hello there. Nice day.
Are you sure about that?
This is it.
This is the end.
The value of $ARGV[0] is .
```

EXPLANATION

1. This will print the contents of all the files named at the command line. Once used, the argument is shifted off. The contents of *f1*, *f2*, and *f3* are read and then printed, respectively.
2. Since the arguments were all shifted off, *$ARGV[0]* has no value and, therefore, nothing is printed.

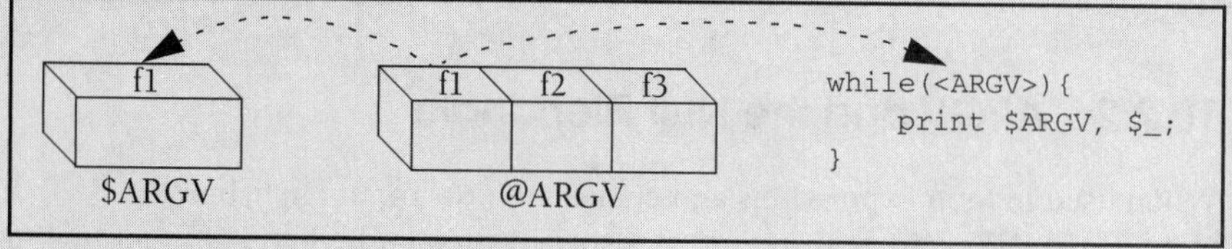

EXAMPLE 10.29

```
(The Text File: emp.names)
Steve Blenheim
Betty Boop
Igor Chevsky
Norma Cord
Jon DeLoach
Karen Evich
```

EXAMPLE 10.29 (CONTINUED)

```
(The Script)
     # Scriptname: grab.pl
     # Program will behave like grep -- will search for a pattern
     # in any number of files.
1    if ( ($#ARGV  < 1 ) {die "Usage: $0 pattern filename(s) \n";}
2    $pattern = shift;
3    while($line=<ARGV>){
         print "$ARGV: $.:  $line" if $line =~ /$pattern/i;
         close(ARGV) if eof;
     }

(Output)
     $ grab.pl
1    Usage: grab.pl pattern filenames(s)
     $ grab.pl 'norma' db
2    db:5: Norma Cord
     $ grab.pl 'Sir Lancelot' db
3    db:4: Sir Lancelot
     $ grab.pl '^.... ' db
4    db:3: Lori Gortz
     $ grab.pl Steve d*
5    datebook.master:12: Johann Erickson:Stevensville, Montana
     datafile:8: Steven Daniels:496-456-5676:83755:11/12/56:20300
     db:1: Steve Blenheim
```

EXPLANATION

1. If there are no command-line arguments, the *die* function is executed.
2. The first argument is shifted from the *@ARGV* array. This should be the pattern that will be searched for.
3. Since the first argument was shifted off the *@ARGV* array and assigned to the scalar *$pattern*, the remaining arguments passed in from the command line are assigned in turn to the *ARGV* filehandle. When the *while* loop is entered, a line is read and assigned to *$line*.
4. The *$ARGV* scalar holds the name of the file that is currently being processed. The $. variable holds the current line number. If the value in *$pattern* is matched, the filename where it was found, the number of the line where the pattern was found, and the line itself are printed. The *i* after the last delimiter in the pattern turns off case sensitivity.
5. When the file being processed reaches the end of file (EOF), the *ARGV* filehandle is closed. This causes the $. variable to be reset. If *ARGV* is not closed explicitly here, the $. variable will continue to increment and not be set back to *1* when the next file is read.

EXAMPLE 10.30

```
(The Script)
1   unless ( $#ARGV == 0 ){ die "Usage: $0 <argument>: $!"; }
2   open(PASSWD, "etc/passwd") || die "Can't open: $!";
3   $username=shift(@ARGV);
4   while( $pwline = <PASSWD>){
5       unless ( $pwline =~ /$username:/){ die "$username is not
                                           a user here.\n";}

    }
6   close PASSWD;
7   open(LOGGEDON, "who |" ) || die "Can't open: $!" ;
8   while($logged = <LOGGEDON> ){
       if ( $logged =~ /$username/){ $logged_on = 1; last;}
    }
9   close LOGGEDON;
    die "$username is not logged on.\n" if ! $logged_on;
    print "$username is logged on and running these processes.\n";
10  open(PROC, "ps -aux|" ) || die "Can't open: $! ";
    while($line=<PROC>){
       print "$line" if  $line =~ /$username:/;
    }
11  close PROC;
    print '*' x 80; "\n";
    print "So long.\n";

(Output)
    $ checkon
1   Usage: checkon <argument>:  at checkon line 6.
    $ checkon joe
5   Joe is not a user here.
    $ checkon ellie
8   ellie is logged on and running these processes:
ellie   3825  6.4  4.5  212  464 p5 R    12:18    0:00 ps -aux
ellie   1383  0.8  8.4  360  876 p4 S    Dec 26 11:34 /usr/local/OW3/bin/xview
ellie   173   0.8 13.4 1932 1392 co S    Dec 20389:19 /usr/local/OW3/bin/xnews
ellie   164   0.0  0.0  100    0 co IW   Dec 20   0:00 -c
                < some of the output was cut to save space >
ellie   3822  0.0  0.0    0    0 p5 Z    Dec 20   0:00 <defunct>
ellie   3823  0.0  1.1   28  112 p5 S    12:18    0:00 sh -c ps -aux | grep '^'
ellie   3821  0.0  5.6  144  580 p5 S    12:18    0:00 /bin/perl checkon ellie
ellie   3824  0.0  1.8   32  192 p5 S    12:18    0:00 grep ^ellie
ellie   3815  0.0  1.9   24  196 p4 S    12:18    0:00 script checkon.tsc
********************************************************************************
```

EXPLANATION

1 This script calls for only one argument. If *ARGV* is empty (i.e., no arguments are passed at the command line), the *die* function is executed and the script exits with an error message. (Remember: *$#ARGV* is the number of the last subscript in the *ARGV* array, and *ARGV[0]* is the first argument, not counting the name of the script, which is *$0*.) If more than one argument is passed, the script will also exit with the error message.
2 The */etc/passwd* file is opened for reading via the *PASSWD* filehandle.
3 The first argument is shifted from *@ARGV* and assigned to *$username*.
4 Each time the *while* loop is entered, a line of the */etc/passwd* file is read via the *PASSWD* filehandle.
5 The =~ is used to test if the first argument passed matches the *$username*. If a match is not found, the loop is exited.
6 The filehandle is closed.
7 The filehandle *LOGGEDON* is opened as an input filter. Output from the UNIX *who* command will be piped to the filehandle.
8 Each line of the input filter is tested. If the user is logged on, the scalar *$logged_on* is set to *1*, and the loop is exited.
9 The input filter is closed.
10 The filehandle *PROC* is opened as an input filter. Output from the UNIX *ps* command will be piped to the filehandle. Each line from the filter is read in turn and placed in the scalar *$line*. If *$line* contains a match for the user, that line will be printed to *STDOUT*, the screen.
11 The filter is closed.

10.2.3 The *eof* Function

The *eof* function can be used to test if end of file has been reached. It returns *1* if either the next read operation on a *FILEHANDLE* is at the end of the file or the file was not opened. Without an argument, the *eof* function returns the *eof* status of the last file read. The *eof* function with parentheses can be used in a loop block to test the end of file when the last filehandle has been read. Without parentheses, each file opened can be tested for end of file.

FORMAT

```
eof(FILEHANDLE)
eof()
eof
```

EXAMPLE 10.31

```
(The Text File: emp.names)
Steve Blenheim
Betty Boop
Igor Chevsky
Norma Cord
Jon DeLoach
Karen Evich

(In Script)
1   open ( DB, "emp.names") || die "Can't open emp.names: $!";
2   while(<DB>){
3       print if (/Norma/ .. eof);        # .. is the range operator
    }

(Output)
Norma Cord
Jonathan DeLoach
Karen Evitch
```

EXPLANATION

1. The file *emp.names* is opened via the *DB* filehandle.
2. The *while* loop reads a line at a time from the filehandle *DB*.
3. When the line containing the regular expression *Norma* is reached, that line and all lines in the range from *Norma* until *eof* (the end of file) are printed.

EXAMPLE 10.32

```
(The Text Files)
$ cat file1
abc
def
ghi

$ cat file2
1234
5678
9101112

(The Script)
    #!/usr/bin/perl
    # eof.p script
```

EXAMPLE 10.32 (CONTINUED)

```
1   while(<>){
2       print "$.\t$_";
3       if (eof){
            print "-" x 30, "\n";
4           close(ARGV);
        }
    }

(Output)
$ eof.p file1 file2
1   abc
2   def
3   ghi
    ------------------------------
1   1234
2   5678
3   9101112
    ------------------------------
```

EXPLANATION

1. The first argument stored in the *ARGV* array is *file1*. The null filehandle is used in the *while* expression. The file *file1* is opened for reading.
2. The $. variable is a special variable containing the line number of the currently opened filehandle. It is printed, followed by a tab and then the line itself.
3. If end of file is reached, print a row of 30 dashes.
4. The filehandle is closed in order to reset the $. value back to *1* for the next file that is opened. When *file1* reaches end of file, the next argument, *file2*, is processed, starting at line 1.

10.2.4 The *-i* Switch—Editing Files in Place

The *-i* option is used to edit files in place. The files are named at the command line and stored in the *@ARGV* array. Perl will automatically rename the output file to the same name as the input file. The output file will be the selected default file for printing. To ensure that you keep a backup of the original file, you can specify an extension to the *-i* flag, such as *-i.bak*. The original file will be renamed *filename.bak*. The file must be assigned to the *ARGV* filehandle when it is being read from. Multiple files can be passed in from the command line and each in turn will be edited in place.

EXAMPLE 10.33

```
(The Text File)
1   $ more names
    igor chevsky
    norma corder
    jennifer cowan
    john deloach
    fred fardbarkle
    lori gortz
    paco gutierrez
    ephram hardy
    james ikeda

(The Script)
2   #!/usr/bin/perl -i.bak
    # Scriptname: inplace

3    while(<ARGV>){    # Open ARGV for reading
4      tr/a-z/A-Z/;
5      print;     # Output goes to file currently being read in-place
6      close ARGV if eof;
    }

(Output)
7   $ inplace names
    $ more names
    IGOR CHEVSKY
    NORMA CORDER
    JENNIFER COWAN
    JOHN DELOACH
    FRED FARDBARKLE
    LORI GORTZ
    PACO GUTIERREZ
    EPHRAM HARDY
    JAMES IKEDA

8   $ more names.bak
    igor chevsky
    norma corder
    jennifer cowan
    john deloach
    fred fardbarkle
    lori gortz
    paco gutierrez
    ephram hardy
    james ikeda
```

EXPLANATION

1 The contents of the original text file, called *names*, is printed.
2 The *-i* in-place switch is used with an extension. The *names* file will be edited in place and the original file will be saved in *names.bak*.
3 The *while* loop is entered. The *ARGV* filehandle will be opened for reading.
4 All lowercase letters are translated to uppercase letters in the file being processed (*tr* function).
5 The *print* function sends its output to the file being processed in place.
6 The *ARGV* filehandle will be closed when the end of file is reached. This makes it possible to reset line numbering for each file when processing multiple files or to mark the end of files when appending.
7 The *names* file has been changed, illustrating that the file was modified in place.
8 The *names.bak* file was created as a backup file for the original file. The original file has been changed.

10.3 File Testing

Like the shells, Perl provides a number of file test operators (see Table 10.3) to check for the various attributes of a file, such as existence, access permissions, directories, files, and so on. Most of the operators return *1* for true and "" (null) for false.

A single underscore can be used to represent the name of the file if the same file is tested more than once. The *stat* structure of the previous file test is used.

Table 10.3 File Test Operators[a]

Operator	*Meaning*
–r $file	True if *$file* is a readable file.
–w $file	True if *$file* is a writeable file.
–x $file	True if *$file* is an executable file.
–o $file	True if *$file* is owned by effective uid.
–e $file	True if file exists.
–z $file	True if file is zero in size.
–s $file	True if *$file* has nonzero size. Returns the size of the file in bytes.
–f $file	True if *$file* is a plain file.
–d $file	True if *$file* is a directory file.

Continues

Table 10.3 File Test Operators[a] **(continued)**

Operator	Meaning
–l $file	True if *$file* is a symbolic link.
–p $file	True if *$file* is a named pipe or *FIFO*.
–S $file	True if *$file* is a socket.
–b $file	True if *$file* is a block special file.
–c $file	True if *$file* is a character special file.
–u $file	True if *$file* has a *setuid* bit set.
–g $file	True if *$file* has a *setgid* bit set.
–k $file	True if *$file* has a sticky bit set.
–t $file	True if filehandle is opened to a *tty*.
–T $file	True if *$file* is a text file.
–B $file	True if file is a binary file.
–M $file	Age of the file in days since modified.
–A $file	Age of the file in days since last accessed.
–C $file	Age of the file in days since the inode changed.

a. If a filename is not provided, $_ is the default.

EXAMPLE 10.34

```
(At the Command Line)
1   $ ls -l perl.test
    -rwxr-xr-x  1 ellie          417 Apr 23 13:40 perl.test
2   $ ls -l afile
    -rws--x--x  1 ellie            0 Apr 23 14:07 afile

(In Script)
    #!/usr/bin/perl
    $file=perl.test;

3   print "File is readable\n" if -r  $file;
    print "File is writeable\n" if -w  $file;
    print "File is executable\n" if -x  $file;
    print "File is a regular file\n" if -f  $file;
    print "File is a directory\n" if -d $file;
    print "File is text file\n" if -T $file;
    printf "File was last modified %f days ago.\n", -M $file;
    print "File has been accessed in the last 12 hours.\n" if -M <= 12;
```

EXAMPLE 10.34 (CONTINUED)

```
4   print "File has read, write, and execute set.\n"
            if -r $file && -w _ && -x _;
5   stat("afile");   # stat another file
    print "File is a set user id program.\n" if  -u _;
                     # underscore evaluates to last file stat'ed
    print "File is zero size.\n" if -z _;

(Output)
3   File is readable
    File is writeable
    File is executable
    File is a regular file
    *** No print out here because the file is not a directory ***
    File is text file
    File was last modified 0.000035 days ago.
    File has read, write, and execute set.
    File is a set user id program.
    File is zero size.
```

EXPLANATION

1. The permissions, ownership, file size, etc., on *perl.test* are shown.
2. The permissions, ownership, file size, etc., on *afile* are shown.
3. The *print* statement is executed if the file is readable, writeable, executable, etc.
4. Since the same file is checked for more than one attribute, an underscore is appended to the file test flag. The underscore references the *stat*[a] structure, an array that holds information about the file.
5. The *stat* function returns a 13-element array containing the statistics about a file. As long as the underscore is appended to the file test flag, the statistics for *afile* are used in the tests that follow.

a. Read more about the *stat* structure in Chapter 18, "Interfacing with the System."

10.4 What You Should Know

1. What is a filehandle?
2. What does it mean to open a file for reading?
3. When opened for writing, if the file exists, what happens to it?
4. What is the purpose of the *select()* function?
5. What is binmode?
6. What does the *die()* function accomplish when working with files?
7. How do Windows and UNIX differ in how they terminate a line?

8. What is an exclusive lock?
9. What does the *tell()* function return?
10. What is the difference between the +< and +> symbols?
11. What does the *stat()* function do?
12. How do you reposition the file pointer in a file?
13. How does the -M switch work when testing a file?

10.5 What's Next?

Until this point, all the functions you have used were provided by Perl. The *print()* and *printf()*, *push()*, *pop()*, *chomp()* functions are all examples of built-in functions. All you had to know was what they were supposed to do and how to use them. You did not have to know what the Perl authors did to make the function work; you just assumed they knew what they were doing. In the next chapter, you will write your own functions, also called subroutines, and learn how to send messages to them and return some result.

EXERCISE 10
Getting a Handle on Things

Exercise A

1. Create a filehandle for reading from the *datebook* file (on the CD); print to another filehandle the names of all those who have a salary greater than $50,000.

2. Ask the user to input data for a new entry in the *datebook* file. (The name, phone, address, etc., will be stored in separate scalars.) Append the newline to the *datebook* file by using a user-defined filehandle.

Exercise B

1. Sort the *datebook* file by names, using a pipe.

2. Create a filehandle with the *open* function that uses a pipe to list all the files in your current directory and will print only those files that are readable text files. Use the *die* function to quit if the *open* fails.

3. Rewrite the program to test if any of the files listed have been modified in the last 12 hours. Print the names of those files.

Exercise C

1. Create a number of duplicate entries in the *datebook* file. *Fred Fardbarkle*, for example, might appear five times, and *Igor Chevsky* three times, etc. In most editors, this will be a simple copy/paste operation.

   Write a program that will assign the name of the *datebook* file to a scalar and check to see if the file exists. If it does exist, the program will check to see if the file is readable and writeable. Use the *die* function to send any errors to the screen. Also tell the user when the *datebook* was last modified.

   The program will read each line of the *datebook* file giving each person a 10% raise in salary. If, however, the person appears more than once in the file (assume having the same first and last name means it is a duplicate), he will be given a raise the first time, but if he appears again, he will be skipped over. Send each line of output to a file called *raise*. The *raise* file should not contain any person's name more than once. It will also reflect the 10% increase in pay.

Display on the screen the average salary for all the people in the *datebook* file. For duplicate entries, print the names of those who appeared in the file more than once and how many times each appeared.

2. Write a script called *checking* that will take any number of filenames as command-line arguments and will print the names of those files that are readable and writeable text files. The program will print an error message if there are no arguments, and exit.

chapter

11

How Do Subroutines Function?

11.1 Subroutines/Functions

In addition to the large number of Perl functions already available, you can create your own functions or subroutines. Some languages distinguish between the terms **function** and **subroutine**. Perl doesn't. If you say "subroutine," everyone will know you are talking about a "function," and if you say "function," everyone will know you are talking about a "subroutine."[1] Technically, a function is a block of code that returns a value, whereas a subroutine is a block of code that performs some task, but doesn't return anything. Perl subroutines and functions can do both, so we'll use the two terms interchangeably in this text. For now, we'll use the term "subroutine" when referring to user-defined functions.

Subroutines are self-contained units of a program designed to accomplish a specified task, such as calculating a mortgage payment, retrieving data from a database, or checking for valid input. When a subroutine is called in a program, it is like taking a detour from the main part of the program. Perl starts executing the instructions in the subroutine and when finished, returns to the main program and picks up where it left off. Subroutines can be used over and over again and thus save you from repetitious programming. They are also used to break up a program into smaller modules to keep it better organized and easier to maintain.

The subroutine declaration consists of one or more statements enclosed in a block, independent of your program and not executed until it is called. It is often referred to as a "black box." Information goes into the black box as input (like the calculator or remote control when you push buttons), and the action or value returned from the box is its output (such as a calculation or a different channel). What goes on inside the box is transparent to the user. The programmer who writes the subroutine is the only one who cares about those details. When you use Perl's built-in functions, such as *print()* or *rand()*, you send a string of text or a number to the function, and it sends something back.

---

1. You could even change the title of this chapter to, "How Do Functions Subroutine?" but some people might frown.

You don't care how it does its job; you just expect it to work. If you send bad input, you get back bad output or maybe nothing; hence the expression "Garbage in, garbage out."

The scope of a subroutine is where it is visible in the program. Subroutines are global and can be placed anywhere in the script, even in another file. When coming from another file, they are loaded into the script with the *do*, *require*, or *use* keywords. All variables created within a subroutine or accessed by it are also global unless specifically made local with either the *local* or *my* operators.

The subroutine is called, or invoked, by prefixing the subroutine name with an ampersand (&), by prefixing the subroutine with the *do* function,[2] or by appending a set of empty parentheses to the subroutine name. If a forward reference is used, neither ampersands nor parentheses are needed to call the subroutine.

If a nonexistent subroutine is called, the program quits with an error message: *Undefined subroutine in "main::prog"* .... If you want to check whether the subroutine has been defined, you can do so with the built-in *defined* function.

The return value of a subroutine is the value of the last expression evaluated (either a scalar or an array). The *return* function can be used explicitly to return a value or to exit from the subroutine early due to the result of testing some condition.

If the call to the subroutine is made part of an expression, the returned value can be assigned to a variable, thus emulating a function call.

FORMAT

```
Subroutine declaration:
    sub subroutine_name;
Subroutine definition:
    sub subroutine_name { Block }
Subroutine call:
    do subroutine_name;
    &subroutine_name;
    subroutine_name();
    subroutine_name;
Subroutine call with parameters:
    &subroutine_name(parameter1, parameter2, ... )
    subroutine_name(parameter1, parameter2, ... )
```

11.1.1 Defining and Calling a Subroutine

A **declaration** simply announces to the Perl compiler that a subroutine is going to be defined in the program and may take specified arguments. Declarations are global in scope; in other words, they are visible no matter where you put them in the program although it is customary to put declarations at the beginning or end of the program, or in another file. A subroutine **definition** is a block of statements that follows the subroutine name. A subroutine that has not been explicitly declared is declared at the same time it is defined.

---

2. The primary use of the *do* function was to include Perl subroutines from the Perl 4 library (e.g., *do'pwd.pl'*).

Declaration: *sub name_of_subroutine;*
Definition: *sub name_of_subroutine { statement; statement; }*

A subroutine can be defined anywhere in your program or even in another file. The subroutine consists of the keyword *sub* followed by an opening curly brace, a set of statements, and ending in a closing curly brace.

The subroutine and its statements are not executed until called. You can call a subroutine by preceding its name with an ampersand or by attaching a set of empty parentheses after its name or by doing neither and calling it as a built-in function. If you call the subroutine with neither the ampersand nor parentheses, then you must declare it first.

EXAMPLE 11.1

```
(The Script)
1   sub greetme { print "Welcome, Välkommen till, Bienvenue!\n";}
2   &greetme if defined &greetme;
3   print "Program continues....\n";
4   &greetme;   # Call to subroutine
5   print "More program here.\n";
6   &bye;
7   sub bye { print "Bye, adjo, adieu.\n"; }
8   &bye;

(Output)
2   Welcome, Välkommen till, Bienvenue!
3   Program continues....
4   Welcome, Välkommen till, Bienvenue!
5   More program here.
    Bye, adjo, adieu.
    Bye, adjo, adieu.
```

EXPLANATION

1. This is a subroutine definition consisting of the keyword *sub*, followed by the name of the subroutine, *greetme*, and a block of statements that will be executed when the subroutine is called. Officially, the subroutine name is preceded by an ampersand (&), but the only time you really need the ampersand is when calling the subroutine or when using its name to create a reference or as an argument to a function, such as *defined*. This definition can be placed anywhere in your program and will do nothing until it is called. In this example, there is only one *print* statement that will be executed when the function is called.
2. The subroutine *greetme* is called by placing an ampersand (&) in front of its name. The term "invoke" a subroutine is often used to mean "call" the subroutine.The *defined* built-in function is used to check that the subroutine has been defined. When using the subroutine's name, the ampersand is required. When called, the program will jump into the subroutine and start executing the statements defined there; in this case, the *Welcome* statement.

EXPLANATION (CONTINUED)

3 After the subroutine is called (invoked), program execution starts at the line right after where it was called and continues from there.
4 The subroutine *greetme* is called again.
5 The program resumes execution after the subroutine exits on line 4.
6 The subroutine *bye* is called. The definition is found later on line 7.
7 Subroutine *bye* is defined. No matter where subroutines are placed, the compiler sees them.
8 Subroutine *bye* is called.

A Null Parameter List. If the subroutine name is followed by parentheses (null parameter list), it can also be called without the ampersand.

EXAMPLE 11.2

```
  #!/usr/bin/perl
1 $name="Ellie";
2 print "Hello $name.\n";

3 bye();     # Without parens or an ampersand, bye would be a bareword
             # causing a warning message when -w is used.
4 sub bye{
5    print "Bye $name.\n";
  }
```

Forward Reference. A forward reference announces to the compiler that the subroutine has been defined somewhere in the program. The ampersand is not needed to call a subroutine if it has been forward referenced.

EXAMPLE 11.3

```
  #!/usr/bin/perl
1 sub bye;   # Forward reference

  $name="Ellie";
2 print "Hello $name.\n";

3 bye;       # Call subroutine without the ampersand

4 sub bye{
5    print "Bye $name\n";
  }
```

EXAMPLE 11.3 (CONTINUED)

```
(Output)
2   Hello Ellie.
5   Bye Ellie
```

Scope of Variables. Scope describes where a variable is visible in your program. Perl variables are global in scope. They are visible throughout the entire program, even in subroutines. If you declare a variable in a subroutine, it is visible to the entire program. If you change the value of an already existing variable from within a subroutine, it will be changed when you exit the subroutine. A local variable is private to the block, subroutine, or file where it is declared. You must use either the *local* or *my* built-in functions to create local variables, since, by default, Perl variables are global in scope. (See "Call-by-Value with *local* and *my*" on page 332.)

EXAMPLE 11.4

```
(The Script)
    # Script: perlsub_sub2
    # Variables used in subroutines are global by default
1   sub bye { print "Bye $name\n"; $name="Tom";}
                                   # Subroutine definition
2   $name="Ellie";
3   print "Hello to you and yours!\n";
4   &bye;
5   print "Out of the subroutine. Hello $name.\n";
                                   # $name is now Tom
6   &bye;

(Output)
3   Hello to you and yours!
1   Bye Ellie
5   Out of the subroutine. Hello Tom.
1   Bye Tom
```

EXPLANATION

1 The subroutine *bye* is defined. Within the subroutine block, the variable *$name* is assigned the value *Tom*. *$name* is a global variable; in other words, it is visible throughout the program.[a]
2 Program execution starts here. Global variable *$name* is assigned the value *Ellie*.
3 This line is here just to show you the flow of execution.

a. We are assuming that the program was compiled into one package, *main*. For more on packages and scope, see Chapter 12, "Modularize It, Package It, and Send It to the Library!"

EXPLANATION (CONTINUED)

4 The subroutine *&bye* is called. The program jumps into the subroutine on line 1. The value of *$name* is still *Ellie*. After the line *Bye, Ellie* is printed, and the variable *$name* is assigned a new value, *Tom*. The subroutine exits and the program resumes execution at line 5.
5 The value of the global variable *$name* was changed in the subroutine.
6 The subroutine is called again. The value of *$name* is *Tom*.

11.2 Passing Arguments

If a user wants to send values to a subroutine, he calls the function with a comma-separated list of arguments enclosed in parentheses.

```
The feed_me function below takes 3 arguments when called:

@fruit=qw(apples pears peaches plums);  # Declare variables
$veggie="corn";

&feed_me( @fruit, $veggie, "milk" );  # Call subroutine with arguments
```

The arguments can be a combination of numbers, strings, references, variables, etc. They are received by the function in a special Perl array, called the @_ array, as a list of corresponding values called parameters.

```
sub feed_me{ print join(",", @_),"\n"; }
# Subroutine gets arguments in @_ array

Output:  apples, pears, peache, plums, corn, milk
```

Call-by-Reference and the @_ Array. Arguments, whether scalar values or lists, are passed into the subroutine and stored in the @_ array. The @_ array is a local array whose values are implicit references to the actual parameters. If you modify the @_ array, you will modify the actual parameters. However, if you shift or pop off elements of the @_ array, you merely lose the reference to the actual parameters. (See "Call-by-Value with *local* and *my*" on page 332.)

When arrays or scalars are passed to a subroutine, the default in Perl is **call-by-reference**. The @_ is a special local array used for referencing the names of the formal arguments. Its values can be changed, thus changing the value of the actual parameters. The elements of the @_ array are *$_[0]*, *$_[1]*, *$_[2]*, and so on. If a scalar variable is passed, its value is the first element of the @_ array, *$_[0]*. Perl doesn't care if you don't use all the parameters passed or if you have an insufficient number of parameters. If you shift or pop the @_ array, you merely lose your reference to the actual arguments. If you want to modify the global copy rather than the local @_ array, then you can use either **typeglobs** (symbolic references) or **pointers** (hard references). Hard references are discussed briefly in section 11.3.2 on page 349 and in more detail in Chapter 13, "Does This Job Require a Reference?"

EXAMPLE 11.5

```
(The Script)
    # Passing arguments
1   $first="Charles";
    $last="Dobbins";
2   &greeting ( $first, $last );
3   sub greeting{
4       print "@_", "\n";
5       print "Welcome to the club, $_[0] $_[1]!\n";
6   }

(Output)
4   Charles Dobbins
5   Welcome to the club, Charles Dobbins!
```

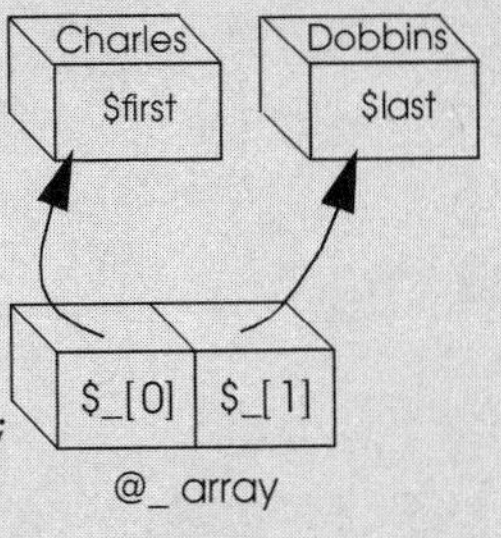

EXPLANATION

1 Scalars are assigned values.
2 The *greeting* subroutine is called with two parameters, *$first* and *$last*.
3 The subroutine is declared.
4 The parameters are stored in the @_ array, a local array that is created when the subroutine is entered and is removed when the subroutine exits. It contains references to the *$first* and *$last*.
5 The first two elements of the @_ array are printed. The individual elements are represented as scalars *$_[0]* and *$_[1]*.
6 The closing curly brace marks the end of the subroutine definition. @_ will disappear.

EXAMPLE 11.6

```
(The Script)
    # Program to demonstrate how @_ references values.
1   sub params{
2       print 'The values in the @_ array are ', "@_\n";
3       print "The first value is $_[0]\n";
4       print "The last value is ", pop(@_),"\n";
5       foreach $value ( @_ ) {
6           $value+=5;
            print "The value is $value", "\n";
        }
    }

    print "Give me 5 numbers : ";
7   @n=split(' ',<STDIN>);
8   &params(@n);
    print "Back in main\n";
9   print "The new values are @n \n";
```

EXAMPLE 11.6 (CONTINUED)

```
(Output)
    Give me 5 numbers: 1 2 3 4 5
2   The values in the @_ array are 1 2 3 4 5
3   The first value is 1
4   The last value is 5
    The value is 6
    The value is 7
    The value is 8
    The value is 9
9   Back in main
10  The new values are 6 7 8 9 5
```

EXPLANATION

1 The subroutine *params* is defined.
2 The value of @_, the actual parameter list, is printed. @_ is a local array referencing any arguments passed to the subroutine.
3 The first value of the @_ array is printed.
4 The last element of the array is removed with the *pop* function and then printed.
5 The *foreach* loop assigns, in turn, to scalar *$value* each element of the @_ array.
6 Each element of the array is incremented by 5 and stored in the scalar *$value.*
7 After the user has typed five numbers, the *split* function returns an array consisting of each of the numbers read from *STDIN.*
8 The subroutine is called, passing the array as a parameter.
9 The values printed illustrate that those values changed in the function were really changed. The only value that wasn't changed is the last element of the original array. The reference to it was popped in line 4 of the subroutine.

Call-by-Value with *local* and *my*. Most programming languages provide a way for you to pass arguments so that the original values are not altered by the subroutine. When an argument is passed using a **call-by-value**, a copy of the value of the argument is sent to the subroutine. If the copy is modified, the original value is untouched. To make copies of values in Perl, the arguments are copied from the @_ array and assigned to local variables. Perl provides two built-in functions, *local* and *my,* to create local copies.

The *local* Function

The *local* function was used to turn on call-by-value in Perl programs prior to the Perl 5 release. Now the *my* operator is used, which further ensures the privacy of variables within a function block.

The *local* function creates local variables from its list. Any variable declared with *local* is said to be dynamically scoped, which means it is visible from within the block where it was created and visible to any functions called from within this block or any blocks (or subroutines) nested within the block where it is defined. If a local variable has the same name as a global variable, the value of the global one is saved and a new local variable is

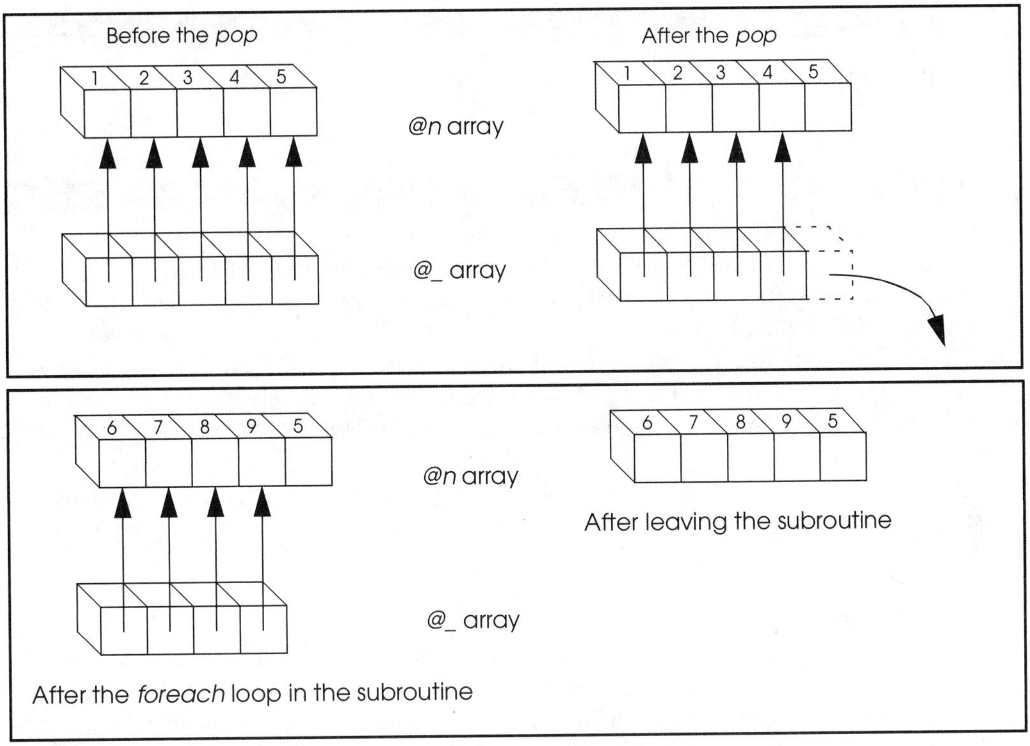

Figure 11.1 The @_ references the actual scalar parameters.

temporarily created. When the local variable goes out of scope, the global variable becomes visible again with its original value(s) restored. After the last statement in a subroutine is executed, its local variables are discarded. It is recommended that all local variables be set at the beginning of the subroutine block.

EXAMPLE 11.7

```
(The Script)
$first="Per";
$last="Lindberg";
&greeting ( $first, $last ) ;     # Call the greeting subroutine
print "---$fname---\n" if defined $fname;    # $fname is local to
                                             # sub greeting

# Subroutine defined
sub greeting{
    local ($fname, $lname) = @_ ;   # Call by value
    print "Welcome $fname!!\n";
}
```

EXAMPLE 11.7 (CONTINUED)

```
(Output)
3   <no output>
5   Welcome Per!!
```

EXPLANATION

1. The scalar variables are assigned values.
2. A call is made to the *greeting* subroutine. Two arguments are passed.
3. The *print* statement is not executed, because *$fname* is not defined here. It was defined as a local variable in the subroutine. It is local to the *greeting* subroutine.
4. The *local* function takes a list of arguments from the @_ array and creates two local variables, *$fname* and *$lname*, from that list. The values in the local variables are **copies** of the values that were passed. This mechanism is called "pass by value."
5. The *print* statement is executed. The contents of the local variable *$fname* are printed, which is a copy of what is in *$first*.

The *my* Operator

The *my* operator is also used to turn on *call-by-value* and is said to be lexically scoped. This means that variables declared as *my* variables are visible from the point of declaration to the end of the innermost enclosing block. That block could be a simple block enclosed in curly braces, a subroutine, *eval*, or a file. A variable declared with the *my* operator is created on a special scratch pad that is private to the block where it was created.[3]

Unlike the variables declared with the *local* function, any variables declared as *my* variables are visible only within the subroutine in which they are declared, not in any subroutines called from this subroutine. If more than one variable is listed, the list must be enclosed in parentheses. So, the subroutine in Example 11.7 could have been written as follows:

```
sub greeting{
    my ($fname, $lname) = @_ ;   # $fname and $lname are private
    print "Welcome $fname!!\n";
}
```

EXAMPLE 11.8

```
    (The Script)
    #  The scope of my variables
1   my $name = "Raimo";
```

3. See Chapter 12 for more on the *my* variables.

EXAMPLE 11.8 (CONTINUED)

```
2   print "$name\n";
3       {  # Enter block
4           print "My name is $name\n";
5           my $name = "Elizabeth";
6           print "Now name is $name\n";
7           my $love = "Christian";
8           print "My love is $love.\n";
9       }  # Exit block
10  print "$name is back.\n";
11  print "I can't see my love,$love, out here.\n";

(Output)
2   Raimo
5   My name is Raimo
6   Now name is Elizabeth
8   My love is Christian.
10  Raimo is back.
11  I can't see my love,, out here.
```

EXPLANATION

1. The *my* operator is used to create a lexical variable *$name* assigned the value *Raimo*. The variable is visible from the place where it is created and within any inner blocks. It is placed on its own private scratch pad.
2. The value of the lexical variable is printed.
3. A new block is entered.
4. The lexical variable, *$name*, is still in scope; i.e., visible.
5. A new lexical variable is declared. It gets its own private scratch pad.
6. The new variable, *$name*, is visible and its value is printed.
7. Another lexical variable is declared within the block and given its private scratch pad.
8. The value of *$love, Christian,* is printed. It is visible within this block.
9. The block ends here. The *my* variables will go out of scope.
10. The value of the *$name* variable is now visible. *Raimo* is printed.
11. The *$love* variable has gone out of scope.

EXAMPLE 11.9

```
(The Script)
    # Difference between my and local
    $friend="Louise";           # Global variables
    $pal="Danny";
    print "$friend and $pal are global.\n";
```

EXAMPLE 11.9 (CONTINUED)

```
4   sub guests {
5       my $friend="Pat"; # Lexically scoped variable
6       local $pal="Chris";  # Dynamically scoped variable
7       print "$friend and $pal are welcome guests.\n";
8       &who_is_it;          # Call subroutine
    }

9   sub who_is_it {
10      print "You still have your global friend, $friend, here.\n";
11      print "But your pal is now $pal.\n";  # Dynamically scoped
    }

12  &guests;                 # Call subroutine
13  print "Global friends are back: $friend and $pal.\n";
```

```
(Output)
3   Louise and Danny are global.
7   Pat and Chris are welcome guests.
10  You still have your global friend, Louise, here.
11  But your pal is now Chris.
12  Global friends are back: Louise and Danny.
```

EXPLANATION

1 The variable *$friend* is assigned a value, *Louise*. All variables are global within *main*.

2 The variable *$pal* is assigned a value, *Danny*. It is also global.

3 The values of the global variables are printed.

4 The subroutine *guests* is defined.

5 The *my* operator localizes the scalar *$friend* to this subroutine.

6 The *local* function localizes the variable *$pal* to this and all subroutines called from here.

7 The *$friend* and the *$pal* variables are printed in the *guests* subroutine.

8 The subroutine *who_is_it* is called.

9 The subroutine *who_is_it* is defined.

10 In the subroutine *who_is_it*, the global variable *$friend(Louise)* is visible. The lexical variable *$friend (Pat)* is declared as a *my* variable in the calling subroutine and is not visible in this subroutine.

11 The *local* scalar variable *$pal (Chris)*, on the other hand, was defined in the *guests* subroutine and is still visible in this subroutine, *who_is_it*.

12 The *guests* subroutine is called.

13 After exiting the subroutines, the global variables are back in scope and their values printed.

Using the *strict* Pragma (*my* and *our*). A pragma is a module that triggers a compiler to behave in a certain way. For example, if it detects something in your program it doesn't like, your program may be aborted. The *strict* pragma can be used to prevent the use of global variables in a program. When you use a global variable, even a variable declared with *local*, the compiler will complain if *strict* has been declared. Only lexically scoped variables are allowed. They are variables that are declared with either the *my* or *our* built-in functions. The *our* built-in (Perl 5.6+) is used when you need a global variable but still want to use the *strict* pragma to protect from the accidental use of global variables elsewhere in the program. (For more information about *strict* and packages, see "The *strict* Pragma" on page 403.)

EXAMPLE 11.10

```
(The Script)
1   use strict "vars";
2   my $name = "Ellie";              # my (lexical) variables are okay
3   @friends = qw(Tom Stefan Bin Marie);
                                     # global variables not allowed
4   local $newspaper = "The Globe"; # local variables are not allowed
5   print "My name is $name and our friends are @friends.\n";

(Output)
3   Global symbol "@friends" requires explicit package name at
       rigid.pl line 3.
4   Global symbol "$newspaper" requires explicit package name at
       rigid.pl line 4.
    In string, @friends now must be written as \@friends at rigid.pl
       line 5, near "$name and our friends our @friends"
    Global symbol "@friends" requires explicit package name at
       rigid.pl line 5.
    Execution of rigid.pl aborted due to compilation errors.
```

EXPLANATION

1. The *strict* pragma is used with *vars* as its argument. This tells the compiler to complain if it spots any global variables. The *strict* module, *strict.pm*, is part of the standard Perl distribution.
2. The variable *$name* is a lexically scoped *my* variable, which means it is private to the block where it is created. The *strict* pragma likes *my* variables.
3. The array *@friends* is a global variable. The compiler will complain when it sees global variables as shown in line 3 of the output. By *explicit package name*, the message is saying that you can still use this global variable if you precede its name with the package name and two colons; in other words, *@main::friends* is acceptable.
4. Perl classifies variables declared with the *local* function as dynamically allocated global variables. The compiler again complains because the variable is not declared with *my*. To still use the local variable, explicit means *local $main::newspaper.*
5. Due to compiler errors, the program never gets this far.

EXAMPLE 11.11

```
(The Script)
1   use strict "vars";
2   my $name = "Ellie";        # All variables are lexical in scope
3   our @friends = qw(Tom Stefan Bin Marie);
4   our $newspaper = "The Globe";
5   print "$name and $friends[0] read the $newspaper.\n";

(Output)
5   Ellie and Tom read the The Globe.
```

EXPLANATION

1. The *strict* pragma is declared with *vars* as its argument. This tells the compiler to complain if it spots any global variables. The *strict* module, *strict.pm*, is part of the standard Perl distribution.
2. The variable *$name* is a lexically scoped *my* variable; in other words, it is private to the block where it is created. The *strict* pragma likes *my* variables.
3. An *our* variable (Perl 5.6.0+) is disguised as a lexically scoped variable,[a] so the *strict* pragma overlooks it. This allows you to get away with using a global variable if you really need one.
4. The scalar is also an *our* variable. It is global and lexical, bypassing compiler warnings caused by the *strict* pragma.
5. The *print* function displays the values of the lexical variables.

a. Wall, L., Christianson, T., and Orwant, J., *Programming Perl*, 3rd ed., O'Reilly & Associates: Sebastopol, CA, 2000, p. 138.

11.2.1 Prototypes

A **prototype**, also described as a template, tells the compiler how many and what types of arguments the subroutine should get when it is called. It lets you treat your subroutine just like a Perl built-in function. The prototype is made part of a declaration and is handled at compile time. To call subroutines that have been declared with a prototype, the ampersand (&) must be omitted, or the subroutine will be treated like a normal user-defined subroutine rather than as a built-in, and the compiler will ignore the prototype.

```
Prototype: (Perl 5.003+)
    sub subroutine_name($$);
    Takes two scalar arguments

    sub subroutine_name(\@);
    Argument must be an array, preceded with an @ symbol

    sub subroutine_name($$;@)
    Takes two scalar arguments and an optional array.
    Anything after the semi-colon is optional.
```

EXAMPLE 11.12

```
    # Filename: prototypes
    # Testing prototyping
1   my $a=5;
    my $b=6;
    my $c=7;
2   @list=(100,200,300);
3   sub myadd($$) {        # myadd requires two scalar arguments
       my($x, $y)=@_;
       print $x + $y,"\n";
    }
4   myadd($a, $b);         # Okay
5   myadd(5, 4);           # Okay
6   myadd($a, $b, $c);     # Too many arguments

(Output)
6   Too many arguments for main::myadd at prototypes line 14,
       near "$c)" Execution of prototypes aborted due to compilation
       errors.11
```

EXPLANATION

1. Three scalar variables are declared and assigned values.
2. The array *@list* is assigned values.
3. The subroutine *myadd* is prototyped. Two scalar values are expected as parameters. Any more or less will cause a compiler error.
4. The subroutine is passed two scalar variables. This is okay.
5. The subroutine is passed two numbers. This is okay.
6. The subroutine was prototyped to take two scalars, but three are being passed here. The compiler sends an error message.

EXAMPLE 11.13

```
    # Prototypes
1   sub mynumbs(@$;$);        # Declaration with prototype
2   @list=(1,2,3);
3   mynumbs(@list, 25);
4   sub mynumbs(@$;$) {       # Match the prototypes
5      my ($scalar)=pop(@_);
6      my(@arr) = @_;
7      print "The array is: @arr","\n";
8      print "The scalar is $scalar\n";
    }

(Output)
7   The array is: 1 2 3
8   The scalar is: 25
```

EXPLANATION

1 This is a declaration with a prototype, asking for an array, a scalar, and an optional scalar. The semicolon is used to indicate that the argument is optional.
2 The array *@list* is assigned values.
3 The *mynumbs* subroutine is called with a list and a scalar value, *25*. Don't use an ampersand when calling prototyped subroutines.
4 The subroutine is defined. Even though the declaration of the subroutine on line 1 established the prototype, it must be repeated again here or the following error will appear:

   Prototype mismatch: sub main::mynumbs (@$;$) vs none at prototype line 19.

5 The last element from the @_array is popped off and assigned to *$scalar.*
6 The rest of the @_array is assigned to *@arr.*
7 The values of the array *@arr* are printed.
8 The value of *$scalar* is printed.

11.2.2 Return Value

The subroutine can act like a function when it is called; the function returns a scalar or a list. For example, a subroutine may be called from the right-hand side of an assignment statement. The subroutine can then send back a value to be assigned to a variable, either scalar or array.

```
$average = &ave(3, 5, 6, 20);
returned value   call to subroutine
```

The value returned is really the value of the last expression evaluated within the subroutine.

The *return* function can also be used to return a specified value or to return early from the subroutine based on some condition. If used outside a subroutine, the *return* function causes a fatal error. You could say that the *return* is to a subroutine what an *exit* is to a program. If you use the *exit* function in a subroutine, you will exit the entire program and return to the command line.

EXAMPLE 11.14

```
(The Script)
    #!/bin/perl
    sub MAX {
1       my($max) = shift(@_);
2       foreach $foo ( @_ ){
3           $max = $foo if $max < $foo;
            print $max,"\n";
        }
        print "------------------------------\n";
4       $max;
    }
    sub MIN {
        my($min) = pop( @_ );
        foreach $foo ( @_ ) {
            $min = $foo if $min > $foo;
            print $min,"\n";
        }
        print "------------------------------\n";
        return $min;
    }

5   my $biggest = &MAX ( 2, 3, 4, 10, 100, 1 );
6   my $smallest= &MIN ( 200, 2, 12, 40, 2, 20 );
7   print "The biggest is $biggest and the smallest is $smallest.\n";

(Output)
    3
    4
    10
    100
    100
    ------------------------------
    200
    2
    2
    2
    2
    ------------------------------
7   The biggest is 100 and the smallest is 2.
```

EXPLANATION

1. The scalar *$max* is assigned the value of the first element in the array @_. The *my* operator makes *$max* local to this subroutine. If *$max* is modified, the original copy is not affected.
2. For each element in the list, the loop will assign, in turn, an element of the list to the scalar *$foo*.

EXPLANATION (CONTINUED)

3 If *$max* is less than *$foo*, *$max* gets *$foo*.

4 Since the **last statement** executed in subroutine *MAX* is *$max*, the value of *$max* is returned and assigned to *$biggest* at line 5.

5 The scalar *$biggest* is assigned the value of the last expression in the *MAX* subroutine.

6 The scalar *$smallest* is assigned the return value from function *MIN*. The return function is explicitly used in subroutine *MIN*.

11.2.3 Context and Subroutines

We introduced "context" when discussing variables and operators. Now we will see how context applies to subroutines. There are two main contexts: *scalar* and *list*. When mixing data types, results differ when an expression is evaluated in one or the other context.

A good example of context is in array or scalar assignment. Consider the following statements:

```
@list = qw( apples pears peaches plums );   # List context
$number = @list;     # Scalar context
```

In list context, @list is assigned an array of the elements, but in scalar context, *$number*, produces the number of items in the array *@list*.

We have also seen context when using built-in Perl functions. Consider the *localtime* function. If the return value is assigned to a scalar, the date and time are returned as a string, but if the return value is assigned to an array, each element of the array represents a numeric value for the hour, minute, second, etc. The *print* function, on the other hand, expects to receive a list of arguments, list context. The built-in *scalar* function can be used to explicitly evaluate an expression in a scalar context as shown in Example 11.15.

EXAMPLE 11.15

```
   # Context
@now = localtime;   # List context
print "@now\n";    # Scalar context

$now = localtime;
print "$now\n";

print localtime, "\n"; # prints in list context
print scalar localtime,"\n"; # Forced to scalar context
```

EXAMPLE 11.15 (CONTINUED)

```
(Output)
2  30 40 9 23 3 107 1 112 1
4   Mon Apr 23 09:40:30 2007
5   2021123310711121
6   Mon Apr 23 11:02:20 2007
```

EXAMPLE 11.16

```
    # Context
1 print "What is your full name? ";

2 ($first, $middle, $last)=split(" ", <STDIN>);# STDIN scalar context

3 print "Hi $first $last.\n";

(Output)
2 What is your full name? Daniel Leo Stachelin
3 Hi Daniel Stachelin.
```

The *wantarray* Function and User-Defined Subroutines. "He took that totally out of context...." something you might say after hearing an argument based on a news story, the Bible, or a political speech. In Chapter 5, we discussed context, in Perl, which refers to how a variable and values are evaluated. For example, is the context list or scalar? There may be times when you want a subroutine to behave in a certain way based on the context in which it was called. This is where the built-in *wantarray* function can be used. You can use this function to determine whether the subroutine should be returning a list or a scalar. If your subroutine is called in list context (i.e., the return value will be assigned to an array), then *wantarray* will return true; otherwise, it will return false. If the context is to return no value (void context), *wantarray* returns the undefined value.

EXAMPLE 11.17

```
#!/usr/bin/perl

  print "What is your full name? ";
  chomp($fullname=<STDIN>);

1 @arrayname = title($fullname); # Context is array
  print "Welcome $arrayname[0] $arrayname[2]!\n";
```

EXAMPLE 11.17 (CONTINUED)

```
   print "What is the name of that book you are reading? ";
   chomp($bookname=<STDIN>);
2  $scalarname = title($bookname);   # Context is string
   print "The book $arrayname[0] is reading is $scalarname.\n";


3  sub title{
      # Function to capitalize the first character of each word
      # in a name and to return a string or an array of words
4     my $text=shift;
      my $newstring;
5     my$text=lc($text);
6     my @newtext=split(" ", $text); # Create a list of words
      foreach my $word ( @newtext ){
         $word = ucfirst($word); # Capitalize the first letter
7        $newstring .= "$word "; # Create a title string
      }
      @newarray = split(" ", $newstring);
8     # Split the string into an array
      chop($newstring); # Remove trailing whitespace

9     return wantarray ? @newarray : $newstring;  # Return either array
      # or scalar based on how the subroutine was called

   }
(Output)
   What is your full name? robert james taylor
   Welcome Robert Taylor!
   What is the name of that book you are reading? harry potter half
blood prince
   The book Robert is reading is Harry Potter Half Blood Prince.
```

11.3 Call-by-Reference

11.3.1 Symbolic References—Typeglobs

Definition. A **typeglob** is an alias for a variable; i.e., another name for a variable. It is called a **symbolic reference** and is analogous to a soft link in the UNIX filesystem. You can create an alias by prefixing the name of a Perl variable with a "*". The "*" represents all the different types of variables: scalar, array, hash, filehandle, subroutine, etc. It is another name for all identifiers on the symbol table with the same name. The name typeglob comes from the fact that it "globs" onto all datatypes with the same name. For example, **name* would represent *$name*, *@name*, *%name*, *&name*, etc.

Aliases were used predominantly in early (Perl 4) programs as a mechanism to pass parameters by reference and can still be used, although with the advent of hard references (see Chapter 13, "Does This Job Require a Reference?"), the practice of using typeglobs and aliases is much a thing of the past. Since there are a number of library routines that evolved during the early years of Perl, where typeglobs are still often found, and because they are used by Perl to build the symbol table for your program (see Chapter 12), they will be introduced here. (To see an example of how hard references are used with subroutines, see "Hard References—Pointers" on page 349, and for a complete discussion, see Chapter 13.)

Passing by Reference with Aliases. Aliases (or typeglobs) can be passed to functions to ensure true call-by-reference so that you can modify the global copy of the variable rather than the local copy stored in the @_ array. If you are passing an array or multiple arrays to a subroutine, rather than copying the entire array into the subroutine, you can pass an alias or a pointer. (See "Hard References—Pointers" on page 349.) To create an alias for a variable, an asterisk is prepended to the alias name, as in

```
*alias=*variable;
```

The asterisk represents all of the funny characters that prefix variables, including subroutines, filehandles, and formats. Typeglobs produce a scalar value that represents all objects with the same name; i.e., it "globs" onto all the symbols in the symbol table that have that name.[4] It is your job to determine what symbol you want the alias to reference. This is done by prepending the correct funny character to the alias name when you want to access its underlying value. For example:

Given: **alias = *var*
Then: *$alias* refers to the scalar *$var*
@alias refers to the array *@var*
$alias{string} refers to an element of a hash *%var*

If a filehandle is passed to a subroutine, a typeglob can be used to make the filehandle local.

Perl 5 improved the alias mechanism so that the alias can now represent one funny character rather than all of them and introduced an even more convenient method for passing by reference, the hard reference, or what you may recognize as a C-like pointer.

Making Aliases Private—*local* versus *my*. The names of variables created with the *my* operator are not stored on the symbol table but within a temporary scratch pad. The *my* operator creates a new variable that is private to its block. Since typeglobs are associated with the symbol table of a particular package, they cannot be made private with the *my* operator. To make typeglobs local, the *local* function must be used.

---

4. This is not the same as the globbing done for filename substitution, as in <*p**>.

EXAMPLE 11.18

```
(The Script)
    #!/usr/bin/perl
1   $colors="rainbow";
2   @colors=("red", "green", "yellow" );
3   &printit(*colors);                  # Which color is this?
4   sub printit{
5       local(*whichone)=@_;           # Must use local, not my with globs
6       print *whichone, "\n";          # The package is main
7       $whichone="Prism of Light";     # Alias for the scalar
8       $whichone[0]="PURPLE";          # Alias for the array
    }
9   print "Out of subroutine.\n";
10  print "\$colors is $colors.\n";
11  print "\@colors is @colors.\n";

Output)
6   *main::colors
9   Out of subroutine.
10  $colors is Prism of Light.
11  @colors is PURPLE green yellow.
```

EXPLANATION

1. The scalar *$colors* is assigned *rainbow.*
2. The array *@colors* is assigned three values: *red*, *green*, and *yellow.*
3. The *printit* subroutine is called. An alias for all symbols named *colors* is passed as a parameter. The asterisk creates the alias (typeglob).
4. The *printit* subroutine is defined.
5. The @_ array contains the alias that was passed. Its value is assigned with the local alias, **whichone. *whichone* is now an alias for any *colors* symbol.
6. Attempting to print the value of the alias itself tells you only that it is in the *main* package and is a symbol for all variables, subroutines, and filehandles called *colors.*
7. The scalar represented by the alias is assigned a new value.
8. The array represented by the alias, the first element of the array, is assigned a new value.
9. Out of the subroutine.
10. Out of the subroutine, the scalar *$colors* has been changed.
11. Out of the subroutine, the array *@colors* has also been changed.

EXAMPLE 11.19

```
(The Script)
    # Revisiting Example 11.6 -- Now using typeglob
1   print "Give me 5 numbers: ";
2   @n = split(' ', <STDIN>);
3   &params(*n);
```

EXAMPLE 11.19 (CONTINUED)

```
4   sub params{
5       local(*arr)=@_;
6       print 'The values of the @arr array are ', @arr, "\n";
7       print "The first value is $arr[0]\n";
8       print "the last value is ", pop(@arr), "\n";
9       foreach $value(@arr){
10          $value+=5;
11          print "The value is $value.\n";
        }
    }
    print "Back in main\n";
12  print "The new values are @n.\n";
```

```
(Output)
1   Give me 5 numbers: 1 2 3 4 5
6   The values in the @arr array are 12345
7   The first value is 1
8   The last value is 5
11  The value is 6
    The value is 7
    The value is 8
    The value is 9
    Back in main
12  The new values are 6 7 8 9  <--- Look here. Got popped this time!
```

EXPLANATION

1 The user is asked for input.
2 The user input is *split* on whitespace and returned to the @*n* array.
3 The subroutine *params* is called. An alias for any *n* in the symbol table is passed as a parameter.
4 The *params* subroutine is defined.
5 In the subroutine, the alias was passed to the @_ array. This value is assigned to a local typeglob, **arr*.
6 The values in the @*arr* array are printed. Remember, @*arr* is just an alias for the array @*n*. It refers to the values in the @*n* array.
7 The first element in the array is printed.
8 The last element of the array is popped, not just the reference to it.
9 The *foreach* loop assigns, in turn, each element of the @*arr* array to the scalar *$value*.
10 Each element of the array is incremented by 5 and stored in the scalar *$value*.
11 The new values are printed.
12 The values printed illustrate that those values changed in the function by the alias really changed the values in the @*n* array. See Example 11.6.

Passing Filehandles by Reference. The only way to pass a filehandle directly to a subroutine is by reference. You can use typeglob to create an alias for the filehandle or use a hard reference. (See Chapter 13, "Does This Job Require a Reference?" for more on hard references.)

EXAMPLE 11.20

```
(The Script)
    #!/bin/perl
1   open(READMEFILE, "f1") || die;
2   &readit(*READMEFILE);       # Passing a filehandle to a subroutine
    sub readit{
3       local(*myfile)=@_;      # myfile is an alias for READMEFILE
4       while(<myfile>){
            print;
        }
    }
```

EXPLANATION

1. The *open* function opens the UNIX file *f1* for reading and attaches it to the *READMEFILE* handle.
2. The *readit* subroutine is called. The filehandle is aliased with typeglob and passed as a parameter to the subroutine.
3. The local alias *myfile* is assigned the value of @_; i.e., the alias that was passed into the subroutine.
4. The alias is another name for *READMEFILE*. It is enclosed in angle brackets, and each line from the filehandle will be read and then printed as it goes through the *while* loop.

Selective Aliasing and the Backslash Operator. Perl 5 references allow you to alias a particular variable rather than all variable types with the same name. For example:

```
*array=\@array;
*scalar=\$scalar;
*hash=\%assoc_array;
*func=\&subroutine;
```

EXAMPLE 11.21

```
(The Script)
    # References and typeglob
1   @list=(1, 2, 3, 4, 5);
2   $list="grocery";
3   *arr = \@list;        # *arr is a reference only to the array @list
4   print @arr, "\n";
```

EXAMPLE 11.21 (CONTINUED)

```
5   print "$arr\n";          # Not a scalar reference
    sub alias {
6       local (*a) = @_;     # Must use local, not my
7       $a[0] = 7;
8       pop @a;
    }
9   &alias(*arr);         # Call the subroutine
10  print "@list\n";
11  $num=5;
12  *scalar=\$num;        # *scalar is a reference to the scalar $num
13  print "$scalar\n";

(Output)
4   1 2 3 4 5
5
10  7 2 3 4
13  5
```

EXPLANATION

1. The *@list* array is assigned a list of values.
2. The *$list* scalar is assigned a value.
3. The **arr* alias is another name for the array *@list*. **It is not an alias for any other type.**
4. The alias **arr* is used to refer to the array *@list*.
5. The alias **arr* does not reference a scalar. Nothing prints.
6. In the subroutine, the local alias **a* receives the value of the alias passed in as a parameter and assigned to the @_ array.
7. The array is assigned new value via the alias.
8. The last value of the array is popped off via the alias.
9. The subroutine is called, passing the alias **arr* as a parameter.
10. The *@list* values are printed reflecting the changes made in the subroutine.
11. The scalar *$num* is assigned a value.
12. A new alias is created. **scalar* refers only to the scalar *$num*.
13. The alias is just another name for the scalar *$num*. Its value is printed.

11.3.2 Hard References—Pointers

Passing values to a subroutine by reference with pointers is now a more common practice than using typeglobs. Before demonstrating how to do this, we will define a pointer, its syntax, and how to use it and then provide examples. For more on pointers and other uses for them, see Chapter 13.

Definition. A hard reference, commonly called a **pointer**, is a scalar variable that contains the address of another variable. The backslash operator (\) is used to create the pointer. When printing the value of the pointer, you see not only a hexadecimal address stored there but also the data type of the variable that resides at that address.

For example, if you write

```
$p = \$name;
```

then *$p* will be assigned the address of the scalar *$name*. *$p* is a reference to *$name*. The value stored in *$p*, when printed, looks like *SCALAR(0xb057c)*.

Since pointers contain addresses, they can be used to pass arguments by reference to a subroutine; and, because the pointer is simply a scalar variable, not a typeglob, it can be made a private, lexical *my* variable.

```
my $arrayptr=\@array;         # creates a pointer to an array
my $scalarptr=\$scalar;       # creates a pointer to a scalar
my $hashptr=\%assoc_array;    # creates a pointer to a hash
my $funcptr=\&subroutine;     # creates a pointer to a subroutine
```

Dereferencing the Pointer. If you print the value of the reference, you will see an address. If you want to go to that address and get the value stored there—i.e., dereference the pointer—the pointer must be prefaced by two funny symbols: one is the dollar sign because the pointer itself is a scalar, and preceding that, the funny symbol representing the type of data it points to. For example, if *$p* is a reference to a scalar *$x*, then *$$p* will get the value of *$x*, and if *$p* is a reference to an array *@x*, then *@$p* would get the values in *@x*. In both examples, the reference *$p* is preceded by the funny symbol representing the data type of the variable it points to. When using more complex types, the arrow (infix) operator can be used. (See "References and Anonymous Variables" on page 406 for more on the arrow operator.) Table 11.1 shows examples of creating and de-referencing pointers.

Table 11.1 Creating and Dereferencing Pointers

Assignment	***Create a Reference***	***Dereference***	***Dereference with Arrow***
$sca= 5;	*$p = \$sca;*	*print $$p;*	
@arr=(4,5,6);	*$p = \@arr;*	*print @$p;* *print $$p[0];*	*$p->[0]*
%hash=(key=>'value');	*$p = \%hash;*	*print %$p;* *print $$p{key};*	*$p->{key}*

EXAMPLE 11.22

```
(The Script)
    #!/bin/perl
1   $num=5;
2   $p = \$num;         # The backslash operator means "adddress of"
3   print 'The address assigned $p is ', $p, "\n";
4   print "The value stored at that address is $$p\n";
```

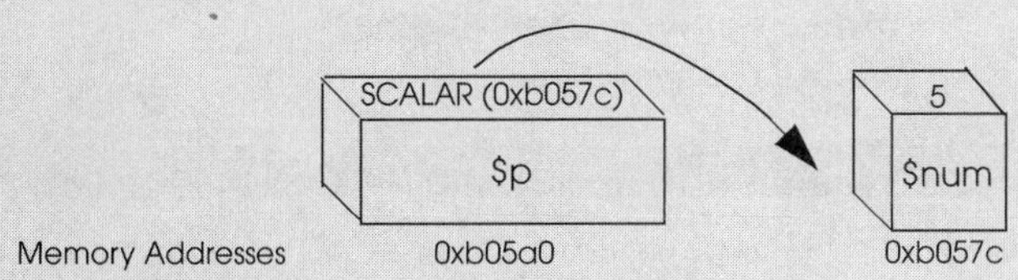


```
(Output)
3   The address assigned $p is SCALAR(0xb057c)
4   The value stored at that address is 5
```

EXPLANATION

1. The scalar *$num* is assigned the value 5.
2. The scalar *$p* is assigned the address of *$num*. The function of the backslash operator is to create the reference. *$p* is called either a **reference** or a **pointer** (the terms are interchangeable).
3. The address stored in *$p* is printed. Perl also tells you the data type is *SCALAR*.
4. To dereference *$p*, another dollar sign is prepended to *$p*. This dollar sign tells Perl that you are looking for the value of the scalar that *$p* references, which is *$num*.

EXAMPLE 11.23

```
(The Script)
1   @toys = qw( Buzzlightyear Woody Thomas Pokemon );
2   $num = @toys;
3   %movies=("Toy Story"=>"US",
             "Thomas"=>"England",
             "Pokemon"=>"Japan",
            );
4   $ref1 = \$num;          # Scalar pointer
5   $ref2 = \@toys;         # Array pointer
6   $ref3= \%movies;        # Hash pointer
7   print "There are $$ref1 toys.\n";    # Dereference pointers
8   print "They are: @$ref2.\n";
9   while( ($key, $value) = each ( %$ref3 )){
10     print "$key--$value\n";
    }
11  print "His favorite toys are $ref2->[0] and $ref2->[3].\n";
12  print "The Pokemon movie was made in $ref3->{'Pokemon'}.\n";
```

EXAMPLE 11.23 (CONTINUED)

```
(Output)
7   There are 4 toys.
8   They are: Buzzlightyear Woody Thomas Pokemon.
10  Thomas--England
    Pokemon--Japan
    Toy Story--US
11  His favorite toys are Buzzlightyear and Pokemon.
12  The Pokemon movie was made in Japan.
```

EXPLANATION

1 The array *@toys* is assigned a list.
2 The array *@toys* is assigned to the scalar variable *$num*, returning the number of elements in the array.
3 The hash *%movies* is assigned key/value pairs.
4 The reference *$ref1* is a scalar. It is assigned the address of the scalar *$num*. The backslash operator allows you to create the reference.
5 The reference *$ref2* is a scalar. It is assigned the address of the array *@toys*.
6 The reference *$ref3* is a scalar. It is assigned the address of the hash *%movies*.
7 The reference is dereferenced, meaning: Go to the address that *$ref1* is pointing to and print the value of the scalar stored there.
8 The reference is again dereferenced, meaning: Go to the address that *$ref2* is pointing to, get the array, and print it.
9 The built-in *each* function gets keys and values from the hash. The hash pointer, *$ref3*, is preceded by a percent sign; in other words, dereference the pointer to the hash.
10 Key/value pairs are printed from the hash *%movies*.
11 Dereference the pointer and get the first element and the fourth elements of the array. To dereference a pointer to an array, use the arrow (infix operator) and the subscript of the array element you are fetching. You could also use the form *$$ref2[0]* or *$$ref2[3]*, but it's not as easy to read or write.
12 The pointer is dereferenced using the arrow notation. Curly braces surround the hash key. You could also use the form *$$ref3{Pokemon}*.

Pointers as Arguments. When a subroutine receives parameters, they are stored in the special @_ array. For example, if you send two arrays to a subroutine, both arrays are stored in the @_ as a single list. There is really no way to separate the two arrays without knowing at least the size of the first one. However, if you send two pointers to the subroutine, they can/will contain the addresses of the original arrays and allow easy separation and dereferencing of those arrays. See Example 11.24.

EXAMPLE 11.24

```
(The Script)
# Passing by reference with pointers
@list1= (1..100);
@list2 = (5..200);

display(@list1, @list2); # Pass two arrays

print "-" x 35,"\n";

display(\@list1, \@list2); # Pass two pointers


sub display{
   print "@_\n";
}

(Output)
3   1 2 3 4 5 6 7 8 9 10 11 12 13 14 15 16 17 18 19 20 21 22 23 24
25 26 27 28 29 30 31 32 33 34 35  36 37 38 39  40 41 42 43 44 45 46 47
48 49 50 51  52 53 54 55  56 57 58 59 60 61 62 63 64 65 66 67

                    <continues>

  177 178 179 180 181 182 183 184 185 186 187 188 189 190 191 192
193 194 195 196 197 198 199 200
  -----------------------------------
4   ARRAY(0x182e048) ARRAY(0x182ea38)
```

Passing Pointers to a Subroutine

EXAMPLE 11.25

```
(The Script)
   # This script demonstrates the use of hard references
   # when passing arrays. Instead of passing the entire
   # array, a hard reference (pointer) is passed.
   # The value of the last expression is returned.

   my @list1=(1 .. 100);
   my @list2=(5, 10, 15, 20);

   print "The total is :  ", &addemup( \@list1, \@list2) , ".\n";
         # two pointers

   sub addemup{
      my( $arr1, $arr2) = (shift, shift) ;    # The two pointers
                                              # are shifted from @_
```

EXAMPLE 11.25 (CONTINUED)

```
6        my $total = 0;
7        print $arr1, "\n" ;
8        print $arr2, "\n";
9        foreach $num ( @$arr1, @$arr2 ){   # dereference the pointers
10           $total+=$num;
         }
11       $total;     # The expression is evaluated and returned
    }

(Output)
7   ARRAY(0x8a62d68)
8   ARRAY(0x8a60f2c)
3   The total is:  5100.
```

EXPLANATION

1 The array *@list1* is assigned values between *1* and *100*.
2 The array *@list2* is assigned four values.
3 The *&addemup* subroutine is called with two arguments. The backslash is used to create the pointers. The addresses of *@list1* and *@list2* are being passed.
4 The subroutine *&addemup* is declared.
5 The @_ array contains the two arguments just passed in. The arguments are shifted from the @_ into *my* variables *$arr1* and *$arr2*. They are pointers.
6 *$total* is assigned an initial value of *0*.
7 The value of the pointer is printed. It points to the array *@list1*.
8 The value of the pointer is printed. It points to the array *@list2*.
9 The *foreach* loop is entered and, by using the dereferenced pointers, each element from *@list1* and *@list2* assigned, in turn, to *$num* until all of the elements in both arrays have been processed.
10 Each value of *$num* is added on and assigned to the value in *$total* until the loop ends.
11 The sum of *$total* is returned to line 3, where it is passed as an argument to the *print* function and then printed.

11.3.3 Autoloading

The Perl *AUTOLOAD* function lets you check to see if a subroutine has been defined. The *AUTOLOAD* subroutine is called whenever Perl is told to call a subroutine and the subroutine can't be found. The special variable *$AUTOLOAD* is assigned the name of the undefined subroutine.

The *AUTOLOAD* function can also be used with objects to provide an implementation for calling unnamed methods. (A **method** is an object-oriented name for a subroutine.)

EXAMPLE 11.26

```
(The Script)
   #!/bin/perl
1  sub AUTOLOAD {
2      my(@arguments)=@_;
3      $args=join(', ', @arguments);
4      print "$AUTOLOAD was never defined.\n";
5      print "The arguments passed were $args.\n";
   }

6  $driver="Jody";
   $miles=50;
   $gallons=5;

7  &mileage($driver, $miles, $gallons);   # Call to an undefined
                                           # subroutine
(Output)
4  main::mileage was never defined.
5  The arguments passed were Jody, 50, 5.
```

EXPLANATION

1 The subroutine *AUTOLOAD* is defined.
2 The *AUTOLOAD* subroutine is called with the same arguments as would have been passed to the original subroutine called on line 7.
3 The arguments are joined by commas and stored in the scalar *$args*.
4 The name of the package and the subroutine that was originally called are stored in the *$AUTOLOAD* scalar. (For this example, *main* is the default package.)
5 The arguments are printed.
6 The scalar variables are assigned values.
7 The *mileage* subroutine is called with three arguments. Perl calls the *AUTOLOAD* function if there is a call to an undefined function, passing the same arguments as would have been passed in this example to the *mileage* subroutine.

EXAMPLE 11.27

```
    #!/bin/perl
    # Program to call a subroutine without defining it
1   sub AUTOLOAD {
2       my(@arguments) = @_;
3       my($package, $command)=split("::",$AUTOLOAD,  2);
4       return '$command @arguments';    # Command substitution
    }

5   $day=date("+%D");       # date is an undefined subroutine
6   print "Today is $day.\n";
7   print cal(3,2007);      # cal is an undefined subroutine
```

```
(Output)
Today is 03/26/07.

     March 2007
Su Mo Tu We Th Fr Sa
             1  2  3
 4  5  6  7  8  9 10
11 12 13 14 15 16 17
18 19 20 21 22 23 24
25 26 27 28 29 30 31
```

EXPLANATION

1. The subroutine *AUTOLOAD* is defined.
2. The *AUTOLOAD* subroutine is called with the same arguments as would have been passed to the original subroutine on lines 5 and 7.
3. The *$AUTOLOAD* variable is *split* into two parts by a double colon delimiter (::). The array returned consists of the package name and the name of the subroutine that was called.
4. The value returned is the name of the function called, which in the first case happens to be a UNIX command and its arguments. The backquotes cause the enclosed string to be executed as a UNIX command. Tricky!
5. The *date* function has never been defined. *AUTOLOAD* will pick its name and assign it to *$AUTOLOAD* in the *AUTOLOAD* function. The *date* function will pass an argument. The argument, *+%D*, is also an argument to the UNIX *date* command. It returns today's date.
6. The returned value is printed.
7. The *cal* function has never been defined. It takes two arguments. *AUTOLOAD* will assign *cal* to *$AUTOLOAD*. The arguments are *3* and *2003* assigned to *@arguments*. They will be passed to the *AUTOLOAD* function and used in line 4. After variable substitution, the backquotes cause the string to be executed. The UNIX command *cal 3 2003* is executed and the result returned to the *print* fucntion.

11.3.4 *BEGIN* and *END* Subroutines (Startup and Finish)

The *BEGIN* and *END* subroutines may remind UNIX programmers of the special *BEGIN* and *END* patterns used in the *awk* programming language. For *C++* programmers, the *BEGIN* has been likened to a constructor, and the *END* a destructor. The *BEGIN* and *END* subroutines are similar to both in functionality.

A *BEGIN* subroutine is executed immediately, before the rest of the file is even parsed. If you have multiple *BEGIN*s, they will be executed in the order they were defined.

The *END* subroutine is executed when all is done; that is, when the program is exiting, even if the *die* function caused the termination. Multiple *END* blocks are executed in reverse order.

The keyword *sub* is not necessary when using these special subroutines.

EXAMPLE 11.28

```
     #!/bin/perl
     # Program to demonstrate BEGIN and END subroutines
1    chdir("/stuff") || die "Can't cd: $!\n";
2    BEGIN{ print "Welcome to my Program.\n"};
3    END{ print "Bailing out somewhere near line ",__LINE__,
                                             " So long.\n"};

(Output)
Welcome to my Program.
Can't cd: No such file or directory
Bailing out somewhere near line 5. So long.
```

EXPLANATION

1. An effort is made to change directories to */stuff*. The *chdir* fails and the *die* is executed. Normally, the program would exit immediately, but this program has defined an *END* subroutine. The *END* subroutine will be executed before the program dies.
2. The *BEGIN* subroutine is executed as soon as possible; that is, as soon as it has been defined. This subroutine is executed before anything else in the program happens.
3. The *END* subroutine is always executed when the program is about to exit, even if a *die* is called. The line printed is there just for you *awk* programmers.

11.3.5 The *subs* Function

The *subs* function allows you to predeclare subroutine names. Its arguments are a list of subroutines. This allows you to call a subroutine without the ampersand or parentheses and to override built-in Perl functions.

EXAMPLE 11.29

```
   #!/bin/perl
   # The subs module
1  use subs qw(fun1 fun2 );

2  fun1;
3  fun2;

4  sub fun1{
       print "In fun1\n";
   }

5  sub fun2{
       print "In fun2\n";
   }

(Output)
In fun1
In fun2
```

EXPLANATION

1 The *subs* module is loaded (see "The *use* Function (Modules and Pragmas)" on page 378) into your program and given a list of subroutines.
2 *fun1* is called with neither an ampersand nor parentheses, because it was in the *subs* list. The function is not defined until later.
3 *fun2* is also called before it is defined.

11.4 What You Should Know

1. How to define and call a subroutine.
2. The difference between a function and a subroutine.
3. Where to put a subroutine definition in your Perl script.
4. How to pass arguments to a subroutine.
5. How Perl retrieves its parameter list.
6. Local versus global variables.

7. Difference between pass by value and pass by reference.
8. What is another name for a hard reference?
9. What is a typeglob?
10. The significance of the return statement.
11. What is prototyping?
12. What is autoloading?

11.5 What's Next?

In the next chapter, you will expand your horizons and go from the "introverted" Perl programmer to the "extroverted" programmer. Instead of writing stand-alone scripts, you will start learning how to use the libraries and modules already provided by Perl. You will explore CPAN and learn how to download and use modules that have been written my other programmers.

You will understand packages and namespaces and how to export and import symbols how to use the standard Perl library, and how to create your own. You will learn how to create procedural modules and how to store and use them.

EXERCISE 11
I Can't Seem to Function without Subroutines

1. Write a program called *tripper* that will ask the user the number of miles he has driven and the amount of gas he used. In the *tripper* script, write a subroutine called *mileage* that will calculate and return the user's mileage (miles per gallon). The number of miles driven and the amount of gas used will be passed as arguments. All variables should be *my* variables. Print the results. Prototype *tripper*.

2. Hotels are often rated by using stars to represent their score. A five-star hotel may have a king-size bed, a kitchen, and two TVs; a one-star hotel may have cockroaches and a leaky roof. Write a subroutine called *printstar* that will produce a histogram to show the star rating for hotels shown in the following hash. The *printstar* function will be given two parameters: the name of the hotel and the number of its star rating. (Hint: sort the hash keys into an array. Use a loop to iterate through the keys, calling the *printstar* function for each iteration.)

```
%hotels=("Pillowmint Lodge" => "5",
         "Buxton Suites"    => "5",
         "The Middletonian" => "3",
         "Notchbelow"       => "4",
         "Rancho El Cheapo" => "1",
         "Pile Inn"         => "2",
        );
```

```
(OUTPUT)
Hotel                   Category
-------------------------------------------
Notchbelow          |****          |
The Middletonian    |***           |
Pillowmint Lodge    |*****         |
Pile Inn            |**            |
Rancho El Cheapo    |*             |
Buxton Suites       |*****         |
-------------------------------------------
```

Sort the hotels by stars, five stars first, one star last.

3. Write the *grades* program to take the course number and the name of a student as command-line arguments. The course numbers are *CS101*, *CS202*, and *CS303*. The program will include three subroutines:
   a. Subroutine *ave* to calculate the overall average for a set of grades.
   b. Subroutine *highest* to get the highest grade in the set.
   c. Subroutine *lowest* to get the lowest grade in the set.

Print the average, the highest score, and the lowest score. If there were any failures (average below 60), print the name, course number, and a warning to *STDERR* such as: *Be advised: Joe Blow failed CS202*. Send the name of the failing student and the course number to a file called *failures*. Sort the file by course number.

Use the *AUTOLOAD* function to test that each of the subroutines has been defined.

chapter

12

Modularize It, Package It, and Send It to the Library!

12.1 Packages and Modules

12.1.1 Before Getting Started

In the following sections, we discuss packages and modules found in the standard Perl library and how to use them. Many of today's modules use an object-oriented approach to programming, discussed in Chapter 14, which will include terms such as classes, objects, and methods. This chapter will focus on function-oriented modules and libraries and how to use and create them. We will also show you how to get modules from CPAN, the Comprehensive Perl Archive Network, but will go into more detail on installing and using CPAN modules in Chapters 14, 15, and 18.

12.1.2 An Analogy

Two boys each have a box of Legos building blocks. One set of Legos blocks will build a toy boat, the other a toy plane. The boys open their boxes and throw the contents on the floor, mixing them together. The Legos blocks are different shapes and colors. There are yellow square pieces, red triangular pieces, and blue rectangular pieces from both boxes, but now they are mixed up so it is difficult to tell which Legos blocks should be used to build the toy boat or the toy plane. If the pieces had been kept in their separate boxes, this confusion never would have happened.

In Perl, the separate boxes are called packages, and the Legos blocks are called symbols; i.e., names for variables and constants. Keeping symbols in their own private packages makes it possible to include library modules and routines in your program without causing a conflict between what you named your variables and what they are named in the module or library file you have included.

12.1.3 Definition

The bundling of data and functions into a separate namespace is termed **encapsulation** (to C++ programmers, this is called a **class**, and to object-oriented Perl programmers it can also be called a class). The separate namespace is termed a **package**. A separate namespace means that Perl has a separate symbol table for all the variables in a named package. By default, the current package is called package *main*. All the example scripts up to this point are in package *main*. By default, all variables are global within the package. The package mechanism allows you to switch namespaces, so that variables in the package are private, even if they have the same name somewhere outside of the package. (See Figure 12.1.)

The scope of the package is from the declaration of the package to the end of the file, end of the innermost enclosing block, or until another package is declared. Normally, a package is of file scope. To reference a package variable in another package, the package name is prefixed by the funny character representing the data type of the variable, followed by two colons and the variable name. In ancient Perl 4, an apostrophe is used instead of the colon.[1] (The double colons are reminiscent of the C++ scope resolution operator.) When referring to the *main* package, the name of the package can be eliminated.

Perl 5 extends the notion of packages to that of **modules**. A module is a package that is usually defined in a library and is reusable. Modules are more complex than simple packages. They have the capability to export symbols to other packages and to work with classes and methods. A module is a package stored in a file, where the basename of the file is given the package name appended with a *.pm* extension. The *use* function takes the module name as its argument and loads the module into your script.

```
$package'variable
$package::variable
$main::variable
$::variable
```

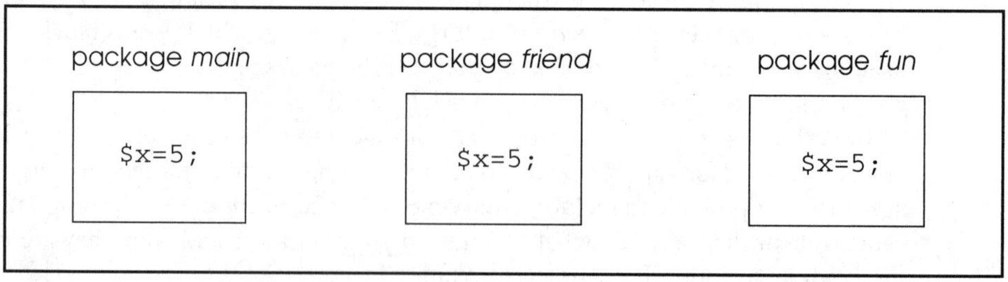

Figure 12.1 Each package has its own namespace (symbol table).

1. The apostrophe is still acceptable in Perl 5 scripts as of version 5.003.

12.1.4 The Symbol Table

To compile a program, the compiler must keep track of all the names for variables, filehandles, directory handles, formats, and subroutines that are used. Perl stores the names of these symbols as keys in a hash table for each package. The name of the hash is the same name as the package. The values associated with the hash keys are the corresponding typeglob values, know as aliases. The typeglob "globs" onto all types that could be represented by the name of the symbol. (See aliases and typeglobs, Chapter 11.) Perl actually creates separate internal pointers for each of the values represented by the same name. (See Figure 12.2.)

Each package has its own symbol table. Any time you use the package declaration, you switch to the symbol table for that package.

A variable assigned using the *local* function can be accessed in another package by using a :: to qualify it by package name. It is still within scope and accessible from the main symbol table.

The variables assigned using the *my* function are not accessible outside their own packages. They are not stored in a package symbol table but are stored in a private scratch pad created for each subroutine called. So when we use "my" variables, they cannot be accessed via the package symbol table, because they aren't there!

In the following example, you will notice that the *main* package stores not only symbols that are provided by the program but also other symbols, such as *STDIN, STDOUT, STDERR, ARGV, ARGVOUT, ENV,* and *SIG*. These symbols and special variables such as *$_* and *$!* are forced into package *main*. Other packages refer to these symbols unless qualified. Example 12.1 shows the contents of the symbol table for the *main* package.

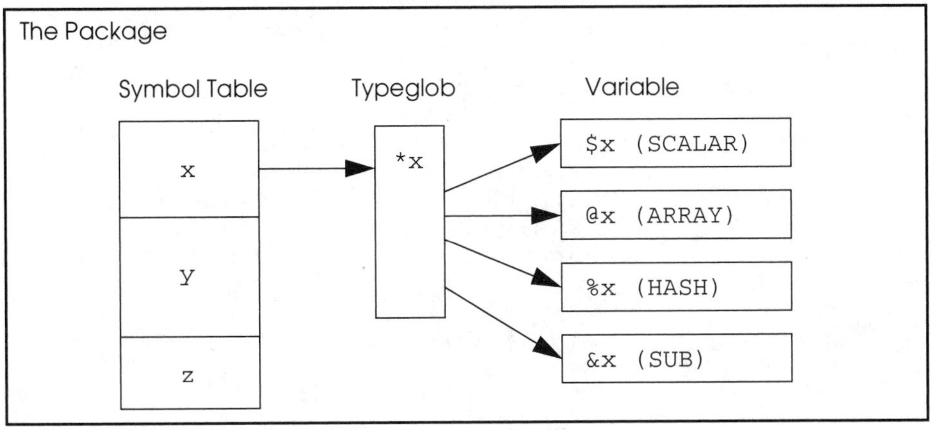

Figure 12.2 Each symbol is assigned a typeglob, *x, which represents all types named *x*.

EXAMPLE 12.1

```
(The Script)
   #!/bin/perl
   # Package main
   use strict "vars";
   use warnings;
   our ( @friends, @dogs, $key, $value );    # Declaring variables
   my($name,$pal,$money);
   $name="Susanne";
   @friends=qw(Joe Jeff Jan );
   @dogs = qw(Guyson Lara Junior);
   local $main::dude="Ernie";     # Keep strict happy
   my $pal = "Linda";             # Not in the symbol table
   my $money = 1000;
   while(($key, $value) = each (%main::)){
                                   # Look at main's symbol table
       print "$key:\t$value\n";
   }

(Output)
Name "main::dude" used only once: possible typo at packages line 10.
STDOUT:          *main::STDOUT
@:               *main::@
ARGV:            *main::ARGV
STDIN:           *main::STDIN
:                *main::
dude:            *main::dude
attributes:::    *main::attributes::
DB:::            *main::DB::
key:             *main::key
_<..\xsutils.c:  *main::_<..\xsutils.c
_<perllib.c:     *main::_<perllib.c
UNIVERSAL:::     *main::UNIVERSAL::
?:               *main::?
value:           *main::value
DynaLoader:::    *main::DynaLoader::
?:               *main::?
?ARNING_BITS:    *main::?ARNING_BITS
SIG:             *main::SIG
Exporter:::      *main::Exporter::
Win32:::         *main::Win32::
warnings:::      *main::warnings::
BEGIN:           *main::BEGIN
stderr:          *main::stderr
INC:             *main::INC
_:               *main::_
":               *main::"
DATA:            *main::DATA
_<.\win32.c:     *main::_<.\win32.c
```

EXAMPLE 12.1 (CONTINUED)

```
$:                    *main::$
stdout:               *main::stdout
IO:::                 *main::IO::
ENV:                  *main::ENV
dogs:                 *main::dogs
strict:::             *main::strict::
stdin:                *main::stdin
Carp:::               *main::Carp::
CORE:::               *main::CORE::
/:                    *main::/
0:                    *main::0
friends:              *main::friends
_<..\universal.c:     *main::_<..\universal.c
STDERR:               *main::STDERR
main:::               *main::main::
```

EXPLANATION

1. The *strict* pragma is turned on, barring any global variables.
2. The *warnings* pragma issues warnings if there are barewords, uninitialized variables, etc.
3. Lexically global *our* variables are declared. They will not be picked up as global variables by the *strict* pragma.
4. Lexically scoped *my* variables are declared.
5. The *my* variable, *$name*, is assigned *Susanne.*
6. The array *@friends* is assigned a list of names.
7. The array *@dogs* is assigned a list.
8. In order to keep the *strict* pragma from complaining, the *local* variable *$dude* must be fully qualified with the package name.
9. The lexically scoped *my* variable is assigned a value. This variable will not show up on the symbol table. It is stored in a special scratch pad within the block.
10. This *my* variable will also be absent from the symbol table.
11. The keys and values from the *main* symbol table are printed. The key is the name of the identifier, and the value is the corresponding typeglob value.

EXAMPLE 12.2

```
(The Script)
    # Default package is main
1   @town = qw(Boston Chico Tampa);
2   $friend="Mary";

3   print "In main: \$friend is $friend\n";
```

EXAMPLE 12.2 (CONTINUED)

```
4  package boy;           # Package declaration
5  $name="Steve";
6  print "In boy \$name is $name.\n";
7  $main::friend="Patricia";
8  print "In boy \@town is @::town\n";
9  package main;          # Package declaration
10 print "In main: \$name is $name\n";
11 print "In main: \$name is $boy::name\n";
12 print "In main: \$friend is $friend.\n";

(Output)
3  In main: $friend is Mary
6  In boy $name is Steve.
8  In boy @town is Boston Chico Tampa
10 In main: $name is
11 In main: $name is Steve
12 In main: $friend is Patricia
```

EXPLANATION

1. The default package is called *main*. In the *main* package an array, *@town*, is assigned values. *@town* is in *main*'s symbol table.
2. In package *main*, the scalar *$friend* is assigned *Mary*. *$friend* is in *main*'s symbol table.
3. The value of *$friend* is printed.
4. The package *boy* is declared. We now switch from the *main* package to the *boy* package. This package has its own symbol table. From this point on until the program ends or another package is declared, the *boy* package is in scope. Variables created in this package are global within this package but not part of the *main* package.
5. The scalar *$name* is assigned *Steve*.
6. The value in *$name* is printed.
7. To access the variable *$friend* in package *main*, first the dollar sign is prepended to the package name to indicate that the type of the variable is a scalar, followed by the name of the package, *main*, two colons, and the variable name, *friend*. This allows you to switch namespaces from within this package. *Patricia* is assigned to *main*'s variable *$friend*.
8. Since *main* is the default package, it is not necessary to use its name when switching namespaces. *@::town* tells Perl to switch namespaces back to the array *@town* in the *main* package.
9. Package *main* is declared. We will now switch back into the *main* package.
10. In the *main* package, *$name* is not defined.
11. The value of the variable *$name* from the *boy* package is printed.
12. The *$friend* scalar was changed in package *boy* because it was fully qualified with *main*'s package *main*, meaning that the program was temporarily switched to package *main* when this variable was assigned. Its value is printed.

EXAMPLE 12.3

```
(The Script)
   # Package declarations
1  $name="Suzanne";      # These variables are in package main
2  $num=100;
3  package friend;       # Package declaration
4  sub welcome {
5     print "Who is your pal? ";
6     chomp($name=<STDIN>);
7     print "Welcome $name!\n";
8     print "\$num is $num.\n";     # Unknown to this package
9     print "Where is $main::name?\n\n";
   }
10 package main;          # Package declaration; back in main
11 &friend::welcome;      # Call subroutine
12 print "Back in main package \$name is $name\n";
13 print "Switch to friend package, Bye ",$friend::name,"\n";
14 print "Bye $name\n\n";

15 package birthday;      # Package declaration

16 $name="Beatrice";
17 print "Happy Birthday, $name.\n";
18 print "No, $::name and $friend::name, it is not your birthday!\n";

(Output)
5  Who is your pal? Tommy
7  Welcome Tommy!
8  $num is .
9  Where is Suzanne?

12 Back in main package $name is Suzanne
13 Switch to friend package, Bye Tommy
14 Bye Suzanne

17 Happy Birthday, Beatrice!!
18 No, Suzanne and Tommy, it is not your birthday!
```

EXPLANATION

1. Scalar *$name* is assigned *Suzanne* for the default package, *main.*
2. Scalar *$num* is assigned *100.*
3. Package *friend* is declared. It is in scope until line 10.
4. The subroutine *welcome* is defined within the *friend* package.
5. The user is asked for input.
6. *$name* is assigned a value. The package is *friend.*
7. The value of *$name* is printed.
8. The scalar *$num* was local to the *main* package; it's not defined here. Nothing is printed.

EXPLANATION (CONTINUED)

9 To access the *$name* variable from the *main* package, the name of the package, *main*, is followed by two colons and the variable name. Note that the $ precedes the package name, not the variable.

10 Out of the subroutine, the package *main* is declared.

11 The subroutine *welcome* cannot be called unless qualified by its package name.

12 *$name* is *Suzanne* in package *main*.

13 To access a variable from the package *friend*, the package has to precede the variable name. This causes a switch in namespaces.

14 *$name* is *Suzanne* in package *main*.

15 A new package called *birthday* is declared. It remains in effect until the block ends—in this case, when the script ends.

16 The *$name* variable in package *birthday* is assigned.

17 *$name* is *Beatrice* in package *birthday.*

18 In order to access variables from the previous packages, the package name and a double colon must precede the variable.

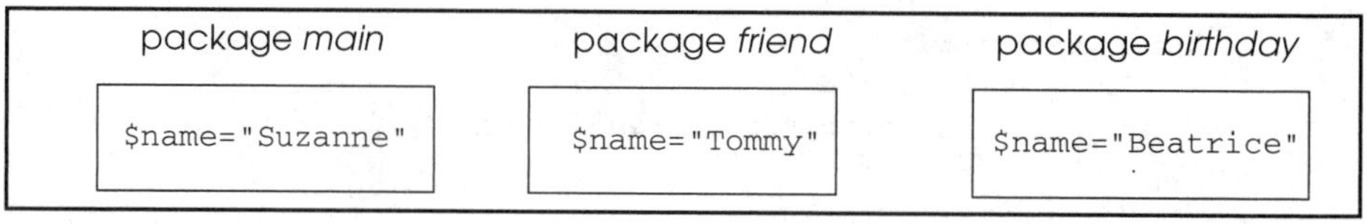

Figure 12.3 Packages create separate namespaces, as shown in Example 12.3.

12.2 The Standard Perl Library

The Perl distribution comes with a number of standard Perl library functions and packages. The Perl 4 library routines are procedural programs and their names end in a *.pl* extension. The Perl 5 modules end with a *.pm* extension. In Perl 5, the *.pm* files are called **modules**. The *.pm* files are modules written in two programming styles: procedural and object oriented. The module filenames start with a capital letter. The *.pm* filenames starting with a lowercase letter are a special type of module, called a pragma. A **pragma** is a module that tells the compiler that certain conditions must be checked in a Perl program before it can run. Files that have no extension at all are subdirectories. They contain common modules that are divided into several *.pm* files; for example, the *Math* subdirectory contains *BigFloat.pm*, *BigInt.pm*, *Complex.pm*, and *Trig.pm*.

Here is a sample listing from the standard Perl 5 library:[2]

2. The pathname to the standard Perl library is determined at the time Perl is installed. This can be assigned either a default value or a pathname designated by the person installing Perl.

AnyDBM_File.pm
AutoLoader.pm
AutoSplit.pm
B
B.pm
Benchmark.pm
ByteLoader.pm
CGI
CGI.pm
CORE
CPAN
CPAN.pm
Carp
Carp.pm
Class
Config.pm
Config.pm~
Cwd.pm
DB.pm
Data
Devel
DirHandle.pm
Dumpvalue.pm
DynaLoader.pm
English.pm
Env.pm
Errno.pm
Exporter
Exporter.pm
ExtUtils
Fatal.pm
Fcntl.pm
File
FileCache.pm
FileHandle.pm
FindBin.pm
Getopt
I18N
IO
IO.pm
IPC
Math
Net
O.pm
Opcode.pm
POSIX.pm
POSIX.pod
Pod
SDBM_File.pm
Safe.pm
Search
SelectSaver.pm
SelfLoader.pm
Shell.pm
Socket.pm
Symbol.pm
Sys
Term
Test
Test.pm
Text
Thread
Thread.pm
Tie
Time
UNIVERSAL.pm
User
XSLoader.pm
abbrev.pl
assert.pl
attributes.pm
attrs.pm
auto
autouse.pm
base.pm
bigfloat.pl
bigint.pl
bigrat.pl
blib.pm
bytes.pm
bytes_heavy.pl
cacheout.pl
charnames.pm
chat2.pl
complete.pl
constant.pm
ctime.pl
diagnostics.pm
dotsh.pl
dumpvar.pl
exceptions.pl
fastcwd.pl
fields.pm
filetest.pm
find.pl
finddepth.pl
flush.pl
ftp.pl
getcwd.pl
getopt.pl
getopts.pl
hostname.pl
importenv.pl
integer.pm
less.pm
lib.pm
locale.pm
look.pl
network.pl
newgetopt.pl
open.pm
open2.pl
open3.pl
ops.pm
overload.pm
perl5db.pl
perllocal.pod
ppm.pm
pwd.pl
re.pm
shellwords.pl
sigtrap.pm
stat.pl
strict.pm
subs.pm
syslog.pl
tainted.pl
termcap.pl
timelocal.pl
unicode
utf8.pm
utf8_heavy.pl
validate.pl
vars.pm
warnings
warnings.pm

12.2.1 The *@INC* Array

The special array *@INC* contains the directory path to where the library routines are located. To include directories not in the *@INC* array, you can use the *-I* switch[3] at the command line, or set the *PERL5LIB* environment variable to the full pathname. Normally, this variable is set in one of your shell initialization files, either *.login* or *.profile* if using UNIX. See Figure 12.4 if using Windows.

EXAMPLE 12.4

```
1   $ perl -V   (Windows Command Line)
    Summary of my perl5 (revision 5 version 8 subversion 8)
    configuration:
  Platform:
    osname=MSWin32, osvers=4.0, archname=MSWin32-x86-multi-thread
    uname=''
    config_args='undef'
      hint=recommended, useposix=true, d_sigaction=undef
    usethreads=define use5005threads=undef useithreads=define
    usemultiplicity=define
```

3. See Table A.18 in Appendix A for a description of the *-I* switch.

EXAMPLE 12.4 (CONTINUED)

```
      useperlio=define d_sfio=undef uselargefiles=define usesocks=undef
      use64bitint=undef use64bitall=undef uselongdouble=undef
      usemymalloc=n, bincompat5005=undef
    Compiler:
      cc='cl', ccflags ='-nologo -GF -W3 -MD -Zi -DNDEBUG -O1 -DWIN32
          -D_CONSOLE -DNO_STRICT -DHAVE_DES_FCRYPT -DNO_HASH_SEED
          -DUSE_SITECUSTOMIZE -DPERL_IMPLICIT_CONTEXT -DPERL_IMPLICIT_SYS
          -DUSE_PERLIO -DPERL_MSVCRT_READFIX',
      optimize='-MD -Zi -DNDEBUG -O1',
        ... output continues here
2     @INC:

--------------------------------------------------

3     $ perl -e 'print "@INC\n"'      (Windows)
       @INC:
       C:/perl/site/lib
       C:/perl/lib
       .

 -----------------------------------------------------------
4 $ perl -V  (Linux)
     @INC:
     /usr/local/lib/perl5/5.8.6/i686-linux
     /usr/local/lib/perl5/5.8.6
     /usr/local/lib/perl5/site_perl/5.8.6/i686-linux
     /usr/local/lib/perl5/site_perl/5.8.6
     /usr/local/lib/perl5/site_perl/5.8.5/i686-linux
     /usr/local/lib/perl5/site_perl/5.8.5
     /usr/local/lib/perl5/site_perl
       .
```

EXPLANATION

1. Perl with the *-V* option displays version, configuration, and library information.
2. The *@INC* array contains the directories where the Perl libraries are located.
3. At the Windows command-line prompt, the *@INC* array is printed. The first element in the colon-separated path is *C:/Perl/site/lib*, where Windows-specific library functions are stored, and the second element is *C:/Perl/lib*, the standard Perl library. The final dot is important. Any libraries stored in the current working directory (folder) will be included when Perl searches for these files.
4. The pathnames containing the word *site* are site-specific and contain library routines that have been downloaded for this particular site or architecture. Some of the site-specific libraries come with the standard distribution. Those pathnames with the word *site* or *linux* (*solaris* if you are using Solaris UNIX) are for Linux-specific library routines and modules. */usr/local/lib/perl5/5.8.6* is where the standard Perl library resides, and the final dot represents the current working directory.

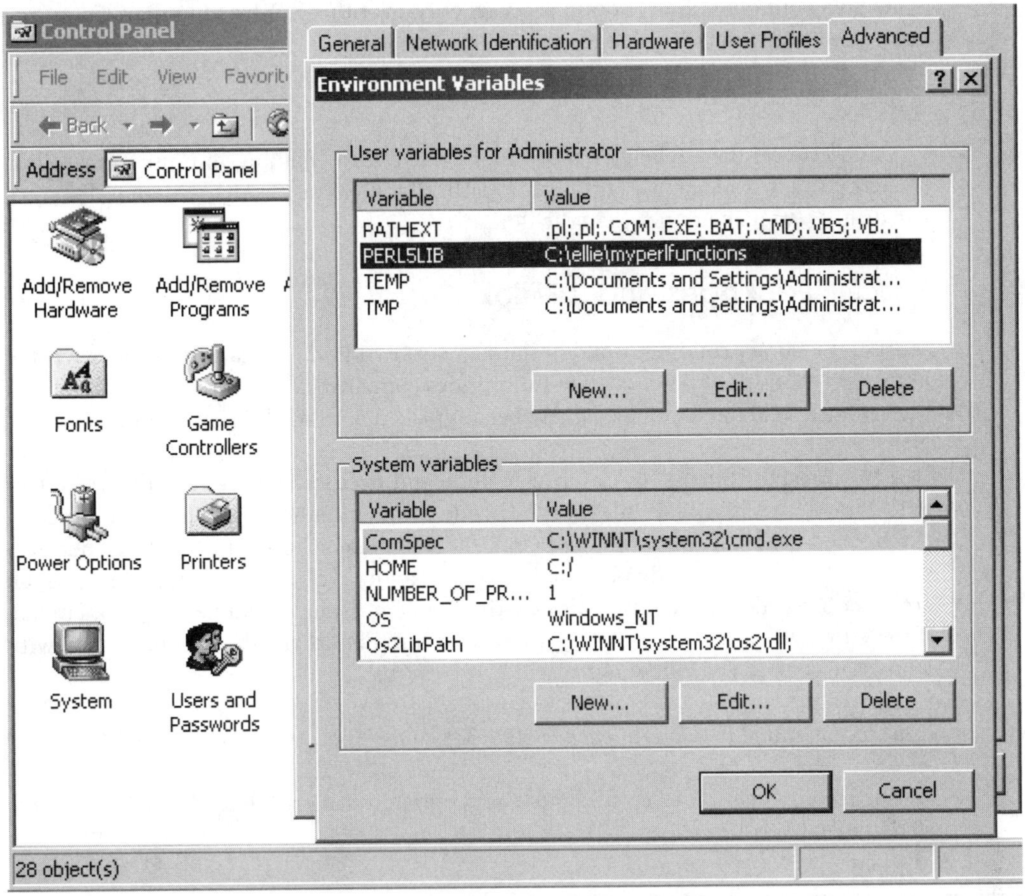

Figure 12.4 Setting the *PERL5LIB* environment variable in Windows.

Setting the *PERL5LIB* Environment Variable. If you are using UNIX/Linux operating systems, to add new path elements to the *@INC* array, the *PERL5LIB* environment variable can be set in your startup initialization files.

In *.login* for the *C* and *TC* shells:

```
setenv PERL5LIB "directory path"
```

In *.profile* for the *Bourne*, *Korn*, and *Bash* shells:

```
PERL5LIB="directory path"; export PERL5LIB
```

If you are using Windows, go to the *Start* menu, then to *Settings*, then *System Properties*, then *Environment Variables*, and finally *New*. Refer back to Figure 12.4.

To give your own library routines precedence over those in listed in the *@INC* array, you can put the following line in your program:

```
unshift(@INC,".");
```

Unshift causes the . to be prepended to the *@INC* array, making your present working directory the first element in the search path. If your library is in a different directory, use its full pathname rather than the dot.

12.2.2 Packages and *.pl* Files

Most of the library routines found in the standard Perl library ending in *.pl* were written in the Perl 4 days. They consisted of subroutines contained within a package. The library files are still available but have largely been replaced with modules or *.pm* files.

The *require* Function. In order to include and execute routines from the standard Perl library (specifically *.pl* files) or Perl code from any other file, the *require* function can be used, which is similar to the *C #include* statement. The *require* function checks to see if the library has already been included, unlike the *eval* and the *do* functions, which are older methods for including files. Without an argument, the value of $_ is included. If the *@INC* array does not have the correct path to the library, the *require* will fail with a message such as the following:

Can't locate pwd.pl in @INC at package line 3.

The *require* function loads files into the program during runtime. The *@INC* array is also updated at runtime.

FORMAT

```
require (Expr)
require Expr
require
```

Including Standard Library Routines. To see an example of a library routine in Perl's library, the *pwd.pl* routine (written by Larry Wall) is shown in Example 12.5. The *pwd* package consists of two subroutines that update the *PWD* environment variable after the *chdir* function has been executed. The value of *$ENV{PWD}* is the present working directory.

Notice that in the following Perl library function, the package *pwd* is declared before the subroutines are defined, thus placing the rest of the file within the *pwd* package. All variables belong to the package. The **names** of the subroutines are explicitly switched to package *main*. They may be called from your *main* package, but the variables remain local to the *pwd* package. (The apostrophe is used here instead of the two colons to switch namespaces. The apostrophe is the Perl 4 symbol for switching namespaces.)

The following example is a sample *.pl* routine from Perl's standard library.

EXAMPLE 12.5

```
  (The pwd package)
     #
1    # Usage:
2    #     require "pwd.pl";
     #     &initpwd;
     #     ...
     #     &chdir($newdir);
3    package pwd;
4    sub main'initpwd {
         if ($ENV{'PWD'}) {
         local($dd,$di) = stat('.');
         local($pd,$pi) = stat($ENV{'PWD'});
         return if $di == $pi && $dd == $pd;
     }
     chop($ENV{'PWD'} = 'pwd');
     }
5    sub main'chdir {
         local($newdir) = shift;
         if (chdir $newdir) {
             if ($newdir =~ m#^/#) {
                 $ENV{'PWD'} = $newdir;
             }
             else {
                 local(@curdir) = split(m#/#,$ENV{'PWD'});
                 @curdir = '' unless @curdir;
                 foreach $component (split(m#/#, $newdir)) {
                     next if $component eq '.';
                     pop(@curdir),next if $component eq '..';
                 }
                 $ENV{'PWD'} = join('/',@curdir) || '/';
             }
         }
         else {
             0;
         }          # Return value
     }

6    1;     <---IMPORTANT
```

EXPLANATION

1. The usage message tells you how you're supposed to use this package.
2. In the usage message, you are being told to be sure to require the file *pwd.pl*. The two subroutines that will be called are *initpwd* and *chdir*. The *chdir* function requires an argument, which is a directory name.

EXPLANATION (CONTINUED)

3 The package *pwd* is declared. This is the only package in the file.
4 The subroutine *initpwd* is defined. Notice that its name is qualified as a symbol for the *main* package. This means that when you call *initpwd* from your *main* package, you won't have to mention the package *pwd* at all.
5 The *chdir* subroutine is defined.
6 The *1* is required at the end of this package for the *require* function. If the last expression evaluated in this file is not true, the *require* function will not load the file into your program.

The following example uses a library routine in the script.

EXAMPLE 12.6

```
(The Script)
   #!/bin/perl
1  require "ctime.pl";
2  require "pwd.pl";
3  &initpwd;          # Call the subroutine
4  printf "The present working directory is %s\n", $ENV{PWD};
5  &chdir ("../..");
6  printf "The present working directory is %s\n", $ENV{PWD};
7  $today=&ctime(time);
8  print "$today";

(Output)
4  The present working directory is /home/jody/ellie/perl
6  The present working directory is /home/jody
8  Wed  Mar 14 11:51:59 2007
```

EXPLANATION

1 The *ctime.pl* Perl standard library function is included here.
2 The *pwd.pl* Perl standard library function is included.
3 The *initpwd* subroutine is called for the *pwd.pl* function. It initializes the value of *PWD*.
4 The present value of the environment variable *PWD* is printed.
5 A call to *chdir* changes the present working directory.
6 The present updated value of the environment variable *PWD* is printed.
7 Today's date is set in a human-readable format by the subroutine *ctime*, from *ctime.pl*.
8 Today's date is printed in its new format.

Using Perl to Include Your Own Library. The following example shows you how to create your own library functions and include them into a Perl script with the *require* function. When including user-defined routines or adding routines to a library, make sure to include *1;* (a nonzero value) as the last line of the routine. If you do not return a true value as the last line of your library file, this is the type of error you will get from the *require* function:

average.pl ***did not return a true value*** *at user.plx line 3.*

EXAMPLE 12.7

```
(The midterms Script)
    #!/bin/perl
    # Program name: midterms
    # This program will call a subroutine from another file
1   unshift(@INC, "/home/jody/ellie/perl/mylib");
2   require "average.pl";
    print "Enter your midterm scores.\n";
    @scores=split(' ', <STDIN>);
3   printf "The average is %.1f.\n", average::ave(@scores);
    # The ave subroutine is found in a file called average.pl
------------------------------------------------------------
4   $ cd mylib          # Directory where library is located
------------------------------------------------------------

(The Script)
5   $ cat average.pl    # File where subroutine is defined
6   package average; # Declare a package
     # Average a list of grades
7   sub ave {
8       my(@grades)=@_;
        my($num_of_grades)=$#grades + 1;
        foreach $grade ( @grades ){
             $total += $grade;
        }
9       $total/$num_of_grades;    # What gets returned
    }
10  1; # Make sure the file returns true or require will not succeed!
```

EXPLANATION

1 The *unshift* function prepends the *@INC* array with the pathname to your personal directory, *mylib*.

2 The *require* function first checks the *@INC* array to get a listing of all directories in which it will search for the *.pl* file. The *require* function includes the Perl function *average.pl*.

3 The *ave* function is called and returns a value to be stored in the scalar *$average*. Since the subroutine *ave()* is defined in a package called *average* in the library file, the package name (and two colons) must precede the call to *ave()*. If not, Perl will try to find *ave()* in *main*, the current package.

EXPLANATION (CONTINUED)

4 We will change directories to *mylib* from the command line. The dollar sign is the shell prompt.
5 Now we look at the contents of the file *average.pl*.
6 A package called *average* is declared.
7 A subroutine called *ave()* is defined.
8 It will accept a list of grades as parameters. The list is made local with the *my* function.
9 The expression is evaluated and returned.
10 This statement evaluates to true and is located at the end of the file. The *require* function needs a true return value in order to load this file when asked.

12.2.3 Modules and *.pm* Files

When using one of the modules (those files ending in *.pm*) provided in the standard Perl library, you must first make sure the *@INC* array contains the full pathname to your library distribution and that you include the *use* function with the module name.

If you are trying to find out how a particular library module works, you can use the *perldoc* command to get the documentation. (The *perldoc* command does not work for *.pl* files from the library.) For example, if you want to know about the *CGI.pm* module, type at the command line

```
perldoc CGI
```

and the documentation for the *CGI.pm* module will be displayed. If you type

```
perldoc English
```

the documentation for the *English.pm* module will be displayed.

The *use* Function (Modules and Pragmas). The *use* function allows Perl modules and pragmas to be imported into your program at **compile** time. The *use* function will not import a module if the module's filename does not have the *.pm* extension. The *require* function does the same thing but does not do imports and loads the module at **runtime**.

A **module** is a file in a library that behaves according to certain set of conventions. The modules in the standard Perl library are suffixed with the *.pm* extension. They can also be found in subdirectories. For example, the module *Bigfloat.pm* is found in a subdirectory called *Math*. To use a module found in a subdirectory, the directory name is followed by two colons and the name of the module, such as *Math::Bigfloat.pm*. (Although using the two colons makes it appear that *Bigfloat.pm* is in a package called "Math," in this context the two colons are used to separate the *Math* directory/folder from the module. The colon then will be translated to a forward slash for UNIX-type operating systems and a backslash for Windows sytems.)

A **pragma**, spelled in lowercase letters, is a directive to the compiler that your program should behave in a certain way and, if it doesn't, the program will abort. Some common pragmas are *lib, strict, subs*, and *diagnostics*. For a list of modules and pragmas, see Tables A.4 and A.5 in Appendix A.

In object-oriented terminology, subroutines are called **methods**. If you receive diagnostics using the term *method*, for now just think of methods as glorified subroutines. Many of the modules in the library use object-oriented Perl. The modules discussed in this chapter do not require any understanding of objects. For a complete discussion on how to use the object-oriented modules, see Chapter 14, "Bless Those Things! (Object-Oriented Perl)."

FORMAT

```
use Module;
use Module ( list );
use Directory::Module;
use pragma (list);
no pragma;
```

12.2.4 Exporting and Importing

In the export/import business, someone exports his goods and the someone who imports them is waiting on the other side. Let's say a wine maker in California has four great-tasting wines in his cellar, and he decides to export three of the wines to buyers but keep the best ones for himself. So he creates an export list and tacks it to the wall of his cellar, and, when the buyer comes, the buyer selects only those wines on the export list. The buyer is the importer. There's nothing preventing the importer from taking all four of the wines, but if he follows the guidelines of the export list, he will take only those listed.

When you use a Perl module, you are like the buyer. You import symbols (subroutines, variables, etc.) from the export list provided by the module. You take symbols from another package and add them to your own symbol table. You can take what's on the export list by default, you can ask for specific symbols from the list, or you can even exclude some or all of the symbols on the list. The business of exporting and importing is really just a way of getting symbols into the namespace of your program package so you don't have to fully qualify all the imported names with the module package name and two colons, such as *Module::fun1*. What you import can be listed after the *use* directive, such as *use Module qw(fun1 fun2);* .

The *Exporter* Module. The exporting module sends symbols to the user of the module. The *Exporter.pm* module found in the standard Perl library supplies the necessary semantics for modules to be able to export symbols. It implements an import method that allows a module to export functions and variables to its users' namespaces. As we discussed earlier, symbols are stored as a hash of typeglobs on the symbol table for the package. The import routine creates an alias for the symbol that is being taken from one package and used in another. Consider the statement:

```
*Package_mine::somefunction = \&Package_exporter::somefunction
```

The package called "Package_mine" is importing a symbol called "somefunction" from "Package_exporter". The symbol is the name of a subroutine called "somefunction". A reference to "somefunction" in the exporting package is assigned to a typeglob in "Package_mine"; i.e., put on the symbol table of "Package_mine".

The *Exporter* module implements an import routine that uses similar semantics as shown previously. Although you can write your own import function, many modules use *Exporter* because it provides a highly flexible interface and is easy to use.

Perl automatically calls the import method when processing a *use* statement for a module. Modules and *use* are documented in *perlfunc* and *perlmod*. Understanding the concept of modules and how the *use* statement operates is important to understanding the *Exporter*. The *Exporter.pm* module is an object-oriented module that functions as a class. Other modules inherit from the *Exporter* class the capability to export symbols. (See Chapter 14 for more on object-oriented programs.) Inherited classes must be listed in the *@ISA* array.

```
require Exporter;
our @ISA=qw(Exporter);4
```

The names listed in the *@EXPORT* array are by default switched into the namespace of the program using the module; the names on the *@EXPORT_OK* array are added to the user's namespace only if requested. The *@EXPORT_FAIL* array lists those symbols that cannot be exported. The *%EXPORT_TAGS* hash contains groups of symbols. If the module is imported with *use* and parentheses are added to the module name, as in *use Module()*, none of the symbols is exported to the module. Table 12.1 describes the exporting modules and the users of the modules.

---

4. Note that the *Exporter* module is not enclosed in double quotes when used as an argument to *require* and that *.pm* is missing. This tells the compiler two things: if, for example, the module is *Math::BigFloat*, that will be translated to *Math/BigFloat*, and if there are indirect method calls within the module, they will be treated as object-oriented method calls, not ordinary subroutine calls.

Table 12.1 Exporting Symbols

The Exporting Module	***What It Means***
package Testmodule;	Package declaration.
require Exporter;	Use the *Exporter.pm* module to export symbols from package to package.
our @ISA = qw(Exporter);	*@ISA* contains the names of base classes needed to do the exporting.
our @EXPORT = qw($x @y z);	Symbols in this list are automatically exported to the user of this module.
our @EXPORT_OK = qw(fun b c);	Symbols in this list are exported only if requested by the user of this module.
our @EXPORT_FAIL=qw(fun3 e);	These symbols are not to be exported.[a]
our %EXPORT_TAGS= (*':group1' => [qw(a b c)],* *':group2' => [qw($x @y %c)]* *);*	The key '*:group1*' represents the symbols *a, b,* and *c* (function names), collectively; '*:group2*' represents the symbols *$x, @y,* and *%c,* collectively.
The Importing Module	***What It Means***
use Testmodule;	*Testmodule* is loaded.
use Testmodule qw(fun2);	*Testmodule* is loaded; *fun2* is imported.
use Testmodule();	*Testmodule* is loaded, no symbols imported.
use Testmodule qw(:group1 !:group2);	*Testmodule* imports symbols from *group1* (See:*%EXPORT_TAGS* hash, above) but not symbols from *group2.*
use Testmodule qw(:group1 !fun2);	*Testmodule* imports symbols from *group1*, not the symbol *fun2.*
use Testmodule qw(/^fu/);	*Testmodule* imports symbols whose names start with *fu.*
SomeModule.pm	***User of the Module***
package SomeModule.pm;	*use SomeModule;*
use Exporter;	*&a;*
our @ISA = qw(Exporter);	*&b;*
our @EXPORT=qw(a b c);	*&c;* *# functions and variables automatically* *# imported from the @EXPORT array*
sub a { }	*&SomeModule::d;* *# d isn't on the @EXPORT list;* *# its name must be fully qualified*
sub b { }	
sub c { }	
sub d { }	
1;	
package SomeModule.pm;	*use SomeModule qw(a c);* *# must ask for symbols*
use Exporter;	*&a;* *# or they won't be imported*
our @ISA = qw(Exporter);	*&c;*
our @EXPORT_OK=qw(a b c);	*&SomeModule::c;* *# must fully qualify names of symbols*
sub a { }	*SomeModule::d;* *# not asked for from @EXPORT_OK list*
sub b { }	
sub c { }	
sub d { }	
1;	

a. Variables have the funny symbol preceding their name; subroutines don't have a funny symbol. *a, b,* and *c* refer to subroutines with those names.

Using *perldoc* to Get Documentation for a Perl Module. When you are ready to start using Perl modules, you can use the built-in *perldoc* command to retrieve the documentation from Perl 5 modules that were formatted with special *pod* directives (see Chapter 15 for details on this type of formatting). The following excerpt was taken from the *CGI.pm* documentation.

Note: If you are interested in testing the code displayed in the *CGI.pm* module, cut and paste the following text, highlighted in bold, and put it into a file. Save the file in the *cgi-bin* directory under your Web server's root. If using UNIX, turn on execute permission with *chmod*. Then execute the script in your browser. If you are unfamiliar with how to execute CGI programs, go to Chapter 16 in this book for detailed instructions.

EXAMPLE 12.8

```
(At the Command Line)
1  perldoc CGI
(Output)
NAME
    CGI - Simple Common Gateway Interface Class

SYNOPSIS
      # CGI script that creates a fill-out form
      # and echoes back its values.

2      use CGI qw/:standard/;
3      print header,
           start_html('A Simple Example'),
           h1('A Simple Example'),
           start_form,
           "What's your name? ",textfield('name'),p,
           "What's the combination?", p,
           checkbox_group(-name=>'words',
                          -values=>['eenie','meenie','minie','moe'],
                          -defaults=>['eenie','minie']), p,
           "What's your favorite color? ",
                popup_menu(-name=>'color',
                -values=>['red','green','blue','chartreuse']),p,
          submit,
           end_form,
           hr;

       if (param()) {
           my $name      = param('name');
           my $keywords  = join ', ',param('words');
           my $color     = param('color');
           print "Your name is",em(escapeHTML($name)),p,
                 "The keywords are: ",em(escapeHTML($keywords)),p,
                 "Your favorite color is ",em(escapeHTML($color)),
                 hr;
       }
```

EXAMPLE 12.8 (CONTINUED)

```
ABSTRACT
    This perl library uses perl5 objects to make it easy to create Web
    fill-out forms and parse their contents. This package defines CGI
-- More  --
```

EXPLANATION

1. The *perldoc* command produces documentation for modules using Perl's POD directives. (See Chapter 15 for details on how to use Plain Ole Documentation, POD.)
2. This line is used to load the CGI module, function-oriented style, and import all of its standard symbols for creating CGI scripts containing HTML and Perl functions. In the *CGI.pm* module, itself, the list of symbols is defined using the *%EXPORT_TAGS* hash, where "standard" is the key, followed by list of values (also tags to include a huge array of function names): *':standard' => [qw/:html2 :html3 :html4 :form :cgi/]*. These symbols will automatically be imported by the user of the module.
3. This section of the documentation shows you how to use some of the features of *CGI.pm*. For more on CGI, see Chapter 16.

Using a Perl 5 Module from the Standard Perl Library. The following module, *English.pm*, provides aliases for built-in variables, such as $_ and $/. For any variables that are also part of the *awk* programming language, there are both long and short English names for the variable. For example, the number of the current record is represented as $. in Perl and *NR* in *awk*. The English names are either *$RS* (*awk*) or *$INPUT_RECORD_SEPARATOR* (Perl).

EXAMPLE 12.9

```
(The Script)
    #!/usr/bin/perl
1   use English;     # Use English words to replace
                     # special Perl variables
2   print "The pid is $PROCESS_ID.\n";
3   print "The pid is $PID.\n";
4   print "The real uid $REAL_USER_ID.\n";
5   print "This version of perl is $PERL_VERSION.\n";

(Output)
2   The pid is 948.
3   The pid is 948.
4   The real uid 9496.
5   5.6.0.
```

EXPLANATION

1 The *English.pm* module is loaded in at compile time with the *use* directive.
2 The process ID number of this process is printed.
3 The *$PID* variable is the same as *$PROCESS.ID*.
4 The real user ID for the user of this program is printed.
5 The version of Perl is 5.6.0.

The following example is a sample *.pm* file from Perl's standard library.

EXAMPLE 12.10

```
(A Module from the Standard Perl Library)[a]
1   package Carp;
    # This package implements handy routines
    # for modules that wish to throw
    # exceptions outside of the current package
2   require Exporter;
3   @ISA = Exporter;
4   @EXPORT = qw(confess croak carp);
5   sub longmess {
6       my $error = shift;
        my $mess = "";
        my $i = 2;
    my ($pack,$file,$line,$sub);
    while (($pack,$file,$line,$sub) = caller($i++)) {
        $mess .= "\t$sub " if $error eq "called";
        $mess .= "$error at $file line $line\n";
        $error = "called";
    }
    $mess || $error;
    }
    sub shortmess {
        my $error = shift;
        my ($curpack) = caller(1);
        my $i = 2;
        my ($pack,$file,$line,$sub);
        while (($pack,$file,$line,$sub) = caller($i++)) {
            return "$error at $file line $line\n"
                        if $pack ne $curpack;
    }
    longmess $error;
    }
7   sub confess { die longmess @_; }
8   sub croak { die shortmess @_; }
9   sub carp { warn shortmess @_; }
```

a. The *Carp.pm* module has been rewritten and is much larger with an additional function, called *cluck*, but this version is used here because it is easier to see how the exporting of subroutines works.

EXPLANATION

1 This is the package declaration. The package is named after the file it resides in, *Carp.pm*. The functions *carp, croak,* and *confess* generate error messages, such as *die* and *warn*. The difference is that with *carp* and *croak*, the error is reported at the line in the calling routine where the error was invoked, whereas *confess* prints out the stack backtrace showing the chain of subroutines that was involved in generating the error. It prints its message at the line where it was invoked.
2 The *Exporter* module is required so that subroutines and variables can be made available to other programs.
3 The *@ISA* array contains the names of packages this module will use. Perl implements inheritance by listing other modules this package will use in the *@ISA* array.
4 The *@EXPORT* array lists the subroutines from this module that will be exported by default to any program using this module. The subroutines *confess*, *croak*, and *carp* are now available to you if you want to use this module. Since *longmess* and *shortmess* are not on the list to be exported, you cannot directly use these subroutines.
5 This is a subroutine definition for this module.
6 The error message provided as an argument to *confess* is passed here and shifted into the *$error* scalar.
7 The definition for subroutine *confess* is to call *die* with the return value of *longmess*.
8 The definition for subroutine *croak* is to call *die* with the return value of *shortmess*.
9 The definition for subroutine *carp* is to call *warn* with the return value of *shortmess*.

12.2.5 How to "use" a Module from the Standard Perl Library

The following example demonstrates how to use the *Carp* module from the standard Perl library. The first step in using a module is to read the documentation. This can be done with the *perldoc* command.

```
$ perldoc Carp

NAME
    carp - warn of errors (from perspective of caller)

    cluck - warn of errors with stack backtrace (not exported by default)

    croak - die of errors (from perspective of caller)

    confess - die of errors with stack backtrace

    shortmess - return the message that carp and croak produce

    longmess - return the message that cluck and confess produce
```

```
SYNOPSIS
    use Carp;
    croak "We're outta here!";

    use Carp qw(cluck);
    cluck "This is how we got here!";

    print FH Carp::shortmess("This will have caller's details added");
    print FH Carp::longmess("This will have stack backtrace added");

DESCRIPTION
    The Carp routines are useful in your own modules because they act
    like die() or warn(), but with a message which is more likely to be
    useful to a user of your module. In the case of cluck, confess, and
    longmess that context is a summary of every call in the call-stack.
    For a shorter message you can use carp, croak or shortmess which
    report the error as being from where your module was called. There
    is no guarantee that that is where the error was, but it is a good
    educated guess.
        <continues here>
```

The "use" directive makes sure the requested module is loaded at compile time. If there is a list following the module name, that list represents symbols that will be exported from the module to be used (imported) in your program. In the *Carp.pm* module, one of the functions is called *croak*. If requested, the user can call the *croak* function without fully qualifying the symbol name with the :: syntax (*Carp::croak*).

EXAMPLE 12.11

```
(Using a Module from the Standard Perl Library in a Script)
    #!/bin/perl
1   use Carp qw(croak);

2   print "Give me a grade: ";
    $grade = <STDIN>;
3   try($grade);      # Call subroutine

4   sub try{
5       my($number)=@_;
6       croak "Illegal value: " if $number < 0 || $number > 100;
    }

(Output)
2   Give me a grade: 200
6   Illegal value:  at expire line 13
        main::try called at expire line 8
```

EXPLANATION

1 The *Carp* module is used (loaded into) in the current package, *main*. Because *croak* is listed after the module name, it is the only function name that can be used in this script without fully qualifying its name. If, for example, you try to use *confess* rather that *Carp::confess*, the program will be aborted with an error message such as: *String found where operator expected at cluck.plx line 9, near "confess "Illegal value: ""   (Do you need to predeclare confess?)...*
2 The user is asked for input.
3 The subroutine *try* is called and passed the scalar *$grade*.
4 The *if* subroutine *try* is defined.
5 The argument passed in is assigned to *$number*.
6 The *croak* function is called with an error message. The *croak* function was exported by the *Carp* module. The program will die if the value of *$number* is not in the range between *0* and *100*. The error message reports the line where the program died, as well as the name of the package, subroutine name, and the number of the line where the subroutine was invoked.

EXAMPLE 12.12

```
(Using a Module from the Standard Perl Library in a Script)
   #!/bin/perl
1  use Carp qw(cluck);   # cluck not exported by default

  print "Give me a grade: ";
  $grade = <STDIN>;
2  try($grade);      # Call subroutine

   sub try{
      my($number)=@_;
      cluck "Illegal value: " if $number < 0 || $number > 100;
   }
  print "That was just a warning. Program continues here.\n";

(Output)
2   Give me a grade: 200
6   Give me a grade: 200
    Illegal value:  at cluck.plx line 9
        main::try('200\x{a}') called at cluck.plx line 5
    That was just a warning. Program continues here.
```

EXPLANATION

1. The *Carp* module is used (loaded into) in the current package, *main*. The *cluck* function will be used in this script. If you look at the documentation for *cluck*, that symbol is not exported by default into the user's namespace. This program explicitly imports it.
2. The user is asked for input.
3. The subroutine *try* is called and passed the scalar *$grade*.
4. The *if* subroutine *try* is defined.
5. The argument passed in is assigned to *$number*.
6. The *cluck* function is called with an error message. The *cluck* function was requested and imported from the *Carp* module. The program will send a warning if the value of *$number* is not in the range between *0* and *100*. Now if you try to use any of the other *Carp* functions, the program will die. You will have to explicitly import any of those functions or use the fully qualified name; e.g., *Carp::confess*.

12.2.6 Using Perl to Create Your Own Module

The following example illustrates how to create a module in a separate *.pm* file and use the module in another program. Although this module itself looks like any other package, it must additionally include the *Exporter* module, the *@ISA* array, and the *@EXPORT* array for it to really behave as a module. The ability to export specific symbols to other programs and to import other modules is what differentiates a module from a *.pl* file. To see a skeletal module for creating modules for CPAN, see "Creating Extensions and Modules for CPAN with the *h2xs* Tool" on page 395.

EXAMPLE 12.13

```
(The Me.pm Module)
package Me;
use strict;  use warnings;
require 5.6;         # Make sure we're a version of Perl no
                     # older than 5.6
require Exporter;    # Exporter.pm allows symbols to be imported
                     # by others
our @ISA=qw(Exporter); # ISA is a list of base packages needed
                       # by this module
our @EXPORT_OK=qw(hello goodbye );  # List of your subroutines
                                    # to export

sub hello { my($name)=shift;
   print "Hi there, $name.\n" };
sub goodbye { my($name)=shift;
   print "Good-bye $name.\n";}
```

EXAMPLE 12.13 (CONTINUED)

```
9   sub do_nothing { print "Didn't print anything.
                              Not in EXPORT list\n";}
    1;
------------------------------------------------------------

    #!/usr/bin/perl
    # Program name: main.perl
10  use lib ("/home/ellie/Modules");    # A pragma to update @INC.
11  use Me  qw(hello goodbye);          # Import package
12  &hello ("Daniel");
13  &goodbye ("Steve");
14  &do_nothing;          # This was not on the Export list
                          # in Me.pm so cannot be imported unless
                          # explicitly with &Me::do_nothing
(Output)
12  Hi there, Daniel.
13  Good-bye Steve.
14  Undefined subroutine &main::do_nothing
```

EXPLANATION

1 The file is called *Me.pm*. It contains a package of the same name without the extension. The *Me* package is declared.

2 The *strict* pragma bars global variables, and the *warnings* pragma issues the appropriate warning messages if there are variables used only once, undefined values, etc.

3 The *require* is used to make sure the Perl version being used is not less than 5.6. If it is, the script will abort.

4 The *Exporter* module is a special Perl module that allows the *use* function to import subroutines (called "methods") from a particular module.

5 The *@ISA* array lists any packages containing subroutines (methods) that will be used by this package. This is how Perl implements inheritance from one module to another. (See Chapter 14, "Bless Those Things! (Object-Oriented Perl).")

6 The *@EXPORT* array lists all subroutines (methods) that can be exported by default. The *@EXPORT_OK* array lists subroutines (methods) that can be exported if the user of the module requests them in his *use* statement. If he doesn't ask, he won't get them. Those subroutines on the export list are *hello* and *goodbye,* defined below.

7 The subroutine *hello* is defined.

8 The subroutine *goodbye* is defined.

9 The subroutine *do_nothing* is defined. Note: the name of this subroutine is not on the export list; that is, it is not in the *@EXPORT_OK* arrray. If not on the export list, Perl will look in the current package, *main*, for it.

10 The *lib* pragma tells the compiler to update the *@INC* array at compile time. It is the same as saying: *BEGIN{ require "/home/ellie/Module"; import Module;}*.

11 The *use* function causes Perl to include the *Me.pm* module into this package.

EXPLANATION (CONTINUED)

12 The subroutine *hello* is called with an argument. This subroutine name was imported.
13 The subroutine *goodbye* is called with an argument. It was also imported.
14 This subroutine was not imported. It was not on the export list (*@EXPORT*) in *Me.pm*. An error message is printed indicating that package *main* does not recognize this subroutine. If the explicit package name, *&Me::goodbye*, is given, the subroutine can be used from package *Me*.

12.3 Modules from CPAN

CPAN (the Comprehensive Perl Archive Network) is the central repository for a collection of hundreds of Perl modules. To find the CPAN mirror closest to you, go to *http://www.perl.com/CPAN*. (In Chapter 16, we show you how to download database modules from CPAN and how to use those modules in a program.)

Perl modules that depend on each other are bundled together by name, author, and category. These modules can be found under the CPAN *modules* directory or by using the CPAN search engine under *http://search.cpan.org*. If you need to install these modules, the CPAN documentation gives you easy-to-follow instructions. The Web page shown here displays how the information is catalogued and gives a partial list of the modules.

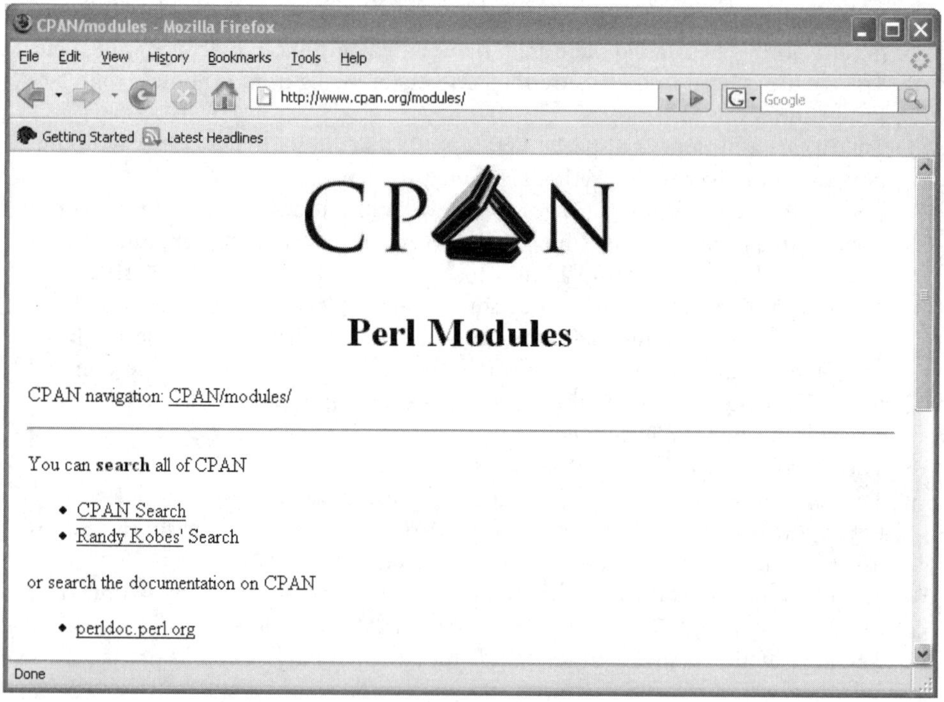

Figure 12.5 The Perl 5 module list at the CPAN Web site.

ActivePerl, available for the Linux, Solaris, Mac OS, and Windows operating systems, contains the Perl Package Manager (for installing packages of CPAN modules) and complete online help. PPM allows you to access package repositories and install new packages or update old ones you already have with relative ease.

Go to *www.activestate.com/ppm packages/5.6* to access the ActiveState Package repository.

The *Cpan.pm* Module. The *Cpan.pm* module allows you to query, download, and build Perl modules from CPAN sites. It runs in both interactive and batch mode and is designed to automate the installation of Perl modules and extensions. The modules are fetched from one or more of the mirrored CPAN sites and unpacked in a dedicated directory. To learn more about this module, at your system command line type

```
$ perldoc Cpan
```

to read the following:

```
NAME
    CPAN - query, download and build perl modules from CPAN sites

SYNOPSIS
   Interactive mode:

      perl -MCPAN -e shell;

   Batch mode:

      use CPAN;

      autobundle, clean, install, make, recompile, test

DESCRIPTION
    The CPAN module is designed to automate the make and install of perl
    modules and extensions. It includes some searching capabilities and
    knows how to use Net::FTP or LWP (or lynx or an external ftp client) to
    fetch the raw data from the net.

    Modules are fetched from one or more of the mirrored CPAN
    (Comprehensive Perl Archive Network) sites and unpacked in a
    dedicated directory.

    The CPAN module also supports the concept of named and versioned
    *bundles* of modules. Bundles simplify the handling of sets of related
    modules. See Bundles below.

    The package contains a session manager and a cache manager. There is no
    status retained between sessions. The session manager keeps track of
    what has been fetched, built and installed in the current session. The
    cache manager keeps track of the disk space occupied by the make
    processes and deletes excess space according to a simple FIFO
    mechanism.
```

```
For extended searching capabilities there's a plugin for CPAN available,
the CPAN::WAIT manpage. 'CPAN::WAIT' is a full-text search engine that
indexes all documents available in CPAN authors directories. If
'CPAN::WAIT' is installed on your system, the interactive shell of
<CPAN.pm> will enable the 'wq', 'wr', 'wd', 'wl', and 'wh' commands
which send queries to the WAIT server that has been configured for your
installation.
```

<continues>

EXAMPLE 12.14

```
1   $ h2xs -A -n Exten.dir
    Writing Exten.dir/Exten.dir.pm
    Writing Exten.dir/Exten.dir.xs
    Writing Exten.dir/Makefile.PL
    Writing Exten.dir/test.pl
    Writing Exten.dir/Changes
    Writing Exten.dir/MANIFEST

2   $ cd Exten.dir

3   $ ls

4   $ more Exten.dir.pm
    package Exten.dir;

    require 5.005_62;
    use strict;
    use warnings;

    require Exporter;
    require DynaLoader;

    our @ISA = qw(Exporter DynaLoader);

    # Items to export into callers namespace by default.
    # Note: do not export names by default without
    # a very good reason. Use EXPORT_OK instead.
    # Do not simply export all your public
    # functions/methods/constants.

    # This allows declaration use Exten.dir ':all';
    # If you do not need this, moving things directly
    # into @EXPORT or @EXPORT_OK will save memory.
```

EXAMPLE 12.14 (CONTINUED)

```
perl -MCPAN -e shell

cpan shell -- CPAN exploration and modules installation (v1.7602)
ReadLine support enabled

cpan> h

Display Information
 command  argument           description
 a,b,d,m  WORD or /REGEXP/   about authors, bundles, distributions, modules
 i        WORD or /REGEXP/   about anything of above
 r        NONE               reinstall recommendations
 ls       AUTHOR             about files in the author's directory

Download, Test, Make, Install...
 get                         download
 make                        make (implies get)
 test      MODULES,          make test (implies make)
 install   DISTS, BUNDLES    make install (implies test)
 clean                       make clean
 look                        open subshell in these dists' directories
 readme                      display these dists' README files

Other
 h,?           display this menu       ! perl-code    eval a perl command
 o conf [opt]  set and query options   q              quit the cpan shell
 reload cpan   load CPAN.pm again      reload index   load newer indices
 autobundle    Snapshot                force cmd      unconditionally do
cmd

cpan>
```

12.3.1 Using PPM

PPM is a program manager that comes with ActivePerl (*www.activestate.com*). It is very easy to use and runs on Linux, Windows, and Mac OS. It comes in both a GUI and command-line interface. When the Perl Package Manager is activated, it brings up a window with all the currently installed packages. You can search for specific modules and install, upgrade, and remove modules using this graphical interface. For everyday use, this is much easier than using CPAN.

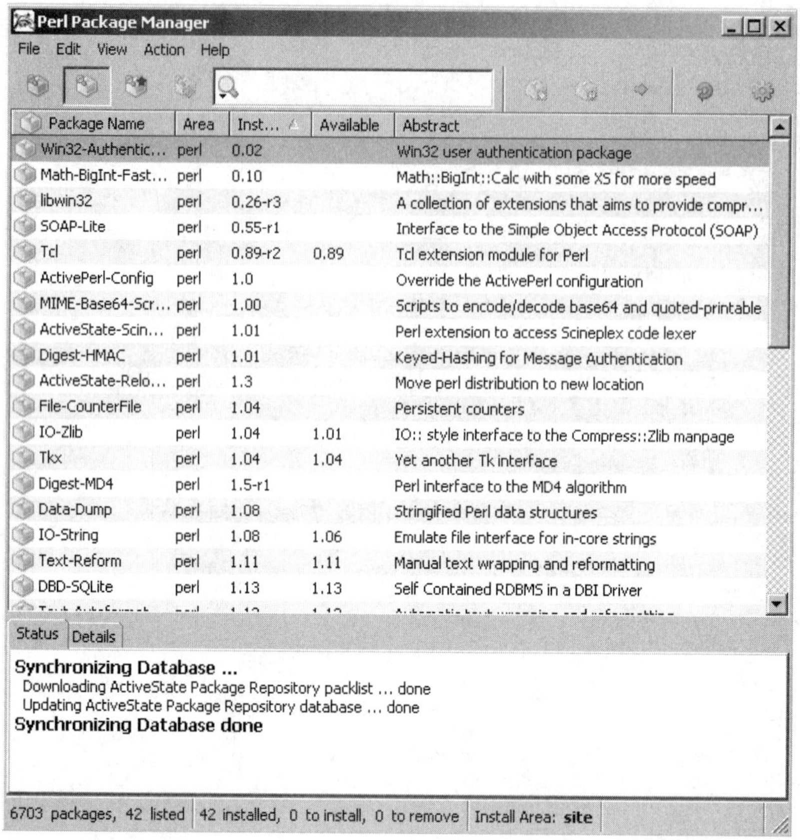

Figure 12.6 PPM GUI.

All packages: Displays all packages installed locally and available in the repository.

Installed packages: Displays all installed packages.

Upgradable packages: Displays packages for which an upgrade is available from the repository.

Packages to install/remove: Displays packages marked for installation or removal.

Mark for install: Marks the selected packages for installation or upgrade.

Mark for remove: Marks the selected packages for removal.

Run marked actions: Runs all marked actions (i.e. install, upgrade, remove)

Refresh all data: Refreshes the list view.

PPM Preferences: Opens the PPM Preferences dialog box.

Figure 12.7 What the icons mean in the PPM window.

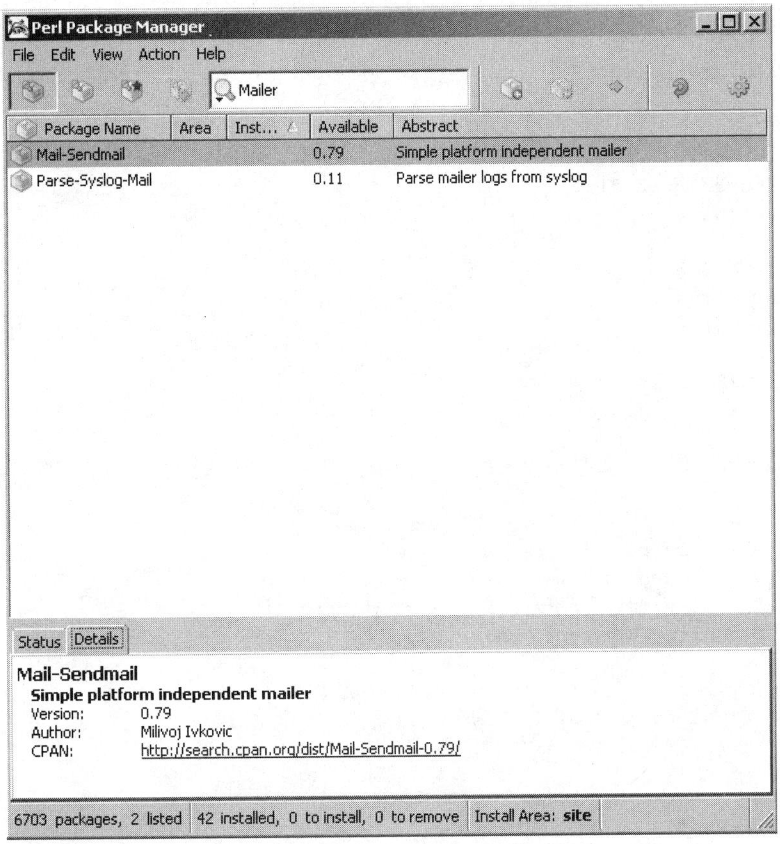

Figure 12.8 Searching for a Perl module to Sendmail.

Creating Extensions and Modules for CPAN with the *h2xs* Tool. The *h2xs* tool is a standard application that comes with the regular Perl distribution. It creates a directory and a set of skeleton files to use when creating a module or adding *C* language extensions. To get a full description, type at your system prompt

```
$ perldoc h2xs
```

EXAMPLE 12.15

```
$ h2xs -A -n Exten.dir
Writing Exten.dir/Exten.dir.pm
Writing Exten.dir/Exten.dir.xs
Writing Exten.dir/Makefile.PL
Writing Exten.dir/test.pl
Writing Exten.dir/Changes
Writing Exten.dir/MANIFEST
```

EXAMPLE 12.15 (CONTINUED)

```
2  $ cd Exten.dir

3  $ ls

4  $ more Exten.dir.pm
   package Exten.dir;

   require 5.005_62;
   use strict;
   use warnings;

   require Exporter;
   require DynaLoader;

   our @ISA = qw(Exporter DynaLoader);

   # Items to export into callers namespace by default.
   # Note: do not export names by default without
   # a very good reason. Use EXPORT_OK instead.
   # Do not simply export all your public
   # functions/methods/constants.

   # This allows declaration use Exten.dir ':all';
   # If you do not need this, moving things directly
   # into @EXPORT or @EXPORT_OK will save memory.
   our %EXPORT_TAGS = ( 'all' => [ qw() ] );

   our @EXPORT_OK = ( @{ $EXPORT_TAGS{'all'} } );

   our @EXPORT = qw();
   our $VERSION = '0.01';

   bootstrap Exten.dir $VERSION;

   # Preloaded methods go here.

   1;
   _ _END_ _
   # Below is stub documentation for your module.
   # You'd better edit it!

   =head1 NAME

   Exten.dir - Perl extension for blah blah blah

   =head1 SYNOPSIS
```

EXAMPLE 12.15 (CONTINUED)

```
    use Exten.dir;
    blah blah blah

    =head1 DESCRIPTION

    Stub documentation for Exten.dir, created by h2xs. It looks like
the author of the extension was negligent enough to leave the stub
unedited.

    Blah blah blah.

    =head2 EXPORT

    None by default.

    =head1 AUTHOR

    A. U. Thor, a.u.thor@a.galaxy.far.far.away

    =head1 SEE ALSO

    perl(1).

    =cut
```

EXPLANATION

1 The *h2xs* tool creates a subdirectory (this one is called *Exten.dir*) consisting of six files that will be used in the creation of a CPAN-style module. Before creating a module for CPAN, you should go to *www.cpan.org/modules/00modlist.long.html* to make sure someone else hasn't already written it, which could save you some work.

2 We change into the new directory created by *h2xs.*

3 This is a listing of the files created by *h2xs* (not shown). The *MANIFEST* file contains a list of all files just created in this directory and where any additional files should be listed that will be distributed with the module. The *Makefile.PL* file generates a *Makefile. Exten.dir.pm* is the skeletal module, which will contain extensions, and *Exten.dir.xs* will contain the *XSUB* routines for loading *C* extensions.

4 This is the skeleton module used to help set up the module correctly.

12.4 What You Should Know

1. What is the default package in a Perl program?
2. What is the symbol table?
3. How can you view the symbol table?
4. What is the *@INC* array?
5. What is a pragma?
6. What is the *PERL5LIB* environment variable for?
7. When should you use *require*?
8. How does *require* differ from *use*?
9. What is the *Exporter* module?
10. What is the *EXPORT_OK* array? The *%EXPORT_TAGS* hash?
11. What is the meaning of putting a "1" at the end of a *.pl* or *.pm* file?
12. How do you update the *@INC* array?
13. How do you access subroutines from another package?
14. How do you keep variables private?
15. What is the easiest way to install modules from CPAN?

12.5 What's Next?

The next chapter focuses on pointers, also called references. You will learn how to create complex data structures using pointers, how to create anonymous variables, how to dereference pointers, and how to pass them to subroutines.

You will learn the reasons for using pointers in Perl.

EXERCISE 12
I Hid All My Perls in a Package

1. Write a script called *myATM*. It will contain two packages: *Checking* and *main*. Later, this file will be broken into a user file and a module file.

2. In the *myATM* script, declare a package called *Checking*.
   It will contain a *my* variable called *balance* set to *0*.
   It will initially contain three subroutines:
   a. *get_balance*
   b. *deposit*
   c. *withdraw*

3. In package *main* (in the same file), create a *here document* that will produce the following output:

   1) Deposit
   2) Withdraw
   3) Current Balance
   4) Exit

   Ask the user to select one of the menu items. Until he selects number 4, the program will go into a loop to redisplay the menu and wait for the user to select another transaction.

   The subroutines will be called in the *main* package by qualifying the *Checking* package name with double colons.

   If the user chooses number 4, before the program exits, print today's date and the current balance to a file called *register*.

   Can you print the value of the balance without calling the *get_balance* subroutine from the user script?

4. Rewrite the *Checking* package so it gets the balance from the file *register* if the file exists; otherwise, it will start at a zero balance. Each time the program exits, save the current balance and the time and date in the *register* file.

5a. In Exercise 11 of Chapter 11, you wrote a program called *tripper* that contained a subroutine called *mileage*. It asked the user the number of miles he drove and the amount of gas he used. The subroutine was to calculate and return the user's mileage (miles per gallon). The arguments passed to the subroutine are the number of miles driven and the amount of gas used. These values are assigned to *my* variables. If you haven't written the *tripper* program, now is a good time to do so.

b. If the input is a non-number, a negative number, or zero for the amount of gas, use the *croak* function to print the error message.

Now create a directory called *myfunctions*. Change to that directory and create a file called *mileage.pl*. Put the subroutine *mileage* in the file *mileage.pl*.

c. In your *tripper* script, update the @*INC* array and use the *require* function to include the *mileage* subroutine. (Be sure that the last line after the closing curly brace of the subroutine is *1*.)

6. Move the *Checking* package from the *myATM* script into a file called *Checking.pm*. Now move the *Checking.pm* module into a directory called "myModules". Update the @*INC* array in the *myATM* script that will *use* the module. Use the *Checking* module in the *myATM* script.

chapter

13

Does This Job Require a Reference?

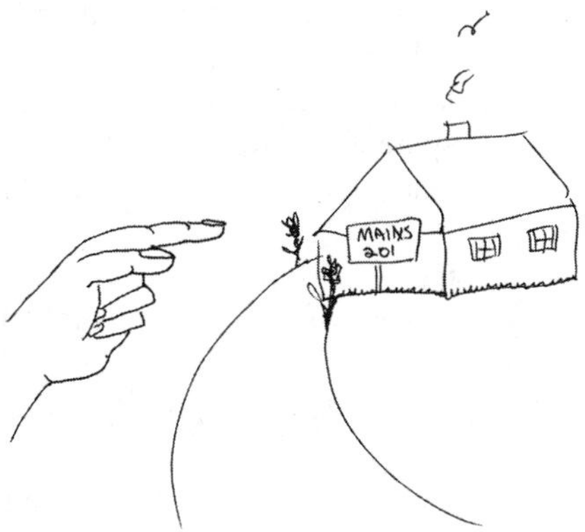

13.1 What Is a Reference? What Is a Pointer?

You can use the terms "reference" and "pointer" interchangeably in Perl. A reference is a variable that refers to another one. In short, it contains the address of another variable. We have seen the usefulness of references when passing values to a subroutine (Chapter 11). We can also use references, or pointers, to create more complex data types, such as a hash that contains a key followed by a list of values, or an array of arrays, etc. and we will need references in the next chapter when creating Perl objects.

13.1.1 Symbolic versus Hard References

A **hard reference** is a scalar variable that holds the address of another type of data. It is similar to a **pointer** found in the *C* programming language.[1] This chapter will focus on hard references.

A Perl variable resides in a symbol table and holds **only one** hard reference to its underlying value. Its value may be as simple as a single number or as complex as a hash. There may be other hard references that point to the same value, but the variable that actually holds the value is unaware of them.

A **symbolic reference** names another variable rather than just pointing to a value.[2] Typeglobs, variable names preceded by *, are a kind of symbolic reference. They are aliases.

You may remember using typeglobs in previous examples. In Chapter 11, we discussed how typeglobs were used in the early days of Perl to pass arguments to subroutines by reference. In Chapter 12, typeglobs were used to import symbols onto the symbol table of a package. The following statement uses typeglobs:

```
*town = *city;    # Any type called city can also be referenced as town
```

1. Unlike C pointers, Perl pointers are strings and you cannot perform pointer arithmetic with them.
2. Wall, L., *Programming Perl*, O'Reilly & Associates: Sebastopol, CA, 1996, p. 244.

The asterisk represents all of the funny characters that prefix variables, including subroutines, filehandles, and formats; i.e., it "globs" onto all the symbols in the symbol table that have that name.[3] **town* is an alias for **city*. It is your job to determine what symbol you want the alias to reference. This is done by prepending the correct funny character to the alias name when you want to access its underlying value. For example:

Given: **town = *city*
Then: *$town* refers to the scalar *$city*
@town refers to the array *@city*
$town{"mayor"}* refers to an element of a hash *$city{"mayor"}

Example 13.1 demonstrates another type of symbolic reference where the value of one variable references the name of another variable.

EXAMPLE 13.1

```
   #!/bin/perl
   # Program using symbolic references
1  $animal="dog";
2  $dog="Lady";
3  print "Your dog is called ${$animal}\n";# Symbolic reference
4  eval "\$$animal='Lassie';";
5  print "Why don't you call her ${$animal}?\n";

(Output)
3  Your dog is called Lady
5  Why don't you call her Lassie?
```

EXPLANATION

1 The scalar *$animal* is assigned the value "*dog*". The name *animal* is stored in the symbol table along with a reference to its value *dog*.
2 The scalar *$dog* is assigned the string "*Lady*".
3 The variable *${$animal}* evaluates to *Lady*. This is a symbolic reference. *$animal*, one variable, is evaluated to *dog*. The second dollar sign causes another variable, *$dog*, to be evaluated to its underlying value, "*Lady*". One variable has referenced another.
4 The *eval* function evaluates the statement as if in a separate little Perl program. The first dollar sign is escaped. *$animal* will be evaluated to its value, *dog*. The literal dollar sign, prepended to the result of the evaluation, leaves *$dog="Lassie"* as the statement.
5 After the *eval*, the value of *${$animal}*; i.e., $dog is "Lassie". It is printed.

3. This is not the same as the globbing done for filename substitution, as in <*p**>.

The *strict* Pragma. To protect yourself from inadvertently using symbolic references in a program, use the *strict* pragma with the *refs* argument. This causes Perl to check that symbolic references are **not** used in the program. Here, we reexecute the previous example using the *strict* pragma.

EXAMPLE 13.2

```
   #!/bin/perl
   # Program using symbolic references
1  use strict "refs";
2  $animal="dog";
3  $dog="Lady";
4  print "Your dog is called ${$animal}\n";
5  eval "\$$animal='Lassie';";
6  print "Why don't you call her ${$animal}?\n";

(Output)
Can't use string ("dog") as a SCALAR ref while "strict refs" in use at
symbolic.plx line 4.
```

EXPLANATION

1 The *strict* pragma ensures that the program uses only hard references and, if it doesn't, will abort during compilation and print an error message as shown in the output of this script.

3 This is line number 10 in the script. The program died at this point because of the first use of a symbolic reference, *${$language}*.

4 This line also includes a symbolic reference but is never reached, because the program had already aborted because *strict* caught it.

13.1.2 Hard References, Pointers

We discussed pointers in Chapter 11 when passing references to a subroutine. To reiterate: A **hard reference** is a scalar that holds the address of another data type. A variable that is assigned an address can also be called a **pointer** because it points to some other address or to another reference. This type of reference can point to a scalar, array, associative array, or a subroutine. The pointer was introduced in Perl 5 to give you the ability to create complex data types, such as arrays of arrays, arrays of hashes, hashes of hashes, etc. In all of the examples where typeglobs were used, we can now opt for pointers instead. Pointers provide a way to pass parameters to subroutines by reference.

The Backslash Operator. The backslash unary operator is used to create a hard reference, similar to the *&* used in *C* to get the "address of." In the following example, *$p* is the reference. It is assigned the address of the scalar *$x*.

```
$p = \$x;
```

An example of hard references from the Perl *man* page *perlref*:

```
$scalarref = \$foo;        # reference to scalar $foo
$arrayref  = \@ARGV;       # reference to array @ARGV
$hashref   = \%ENV;        # reference to hash %ENV
$coderef   = \&handler;    # reference to subroutine handler
$globref   = \*STDOUT;     # reference to typeglob STDOUT
$reftoref  = \$scalarref;  # reference to another reference
                             (pointer to pointer, ugh)
```

Dereferencing the Pointer. If you print the value of a reference (or pointer), you will see an address. If you want to go to that address and get the value stored there—that is, dereference the pointer—the pointer must be prefaced by two "funny" symbols. The first is the dollar sign, because the pointer itself is a scalar, and preceding that goes the funny symbol representing the type of data to which it points. When using more complex types, the arrow (infix) operator can be used.

EXAMPLE 13.3

```
(The Script)
    #!/bin/perl
1   $num=5;
2   $p = \$num;        # $p gets the address of $num
3   print 'The address assigned $p is ', $p, "\n";
4   print "The value stored at that address is $$p\n"; # dereference

(Output)
3   The address assigned $p is SCALAR(0xb057c)
4   The value stored at that address is 5
```

EXPLANATION

1. The scalar *$num* is assigned the value 5.
2. The scalar *$p* is assigned the address of *$num*. This is the function of the backslash operator. *$p* is called either a reference or a pointer; the terms are interchangeable.
3. The address stored in *$p* is printed. Perl also tells you the data type is *SCALAR*.
4. To dereference *$p*, another dollar sign is prepended to *$p*. This dollar sign tells Perl that you are looking for the value of the scalar that *$p* references; i.e., *$num*.

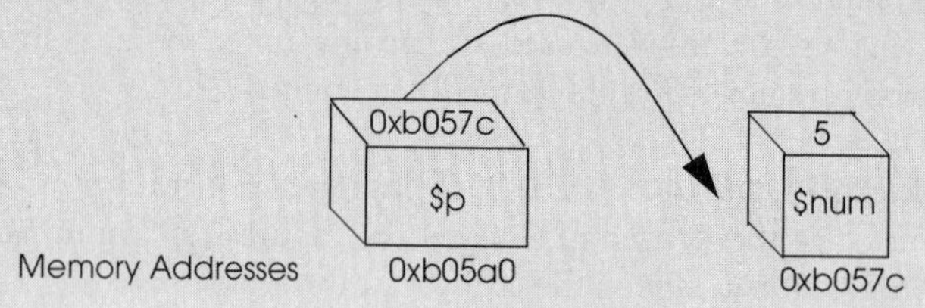

EXAMPLE 13.4

```
   #!/bin/perl
1  @toys = qw( Barbie Elmo Thomas Barney );
2  $num = @toys;
3  %games=("Nintendo"  => "Wii",
           "Sony"      => "PlayStation 3",
           "Microsoft" => "XBox 360",
         );
4  $ref1 = \$num;  # Create pointers
5  $ref2 = \@toys;
6  $ref3 = \%games;

7  print "There are $$ref1 toys.\n"; # dereference pointers
8  print "They are: ",join(",",@$ref2), ".\n";
9  print "Jessica's favorite toy is $ref2->[0].\n";
10 print "Willie's favorite toy is $ref2->[2].\n";

11 while(($key,$value)=each(%$ref3)){
      print "$key => $value\n";
   }
12 print "They waited in line for a $ref3->{'Nintendo'}\n";

(Output)
There are 4 toys.
They are: Barbie,Elmo,Thomas,Barney.
Jessica's favorite toy is Barbie.
Willie's favorite toy is Thomas.
Microsoft => XBox 360
Sony => PlayStation 3
Nintendo => Wii
They waited in line for a Wii
```

EXPLANATION

1. A list is assigned to the array *@toys*.
2. The array *@toys* is assigned to the scalar variable *$num*, returning the number of elements in the array.
3. The hash *%games* is assigned key/value pairs.
4. The pointer *$ref1* is a pointer. It is assigned the address of the scalar *$num* by using the backslash operator.
5. The pointer *$ref2* is assigned the address of the array *@toys*.
6. The pointer *$ref3* is assigned the address of the hash *%games*.
7. The pointer is dereferenced, meaning: Go to the address that *$ref1* is pointing to and print the value of the scalar stored there.
8. The pointer is again dereferenced, meaning: Go to the address that *$ref2* is pointing to, get the array, and print it.

EXPLANATION

9 The -> arrow operator is used to dereference the pointer and get the first element of the array. (This could also be written as *$$ref2[0]*.)

10 Again the -> arrow operator is used to dereference the pointer and retrieve the third element of the array.

11 The *each* function is used to retrieve the keys and values from the hash via its pointer. To dereference a hash, the % sign precedes the pointer variable.

12 The -> arrow operator is used to dereference the pointer and get the value of the hash where the key is "Nintendo". (This could also be written as *$$ref3{"Nintendo"}*.)

13.1.3 References and Anonymous Variables

It is not necessary to name a variable to create a reference (pointer) to it. If a variable or subroutine has no name, it is called **anonymous**. If an anonymous variable (or subroutine) is assigned to a scalar, then the scalar is a reference to that variable (subroutine).

The **arrow operator** (–>), also called the **infix operator**, is used to dereference the reference to anonymous arrays and hashes. Although not really necessary, the arrow operator makes the program easier to read.

Anonymous Arrays. Anonymous array elements are enclosed in square brackets (*[]*). These square brackets are not to be confused with the square brackets used to subscript an array. Here they are used as an expression to be assigned to a scalar. The brackets will not be interpolated if enclosed within quotes. The arrow (infix) operator is used to get the individual elements of the array.

EXAMPLE 13.5

```
(The Script)
   #!/bin/perl
1  my $arrayref = [ 'Woody', 'Buzz', 'Bo', 'Mr. Potato Head' ];
2  print "The value of the reference, \$arrayref is ",
                                         $arrayref, "\n";
   # All of these examples dereference $arrayref
3  print "$arrayref->[3]", "\n";
4  print $$arrayref[3], "\n";
5  print ${$arrayref}[3], "\n";
6  print "@{$arrayref}", "\n";

(Output)
2  The value of the reference, $arrayref is ARRAY(0x8a6f134)
3  Mr. Potato Head
4  Mr. Potato Head
5  Mr. Potato Head
6  Woody Buzz Bo Mr. Potato Head
```

EXPLANATION

1. The anonymous array elements are assigned to the array reference *$arrayref*.
2. The array reference contains the data type and the hexadecimal address of the anonymous array.
3. The fourth element of the array is printed. The pointer variable *$arrayref* is followed by the arrow operator pointing to the index value that will be retrieved.
4. The arrow operator is not really needed here. Instead, the element can be accessed by the two methods in lines 4 and 5.
6. The entire array is printed after dereferencing the pointer. Curly braces are required.

Anonymous Hashes. An **anonymous hash** is created by using curly braces (*{}*). You can mix array and hash composers to produce complex data types. These braces are not the same braces that are used when subscripting a hash. The anonymous hash is assigned to a scalar reference.

EXAMPLE 13.6

```
(The Script)
   #!/bin/perl
1  my $hashref = { "Name"=>"Woody",
                   "Type"=>"Cowboy"
                 };
2  print $hashref->{"Name"}, "\n\n";
3  print keys %$hashref, "\n";
4  print values %$hashref, "\n";

(Output)
2  Woody

3  NameType
4  WoodyCowboy
```

EXPLANATION

1. The anonymous hash contains a set of key/value pairs enclosed in curly braces. The anonymous hash is assigned to the reference *$hashref*.
2. The hash pointer *$hashref* uses the arrow operator to dereference the hash. The key *Name* is associated with the value *Woody*.
3. The *keys* function returns all the keys in the anonymous hash via the reference (pointer).
4. The *values* function returns all the values in the anonymous hash via the reference (pointer).

13.1.4 Nested Data Structures

The ability to create references (pointers) to anonymous data structures lends itself to more complex types. For example, you can have hashes nested in hashes or arrays of hashes or arrays of arrays, etc.

Just as with simpler references, the anonymous data structures are dereferenced by prepending the reference with the correct funny symbol that represents its data type. For example, if *$p* is a pointer to a scalar, you can write *$$p* to dereference the scalar, and if *$p* is a pointer to an array, you can write *@$p* to dereference the array or *$$p[0]* to get the first element of the array. You can also dereference a pointer by treating it as a block. *$$p[0]* could also be written *${$p}[0]* or *@{p}[0..3]*. Sometimes, the braces are used to prevent ambiguity, and sometimes they are necessary so that the funny character dereferences the correct part of the structure.

Lists of Lists. A list may contain another list or set of lists, most commonly used to create a multidimensional array. A reference is assigned an anonymous array containing another anonymous array in Examples 13.7 and 13.8.

EXAMPLE 13.7

```
   #!/bin/perl
   # Program to demonstrate a reference to a list with a
   # nested list
1  my $arrays = [ '1', '2', '3', [ 'red', 'blue', 'green' ]];
2  for($i=0;$i<3;$i++){
3      print $arrays->[$i],"\n";
   }

4  for($i=0;$i<3;$i++){
5      print $arrays->[3]->[$i],"\n";
   }
6  print "@{$arrays}\n";
7  print "--@{$arrays->[3]}--", "\n";

(Output)
3  1
   2
   3
5  red
   blue
   green

6  1 2 3 ARRAY(0x8a6f134)
7  --red blue green--
```

EXPLANATION

1 *$arrays* is a reference (pointer) to a four-element array that contains another anonymous three-element array whose elements are *red*, *blue*, and *green*.
2 The *for* loop is used to get the values of the first array, consisting of elements *1*, 2, and 3.
3 The arrow operator is used here to dereference *$arrays*.
4 The second *for* loop is used to iterate through the nested anonymous array. Since this array is the fourth element of the first array, starting at subscript 0, the first index is *3* and the second index references each of its elements.
5 Each of the elements (*red, blue, green*) of the nested anonymous array is printed.
6 By prepending the @ symbol to the block containing the reference, the elements of the anonymous array are retrieved and printed. The third element of the array is a reference (pointer) to another anonymous hash. Its address is printed.
7 The second nested array is dereferenced and printed.

EXAMPLE 13.8

```
(The Script)
    #!/bin/perl
    # Program to demonstrate a pointer to a two-dimensional array.
1   my $matrix = [
                   [ 0, 2, 4 ],
                   [ 4, 1, 32 ],
                   [ 12, 15, 17 ]
                 ] ;

2   print "Row 3 column 2 is $matrix->[2]->[1].\n";

3   print "Dereferencing with two loops.\n";
4   for($x=0;$x<3;$x++){
5       for($y=0;$y<3;$y++){
6           print "$matrix->[$x]->[$y] ";
        }
        print "\n\n";
    }
    print "\n";
7   print "Derefencing with one loop.\n";
8   for($i = 0; $i < 3; $i++){
9       print "@{$matrix->[$i]}", "\n\n";
    }
10  $p=\$matrix;        # Reference to a reference
11  print "Dereferencing a reference to reference.\n"
12  print ${$p}->[1][2], "\n";
```

EXAMPLE 13.8 (CONTINUED)

```
(Output)
2   Row 3 column 2 is 15.
3   Dereferencing with two loops.
6   0 2 4
    4 1 32
    12 15 17

7   Dereferencing with one loop.
9   0 2 4
    4 1 32
    12 15 17

11  Dereferencing a reference to reference.
12  32
```

EXPLANATION

1. The reference (pointer) *$matrix* is assigned an anonymous array of three anonymous arrays; that is, a two-dimensional array (list of lists).
2. The arrow operator is used to access the first element of the array. An arrow is implied between adjacent subscript brackets and is not needed. It could have been written as *$matrix–>[2][1]*.
4. The outer *for* loop is entered. This will iterate through the rows of the array.
5. The inner *for* loop is entered. This loop iterates through the columns of the array.
6. Each element of the two-dimensional array is printed via the reference (pointer).
8. This time, only one *for* loop will be used to print out the contents of the matrix.
9. The block format is used to dereference the pointer. All elements of each list are printed.
10. *$p* is a reference assigned another reference, *$matrix*. This is more commonly called a pointer to a pointer.
12. If you want to access the array elements—that is, dereference *$p*—an additional dollar sign is needed, one for *p* and one for *matrix*. The arrow is implied between the adjacent subscripts; for example, this line could have been written *$p–>[1]–>[2]*.

Array of Hashes. A list may contain a hash or a set of hashes. In Example 13.9, a reference is assigned an anonymous array containing two anonymous hashes.

EXAMPLE 13.9

```
1   my $petref = [   { "name"  => "Rover",
                       "type"  => "dog",
                       "owner" => "Mr. Jones",
                     },
2                    { "name"  => "Sylvester",
                       "type"  => "cat",
                       "owner" => "Mrs. Black",
                     }
3                ];

4   print "The first pet's name is $petref->[0]->{name}.\n";
    print "Printing an array of hashes.\n";
5   for($i=0; $i<2; $i++){
6       while(($key,$value)=each %{$petref->[$i]} ){
7           print "$key -- $value\n";
        }
        print "\n";
    }
    print "Adding a hash to the array.\n";

8   push @{$petref},{ "owner"=>"Mrs. Crow", "name"=>"Tweety",
                      "type"=>"bird" };

9   while(($key,$value)=each %{$petref->[2]}){
10      print "$key -- $value\n";
    }
```

```
(Output)
4   The first pet's name is Rover.
    Printing an array of hashes.
7   owner -- Mr. Jones
    type -- dog
    name -- Rover

    owner -- Mrs. Black
    type -- cat
    name -- Sylvester

    Adding a hash to the array.
10  type -- bird
    owner -- Mrs. Crow
    name -- Tweety
```

EXPLANATION

1. The reference (pointer) *$petref* is assigned the address of an anonymous array containing two anonymous hashes.
2. This is the second element of the list, an anonymous hash with its key/value pairs.

EXPLANATION (CONTINUED)

3 This is the closing square bracket for the anonymous array.
4 The pointer *$petref* is used to dereference the list, first by selecting the zeroth element of the array and, with the arrow operator, selecting the key in the hash. The value associated with the key *name* is displayed.
5 The *for* loop is entered to loop through the list.
6 The *while* loop is entered. Each time through the loop, a key and a value are extracted from the hash pointed to by *$petref–>[$i]* and assigned to *$key* and *$value*, respectively.
7 The key/value pairs are displayed.
8 A new hash is pushed onto the array, *@{$petref}*, with the *push* function.
9 The *while* loop is entered. Each time through the loop, a key and a value are extracted from the hash pointed to by *$petref–>[0]* and assigned to *$key* and *$value*, respectively. The new hash that was pushed on will be displayed.
10 After dereferencing *$petref*, the second element of the array, *$petref–>[0]*, is dereferenced, and each of the key/value pairs of the nested hash is displayed.

Hash of Hashes. A hash may contain another hash or a set of hashes. In Example 13.10, a reference is assigned an anonymous hash consisting of two keys, each of which is associated with a value that happens to be another hash (consisting of its own key/value pairs).

EXAMPLE 13.10

```
#!/bin/perl
# Program to demonstrate a hash containing anonymous hashes.
my $hashref = {
               Math     => {                    # key
                     "Anna"  => 100,
                     "Hao"   => 95,             # values
                     "Rita"  => 85,
                   },
               Science => {                     # key
                     "Sam"   => 78,
                     "Lou"   => 100,            # values
                     "Vijay" => 98,
                   },
          };

print "Anna got $hashref->{'Math'}->{'Anna'} on the Math test.\n";
$hashref->{'Science'}->{'Lou'}=90;
print "Lou's grade was changed
 to $hashref->{'Science'}->{'Lou'}.\n";
print "The nested hash of Math students and grades is: ";
print %{$hashref->{'Math'}}, "\n";    # Prints the nested hash, Math
```

EXAMPLE 13.10 (CONTINUED)

```
10 foreach $key (keys %{$hashref}){
11     print "Outer key: $key \n";
12     while(($nkey,$nvalue)=each(%{$hashref->{$key}})){
13        printf "\tInner key: %-5s -- Value: %-8s\n",
                                          $nkey,$nvalue;
       }
   }
```

```
(Output)
5  Anna got 100 on the Math test.
7  Lou's grade was changed to 90.
8  The nested hash of Math students and grades is: Rita85Hao95Anna100
11 Outer key: Science
13 Inner key: Lou   -- Value: 90
   Inner key: Sam   -- Value: 78
   Inner key: Vijay -- Value: 98
11 Outer key: Math
13 Inner key: Rita  -- Value: 85
   Inner key: Hao   -- Value: 95
   Inner key: Anna  -- Value: 1005
   Anna got 100 on the Math test.
```

EXPLANATION

1 The anonymous hash is defined. It consists of two hash keys, *Math* and *Science*, whose values are themselves a hash (key/value pair). The address of the hash is assigned to *$hashref*. *$hashref* is a hard reference (pointer).

2 *Math* is the key for its value, a nested hash.

3 *Science* is the key for its value, also a nested hash.

4 This is the closing curly brace of the anonymous hash.

5 To access Anna's grade, first the key *Math* is dereferenced, followed by the arrow operator and the nested key *Anna*. The second arrow is not necessary but may make the construct easier to follow. In fact, you don't need to use the arrow operator at all. This could have been written as *$$hashref{Math} {Anna}*.

6 Using the *$hashref* reference, you can also change or add new values to the hash. Lou's grade is changed.

7 The new grade is printed by dereferencing *$hashref*.

8, 9 The nested hash *Math* is printed by enclosing the reference *$hashref–>Math* in curly braces prepended by a %. The % represents the unnamed hash, both keys and values.

10 The *foreach* loop iterates through the list (produced by the *keys* function) of outer keys in the anonymous hash.

11 Each of the outer keys is printed.

12 Since each of the outer keys is associated with a value that happens to be another hash, the reference *$hashref* is dereferenced by placing *$hashref–>{$key}* in a block prepended by a percent sign.

13 The nested keys and their associated values are printed.

Hash of Hashes with Lists of Values. A hash may contain nested hash keys associated with lists of values. In Example 13.11, a reference is assigned two keys associated with values that are also keys into another hash. The nested hash keys are, in turn, associated with an anonymous list of values.

EXAMPLE 13.11

```
(The Script)
    # A hash with nested hash keys and anonymous arrays of values
1   my $hashptr = { "Teacher"=>{"Subjects"=>[ qw(Science Math English)]},
                    "Musician"=>{"Instruments"=>[ qw(piano flute harp)]},
                  };
                  # Teacher and Musician are keys.
                  # The values consist of nested hashes.
2   print $hashptr->{"Teacher"}->{"Subjects"}->[0],"\n";
3   print "@{$hashptr->{'Musician'}->{'Instruments'}}\n";

(Output)
2   Science
3   piano flute harp
```

EXPLANATION

1 The pointer *$hashptr* is assigned an anonymous hash consisting of two keys, *Teacher* and *Musician*. The values for *Teacher* consist of another anonymous hash with a key, *Subjects*, associated with an anonymous array of values, *Science*, *Math*, and *English*. The key *Musician* also consists of an anonymous hash with a key, *Instruments*, associated with an anonymous array of values, *piano*, *flute*, and *harp*.

2 To dereference the pointer, the arrow operator is used to separate the nested keys. The final arrow refers to the first element of the array of values associated with *Subjects*, *Science*.

3 To get all the values from the anonymous array associated with the key, the @ symbol precedes the pointer and its nested keys, each key separated with the arrow operator. If a variable has no name, you can replace its name with a block preceded by the symbol for the correct data type. Here, the curly braces enclosing the entire structure allow you to dereference the whole block as an array.

13.1.5 References and Subroutines

Anonymous Subroutines. An anonymous subroutine is created by using the keyword *sub* without a subroutine name. The expression is terminated with a semicolon. For more on using anonymous subroutine, see "Closures" in Chapter 14.

EXAMPLE 13.12

```
(The Script)
   #!/bin/perl
1  my $subref = sub { print @_ ; };
2  &$subref('a','b','c');
   print "\n";

(Output)
1  abc
```

EXPLANATION

1 The scalar *$subref* is assigned an anonymous subroutine by reference. The only function of the subroutine is to print its arguments stored in the @_ array.
2 The subroutine is called via its reference and passed three arguments.

Subroutines and Passing by Reference. When passing arguments to subroutines, they are sent to the subroutine and stored in the @_ array. If you have a number of arguments, say an array, a scalar, and another array, the arguments are all flattened out onto the @_ array. It would be hard to tell where one argument ended and the other began unless you also passed along the size of each of the arrays, and then the size would be pushed onto the @_ array and you would have to get that to determine where the first array ended, and so on. The @_ could also be quite large if you are passing a 1,000-element array. So, the easiest and most efficient way to pass arguments is by address, as shown in Example 13.13.

EXAMPLE 13.13

```
(The Script)
1  @toys = qw(Buzzlightyear  Woody  Bo);
2  $num = @toys;  # Number of elements in @toys is assigned to $num
3  gifts( \$num, \@toys );    # Passing by reference

4  sub gifts {
5     my($n, $t) = @_;    # Localizing the reference with 'my'
6     print "There are $$n gifts: ";
7     print "@$t\n";
8     push(@$t, 'Janey', 'Slinky');
   }
9  print "The original array was changed to: @toys\n";

(Output)
6,7 There are 3 gifts: Buzzlightyear Woody Bo
9   The original array was changed to: Buzzlightyear Woody Bo Janey
     Slinky
```

EXPLANATION

1. The array *@toys* is assigned three values.
2. The scalar *$num* is assigned the number of elements in the *@toys* array. (Remember, a scalar contains only one value, so when you assign an array to a scalar, the number of elements in the array is assigned to the scalar.)
3. The subroutine *gifts* is called with two pointers as parameters.
4. The subroutine is entered.
5. The @_ array contains the two pointer variables. The values of the pointers are copied into two lexical variables, *$n* and *$t*.
6. The pointer to the scalar is dereferenced. It points to the scalar *$n*.
7. The pointer to the array is dereferenced. It points to the array *@toys*.
8. The *push* function adds two new elements to the array pointed to by *$t*.
9. After exiting the subroutine, *@toys* is printed with its new values.

EXAMPLE 13.14

```
(The Script)
    # This script demonstrates the use of references
    # to pass arrays. Instead of passing the entire
    # array, a reference is passed.
    # The value of the last expression is returned.

    my @list1=(1 .. 100);
    my @list2=(5, 10, 15, 20);

    print "The total is :  ",  &addemup( \@list1, \@list2) , ".\n";
              # Two pointers are passed
    sub addemup{
        my( $arr1, $arr2) = @_;
              # @_ contains two pointers (references)
        my ($total);
        print $arr1, "\n" ;
        print $arr2, "\n";

        foreach $num ( @$arr1, @$arr2 ){
            $total+=$num;
        }

        return $total;  # The expression is evaluated and returned
    }

(Output)
    ARRAY(0x8a62d68)
    ARRAY(0x8a60f2c)
    The total is:  5100.
```

EXPLANATION

1. The array *@list1* is assigned a list of numbers between *1* and *100*.
2. The array *@list2* is assigned the list of numbers *5*, *10*, *15*, and *20*.
3. The *addemup* subroutine is called. Two parameters are passed. The backslash preceding each of the arrays causes the addresses (pointers) to be passed.
4. The subroutine *addemup* is declared and defined.
5. The pointers are passed to the @_ array and assigned to *my* variables *$arr1* and *$arr2*, respectively.
6. The *my* variable *$total* is declared.

7, 8 The addresses of the pointers are printed.

9. The *foreach* loop is entered. *@$arr1* and *@$arr2* dereference the pointers, creating a list of array elements to be processed, one at a time.
10. Each time through the loop, *$total* accumulates the sum of *$total* + *$num*.
11. The sum is returned to where the subroutine was called on line 3. Since the subroutine was called as an argument to the *print* function, the results will be printed after they are returned from the subroutine.

13.1.6 Filehandle References

One of the only ways to pass a filehandle to a subroutine is by reference. You can use a typeglob to create an alias for the filehandle and then use the backslash to create a reference to the typeglob. Wow…

EXAMPLE 13.15

```
(The Script)
    #!/bin/perl
1   open(README, "/etc/passwd") || die;

2   &readit(\*README);        # Reference to a typeglob

3   sub readit {
4       my ($passwd)=@_;
5       print "\$passwd is a $passwd.\n";
6       while(<$passwd>){
7           print;
        }
    }

9   seek(README,0,0) || die "seek: $!\n";
                            # Reset back to begining of job
```

EXAMPLE 13.15 (CONTINUED)

```
(Output)
5   $passwd is a GLOB(0xb0594).
7   root:x:0:1:Super-User:/:/usr/bin/csh
    daemon:x:1:1::/:
    bin:x:2:2::/usr/bin:
    sys:x:3:3::/:
    adm:x:4:4:Admin:/var/adm:
    lp:x:71:8:Line Printer Admin:/usr/spool/lp:
    smtp:x:0:0:Mail Daemon User:/:
    uucp:x:5:5:uucp Admin:/usr/lib/uucp:
    nuucp:x:9:9:uucp Admin:/var/spool/uucppublic:/usr/lib/uucp/uucico
    listen:x:37:4:Network Admin:/usr/net/nls:
    nobody:x:60001:60001:Nobody:/:
    noaccess:x:60002:60002:No Access User:/:
    nobody4:x:65534:65534:SunOS 4.x Nobody:/:
    ellie:x:9496:40:Ellie Quigley:/home/ellie:/usr/bin/csh
9   seek: Bad file number
```

EXPLANATION

1 The */etc/passwd* file is attached to the *README* filehandle and opened for reading.

2 The *readit* subroutine is called. The filehandle is passed by creating a reference to a typeglob. First, the filehandle symbol is globbed with the asterisk. Then, the reference to the typeglob is created by prefixing the typeglob with a backslash.

3 The *readit* subroutine is defined.

4 The @_ variable contains the reference. It is assigned to a local scalar variable called *$passwd*. *$passwd* is a reference to the filehandle.

5 The reference *$passwd*, when printed, shows that it contains the address of a typeglob (alias).

6, 7 The expression in the *while* loop causes a line to be read from the */etc/passwd* file and assigned to the $_ variable. The line is printed to the screen. The loop will continue until all the lines have been read and printed.

9 The *seek* function resets the read pointer for this file back to the begining of the file.

13.1.7 The *ref* Function

The *ref* function is used to test for the existence of a reference. If the argument for *ref* is a pointer variable, *ref* returns the type of data the reference points to; e.g., *SCALAR* is returned if the reference points to a scalar, and *ARRAY* is returned if it points to an array. If the argument is not a reference, the null string is turned. Table 13.1 lists the values returned by the *ref* function

Table 13.1 Return Values from the *ref* Function

What Is Returned	***Meaning***
REF	Pointer to pointer
SCALAR	Pointer to scalar
ARRAY	Pointer to array
HASH	Pointer to hash
CODE	Pointer to subroutine
GLOB	Pointer to typeglob

EXAMPLE 13.16

```
(The Script)
1   sub gifts;      # Forward declaration
2   $num = 5;
3   $junk = "xxx";
4   @toys = qw/Budlightyear Woody Thomas/ ;
5   gifts( \$num, \@toys, $junk );
6   sub gifts {
7       my( $n, $t, $j) = @_;
8       print "\$n is a reference.\n" if ref($n);
        print "\$t is a reference.\n" if ref($t);
9       print "\$j is a not a reference.\n" if ref($j);
10      printf "\$n is a reference to a %s.\n", ref($n);
11      printf "\$t is a reference to an %s.\n", ref($t);
    }

(Output)
8   $n is a reference.
    $t is a reference.
9
10  $n is a reference to a SCALAR.
11  $t is a reference to an ARRAY.
```

EXPLANATION

1. The subroutine *gifts* is a forward declaration, allowing Perl to know it is a subroutine defined somewhere in the program. You will not need an ampersand to call the subroutine if it is declared before it is defined.
2. The scalar *$num* is assigned 5.
3. The scalar *$junk* is assigned the string *xxx*.

EXPLANATION (CONTINUED)

4 The array *@toys* is assigned a list.
5 The subroutine *gifts* is called. The first two variables are passed as references by preceding them with a backslash. The last variable, *$junk,* is not passed as a reference.
6 The subroutine *gifts* is defined.
7 The values assigned to the @_ array, in this case, two references (addresses) and one nonreference, will be assigned to *$n, $t,* and *$j,* respectively, and made local with the *my* function.
8 The *ref* function is called with a reference, *$n*, as its argument. The line will be printed only if the variable *$n* is a reference.
9 *$j* is not a reference. The return value for the *ref* function is null.
10 The *printf* function prints the value of the data type returned from *ref*, a scalar.
11 The *printf* function prints the value of the data type returned from *ref*, an array.

13.2 What You Should Know

1. What is the difference between a symbolic and hard reference?
2. What is a typeglob?
3. How do you create a pointer to a hash?
4. How can you tell an anonymous array from a named array?
5. Show two ways to dereference this pointer: *$ptr = { 'Name' => "John"; }*
6. How do you dereference this pointer? *$p = \$x;*
7. What is meant by a nested hash?
8. How do you create a two-dimensional array?
9. What is the advantage of passing by reference?
10. What is the purpose of the *ref* function?

13.3 What's Next?

Now that you understand pointers, you will be ready learn how to create objects in Perl. The next chapter focuses on object-oriented Perl. It is a big chapter and extremely important if you are going to use modules from other libraries or CPAN, etc. You will learn how to create objects, assign properties to objects, use methods to manipulate objects, and how to destroy and reuse them. You will learn about *@ISA* and inheritance, closure, and garbage collection, etc. You will also learn how to document your modules with POD, Plain Old Documentation.

EXERCISE 13
It's Not Polite to Point!

1. Rewrite *tripper* (from Chapter 11) to take two pointers as arguments and copy the arguments from the @_ in the subroutine into two *my* pointer variables.

2. Create a hash **named** *employees* with the following three keys:
   Name
   Ssn
   Salary

   The values will be assigned as undefined (*undef* is a built-in Perl function). For example: *Name => undef,*

   a. Create a reference to the hash.
   b. Assign values to each of the keys using the reference.
   c. Print the keys and values of the hash using the built-in *each* function and the reference.
   d. Print the value of the reference; in other words, what the reference variable contains, not what it points to.

3. Rewrite the above exercise so the hash is anonymous, and assign the anonymous hash to a reference (pointer). Delete one of the keys from the hash using the reference (use the *delete* function).
4. Write a program that will contain the following structure:

```
$student = { Name    => undef,
             SSN     => undef,
             Friends => [],
             Grades  => { Science => [],
                          Math    => [],
                          English => [],
                          }
           };
```

   Use the pointer to assign and display output resembling the following:

```
Name is John Smith.
Social Security Number is 510-23-1232.
Friends are Tom, Bert, Nick.
Grades are:
         Science--100, 83, 77
         Math--90, 89, 85
         English--76, 77, 65
```

chapter

14

Bless Those Things! (Object-Oriented Perl)

14.1 The OOP Paradigm

14.1.1 Packages and Modules Revisited

The big addition to Perl 5 was the ability to do object-oriented programming, called OOP for short. OOP is centered on the way a program is organized. Object-oriented languages, such as *C++* and *Java,* bundle up data into a variable and call it an **object**. An object can be described as a noun in English: a person, place, or thing. A cat, a computer, and an employee are objects. Adjectives describe nouns. For example, the cat is sneaky, the computer is fast, the employee is called "John." In OO languages, the adjectives that describe the object are called **properties**, also called **attributes**. Verbs that describe what the object can do or what can be done to it are called **methods** in OO. The cat eats, the computer crashes, the employee works. Perl methods are just specialized subroutines.

The object's data is normally kept **private**. Messages are sent to the object through its **methods**. The methods are normally **public**. The only way that a user of the program should access the data is through these public methods. If you have an object called "money", the methods might be *earnit(), findit(), stealit()*, etc.

The data and the methods are packaged up into a data structure called a **class**. A Perl package will function as a class when using the object-oriented approach. This is not really a new idea for Perl, since data is already encapsulated in packages. Recall from our short discussion of packages that a package gives a sense of privacy to your program. Each package has its own symbol table, a hash that contains all the names in the "current" package. This makes it possible to create variables and subroutines that have their own namespace within a package. When using different packages within your program, each package has its own namespace, thus protecting the accidental clobbering of variables with the same name. The idea of hiding data in packages, then, is inherently part of Perl and also happens to be one of the basic tenets of object-oriented programming.

Every Perl program has at least one package called *main*, where Perl statements are internally compiled. The standard Perl library consists of a number of files containing packages. Most of these files are called **modules**. A module is really just a fancy package that is reusable. The reuse of code is done through **inheritance**; that is, a package can inherit characteristics from a parent, or base, class and thus extend or restrict its own capabilities. The ability to extend the functionality of a class is called **polymorphism**. Hiding data (encapsulation), inheritance, and polymorphism are considered the basic tenets of the object-oriented philosophy.

To create a Perl module, you still use the *package* keyword, and the scope is from the declaration of the package to the end of the enclosing block or file. Packages normally are the size of one file. The files can be recognized as modules if their names end with a *.pm* extension and if the first letter of the module is capitalized. **Pragmas** are another special kind of module (the name is spelled in lowercase but still has the *.pm* extension) that directs the compiler to behave in a specified way. Whether the package is called a module or a pragma, it has some special features that differentiate it from an ordinary package. Those special features introduced in Perl 5 give you the ability to model your programs with the object-oriented way of abstract thinking. You can think of procedural languages as action-oriented and OO languages as object-oriented.

Tom Christianson, discussing Perl and objects on his Web page "Easy Perl5 Object Intro," says that people tend to shy away from highly convenient Perl 5 modules because some of them deal with objects. Unfortunately, some problems very much lend themselves to objects. Christianson says that people shouldn't be scared by this, because merely knowing enough OO programming to use someone else's modules is not nearly as difficult as actually designing and implementing one yourself.[1] Even if you are not interested in writing programs that take advantage of the OOP features of Perl but still need to use Perl modules that do utilize objects, reading through this chapter should greatly enhance your understanding of how these modules work.

14.1.2 Some Object-Oriented Lingo

Object-oriented programming is a huge subject. Thousands of books have been written on OO programming, design, and methodology. Many programmers of the 1990s moved away from traditional top-down structured programming and toward object-oriented programming languages for building complex software. This is not a book on object-oriented design or programming. However, there are some basic key words associated with OOP that should be mentioned before tackling Perl's OOP features. They are listed in Table 14.1.

1. Go to *www.perl.com/CPAN-local/doc/FMTEYEWTK/easy_objects.html* to see Tom Christianson's Web page.

Table 14.1 Key OOP Words

Word	Perl Meaning
Data encapsulation	Hiding data and subroutines from the user, as in a package
Inheritance	The reuse of code, usually from a library where a package inherits from other packages
Polymorphism	Literally "many forms" and specifically, the ability to extend the functionality of a class
Object	A referenced type that knows what class it belongs to; an instance of a class
Method	A special subroutine that manipulates objects
Class	A package that contains data and methods
Constructor	A method that creates and initializes an object
Destructor	A method that destroys an object
Setters/Getters	Methods that store data in an object or fetch data from an object

14.2 Classes, Objects, and Methods

14.2.1 Real World

Suppose you want to build a house. First, you would buy a piece of property located at a specific address. Then you would hire an architect or buy a program for your computer to help design the house. You would decide what type, style, how many rooms, doors, windows, etc. After you design the house, you will hire a contractor to build the house. Once it's built, you have access to your new house, you can go inside, set up housekeeping, paint it, clean it, furnish it, remove trash, landscape it, whatever. But before you can really do anything in or around your house, you must build it. Later you may want to add a new room, show it for sale, demolish it, etc. Since you have the blueprints, you could find another piece of property and build a house just like yours, maybe paint it a different color, change the landscaping, etc. In fact, you could build a whole development with houses like yours from the same design, each house identified by its unique address.

In an object-oriented language, the house would be the object, a noun. The style, number of rooms, type, etc., would be the properties that describe the object, like adjectives, and the verbs, such as paint the house, move into the house, show the house, describe the "behaviors" for the object.

All of this will become clearer as we examine a number of examples and discuss how Perl creates, maniuplates, and destroys objects.

14.2.2 The Steps

This chapter will discuss a number of topics in detail. For the big picture, the following steps are necessary to create the new data type called object and define what it can do:

1. Determine what your object is and what it is supposed to accomplish (design).
2. Create the new object (constructor) in a package, called a class.
3. Describe the object; i.e., give it properties, attributes (adjectives).
4. Bless the object (make the data type an object).
5. Define the functions (verbs), what it can do or what can be done to it (methods).
6. Use the object (define the user interface, call the methods).
7. Reuse the object (inheritance).
8. Destroy the object (remove the object from memory).

14.2.3 Classes and Privacy

A Perl class is just a package. The terms are interchangeable. A class is stored in a *.pm* module, and the class name is the same as the module (minus the *.pm* extension). If you want to distinguish between the two terms, a class is a package containing special subroutines called **methods** that manipulate objects. A Perl class normally consists of:

1. The data that describes the object.
2. A function, called "bless," that creates the object.
3. Special subroutines, called "methods," that know how to create, access, manipulate, and destroy the object.

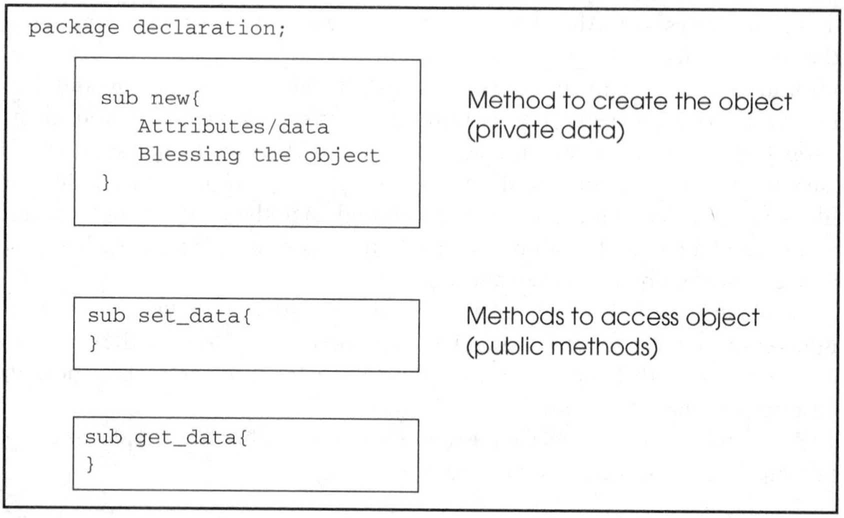

Figure 14.1 What makes up a class? The *.pm* file.

Since a class is really just a package, it has its own symbol table, and the data or routines in one class can be accessed in another via the double colon (Perl 5) or the single apostrophe (Perl 4).

Unlike other languages, Perl does not strictly monitor public/private borders within its modules.[2] To keep variables private, the *my* function is used. The *my* variables exist only within the innermost enclosing block, subroutine, *eval*, or file. The *my* variables cannot be accessed from another package by using the double colon (or single apostrophe), because *my* variables are not related to any package; they are not stored in the symbol table of the package in which they are created.

EXAMPLE 14.1

```
   #!/bin/perl
1  package main;

2  $name = "Susan";
3  my $birthyear = 1942;

4  package nosy;
5  print "Hello $main::name.\n";
6  print "You were born in $main::birthyear?\n";

(Output)
5  Hello Susan.
6  You were born in ?
```

EXPLANATION

1. The package is *main*.
2. The scalar *$name* is global in scope within this package.
3. The scalar *$birthyear* is local to this and any enclosing inner blocks.
4. The package *nosy* is declared. Its scope is from the declaration to the bottom of the file.
5. The global variable *$name* can be accessed by qualifying it with its package name and two colons.
6. The scalar *$birthyear* is inaccessible to this package via the symbol table. It was declared with the *my* function in a different package, *main*, and is not associated with any symbol table but is stored in a private scratch pad created within the enclosing block.

2. Wall, L., and Schwartz, R. L., *Programming Perl*, 2nd ed., O'Reilly & Associates: Sebastopol, CA, 1998, p. 287.

14.2.4 Objects

To begin with, an object in Perl is created by using a reference. A reference, if you recall, is a scalar that holds the address of some variable. It's a pointer. A reference might also point to a variable or subroutine that has no name, called an anonymous variable. For example, here is a reference, called *$ref*, to an anonymous hash consisting of two key/value pairs:

```
my $ref  = { "Owner"=>"Tom",   "Price"=>"25000" };
```

To access a value in the anonymous hash, the reference (pointer) *$ref* can be dereferenced by using the arrow operator as follows:

```
$ref->{"Owner"}
```

To make a Perl object, first a reference is created. The reference normally is assigned the address of an anonymous hash (although it could be assigned the address of an array or scalar or subroutine). The hash will contain the data members, properties, of the object. In addition to storing the address of the hash, the reference must know what package it belongs to. This is done by creating the reference and then "blessing" it into a package. The *bless* function acts on the "thing" being referenced in the package, not the reference itself. It creates an internal pointer to track what package the thing (object) belongs to. The object is the thing (usually a hash) that was blessed into the class (package). If the package is not listed as the second argument, the *bless* function assumes the current package. It returns a reference to the blessed object. (See "The *bless* Function" for a complete discussion of *bless*.)

```
my $ref  = { Owner => "Tom",  Price => 250000 };    # This is the object
bless( $ref, Class);    # The object is blessed into the package named Class
return $ref;            # A reference to the object is returned
```

Once an object has been blessed, you don't have to export symbols with the *@EXPORT_OK* or *@EXPORT* arrays. In fact, as a general rule, if the module is trying to be object-oriented, then export nothing.

The *House* Class. Figure 14.2 demonstrates how you might visualize a *House* class. First you would create a package. This package is called *House* and is found in a file called *House.pm*. In OO lingo, the package will now be called a **class**. (Note the class name must be same as the filename without the *.pm* extension.) To illustrate encapsulation, the house object is enclosed around the data that describes it. The properties, or attributes, describe characteristics of the object, such as its owner, style, size, color, and so forth. In our example, the house properties are *Owner*, *Style*, and *Price*. In Perl, the object is often described with an anonymous hash, where the key/value pairs are the properties of the object. Outside of the house, subroutines are listed. In the OO world, these subroutines are called public methods, and they are the way you get access to the object. They can get access to the object but not until it exists. They often describe "behaviors" of the object; i.e., what it can do or what can be done to it. In fact, the methods should be the only way to get access to the object. For our house object, one method to access the house might be to move in, another to clean it, another to display it, and so on. Methods in Perl are just glorified subroutines.

There are no special Perl keywords called *private*, *public*, or *protected* as in other OO languages. Perl's package mechanism makes up the class where the data and subroutines, called methods, are stored. The *my* function keeps variables lexically scoped, and the *bless* function guarantees that when the object is created, it will know to which class it belongs. In summary, the object is usually a pointer to an anonymous hash, array, or scalar and is manipulated by special functions called methods that have access to the object via the pointer.

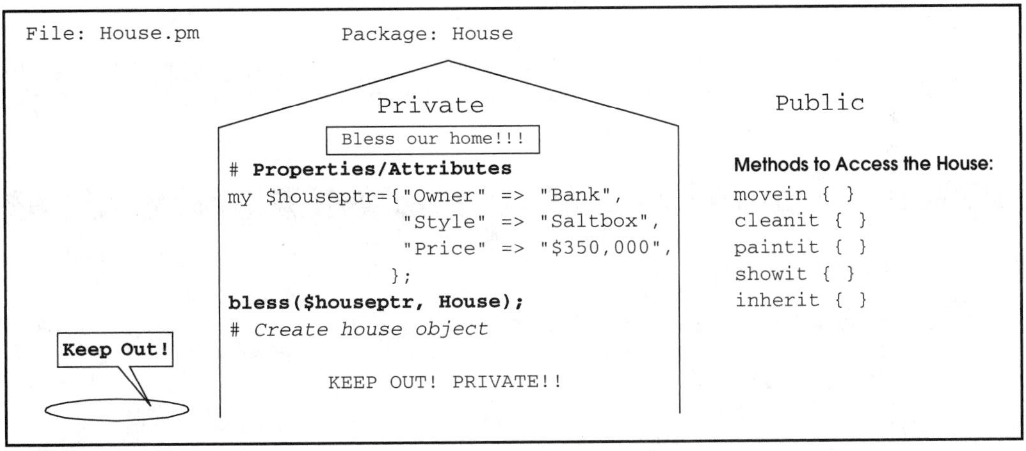

Figure 14.2 A *House* class.

14.2.5 The *bless* Function

Think of the *bless* function as creating a new data type called an object. In Figure 14.2 the *House* object is created by first giving it properties with an anonymous hash and getting back a pointer, an address. Think of it as the address where the house is located, only in our program, the memory address. The *bless* goes to that address and creates a *House* object. Once you've blessed a scalar, array, hash, etc., it is transformed into an object. To be more technical, the first argument to the *bless* function must be pointer. The *bless* function internally tags whatever the pointer is pointing at (called the referent) with a reference to the package where it belongs. This is how an **object** is created. If the package (class) is not listed as the second argument, the *bless* function tags the object as belonging to the current package. The *bless* function uses the reference to find the object and returns a reference to the object. Since the blessing associates the object with a particular package (class), Perl will always know to what package the object belongs. An object can be blessed into one class and then *reblessed* into another and then another, and so on, but an object can belong to only one class at a time.

FORMAT

```
bless REFERENCE, CLASSNAME
bless REFERENCE
```

EXAMPLE 14.2

```
my $reference = {};
return bless( $reference, $class);
```

Example 14.3 illustrates how to create an object. First we create an anonymous hash, then bless it into a package, and use the *ref* function to see if the object is truly in the package.

EXAMPLE 14.3

```
(The Script)
1   package House;            # Package declaration

2   my $ref = { "Owner"=>"Tom", #Anonymous hash; data for the package
                "Price"=>"25000", # Properties/attributes
              };
3  bless($ref, House);

    # The bless function creates the object. The hash referenced by
    # $ref  is the object. It is blessed into
    # the package; i.e., an internal pointer is created to keep track
    # of the package where it belongs.

4   print "The bless function tags the hash with its package
        name.\n";
5   print "The value of \$ref is: $ref.\n";
6   print "The ref function returns the class (package) name:",
        ref($ref), ".\n";

(Output)
4   The bless function tags the hash with its package name.
5   The value of $ref is: House=HASH(0x5a08a8).
6   The ref function returns the class (package) name: House.
```

EXPLANATION

1 The *House* package is declared. It is the class.
2 A reference, *$ref*, is assigned the address of an anonymous hash, consisting of two key/value pairs. These values represent the properties that describe the object.
3 The *bless* function takes either one or two arguments. The first argument is a reference and the second argument is the name of the package. If the second argument is missing, the current package is assumed.[a] In this example, the current package is called *House*. Now the reference knows that the object it references (the object) is in the *House* package.
5 The value of the reference (the address of the object) is printed. It is a reference to a hash in the *House* package; simply put, it is a pointer to the new *House* object.
6 The *ref* function returns the name of the package if its argument, a pointer, is an object; i.e., it has been blessed.

a. It is recommended that the two-argument form for the *bless* function be used, especially with inheritance. (See "Inheritance" on page 460.)

14.2.6 Methods

Definition. A **method** is a subroutine that operates on an object. It is a special subroutine that belongs to a class and expects its first argument to be either a package name or a reference to an object. This argument is sent by Perl implicitly. Otherwise, it looks like any other subroutine. A method is used primarily to create an object, to assign or change the data in the object, or to retrieve data from an object.[3]

Types of Methods. There are two types of methods: class (or static) methods and instance (or virtual) methods.[4] The class method expects a class name as its first argument, and the instance method expects an object reference as its first argument.

A **class method** is a subroutine that affects the class as a whole; for example, it can create an object or act on a group of objects. The class method expects a class name as its first argument. In object-oriented programs, a **constructor** function is a class method used to create an object. In Perl, this method is commonly called *new*, although you can call it anything you like. The creation of the object is often called the **instantiation** of the object, or instance, of the class.

Object-oriented programs use **instance methods** (also called **access methods**) to control the way the object's data is assigned, modified, and retrieved. You can't use an instance method until you have created the object. The method that creates the object is called a constructor. It returns a reference to the object. Once the reference to the

3. Unlike C++, Perl doesn't provide any special syntax for a method definition.
4. What you call a method type depends on what book you read. Larry Wall categorizes methods as **class methods**, **instance methods**, and **dual-nature methods**.

newly created object is returned, the instance method uses that reference, often called *$this* or *$self*, to get at the object. The instance method expects a reference to the object as its first argument. It then manipulates an object by using the reference to it.

Invoking Methods. Perl provides a special syntax for invoking methods. Instead of using the *package::function* syntax, methods are invoked in one of two ways: class method invocation or instance method invocation. There are two types of syntax for each method call: **object-oriented syntax** and **indirect syntax**. If you are using objects, either syntax for these method calls is acceptable. The older way of calling methods with the double colons is not recommended.

Something to remember: A method, unlike an ordinary subroutine, is always sent one argument implicitly, either the name of the class or a reference to the object. If, for example, you call a method with three arguments, four arguments are really sent, the first one being the value found on the left-hand side of the arrow when using the object-oriented style.

Class Method Invocation

Assume the method name is called *new* and the return value, *$ref*, is a pointer to the object.

```
1) $ref = class->new( list of arguments );    # object-oriented syntax
2) $ref = new class ( list of arguments );    # indirect syntax
```

If the class is called *House*, Perl translates

```
$ref = House->new();
```

to

```
$ref = House::new(House);
```

Instance Method Invocation

Assume the method name is called *display* and the reference to the object is called *$ref*.

```
1) $ref->display( list of arguments );    # object-oriented syntax
2) display $ref ( list of arguments );    # indirect syntax
```

The first example for each method is called the object-oriented; the second example, using the arrow operator, is called the indirect syntax syntax.

When Perl sees one of the preceding methods being invoked, it knows what class the object belongs to, because the object was blessed (an internal pointer is tracking where it is).[5]

---

5. The capability of Perl to call the appropriate module's function is called **runtime binding**, according to Srinivasan, S., *Advanced Perl Programming*, O'Reilly & Associates: Sebastopol, CA, 1997.

If you call either

```
display $ref (arguments...);
```

or

```
$ref->display(arguments...);
```

and *$ref* points to an object in a class called *House*, Perl translates that to

```
House::display($ref, arguments...);
```

14.2.7 What an Object-Oriented Module Looks Like

Figure 14.3 illustrates the layout of a typical object-oriented module. The file where the module is created is a *.pm* file. In this example, the *.pm* file is *House.pm*. The file consists of one package declaration. The package will be called a *class*; so, this is the *House* class. The class consists of subroutines, now called *methods*. The first type of method, called *new*, is a constructor method. It is the method that will define and create (construct) the object. When a user of this module calls the method *new*, he will get back a reference to the newly created *House* object (the address of the house). The *new* method gets the name of the class as it first argument. This method not only creates the object but also blesses the object so that the object always knows what class (package) it belongs to. (See "The *bless* Function" on page 429.) The second two methods are called access, or instance, methods. These are the methods that store and fetch the data from the object. You can't use these methods until you have created an instance of the object. (You can't move into the house or show it off until you have built it.) Once you, the user, have a reference to the object, the reference is used to call the instance methods.

Continuing in Figure 14.3, we see that the object's data will be described in an empty anonymous hash (although any other data type might be used), and the address of the object will be assigned to a local (*my*) reference. (The object's data will be assigned later with an instance method called *set_data*.) The *bless* function will tag the object with the name of the class where it belongs and return a pointer to the object; i.e., when the user of the module calls the constructor, he gets back a pointer to the newly created object. The constructor is said to "instantiate" the object (create a new house). The user can create as many objects as he wants, and Perl will give him a unique address for each. Once an object is created, the instance methods (often called **setters** and **getters**) will be used to manipulate the object. The user calls the instance methods to store data in the object and to retrieve data from the object. The instance methods **must** have a reference to the object in order to access the right object. **The instance methods always get a reference to the object as their first argument.**

There are many ways the module can be designed. This is just one simple approach.

The *House.pm* Module

package *House*; *# The House class in the House.pm module*

```
sub new{
    my $class = shift;
    my $ref = { };   # define the object
    bless($ref, $class);
    return $ref;
}
```

Constructor method
Create a pointer
Create the object with the *bless* function
Return a reference to the object

```
sub set_data{
    my   $self = shift;
    $self->{key}=value;
}
```

Access, or instance, methods

Assign or store the object's attributes

```
sub get_data{
    my $self = shift;
    print $self->{key};
}
1;
```

Get, or fetch, the object's attributes

User of the Class

```
#!/usr/bin/perl
# package is main
use House;
$obj1 = House->new(args);# Create the object; a pointer is returned;
            # args refers to any arguments that might be passed
$obj2 = House->new(args);# Create another house object.
$obj1->setdata(args);# Store or assign data to the object
$obj1->getdata(args);# Fetch data from the object

$obj2->setdata(args);# Store or assign data to the object
$obj2->getdata(args);# Fetch data from the object
```

Figure 14.3 A *House* class and the user of the class.

The Class Constructor Method. **Constructor** is an OOP term for a class method that creates and initializes an object into a class. There is no special syntax for a constructor. It is just a method that is used to get a reference blessed into a package. The first method in a Perl class (i.e., the first subroutine in a package) is normally the one that creates the reference (to the object) and blesses it into the package. This method is often called *new*, since it makes a new "thing," but could be called anything you want, such as *create*, *construct*, *initiate*, and so forth.

The object that is blessed into the *new* subroutine is usually an anonymous hash or anonymous array. The anonymous hash or array is assigned the data that describes the object. The data is often described as the **properties**, or **attributes**, of the object. When referred to collectively, the attributes define the **state** of the object.

EXAMPLE 14.4

```
(The Module: House.pm)
1   package House;                      # Class

2   sub new {                           # Class method called a constructor
3       my $class = shift;
4       my $ref={"Owner"=>undef,        # Attributes of the object
                 "Price" =>undef,       # Values will be assigned later
                };
5       bless($ref, $class);
                                # $ref now references an object in this class
6       return $ref;            # A reference to the object is returned
    }
    1;
-----------------------------------------
(The User of the Module)
    #!/usr/bin/perl
7   use House;
8   my $houseref = House->new();
    # call the new method and create the object
9   # my $houseref = new House; another way to call the new method
10  print "\$houseref in main belongs to class ",
            ref($houseref),".\n";
```

```
(Output)
10  $houseref in main belongs to class House.
```

EXPLANATION

1. The package *House* is declared. It can be called a class because it contains a method that will bless a reference.
2. The subroutine *new* is called a **constructor** method in OOP lingo. The primary job of a constructor is to create and initialize an object. In Perl, it doesn't really have any special syntax. This is called a class method, since its first argument is the name of the class. It is a subroutine that blesses a referenced "thing" (object) into a class and returns a reference to it. The subroutine is called a **method** and the "thing" it blessed is an **object**. The package is called a **class**.
3. The first argument received by this type of subroutine is the name of the package or class, in this case *House*. This is another difference between a method and a subroutine. The first argument of a method is the name of either a class or an object.
4. The reference *$ref* is assigned the address of an anonymous hash (object). The keys are assigned *undef*, meaning the values at this time are undefined and will be defined later.

EXPLANATION (CONTINUED)

5 The "thing" *$ref* is pointing at is blessed into the class *$class* and transformed into an object.
6 A pointer to the object is returned to the caller of the constructor method.
7 This is the script where the *House* module will be used. After the *shbang* line, the *use* statement causes the module *House.pm* to be loaded into memory.
8 The *new* constructor method is called with the class/package name *House* as its first argument. It returns a reference, *$houseref,* which points to the anonymous hash, the new object. The name of the class is implicitly sent as the first argument to the *new()* method.
9 Perl translates *$houseref = House–>new()* to *$houseref=House::new(House);* . This line is commented out. It demonstrates another way, called the indirect syntax, in which to invoke a method. You can use either style.
10 The *ref* function returns the name of the class (package) if the reference has been blessed into that class.

The Class and Instance Methods. To review: The **class methods**, also called **static methods**, are methods, or subroutines, that don't require the instance of an object in order to function. They are independent functions that act on behalf of the class. A function that calculates a paycheck or gets a list of names from a database is an example of a class method. The most common class method is called a constructor method, a method used to create the object. It takes a class (package) name as its first argument and functions for the entire class.

Object-oriented programs often use **access**, or **instance**, **methods** to control the way data is modified, retrieved, and displayed. In order to manipulate an object, the instance, or access, methods require an **instance** of an object; that is, a reference to an object that has already been created.

If the data need to be represented in a different way in one of the methods, the other methods needs not be affected, as long as the interface provided to the user remains the same. The instance methods in the following examples are used as access functions that display the data members of the class. Instance methods take an object reference as their first argument. Look at the value on the left-hand side of the -> where the method is being called. That value is the object, and it is implicitly sent as the first argument to the method being called. (If the value on the left-hand side of the -> is a class name, then the class name is sent as the first argument to the method; e.g., a constructor sends the class as its first argument.)

EXAMPLE 14.5

```
   #!/usr/bin/perl
1  package House;
```

EXAMPLE 14.5 (CONTINUED)

```
2   sub new{            # Class/Static method
3       my $class = shift;
4       my $ref={};     # Anonymous and empty hash
5       bless($ref);
6       return $ref;
    }
7   sub set_owner{      # Instance/Virtual method
8       my $self = shift;
9       print "\$self is a class ", ref($self)," reference.\n";
10      $self->{"Owner"} = shift;
    }
11  sub display_owner {
12      my $self = shift;
                    # The object reference is the first argument
13      print $self->{"Owner"},"\n";
    }
    1;
-------------------------------------------------------------------

(The Script)
    #!/usr/bin/perl
    # The user of the class
14  use House;
15  my $house = House->new;               # Call class method
16  $house->set_owner ("Tom Savage");     # Call instance method
17  $house->display_owner;                # Call instance method

(Output)
9   $self is a class House reference.
13  Tom Savage
```

EXPLANATION

1. The package *House* is declared. This can also be called the class *House*.
2. The class method *new* is a constructor. It creates a reference and blesses it into the class *House*.
3. The *$class* variable is assigned the name of the class, the first argument to the new constructor.
4. The reference *$ref* is assigned an anonymous, empty hash.
5. The "thing" (anonymous hash) referenced by *$ref* is blessed into the class *House*. The "thing" becomes the new object.
6. A reference to the object will be returned to the caller.
7. The instance method *set_owner* is defined.
8. A reference to the object is shifted from the @_ array into *$self*. Now the instance method can manipulate the object because it has a reference to it.
9. The return from the *ref* function is the name of the class *House*. The class name is returned by *ref* only if the object has been blessed.

EXPLANATION (CONTINUED)

10 The second argument is shifted from the @_ array. *Tom Savage* is assigned as a value to the key *Owner*. This instance method is then used to assign data to the object (called a "setter").

11 The instance method *display_owner* is called to access the object's data; in this example, to print the value in the *Owner* field of the anonymous hash.

12 The object reference is the first argument to the method. It is shifted from the @_ array into *$self*.

13 The value in the key *Owner* field is displayed.

14 This program uses the *House.pm* module.

15 The *new* constructor method is called and a reference to a *House* object is returned; that is, a reference to an anonymous hash in the *House* class. The constructor method, *new*, always passes at least one argument, the name of the class. *House–>new()* translates to *House::new(House)*.

16 The instance method *set_owner* is called with the argument *Tom Savage*. Remember, the first argument passed to an instance method is always a reference to the object, making *Tom Savage* the second argument:
$house–>set_owner ("Tom Savage") translates to *House::set_owner($house, "Tom Savage");*

17 The *display* method is called, which displays the value of the anonymous hash, *Tom Savage*.

Passing Parameters to Constructor Methods. Instance variables are used to initialize the object when it is created. In this way, each time the object is created, it can be customized. The properties that describe the object may be passed as arguments to the constructor method and assigned to instance variables. They are called **instance variables** because they come into existence when the object is created, or instantiated. Either an anonymous hash or an anonymous array is commonly used to hold the instance variables. In the following example, the object "has a" or "contains a" owner and a price.

EXAMPLE 14.6

```
(The Module: House.pm)
package House;
sub new{              # Constructor  method
    my $class = shift;
    my ($owner, $salary) = @_;        # Instance variables
    my $ref={"Owner"=>$owner,         # Instance variables to
             "Price"=>$price,         # initialize the object
    };
    bless($ref, $class);
    return $ref;
}
```

EXAMPLE 14.6 (CONTINUED)

```
8   sub display_object {        # An instance method
9      my $self = shift;       # The name of the object is passed
10     while( ($key, $value)=each %$self){
          print "$key: $value \n";
       }
    }
    1;
-------------------------------------------------------------------

(The Script)
    #!/usr/bin/perl
    # User of the class; another program
11  use House;
    # Documentation explaining how to use the House
    # package is called the public interface.
    # It tells the programmer how to use the class.
    # To create a House object requires two arguments,
    # an owner and a price.
    # See "Public User Interface—Documenting Classes" on page 474
    # to create documentation.

    # my $house1 = new House("Tom Savage", 250000);
    # Invoking constructor--two ways.
12  my $house1  = House->new("Tom Savage", 250000);
13  my $house2 = House->new("Devin Quigley", 55000);
    # Two objects have been created.
14  $house1->display_object;
15  $house2->display_object;
16  print "$house1, $house2\n";

(Output)
14  Owner: Tom Savage
    Price: 250000
15  Owner: Devin Quigley
    Price: 55000
16  House=HASH(0x9d450), House=HASH(0xa454c)
```

EXPLANATION

1. The package *House* is declared.
2. The class method *new* is defined as a constructor.
3. The first argument to the class method is the name of the class (package).
4. The instance variables are created from the remainder of the argument list.
5. The address of an anonymous array is assigned to the reference *$ref*. The keys are hard coded and the values are supplied from the instance variables.
6. The "thing" the reference *$ref* points to is blessed into the class and becomes the new object.

EXPLANATION (CONTINUED)

7 The value of the reference *$ref* will be returned when the method is called.

8 The subroutine *display_object* is an instance method. It is defined in this class.

9 The first argument to the instance method is the reference to the object.

10 The *while* loop is used with the *each* function to get both keys and values from the hash (object) referenced by *$self*.

11 The user of the class loads *House.pm* into his namespace.

12 The *new* method is called with three arguments, *House*, *Tom Savage*, and *250000*. The first argument is the name of the class. You don't see it, but Perl implictly sends it to the constructor. The next two arguments are sent explicitly by the user of the class. The only request here is that the *Owner* value is the first argument and the *Price* value is the second argument. There is no error checking. The example simply shows how to pass arguments to a constructor. The value returned to *$house1* is a reference to the hash object.

13 The *new* method is called again with different arguments, *Devin Quigley* and *55000*. The value returned to *$house2* is a reference to another object. The *new* method has been used to create two *House* objects. You can create as many objects as you want. They will all have unique addresses, as shown in the output at line 16. Since the objects were blessed in the constructor, Perl knows that the objects are in the *House* class.

14 The instance method is called to display the data for the object referenced by *$house1*.

15 The instance method is called again but to display the data of the object referenced by *$house2*.

16 The addresses of the two objects are printed.

Passing Parameters to Instance Methods. The first argument to an instance method is always a reference to the object. In the called method, this value is typically shifted from the @_ array and stored in a *my* variable called *$self* or *$this*, although it doesn't matter what you call the variable. The remaining arguments are then processed as they are in any regular subroutine.

EXAMPLE 14.7

```
   #!/bin/perl
   # Program to demonstrate passing arguments to an instance method.
   # When method is called, user can select what he wants returned.
1  package House;

2  sub new{      # Constructor, class method
       my $class = shift;
       my ($owner, $salary, $style) = @_;
```

EXAMPLE 14.7 (CONTINUED)

```
       my $ref={ "Owner"=>$name,
                 "Price"=>$salary,
                 "Style"=>$style,
               };
       return bless($ref, $class);
   }
3  sub display {              # Instance method
4      my $self = shift;     # Object reference is the first argument
5      foreach $key ( @_){
6          print "$key: $self->{$key}\n";
       }
   }
   1;

---------------------------------------------------------------------

(The Script)
   #!/bin/perl
   # User of the class--Another program
7  use House;
8  my $house = House->new("Tom Savage", 250000, "Cape Cod");
9  $house->display ("Owner", "Style");
                            # Passing arguments to instance method

(Output)
Owner: Tom Savage
Style: Cape Cod
```

EXPLANATION

1. The package *House* is declared. Since this package deals with blessed references and methods, call it a **class**.
2. The *new* method is a constructor. The object is an anonymous hash consisting of three key/value pairs. The key/value pairs are called the **properties**, or **attributes**, of the object. The values are passed in as arguments to the constructor. The blessing creates an object. The object, referenced by *$ref*, is blessed into the *House* class so Perl can keep track of the package where the object belongs.
3. The instance method *display* is defined.
4. The first argument to the *display* instance method is a reference to a *House* object. It is shifted and assigned to *$self*.
5. The *foreach* loop iterates through the remaining arguments in the @_ array, one at a time, assigning each argument in turn to the variable *$key*. The variable *$key* is a key in the anonymous array.
6. The selected values from the associative array are printed.
7. The user of the class loads the module into his program.

EXPLANATION (CONTINUED)

8 The constructor method is called to create a new *House* object.

9 The instance method is called with arguments. The first argument is a pointer to the object, *$house*, even though you can't see it. The rest of the arguments, provided by the user, are in parentheses.

Named Parameters. All of the examples so far have used a *House* object. In the next example, we will create an *Employee* object. The *Employee* constructor will take parameters to be used as properties of an employee. If a constructor method is expecting a name, address, and salary to be passed in that order, it would be easy to send the parameters in the wrong order, causing the address to be assigned to the name, or the name to the salary, and so on. Using named parameters provides a method to ensure that parameters can be passed to a method in any order and still result in the values, getting assigned to the correct attributes. The arguments are passed by the calling, or driver, program as key/value pairs (hash) and received by the constructor as a hash. The following example demonstrates how named parameters are passed to a method and by a method.

The *user/driver* Program

EXAMPLE 14.8

```
     #!/usr/bin/perl
     # User of Employee.pm--See Example 14.9 for module
1    use Employee;
2    use warnings;
     use strict;
3    my($name, $extension, $address, $basepay, $employee);
4    print "Enter the employee's name. ";
     chomp($name=<STDIN>);
     print "Enter the employee's phone extension. ";
     chomp($extension=<STDIN>);
     print "Enter the employee's address. ";
     chomp($address=<STDIN>);
     print "Enter the employee's basepay. ";
     chomp($basepay=<STDIN>);

     # Passing parameters as a hash
5    $employee = Employee->new( "Name"=>$name,
                                "Address"=>$address,
                                "Extension"=>$extension,
                                "PayCheck"=>$basepay,
                              );
     print "\nThe statistics for $name are: \n";

6    $employee->get_stats;
```

EXAMPLE 14.8 (CONTINUED)

```
(Output)
Enter the employee's name. Daniel Savage
Enter the employee's phone extension. 2534
Enter the employee's address. 999 Mission Ave, Somewhere, CA
Enter the employee's basepay. 2200

The statistics for Daniel Savage are:
Address = 999 Mission Ave, Somewhere, CA
PayCheck = 2200
IdNum = Employee Id not provided!
Extension = 2534
Name = Daniel Savage
```

EXPLANATION

1. The *Employee.pm* module will be used by this program.
2. Warnings will be issued for possible errors, and the *strict* pragma will track global and undefined variables, barewords, etc.
3. A list of lexical private variables is created.
4. The user of the program will be asked for the information that will be passed to the *Employee* module.
5. The constructor is called to pass arguments as key/value pairs; that is, a hash is passed to the constructor in the *Employee* module. (See Example 14.9.) A reference to the object is returned and assigned to *$employee*.
6. The instance method *get_stats* is called to display the employee's attributes.

The Object-Oriented Module

EXAMPLE 14.9

```
# Module Employee.pm--See Example 14.8 to use this module.
package Employee;
use Carp;
sub new {
    my $class = shift;
    my(%params)=@_;    # Receiving the hash that was passed
    my $objptr={
        "Name"=>$params{"Name"} || croak("No name assigned"),
        "Extension"=>$params{"Extension"},
        "Address"=>$params{"Address"},
        "PayCheck"=>$params{"PayCheck"} ||
                croak("No pay assigned"),
        ((defined $params{"IdNum"})?("IdNum"=>$params{"IdNum"}):
            ("IdNum"=>"Employee's id was not provided!"
        )),

    };
```

EXAMPLE 14.9 (CONTINUED)

```
10      return bless($objptr,$class);
    }
11  sub get_stats{
12      my $self=shift;
13      while( ($key, $value)=each %$self){
            print $key, " = ", $value, "\n";
        }
        print "\n";
    }
    1;
```

EXPLANATION

1 The class (package) *Employee* is declared.

2 The *Carp* module from the standard Perl library is used to handle error messages. Instead of using the built-in *die* function, we can use the *croak* method from the *Carp* module to exit when there is an error with a little more detail on what caused the error.

3 The constructor method *new* is defined.

4 The first argument to the constructor method is the name of the class. It is shifted from the @_ array and assigned to *$class*.

5 The rest of the arguments in the @_ array are assigned to the hash *%params*. They were sent to the constructor as a set of key/value pairs.

6 A reference, *$objptr*, is assigned the address of an anonymous hash.

7 The key *Name* is assigned a value, retrieved from the *%params* hash. Error checking is done here. If a corresponding value for the key *Name* is not provided, the *croak* function will be executed, letting the user know that he did not assign a value to the *Name*, and the program will exit.

8 The *Address* property is assigned by getting its value from the *%params* hash.

9 This is an example of how you can make sure the user of the module passed the expected arguments. The conditional statement reads: If the *%params* has a key called *IdNum* defined, then get its value and assign it to *IdNum*; otherwise, when the program runs, tell the user he forgot to include this parameter. In the examples using *croak*, the program will die if the user doesn't provide input when asked for it, whereas in this form of checking, the program will continue to run.

10 After assigning properties, a reference to the object is blessed into the class and returned to the caller.

11 The instance method *get_stats* is defined.

12 The first argument is shifted from the @_ array and assigned to *$self*. It is a pointer to the object.

13 The *while* loop is entered. Each key/value pair from the object is returned by the *each* function and displayed.

14.2.8 Polymorphism and Dynamic Binding

Webster's Dictionary defines polymorphism as

> polymorphism: *n.* 1. the state or condition of being polymorphous.[6]

There, that should clear things up! Here's another definition:

> Having many forms or the ability to take several forms . . . The same operation may behave differently on different classes.

Polymorphism can be described in many ways, and it's a word that is inherently part of the OO lingo. In Perl, it means that you can provide a method with the same name in different classes and when you call the method, it will do the right thing; in other words, when the reference to the object invokes the method, it will go to the class where the object belongs.

In Example 14.10, polymorphism is demonstrated. Two modules, *Cat.pm* and *Dog.pm*, each have three functions with the same names: *new*, *set_attributes*, and *get_attributes*. The driver, or user, program in Example 14.11 will use both of the modules. A reference to the *cat* or *dog* object is returned when it's respective class constructors are called. When the access methods are called with an object reference, Perl knows which method to call and to which class it belongs even though the methods have the same name. Perl determines which class the invoking object belongs to and looks in that class (package) for the method being called. The ability to call the right method demonstrates polymorphism. Dynamic, or **runtime**, **binding** allows the program to defer calling the correct method until the program is running and, along with polymorphism, to tie the correct method to its associated class without using *if* statements to determine which method to call. This provides a great deal of flexibility and is necessary for inheritance to work properly.

To take advantage of polymorphism and runtime binding, the object-oriented syntax must be used rather than the :: syntax. If, for example, you have two classes, *Director* and *Rifleman*, and both classes contain an access method called *shoot*, you can write *$object->shoot*, and Perl will know which class the object belongs to. It determined the correct class at compile time. In this way, the *Director* will not shoot bullets at his cast, and the *Rifleman* will not try to take movies of the rifle range. It is also possible to add another class, such as a *BasketballPlayer* class, with a different *shoot* method and be sure that the appropriate method will be called for that class. Without runtime binding and polymorphism, the correct class will be determined based on the outcome of some condition, as shown here:

---

6. *Webster's Encyclopedic Unabridged Dictionary of the English Language*, Random House Value Publishing: Avenel, NJ, 1996, p. 1500. Reprinted by permission.

```
if ( ref($object1) eq "Director") {
    Director::shoot($object1);
elsif ( ref($object2) eq "Rifleman" ){
    Rifleman::shoot($object2);
else{
    BasketballPlayer::shoot($object3);
}
```

With the object-oriented syntax, a reference to the object is implicitly passed to the method. Since Perl sends the object to the access method as its first argument and the object has been blessed into the proper class, Perl can implement polymorphism and do the right thing! Assume in Example 14.10 that *$object1* was created as an object in the *Director* class, *$object2* object in the *Rifleman* class, and *$object3* in the *BasketballPlayer* class.

```
$object1->shoot;evaluates to  Director::shoot($object1);
$object2->shoot;evaluates to  Rifleman::shoot($object2);
$object3->shoot;evaluates to  BasketballPlayer::shoot($object3)
```

EXAMPLE 14.10

```
( File: Cat.pm)
1   package Cat;
2   sub new{        # Constructor
        my $class=shift;
        my $dptr={};
        bless($dptr, $class);
    }
3   sub set_attributes{                # Access Methods
        my $self= shift;
4       $self->{"Name"}="Sylvester";
        $self->{"Owner"}="Mrs. Black";
        $self->{"Type"}="Siamese";
        $self->{"Sex"}="Male";
    }
5   sub get_attributes{
        my $self = shift;
        print "-" x 20, "\n";
        print "Stats for the Cat\n";
        print "-" x 20, "\n";
        while(($key,$value)=each( %$self)){
            print "$key is $value. \n";
    }
    print "-" x 20, "\n";
    1;
------------------------------------------------------------------
```

EXAMPLE 14.10 (CONTINUED)

```
(File: Dog.pm)
6   package Dog;
7   sub new{                    # Constructor
        my $class=shift;
        my $dptr={};
        bless($dptr, $class);
    }
8   sub set_attributes{
        my $self= shift;
9       my($name, $owner, $breed)=@_;
10      $self->{"Name"}="$name";
        $self->{"Owner"}="$owner";
        $self->{"Breed"}="$breed";
    }
11  sub get_attributes{
        my $self = shift;
        print "x" x 20, "\n";
        print "All about $self->{Name}\n";
        while(($key,$value)= each( %$self)){
            print "$key is $value.\n";
        }
        print "x" x 20, "\n";
    }
    1;
-----------------------------------------------------------------------
```

EXPLANATION

1 This is the package declaration for a class called *Cat* in module *Cat.pm*.
2 The constructor method for the *Cat* class is called *new*. A *Cat* object is blessed into the class.
3 The access method *set_attributes* will define data properties of the *Cat* object.
4 The object pointer *$self* is used to assign a key/value pair to give the cat a name.
5 Another access method, *get_attributes*, is used to display the *Cat* object.
6 In another file, *Dog.pm*, a package is declared for a class called *Dog*.
7 Like the *Cat* class, the *Dog* class has a constructor called *new*. A *Dog* object is blessed into the class.
8 The access method *set_attributes* will define data properties of the *Dog* object.
9 The properties of the *Dog* object are being passed from the driver program and assigned to the @_ array.
10 The object pointer *$self* is used to assign a key/value pair to give the dog a name.
11 Like the *Cat* class, another access method, *get_attributes*, is used to display the *Dog* object.

EXAMPLE 14.11

```
(The Script: driver program for Example 14.10)
#!/bin/perl
1   use Cat;    # Use the Cat.pm module
2   use Dog;    # Use the Dog.pm module

3   my $dogref = Dog->new;      # Polymorphism
4   my $catref= Cat->new;

5   $dogref->set_attributes("Rover", "Mr. Jones", "Mutt");
6   $catref->set_attributes;    # Polymorphism

7   $dogref->get_attributes;
8   $catref->get_attributes;

(Output)
xxxxxxxxxxxxxxxxxxxx
All about Rover
Owner is Mr. Jones.
Breed is Mutt.
Name is Rover.
xxxxxxxxxxxxxxxxxxxx
--------------------
Stats for the Cat
--------------------
Sex is Male.
Type is Siamese.
Owner is Mrs. Black.
Name is Sylvester.
--------------------
```

EXPLANATION

1. The *use* directive loads in the *Cat.pm* module.
2. The *use* directive loads in the *Dog.pm* module. Now we have access to both classes.
3. The *new* constructor method is called.[a] The first argument is the name of the class, *Dog*, which is translated to *Dog::new(Dog)*. A reference to a *Dog* object is returned. Perl knows the reference belongs to the *Dog* class because it was blessed in the constructor method. An instance of the *Dog* class has been created.
4. The *new* constructor method is called. It passes the name of the class as its first argument. A reference to a *Cat* object is returned. Perl translates the method call to *Cat::new(Cat)*. Two classes have used the *new* function, but because Perl knows to which class the method belongs, it always calls the correct version of *new*. This is an example of polymorphism.
5. Now that we have a reference to the object, we use it to call the access (instance) methods. Perl translates the *$dogref->set_attributes* method to *Dog::set_attributes($dogref, "Rover", "Mr. Jones", "Mutt")*.

a. The new constructor could also be called by using the indirect method *new Dog*.

EXPLANATION (CONTINUED)

6 This time, the *set_attributes* method for the cat is called. The *Cat* class sets the attributes for the cat.
7 The *get_attributes* method is called to display the data attributes of the *Cat* class.
8 The *get_attributes* method is called to display the data attributes of the *Dog* class.

The :: versus -> Notation. The –> arrow syntax is used in object-oriented programs that use polymorphism, dynamic binding, and inheritance. The :: syntax is allowed, but it is not flexible and can lead to problems unless conditional statements are used. The following example demonstrates how the :: syntax can be a disadvantage. With the object-oriented syntax, the problem would not occur.

EXAMPLE 14.12

```
# The Cat class
package Cat;
sub new{         # The Cat's constructor
    my $class = shift;
    my $ref = {};
    return bless ($ref, $class);
}
sub set_attributes{    # Giving the Cat some attributes,
                       # a name and a voice
    my $self = shift;
    $self->{"Name"} = "Sylvester";
    $self->{"Talk"}= "Meow purrrrrr.... ";
}
sub speak {            # Retrieving the Cat's attributes
    my $self = shift;
    print "$self->{Talk} I'm the cat called $self->{Name}.\n";
}
1;
----------------------------------------------------------------------
# The Dog class
package Dog;    # The Dog's Constructor
sub new{
    my $class = shift;
    my $ref = {};
    return bless ($ref, $class);
}
sub set_attributes{     # Giving the Dog some attributes
    my $self = shift;
    $self->{"Name"} = "Lassie";
    $self->{"Talk"}= "Bow Wow, woof woof.... ";
}
```

EXAMPLE 14.12 (CONTINUED)

```
    sub speak {              # Retrieving the Dog's attributes
        my $self = shift;
        print "$self->{'Talk'} I'm the dog called $self->{'Name'}.\n";
    }
    1;
---------------------------------------------------------------------------
    #!/bin/perl
    # User Program
    # This example demonstrates why to use the object-oriented
    # syntax rather than the colon-colon syntax when passing
    # arguments to methods.
    use Cat;
    use Dog;
    $mydog = new Dog;      # Calling the Dog's constructor
    $mycat = new Cat;      # Calling the Cat's constructor

    $mydog->set_attributes;  # Calling the Dog's access methods
    $mycat->set_attributes;  # Calling the Cat's access methods

1   $mydog->speak;
2   $mycat->speak;

3   print "\nNow we make a mistake in passing arguments.\n\n";

4   Cat::speak($mydog); # Perl goes to the Cat class to find the
                          # method, even though attributes have been
                          # set for the dog!

(Output)
1   Bow Wow, woof woof.... I'm the dog called Lassie.
2   Meow purrrrrr.... I'm the cat called Sylvester.

3   Now we make a mistake in passing arguments.

4   Bow Wow, woof woof.... I'm the cat called Lassie.
```

EXPLANATION

1. The object-oriented approach of calling the *speak* method guarantees that Perl will bind the method to the class where it was blessed.

   A reference to the *Dog* object is passed as the first argument to the *speak* method. It breaks down to *Dog::speak($mydog)*. Perl determines what class to use at compile time so that when the *speak* method is called at runtime, it will be bound to the right class.
2. A reference to the *Cat* object is passed as the first argument to the *speak* method. It breaks down to *Cat::speak($mydog)*.

EXPLANATION (CONTINUED)

3 The following line passes a dog reference to the *Cat* package. This mistake will not occur when using the object-oriented approach, because Perl will be able to determine to which class the method belongs and make the correct method call. This feature is called **polymorphism** and **runtime binding**.

4 By using the :: notation, Perl will figure out the class at runtime and use the *speak* method found in the *Cat* class, even though a reference to the *Dog* object is passed. And we wind up with a cat that barks!

14.2.9 Destructors and Garbage Collection

Perl keeps track of the number of references to an object, and when the count reaches *0*, the object is automatically destroyed. If a reference goes out of scope or your program exits, Perl handles the garbage collection by destroying every object associated with a reference and deallocating any memory that was used. So, you don't have to worry about cleaning up memory.[7] However, you can define a *DESTROY* method in your program to get control of the object just before it goes away.

EXAMPLE 14.13

```
(The Class)
1 package Employee;
  sub new{
         my $class = shift;
         $ref={};
         bless($ref, $class);
         return $ref;
}

2 sub DESTROY{
         my $self = shift;
3         print "Employee $self->{Name} is being destroyed.\n";
         }

  1;
-----------------------------------------------------------------

(The Script)
  #!/usr/bin/perl
  # User of the class
4 use Employee;
5 my $emp1 = Employee->new;   # Create the object
```

7. If you use self-referencing data structures, you will be responsible for destroying those references.

EXAMPLE 14.13 (CONTINUED)

```
6 { my $emp2 = Employee->new;
    $emp2->{"Name"}="Christian Dobbins";
    print "\t\t$emp2->{'Name'}\n";
  } # Create the object

7  my $emp3 = Employee->new;  # Create the object

8  $emp1->{"Name"}="Dan Savage";
   $emp3->{"Name"}="Willie Rogers";

   print "Here are our remaining employees:\n";
   print "\t\t$emp1->{'Name'}\n";
   print "\t\t$emp3->{'Name'}\n";

(Output)
                  Christian Dobbins
 Employee Christian Dobbins is being destroyed.
 Here are our remaining Employees:
                 Dan Savage
                 Willie Rogers
 Employee Dan Savage is being destroyed.
 Employee Willie Rogers is being destroyed.
```

EXPLANATION

1 The *Employee* class is declared and its constructor method defined.

2 When an *Employee* object is no longer in scope, the *DESTROY* method is called and this line is printed. The object on line 6 is defined within a block. It goes out of scope when the block exits. The other objects go out of scope when the program ends.

3 Each time an object goes out of scope, this line is printed.

4 The *Employee* module will be used.

5 A new *Employee* object, referenced by *$emp1*, is being created by calling the constructor method.

6 Another *Employee* object is created within a block. The object is assigned a "Name" with a value, *Christian Dobbins*. Since it is a "my" variable, it is lexically scoped, meaning the object will go out of scope when the block is exited, at which time the *DESTROY* method will be called and remove it from memory.

7 A third *Employee* object, referenced by *$emp3*, is being created by calling the constructor method.

8 The *Employee* objects are assigned key/value pairs.

14.3 Anonymous Subroutines, Closures, and Privacy

One of the problems with the object-oriented examples we have used thus far is that a user can manipulate the object directly once he gets a reference to it. Even if he is supposed to use the methods provided by the module, there is nothing to stop him from accessing the object's data directly, since Perl does not specifically provide a private section for the class data. But for those who feel this lack of guaranteed privacy is an affront to the object-oriented approach, the paranoid, the sensible, etc., Perl provides several solutions. One of them is the use of closures.

14.3.1 What Is a Closure?

Larry Wall describes closures as just anonymous subroutines with an attitude.[8] Barrie Slaymaker calls closures "inside-out objects": objects are data that have some subroutines attached to them, and closures are subroutines that have some data attached to them.

A closure is an anonymous subroutine that has access to "my" (lexical) variables even if it is called from outside the block where the variables were defined and it seems as though those variables should no longer be in scope. The subroutine clings to the lexical variables it references. Each time the subroutine is called via its reference, a new lexical variable with the same name is created for that call. The lexical variables stay in scope until they are no longer being referenced.

EXAMPLE 14.14

```
(The Script)
my $name="Tommy";

{   my $name = "Grandfather";   # Lexical variables
    my $age = 86;
    $ref = sub{ return "$name is $age.\n"; }  # anonymous subroutine
}
    print "$name is back\n";
    print &{$ref};   # Call to subroutine outside the block

(Output)
    Tommy is back.
    Grandfather is 86.
```

8. Wall, L., Christianson, T., and Orwant, J., *Programming Perl, 3rd ed.*, O'Reilly & Associates: Sebastopol, CA, 2000, p. 262.

EXPLANATION

1 The lexical variable *$name* is assigned *Tommy*. The variable is visible from here to the end of the file.

2 A block is entered. A new lexical variable, *$name*, is assigned *Grandfather*. It is visible from here to the end of its block.

3 Another lexical variable, *$age*, is defined. It is visible from here to the end of the enclosing block.

4 An anonymous subroutine is defined within the same block as the two lexical variables (*my* variables), *$name* and *$age*. The address of the subroutine is assigned to *$ref*. The subroutine has access to those variables even if it is called from outside the block. The subroutine is called a closure because the variables referenced within the subroutine are enclosed there until they are no longer needed.

5 The value of *$name*, *Tommy*, is now visible.

6 The anonymous subroutine is called via the pointer *$ref*. The lexical variables are still available even though they appear to be out of scope. They remain in scope because the reference still needs access to them. Perl doesn't clean up the variables until they are no longer referenced.

EXAMPLE 14.15

```
(The Script)
    # Closure
1       sub paint {
2           my $color = shift;     # @_ array is shifted
3           my $ref = sub {        # Pointer to an anonymous subroutine
4               my $object=shift;
5               print "Paint the $object $color.\n"; # $color still
                                                     # in scope
            };
6       return $ref;     # Returns a closure
        }

7       my $p1=paint("red");    #  Creates a closure
        my $p2=paint("blue");   #  Creates a closure

8       $p1->("flower");  # Call to anonymous subroutine
9       $p2->("sky");

(Output)
Paint the flower red.
Paint the sky blue.
```

EXPLANATION

1 The *paint()* subroutine is defined.
2 The lexical scalar *$color* is assigned the value shifted from the @_ array.
3 The value in *$ref* is assigned the address of an anonymous subroutine.
4 The anonymous subroutine takes one argument from the @_ array. In this example, the value of object will be "flower" the first time this subroutine is called and "sky" the next time. See lines 8 and 9.
5 Here is where we see a closure in action. The lexical variable *$color* is still in scope. The lexical variable *$color* doesn't go out of scope even after the subroutine called *paint()* is called and exited, because the anonymous subroutine still needs it.
6 *$color* is still available here even though the *paint()* function was called and exited.
7 The *paint()* subroutine returns a reference to the anonymous subroutine. The reference forms the closure; it keeps the lexical variables, in this case *$color*, around until they are no longer being referenced.
8 The *paint()* subroutine is called twice with different arguments. Each time *paint()* is called, Perl creates a new lexical scalar, *$color*, with it own value. The *$color* variable gets wrapped up in the closure that is returned. So *$p1* encloses one *$color*, which is initialized to "red", and *$p2* encloses a totally different *$color*, initialized to "blue".
9 The pointers *$p1* and *$p2* are references to the anonymous subroutine defined on line 3. They have formed a "closure" around the variable *$color* defines in *paint()* and will have access to their own copy of that variable until it is no longer being referenced.

14.3.2 Closures and Objects

Closures provide a way to encapsulate the object's data and thereby prevent the user from directly accessing the object. This can be done by defining the constructor with the object's data and an anonymous subroutine that will act as the closure. The anonymous subroutine will be the only way to set and get data for the object. Instead of blessing the data (e.g., anonymous hash into the class), the anonymous subroutine will be blessed. The pointer to the anonymous subroutine will be returned and serve as the only way to access the private data defined in the constructor. The blessed anonymous subroutine will have access to the object's data because it was declared within the same lexical scope. It encapsulates the data with the subroutine; i.e., forms a closure. As long as the anonymous subroutine refers to the object's data, the data will be accessible.

Example 14.16 will demonstrate how to use a closure to encapsulate the data for an object by following these steps.

1. A constructor method is defined for a *Student* class. The constructor will define an empty anonymous hash that will be used to set properties for each new *Student*

object, a global class variable to keep track of the number of students, and an anonymous subroutine to encapsulate the data to be assigned to and retrieved from the object. The blessing will return a pointer to the anonymous subroutine.

2. The instance methods will be defined for the object for setting and getting the data. Instead of getting back a pointer to the object's data, these methods will get back a pointer to the anonymous subroutine. The only way they can access the data is by calling this anonymous subroutine with the appropriate arguments.
3. A destructor method will be defined to display each *Student* object as it is being destroyed.

EXAMPLE 14.16

```
1    package Student;
2    sub new {   # Constructor
        my $class = shift;
3       my $data={};
4       our $students;

5       my $ref = sub { # Closure
           my ($access_type, $key, $value) = @_;

7          if ($access_type eq "set"){
              $data->{$key} = $value;   # $data still available here
           }
           elsif ($access_type eq "get"){
              return $data->{$key};
           }
           elsif ($access_type eq "keys"){
              return (keys %{$data});
           }
8          elsif ($access_type eq "destroy"){
9             $students--;
              return $students;
           }
           else{
              die "Access type should be set or get";
           }
10         print "New student created, we have ", ++$students,
              " students.\n";
11         bless ($ref, $class);   # bless anonymous subroutine
        }
     } # End constructor
```

EXAMPLE 14.16 (CONTINUED)

```
12  sub set{
13      my ($self,$key,$value) = @_; # $self references anonymous sub
14      $self->("set",$key,$value);
    }
15  sub get{
        my ($self,$key) = @_;
        return $self->("get", $key);
    }
16  sub display{
        my $self = shift;
        my @keys = $self->("keys");
        @keys=reverse(@keys);
        foreach my $key (@keys){
            my $value = $self->("get",$key);
            printf "%-25s%-5s:%-20s\n",$self, $key,$value ;
        }
        print "\n";
    }
17  sub DESTROY{
        my $self = shift;
        print "Object going out of scope:\n";
        print "Students remain: ", $self->("destroy"), "\n";
    }

1;
```

EXPLANATION

1 The package *Student* is declared.

2 The constructor will be used to create the object.

3 A reference, *$data*, to an anonymous hash is declared. This will be used to assign properties to the object.

4 The global class variable *$student* will be used to count the number of *Student* objects created by this script.

5 Here is the closure, a pointer to an anonymous subroutine. This subroutine will be blessed into the class and will be used to set and get the data for the *Student* object.

6 The subroutine takes three arguments, the access type, which is "set", "get", "keys", or "destroy"; a key for the object; and a value for the object.

7 If the access type is "set", then a property is set for the object's data. When the *set()* method is called by the user, it gets a pointer to this anonymous subroutine and calls it from line 15.

8 If the access type is "destroy", the *DESTROY* method has been called; i.e., a *Student* object is going out of scope.

9 Each time an object is removed, the value of the class variable *$student* is decremented by 1.

EXPLANATION (CONTINUED)

10 Each time a new *Student* object is created, the class variable *$student* is incremented by 1.

11 The anonymous subroutine, referenced by *$ref*, is blessed into the *Student* class.

12 This method is used to put data into the object; i.e., assign properties to the student.

13 Its first parameter, *$self*, is a pointer to the anonymous subroutine blessed into the class, then a key, and a value. The data for the object has been "enclosed" in the anonymous subroutine.

14 When the anonymous subroutine is called, it gets three arguments, the access type, "set" a key; and a value to be assigned to the object. This is the only way the user can "set" data for the *Student* object and will "stick around" until there is no longer any reference to it.

15 The *get* method will call the closure with a specified access method, "get", and a key. It will return one value to the caller.

16 This method is used to fetch data in the *Student* object. It calls the closure on line 5 with the key that will be used to get the value for the object. This is the only way to "get" data from the object.

17 This method will display all the object's data by calling the closure to get a list of all the keys in the object's hash, and then from within a *foreach* loop, the list of keys is used to display all of the object's data.

18 Perl's special *DESTROY* method is called when an object is about to be removed from memory; i.e., when it goes out of scope or the program ends. When this method is called, it will, in turn, call the closure and send it the access type, "destroy". See line 8.

User of the Module.

EXAMPLE 14.17

```
  use lib("lib");
1 use Student;

2 $ptr1 = Student->new();   # Create new students
  $ptr2 = Student->new();
  $ptr3 = Student->new();

3 $ptr1->set("Name", "Jody Rogers"); # Set data for object
  $ptr1->set("Major", "Law");

  $ptr2->set("Name", "Christian Dobbins");
  $ptr2->set("Major", "Drama");

  $ptr3->set("Name", "Tina Savage");
  $ptr3->set("Major", "Art");
```

EXAMPLE 14.17 (CONTINUED)

```
4 $ptr1->display();  # Get all data for object
  $ptr2->display();
  $ptr3->display();

5 print "\nThe major for ", $ptr1->get("Name"),
       " is ", $ptr1->get("Major"), ".\n\n";

(The Output)
 New student created, we have 1 students.
 New student created, we have 2 students.
 New student created, we have 3 students.

Student=CODE(0x225420)   Name :Jody Rogers
Student=CODE(0x225420)   Major:Law

Student=CODE(0x183192c)  Name :Christian Dobbins
Student=CODE(0x183192c)  Major:Drama

Student=CODE(0x1831a04)  Name :Tina Savage
Student=CODE(0x1831a04)  Major:Art

The major for Jody Rogers is Law.

Object going out of scope:
Students remain: 2
Object going out of scope:
Students remain: 1
Object going out of scope:
Students remain: 0

--------Try to get direct Access----------------------------------
  use lib("lib");
  use Student;

$ptr1 = Student->new();  # Create new students
$ptr2 = Student->new();
$ptr3 = Student->new();
$ptr1->("Name", "Jody Rogers");  # Direct Access Not Allowed
$ptr1->set("Name", "Jody Rogers");
$ptr1->set("Major", "Law");
 ----------------------------------------------------
(Output)
New student created, we have 1 students.
New student created, we have 2 students.
New student created, we have 3 students.
Access type should be set or get at Student.pm line 25.
...
```

14.4 Inheritance

Inheritance means that a new class can inherit methods from an existing class. The new class can then add to or modify existing code in order to customize the class without having to reinvent what has already been done. The principle is that a class may be subdivided into a number of subclasses that all share common features, but each subclass may provide its own additional features, refining what it borrows to a more specific functionality. The idea of this kind of organization is not new. You may have seen it in a biology class when learning about the plant and animal kingdoms and the breakdown of each phylum, kingdom, class, order, family, species, and variety or in procedural programs with the use of functions to combine the common elements of a program into specific tasks.

In object-oriented programming, once a class has been written and debugged, it can be stored in a library and reused by other programmers. The programmer can then add features and capabilities to the existing class without rewriting the whole thing. This is done through inheritance; that is, by deriving a new class from an already existing class. The reuse of software and the increased use of library classes where all this software is stored and organized have contributed to the wide popularity of OOP languages. Let's see how Perl implements inheritance.

14.4.1 The *@ISA* Array and Calling Methods

The classes (packages) listed in the *@ISA* array are the **parent**, or **base**, **classes** of the current class. This is how Perl implements inheritance. The *@ISA* array contains a list of packages (classes) where Perl will search for a method if it can't find it in the current package (class). If the method still isn't found, then Perl searches for an *AUTOLOAD* function and calls that method instead. And if that isn't found, then Perl searches for the last time in a special predefined package called *UNIVERSAL*. The *UNIVERSAL* class is a global base class for all packages, the highest class in the hierarchy of classes.

The *@ISA* array is not searched in a call to a normal subroutine but in a call to a subroutine if it is called with the method invocation syntax.

EXAMPLE 14.18

```
   #!/bin/perl
   # Example of attempting inheritance without updating
   # the @ISA array
1  { package Grandpa;
2    $name = "Gramps";
3    sub greetme {
       print "Hi $Child::name I'm your $name from package Grandpa.\n";
     }
   }
4  { package Parent;
     # This package is empty
   }
```

EXAMPLE 14.18 (CONTINUED)

```
5  { package Child;
6     $name = "Baby";
7     print "Hi I'm $name in the Child Package here.\n";
8     Parent->greetme();     # Use method invocation syntax
   }

(Output)
7  Hi I'm Baby in the Child Package here.
8  Can't locate object method "greetme" via package "Parent" at inher2
line 23.
```

EXPLANATION

1 The package *Grandpa* is declared.
2 The scalar *$name* is assigned *Gramps* in package *Grandpa.*
3 The subroutine *greetme* is defined and when called, the *print* statement will be executed. *$Child::name* refers to the scalar *$name* in the *Child* package.
4 The package *Parent* is declared. It is empty.
5 The package *Child* is declared. This package will try to call a method from another package. Although objects and methods aren't being used here, the purpose of this example is to show you what happens if you try to inherit a method from a class that this package doesn't know about.
8 Perl can't find the method *greetme* in package *Parent* and prints the error message.

EXAMPLE 14.19

```
   #!/bin/perl
   # Example of attempting inheritance by updating the @ISA array
1  { package Grandpa;
     $name = "Gramps";
2    sub greetme {
        print "Hi $Child::name I'm your $name from package Grandpa.\n";
     }
   }

3  { package Parent;
4    @ISA=qw(Grandpa);    # Grandpa is a package in the @ISA array.
                          # This package is empty.
   }

5  { package Child;
     $name = "Baby";
6    print "Hi I'm $name in the Child Package here.\n";
7    Parent->greetme();     # Parent::greetme() will fail
   }
```

EXAMPLE 14.19 (CONTINUED)

```
(Output)
6  Hi I'm Baby in the Child Package here.
7  Hi Baby I'm your Gramps from package Grandpa.
```

EXPLANATION

1 The package *Grandpa* is declared.
2 The subroutine *greetme* is defined and, when called, the *print* statement will be executed. *$Child::name* refers to the scalar *$name* in the *Child* package.
3 The *Parent* package is declared.
4 The *@ISA* array is assigned the name of the package *Grandpa*. Now if a method is called from this *Child* package and Perl can't find it, it will try the *Grandpa* package listed in the *@ISA* array. If you try to call a normal subroutine without method invocation, Perl won't consult the *@ISA* array, because it uses the *@ISA* array only when methods are being called. Even though the subroutines used here are not technically methods, by calling *greetme* as a class method, Perl will search the *@ISA* array.
5 The *Child* package is declared.
6 This line will be printed from the *Child* package.
7 The class method *greetme* is called in the *Parent* package. The *@ISA* array tells Perl to look in the *Grandpa* package if the method isn't in the *Parent* package.

14.4.2 *$AUTOLOAD, sub AUTOLOAD,* and *UNIVERSAL*

If a subroutine (or method) cannot be found in the current package or in the *@ISA* array, the *AUTOLOAD* function will be called. The *$AUTOLOAD* variable is assigned the name of the missing subroutine if it is used with the *AUTOLOAD* function. Arguments passed to the undefined subroutine are stored in the *AUTOLOAD* subroutine's *@_* array. If you assign a function name to the *$AUTOLOAD* variable, that subroutine will be called if the *AUTOLOAD* subroutine is provided in place of the missing subroutine. If the *$AUTOLOAD* variable is used with the *AUTOLOAD* subroutine, either the method or regular subroutine syntax can be used. If all fails and Perl still can't find the subroutine, a final package (class) called *UNIVERSAL* is searched for the missing method. The *UNIVERSAL* method contains three methods that all classes inherit. They are *isa()*, *can()*, and *VERSION()*. (See Table 14.2.)

Table 14.2 *UNIVERSAL* Methods

Method	**What It Does**	**Example**
isa	Returns true if one package inherits from another.	*Salesman–>isa("Employee");*
can	Returns true if a package or any of its base classes contain a specified method.	*Salesman–>can("get_data");*
VERSION	Used to check that the correct modules are loaded for that version number. In the example, Perl calls the *UNIVERSAL* method *Salesman–>VERSION(6.1)*.	*package Salesman;* *use$VERSION=6.1;*

EXAMPLE 14.20

```
   #!/bin/perl
1  { package Grandpa;
     $name = "Gramps";
     sub greetme {
2      print "Hi $Child::name I'm your $name from package Grandpa.\n";
     }
   }

3  { package Parent;
4    sub AUTOLOAD{
5      print "$_[0]: $_[1] and $_[2]\n";
6      print "You know us after all!\n";
7      print "The unheard of subroutine is called $AUTOLOAD.\n"
     }
   }
8  { package Child;
     $name = "Baby";
9    $AUTOLOAD=Grandpa->greetme();
10   print "Hi I'm $name in the Child Package here.\n";
11   Parent->unknown("Mom", "Dad");    # Undefined subroutine
   }
```

```
(Output)
2  Hi Baby I'm your Gramps from package Grandpa.
10 Hi I'm Baby in the Child Package here.
5  Parent: Mom and Dad
6  You know us after all!
7  The unheard of subroutine is called Parent::unknown.
```

EXPLANATION

1. The package *Grandpa* is declared. It contains one subroutine.
2. This line is printed from the *Grandpa* package.
3. The package *Parent* is declared. It contains an *AUTOLOAD* subroutine. An undefined subroutine is called on line 11. It has two arguments, *Mom* and *Dad*. If Perl can't find this subroutine in the *Child* package, it will look in the *@ISA* array, and if it is not there, Perl will look for an *AUTOLOAD* function.
4. The subroutine *AUTOLOAD* is defined.
5. Since this function was called as a class method, the first argument stored in the @_ array is the name of the class. The remaining arguments are *Mom* and *Dad*.
6. This line is printed to show that we got here.
7. The *$AUTOLOAD* variable contains the name of the class and the unnamed subroutine.
8. The package *Child* is declared.
9. If the scalar variable *$AUTOLOAD* is assigned the name of a subroutine, Perl will automatically call that subroutine.

EXPLANATION (CONTINUED)

10 This line is printed to show in what order the lines are executed.

11 The *Child* package wants to access a method in the *Parent* package. The *Parent* package does not contain a method or subroutine called *unknown*. It does, on the other hand, contain an *AUTOLOAD* subroutine that will be executed because this subroutine can't be found.

EXAMPLE 14.21

```
       #!/bin/perl
1      { package Grandpa;
         $name = "Gramps";
2        sub greetme {
             print "Hi $Child::name I'm your $name from package
                  Grandpa.\n";
         }
       }
3      { package Parent;
           # This package is empty
       }
4      { package Child;
       $name = "Baby";
5      print "Hi I'm $name in the Child Package here.\n";
6      Parent->greetme();
       }

7      package UNIVERSAL;
8      sub AUTOLOAD {
9          print "The UNIVERSAL lookup package.\n";
10         Grandpa->greetme();
       }

(Output)
2      Hi I'm Baby in the Child Package here.
9      The UNIVERSAL lookup package.
5      Hi Baby I'm your Gramps from package Grandpa.
```

EXPLANATION

1 The package *Grandpa* is declared.

2 The subroutine *greetme* is defined in this package.

3 The package *Parent* is declared. It is empty.

4 The package *Child* is declared.

5 This line is printed to show the flow of execution in the program.

6 The *greetme* subroutine is called as one of the *Parent* package methods.

7 Since the method could not be found in its own class or in the *@ISA* array, and an *AUTOLOAD* function is not supplied in the *Parent* package, Perl looks for package *UNIVERSAL* as a last resort. Here the subroutine *AUTOLOAD* calls *greetme*.

14.4.3 Derived Classes

As already discussed, **inheritance** is when one class can inherit methods from an existing class. The existing class is called the **base**, or **parent**, **class**, and the new class that inherits it is called the **derived**, or **child**, **class**. The base class has capabilities that all its derived classes inherit, and the derived class can then go beyond those capabilities. If a derived class inherits from one base class, it is called **single inheritance**. For example, single inheritance in real life might be that a child inherits his ability to draw from his father. If a derived class inherits from more than one base class, this is called **multiple inheritance**. To continue the analogy, the child inherits his ability to draw from his father and his ability to sing from his mother. In Perl, the derived class inherits methods from its base class (package) and can add and modify these methods when necessary.

The classes are inherited by putting them in the *@ISA* array. The methods to be exported to other modules can be specified in either the *@EXPORTER* or the *@EXPORTER_OK* arrays. The data itself is inherited by referencing keys and values in the anonymous hash where the data was initially assigned. These variables are called **instance variables** and are defined in the constructor method.

In Chapter 12, we looked at modules from the Perl standard library and modules you could create yourself. In order to include a module or pragma into your program, the *use* function was called with the module name (minus the *.pm* extension). The module had the capability to export symbols to other packages that might need to use the module. A special module called *Exporter.pm* handled the details for exporting and importing symbols between modules. This module also needs to be included in the *@ISA* array. If a module functions as a class, then its methods can be called without explicitly listing them in the *@EXPORT* array. Note in the following examples, the class methods and the instance methods are not exported.

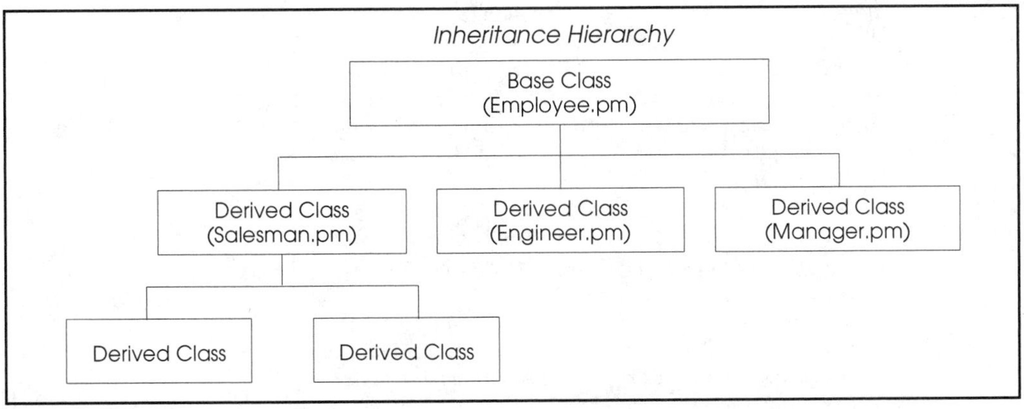

Figure 14.4 Deriving classes from a base class.

The following examples demonstrate inheritance. Example 14.22 is the user of the *Salesman.pm* class. The user program need not make any reference to the base class,

Employee.pm (see Example 14.23). The *Salesman.pm* class is derived from *Employee.pm*. The *Salesman.pm* class "uses" the *Employee.pm* class.

EXAMPLE 14.22

```
# The Driver (user) Program
use Salesman;
use strict;
use warnings;
# Create two salesman objects
print "Entering data for the first salesman.\n";
my $salesguy1=Salesman->new;
$salesguy1->set_data;
print "\nEntering data for the second salesman.\n";

my $salesguy2=Salesman->new;
$salesguy2->set_data;

print "\nHere are the statistics for the first salesman.\n";
$salesguy1->get_data;
print "\nHere are the statistics for the second salesman.\n";
$salesguy2->get_data;
```

(Output)

```
The salesman is an employee.
The salesman can display its properties.
Entering data for the first salesman.
Enter the name of the employee. Russ Savage
Enter the address of Russ Savage. 12 Main St., Boston, MA
Enter the monthly base pay for Russ Savage. 2200
Before blessing package is: Employee
After blessing package is: Salesman
Enter Russ Savage's commission for this month. 1200
Enter Russ Savage's bonuses for this month. 500.50
Enter Russ Savage's sales region. northeast

Entering data for the second salesman.
Enter the name of the employee. Jody Rodgers
Enter the address of Jody Rodgers. 2200 Broadway Ave, Chico, CA
Enter the monthly base pay for Jody Rodgers. 34500
Before blessing package is: Employee
After blessing package is: Salesman
Enter Jody Rodgers's commission for this month. 2300
Enter Jody Rodgers's bonuses for this month. 1400
Enter Jody Rodgers's sales region. northwest
```

EXAMPLE 14.22 (CONTINUED)

```
8   Here are the statistics for the first salesman.
    Name = Russ Savage.
    Bonuses = 500.50.
    Commission = 1200.
    BasePay = 2200.
    Address = 12 Main St., Boston, MA.
    PayCheck = 3900.5.
    Region = northeast.


10  Here are the statistics for the second salesman.
    Name = Jody Rodgers.
    Bonuses = 1400.
    Commission = 2300.
    BasePay = 34500.
    Address = 2200 Broadway Ave, Chico, CA.
    PayCheck = 38200.
    Region = northwest.
```

EXPLANATION

1 This *use* directive loads the *Salesman* module into this package, *main*. The program that contains the user interface is often called the **driver** program. It will be using the *Salesman* module to create a new salesman employee. Even though the *Salesman* class was derived from the *Employee* class, this program doesn't have to know that. All this program needs to do is call the *Salesman* constructor with the correct arguments (if any) and ask the user for input.

2 The *strict* and *warnings* pragmas are turned on to help keep the program from using unsafe constructs and from making compile or runtime errors.

3 The *Salesman* class constructor is called and returns a reference to a *Salesman* object, *$salesguy1*.

4 The *set_data* method is called. The user is asked for input for the first salesman. This method is called from *Salesman.pm*.

6 The constructor method for the *Salesman* module is called. A reference to the new *Salesman* object is returned and assigned to *$salesguy2*.

7 The *set_data* method is called for the second salesman. This method is called from *Salesman.pm*.

9 Inheritance is used here. The *get_data* method is called, but it is not implemented in the *Salesman* module. Perl searches the *@ISA* array in *Salesman.pm* and goes to the base class listed there, *Employee*. Since the *get_data* method is there, it will be called. The statistics for the first salesman are displayed.

11 The *get_data* method is called for the second salesman.

EXAMPLE 14.23

```
     # Module Employee.pm
     # The Base Class
1    package Employee;
2    use strict;
3    use warnings;
     # Constructor method
4    sub new {
5        my $class = shift;
6        my $self = {_Name=>undef,
                     _Address=>undef,
                     _BasePay=>undef,
                    };
7        return bless($self, $class);
     }

     # Instance/access methods
8    sub set_data{
9        my $self=shift;
10           print "Enter the name of the employee. ";
11           chomp($self->{_Name}=<STDIN>);
             print "Enter the address of $self->{_Name}. ";
             chomp($self->{_Address}=<STDIN>);
             print "Enter the monthly base pay for $self->{_Name}. ";
             chomp($self->{_BasePay}=<STDIN>);

         }
12   sub get_data{
13       my $self=shift;
14       my ($key,$value);
15       print "Name = $self->{_Name}.\n";
16       while(($key,$value)=each(%$self)){
17           $key =~ s/_//;
18           print "$key = $value.\n" unless $key eq "Name";
         }
         print "\n";
     }
     1;
```

EXPLANATION

1 The package is declared with the same name as the file, *Employee.pm*, minus the *.pm* extension. This is the base class. All employees have some common characteristics. In this example, they all have a name, an address, and a paycheck.

2 The *strict* pragma will do strict error checking; in other words, restrict unsafe constructs, such as the use of global variables, barewords, etc.

3 The *warnings* pragma will send warnings for probable compile or runtime errors.

EXPLANATION (CONTINUED)

4 The *Employee* constructor method is defined. It is called *new* by convention.

5 The name of the class will be shifted from the @_ array. This is a class method because it acts on behalf of the class and does not require an instance of the object.

6 An anonymous hash will be assigned the attributes/properties for the object as key/value pairs. The values are undefined, to be assigned later. A reference to the hash is returned and assigned to *$self*. (The leading underscore on the keys is a convention used to indicate that this is private data for the object.)

7 The object referenced by *$self* will be blessed into this class, *Employee*, and a reference to it will be returned to the caller.

8 The subroutine *set_data* is an access method for the *Employee* class. When called, it will be used to assign data to the object; that is, add values to the keys in the anonymous hash.

9 A reference to the object is shifted from the @_ array and assigned to *$self*.

10 The user of the module is asked for input.

11 The reference *$self* is used to assign values to the keys *_Name*, *_Address*, *_BasePay*.

12 This access method is used to retrieve and display the object's data.

13 A reference to the object is shifted from the @_ array and assigned to *$self*.

14 Two lexical variables are declared.

15 Because hash values are pulled in random order, this line guarantees that the name of the employee is displayed first.

16 The *while* loop is entered, and the *each* function will extract the key/value pairs from the object by using the reference to the object (*$%self*).

17 The leading underscore is removed from the key.

18 The rest of the properties for the object are displayed.

EXAMPLE 14.24

```
    # The Derived Class
1   package Salesman;
2   use strict;
    use warnings;
3   BEGIN{unshift(@INC, "./Baseclass");};
4   our @ISA=qw( Employee);
5   use Employee;
6   print "The salesman is an employee.\n"
            if Salesman->isa('Employee');
7   print "The salesman can display its properties.\n"
            if Salesman->can('get_data');
```

EXAMPLE 14.24 (CONTINUED)

```
8    sub new   {           # Constructor for Salesman
9        my ($class)= shift;
10       my $emp = new Employee;
11       $emp->set_data;
12       print "Before blessing package is: ", ref($emp), "\n";
         bless($emp, $class);
13       print "After blessing package is: ", ref($emp), "\n";
         return $emp;
     }
14   sub set_data{
         my $self=shift;
15       my $calc_ptr = sub{ my($base, $comm, $bonus)=@_;
                        return $base+$comm+$bonus; };
16       print "Enter $self->{_Name}'s commission for this month. ";
         chomp($self->{_Commission}=<STDIN>);
         print "Enter $self->{_Name}'s bonuses for this month. ";
         chomp($self->{_Bonuses}=<STDIN>);
         print "Enter $self->{_Name}'s sales region. ";
         chomp($self->{_Region}=<STDIN>);
17       $self->{_PayCheck}=&$calc_ptr( $self->{_BasePay},
                                        $self->{_Commission},
                                        $self->{_Bonuses}
                                      );
     }
     1;
```

EXPLANATION

1. The package (class) *Salesman* is declared.
2. The *strict* and *warnings* pragmas are loaded.
3. The *BEGIN* block is used to make sure the *@INC* array is updated at compile time so it will be available in the search for the base classes. The *Employee.pm* module is located in a subdirectory called *Baseclass*.
4. The *@ISA* array contains the names of packages that will be used by this package. The *Employee* module is the base class needed by this *Salesman* module. The *our* function makes the *@ISA* array a lexical, global array. Without *our*, the *strict* pragma causes the compiler to abort the script because global variables are not allowed (unless you fully qualify their names with the package name and two colons).
5. The *use* function causes the *Employee* module to be loaded into the program.
6. All packages/classes inherit from the superclass called *UNIVERSAL*, which provides the *isa* method The *isa* method returns true if the *Salesman* module inherits from the *Employee* module.
7. All packages/classes also inherit from the super class *UNIVERSAL*, which provides the *can* method. The *can* method returns true if the *Salesman* module or any of its parent classes contain a method called *get_data*, and *undef* if not.

EXPLANATION (CONTINUED)

8 The *Salesman* class defines a constructor method called *new.*
9 Arguments passed in are taken from the @_. The name of the class is assigned to *$class.*
10 The constructor *new* for the *Employee* base class is called. A reference to the object *$emp* is returned.
11 The *Salesman* class constructor calls *set_data* to add properties to the object.
12 Before the blessing, the *ref* function returns the name of the class (package) the object belongs to, the *Employee* base class. The object, with its new properties, is now blessed into the *Salesman* class.
13 After the blessing, the *ref* function returns the name of the class where the object was blessed, *Salesman.* A blessed reference to the object is returned to the caller.
14 The instance method *set_data* is defined for the *Salesman* class.
15 An anonymous subroutine is created to calculate the paycheck; a reference is returned. The subroutine should not be called by a user of the class. Only the class should be able to calculate the paycheck.
16 New properties are added to the *Employee* class.
17 The function to calculate the paycheck is called.

14.4.4 Multiple Inheritance

When a class inherits methods from more than one base, or parent, class, it is called **multiple inheritance**. In Perl, multiple inheritance is accomplished by adding more than one class to the *@ISA* array.

```
package  Child;
@ISA = qw (Mother Father Teacher);
```

The search is depth-first, meaning that Perl will search for classes in *Mother* and the hierarchy of classes it descends from, then *Father* and the hierarchy of classes it descends from, and finally *Teacher* and all its ancestors.

14.4.5 Overriding a Parent Method

There are times when two classes may have a method with the same name. If a derived class has a method with the same name as the base class, its method will take precedence over the base method. To override the method in the derived class so you can access the method in the base class, the name of the method must be fully qualified with the class name and two colons.

EXAMPLE 14.25

```
1   package Employee;  # Base class
    use strict;
    use warnings;
    sub new {           # Employee's constructor is defined
        my $class = shift;
        my %params = @_;
        my $self = { Name=>$params{"Name"},
                     Salary=>$params{"Salary"},
                   };
        bless ($self, $class);
        }
2   sub display {        # Instance method
        my $self = shift;
        foreach my $key ( @_){
3           print "$key: $self->{$key}\n";
        }
4       print "The class using this display method is ",
              ref($self),"\n";
    }
    1;
------------------------------------------------------------------
5   package Salesman;  # Derived class
    use strict;
    use warnings;
    use Employee;
6   our @ISA=qw (Exporter Employee);
7   sub new {           # Constructor in derived Salesman class
        my $class = shift;
        my (%params) = @_;
        my $self = new Employee(%params);  # Call constructor
                                           # in base class
        $self->{Commission} = $params{Commission};
        bless ( $self, $class );      # Rebless the object into
                                      # the derived class
    }
    sub set_Salary {
        my $self = shift;
        $self->{Salary}=$self->{Salary} + $self->{Commission};
    }
8   sub display{        # Override method in Employee class
        my $self = shift;
        my @args = @_;
9       print "Stats for the Salesman\n";
        print "-" x 25, "\n";
10      $self->Employee::display(@args);  # Access to the
                                          # overridden method
    }
    1;
    ----------------------------------------
```

EXAMPLE 14.25 (CONTINUED)

```
    # User or Driver Program
    #!/bin/perl
11  use Salesman;
    use strict;
    use warnings;
12  my $emp = new Salesman ( "Name", "Tom Savage",
                             "Salary", 50000,   # Call to constructor
                             "Commission", 1500,
                           );
    $emp->set_Salary;  # Call to the access method
13  $emp->display( "Name" , "Salary", "Commission");
                       # Call Salesman's display method
```

```
(Output)
9   Stats for the Salesman
    -------------------------
    Name: Tom Savage
    Salary: 51500
    The class using this display method is Salesman
```

EXPLANATION

1. The class *Employee* is declared. It contains a constructor method called *new* and an instance method called *display.*
2. The *display* access method is defined for the *Employee* class.
3. The attributes for the employee are displayed.
4. The *ref* function returns the name of the class of a blessed object.
5. The *Salesman* class is declared. It will inherit from the *Employee* class and is called a derived class.
6. The *@ISA* array includes the names of the classes it needs: the *Exporter* class and the base class, *Employee.*
7. This is the *Saleman's* constructor.
8. This *display* method takes precedence here in the derived class because it belongs to class *Salesman.* It is called in the driver program passing a reference to a *Salesman* object.
9. The printout is coming from the derived class (*Salesman*) subroutine, *display.*
10. By qualifying the name of the method to be of class *Employee*, this *display* method will override the current display method in package *Salesman.*
11. This is the driver program. It uses the *Salesman* module.
12. A new *Salesman* object is created, using the indirect method to call the constructor.
13. The *display* method is called. Since there is a *display* subroutine in the *Salesman* class, it is the one that will be called.

14.5 Public User Interface—Documenting Classes

One of the most important phases in creating a useful class is providing the user with good documentation describing how the class should be used. This is called the **public user interface**. Whether a module is object oriented or not, there must be some published user interface—the written documentation—available describing how the programmer (client) should use a class (e.g., what arguments will be passed to a method). The publicly defined interface should not change, even if something in the class is changed. Perl 5 introduced *pod* commands as a way to document modules. This is done by interspersing the program with *POD* (Plain Ole Documentation) instructions, similar to embedding HTML or *nroff* instructions within the text of a file. Then the program is run through a Perl filtering program, which translates the commands into manual pages in a number of different formats.

14.5.1 *pod* Files

If you look in the standard Perl library, you will find that the modules contain documentation explaining what the module is supposed to do and how to use it. The documentation is either embedded within the program or placed at the end of the program right after the special literal *__END__*. This documentation is called *POD*, short for Plain Ole Documentation. A *pod* file is just an ASCII text file embedded with special commands that can be translated by one of Perl's special interpreters, *pod2html*, *pod2latex*, *pod2text*, or *pod2man*. The purpose is to create formatted documents that can be represented in a number of ways. The UNIX *man* pages are an example of documentation that has been formatted with *nroff* instructions. It is now easy to embed a set of *pod* formatting instructions in your scripts to provide documentation in any of the four formats: text, HTML, LaTeX, or nroff.

The first line of the *pod* documentation starts with an equal sign (=). Each word starting with an equal sign is a formatting instructions for the *pod* translator. **Each formatting instruction must be followed by a blank line.**

EXAMPLE 14.26

```
(Here is the documentation found at the end of the BigFloat.pm module
in the standard Perl library, under the subdirectory Math.)

=head1 NAME

Math::BigFloat - Arbitrary length float math package

=head1 SYNOPSIS

  use Math::BigFloat;
  $f = Math::BigFloat->new($string);
```

EXAMPLE 14.26 (CONTINUED)

```
  $f->fadd(NSTR) return NSTR                addition
  $f->fsub(NSTR) return NSTR                subtraction
  $f->fmul(NSTR) return NSTR                multiplication
  $f->fdiv(NSTR[,SCALE]) returns NSTR       division to SCALE places
  $f->fneg() return NSTR                    negation
  $f->fabs() return NSTR                    absolute value
  $f->fcmp(NSTR) return CODE                compare undef,<0,=0,>0
  $f->fround(SCALE) return NSTR             round to SCALE digits
  $f->ffround(SCALE) return NSTR            round at SCALEth place
  $f->fnorm() return (NSTR)                 normalize
  $f->fsqrt([SCALE]) return NSTR            sqrt to SCALE places

=head1 DESCRIPTION

All basic math operations are overloaded if you declare your big
floats as

   $float = new Math::BigFloat "2.123123123123123123123123123123123";

=over 2

=item number format

canonical strings have the form /[+-]\d+E[+-]\d+/ . Input values can
have inbedded whitespace.

=item Error returns 'NaN'

An input parameter was "Not a Number" or divide by zero or sqrt of
negative number.

=item Division is computed to

C<max($div_scale,length(dividend)+length(divisor))> digits by default.
Also used for default sqrt scale.

=back

=head1 BUGS

The current version of this module is a preliminary version of the
real thing that is currently (as of perl5.002) under development.

=head1 AUTHOR

Mark Biggar

=cut
```

EXPLANATION

The preceding text is a *pod* file. It consists of lines starting with an equal sign and a *pod* command, then a blank line, and text. Perl provides a special translator program that reads the *pod* file and translates it into a readable file in plain text, HTML format, *nroff* text, or LaTeX. The next section describes how to use the *pod* filter programs to make the translation for you.

14.5.2 *pod* Commands

It's easy to embed *pod* instructions in a text file. Commands are placed at the beginning of a line, starting with *=pod* (or any other *pod* command) and ending with *=cut*. Everything after the first *=pod* instruction to the *=cut* instruction will be ignored by the compiler, just as comments are ignored. The nice thing about using the commands is that they allow you to create bold, italic, or plain text to indent to create headings and more. Table 14.3 contains a list of instructions.

Table 14.3 *pod* Commands

Paragraph Commands	***What They Do***
=pod	Marks the start of *pod*, but an equal sign, followed by any pod instruction starts the documentation
=cut	Marks the end of *pod*
=head1 heading	Creates a level1 heading
=head2 heading	Creates a level2 heading
*=item **	Starts a bulleted list
=over N	Moves over *N* number of spaces, usually set to *4*
=back	Returns indent back to default, no indent
Formatting Commands	***What They Do***
I<text>	Italic text
B<text>	Bold text
S<text>	Contains text nonbreaking spaces
C<code>	Contains typed text, literal source code
L<name>	Creates a link (cross reference) to name
F<file>	Used for listing filenames
X<index>	An index entry
Z<>	A zero-width character

Table 14.3 *pod* Commands *(continued)*

Filter Specific Commands	***What They Do***
=for	For HTML-specific commands; e.g., *=for html* *<IMG SRC=file.gif>* *<B>Figure a.>/B>>* For text-specific commands; e.g., *=for text* text to represent what the above image means For *manpage*-specific commands; e.g., *=for man* *.ce 3* *<center next three lines>*

14.5.3 How to Use the *pod* Interpreters

The *pod* interpreters come with the Perl distribution and are located in the *bin* directory under the main Perl directory; for example, in */usr/bin/perl5/bin.*

The four interpreters are

`pod2html`	(translate to HTML)
`pod2text`	(translate to plain text)
`pod2man`	(translate to *nroff*, like UNIX *man* pages)
`pod2latex`	(translate to LaTeX)

The easiest way to use the interpreters is to copy the one you want into your own directory. For example:

```
$ cp /usr/bin/perl5/bin/pod2text
```

You may also copy the library routine into your directory:

```
$ cp /usr/bin/perl5/lib/BigFloat.pm
```

Now when you list the contents of the directory, you should have both the *pod* interpreter and the library module.

```
$ ls
BigFloat.pm
pod2text
```

14.5.4 Translating *pod* Documentation into Text

The easiest way to translate the *pod* commands to text for your terminal screen is to use the *perldoc* command that comes with the Perl distribution. It may not be in your search path, but it is usually found in the *bin* directory under *perl.* The following command would display all the documentation for the *BigFloat.pm* module.

```
perldoc Math::BigFloat
```

Another way to translate *pod* directives to text is to let the *pod* interpreter filter through the module and create an output file to save the translated text. If you don't redirect the output to a file, it will simply go to the screen.

```
$ pod2text BigFloat.pm > BigFloat.Text
$ cat BigFloat.Text   (The output file after pod commands have been
                       translated into text.)

NAME
    Math::BigFloat - Arbitrary length float math package

SYNOPSIS
      use Math::BogFloat;
      $f = Math::BigFloat->new($string);

      $f->fadd(NSTR) return NSTR                   addition
      $f->fsub(NSTR) return NSTR                   subtraction
      $f->fmul(NSTR) return NSTR                   multiplication
      $f->fdiv(NSTR[,SCALE])    returns NSTR       division to SCALE places
      $f->fneg() return NSTR                       negation
      $f->fabs() return NSTR                       absolute value
      $f->fcmp(NSTR) return CODE                   compare undef,<0,=0,>0
      $f->fround(SCALE) return NSTR                round to SCALE digits
      $f->ffround(SCALE) return NSTR               round at SCALEth place
      $f->fnorm() return (NSTR)                    normalize
      $f->fsqrt([SCALE]) return NSTR               sqrt to SCALE places

DESCRIPTION
    All basic math operations are overloaded if you declare your big
    floats as

$float=newMath::BigFloat"2.123123123123123123123123123123123";

     number format
     canonical strings have the form /[+-]\d+E[+-]\d+/ . Input
     values can have inbedded whitespace.

 Error returns 'NaN'
      An input parameter was "Not a Number" or divide by zero or
      sqrt of negative number.

 Division is computed to
      `max($div_scale,length(dividend)+length(divisor))' digits by
      default. Also used for default sqrt scale.
```

```
BUGS
    The current version of this module is a preliminary version of
    the real thing that is currently (as of perl5.002) under
    development.

AUTHOR
    Mark Biggar
```

14.5.5 Translating *pod* Documentation into HTML

To create an HTML document, copy *pod2html* into your directory and type

```
$ pod2html BigFloat.pm > BigFloat.pm.html
```

The *pod2html* translator will create a file called *BigFloat.pm.html.* Now open your browser window and assign *BigFloat.pm.html* to a file protocol in the URL location box; e.g., *<file:/yourdirectory path/BigFloat.pm.html>.*[9]

14.6 Using Objects from the Perl Library

In Chapter 12, "Modularize It, Package It, and Send It to the Library!" we first looked into the standard Perl library that was provided with this distribution, Perl 5.6. In that library were a number of *.pl* and *.pm* files. The examples covered dealt with packages that did not require knowledge about Perl's use of objects. Those files utilized standard subroutines, not methods. Now that you know how objects and methods are used in Perl, the following examples will demonstrate how to use those modules that require the OOP methodology.

14.6.1 Another Look at the Standard Perl Library

The *@INC* array contains the pathnames to the libraries Perl will search. After looking at the library listings, we will *cd* into the standard Perl library and list the files found there. You'll notice that some of the files end with the *.pm* extension and some end with the *.pl* extension. The files that utilize objects (ending in *.pm)* were introduced in Perl 5 and are the modules that support OOP. The files that do not have an extension are the names of directories where Perl has stored modules that fit into that category. For example, the *File* and *Math* subdirectories contain modules that pertain to those respective subjects.

---

9. If you receive some obscure diagnostic messages, it may be that the documentation for the *.pm* file contains links to some other page that cannot be resolved by the *pod* filter.

EXAMPLE 14.27

```
1   $ perl -e "print join qq/\n/,@INC;"
    c:/Perl/lib
    c:/Perl/site/lib

2   $ ls /Perl/lib
AnyDBM_File.pm   Exporter.pm      Symbol.pm        cacheout.pl      newgetopt.pl
AutoLoader.pm    ExtUtils         Sys              charnames.pm     open.pm
AutoSplit.pm     Fatal.pm         Term             chat2.pl         open2.pl
B                Fcntl.pm         Test             complete.pl      open3.pl
B.pm             File             Test.pm          constant.pm      ops.pm
Benchmark.pm     FileCache.pm     Text             ctime.pl         overload.pm
ByteLoader.pm    FileHandle.pm    Thread           diagnostics.pm   perl5db.pl
CGI              FindBin.pm       Thread.pm        dotsh.pl         perllocal.pod
CGI.pm           Getopt           Tie              dumpvar.pl       pwd.pl
CORE             I18N             Time             exceptions.pl    re.pm
CPAN             IO               UNIVERSAL.pm     fastcwd.pl       shellwords.pl
CPAN.pm          IO.pm            User             fields.pm        sigtrap.pm
Carp             IPC              Win32.pod        filetest.pm      stat.pl
Carp.pm          Math             XSLoader.pm      find.pl          strict.pm
Class            Net              abbrev.pl        finddepth.pl     subs.pm
Config.pm        O.pm             assert.pl        flush.pl         syslog.pl
Cwd.pm           Opcode.pm        attributes.pm    ftp.pl           tainted.pl
DB.pm            POSIX.pm         attrs.pm         getcwd.pl        termcap.pl
Data             POSIX.pod        auto             getopt.pl        timelocal.pl
Devel            Pod              autouse.pm       getopts.pl       unicode
DirHandle.pm     SDBM_File.pm     base.pm          hostname.pl      utf8.pm
Dumpvalue.pm     Safe.pm          bigfloat.pl      importenv.pl     utf8_heavy.pl
DynaLoader.pm    Search           bigint.pl        integer.pm       validate.pl
English.pm       SelectSaver.pm   bigrat.pl        less.pm          vars.pm
Env.pm           SelfLoader.pm    blib.pm          lib.pm           warnings
Errno.pm         Shell.pm         bytes.pm         locale.pm        warnings.pm
Exporter         Socket.pm        bytes_heavy.pl   look.pl

3   $ cd Math
4   $ ls
    BigFloat.pm  BigInt.pm    Complex.pm    Trig.pm
```

EXPLANATION

1. The elements of the *@INC* array are printed to ensure that the standard Perl library is included in Perl's library search path.
2. The library routines are listed.
3. Any file not ending in *.pl* or *.pm* is a subdirectory. We change to the *Math* subdirectory.
4. The contents of the directory are listed, showing three *Math* modules.

14.6.2 An Object-Oriented Module from the Standard Perl Library

The following module, *BigFloat.pm*, allows the use of floating point numbers of arbitrary length. Number strings have the form */[+-]\d*\.?\d*E[+-]\d+/*. When *NaN* is returned, it means that a non-number was entered as input, that you tried to divide by zero, or that you tried to take the square root of a negative number. *BigFloat* uses the *overload* module, which allows Perl's built-in operators to be assigned methods that will cause the operators to behave in a new way. The operator is the key and the method assigned is the value. (See *overload.pm* in the standard Perl library.)

EXAMPLE 14.28

```
(The File: BigFloat.pm)

1   package Math::BigFloat;
2   use Math::BigInt;

    use Exporter;  # Just for use to be happy
    @ISA = (Exporter);

3   use overload
4   '+'    =>  sub {new Math::BigFloat &fadd},
    '-'    =>  sub {new Math::BigFloat
                  $_[2]? fsub($_[1],${$_[0]}) : fsub(${$_[0]},$_[1])},
    '<=>'  =>  sub {new Math::BigFloat
                  $_[2]? fcmp($_[1],${$_[0]}) : fcmp(${$_[0]},$_[1])},
    'cmp'  =>  sub {new Math::BigFloat
                  $_[2]? ($_[1] cmp ${$_[0]}) : (${$_[0]} cmp $_[1])},
    '*'    =>  sub {new Math::BigFloat &fmul},
    '/'    =>  sub {new Math::BigFloat
                  $_[2]? scalar fdiv($_[1],${$_[0]}) :
                    scalar fdiv(${$_[0]},$_[1])},
    'neg'  =>  sub {new Math::BigFloat &fneg},
    'abs'  =>  sub {new Math::BigFloat &fabs},
    qw(
        ""   stringify
        0+   numify)     # Order of arguments unsignificant
        ;

5   sub new {
        my ($class) = shift;
        my ($foo) = fnorm(shift);
6       panic("Not a number initialized to Math::BigFloat")
                if $foo eq "NaN";
```

EXAMPLE 14.28 (CONTINUED)

```
7      bless \$foo, $class;
   }

    < Methods continue here. Module was too long to put here>

   # addition
8  sub fadd { #(fnum_str, fnum_str) return fnum_str
       local($x,$y) = (fnorm($_[$[]),fnorm($_[$[+1]));
       if ($x eq 'NaN' || $y eq 'NaN') {
           NaN';
       } else {
           local($xm,$xe) = split('E',$x);
           local($ym,$ye) = split('E',$y);
           ($xm,$x e,$ym,$ye) = ($ym,$ye,$xm,$xe) if ($xe < $ye);
           &norm(Math::BigInt::badd($ym,$xm.('0' x ($xe-$ye))),$ye);
       }
   }

    < Methods continue here>

   # divisionbb
   # args are dividend, divisor, scale (optional)
   # result has at most max(scale, length(dividend),
   # length(divisor)) digits
9  sub fdiv    #(fnum_str, fnum_str[,scale]) return fnum_str
   {
       local($x,$y,$scale) = (fnorm($_[$[]),
                             fnorm($_[$[+1]),$_[$[+2]);
       if ($x eq 'NaN' || $y eq 'NaN' || $y eq '+0E+0') {
           'NaN';
       } else {
           local($xm,$xe) = split('E',$x);
           local($ym,$ye) = split('E',$y);
           $scale = $div_scale if (!$scale);
           $scale = length($xm)-1 if (length($xm)-1 > $scale);
           $scale = length($ym)-1 if (length($ym)-1 > $scale);
           $scale = $scale + length($ym) - length($xm);
           &norm(&round(Math::BigInt::bdiv($xm.('0' x $scale),$ym),
                                          $ym),$xe-$ye-$scale);
       }
   }
```

EXPLANATION

1 The *BigFloat* class is declared. It resides in the *Math* subdirectory of the standard Perl library.
2 The *BigFloat* class also needs to use the *BigInt* module.
3 The *overload* function allows you to change the meaning of the built-in Perl operators. For example, when using *BigFloat.pm*, the + operator is a key and its value an anonymous subroutine that creates an object and calls the *&fadd* subroutine.
4 The + operator is overloaded. See previous explanation.
5 This is *BigFloat*'s constructor method for creating an object.
6 If the value is not a number, this panic message is printed.
7 The object is blessed into the class.
8 This is the subroutine that performs addition on the object.
9 This is the subroutine that performs division on the object.

14.6.3 Using a Module with Objects from the Standard Perl Library

EXAMPLE 14.29

```
1   #!/bin/perl
2   use Math::BigFloat;   # BigFloat.pm is in the Math directory

3   $number = "000.95671234e-21";
4   $mathref = new Math::BigFloat("$number");  # Create the object

5   print "\$mathref is in class ", ref($mathref), "\n";
                        # Where is the object

6   print $mathref->fnorm(), "\n";  # Use methods from the class

7   print "The sum of $mathref + 500 is: ", $mathref->fadd("500"),
                                         "\n";
8   print "Division using overloaded operator: ", $mathref / 200.5,
                                         "\n";
9   print "Division using fdiv method:", $mathref->fdiv("200.5"),
                                         "\n";

10  print "Enter a number ";
    chop($numstr = <STDIN>);

11  if ( $mathref->fadd($numstr) eq "NaN" ){
                     print "You didn't enter a number.\n"};

# Return value of NaN means the string is not a number,
# or you divided by zero, or you took the square root
# of a negative number.
```

EXAMPLE 14.29 (CONTINUED)

```
(Output)
5  $mathref is in class Math::BigFloat
6  +95671234E-29
7  The sum of .00000000000000000000095671234 + 500 is:
   +50000000000000000000000095671234E-29
8  Division using overloaded operator:
   .000000000000000000000004771632618453865336658354114713216957606
9  Division using fdiv method:
   +4771632618453865336658354114713216957606E-63
10 Enter a number hello
11 You didn't enter a number.
```

EXPLANATION

1 The *shbang* line to the Perl interpreter.

2 The *use* function loads the module *BigFloat.pm* into the program. Since this module is in a subdirectory of the library called *Math*, that subdirectory is included by prepending its name to the module with two colons.

3 A large number (*e* notation) is assigned to *$number*.

4 Now the methods from the module are utilized. The *BigFloat* constructor is called. A reference to the object is returned and assigned to *$mathref*.

5 The *ref* function returns the name of the class.

6 The *fnorm* method returns the "normal" value of *$number* in signed scientific notation. Leading zeros are stripped off.

7 The *fadd* method adds *500* to the number.

8 In this example, an overloaded operator is used. The / operator is assigned a class method, *fdiv*, to perform the division. See code from *BigFloat.pm* shown above.

9 This time the *fdiv* method is called directly without using overloading to perform the division. The output is slightly different.

10 The user is asked to enter a number.

11 If *NaN* (not a number) is returned from the *fadd* method, the message is printed. This is a way you could check that user input is a valid numeric value.

14.7 What You Should Know

1. What does OOP mean?
2. What is the difference between a package and a class?
3. What is a method?
4. What is the first parameter received by a class method?
5. What function creates an object?

6. What are properties?
7. What is an instance method?
8. Does Perl have a "private" keyword?
9. How do you name a class? Where do you put a class?
10. What is meant by class method invocation?
11. What is polymorphism?
12. What is the *@ISA* array used for?
13. What is a derived class?
14. What is a closure used for?
15. How do you document a class?
16. What is a *pod* filter?
17. How is a *pod* directive used?

14.8 What's Next?

In the next chapter, you will learn about Perl's built-in predefined methods to tie a variable to a class and how this applies to using DBM, the database management library for storing large binary files.

EXERCISE 14
What's the Object of This Lesson?

Part 1. Intro to Objects

1. Write a module called *Rightnow.pm* that contains three methods:
   a. A constructor called "new".
   b. A method called "set_time" to set the time. Use the *localtime* function.
   c. A method called "print_time" to print the time.
      This method will take an argument to determine whether the time is printed in military or standard time; e.g., print_time("Military");
   d. In another Perl script, use the *Rightnow* module to create a *Rightnow* object, and call the "print_time" method to produce output as follows:

      Time now: 2:48:20 PM
      Time now: 14:48:20

Part 2. More Objects

1. In a class, create a *Student* object. The attributes for the *Student* object will be sent as arguments to the constructor method. The *Student* object will have three attributes: the name of the student, the student's major, and a list of courses he is taking.

   Create an instance method called "show_student" that will display a *Student* object.

   The user of the module will create two *Student* objects and display each.

2. Add three new attributes to the *Student* object: the student's address, the student's ID number, the start date, and tuition; e.g.,

   Address: 140 Kennedy Drive,
   Luxembourg City, Luxembourg
   ID: 123A
   StartDate: 01/10/07
   Tuition: 5400.55

   How will you manage this? If the user has so much information to pass to the constructor, it may be a good time to create an access method called "set_student".

   Create three new *Student* objects.

3. Create two new access methods that take arguments. One is called "add_courses" and the other is called "drop_courses".

   The user interface will allow the user to add or drop any number of courses by sending a list of parameters to the methods; e.g., $ptr->add_courses(["C++", "Java"]);

4. You will use a "class" variable to keep track of the number of new students. Each time you add a student, update the counter. Before exiting the program, print the number of new students. Use the *DESTROY* method.

5. From now on, send the data for each student to a file. It should contain a line that looks like this:

   John Doe:14 Main St:3456IX:Math:Trigonometry,Calculus, French:01/01/06:4500

6. Create another file that keeps track of the number of students. Each time you start your script, read the number from the file. When you add a new student, tell him "Welcome, John D.

Part 3. Create an Object-Oriented Module

1. Make *Checking.pm* object oriented. The object will be "the balance" and the subroutines will be "methods." The constructor will contain at least two attributes: the balance, account number. The account number will be passed to the constructor as an argument. The balance will be retrieved from the register, initially set to 0.

   When you create the register file, append the account number to the filename. Include the account number, balance, and date in the register file.

   Use the *Checking* module in the ATM user script you created earlier.

2. Can you make more that one instance of the *Checking* object and keep track of the balance for each account?

Part 4. Using *@ISA* and Inheritance

1. Create a *Pet* class with a constructor and one access method.
   The constructor provides attributes for a generic pet, such as:
      owner
      name
      sex

   a. The access method is called *eat()*. It takes one argument: the type of food a specific pet eats. For example, the dog eats Alpo. The dog will not have an *eat()* method and will inherit from this class.
   b. Create two classes that will inherit from the *Pet* class; for example, a *Dog* and a *Cat* class. They will use the *Pet*'s constructor and add new attributes of their own. They will have a *speak()* method but not an *eat()* method.

2. Now we will create a base class called *Bank.pm* and two modules that use it: *Checking.pm* and *Savings.pm*.

   a. The *Bank.pm* parent class may or may not have a constructor but will contain the *deposit()*, *withdraw()*, and *get_balance()* methods from the *Checking.pm* module.
   b. Remove *deposit()* and *withdraw()* from *Checking.pm*. The program that uses *Checking.pm* will inherit these methods from *Bank.pm* via *@ISA*.
   c. Create another module called *Savings.pm*.
   d. Both *Checking.pm* and *Savings.pm* will use the *Bank* module and inherit its methods. Each will gave its own constructor and attributes. One attribute is the status of the account. It can be "active" or "closed."
      The *Savings* account accrues compounded daily interest 1% and must start with a minimum balance of $200.
      The *Checking* account has overdraft protection and charges $35 for each bounced check. It will not allow an overdraft of over $300. It can be opened with a starting balance of $25.
   e. The *Checking.pm* and *Savings.pm* modules will each have its own account numbers and registers.
   f. The ATM script will use both modules. The user script will have a main menu allowing the user to select either of the two accounts. After getting a new account object, the user can select from the types of transactions (submenu in your original *Checking.pm* module) for that account and continue transactions until he is ready to quit. When he exits, his account register will be updated and he will be asked if he wants to return to the main menu. If he says "yes," he will see the main menu again, and if he says "no," the program will exit. You will have to uniquely name the register for each account so you can differentiate between savings and checking accounts.

Example:

perl user.pl

```
      Welcome!
Select an account type:
  1) Checking
  2) Savings
1
Select a function:
 1) deposit
 2) withdraw
 3) get balance
 4) exit
1
How much do you want to deposit? 5
Select a function:
 1) deposit
 2) withdraw
 3) get balance
 4) exit
3
Your balance is $30.00
Select a function:
 1) deposit
 2) withdraw
 3) get balance
 4) exit
2
```

perl user.pl

```
      Welcome!
Select an account type:
  1) Checking
  2) Savings
1
Select a function:
 1) deposit
 2) withdraw
 3) get balance
 4) exit
1
How much do you want to deposit? 5
Select a function:
 1) deposit
 2) withdraw
 3) get balance
```

```
 4) exit
3
Your balance is $30.00
Select a function:
 1) deposit
 2) withdraw
 3) get balance
 4) exit
2
Return to the main menu? y
      Welcome!
Select an account type:
  1) Checking
  2) Savings
2
Select a function:
 1) deposit
 2) withdraw
 3) get balance
 4) exit
3
Your balance is $100.00
Select a function:
 1) deposit
 2) withdraw
 3) get balance
 4) exit
1
How much do you want to deposit? 25
Select a function:
 1) deposit
 2) withdraw
 3) get balance
 4) exit
4
After interest balance is 127.50
```

Part 5.

Go to the *pod* directory in the standard Perl library. Look for *perlpod.html*. The file contains Larry Wall's user interface for using *pod* commands to document your Perl programs.

Go to your browser and in the Location box, type:

```
file:/<directory-to -your-library-file>/Pod/pod.html
```

Now you have the instructions for creating *pod* documentation.

Create a published interface for your *Checking.pm* module. Embed *pod* commands in your *Checking.pm* script explaining how the module should be used. Follow the guidelines of the modules in the library; for example, there should be a NAME, SYNOPSIS, DESCRIPTION, AUTHOR, etc. Run the *pod* file through the *pod2html* filter and display the documentation in your browser. Use the *perldoc* command to print your documentation on the terminal screen.

chapter

15

Those Magic Ties and DBM Stuff

15.1 Tying Variables to a Class

Normally when you perform some operation on a variable, such as assigning, changing, or printing the value of the variable, Perl performs the necessary operations on that variable internally. For example, you don't need a constructor method just to create a variable and assign a value to it, and you don't have to create access methods to manipulate the variable. The assignment statement *$x=5;* doesn't require any tricky semantics. Perl creates the memory location for *$x* and puts the value 5 in that location.

It is now possible to bind an ordinary variable to a class and provide methods for that variable so that, as if by magic, the variable is transformed when an assignment is made or a value is retrieved from it. A scalar, array, or hash, then, can be given a new implementation. Unlike objects, where you must use a reference to the object, tied variables, once created, are treated like any other variable. All of the details are hidden from the user. You will use the same syntax to assign values to the variable and to access the variable as you did before tying.[1] The magic goes on behind the scenes. Perl creates an object to represent the variable and uses predefined method names to construct, set, get, and destroy the object that has been tied to the variable. The programmer who creates the class uses the predefined method names, such as *FETCH* and *STORE,* to include the statements necessary to manipulate the object. The user ties the variable and, from that point on, uses it the same way as he would any other variable in his program.

15.1.1 The *tie* Function

The *tie* function binds a variable to a package or class and returns a reference to an object. All the details are handled internally. The *tie* function is most commonly used with associative arrays to bind key/value pairs to a database; for example, the DBM modules provided

1. DBM databases use the *tie* mechanism to automatically perform database operations on data.

with the Perl distribution use tied variables. The *untie* function will disassociate a variable from the class to which it was tied. The format for *tie* follows.

FORMAT

```
$object =  tie variable, class, list;
untie variable;

tie variable, class, list;
$object = tied variable;
```

The *tie* function returns a reference to the object that was previously bound with the *tie* function or undefined if the variable is not tied to a package.

15.1.2 Predefined Methods

Tying variables allows you to define the behavior of a variable by constructing a class that has special methods to create and access the variable. The methods will be called automatically when the variable is used. A variable can't be tied to any class but must be tied to a class that has predefined method names. The behavior of the variable is determined by methods in the class that will be called automatically when the variable is used. The constructors and methods used to tie (constructor) and manipulate (access methods) the variable have predefined names. The methods will be called automatically when the tied variables are fetched, stored, destroyed, and so on. All of the details are handled internally. The constructor can bless and return a pointer to any type of object. For example, the reference may point to a blessed scalar, array, or hash. But the access methods **must return** a scalar value if *TIESCALAR* is used, an array value if *TIEARRAY* is used, and a hash value if *TIEHASH* is used.

15.1.3 Tying a Scalar

In order to use a tied scalar, the class must define a set of methods that have predefined names. The constructor *TIESCALAR* is called when the variable is tied, and it creates the underlying object that will be manipulated by the access methods *STORE* and *FETCH*. Any time the user makes an assignment to the tied scalar, the *STORE* method is called, and whenever he attempts to display the tied scalar, the *FETCH* method is called. The *DESTROY* method is not required but if it is defined, will be called when the tied scalar is untied or goes out of scope. Methods provided for a tied scalar are

```
TIESCALAR $classname, LIST
STORE $self, $value
FETCH $self
DESTROY $self
```

There is also a base module in the standard Perl library for tying scalars that provides some skeletal methods for scalar-tying classes. See the *perltie man* page for a list of the functions required in tying scalar to a package. The basic *Tie::Scalar* package provides a *new* method, as well as methods *TIESCALAR*, *FETCH*, and *STORE*. For documentation of this module, type *perldoc Tie::Scalar.*

Example 15.1 demonstrates tying a scalar and how to access the tied scalar.

EXAMPLE 15.1

```
# File is Square.pm
# It will square a number, initially set to 5
package Square;
sub TIESCALAR{
    my $class = shift;
    my $data = shift;
    bless(\$data,$class);    # Blessing a scalar
}
sub FETCH{
    my $self = shift;
    $$self **= 2;
}
sub STORE{
    my $self = shift;
    $$self = shift;
}
1;
-----------------------------------------------------------------------

# User program
use Square;
$object=tie $squared, 'Square', 5;   # Call constructor TIESCALAR
print "object is $object.\n";
print $squared,"\n";        # Call FETCH three times
print $squared,"\n";
print $squared,"\n";
print "----------------------------\n";

$squared=3;                 # Call STORE

print $squared,"\n";        # Call FETCH
print $squared,"\n";
print $squared,"\n";

untie $squared;          # Break the tie that binds the
                         # scalar to the object
```

EXAMPLE 15.1 (CONTINUED)

```
(Output)
14 object is Square=SCALAR(0x1a72da8).
15 25
16 625
   390625
   ----------------------------
18 9
   81
   6561
```

EXPLANATION

1 The package/class *Square* is declared. The file is *Square.pm*.
2 *TIESCALAR* is the constructor for the class. It creates an association between the tied scalar and an object. Look at line 13 of this example. This is where the constructor is called. The variable tied to the object is *$squared*.
3 The first argument to the constructor is the name of the class. It is shifted from the @_ array and assigned to *$class*.
4 Look again at line 13. The tied variable, *$squared*, is followed by the name of the class and then the number 5. The class name is passed first, followed by 5. In the constructor, the number 5 is shifted from the @_ array and assigned to *$data*.
5 A reference to the scalar is created and passed to the *bless* function, which creates the object.
6 The *FETCH* method is defined. This access method will retrieve data from the object.
7 The first argument to the *FETCH* method is a reference to the object.
8 The pointer is dereferenced and its value squared.
9 The *STORE* method is defined. It will be used to assign a value to the object.
10 The first argument to the *STORE* method is a reference to the object.
11 The value to be assigned is shifted off the @_ array and assigned to *$$self*.
12 This is the user/driver program. The *Square* module is loaded into the program.
13 The *tie* function automatically calls the constructor *TIESCALAR*. The *tie* function ties the variable, *$squared*, to the class and returns a reference to the newly created object.
14 The reference, *$object*, points to a scalar variable found in the *Square* class.
15 The *FETCH* method is automatically called and the current value of *$squared* is printed.
16 The *FETCH* method is called again. Each time the method is called, the current value of the tied variable is squared again and returned.
17 The *STORE* method is automatically called. A new value, *3*, is assigned to the tied variable.
18 The *FETCH* method is automatically called and displays the squared value.
19 The *untie* method disassociates the object with the tied variable. If a *DESTROY* method had been defined, it would have been called at this point.

15.1.4 Tying an Array

In order to use a tied array, the class must define a set of methods that have predefined names. The constructor *TIEARRAY* is called when the variable is tied, and it creates the underlying object that will be manipulated by the access methods *STORE* and *FETCH*. Any time the user makes an assignment to the tied array, the *STORE* method is called, and whenever he attempts to display the tied array, the *FETCH* method is called. The *DESTROY* method is not required but, if it is defined, will be called when the tied scalar is untied or goes out of scope. There is also a set of optional methods that can be used with tied arrays. *STORESIZE* sets the total number of items in the array, *FETCHSIZE* is the same as using *scalar(@array)* or *$#array + 1* to get the size of the array, and *CLEAR* is used when the array is to be emptied of all its elements. There are also a number of methods, such as *POP* and *PUSH*, that emulate their like-named Perl functions in manipulating the array. Methods provided for an array are

```
TIEARRAY $classname, LIST
STORE $self, $subscript, $value
FETCH $self, $subscript, $value
DESTROY $self
STORESIZE  $self, $arraysize
FETCHSIZE  $self
EXTEND $self, $arraysize
EXISTS $subscript
DELETE $self, $subscript
CLEAR $self
PUSH $self, LIST
UNSHIFT $self, LIST
POP $self
SHIFT $self
SPLICE $self, OFFSET, LENGTH, LIST
```

There is also a base class called *Tie::Array* in the standard Perl library that contains a number of predefined methods from the preceding list, making the implementation of tied arrays much easier. To see documentation for this module, type *perldoc Tie::Array*.

EXAMPLE 15.2

```
package Temp;
sub TIEARRAY {
   my $class = shift;  # Shifting the @_ array
   my $obj = [ ];
   bless ($obj, $class);
}
```

EXAMPLE 15.2 (CONTINUED)

```
# Access methods
sub FETCH {
    my $self=shift;
    my $indx = shift;
    return $self->[$indx];
}

sub STORE {
    my $self = shift;
    my $indx= shift;
    my $F = shift;     # The Fahrenheit temperature
    $self->[$indx]=($F - 32) / 1.8;    # Magic works here!

}
1;
------------------------------------------------------------------
#!/bin/perl
# The user/driver program
use Temp;
tie @list, "Temp";
print "Beginning Fahrenheit: ";
chomp($bf = <STDIN>);
print "Ending temp: ";
chomp($ef = <STDIN>);
print "Increment value: ";
chomp($ic = <STDIN>);
print "\n";
print "\tConversion Table\n";
print "\t----------------\n";

for($i=$bf;$i<=$ef;$i+=$ic){
    $list[$i]=$i;
    printf"\t$i F. = %.2f C.\n", $list[$i]; }
```

```
(Output)
Beginning Fahrenheit: 32
Ending temp: 100
Increment value: 5

Conversion Table
----------------
2 F. = 0.00 C.
37 F. = 2.78 C.
42 F. = 5.56 C.
47 F. = 8.33 C.
```

EXAMPLE 15.2 (CONTINUED)

```
52 F. = 11.11 C.
57 F. = 13.89 C.
62 F. = 16.67 C.
67 F. = 19.44 C.
72 F. = 22.22 C.
77 F. = 25.00 C.
82 F. = 27.78 C.
87 F. = 30.56 C.
92 F. = 33.33 C.
97 F. = 36.11 C.
```

EXPLANATION

1 This is the package/class declaration. The file is *Temp.pm*.
2 *TIEARRAY* is the constructor for the tied array. It creates the underlying object.
3 The first argument passed into the constructor is the name of the class, *Temp*.
4 A reference to an anonymous array is created.
5 The object is blessed into the class.
6 The access method *FETCH* will retrieve elements from the tied array.
7 The first argument shifted off and assigned to *$self* is a reference to the object.
8 The next argument is the value of the subscript in the tied array. It is shifted off and assigned to *$indx*.
9 The value of the array element is returned when the user/driver program attempts to display an element of the tied array.
10 The access method *STORE* will assign values to the tied array.
11 The first argument shifted off and assigned to *$self* is a reference to the object.
12 The next argument is the value of the subscript in the tied array. It is shifted off and assigned to *$indx*.
13 The value of the Fahrenheit temperature is shifted from the argument list. See line 19 where the assignment is being made in the user/driver program. The value being assigned is what will be stored in *$F* in the *STORE* method.
14 The calculation to convert from Fahrenheit to Celsius is made on the incoming tied array element. The user/driver program never sees this calculation, as though it were done by magic.
15 This is the user's program. The *Temp.pm* module is loaded into the program.
16 The *tie* function ties the array to the class *Temp* and returns an underlying reference to an object that is tied to the array.
17 The user is asked for input. He will provide a beginning Fahrenheit temperature, an ending Fahrenheit temperature, and an increment value.
18 A *for* loop is entered to iterate through the list of temperatures. It charts the Fahrenheit temperature and the corresponding Celsius temperature after the conversion.

EXPLANATION (CONTINUED)

19 The magic happens here. When the assignment is made, the *STORE* method is automatically called, where the formula converts the Fahrenheit temperature to Celsius and assigns it to the array. A reference to the tied object and the array index are passed to *STORE*.

20 When *printf* is used, the *FETCH* method will automatically be called and display an element of the tied array. A reference to the tied object and the array index are passed to *FETCH*.

15.1.5 Tying a Hash

In order to use a tied hash, the class must define a set of methods that have predefined names. The constructor *TIEHASH* is called when the variable is tied, and it creates the underlying object that will be manipulated by the access methods *STORE* and *FETCH*. Any time the user makes an assignment to the tied hash, the *STORE* method is called, and whenever he attempts to display the tied hash, the *FETCH* method is called. The *DESTROY* method is not required but, if it is defined, will be called when the tied hash is untied or goes out of scope. There is also a set of optional methods that can be used with tied hashes. *DELETE* removes a key/value pair, *EXISTS* checks for the existence of a key, and *CLEAR* empties the entire hash. If you use Perl's built-in keys, values, or *each* methods, the *FIRSTKEY* and *NEXTKEY* methods are called to iterate over the hash. Methods provided for an associative array are

```
TIEHASH $classname, LIST
FETCH $self, $key
STORE $self, $key
DELETE $self, $key
EXISTS $self, $key
FIRSTKEY $self
NEXTKEY $self, $lastkey
DESTROY $self
CLEAR $self
```

There is also a base class module called *Tie::Hash* in the standard Perl library that contains a number of predefined methods from the preceding list, making the implementation of tied arrays much easier. To see documentation for this module, type *perldoc Tie::Hash*.

EXAMPLE 15.3

```
(The Script)
    #!/bin/perl
    # Example using tie with a hash
```

EXAMPLE 15.3 (CONTINUED)

```
1   package House;
2   sub TIEHASH {                # Constructor method
3       my $class = shift;       # Shifting the @_ array
        my $price = shift;
        my $color = shift;
        my $rooms = shift;
4       print "I'm the constructor in class $class.\n";
5       my $house =  {  Color=>$color,     # Data for the tied hash
6                       Price=>$price,
                        Rooms=>$rooms,
                     };
7       bless $house, $class;
    }
8   sub FETCH {                  # Access methods
        my $self=shift;
        my $key=shift;
9       print "Fetching a value.\n";
10      return $self->{$key};
    }
11  sub STORE {
        my $self = shift;
        my $key = shift;
        my $value = shift;
        print "Storing a value.\n";
12      $self->{$key}=$value;
    }
    1;
------------------------------------------------------------------------

    # User/driver program
13  use House;
    # The arguments following the package name are
    # are passed as a list to the tied hash
    # Usage: tie hash, package, argument list
    # The hash %home is tied to the package House.
14  tie %home, "House", 155000, "Yellow", 9;
                      # Calls the TIEHASH constructor
15   print qq/The original color of the house: $home{"Color"}\n/;
                      # Calls FETCH method
16  print qq/The number of rooms in the house: $home{"Rooms"}\n/;
17  print qq/The price of the house is: $home{"Price"}\n/;
18  $home{"Color"}="beige with white trim";    # Calls STORE method
19  print "The house has been painted. It is now $home{Color}.\n";
20  untie(%home);     # Removes the object
```

EXAMPLE 15.3 (CONTINUED)

```
(Output)
4   I'm the constructor in class House.
9   Fetching a value.
15  The original color of the house: Yellow
9   Fetching a value.
16  The number of rooms in the house: 9
9   Fetching a value.
17  The price of the house is: 155000
    Storing a value.
    Fetching a value.
    The house has been painted. It is now beige with white trim.
```

EXPLANATION

1. The package/class *House* is declared. The file is *House.pm*.
2. The constructor *TIEHASH* will tie a hash to an object.
3. The first argument is the name of the class, *$class*. The rest of the arguments shifted, and all will be assigned as values to the keys of an anonymous hash, the object.
4. The printout shows that the constructor class is called *House*.
5. A reference to an anonymous hash is created and with key/value pairs assigned. They will become the properties of the object.
6. The values assigned to the keys of the anonymous hash were passed to the constructor *TIEHASH*. (See line 13 in the user program.)
7. The *bless* function returns a reference to the object that is created.
8. The *FETCH* method is an access method that will retrieve a value from the hash object.
9. Each time the user uses the *print* function to display a value from the hash, the *FETCH* method is automatically called and this line will be printed.
10. A value from the hash is returned.
11. The *STORE* method is an access method that will be called automatically when the user attempts to assign a value to one of the keys in the hash.
12. The value to be assigned to the hash came from the argument list passed to the *STORE* method.
13. This is the user/driver program. The *House* module is loaded into the program.
14. The *tie* function calls the *TIEHASH* constructor in *House.pm*. The hash *%home* is tied to an object in the *House* class. The name of the class, *House*, and three additional arguments are passed.
15. This line causes the *FETCH* access method to be called, which will display the value for the hash key *Color*.
16. This line causes the *FETCH* access method to be called, which will display the value for the hash key *Rooms*.
17. This line causes the *FETCH* access method to be called, which will display the value for the hash key *Price*.
18. This line causes the *STORE* access method to be called automatically when a value is assigned to one of the hash keys, in this case the key *Color*.

EXPLANATION (CONTINUED)

19 The *print* function causes the *FETCH* method to be called automatically to display a value for a specified hash key, *Color*.

20 The *untie* function disassociates the hash from the object to which it was tied.

EXAMPLE 15.4

```
   # File is House.pm
1  package House;
2  sub TIEHASH {
       my $class = shift;
       print "I'm the constructor in package $class\n";
       my $houseref = {};
       bless $houseref, $class;
   }
3  sub FETCH {
       my $self=shift;
       my $key=shift;
       return $self->{$key};
   }
4  sub STORE {
       my $self = shift;
       my $key = shift;
       my $value = shift;
       $self->{$key}=$value;
   }

5  sub FIRSTKEY {
       my $self = shift;
6      my $tmp = scalar keys %{$self};
7      return each  %{$self};
   }
8  sub NEXTKEY {
       $self=shift;
       each %{$self};
   }
   1;

--------------------------------------------------------------------

   #!/usr/bin/perl
   # File is mainfile
9  use House;
10 tie %home, "House";
   $home{"Price"} = 55000;  # Assign and Store the data
   $home{"Rooms"} = 11;
   # Fetch the data
```

EXAMPLE 15.4 (CONTINUED)

```
       print "The number of rooms in the house: $home{Rooms}\n";
       print "The price of the house is: $home{Price}\n";
11     foreach $key (keys(%home)){
12        print "Key is $key\n";
       }
13     while( ($key, $value) = each(%home)){
             # Calls to FIRSTKEY and NEXTKEY
14        print "Key=$key, Value=$value\n";
       }
15     untie(%home);
```

```
(Output)
I'm the constructor in package House
The number of rooms in the house: 11
The price of the house is: 55000
Key is Rooms
Key is Price
Key=Rooms, Value=11
Key=Price, Value=55000
```

EXPLANATION

1 The package/class *House* is declared. The file is *House.pm*.

2 The constructor *TIEHASH* will tie a hash to an object.

3 The *FETCH* method is an access method that will retrieve a value from the hash object.

4 The *STORE* method is an access method that will assign a value to the hash object.

5 The *FIRSTKEY* method is called automatically if the user program calls one of Perl's built-in hash functions: *keys*, *value*, or *each*.

6 By calling keys in a scalar context, Perl resets the internal state of the hash in order to guarantee that the next time *each* is called, it will be given the first key.

7 The *each* function returns the first key/value pair.

8 The *NEXTKEY* method knows what the previous key was (*PREVKEY*) and starts on the next one as the hash is being iterated through a loop in the user program.

9 This is the user/driver program. The *House* module is loaded into the program.

10 The *tie* function calls the *TIEHASH* constructor in *House.pm*. The hash *%home* is tied to an object in the *House* class.

11 The *while* loop is used to iterate through the hash with the *keys* function. The first time in the loop, the *FIRSTKEY* method is automatically called.

12 The value for each key is printed. This value is returned from the access methods *FIRSTKEY* and *NEXTKEY*.

13 The *while* loop is used to iterate through the hash with the *each* function. The first time in the loop, the *FIRSTKEY* method is automatically called.

14 Each key and value is printed. These values are returned from the access methods *FIRSTKEY* and *NEXTKEY*.

15.2 DBM Files

The Perl distribution comes with a set of database management library files called DBM, short for database management. The concept of DBM files stems from the early days of UNIX and consists of a set of *C* library routines that allow random access to its records. DBM database files are stored as key/value pairs, an associative array that is mapped into a disk file. There are a number of flavors of DBM support, and they demonstrate the most obvious reasons for using tied hashes.

DBM files are binary. They can handle very large databases. The nice thing about storing data with DBM functions is that the data is persistent; that is, any program can access the file as long as the DBM functions are used. The disadvantage is that complex data structures, indexes, multiple tables, and so forth are not supported, and there is no reliable file locking and buffer flushing, making concurrent reading and updating risky.[2] File locking can be done with the Perl *flock* function, but the strategy for doing this correctly is beyond the scope of this book.[3]

So that you don't have to figure out which of the standard DBM packages to use, the *AnyDBM_File.pm* module will get the appropriate package for your system from the standard set in the standard Perl library. The *AnyDBM_File* module is also useful if your program will run on multiple platforms. It will select the correct libraries for one of five different implementations:

Table 15.1 DBM Implementations

odbm	"Old" DBM implementation found on UNIX systems and replaced by NDBM
ndbm	"New" DBM implementation found on UNIX systems
sdbm	Standard Perl DBM, provides cross-platform compatibility, but not good for large databases
gdbm	GNU DBM, a fast, portable DBM implementation; see *www.gnu.org*
bsd-db	Berkeley DB; found on BSD UNIX systems, most powerful of all the DBMs; see *www.sleepycat.com*

The following table comes from the documentation for *AnyDBM_FILE* and lists some of the differences in the various DBM implementations. At your command-line prompt, type:

2. Although Perl's *tie* function will probably replace the *dbmopen* function, for now we'll use this function because it's easier than *tie*.
3. For details on file locking, see Descartes, A., and Bunce, T., *Programming the Perl DBI*, O'Reilly & Associates, 2000, p. 35.

```
perldoc AnyDBM_File

                          odbm    ndbm     sdbm     gdbm     bsd-db
                          ----    ----     ----     ----     ------
Linkage comes w/ perl     yes     yes      yes      yes      yes
Src comes w/ perl         no      no       yes      no       no
Comes w/ many unix os     yes     yes[0]   no       no       no
Builds ok on !unix        ?       ?        yes      yes      ?
Code Size                 ?       ?        small    big      big
Database Size             ?       ?        small    big?     ok[1]
Speed                     ?       ?        slow     ok       fast
FTPable                   no      no       yes      yes      yes
Easy to build            N/A     N/A       yes      yes      ok[2]
Size limits               1k      4k       1k[3]    none     none
Byte-order independent    no      no       no       no       yes
Licensing restrictions    ?       ?        no       yes      no
```

15.2.1 Creating and Assigning Data to a DBM File

Before a database can be accessed, it must be opened by using the *dbmopen* function or the *tie* function. This binds the DBM file to an associative array (hash). Two files will be created: one file contains an index directory and has *.dir* as its suffix; the second file, ending in *.pag*, contains all the data. The files are not in a readable format. The *dbm* functions are used to access the data. These functions are invisible to the user.

Data is assigned to the hash, just as with any Perl hash, and an element removed with Perl's *delete* function. The DBM file can be closed with the *dbmclose* or the *untie* function.

FORMAT

```
dbmopen(hash, dbfilename, mode);
tie(hash, Module , dbfilename, flags, mode);
```

EXAMPLE 15.5

```
dbmopen(%myhash, "mydbmfile", 0666);
tie(%myhash,SDBM_File, "mydbmfile", O_RDWR|O_CREAT,0640);
```

Perl's report writing mechanism is very useful for generating formatted data from one of the DBM files. The following examples illustrate how to create, add, delete, and close a DBM file and how to create a Perl-style report.

EXAMPLE 15.6

```
(The Script)
    #!/usr/bin/perl
    # Program name: makestates.pl
    # This program creates the database using the dbm functions
```

EXAMPLE 15.6 (CONTINUED)

```
1   use AnyDBM_File;   # Let Perl pick the right dbm for your system
2   dbmopen(%states, "statedb", 0666[a]) || die;
                       # Create or open the database
3   TRY: {
4       print "Enter the abbreviation for your state. ";
        chomp($abbrev=<STDIN>);
        $abbrev = uc $abbrev;  # Make sure abbreviation is uppercase
5       print "Enter the name of the state. ";
        chomp($state=<STDIN>);
        lc $state;
6       $states{$abbrev}="\u$state";  # Assign values to the database
7       print "Another entry? ";
        $answer = <STDIN>;
8       redo TRY  if $answer =~ /Y|y/;
    }
9   dbmclose(%states);         # Close the database
--------------------------------------------------------------------

(The Command line)
10  $ ls
    makestates.pl  statedb.dir  statedb.pag[b]
--------------------------------------------------------------------
(Output)
4   Enter the abbreviation for your state. CA
5   Enter the name of the state. California
7   Another entry? y
    Enter the abbreviation for your state. me
    Enter the name of the state. Maine
    Another entry? y
    Enter the abbreviation for your state. NE
    Enter the name of the state. Nebraska
    Another entry? y
    Enter the abbreviation for your state. tx
    Enter the name of the state. Texas
    Another entry? n
```

a. Permissions are ignored on Win32 systems.

b. On some versions, only one file with a *.db* extension is created.

EXPLANATION

1 The *AnyDBM_File* module selects the proper DBM libraries for your particular installation.

2 The *dbmopen* function binds a DBM file to a hash. In this case, the database file created is called *statedb* and the hash is called *%states*. If the database does not exist, a valid permission mode should be given. The octal mode given here is *0666*, read and write for all, on UNIX-type systems.

3 The labeled block is entered.

EXPLANATION

4 The user is asked for input, the abbreviation of his state. This input will be used to fill the *%states* hash.

5 The user is asked to enter the name of his state.

6 The value *state* is assigned to the *%states* hash where the key is the abbreviation for the state. The \u escape sequence causes the first letter of the state to be uppercase. When this assignment is made, the DBM file will be assigned the new value through a *tie* mechanism that takes place behind the scenes.

7 The user is asked to enter another entry into the DBM file.

8 If the user wants to add another entry to the DBM file, the program will go to the top of the block labeled *TRY* and start over.

9 The *dbmclose* function breaks the tie (by calling the *untie* function), binding the DBM file to the hash *%states*.

10 The listing displays the files that were created with the *dbmopen* function. The first file, *makestates.pl,* is the Perl script. The second file, *statedb.dir*, is the index file, and the last file, *statedb.pg,* is the file that contains the hash data.

15.2.2 Retrieving Data from a DBM File

Once the DBM file has been opened, it is associated with a tied hash in the Perl script. All details of the implementation are hidden from the user. Data retrieval is fast and easy. The user simply manipulates the hash as though it were any ordinary Perl hash. Since the hash is tied to the DBM file, when the data is retrieved, it is coming from the DBM file.

EXAMPLE 15.7

```
(The Script)
    #!/bin/perl
    # Program name: getstates.pl
    # This program fetches the data from the database
    # and generates a report

    use AnyDBM_File;
    dbmopen(%states, "statedb", 0666);   # Open the database
    @sortedkeys=sort keys %states;     # Sort the database by keys
        foreach $key ( @sortedkeys ){
        $value=$states{$key};
        $total++;
        write;
    }
    dbmclose(%states);     # Close the database
    format STDOUT_TOP=
    Abbreviation     State
    ==============================
    .
```

EXAMPLE 15.7 (CONTINUED)

```
10  format STDOUT=
    @<<<<<<<<<<<<<<<@<<<<<<<<<<<<<<<<
    $key,           $value
    .
11  format SUMMARY=
    ==============================
    Number of states:@###
                     $total
    .
    $~=SUMMARY;
    write;
--------------------------------------------------------------------

(Output)
  Abbreviation    State
==============================
  AR              Arizona
  CA              California
  ME              Maine
  NE              Nebraska
  TX              Texas
  WA              Washington
==============================
        Number of states:   6
```

EXPLANATION

1. The *AnyDBM_File* module selects the proper DBM libraries for your particular installation.
2. The *dbmopen* function binds a DBM file to a hash. In this case, the database file opened is called *statedb* and the hash is called *%states*.
3. Now that the DBM file has been opened, the user can access the key/value pairs. The *sort* function combined with the *keys* function will sort out the keys in the *%states* hash.
4. The *foreach* loop iterates through the list of sorted keys.
5. Each time through the loop, another value is retrieved from the *%states* hash, which is tied to the DBM file.
6. After adding one to the *$total* variable (keeping track of how many entries are in the DBM file), the *write* function invokes the report templates to produce a formatted output.
7. The DBM file is closed; that is, the hash *%states* is disassociated from the DBM file.
8. This is the format template that will be used to put a header on the top of each page.
9. The period ends the template definition.

EXPLANATION

10 This is the format template for the body of each page printed to standard output. The picture line below is used to format the key/value pairs on the line below the picture.

11 This is the format template that will be invoked at the bottom of the report.

15.2.3 Deleting Entries from a DBM File

To empty the completed DBM file, you can use the *undef* function; for example, *undef %states* would clear all entries in the DBM file created in Example 15.8. Deleting a key/value pair is done simply by using the Perl built-in *delete* function on the appropriate key within the hash that was tied to the DBM file.

EXAMPLE 15.8

```
(The Script)
    #!/bin/perl
    # dbmopen is an older method of opening a dbm file but simpler
    # than using tie and the SDBM_File module provided
    # in the standard Perl library Program name: remstates.pl
1   use AnyDBM_File;
2   dbmopen(%states, "statedb", 0666) || die;
    TRY: {
        print "Enter the abbreviation for the state to remove. ";
        chomp($abbrev=<STDIN>);
        $abbrev = uc $abbrev;  # Make sure abbreviation is uppercase
3       delete $states{"$abbrev"};
        print "$abbrev removed.\n";
        print "Another entry? ";
        $answer = <STDIN>;
        redo TRY  if $answer =~ /Y|y/;  }
4   dbmclose(%states);

(Output)
5   $ remstates.pl
    Enter the abbreviation for the state to remove. TX
    TX removed.
    Another entry? n
6   $ getstates.pl
    Abbreviation      State
    ==============================
    AR              Arizona
    CA              California
    ME              Maine
    NE              Nebraska
    WA              Washington
    ==============================
    Number of states:    5
```

EXAMPLE 15.8 (CONTINUED)

```
7  $ ls
   getstates.pl    makestates.pl    rmstates.pl    statedb.dir
statedb.pag
```

EXPLANATION

1 The *AnyDBM_File* module selects the proper DBM libraries for your particular installation.
2 The *dbmopen* function binds a DBM file to a hash. In this case, the database file opened is called *statedb* and the hash is called *%states*.
3 Now that the DBM file has been opened, the user can access the key/value pairs. The *delete* function will remove the value associated with the specified key in the *%states* hash tied to the DBM file.
4 The DBM file is closed; in other words, the hash *%states* is disassociated from the DBM file.
5 The Perl script *remstates.pl* is executed to remove Texas from the DBM file.
6 The Perl script *getstates.pl* is executed to display the data in the DBM file. Texas was removed.
7 The listing shows the files that were created to produce these examples. The last two are the DBM files created by *dbmopen*.

EXAMPLE 15.9

```
1  use Fcntl;
2  use SDBM_File;
3  tie(%address, 'SDBM_File', 'email.dbm', O_RDWR|O_CREAT, 0644)
   || die $!;
4  print "The package the hash is tied to: ",ref tied %address,"\n";

5  print "Enter the email address.\n";
   chomp($email=<STDIN>);
6  print "Enter the first name of the addressee.\n";
   chomp($firstname=<STDIN>);
   $firstname = lc $firstname;
   $firstname = ucfirst $firstname;
7  $address{"$email"}=$firstname;
8  while( ($email, $firstname)=each(%address)){
       print "$email, $firstname\n";
   }
9  untie %address;
```

EXPLANATION

1 The file control module is used to perform necessary tasks on the DBM files. It is where the *O_RDWR* and *O_CREAT* flags are defined, flags needed to set up the DBM file.

EXPLANATION (CONTINUED)

2 The *SDBM_File* module is used. It is the DBM implementation that comes with standard Perl and works across platforms.
3 Instead of using the *dbmopen* function to create or access a DBM file, this example uses the *tie* function. The hash *%address* is tied to the package *SDBM_File*. The DBM file is called *email.dbm*. If the database doesn't exist, the *O_CREATE* flag will cause it to be created with read/write permissions (*O_RDWR*).
4 The *tied* function returns true if it was successful, and the *ref* function returns the name of the package where the hash is tied.
5 In this example, an e-mail address is used as the key in *%address* hash, and the value associated with the key will be the first name of the user. Since the keys are always unique, this mechanism will prevent storing duplicate e-mail addresses. The user is asked for input.
6 The value for the key is requested from the user.
7 Here the database is assigned a new entry. The key/value pair is assigned and stored in the DBM file.
8 The *each* function will pull out both the key and value from the hash *%address*, which is tied to the DBM file. The contents of the DBM file are displayed.
9 The *untie* function disassociates the hash from the DBM file.

15.3 What You Should Know

1. You should understand how Perl uses the *tie* mechanism to turn scalars, arrays, and hashes into objects.
2. What does the *tie* function return.
3. Why is DBM useful?
4. Where DBM files are stored.

15.4 What's Next?

Although using DBM files can save a lot of time and space when you are storing a large number of records, you may find that what you really need is a relational database system, like Oracle, Sybase, or MySQL. The next chapter introduces relational databases, specifically MySQL and the way Perl interaces with it. You will learn how to use the DBI module and the methods provided to connect, query, update, and delete entries from the MySQL database.

chapter

16

CGI and Perl: The Hyper Dynamic Duo

16.1 Static and Dynamic Web Pages

Once you start browsing the Internet, you jump from one site to another, viewing all kinds of Web pages from simple home pages to highly developed sites, such as Google or Amazon. Even a simple Web page is a file that normally contains HTML tags and text, formatting instructions, and underlined phrases called **links** that connect you to other documents either on the same machine or on some other machine on the network. The document (called a hypertext document) tells the browser how to display the document; e.g., what fonts, colors, styles will be used. The page may also contain hypermedia, which includes images, sound, movies, and hotlinks to other documents. A Web page is created in a text editor, and the resulting HTML file is called the source file, which can be viewed in the browser by clicking on "View" in the menu bar.

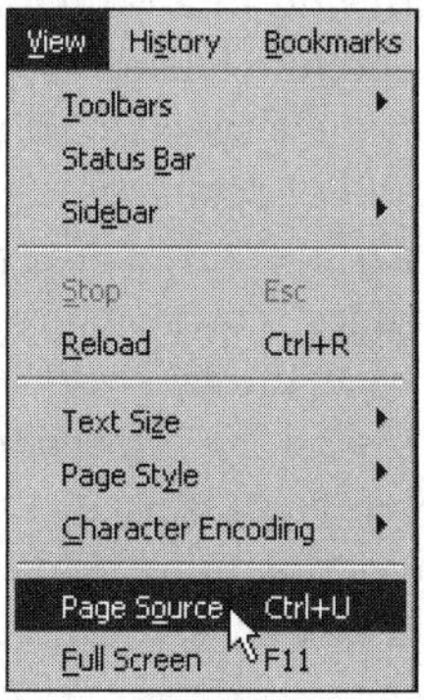

Figure 16.1 To view the source file.

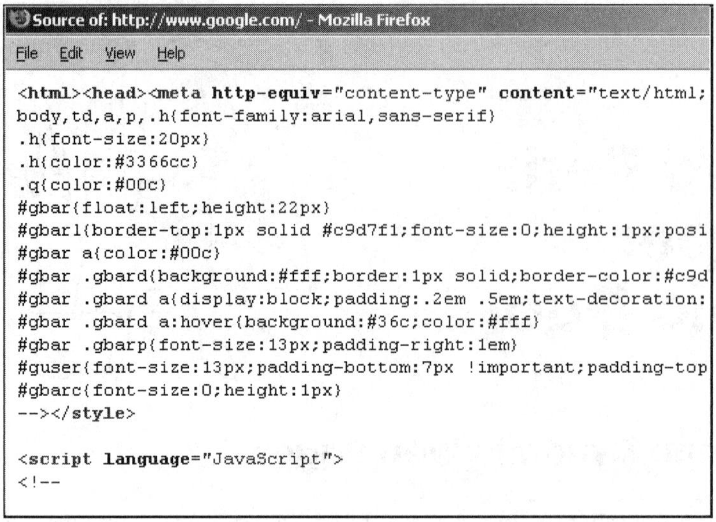

Source of: http://www.google.com/ - Mozilla Firefox

File Edit View Help

```
<html><head><meta http-equiv="content-type" content="text/html;
body,td,a,p,.h{font-family:arial,sans-serif}
.h{font-size:20px}
.h{color:#3366cc}
.q{color:#00c}
#gbar{float:left;height:22px}
#gbar1{border-top:1px solid #c9d7f1;font-size:0;height:1px;posi
#gbar a{color:#00c}
#gbar .gbard{background:#fff;border:1px solid;border-color:#c9d
#gbar .gbard a{display:block;padding:.2em .5em;text-decoration:
#gbar .gbard a:hover{background:#36c;color:#fff}
#gbar .gbarp{font-size:13px;padding-right:1em}
#guser{font-size:13px;padding-bottom:7px !important;padding-top
#gbarc{font-size:0;height:1px}
--></style>

<script language="JavaScript">
<!--
```

Figure 16.2 Viewing partial source page for google.com.

So that the browser recognizes the file, its name ends in either *.html* or *.htm*. The HTML tags tell the browser how to display the document on your screen. Learning the basics of HTML is not difficult, but developing an artistic and interesting design is another story, and there are thousands of companies devoted to creating these masterpieces for other companies doing competitive business over the Web.

There are two types of pages: **static** pages and **dynamic** pages. Static pages do not require interaction with the user. The most they can do is send already existing documents to users. They are analagous to a page in a book and usually describe the services some individual or company offers. They can be very artistic and interesting, but they can't handle information on demand. Dynamic pages, on the other hand, are "alive." They can accept and retrieve information from the user, produce specialized and customized content, search through text, respond with e-mail, query databases, and generate documents on the fly. They can manage information that is continually changing, based on the requests of different users. These dynamic pages require more than an HTML text file. They are driven by programs, or scripts, that interact with the Web server, which then transfers information to your browser. To send the information back and forth between the program and the server, a server-side program is used. The server itself relays user requests to a program, which in turn manages the information, such as parsing the data from a form, retrieving data from a file or database as a result of a user request, and then sending it back to the server.

The CGI (Common Gateway Interface) protocol defines how a server can communicate with programs. Its function is to allow the Web server to go beyond its normal boundaries for retrieving and accessing information from external databases and files. It is, then, a specification that defines how data can be transferred from the script to the server and from the server to the script. Gateway programs, called **CGI scripts**, can be written in any programming language, but Perl has become the de facto standard language, mainly because it is flexible and easy to use.

If you have read the previous chapters, you know that the Perl interpreter is easy to obtain. You know that it is portable. And you know about Perl's capability to handle regular expressions, files, sockets, and I/O. Once you know Perl, writing CGI scripts is relatively easy. The critical part is making sure that the server and Perl have been properly installed and that your scripts are placed in the directory where the server will look for them. The pathnames must also be set correctly so that the server knows where you are storing the scripts and how to reach the necessary libraries. All efforts are for nothing if any of the necessary steps from installation to implementation are incorrect in any way. It is very frustrating to see the browser whining about not finding a requested file or a server scolding that you are forbidden to run a program or that your document contains no data when you know it does.

This chapter is not written to make you a master Web designer; it is to give you some understanding of how Perl fits into the CGI scheme and how dynamic pages for the Web are created. Sometimes, seeing the overall picture is the key to understanding the purpose and plan of the more detailed design. There is a plethora of Web information available on the Internet and in trade books to fill in the details.

Today, PHP and ASP.net are server programming modules embedded in the server itself, eliminating the need for CGI scripts, but due to the popularity of Perl and the fact that there are so many CGI scripts in use, *mod_perl* (dubbed "Perl on steroids") allows you to embed the Perl interpreter right in the Apache server to increase Perl's performance and to accommodate the developers who prefer to use Perl to create dynamic pages and still be able to use CGI scripts with enhanced speed and power. To learn more about *mod_perl*, see Appendix D and *http://perl.apache.org/*.

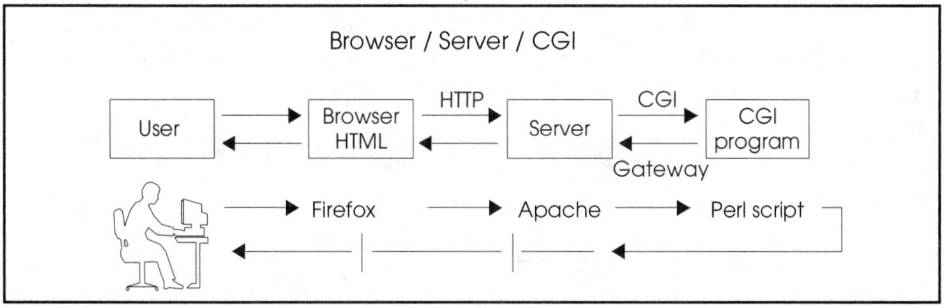

Figure 16.3 The relationship between the browser, server, and CGI program.

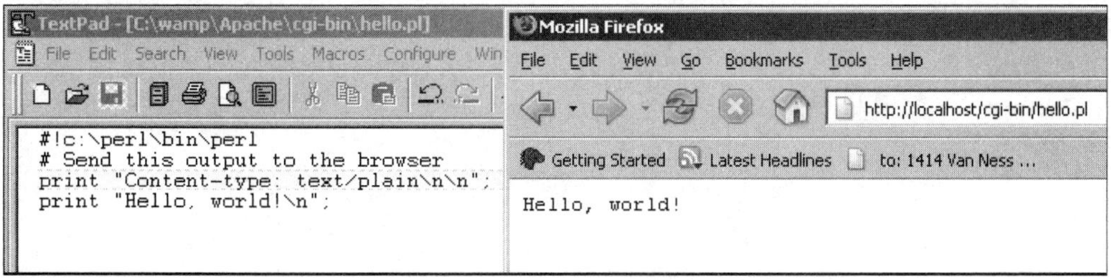

Figure 16.4 A simple CGI program sends output to the browser.

16.2 How It all Works

16.2.1 Internet Communication between Client and Server

The HTTP Server. We discuss the client/server model and the TCP/IP protocols for regulating network operations in Chapter 20, "Send It Over the Net and Sock It to 'Em!" On the Internet, communication is also handled by a TCP/IP connection. The Web is based on this model. The server side responds to client (browser) requests and provides feedback by sending back a document, by executing a CGI program, or by issuing an error message. The network protocol that is used by the Web so that the server and client know how to talk to each other is the Hypertext Transport Protocol, or HTTP. This does not preclude the TCP/IP protocol's being implemented. HTTP objects are mapped onto the transport data units, a process that is beyond the scope of this discussion; it is a simple, straightforward process that is unnoticed by the typical Web user. (See *www.cis.ohio-state.edu/cgi-bin/rfc/rfc2068.html* for a technical description of HTTP.) The HTTP protocol was built for the Web to handle hypermedia information; it is object oriented and stateless. In object-oriented terminology, the documents and files are called **objects**, and the operations that are associated with the HTTP protocol are called **methods**. When a protocol is stateless, neither the client nor the server stores information about each other but manages its own state information.

Once a TCP/IP connection is established between the Web server and client, the client will request some service from the server. Web servers are normally located at well-known TCP port 80. The client tells the server what type of data it can handle, by sending *Accept* statements with its requests. For example, one client may accept only HTML text, whereas another client might accept sounds and images as well as text. The server will try to handle the request (requests and responses are in ASCII text) and send back whatever information it can to the client (browser).

EXAMPLE 16.1

```
(Client's (Browser) Request)
GET /pub HTTP/1.1
Connection: Keep-Alive
User-Agent: Mozilla/4.0 Gold
Host: severname.com
Accept: image/gif, image/x-xbitmap, image/jpeg, image/pjpeg,*/*
```

EXAMPLE 16.2

```
(Server's Response)
HTTP/1.1 200 OK
Server: Apache/1.2b8
Date: Mon, 22 Jan 2007  13:43:22 GMT
Last-modified: Mon, 01 Dec 2007 12:15:33
Content-length: 288
Accept-Ranges: bytes
Connection: close
Content-type: text/html

<HTML><HEAD><TITLE>Hello World!</TITLE>
           ---continue with body---
</HTML>
Connection closed by foreign host.
```

The response confirms what HTTP version was used, the status code describing the results of the server's attempt (did it succeed or fail?), a header, and data. The header part of the message indicates whether the request is okay, what type of data is being returned (for example, the content type may be *html/text*), and how many bytes are being sent. The data part contains the actual text being sent.

The user then sees a formatted page on the screen, which may contain highlighted hyperlinks to some other page. Regardless of whether the user clicks on a hyperlink, once the document is displayed, that transaction is completed, and the TCP/IP connection will be closed. Once closed, a new connection will be started if there is another request. What happened in the last transaction is of no interest to either client or server; in other words, the protocol is stateless.

HTTP is also used to communicate between browsers, proxies, and gateways to other Internet systems supported by FTP, Gopher, WAIS, and NNTP protocols.

HTTP Status Codes and the Access Log File. When the server responds to the client, it sends information that includes the way it handled the request. Most Web browsers handle these codes silently if they fall in the range between 100 and 300. The codes within the 100 range are informational, indicating that the server's request is being processed. The most common status code is 200, indicating success, which means the information requested was accepted and fulfilled.

Check your server's access log to see what status codes were sent by your server after a transaction was completed.[1] The following example consists of excerpts taken from

1. For more detailed information on status codes, see *www.w3.org/Protocols/HTTP/HTRESP.html*.

the Apache server's access log, called *access.log*. This log reports information about a request handled by the server and the status code generated as a result of the request.

Table 16.1 HTTP Status Codes

Status	***CodeMessage***
100	Continue
200	Success, OK
204	No Content
301	Document Moved
304	Document Not Modified, No Message Body
400	Bad Request
401	Unauthorized
403	Forbidden
404	Not Found
405	Method Not Allowed
500	Internal Server Error
501	Not Implemented
503	Service Unavailable

See *http://www.w3.org/Protocols/rfc2616/rfc2616-sec10.html.*

EXAMPLE 16.3

```
(From Apache's Access log)

1  127.0.0.1 - - [22/May/2007:20:50:42 -0700] "GET /cgi-bin/firstc
gi.pl HTTP/1.1" 200 235

2 127.0.0.1 - - [22/May/2007:20:50:43 -0700] "GET /Williewonker.j
pg HTTP/1.1" 304 -

3 127.0.0.1 - - [22/May/2007:20:50:52 -0700] "GET /cgi-bin/env.pl
x HTTP/1.1" 500 623
```

EXPLANATION

1 The server hostname is *127.0.0.1*, followed by two dashes indicating unknown values, such as user ID and password. The time the request was logged, the type of request is *GET* (see "The *GET* Method" on page 541), and the file accessed was *firstcgi.pl*. The protocol is HTTP/1.1. The status code sent by the server was 200, indicating success! The request was fullfilled.

2 The status code 304 indicates that the request was for a document with no message body that has not been modified. The document, in this case, is a jpeg image file.

3 The status code 500 indicates an Internal Server Error, meaning that there was some internal error, such as a syntax error in the Perl program or an incorrect #! line that contains the full path to you. The browser's request was not fulfilled. The number of bytes sent was 623.

The URL (Uniform Resource Locator). URLs are what you use to get around on the Web. You click on a link and you are transported to some new page, or you type a URL in the browser's Location box and a file opens up or a script runs. It is a virtual address that specifies the location of pages, objects, scripts, etc. It refers to an existing protocol, such as HTTP, Gopher, FTP, mailto, file, Telnet, or news (see Table 16.2). A typical URL for the popular Web HTTP protocol looks like this:

```
http://www.comp.com/dir/text.html
```

Table 16.2 Web Protocols

Protocol	***Function***	***Example***
http:	HyperText Transfer Protocol	*http://www.nnic.noaa.gov/cgi-bin/netcast.cgi* open Web page or start CGI script
ftp:	File Transfer Protocol	*ftp://jague.gsfc.nasa.gov/pub*
mailto:	Mail protocol by e-mail address	*mailto:debbiej@aol.com*
file:	Open a local file	*file://opt/apache/htdocs/file.html*
telnet:	Open a Telnet session	*telnet://nickym@netcom.com*
news:	Opens a news session by news server	*news:alt.fan.john-lennon Name or Address*

The two basic pieces of information provided in the URL are the protocol *http* and the data needed by the protocol, *www.comp.com/dir/files/text.html*. The parts of the URL are further defined in Table 16.3.

Table 16.3 Parts of a URL

Part	*Description*
protocol	Service such as HTTP, Gopher, FTP, Telnet, news, etc.
host/IP number	DNS host name or its IP number
port	TCP port number used by server, normally port 80
path	Path and filename reference for the object on a server
parameters	Specific parameters used by the object on a server
query	The query string for a CGI script
fragment	Reference to subset of the object

The default HTTP network port is 80; if an HTTP server resides on a different network port, say *12345* on *www.comp.com*, the URL becomes

```
http://www.comp.com.12345/dir/text.html
```

Not all parts of a URL are necessary. If you are searching for a document in the Locator box in the Netscape browser, the URL may not need the port number, parameters, query, or fragment parts. If the URL is part of a hotlink in the HTML document, it may contain a relative path to the next document, that is, relative to the root directory of the server. If the user has filled in a form, the URL line may contain information appended to a question mark in the URL line. The appearance of the URL really depends on what protocol you are using and what operation you are trying to accomplish.

EXAMPLE 16.4

```
1   http://www.cis.ohio-state.edu/htbin/rfc2068.html
2   http://127.0.0.1/Sample.html
3   ftp://ptgp023@ptgpftp.pearsoned.com/quigley
4   file:///c:/wamp/www/family.jpg
5   http://localhost/cgi-bin/form.cgi?name=Fred+Thompson
```

EXPLANATION

1 The protocol is *http*.
The hostname *www.cis.ohio-state.edu/htbin/rfc2068.html* consists of [a]
The hostname translated to an IP address by the Domain Name Service, DNS.
The domain name is *ohio-state.edu*.
The top-level domain name is *edu*.
The directory where the HTML file is stored is *htbin*.
The file to be retrieved is *rfc20868.html*, an HTML document.

a. Most Web servers run on hostnames starting with *www*, but this is only a convention.

EXPLANATION (CONTINUED)

2 The protocol is *http*.
The IP address is used instead of the hostname; this is the IP address for a local host.
The file is in the server's document root. The file consists of HTML text.

3 The protocol is *ftp*.
The ftp server is *ptgpftp.pearsoned.*
The top-level domain is *com*.
The directory is *quigley*.

4 The protocol is file. A local file will be opened.
The hostname is missing. It then refers to the local host.
The full path to the file *index.html* is listed.

5 The information after the question mark is the query part of the URL, which may have resulted from submitting input into a form. The query string is URL encoded. In this example, a plus sign has replaced the space between *hello* and *there*. The server stores this query in an environment variable called *QUERY_STRING*. It will be passed on to a CGI program called from the HTML document. (See "The *GET* Method" on page 541.)

File URLs and the Server's Root Directory. If the protocol used in the URL is *file*, the server assumes that file is on the local machine. A full pathname followed by a filename is included in the URL. When the protocol is followed by a server name, all pathnames are relative to the document root of the server. The server root is the directory defined in the server's main directory where the configuration, error, and log files are kept. The document root is the directory where you store HTML documents, images, and any other documents that will be served up by the server; e.g., a file called "htdocs" or "www".

The leading slash that precedes the path is not really part of the path as with a UNIX absolute path, which starts at the root directory. Rather, the leading slash is used to separate the path from the hostname. An example of a URL leading to documents in the server's root directory:

```
http://localhost/index.html
```

The full pathname for this might be

```
C:/wamp/www/index.html
```

A shorthand method for linking to a document on the same server is called a partial, or relative, URL. For example, if a document at *http://www.myserver/stories/webjoke.html* contains a link to *images/webjoke.gif*, this is a relative URL. The browser will expand the relative URL to its absolute URL, *http://www.myserver/stories/images/webjoke.gif*, and make a request for that document if asked.

16.3 Creating a Web Page with HTML

In order to write Web pages, you must learn at least some of what makes up the HTML language. There are volumes written on this subject. Here we will cover just enough to introduce you to HTML and give you the basics so you can write some simple dynamic pages with forms and CGI scripts.

As previously stated, Web pages are written as ASCII text files in HTML. HTML consists of a set of instructions called **tags** that tell your Web browser how to display the text in the page.[2] When you type in the URL or click on a hyperlink in a page, the browser (client) communicates to the server that it needs a file and the file is sent back to the browser. The file contains HTML content that may consist of plain text, images, audio, video, and hyperlinks. It's the browser's job to interpret the HTML tags and display the formatted page on your screen. (To look at the source file for a Web page, you can use the View Document menu under View in the Netscape browser or, using Internet Explorer, select the View menu and then select Source to see the HTML tags used to produce the page.)

Creating Tags. The HTML source file can be created with any text editor. Its name ends in *.html* or *.htm* to indicate it is an HTML file. The HTML tags that describe the way the document looks are enclosed in angle brackets < >. The tags are easy to read. If you want to create a title, for example, the tag instruction is enclosed in brackets and the actual text for the title is sandwiched between the marker that starts the instruction, *<TITLE>*, and the tag that ends the instruction, *</TITLE>*. The following line is called a **TITLE element**, consisting of the *<TITLE>* start tag, the enclosed text, and the *</TITLE>* end tag. A tag may also have attributes to further describe its function. For example, a text input area may allow a specified number of rows and columns, or an image may be aligned and centered at the top of the page. The elements and attributes are case insensitive.

```
<TITLE>War and Peace</TITLE>
```

When the browser sees this instruction, the title will be printed in the bar at the top of the browser's window as a title for the page. To put comments in the HTML document, the commented text is inserted between *<!--* and *-->*.

Because HTML is a structured language, there are rules about how to place the tags in a document. These rules are discussed later in the chapter.

A Simple HTML Document. The following HTML file is created in your favorite text editor and consists of a simple set of tagged elements that will be rendered by the browser when the file is displayed. See *http://www.w3.org/MarkUp/Guide/*.

---

2. If you have ever used the UNIX programs *nroff* and *troff* for formatting text, you'll immediately recognize the tags used for formatting with HTML.

EXAMPLE 16.5

```
1   <!DOCTYPE html PUBLIC "-//W3C//DTD HTML 4.01 Transitional//EN"
    "http://www.w3.org/TR/html4/loose.dtd">
2   <html>
3   <head>
4       <title>Simple HTML Template</title>
5   </head>
6   <body bgcolor="silver">
7       <div align="center">
8       <h1>Getting Started</h1>
9       <p>This is a paragraph in the body of my document.
            It starts and ends with a paragraph tag.
10          </br>You can put pictures, links, movies, here,
            whatever you like..
        </p>
        <p>
11          <img src="file:///c:/wamp/www/mexico.jpg" border="1"
                width="200" height="250">
        </p>
        <br/>
        For a great HTML tutorial:
12          <a href="http://www.w3schools.com/html/default.asp">
            <strong>Click here</strong></a>
        </div>
13  </body>
14  </html>
```

EXPLANATION

1 This line declares the DOCTYPE; i.e., what flavor of HTML or XHTML you are using. This declaration can be used later when validating the page for the correct syntax for a particular version. For plain HTML4, we use a DOCTYPE of *transitional*. Other types are *frameset* and *strict*, beyond the scope of this discussion.

2 All of the text for the HTML document is between the *<html>* start tag and the *</html>* end tag. Although HTML is the standard language for creating Web pages, there are other markup languages that look like HTML. The HTML element identifies this as an HTML document. You can omit these tags and your browser will not complain. It is just more official to use them.

3 Between the *<head>* tag and *</head>* tag, information about the document is inserted, such as the title. This information is not displayed with the rest of the document text. The *<head>* tag always comes right after the *<html>* tag.

4 The *<title>* tag is used to create the title shown at the top of the browser window.

5 This is the closing tag for the *<head>* tag.

6 The main part of the document appears in the browser's window and is enclosed between the *<body>* start tag and *</body>* end tag.

7 The *<div>* tag creates a creates a division in the page. All content between the opening and closing *</div>* tags will be centered on the page.

EXPLANATION (CONTINUED)

8 A level 1 heading is enclosed between the *<h1>* and *</h1>* start and end tags.

9 The *<p>* starts a new paragraph. *</p>* marks the end of the paragraph.

10 This line uses a *
* tag to create a line break in the text.

11 The *<img>* tag allows you to place logos, photographs, illustrations, animations, etc., such as a *gif*, *png*, or *jpeg* images within a document. The *src* attribute to the *img* tag states the location of the document on the server. You can also scale the image to a specific size by specifying its height and width in pixels.

12 You can also create links on the page with the *<a href>* tag. When the user clicks on the link, he will be redirected to a tutorial on how to use HTML.

13 This tag marks the end of the body of the document.

14 This tag marks the end of the HTML document.

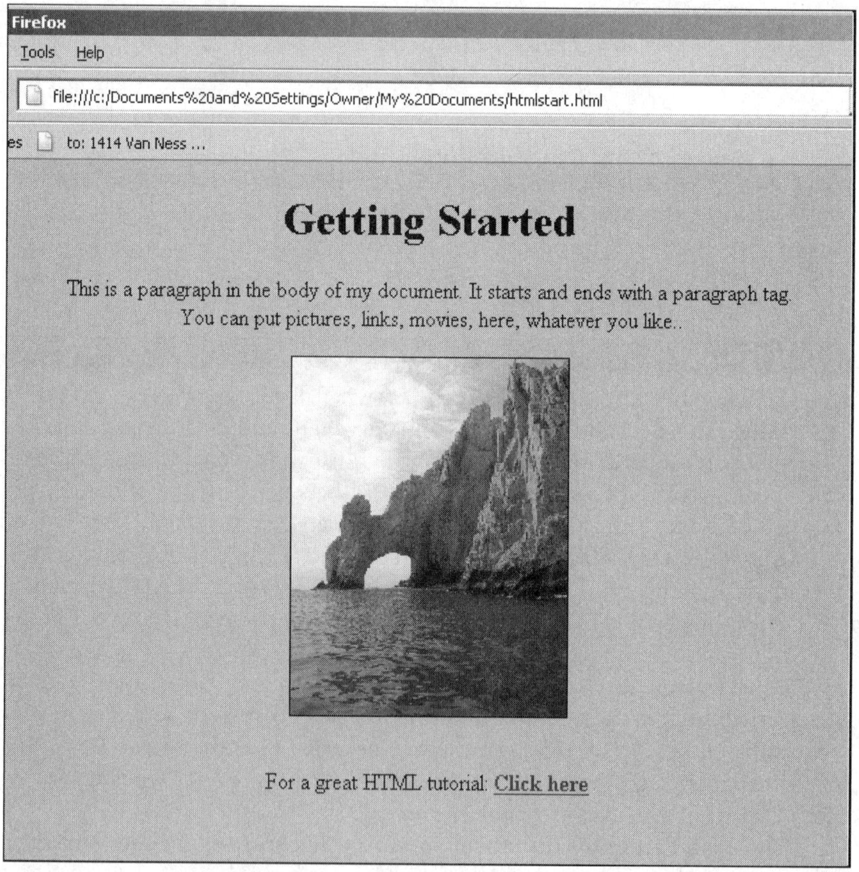

Figure 16.5 The HTML document from Example 16.5, as displayed in Mozilla Firefox.

Table 16.4 Simple HTML Tags and What They Do

Tag Element	*Function*
<!-- *text* -->	Commented text; nothing is displayed.
<*BASE* *HREF="http://www.bus.com/my.html"*>	Where this document is stored.
<*HTML*>document</*HTML*>	Found at the beginning and end of the document, indicating to a browser that this is an HTML document.
<*HEAD*>headinginfo</*HEAD*>	First element inside the document. Contains title, metatags, JavaScript, and CSS. Only the title is displayed directly.
<*TITLE*>title of the document</*TITLE*>	Title of the document; displayed outside the document text in a window frame or top of the screen. Can be placed in the bookmark list.
<*BODY*>document contents</*BODY*>	Contains all the text and other objects to be displayed.
<*H1*>heading type</*H1*>	Creates boldface heading elements for heading levels 1 through 6. The levels elements are: H1, H2, H3, H4, H5, and H6. The largest, topmost heading is H1.
<*P*>text</*P*>	Paragraph tag. Marks the beginning of a paragraph. Inserts a break after a block of text. Can go anywhere on the line. Ending paragraph tags are optional. Paragraphs end when a </*P*> or another <*P*> (marking a new paragraph) is encountered.
<*B*>text</*B*>	Bold text.
<*I*>text</*I*>	Italic text.
<*TT*>text</*TT*>	Typewriter text.
<*U*>text</*U*>	Underlined text.
<*BR*>	Line break.
<*HR*>	Horizontal shadow line.
<*UL*>	Start of an unordered (bulleted) list.
<*LI*>	An item in a list.
<*LI*>	Another item in a list.
</*UL*>	The end of the list.

Continues

Table 16.4 Simple HTML Tags and What They Do *(continued)*

Tag Element	***Function***
<OL>	Start of an ordered list.
<DL>	Descriptive list.
<DT>	An item in a descriptive list.
<DT>	Another item in a descriptive list.
</DL>	End of the descriptive list.
<STRONG>	Bold text.
<EM>	Italic text.
*<BLOCKQUOTE>*text*</BLOCKQUOTE>*	Italicized blocked text with spaces before and after quote.
<A HREF SRC="URL">	Creates a hotlink to a resource at address in URL on the Web.
<IMG SRC="URL">	Loads an image into a Web page. URL is the address of the image file.

16.4 How HTML and CGI Work Together

As previously discussed, HTML is the markup language used to determine the way a Web page will be displayed. CGI is a protocol that allows the server to extend its functionality. A CGI program is executed on behalf of the server mainly to process forms, such as a registration form or a shopping list. If you have purchased a book or CD from Amazon.com, you know what a form looks like. When a browser (client) makes a request of the server, the server examines the URL. If the server sees *cgi-bin* as a directory in the path, it will go to that directory, open a pipe, and execute the CGI program. The CGI program gets its **input from the pipe** and sends its **standard output back through the pipe** to the server. **Standard error** is sent to the server's **error log**. If the CGI program is to talk to the server, it must speak the Web language, since this is the language that is ultimately used by the browser to display a page. The CGI program then will format its data with HTML tags and send it back to the HTTP server. The server will then return this document to the browser, where the HTML tags will be rendered and displayed to the user.

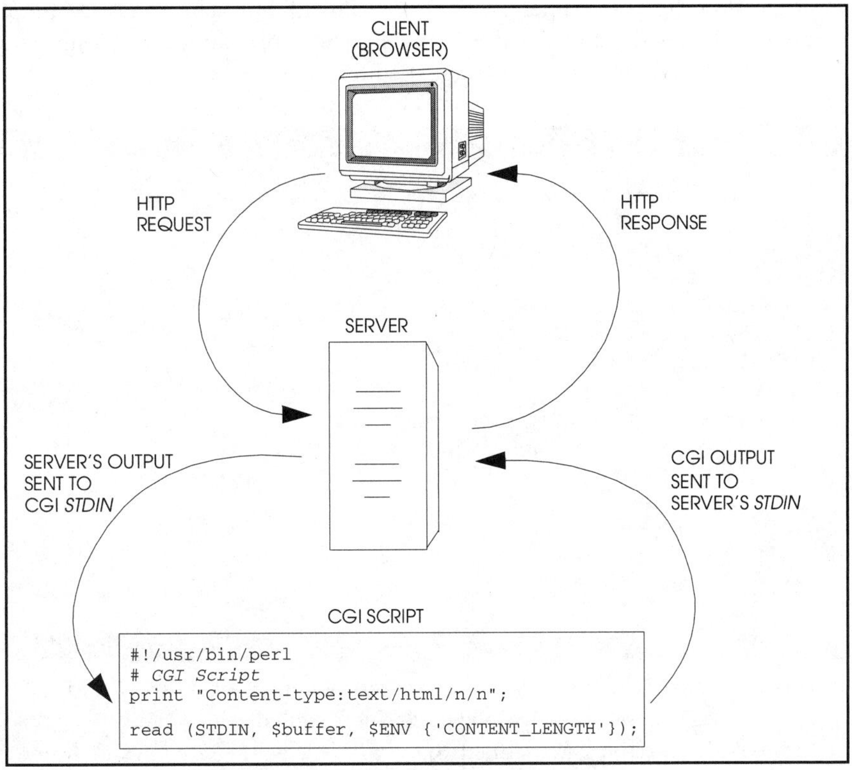

Figure 16.6 The client/server/CGI program relationship.

16.4.1 A Simple CGI Script

Before writing more sophisticated dynamic pages, we will look at a simple CGI script written in Perl and executed by the Apache server. The date and time will change each time this script is executed in the browser. The script consists of a series of print statements, most of which send HTML output back to *stdout* (piped to the server) as depicted in Figure 16.6. Some things to consider that make this script different from ordinary Perl scripts:

This program is executed directly from the CGI directory, *cgi-bin*.

The first line in the script is the called the "shbang" line and tells the server where your Perl interpreter is installed. Any error in this line causes an "Internal Server Error."

The next important line in the CGI script is the header line, called the HTTP MIME header. It tells the browser what type of output the program is sending in this example; "Content-type: text/html" is sent to the browser to announce that both regular text and HTML tags are contained within the document. We will go into more detail later in this chapter.

Right after the header line, there must be a blank line. This can be accomplished by ending the line with "\n\n", or if in a *here document*, providing a blank line as shown in a simple Perl CGI script created in a text editor

EXAMPLE 16.6

```
1 #!c:/ActivePerl/bin/perl.exe
2 $now=localtime;
  $myname="Willie";
3  print <<EOF;
4  Content-type:text/html
5    <body bgcolor="silver">
      <div align="center">
      <font face="arial" size="+2" color="darkblue">
      <b>Welcome,  Wee $myname!<p>
      <img src="/Williewonker.jpg" width="200"
           height="230" border="1">
      <p>
6     Today is $now<br>
    </body>
7 EOF
```

EXPLANATION

1. This first line is critical. Many Web servers will not process a CGI script if this line is missing. It tells the server where Perl is installed.
2. Two scalar variables are defined: *$now* will receive the return value from Perl's *localtime* function. Each time this program is executed, the time will change, making the page dynamic. The variable *$myname* is assigned the string "Willie".
3. This line starts a *here document* (see Chapter 2). The *here document* provides a blocked form of quoting, allowing us to use just one *print* function to print multiple lines. EOF is the user-defined terminator that is matched on line 7. All text between the two EOF markers will be sent as output and displayed in the browser.
4. This line is called the **MIME header**. No matter what programming language you are using, the first output of your CGI program must be a MIME header followed by two newlines. This line indicates what type of data your application will be sending. In this case, the CGI script will be sending HTML text back to the server. The *\n\n* cause a blank line to be printed. The blank line is also crucial to success of your CGI program. All headers require a blank line before the document's content.
5. This is text mixed with HTML tags. The browser will render the tags to provide the HTML page.
6. The value of the variable will change each time this program is executed, indicating the time and date coming from the server side.
7. The EOF marks the end of the *here document*.

Figure 16.7 Output of the Perl CGI script in the browser.

Some servers require that CGI script names end in *.cgi* or *.pl* so they can be recognized as CGI scripts. After creating the script, the execute permission for the file must be turned on for UNIX systems by typing at the shell prompt:

```
chmod 755 <scriptname>
```

or

```
chmod +x <scriptname>
```

The URL entered in the browser Location window includes the protocol, the name of the host machine, the directory where the CGI scripts are stored, and the name of the CGI script. The URL will look like this:

```
http://localhost/cgi-bin/cgisimple.pl
```

The HTTP Headers. The first line of output for most CGI programs is an HTTP header that tells the browser what type of output the program is sending to it. Right after the header line, there must be a blank line and two newlines. The two most common types of headers, also called **MIME** types (which stands for multipurpose Internet extension), are "Content-type: text/html\n\n" and "Content-type: text/plain\n\n". Another type of header is called the **Location** header, which is used to redirect the browser to a different Web page. And finally, **Cookie** headers are used to set cookies for maintaining state; that is, keeping track of information that would normally be lost once the transaction between the server and browser is closed. Right after the header line, there must be a blank line. This is accomplished by ending the line with *\n\n* in Perl.

Table 16.5 HTTP Headers

Header	Type	Value
Content-type:	text/plain	Plain text
Content-type:	text/html	HTML tags and text
Content-type:	image/gif	GIF graphics
Location:	http://www....	Redirection to another Web page
Set-cookie: NAME=VALUE...	Cookie	Set a cookie on a client browser

16.4.2 Error Log Files

Error Logs and *STDERR*. Normally, error messages are sent to the terminal screen (*STDERR*) when something goes wrong in a Perl script, but when launched by a server as a CGI script, the errors are not sent to the screen but to the server's error log file. In the browser you may see "Empty Document" or "Internal Server Error," which tells you nothing about what went wrong in the program.

Always check your syntax at the shell command line with the *-c* switch before handing the script to the server. Otherwise, you will not see your error messages unless you check the log files. **Check the syntax of your Perl scripts with the *-c* switch.**

EXAMPLE 16.7

```
(At the Command line)
1  perl -c perlscript
2  perlscript syntax OK
```

EXAMPLE 16.8

```
(Perl syntax errors shown in the Apache server's error log)

   [Mon Jul 20 10:44:04 2006] access to /opt/apache_1.2b8/
      cgi-bin/submit-form failed for susan, reason: Premature end
      of script headers
```

EXAMPLE 16.8 (CONTINUED)

```
   [Mon Sep 14 11:11:32 2006] httpd: caught SIGTERM, shutting down
   [Fri Sep 25 16:13:11 1998] Server configured -- resuming normal
      operations
1  Bare word found where operator expected at welcome.pl line 21,
       near "/font></TABLE"
   (Missing operator before TABLE?)
2  syntax error at welcome.pl line 21, near "<TH><"
   syntax error at welcome.pl line 24, near "else"
   [Fri Sep 25 16:16:18 2006] access to /opt/apache_1.2b8/
      cgi-bin/visit_count.pl failed for susan, reason:
      Premature end of script headers
```

16.5 Getting Information Into and Out of the CGI Script

The server and the CGI script communicate in four major ways. Once the browser has sent a request to the server, the server can then send it on to the CGI script. The CGI script gets its input from the server as:

1. Environment variables
2. Query strings
3. Standard input
4. Extra path information

After the CGI program gets the input from the server, it parses and processes it and then formats it so that the server can relay the information back to the browser. The CGI script sends output through the gateway by

1. Generating new documents on the fly
2. Sending existing static files to the standard output
3. Using URLs that redirect the browser to go somewhere else for a document

16.5.1 CGI Environment Variables

The CGI program is passed a number of environment variables from the server. The environment variables are set when the server executes the gateway program and are set for all requests. The environment variables contain information about the server, the CGI program, the ports and protocols, path information, etc., and they are always represented in uppercase. User input is normally assigned to the *QUERY_STRING* environment variable. In the following example, this variable has no value, because the user was never asked for input; that is, the HTML document has no *INPUT* tags.

EXAMPLE 16.9

```
(The CGI Perl Script)

#!/bin/perl
print "Content type: text/plain\n\n";
print "CGI/1.1 test script report:\n\n";
# Print out all the environment variables
while(($key, $value)=each(%ENV)){
   print "$key = $value\n";
}
```

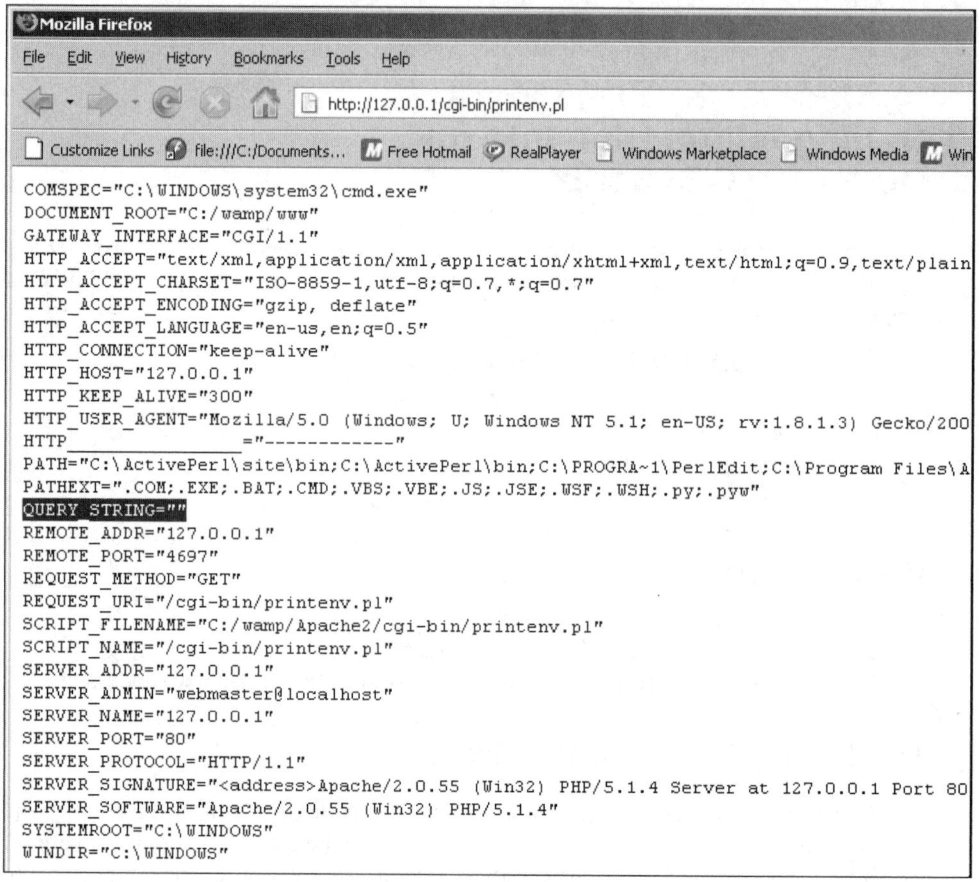

Figure 16.8 The *QUERY_STRING* environment variable.

Have you ever noticed, when performing a search in your browser, you end up with a line that looks like this?

```
http://www.gogle.com/search?hl=en&q=related%3Awww.lynda.com%2Fhexh.ht-
ml&btnG=Search
```

The information after the ? is sent by the browser to the server and assigned to the *QUERY_STRING* environment variable. It is a URL encoded by the browser; i.e., any nonalphanumeric characters in the string are represented by +, &, or a hexadecimal number preceded by a %, such a %2. The program on the server side will be responsible for decoding this string to make it legible. For our discussion, that program is a Perl CGI script, although it could be a C, C++, Tcl, Shell script, etc.

In the next example, we have appended a ? and string of text to the URL of the same CGI script we executed in Example 16.9. This string is encoded by the browser and assigned to the *QUERY_STRING* environment variable, making the information available to the Perl script. The next step would be to remove the %20 (hexadecimal value of a space); i.e., to decode the encoded string. All of this will be explained in detail on page 545, but for now, when you see this type of URL, the string after the ? is sent to your program in the *QUERY_STRING* environment variable.

Table 16.6 CGI Environment Variables (Must Be Uppercase)

Name	***Value***	***Example***
AUTH_TYPE	Validates user if server supports user authentication	
CONTENT_LENGTH	The number of bytes passed from the server to CGI program	*Content-Length=55*
CONTENT_TYPE	The MIME type of the query data	*text/html*
DOCUMENT ROOT	The directory from which the server serves Web documents	*/opt/apache/htdocs/index.html*
GATEWAY_INTERFACE	The revision of the CGI used by the server	CGI/1.1
HTTP_ACCEPT	The MIME types accepted by the client	*image/gif, image/jpeg,* etc.
HTTP_CONNECTION	The preferred HTTP connection type	Keep-Alive

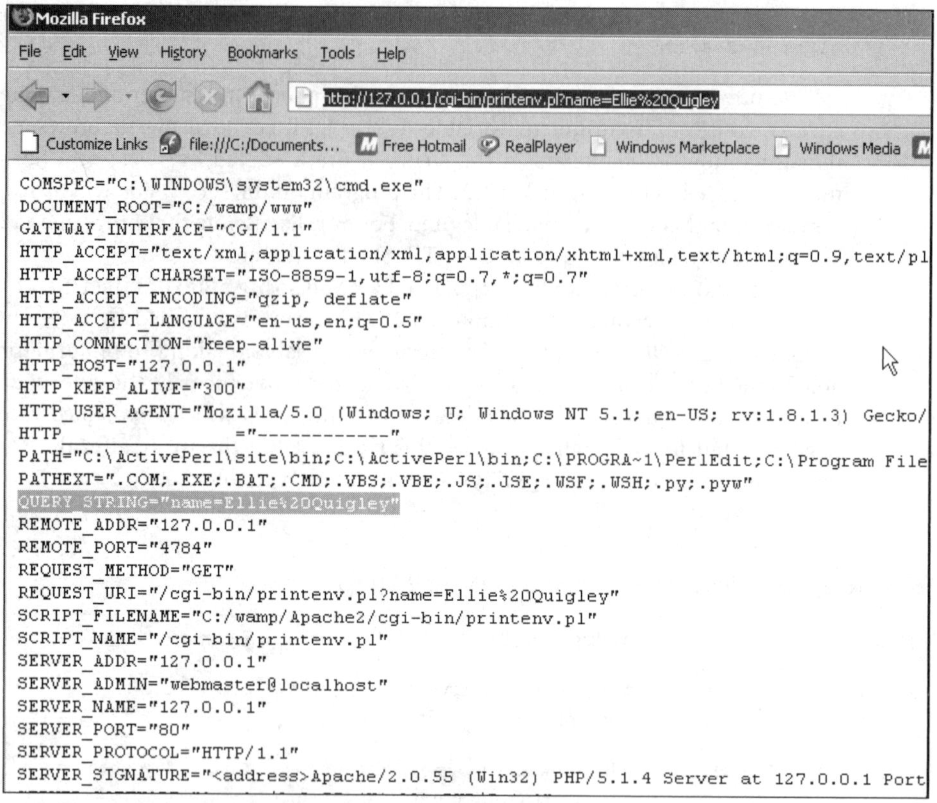

Figure 16.9 Now the *QUERY_STRING* environment variable has a value.

A question mark has been appended to the URL, followed by a string of text.

An HTML File with a Link to a CGI Script. The following example is an HTML file that will allow the user to print out all the environment variables by clicking on a hyperlink. When the browser displays this document, the user can click on the link *here*, and the CGI script *printenv.pl* will then be executed by the server. In the HTML document, the string *here* and the URL *http://localhost/cgi-bin/printenv.pl* are enclosed in the *<A href></A>* tags. If the link is ignored by the user, the browser displays the rest of the document. The following example is the HTML source file that will be displayed in the browser. The browser's output is shown in Figure 16.9.

EXAMPLE 16.10

```
(The HTML file with a hotlink to a CGI script)
1  <html>
2  <head>
3  <title>TESTING ENV VARIABLES</title>
   </head>
   <body>
4  <p>
   <h1> MAJOR TEST </h1>
   <p> if you would like to see the environment variables<br>
   being passed on by the server, click .
5  <a href="http://localhost/cgi-bin/printenv.pl">here</a>
   <p>text continues here...
   </body>
   </html>
```

EXPLANATION

1. The *<HTML>* tag says this document is using the HTML protocol.
2. The *<HEAD>* tag contains the title and any information that will be displayed outside the actual document.
3. The *<TITLE>* tag is displayed in the top bar of the browser window.
4. The *<P>* tag is the start of a paragraph. The *
* tag causes the line to break.
5. The *<A>* tag is assigned the path to the CGI script *printenv.pl* on server *localhost*. The word *here* will be displayed by the browser in blue underlined letters. If the user clicks on this word, the CGI script will be executed by the server. The script will print out all of the environment variables passed to the script from the server. This is one of the ways information is given to a CGI script by a Web server. The actual CGI script is shown in Example 16.9.

16.6 CGI and Forms

Processing user input is one of the most common reasons for using a CGI script. This is normally done with forms. The form offers you a number of methods, called virtual input devices, with which to accept input. These include radio buttons, check boxes, pop-up menus, and text boxes. All forms are in HTML documents and begin with a *<form>* tag and end with a *</form>* tag. A method attribute may be assigned. The method attribute indicates how the form will be processed. The *GET* method is the default, and the *POST* method is the most commonly used alternative.[3] The *GET* method is preferable for operations that will not affect the state of the server; that is, simple document retrieval and database lookups, etc., whereas the *POST* method is preferred for handling operations that may change the state of the server, such as adding or deleting records

3. The HTML tags and form attributes are not case sensitive.

from a database. These methods will be described in the next section. The *ACTION* attribute is assigned the URL of the CGI script that will be executed when the data is submitted by clicking the Submit button.

The browser gets input from the user by displaying fields that can be edited. The fields are created by the HTML *<INPUT TYPE=key/value>* tag. These fields might take the form of check boxes, text boxes, radio buttons, etc. The data that is entered into the form is sent to the server in an encoded string format in a name/value pair scheme. The value represents the actual input data. The CGI programmer must understand how this input is encoded in order to parse it and use it effectively. First, let's see how input gets into the browser, by looking at a simple document and the HTML code used to produce it. The user will be able to click on a button or enter data in the text box. The input in this example won't be processed, thereby causing an error to be sent to the server's error log when the Submit button is selected. Nothing will be displayed by the browser. The default for obtaining input is the *GET* method.

A summary of the steps in producing a form is

1. START: Start the form with the HTML *<form>* tag. The *<form>* tag is nested within HTML *<body> </body>* tags.
2. ACTION: The *action* attribute of the *<form>* tag is the URL of the CGI script that will process the data input from the form.
3. METHOD: Provide a method on how to process the data input. The default is the *get* method.
4. CREATE: Create the form with buttons and boxes and whatever looks nice using HTML tags and fields.
5. SUBMIT: Create a Submit button so the form can be processed. This will launch the CGI script listed in the *ACTION* attribute.
6. END: End the form and the HTML document.

16.6.1 Input Types for Forms

Table 16.7 Form Input Types

Input Type	*Attributes*	*Description*
CHECKBOX	*NAME, VALUE*	Displays a square box that can be checked. Creates name/value pairs from user input. Multiple boxes can be checked.
FILE	*NAME*	Specifies files to be uploaded to the server. MIME type must be multipart/form-data.
HIDDEN	*NAME, VALUE*	Provides name/value pair without displaying an object on the screen.

Table 16.7 Form Input Types (continued)

Input Type	*Attributes*	*Description*
IMAGE	*SRC, VALUE, ALIGN*	Same as the Submit button but displays an image instead of text. The image is in a file found at SRC.
PASSWORD	*NAME, VALUE*	Like a text box, but input is hidden. Asterisks appear in the box to replace characters typed.
RADIO	*NAME, VALUE*	Like check boxes, except only one box (or circle) can be checked at a time.
RESET	*NAME, VALUE*	Resets the form to its original position; clears all input fields.
SELECT	*NAME, OPTION SIZE, MULTIPLE*	Provides pop-up menus and scrollable lists. Only one can be selected. Attribute *MULTIPLE* creates a visibly scrollable list. A *SIZE* of *1* creates a pop-up menu with only one visible box.
SUBMIT	*NAME, VALUE*	When clicked, executes the form; launches CGI.
TEXT	*NAME* *SIZE, MAXLENGTH*	Creates a text box for user input. *SIZE* specifies the size of the text box. *MAXLENGTH* specifies the maximum number of characters allowed.
TEXTAREA	*NAME, SIZE* *ROWS, COLS*	Creates a text area that can take input spanning multiple lines. *ROWS* and *COLUMNS* specify the size of the box.

16.6.2 Creating an HTML Form

A Simple Form with Text Fields, Radio Buttons, Check Boxes, and Pop-up Menus. First, let's see how input gets into the browser, by looking at a simple document and the HTML code used to produce it. The user will be able to click on a button or enter data in the text box. The input in this example won't be processed, thus causing an error to be sent to the server's error log when the Submit button is selected. Nothing will be displayed by the browser. The HTML file is normally stored under the server's root in a directory called *htdocs*. If the HTML file is created on the local machine, then the *file:///* protocol is used in the Location box with the full pathname of the HTML file, which would normally end with an *.html* or *.htm* extension.

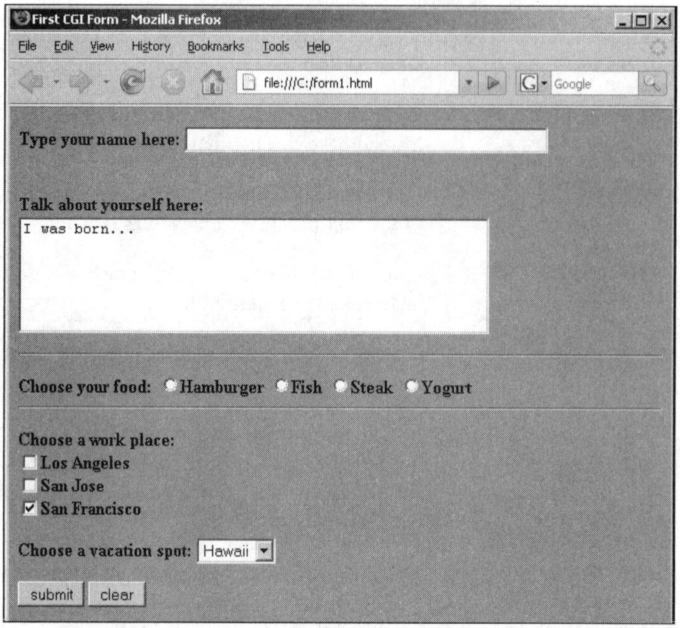

Figure 16.10 A form as it is initially displayed.

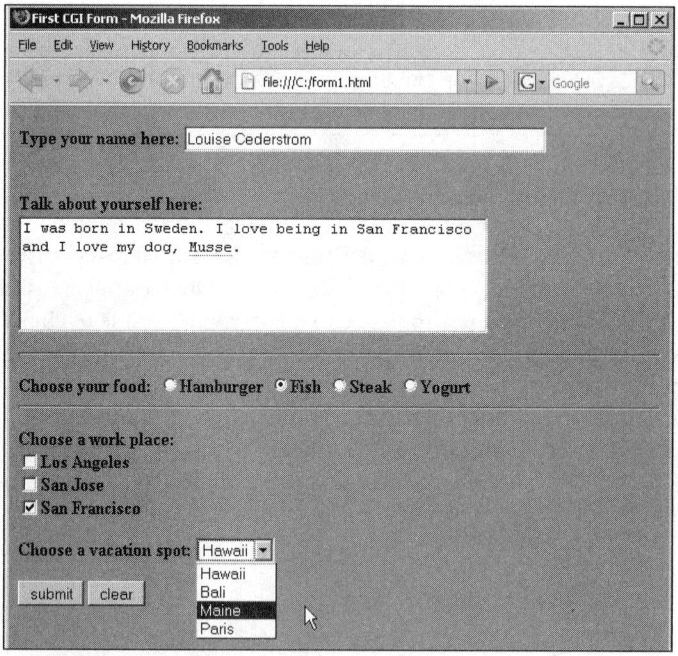

Figure 16.11 A form filled with user input.

EXAMPLE 16.11

```
    (The HTML Form Source File)
1   <html><head>
2   <title>First CGI Form</title></head>

    <body bgcolor="#9999cc">
3   <form action="/cgi-bin/bookstuff/form1.cgi" >
    <p/>
4     <b> Type your name here:
5        <input type="text" name="namestring" size=50>
         <p><br>Talk about yourself here: <br>
7        <textarea name="comments" rows=5 cols=50>I was born...
    </textarea>
    </b>
     <hr>
8   </p><b> Choose your food:
9   <input type="radio" name="choice" value="burger"/>Hamburger
    <input type="radio" name="choice" value="fish"/>Fish
    <input type="radio" name="choice" value="steak"/>Steak
    <input type="radio" name="choice" value="yogurt"/>Yogurt
    <hr>
    </p> <b>Choose a work place:</b> <br>

10  <input type="checkbox" name="place" value="la"/>Los Angeles
    <br>
    <input type="checkbox" name="place" value="sj"/>San Jose
    <br
    <input type="checkbox" name="place" value="sf" checked/>San
Francisco
    </p>
    <b>Choose a vacation spot:</b>
11  <select name="location"> <option selected value="hawaii"/> Hawaii
    <option value="bali"/>Bali
    <option value="maine"/>Maine
    <option value="paris"/>Paris
    </select> <p>

    <input type="submit" value="submit">
    <input type="reset" value="clear">
    </body>
    </form>
    </html>
```

EXPLANATION

1. This tag says that this is the start of an HTML document.
2. The <*TITLE*> tag; the title appears outside of the browser's main window.

EXPLANATION (CONTINUED)

3 The beginning of a *<FORM>* tag, followed by attributes that specify where the browser will send the input data and the HTTP method that will be used to process it. The default method is the *GET* method. When the data is submitted, the CGI script will be executed by the server. The CGI script is located under the server's root directory in the *cgi-bin* directory, the directory where CGI scripts are normally stored. In this example, the *cgi* script is stored in a directory called *bookstuff*, below the *cgi-bin* directory.

4 The *<P>* tag starts a new paragraph. The *<B>* tag says the text that follows will be in bold type. The user is asked for input.

5 The input type is a text box that will hold up to 50 characters. When the user types text into the text box, that text will be stored in the user-defined *NAME* value, *namestring*. For example, if the user types *Louise Cederstrom*, the browser will assign *namestring=Louise Cederstrom* to the query string. If assigned a *VALUE* attribute, the text field can take a default; i.e., text that appears in the text box when it is initially displayed by the browser.

6 The user is asked for input.

7 The text area is similar to the text field but will allow input that scans multiple lines. The *<textarea>* tag will produce a rectangle (name comments) with dimensions in rows and columns (5 rows by 50 columns) and an optional default value (*I was born...*).

8 The user is asked to pick from a series of menu items.

9 The first input type is a list of radio buttons. Only one button can be selected. The input type has two attributes: a *type* and a *name*. The value of the *name* attribute *choice*, for example, will be assigned *burger* if the user clicks on the *Hamburger* option. *choice=burger* is passed onto the CGI program. And if the user selects *Fish*, *choice=fish* will be assigned to the query string, and so on. These key/value pairs are used to build a query string to pass onto the CGI program after the Submit button is clicked.

10 The input type this time is in the form of check boxes. More than one check box may be selected. The optional default box is already checked. When the user selects one of the check boxes, the value of the *name* attribute will be assigned one of the values from the *value* attribute, such as *place=la* if *Los Angeles* is checked.

11 The *<select>* tag is used to produce a pop-up menu (also called a drop-down list) or a scrollable list. The *name* option is required. It is used to define the name for the set of options. For a pop-up menu, the *size* attribute is not necessary; it defaults to 1. The pop-up menu initially displays one option and expands to a menu when that option is clicked. Only one selection can be made from the menu. If a *size* attribute is given, that many items will be displayed. If the *multiple* attribute is given (e.g., *select multiple name=whatever*), the menu appears as a scrollable list, displaying all of the options.

12 If the user clicks the Submit button, the CGI script listed in the form's *action* attribute will be launched. In this example, the script wasn't programmed to do anything. An error message is sent to the server's error log and to the browser.

13 If the Clear button is clicked, all of the input boxes are reset to their defaults.

16.6.3 The *GET* Method

The simplest type of form is created with what is called the *GET* method. It is used every time the browser requests a document. If a method is not supplied, the *GET* method is the default. It is the only method used for retrieving static HTML files and images.

Since HTML is an object-oriented language, you may recall that a method is a name for an object-oriented subroutine. The *GET* method passes data to the CGI program by appending the input to the program's URL, usually as a URL-encoded string. The *QUERY_STRING* environment variable is assigned the value of the encoded string as was demonstrated in Example 16.12.

Servers often have size limitations on the length of the URL. For example, the UNIX size is limited to 1,240 bytes. If a lot of information is being passed to the server, the *POST* method should be used.

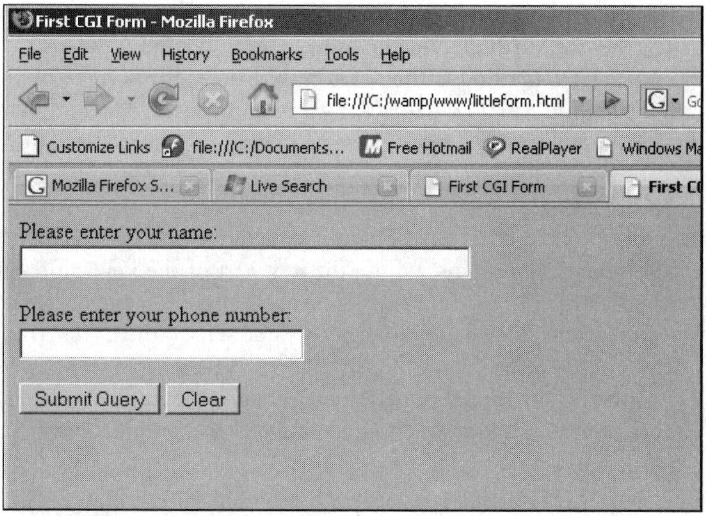

Figure 16.12 The HTML form created in Example 16.12.

EXAMPLE 16.12

```
HTML Source File with a Form Tag and ACTION Attribute
---------------------------------------------------------------------
    <html>
      <head><title>First CGI Form</title></head>
    <body bgcolor=silver>
1     <form action="/cgi-bin/littleform.cgi" method=get>
          <!-- When user presses "submit", cgi script is called to
            process input -->
2           Please enter your name: <br>
3           <input type="text" size=50 name="Name">
            <p/>
```

EXAMPLE 16.12 (CONTINUED)

```
       Please enter your phone number: <br>
4      <input type="text" size=30 name="Phone">
         <p/>
5      <input type=submit>
       <input type=reset value="Clear">
6    </form>
   </body>
```

EXPLANATION

1 A form is created within the *<body>* tags of an HTML document. The *<form>* tag specifies the URL and method that will be used to process a form. When a user submits the form, the browser will send all the data it has obtained from the browser to the Web server. The *action* attribute tells the server to call a CGI script at the location designated in the URL and send the data on to that program to be processed. The *method* attribute tells the browser how the input data is to be sent to the server. The *GET* method is the default, so it does not need to be assigned here. The CGI program can do whatever it wants to with the data and, when finished, will send it back to the server. The server will then relay the information back to the browser for display.

2 The user is asked for input.

3 The input type is a text box that will hold up to 50 characters. The *NAME* attribute is assigned the string *Name*. This will be the key part of the key/value pair. The user will type something in the text box. The value entered by the user will be assigned to the *name* key. This *name=value* pair will be sent to the CGI script in that format; for example, *Name=Christian*.

4 The *name* attribute for the input type is *Phone*. Whatever the user types in the text box will be sent to the CGI program as *Phone=value*; for example, *Phone=543-123-4567*.

5 The *submit* attribute for the input type causes a Submit button to appear with the default string *Send Query* written on the button. If this box is selected, the CGI program will be executed. The input is sent to the CGI program. The *reset* attribute allows the user to clear all the input devices by clicking on the Clear button.

6 The *</form>* tag ends the form.

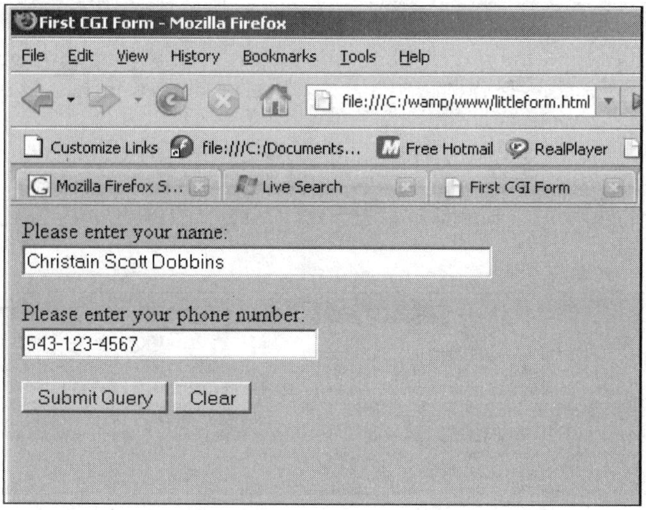

Figure 16.13 Filling out the form from Example 16.13.

The CGI Script

EXAMPLE 16.13

```
(The CGI Script)
1  #!c:/ActivePerl/bin/perl.exe
   # The CGI script that will process the form information sent
   # from the server

2  print "Content-type: text/html\n\n";

print "Processing CGI form :\n\n";
# Print out only the QUERY_STRING environment variable

while(($key, $value)=each(%ENV)){
   print "<h3>$key = <em>$value</em></h3><br>"
   if $key eq "QUERY_STRING";
}
```

EXPLANATION

1. The *#!* line tells the server where to find the Perl interpreter. It must be on the first and topmost line of the program and contain the exact path to the CGI script. One error in this line will result in "Internal Server Error." Always check this line first when debugging.
2. Perl's output goes to the browser rather than the screen. The content type (also called the MIME header) is *text/html*, since there are HTML tags embedded in the text.

EXPLANATION

3 Perl's input comes from the server. The *while* loop is used to loop through all of the environment variables in the *%ENV* hash. These variables were passed into the Perl script from the Web server.

4 This line will be printed only when the value of the *QUERY_STRING* environment variable is found. It wasn't really necessary to loop through the entire list. It would have been sufficient to just type *print "$ENV{QUERY_STRING}
";*.

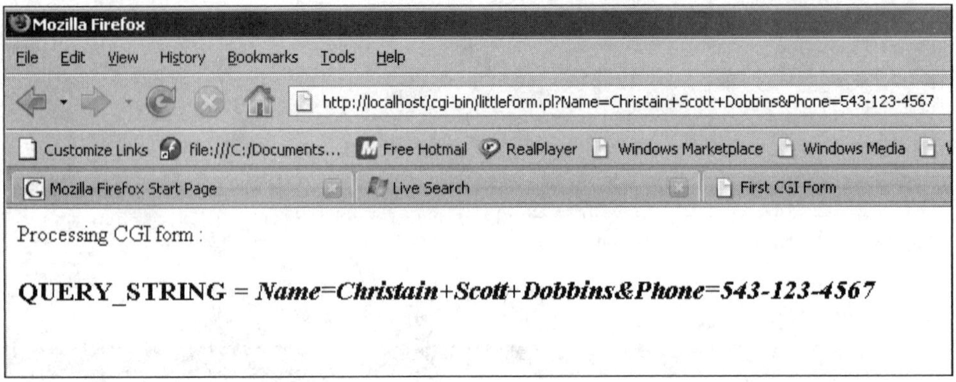

Figure 16.14 Output from CGI script.

16.6.4 Processing the Encoded Data

The Encoded Query String. When using the *GET* method, information is sent to the CGI program in the environment variable *QUERY_STRING*.[4] The string is URL-encoded. In fact, all data contained in an HTML form is sent from the browser to the server in an encoded format. When the *GET* method is used, this encoded data can be seen on the URL line in your browser, preceded by a question mark. The string following the *?* will be sent to the CGI program in the *QUERY_STRING* environment variable. Each key/value pair is separated by an ampersand (*&*), and spaces are replaced with plus signs (+). Any nonalphanumeric values are replaced with their hexadecimal equivalent, preceded by a percent sign (%). After clicking the Submit button in the previous example, you would see the input strings in your browser's Location box (Netscape), appended to the URL line and preceded by a question mark. The highlighted part in the following example is the part that will be assigned to the environment variable, *QUERY_STRING*. The *QUERY_STRING* environment variable will be passed to your Perl script in the *%ENV* hash. To access the key/value pair in your Perl script, add a *print* statement: *print $ENV{QUERY_STRING};* .

4. When using the *POST* method, input is assigned to a variable from *STDIN* and encoded the same way.

EXAMPLE 16.14

```
1   What you see in the Location box of the browser:

http://servername/cgi-bin/
form1.cgi?Name=Christian+Dobbins&Phone=543-123-4567

2   What the server sends to the browser in the ENV hash value,
QUERY_STRING:

QUERY_STRING=Name=Christian+Dobbins&Phone=543-123-4567
```

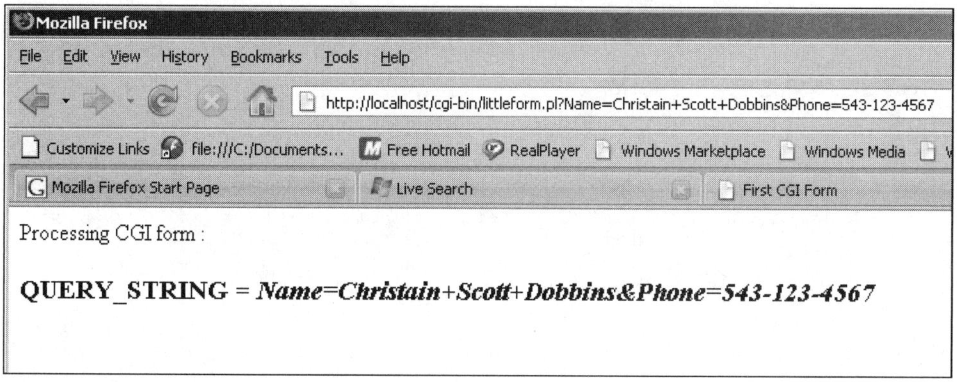

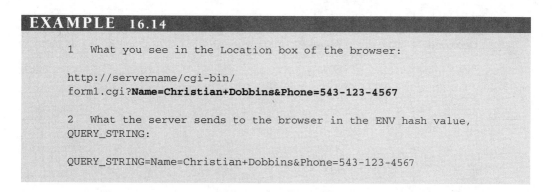

Figure 16.15 Output of the CGI script from Example 16.14.

Decoding the Query String with Perl. Decoding the query string is not a difficult task, because Perl has such a large number of string manipulation functions, such as *tr*, *s*, *split*, *substr*, *pack*, etc. Once you get the query string from the server into your Perl program, you can parse it and do whatever you want with the data. For removing &, +, and = signs from a query string, use the substitution command, *s*, the *split* function, or the translate function, *tr*. To deal with the hexadecimal-to-character conversion of those characters preceded by a % sign, the *pack* function is normally used.

Table 16.8 Encoding Symbols in a Query String

Symbol	*Function*
&	Separates key/value pairs.
+	Replaces spaces.
%xy	Represents any ASCII character with a value of less than 21 hexadecimal (33 decimal) or greater than 7f (127 decimal) and special characters ?, &, %, +, and = . These characters must be escaped with a %, followed by the hexadecimal equivalence (xy) of that character, e.g., *%2F* represents a forward slash, and *%2c* represents a comma.

Table 16.9 URL Hex-Encoded Characters

Character	***Value***
Tab	%09
Space	%20
!	%21
"	%22
#	%23
$	%24
%	%25
&	%26
(	%28
)	%29
,	%2C
.	%2E
/	%2F
:	%3A
;	%3B
<	%3C
=	%3D
>	%3E
?	%3F
@	%40
[	%5B
\	%5C
]	%5D
^	%5E
‘	%60
{	%7B
|	%7C

Table 16.9 URL Hex-Encoded Characters (continued)

Character	*Value*
}	%7D
~	%7E

Parsing the Form's Input with Perl. After the Perl CGI script gets the input from the form, it will be decoded. This is done by splitting up the key/value pairs and replacing special characters with regular text. Once parsed, the information can be used to create a guest book, a database, send e-mail to the user, and so on.

The routines for parsing the encoded string can be stored in subroutines and saved in your personal library, or you can take advantage of the *CGI.pm* library module, part of Perl's standard distribution, which eliminates all the bother.

Decoding the Query String. Steps to decode are handled with Perl functions. The following shows a URL-encoded string assigned to *$ENV{QUERY_STRING}*.

```
Name=Christian+Dobbins&Phone=543-456-1234
```

The key/pair values show that the URL has three pieces of information separated by the ampersand (&): *Name*, *Phone*, and *Sign*:

```
Name=Christian+Dobbins&Phone=543-456-1234
```

The first thing to do would be to split up the line and create an array (see step 1). After splitting up the string by ampersands, remove the + with the *tr* or *s* functions, and split the remaining string into key/value pairs with the split function, using the = as the split delimiter (see step 2).

```
1. @key_value = split(/&/, $ENV{QUERY_STRING});
   print "@key_value\n";

2. Output:
   Name=Christian+Dobbins   Phone=543-456-1234
```

The @key_value array created by splitting the query string:

Name=Christian+Dobbins	Phone=543-456-1234

```
3. foreach $pair ( @key_value){
       $pair =~ tr/+/ /;
       ($key, $value) = split(/=/, $pair);
       print "\t$key: $value\n";
   }
4. Output:
   Name: Christian Dobbins
   Phone: 543-456-1234
```

EXAMPLE 16.15

```
(Another URL-Encoded String assigned to $ENV{QUERY_STRING})

1   $input="string=Joe+Smith%3A%2450%2c000%3A02%2F03%2F77";
2   $input=~s/%(..)/pack("c", hex($1))/ge;
3   print $input,"\n";

    Output:
    string=Joe+Smith:$50,000:02/03/77
```

EXPLANATION

1 This string contains ASCII characters that are less than 33 decimal and greater than 127, the colon, the dollar sign, the comma, and the forward slash.

2 The *pack* function is used to convert hexadecimal-coded characters back into character format.

3 The search side of the substitution, */%(..)/*, is a regular expression that contains a literal percent sign followed by any two characters (each dot represents one character) enclosed in parentheses. The parentheses are used so that Perl can store the two characters it finds in the special scalar *$1*.

  On the replacement side of the substitution, the *pack* function will first use the *hex* function to convert the two hexadecimal characters stored in *$1* to their corresponding decimal values and then pack the resulting decimal values into an unsigned character. The result of this execution is assigned to the scalar *$input*.

  Now you will have to remove the + sign.

16.6.5 Putting It All Together

The *GET* Method. Now it is time to put together a form that will be processed by a Perl CGI program using the *GET* method. The CGI program will decode the query string and display the final results on the HTML page that is returned after the form was filled out and the Submit button clicked.

The following examples demonstrate

1. The HTML fill-out form
2. The HTML source file that produced the form
3. The form after it has been processed by the CGI script
4. The Perl CGI script that processed the form

EXAMPLE 16.16

```
(The HTML source file)
    <html><head><title>cgi form</title></head><body>
    <hr/>
1   <form action="http://127.0.0.1/cgi-bin/getmethod.cgi" method=get>
    <!When user presses "submit", cgi script is called to process input >
```

EXAMPLE 16.16 (CONTINUED)

```
2   Please enter your name: <BR>
3   <input type="text" size=50 name=name>
    <P/>
    Plese enter your salary ($####.##): <BR>
    <INPUT TYPE="text" SIZE=30 NAME=Salary>
    <P/>
    Plese enter your birth date (mm/dd/yy): <BR>
    <input type="text" size=30 name=birthdate>
    <P/>
4   <input type=submit value="Submit Query">
    <INPUT TYPE=RESET VALUE="Reset">
5   </form>
    </body></html>
```

EXPLANATION

1. The form is started with the *<form>* tag. When the user clicks the Submit button on the form, the *action* attribute triggers the HTTP server on this machine (local host is IP address 127.0.0.1) to start up the script called *getmethod.cgi* found under the server's root in the *cgi-bin* directory.
2. The user is asked for information.
3. The user will fill in the text boxes with his name, salary, etc.
4. When the user clicks the Submit button, the CGI script assigned to the *action* attribute will be activated.
5. This is the end of the form tag.

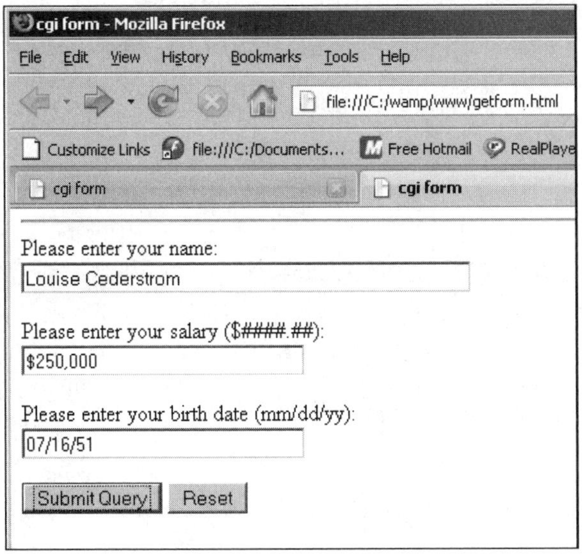

Figure 16.16 The HTML form from Example 16.16.

EXAMPLE 16.17

```
#!c:/perl/bin/perl
# The CGI script that processes the form shown in Example 8.12.
1 print "Content-type: text/html\n\n";
2 print <<HTML;
 <html><title>Decoding the Input Data</title>
 <body bgcolor="lavender">
 <font face="verdana" size="+1">
 HTML
 print "<H3><U>Decoding the query string</U></H3>";
 # Getting the input
3 $inputstring=$ENV{QUERY_STRING}};
  print "<B>Before decoding:</B>";
  print "<P>$inputstring";
  # Extracting the + and & and creating key/value pairs
4 @key_value=split(/&/,$inputstring);
  foreach $pair ( @key_value){
5     ($key, $value) = split(/=/, $pair);
6     $value=~s/%(..)/pack("C", hex($1))/ge;
      $value =~ s/\n/ /g;
 $value =~ s/\r//g;
 $value =~ s/\cM//g;
7     $input{$key}=$value ; # Creating a hash
  }
  # After decoding
  print "<HR>";
  print "<P><B>After decoding:</B><P>";
8     while(($key, $value)=each(%input)){
       print "$key: <I>$value</I><BR>";
  }
  print <<HTML;
   <hr>
   <p>Now what do we want to do with this information? </p>
   </font>
   </body>
   </html>
  HTML
```

EXPLANATION

1 This MIME header line describes the format of the data returned from this program to be HTML text. The two newlines (required!) end the header information.

2 The *%ENV* hash contains the key/value pairs sent to this Perl program by the Web server. The value of the *QUERY_STRING* environment variable is assigned to a scalar, *$inputstring*.

3 The *tr* function translates all + signs to spaces.

4 The *pack* function converts any hexadecimal numbers to their corresponding ASCII characters.

EXPLANATION

5 The value of the scalar *$inputstring* is sent from the Perl script to the server and then on to the browser.
6 The scalar *$inputstring* is now split by ampersands. The output returned is stored in the three-element array *@key_value* as:
Name=Louise Cederstrom&Salary=$200,000&Birthdate=7/16/51
7 The *foreach* loop is used to iterate through the *@key_value* array. The resulting key/value pairs are created by splitting each array element by the = sign.
8 A new hash called *%input* is created with corresponding key/value pairs.
9 The *while* loop is used to iterate through the hash.
10 The new key/value pair is printed and sent back to the Web server. The browser displays the output. Now that the Perl script has parsed and stored the input that came from the form, it is up to the programmer to decide what to do with this data. He may send back an e-mail to the user, store the information in a database, create an address book, etc. The real work is done!

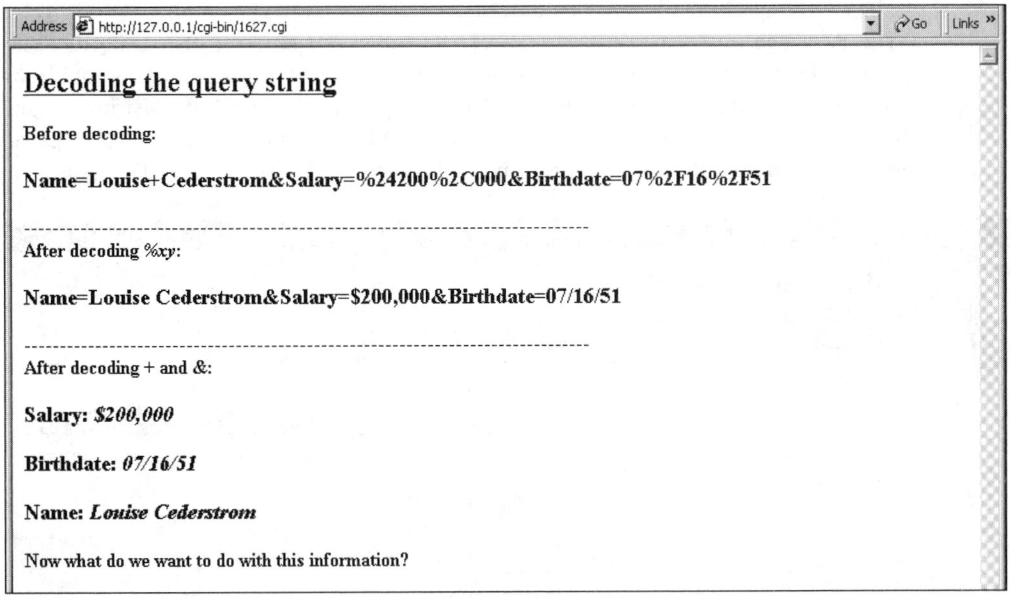

Address http://127.0.0.1/cgi-bin/1627.cgi
Go
Links
Decoding the query string
Before decoding:
Name=Louise+Cederstrom&Salary=%24200%2C000&Birthdate=07%2F16%2F51
After decoding %xy:
Name=Louise Cederstrom&Salary=$200,000&Birthdate=07/16/51
After decoding + and &:
Salary: $200,000
Birthdate: 07/16/51
Name: Louise Cederstrom
Now what do we want to do with this information?

Figure 16.17 Output after CGI/Perl processing, Example 16.17.

16.6.6 The *POST* Method

The only real difference between the *GET* and *POST* methods is the way input is passed from the server to the CGI program. When the *GET* method is used, the server sends input to the CGI program in the *QUERY_STRING* environment variable.

When the *POST* method is used, the CGI program gets input from standard input, *STDIN*. Either way, the input is encoded in exactly the same way. One reason for using the *POST* method is that some browsers restrict the amount of data that can be stored in the *QUERY_STRING* environment variable. The *POST* method doesn't store its data in the query string. Also, the *GET* method displays the input data in the URL line in the Location box of the browser, whereas the *POST* method hides the data. Since the *POST* method does not append input to the URL, it is often used in processing forms where there is a lot of data being filled into forms.

In an HTML document, the *<FORM>* tag starts the form. The *ACTION* attribute tells the browser **where** to send the data that is collected from the user, and the *METHOD* attribute tells the browser **how** to send it. If the *POST* is method used, the output from the browser is sent to the server and then to the CGI program's standard input, *STDIN*. The amount of data, that is, the number of bytes taken as input from the user, is stored in the *CONTENT_LENGTH* environment variable.

Rather than assigning the input to the *QUERY_STRING* environment variable, the browser sends the input to the server in a message body, similar to the way e-mail messages are sent. The server then encapsulates all the data and sends it on to the CGI program.

The CGI program reads input data from the *STDIN* stream via a pipe.

The Perl *read* function reads the *CONTENT_LENGTH* amount of bytes, saves the input data in a scalar, and then processes it the same way it processes input coming from the query string. It's not that the format for the input has changed; it's just **how** it got into the program. Note that after the *POST* method has been used, the browser's Location box does not contain the input in the URL as it did with the *GET* method.

EXAMPLE 16.18

```
    (The HTML source file)
    <HTML>
    <HEAD>
    <TITLE>CGI Form</TITLE>
    <HR>
1   <FORM ACTION="http://127.0.0.1/cgi-bin/postmethod.cgi" METHOD=POST>
    <!When user presses "submit", cgi script is called to process input >
2   Please enter your name: <BR>
3   <INPUT TYPE="text" SIZE=50 NAME=Name>
    <P>
    Please enter your salary ($####.##): <BR>
    <INPUT TYPE="text" SIZE=30 NAME=Salary>
    <P>
    Please enter your birth date (mm/dd/yy): <BR>
    <INPUT TYPE="text" SIZE=30 NAME=Birthdate>
    <P>
4   <INPUT TYPE=SUBMIT VALUE="Submit Query">
    <INPUT TYPE=RESET VALUE="Reset">
5   </FORM>
    </HTML>
```

EXPLANATION

1 The *<FORM>* tag starts the form. The *ACTION* attribute is assigned the URL of the CGI script, *postmethod.cgi*, that will be executed whent the Submit button is clicked by the user, and the *METHOD* attribute is assigned *POST* to indicate how the data coming from the form will be handled.
2 The user is asked for input.
3 Text fields are created to hold the user's name, salary, and birth date.
4 The Submit button is created.
5 The form is ended.

EXAMPLE 16.19

```
#!c:/perl/bin/perl
# The CGI script that processes the form shown in Example 8.12.
1 print "Content-type: text/html\n\n";
2 print <<HTML;
 <html><title>Decoding the Input Data</title>
 <body bgcolor="lavender">
 <font face="verdana" size="+1">
 HTML
 print "<H3><U>Decoding the query string</U></H3>";
 # Getting the input
3 $inputstring=$ENV{QUERY_STRING}};
  print "<B>Before decoding:</B>";
  print "<P>$inputstring";
  # Extracting the + and & and creating key/value pairs
4 @key_value=split(/&/,$inputstring);
  foreach $pair ( @key_value){
5     ($key, $value) = split(/=/, $pair);
6     $value=~s/%(..)/pack("C", hex($1))/ge;
      $value =~ s/\n/ /g;
      $value =~ s/\r//g;
      $value =~ s/\cM//g;
7     $input{$key}=$value ; # Creating a hash
  }
  # After decoding
  print "<HR>";
  print "<P><B>After decoding:</B><P>";
8 while(($key, $value)=each(%input)){
      print "$key: <I>$value</I><BR>";
  }
  print <<HTML;
  <hr>
  <p>Now what do we want to do with this information? </p>
  </font>
  </body>
  </html>
  HTML
```

EXPLANATION

1 This MIME header line describes the format of the data returned from this program to be HTML text. The two newlines (required!) end the header information.

2 The *here document* is used to set up the beginning of the HTML page.

3 The *%ENV* hash contains the key/value pairs sent to this Perl program by the Web server. The value of the *QUERY_STRING* environment variable is assigned to a scalar, *$inputstring*.

4 The scalar *$inputstring* is now split by ampersands. The output returned is stored in the three-element array *@key_value* as:

    Name=Louise+Cederstrom Salary=$200,000 Birthdate=7/16/51
    $key_value[0] *$key_value[1]* *$key_value[2]*

5 The *foreach* loop takes each element of the array, one at a time. Each element is first split up by "=" signs, creating two values, one called *$key* to represent the name of the input device from the HTML form; e.g., "Name"; and the second, *$value*, containing the data that was typed by the user into the input device; e.g., "Louise+Cederstrom".

6 Now the hexidecimal values are decoded with the Perl *pack* function into their respective ASCII values.

7 A new hash called *%input* is created using the decoded key/value pairs.

8 The *while* loop is used to iterate through the hash. The new key/value pair is printed and sent back to the Web server. The browser displays the output. Now that the *perl* script has parsed and stored the input that came from the form, it is up to the programmer to decide what to do with this data. He may send back an e-mail to the user, store the information in a database, create an address book, etc. The real work is done!

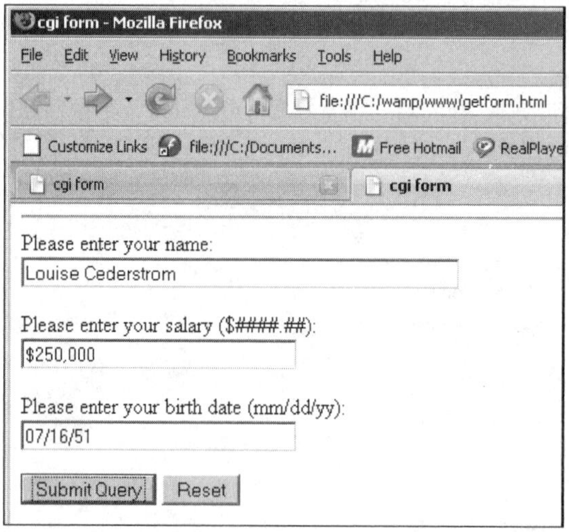

Figure 16.18 The HTML input form from Example 16.18.

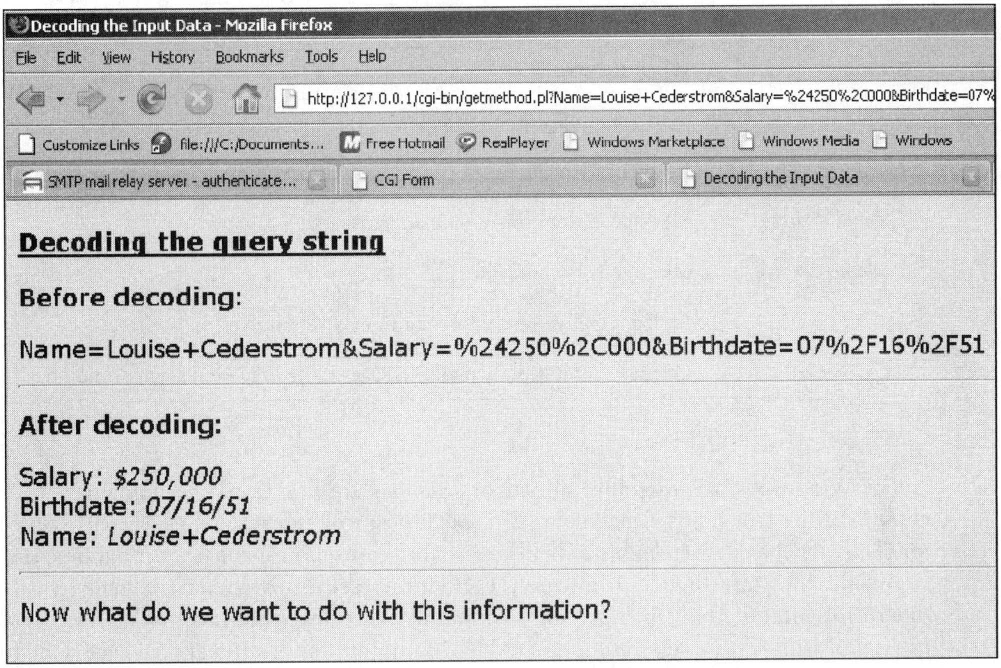

Figure 16.19 The output from the CGI script in Example 16.19.

16.6.7 Handling E-mail

The SMTP Server. When processing a form, it is often necessary to send e-mail before exiting. You may be sending e-mail to the user and/or to yourself with the submitted form data. E-mail cannot be sent over the Internet without a valid SMTP (Simple Mail Transfer Protocol) server.[5]

The SMTP server is an instance of a mail daemon program that listens for incoming mail on Port 25. SMTP is a TCP-based client/server protocol where the client sends messages to the server. UNIX systems commonly use a mail program called *sendmail* to act as the SMTP server listening for incoming mail. Normally, you would run *sendmail* at the command line with the recipient's name as an argument. To end the e-mail message, a period is placed on a line by itself. In a CGI script, the mail will not be sent interactively, so you will probably want to use the *sendmail* options to control these features. See Table 16.10.

5. The format for Internet mail messages is defined by RFC822.

Table 16.10 *sendmail* Options

Option	***What It Does***
-o	A *sendmail* option follows
-t	Reads headers *To*, *From*, *Cc*, and *Bcc* information from message body
-f "email address"	Message is from this e-mail address
-F "name"	Message is from *name*
-i	Periods will be ignored if on a line by themselves
-odq	Queues up multiple e-mail messages to be delivered asynchronously

For Windows, two programs similar to *sendmail* are *Blat*, a public domain Win32 console utility that sends e-mail using the SMTP protocol (see *www.interlog.com/~tcharron/ blat.html*), and *wSendmail*, a small utility that can send e-mail from programs, the command line, or directly from an HTML form (see *http://www.scriptarchive.com/, /Internet/E_Mail/E_Mail_Tools* or *http://www.developertutorials.com/tutorials/cgi-perl/email-with-perl-2/page4.html*). Go to CPAN and find the *MailFolder* package, which contains such modules as *Mail::Folder, Mail::Internet*, and *Net::SMTP* to further simplify sending and receiving e-mail.

EXAMPLE 16.20

```
(From the HTML form where the e-mail information is collected)
<html>
<head><title>Register Now!</title></head>
<body bgcolor="ccff66">
<form method="post" action="http://127.0.0.1/cgi-bin/mailer.pl">
<input type="hidden" name="xemailx"
        value="elizabeth@ellieq.com">
<input type="hidden" name="xsubjext"
        value="course registration">
<input type="hidden"  name="xgoodbyex"
        value="thank you for registering.">
<p>
<a name="registration">
<table cellspacing=5 cellpadding=3>

<tr> <td align=right><b>First name:</b></td>
    <td align=left><input type=text size=30 name="first_name*"
        value=""></td>
</tr>
</p>
```

EXAMPLE 16.20 (CONTINUED)

```
<tr> <td align=right><B>Last Name:</B></TD>
    <td align=left><input type=text size=30 name="last_name*"
        value=""></td>
</tr>
<tr>
    <td align=right><b>Company:</b></td>
    <td align=left><input type=text size=30 name="company*"></td>
</tr>
<tr>
    <td align=right><b>Address:</b></td>
    <td align=left><input type=text size=30 name="address1*"
value=""></td>
</tr>
<tr>
    <td align=right><b>City/Town:</b></td>
    <td align=left><input type=text size=30 name="city*"
        value=""></td>
</tr>
<tr>
    <td align=right><b>State/Province:</b></td>
    <td align=left>
        <select name="state" size="1">
            <option value="AL">Alabama</option>
            <option value="AK">Alaska</option>
            <option value="AZ">Arizona</option>
            <option value="AR">Arkansas</option>
            <option value="CA">California</option>
            <option value="CO">Colorado</option>
            <option value="CT">Connecticut</option>
                  --- continue here ---
            <option value="WA">Washington</option>
            <option value="WV">West Virginia</option>
            <option value="WI">Wisconsin</option>
            <option value="WY">Wyoming</option>
        </select>
    <td align=right><b>Postal/Zip code:</b></td>
    <td align=left><input type=text size=10 name="zip"
        value=""></td>
</tr></b></td>
</table>
<p>
    <input type=submit value="Register now!"></td>
    <input type=reset></td>
</tr>
</form>
</body>
</html>
```

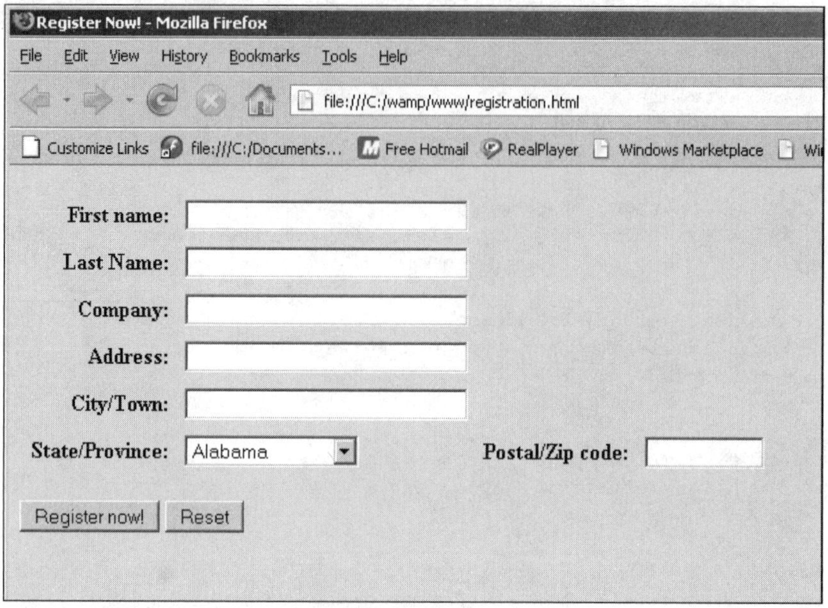

Figure 16.20 Portion of the HTML registration form from Example 16.20.

EXAMPLE 16.21

```
(CGI script to Handle email--only a portion of the script)
# An HTML Form was first created and processed to get the name of the
# user who will receive the e-mail, the person it's from, and the
# subject line.
1   $mailprogram="/usr/lib/sendmail";   # Your mail program goes here
2   $sendto="$input{xemailx}";          # Mailing address goes here
3   $from="$input{xmailx}";
4   $subject="$input{xsubjext}";

5   open(MAIL, "|$mailprogram -t  -oi") || die "Can't open mail
         program: $!\n";
    # -t option takes the headers from the lines following the mail
    # command -oi options prevent a period at the beginning of  a
    # line from meaning end of input
6   print MAIL "To: $sendto\n";
    print MAIL "From: $from\n";
    print MAIL "Subject: $subject\n\n";

7   print MAIL <<EOF;     # Start a "here document"

    Registration Information for $input{$first_name}
        $input{$last_name}:
```

EXAMPLE 16.21 (CONTINUED)

```
      Date of Registration: $today
      ----------------------------------------------
      First Name:           $input{$first_name}
      Last Name:            $input{$last_name}
      Street Address:       $input{$address}
      City:                 $input{$city}
      State/Province:       $input{$state}

      <Rest of message goes here>

8     EOF
9     close MAIL;   # Close the filter
```

EXPLANATION

1. The name of the mail program being used here is *sendmail*, located in the UNIX subdirectory */usr/lib*.
2. This line will be assigned to the *To:* header in the e-mail document.
3. This line will be assigned to the *From:* header in the e-mail document.
4. And this line is the *Subject:* header in the e-mail document.
5. Perl is going to open a filter called *MAIL* that will pipe the user's e-mail message to the *sendmail* program. The *-t* option tells *sendmail* to scan the e-mail document for the *To:*, *From:*, and *Subject:* lines (instead of from the command line), and the *-i* option tells the mail program to ignore any period that may be found on a line by itself.
6. These are the header lines indicating to whom the mail is going, where it's going, and the subject of the mail. These values were pulled from the form.
7. A *here document* is started. The text between EOF and EOF is sent to the *sendmail* program via the *MAIL* filter.
8. EOF marks the end of the *here document*.
9. The *MAIL* filter is closed.

16.7 The *CGI.pm* Module

16.7.1 Introduction

The most popular Perl 5 library for writing dynamic CGI programs, such as guestbooks, page counters, feedback forms, etc., is the *CGI.pm* module written by Lincoln Stein; it is included in the standard Perl library starting with version 5.004. The most recent version of *CGI.pm* can be found at *www.perl.com/CPAN*. *CGI.pm* takes advantage of the object-oriented features that were introduced in Perl 5 and also provides methods (*GET* and *POST*) to interpret query strings, handle forms, and hide the details of HTML syntax.

Lincoln Stein has also written the *Official Guide to Programming with CGI.pm*[6] (*www.wiley.com/compbooks/stein*), an excellent, easy-to-read guide from which much of the following information was gleaned.

16.7.2 Advantages

1. *CGI.pm* allows you to keep a fill-out form (HTML) and the script that parses it, all in one file under the *cgi-bin* directory. In this way, your HTML file (that holds the form) and your CGI script (that reads, parses, and handles the form data) are not so far apart.[7]
2. After the user has filled out a form, the results appear on the same page; in other words, the user doesn't have to backpage to see what was on the form, and the fill-out form does not lose data it maintains its state. Data that doesn't disappear is called "sticky." To override stickiness, see "The *override* Argument" on page 593.
3. All the reading and parsing of form data is handled by the module.
4. Methods are used to replace HTML tags for creating text boxes, radio buttons, menus, etc., to create the form, as well as for assigning standard tags, such as headers, titles, paragraph breaks, horizontal rule lines, breaks, etc.
5. To see what HTML tags are produced by the *CGI.pm* module, from the View menu, select Source (in Internet Explorer) after the form has been displayed.
6. Accepting uploaded files and managing cookies is easier with the *CGI.pm* module.

16.7.3 Two Styles of Programming with *CGI.pm*

The Object-Oriented Style. Using the object-oriented style, you create one or more CGI objects and then use object **methods** to create the various elements of the page. Each CGI object starts out with the list of named parameters that were passed to your CGI script by the server. You can modify the objects and send them to a file or database. Each object is independent; it has its own parameter list. If a form has been filled out, its contents can be saved from one run of the script to the next; that is, it maintains its **state**. (Normally, the HTML documents are **stateless**; in other words, everything is lost when the page exits.)

EXAMPLE 16.22

```
use CGI;
$obj=new CGI;  # Create the CGI object
print $obj->header,      # Use functions to create the HTML page
$obj->start_html("Object oriented syntax"),
$obj->h1("This is a test..."),
$obj->h2("This is a test..."),
$obj->h3("This is a test..."),
$obj->end_html;
```

---

6. Stein, L., *Official Guide to Programming with CGI.pm: The Standard for Building Web Scripts*, Wiley Computer Publishing, 1998.
7. Ibid.

EXPLANATION

The following output can be seen by viewing the source from the browser. It demonstrates the HTML output produced by the *CGI.pm* module.

```
<!DOCTYPE html
PUBLIC "-//W3C//DTD XHTML 1.0 Transitional//EN"
"DTD/xhtml1-transitional.dtd">
<html xmlns="http://www.w3.org/1999/xhtml" lang="en-US">
<head><title>Object oriented syntax</title></head><body>
<h1>This is a test...</h1>
<h2>This is a test...</h2>
<h3>This is a test...</h3>
</body
</html>
```

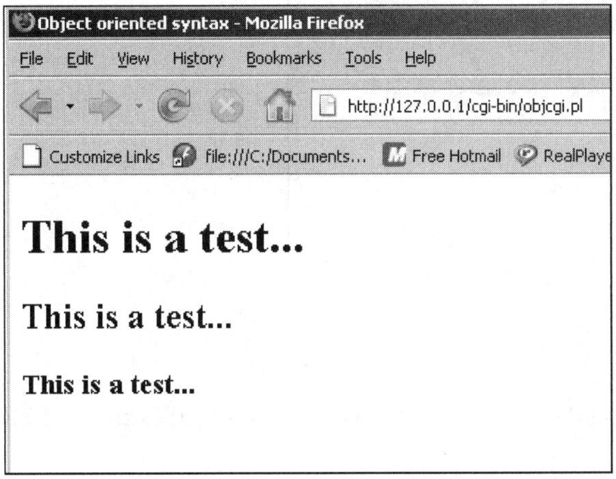

Figure 16.21 Output from the object-oriented CGI script in Example 16.22.

Function-Oriented Style. The function-oriented style is easier to use than the object-oriented style, because you don't create or manipulate the CGI object directly. The module creates a default CGI object for you. You use the same built-in functions to manipulate the object, pass parameters to the functions to create the HTML tags, and retrieve the information passed into the form.

Although the function-oriented style provides a cleaner programming interface, it limits you to using one CGI object at a time.

The following example uses the function-oriented interface. The main differences are that the *:standard* functions must be imported into the program's namespace, and you don't create a CGI object. It is created for you.[8]

8. A default object called *$CGI::Q* is created, which can be accessed directly if needed.

EXAMPLE 16.23

```
#!/usr/bin/perl
use CGI qw(:standard);    # Function-oriented style uses a set of
                          # standard functions
print header,
  start_html("Function oriented syntax"),
  h1("This is a test..."),
  h2("This is a test..."),
  h3("This is a test..."),
end_html;
```

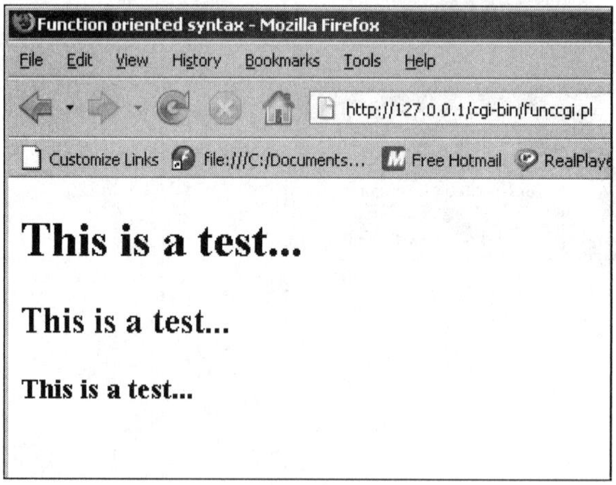

Figure 16.22 Output from the function-oriented CGI script in Example 16.23.

16.7.4 An Important Warning!

Perl's *print* function is used to send output from your script to the server, but in many of the examples, rather than using separate *print* statements on each line, the *print* function is passed multiple strings separated by commas. In fact, in the *CGI.pm* documentation, the sample script shown in Figure 16.23 starts with one *print* function to be continued over 30 lines and finally terminated with a semicolon. It is very easy to prematurely terminate one of the lines with a semicolon. Doing so will break your program and send an "Internal Server Error" message to the browser.

```
NAME
    CGI - Simple Common Gateway Interface Class

SYNOPSIS
      # CGI script that creates a fill-out form
      # and echoes back its values.

      use CGI qw/:standard/;
      print header,
            start_html('A Simple Example'),
            h1('A Simple Example'),
            start_form,
            "What's your name? ",textfield('name'),p,
            "What's the combination?", p,
            checkbox_group(-name=>'words',
                           -values=>['eenie','meenie','
minie','moe'],
                           -defaults=>['eenie','minie']
), p,
            "What's your favorite color? ",
            popup_menu(-name=>'color',
                       -values=>['red','green','blue','
chartreuse']),p,
            submit,
            end_form,
            hr;

       if (param()) {
           my $name      = param('name');
           my $keywords  = join ', ',param('words');
           my $color     = param('color');
           print "Your name is",em(escapeHTML($name)),p
,
                 "The keywords are: ",em(escapeHTML($ke
ywords)),p,
                 "Your favorite color is ",em(escapeHTM
L($color)),
                 hr;
       }

ABSTRACT
    This perl library uses perl5 objects to make it eas
stdin
```

Figure 16.23 *CGI.pm* documentation page.

Another common error is improperly terminating a *here document*. To avoid using multiple *print* lines, the *here document* (see Chapter 4) is often used. The terminating word for a *here document* MUST be on a line by itself and flush against the left margin, with no space surrounding it, and terminated with a carriage return.

```
#!/bin/perl
# The HTML tags are embedded in the here document to avoid using
# multiple print statements
print <<EOF;       # here document in a CGI script
Content-type: text/html

```

```
4   <HTML><HEAD><TITLE>Town Crier</TITLE></HEAD>
    <H1><CENTER>Hear ye, hear ye, Sir Richard cometh!!</CENTER></H1>
    </HTML>
5   EOF
    # The EOF in line 5 cannot have surrounding spaces and must be
    # terminated with a newline.
```

16.7.5 HTML Form Methods

A CGI script consists of two parts: the part that creates the form that will be displayed in the browser and the part that retrieves the input from the form, parses it, and handles the information by sending it back to the browser, to a database, to e-mail, etc.

Creating the HTML Form. Methods are provided to simplify the task of creating the HTML form. For example, there are methods to start and end the HTML form and methods for creating headers, check boxes, pop-up menus, radio buttons, Submit and Reset buttons, etc. Table 16.11 lists the most-used of the HTML methods provided by *CGI.pm*.

When passing arguments to the *CGI.pm* methods, two styles can be used:

Named arguments—passed as key/value pairs. Argument names are preceded by a leading dash and are case insensitive.

EXAMPLE 16.24

```
(Named Arguments)
1   print popup_menu(-name=>'place',
                     -values=>['Hawaii','Europe','Mexico', 'Japan' ],
                     -default=>'Hawaii',
                    );
2   print popup_menu(-name=>'place',
                     -values=> \@countries,
                     -default=>'Hawaii',
                    );
```

EXPLANATION

1 The arguments being passed to the *popup_menu* method are called **named parameters**, or **argument lists**. The argument names in this example are *-name*, *-values*, and *-default*. These arguments are always preceded by a leading dash and are case insensitive. If the argument name might conflict with some built-in Perl function or reserved word, quote the argument. Note that the arguments are passed to the method as a set of key/value pairs. The *-values* key has a corresponding value consisting of an anonymous array of countries.

2 This is exactly like the previous example, except that the value for the *-values* key is a reference to an array of countries. Somewhere else in the program, the array *@countries* was created and given values.

Positional arguments—passed as strings, they represent a value. They are used with simple HTML tags. For example, *CGI.pm* provides the *h1()* method to produce the HTML tags *<H1>* and *</H1>*. The argument for *h1()* is the string of text that is normally inserted between the tags. The method is called as follows:

```
print  h1("This is a positional argument");
```

which translates to

```
<H1>This is a positional argument</H1>
```

If using HTML attributes,[9]and the first argument is a reference to an anonymous hash, the attribute and its values are added after the leading tag into the list. For example:

```
print h1({-align=>CENTER}, "This heading is centered");
```

translates to

```
<H1 ALIGN="CENTER">This heading is centered</H1>
```

If the arguments are a reference to an anonymous list, each item in the list will be properly distributed within the tag. For example:

```
print li( ['apples', 'pears', 'peaches'] );
```

translates to three bulleted list items:

```
<LI>apples</LI> <LI>pears</LI> <LI>peaches</LI>
```

whereas

```
print li( 'apples', 'pears', 'peaches' );
```

translates to one bulleted list item:

```
<LI>apples pears peaches</LI>
```

9. Attributes do not require a leading dash.

EXAMPLE 16.25

```
(The CGI script)
#!c:/ActivePerl/bin/perl.exe
# Shortcut calling styles with HTML methods

1  use CGI qw(:standard);  # Function-oriented style print header
2  print header;
# Note that the following functions are all embedded as a
# comma-separated list of arguments in one print statement.

3  print start_html(-title=>"Testing arguments",
                    -bgcolor=>"#99FF66"),
4     b(),font({-size=>"+2", -color=>"#006600"}),
5     p(),"\n",
6     p("This is a string"),"\n",
7     p({-align=>center}, "red", "green", "yellow"), "\n",
8      p({-align=>left}, ["red","green","yellow"]),
9      end_html;# Shortcut calling styles with HTML methods
```

EXPLANATION

1. The function-oriented style of the *CGI.pm* module is used.
2. The *header* function generates the header information ("Content-type: text/html\n\n").
3. The *start_html* function starts the HTML document, including the title of the page and the background color (a lime green).
4. The *b* function generates a *<b>* tag to create bold, and the *font* function causes the font to be increased by two sizes and to be a dark green color.
5. The *p* function generates a paragraph tag that takes no arguments. It is a start tag only.
6. This *p* function takes a string as its argument, causing the string to be printed as a separate paragraph.
7. The first argument to the *p* function causes the paragraph to be centered on the page. The paragraph's text is displayed as one line in the browser: *red green yellow.*
8. This paragraph tag displays each word, left-justified, on a line by itself. It consists of a start tag, with the attributes for left alignment distributed across each of the listed arguments. The arguments are listed as a reference to an anonymous array.
9. This creates the ending *</body>* and *</html>* tags.

EXAMPLE 16.26

```
<!DOCTYPE html
   PUBLIC "-//W3C//DTD XHTML 1.0 Transitional//EN"
    "http://www.w3.org/TR/xhtml1/DTD/xhtml1-transitional.dtd">
  <html xmlns="http://www.w3.org/1999/xhtml" lang="en-US"
xml:lang="en-US">
  <head>
     <title>Testing arguments</title>
     <meta http-equiv="Content-Type" content="text/html;charset=iso-
   8859-1" />
  </head>
  <body bgcolor="#99FF66">
  <b /><font color="#006600" size="+2" /><p />
  <p>This is a string</p>
  <p align="center">red green yellow</p>
  <p align="left">red</p> <p align="left">green</p> <p
align="left">yellow</p>
  </body>
  </html>
```

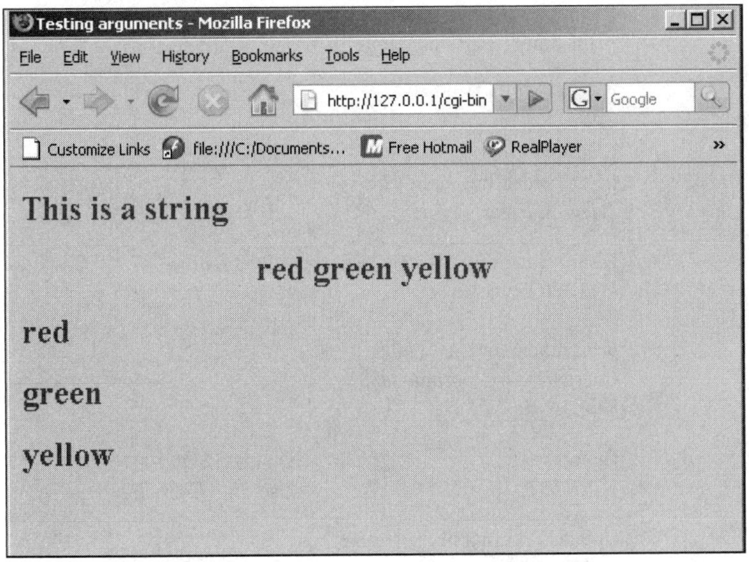

Figure 16.24 Output produced by *CGI.pm* functions.

To avoid conflicts and warnings (-*w* switch), enclose all arguments in quotes.

Table 16.11 HTML Methods

Method	***What It Does***	***Attributes***
a()	Anchor tag *<A>* Example: print a({-href://google.com/'}, "Go Search"};	*-href, -name, -onClick, -onMouseOver,* *-target*
b()	Bold text *<B>* Example: print b("This text is bold");	
basefont() (:html3)	Set size of base font *<FONT>* Example: print basefont({-size=7});	*-size* (sizes 1–7)
big (:netscape group)	Increase text font size *<BIG>* Example: print "Large, big("and larger");	
br()	Creates a line break * * Example: print "Break line here", br, "New line starts here.";	
caption (:html3)	Inserts a caption above a table *<CAPTION>* *print table(caption(b(Table* *Caption)), Tr(continue table* *here...)*	*-align, -valign*
center() (:netscape group)	Center text *<CENTER>*	Doesn't seem to work Use the *<CENTER>* tag.
cite()	Creates text in a proportional italic font *<CITE>*	
checkbox()	Creates a single named check box and label	*-checked, -selected, -on, -label, -name,* *-onClick, -override, -force, -value*

Table 16.11 HTML Methods (continued)

Method	What It Does	Attributes
checkbox_group()	Creates a set of check boxes linked by one name	*-columns, -cols, -colheaders, -default, -defaults, -labels, -linebreak, -name, -nolabels, -onClick, -override, -force, -rows, -rowheaders, -value, -values*
code()	Creates text in a monospace font *<CODE>*	
dd()	Definition item of definition list *<DD>*	
defaults()	Creates a fill-out button for submitting a form as though for the first time; clears the old parameter list	
dl()	Creates a definition list *<DL>*; see *dd()*	*-compact*
dt()	Term part of definition list *<DT>*	
em()	Emphatic (italic) text	
end_form(), endform()	Terminate a form *</FORM>*	
end_html()	Ends an HTML document *</BODY></HTML>*	
font() (:netscape group)	Changes font	*-color, -face, -size*
frame() (:netscape group)	Defines a frame	*-marginheight, -marginwidth, -name, -noresize, -scrolling, -src*
frameset() (:netscape group)	Creates a frameset *<FRAMESET>*	*-cols, -rows*
h1()...h6()	Creates heading levels 1–6 *<H1>, <H2> ... <H6>*	
hidden()	Creates a hidden, invisible text field, uneditable by the user	
hr()	Creates a horizontal rule *<HR>*	*-align, -noshade, -size, -width*

Continues

Table 16.11 HTML Methods (continued)

Method	***What It Does***	***Attributes***
i()	Creates italic text *<I>*	
img()	Creates an inline image *<IMG>*	*-align, -alt, -border, -height, -width, -hspace, -ismap, -src, -lowsrc, -vrspace, -usemap*
image_button()	Produces an inline image that doubles as a form submission button	*-align, -alt.-height, -name, -src, -width*
kbd()	Creates text with keyboard style	
li()	Creates list item for an ordered or unordered list	*-type, -value*
ol()	Start an ordered list	*-compact, -start, -type*
p()	Creates a paragraph *<P>*	*-align, -class*
password_field()	Creates a password field; text entered will be stars	
popup_menu()	Creates a pop-up menu *<SELECT><OPTION>*	*-default, -labels, -name, -onBlur, -onChange, -onFocus, -override, -force, -value, -values*
pre()	Creates preformatted typewriter text for maintaining line breaks, etc. *<PRE>*	
radio_group()	Creates a set of radio buttons all linked by one name	*-columns, -cols, -colheaders, -default, -labels, -linebreak, -name, -nolabels, -onClick, -override, -force, -rows, -rowheaders, -value, -values*
reset()	Creates form's Reset button	
scrolling_list()	Controls a scrolling list box form element	*-default, -defaults, -labels, -multiple, -name, -onBlur, -onChange, -onFocus, -override, -force, -size, -value, -values*

Table 16.11 HTML Methods (continued)

Method	***What It Does***	***Attributes***
Select()	Creates a select tag; note the uppercase "S" to avoid conflict with Perl's built-in *select* function. *<SELECT>*	
small() (:netscape group)	Reduce size of text	
start_form(),startform()	Starts an HTML form *<FORM>*	
start_multipart_form(),	Just like *start_form* but used when uploading files	
strong()	Bold text	
submit()	Creates a Submit button for a form	*-name, -onClick, -value, -label*
sup() (:netscape group)	Superscripted text	
table() (:html3 group)	Creates a table	*-align,bgcolor, -border, -bordercolor, -bordercolor-dark, -bordercolorlight, -cellpadding, -hspace, -vspace, -width*
td() (:html3 group)	Creates a table data cell *<TD>*	*-align, -bgcolor, -bordercolor, -bordercolorlight,-bordercolordark, -colspan, -nowrap, -rowspan, -valign, -width*
textarea()	Creates a multiline text box	*-cols, -columns, -name, -onChange, -onFocus,OnBlur, -onSelect, -override, -force, -value, -default, -wrap*
textfield()	Produces a one-line text entry field	*-maxLength, -name, -onChange, -onFocus, -onBlur, -onSelect, -override, -force, -size, -value, -default*
th() (:html3 group)	Creates a table header *<TH>*	
Tr() (:html3 group)	Defines a table row; note the uppercase "T" to avoid conflict with Perl's *tr* function. *<TR>*	*-align,bgcolor, -bordercolor, -bordercolordark, -bordercolorlight, -valign*
tt()	Typewriter font	
ul()	Start unordered list	

16.7.6 How *CGI.pm* Works with Forms

The *CGI.pm* module makes it possible to create the form and process it all in one Perl script. (You can create a separate HTML form and do just the processing part with *CGI.pm*, but these examples demonstrate combining the whole process in one Perl script.) The module provides methods or functions to handle every aspect of creating a Web page from starting the HTML document to creating a form and its input devices to parsing and decoding the input data. These scripts, where you are producing a form and processing its input on the same page, are self-processing forms, meaning that in the *ACTION* attribute, the address of the same script that printed the form is activated when the user clicks the Submit button. The script simply needs to perform some test to make sure the form was submitted. You will see how all this is done now.

The *start_html* Method. After creating the HTTP header, most CGI scripts will start an HTML document. The *start_html()* method creates the top of the page and options to tailor the appearance and behavior of the page, such as the background color, title, DTD, author, etc. It creates the header line ("Content-type") and also starts the opening *<body>* tag for the document.

The *start_form* Method. The form is created with *start_form* method and its arguments. Each of the field types also a CGI method provided by the module, such as *textfield*, *popup_menu*, *submit*, etc., listed in Table 16.11. Each of these methods is described in detail later in this chapter.

The *submit* Method. Of course, in order to process the form, it must be submitted. The *submit* method provides the form's Submit button.

The *param* Method. This is a very important part of *CGI.pm* After the user has filled in a form, the *CGI.pm* module will take the input from the form, decode it, and store it in name/value pairs. This is all invisible to the user. The names and values can be retrieved with the *param()* function. When *param()* is called, if null is returned, then the form has not yet been filled out. If the *param()* function returns true (non-null), then the form must have been filled out, and the *param()* function can be used to retrieve the form information. If you want an individual value, the *param()* can retrieve it by its name; i.e., the name of the input device in the form.

The following example illustrates the two parts to the CGI program: the HTML form and how to get the information with the *param()* function. For a list of other methods used to process parameters, see Table 16.13.

EXAMPLE 16.27

```
   #!c:/ActivePerl/bin/perl.exe
1  use CGI qw(:standard);
2  print header;
3  print start_html(-title=>'Using the Function-Oriented Syntax',
                    -BGCOLOR=>'yellow');
4  print img({-src=>'/greenballoon.jpg', -align=>LEFT}),
    h1("Let's Hear From You!"),
    h2("I'm interested."),
5   start_form,
       "What's your name? ", textfield('name'),
6      p,
       "What's your occupation? ", textfield('job'),
       p,
7      "Select a vacation spot. ", popup_menu(
           -name=>'place',
           -values=>['Hawaii','Europe','Mexico', 'Japan' ],
                                                  ),
       p,
8      "Do you want a green balloon? ", br,
        checkbox(-name=>'choice',-label=>'If yes, check this box'),
       p,
9      submit("Press here"),
10     end_form;
       print hr;
11     if ( param() ){  # If the form has been filled out,
                        # there are parameters
12          print "Your name is ", em(param('name')),
            p,
             "Your occupation is ", em(param('job')),
            p,
             "Your vacation spot is ", em(param('place')),
            p;
13          if( param('choice') eq "on"){
                print "You will receive a green balloon shortly!"
            }
            else{
                print "Green may not be the best color for you.";
           }
       hr;
     }
```

EXPLANATION

1 The *use* directive says that the *CGI.pm* module is being loaded and will import the *:standard* set of function calls, which use a syntax new in library versions 1.21 and higher. This syntax allows you to call methods without explicitly creating an object with the *new* constructor method; that is, the object is created for you. The *Official Guide to Programming with CGI.pm* by Lincoln Stein contains a complete list of shortcuts.

2 The header method *header* returns the *Content-type: header*. You can provide your own MIME type if you choose; otherwise, it defaults to *text/html*.

3 This will return a canned HTML header and the opening *<BODY>* tag. Parameters are optional and are in the form *-title*, *-author*, and *-base*. Any additional parameters, such as the Netscape unofficial *BGCOLOR* attribute, are added to the *<BODY>* tag; for example, *BGCOLOR=>yellow*.

4 The *img* method allows you to load an image. This GIF image is stored under the document's root in a directory called *Images*. It is aligned to the left of the text. Note: The *print* function here does not terminate until line 11. All of the CGI functions are passed as a comma-separated list to the *print* function.

5 This will produce a level 1 heading tag. It's a shortcut and will produce the *<H1>* HTML tag.

6 This method starts a form. The defaults for the form are the *ACTION* attribute, assigned the URL of this script, and the *METHOD* attribute, assigned the *POST* method.

7 The *textfield* method creates a text field box. The first parameter is the *NAME* for the field the second parameter; representing the *VALUE*, is optional. *NAME* is assigned *name* and *VALUE* is assigned "".

8 The *p* is a shortcut for a paragraph *<P>*.

9 The *popup_menu* method creates a menu. The required first argument is the menu's name (*-name*). The second argument, *-values*, is an array of menu items. It can be either anonymous or named.

10 The *submit* method creates the Submit button.

11 This line ends the form.

12 If the *param* method returns non-null, each of the values associated with the parameters will be printed.

13 The *param* method returns the value associated with *name*; in other words, what the user typed as input for that parameter.

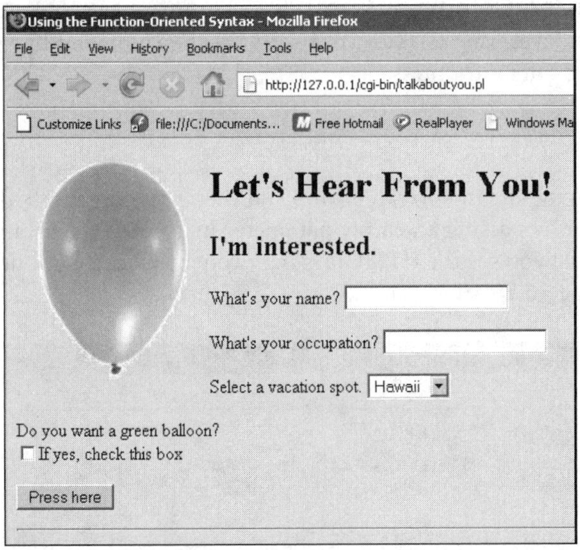

Figure 16.25 Output from lines 1–11 in Example 16.27 before filling out the form.

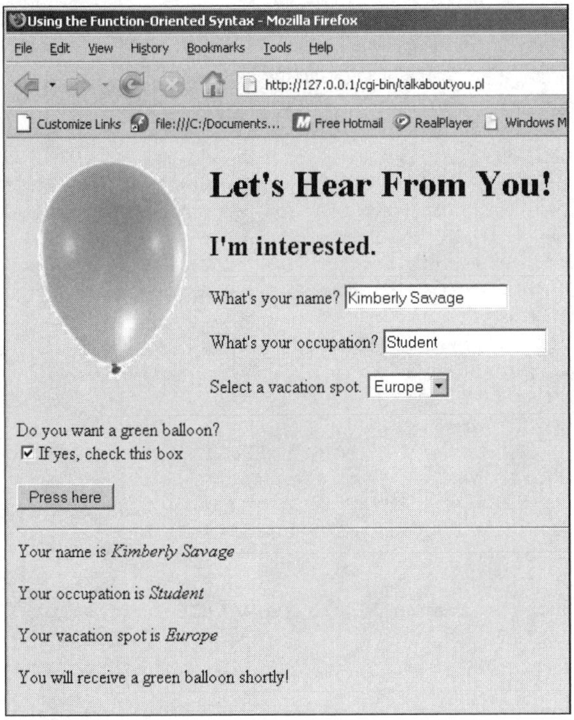

Figure 16.26 The completed form and result of *CGI.pm* processing.

Checking the Form at the Command Line. If you want to see the HTML tags generated by the *CGI.pm* form, you can run your script at the command line, but you will probably see the following error message:

```
(Offline mode: enter name=value pairs on standard input)
```

You can handle this by typing in key/value pairs and then pressing *<Ctrl>-d* (UNIX) or *<Ctrl>-z* (Windows) or by passing an empty parameter list. When the parameter list is empty, the output will let you see the HTML tags that were produced without any values assigned. See Example 16.28.

EXAMPLE 16.28

```
(At the Command Line)
1   $ perl talkaboutyou.pl
    (Offline mode: enter name=value pairs on standard input)
    name=Dan
    job=Father
    place=Hawaii
    <Now press Ctrl-d or Ctrl-z>

(Output)
    Content-Type: text/html

    <!DOCTYPE HTML PUBLIC "-//IETF//DTD HTML//EN">
    <HTML><HEAD><TITLE>Using the Function Oriented Syntax</TITLE>
    </HEAD><BODY BGCOLOR="yellow">
    <H1>Let's Hear From You!</H1>
    <H2>I'm internested.</H2>
    <FORM METHOD="POST"  ENCTYPE="application/x-www-form-urlencoded">
       What's your name? <INPUT TYPE="text" NAME="name"
       VALUE="Dan"><P>What's your occupation? <INPUT TYPE="text"
       NAME="job" VALUE="Father"><P>Select a vacation spot.
       <SELECT NAME="place">
    <OPTION SELECTED VALUE="Hawaii">Hawaii
    <OPTION  VALUE="Europe">Europe
    <OPTION  VALUE="Mexico">Mexico
    <OPTION  VALUE="Japan">Japan
    </SELECT>
    <P><INPUT TYPE="submit" NAME=".submit"></FORM>
       <HR>Your name is <EM>Dan</EM><P>Your occupation is <EM>Father
       </EM><P>Your vacation spot is <EM>Hawaii</EM><HR>

(At the Command Line)
2   $ perl talkaboutyou.pl < /dev/null  or perl talkaboutyou.pl ' '
    Content-Type: text/html
```

EXAMPLE 16.28 (CONTINUED)

```
(Output)
    <!DOCTYPE HTML PUBLIC "-//IETF//DTD HTML//EN">
    <HTML><HEAD><TITLE>Using the Function Oriented Syntax</TITLE>
    </HEAD><BODY BGCOLOR="yellow">
    <H1>Let's Hear From You!</H1>
    <H2>I'm interested.</H2><FORM METHOD="POST"
        ENCTYPE="application/x-wwwform-urlencoded">
        What's your name? <INPUT TYPE="text" NAME="name"
        VALUE=""><P>What's your occupation? <INPUT TYPE="text"
        NAME="job" VALUE=""><P>Select a vacation spot.
        <SELECT NAME="place">
    <OPTION  VALUE="Hawaii">Hawaii
    <OPTION  VALUE="Europe">Europe
    <OPTION  VALUE="Mexico">Mexico
    <OPTION  VALUE="Japan">Japan
    </SELECT>
    <P><INPUT TYPE="submit" NAME=".submit"></FORM><HR>Your name is
        <EM><P>Your occupation is <EM><P>Your vacation spot is <EM><HR>
```

EXPLANATION

1 When running in offline mode, you can enter the key/value pairs as standard input. You need to check the form so that you get the right keys and then supply the values yourself. In this example, *name=Dan, job=Father, place=Hawaii* were supplied by the user. After the user press *<Ctrl>-d* (UNIX) or *<Ctrl>-z* (Windows), the input will be processed by *CGI.pm*.

2 By passing an empty parameter list, you can see the HTML output as it appears without the values assigned. If using UNIX, */dev/null* is the UNIX bit bucket (black hole), and reading from that directory is the same as reading from an empty file. By supplying a set of empty quotes as an argument, the effect is the same.

16.7.7 *CGI.pm* Form Elements

Table 16.12 CGI Methods

Method	*Example*	*What It Does*
append	*$query–>append(-name=>'value');*	Appends values to parameter
checkbox	*$query–>checkbox(-name=>'checkbox_name', -checked=>'checked', -value=>'on', -label=>'clickme');*	Creates a standalone check box
checkbox_group	*$query–>checkbox_group(-name=> 'group_name', -values=>[list], -default=>[sublist], -linebreak=>'true', -labels=>\%hash);*	Creates a group of check boxes

Continues

Table 16.12 CGI Methods *(continued)*

Method	Example	What It Does
cookie	$query–>cookie(-name=>'sessionID', -value=>'whatever', -expires=>'+3h', -path=>'/', -domain=>'ucsc.edu', -secure=>1);	Creates a Netscape cookie
defaults	$query–>defaults;	Creates a button that resets the form to its defaults
delete	$query–>delete('param');	Deletes a parameter
delete_all	$query–>delete;	Deletes all parameters; clears *$query*, the object
endform	$query–>endform;	Ends the *<FORM>* tag
header	$query–>header(-cookie=>'cookiename');	Puts a cookie in the HTTP header
hidden	$query–>hidden(-name=>'hidden', -default=>[list]);	Creates a hidden-from-view text field
image_button	$query–>image_button(-name=>'button', -src=>'/source/URL', -align=>'MIDDLE');	Creates a clickable image button
import_names	$query–>import_names('namespace');	Imports variables into namespace
keywords	@keywords = $query–>keywords;	Obtains parsed keywords from the *Isindex* input string and returns an array
new	$query = new CGI;	Parses input and puts it in object *$query* for both the *GET* and *POST* methods
	$query = new CGI(INPUTFILE);	Reads contents of form from previously opened filehandle
param	@params = $query–>param(-name=>'name', -value=>'value');	Returns an array of parameter names passed into the script
	$value = $query–>('arg');	Returns a value (or list of values) for the *@values = $query–>('arg')* parameter passed
password_field	$query–>password_field(-name=>'secret' -value=>'start', -size=>60, -maxlength=>80);	Creates a password field
popup_menu	$query–>popup_menu(-name=>'menu' -values=>@items, -defaults=>'name', -labels=>\%hash);	Creates a pop-up menu
radio_group	$query–>radio_group(-name=>'group_name', -values=>[list], -default=>'name', -linebreak=>'true', -labels=>\%hash);	Creates a group of radio buttons
reset	$query–>reset;	Creates the Reset button to clear a form's boxes to former values
save	$query–>save(FILEHANDLE);	Saves the state of a form to a file

Table 16.12 CGI Methods *(continued)*

Method	Example	What It Does
scrolling_list	*$query–>scrolling_list(-name=>'listname', -values=>[list], -default=> [sublist], -multiple=>'true', -labels=>\%hash);*	Creates a scrolling list
startform	*$query–>startform(-method=> -action=>, -encoding);*	Returns a <FORM> tag with optional method, action, and encoding
submit	*$query–>submit(-name=>'button', -value=>'value');*	Creates the *Submit* button for forms
textarea		Same as text field but includes multiline text entry box
textfield	*$query–>textfield(-name=>'field', -default=>'start', -size=>50, -maxlength=>90);*	Creates a text field box

Table 16.13 CGI Parameter Methods

Method	What It Does	Example
delete(), Delete()	Deletes a named parameter from parameter list. Delete must be used if you are using the function-oriented style of *CGI.pm*.	*$obj–>delete('Joe');* *$obj–>delete(-name=>'Joe');* *Delete('Joe');* *Delete(-name=>'Joe');*
delete_all(), Delete_all()	Deletes all CGI parameters.	*$obj–>delete_all();* *Delete_all();*
import_names()	Imports all CGI parameters into a specified namespace.	
param()	Retrieves parameters from a fill-out form in key/value pairs. Can return a list or a scalar.	*print $obj–>param();* *@list=$obj–>param();* *print param('Joe');* *$name=$obj–>param(-name=>'Joe');*

16.7.8 Methods Defined for Generating Form Input Fields

The following examples use the object-oriented style and can easily be replaced with the function-oriented style by removing all object references. The *print_form* subroutine will cause the form to be displayed in the browser window, and the *do_work* subroutine will produce output when the *param* method returns a true value, meaning that the form was filled out and processed.

The *textfield()* Method. The *textfield* method creates a text field. The text field allows the user to type in a single line of text into a rectangular box. The box dimensions can be specified with the *-size* argument, where the size is the width in characters, and *-maxlength* (a positive integer) sets an upper limit on how many characters the user can enter. If *-maxlength* is not specified, the default is to enter as many characters as you like. With the *-value* argument, the field can be given a default value, text that will appear in the box when it is first displayed.

FORMAT

```
print $obj->textfield('name_of_textfield');
print $obj->textfield(
    -name=>'name_of_textfield',
    -value=>'default starting text',
    -size=>'60',           # Width in characters
    -maxlength=>'90');     # Upper width limit
```

EXAMPLE 16.29

```
#!/usr/bin/perl
1   use CGI;
2   $query = new CGI;
    # Create a CGI object
3   print $query->header;
4   print $query->start_html("Forms and Text Fields");
5   print  $query->h2("Example: The textfield method");

6   &print_form($query);
7   &do_work($query) if ($query->param);
    print $query->end_html;

8   sub print_form{
9       my($query) = @_;
10      print $query->startform;
        print "What is your name? ";
11      print $query->textfield('name'); # A simple text field
        print  $query->br();
12      print "What is your occupation? ";
13      print $query->textfield(-name=>'occupation',  # Giving values
                                -default=>'Retired',  # to the
                                -size=>60,            # text field
                                -maxlength=>120,
                               );
        print $query->br();
14      print $query->submit('action', 'Enter ');
15      print $query->reset();
16      print $query->endform;
        print $query->hr();
    }
```

EXAMPLE 16.29 (CONTINUED)

```
17  sub do_work{
        my ($query) = @_;
        my (@values, $key);
        print $query->("<H2>Here are the settings</H2>");
18      foreach $key ($query->param){
            print "$key: \n";
19          @values=$query->param($key);
            print join(", ",@values), "<BR>";
        }
    }
```

EXPLANATION

1 The *CGI.pm* module is loaded. It is an object-oriented module.
2 The CGI constructor method, called *new*, is called and a reference to a CGI object is returned.
3 The HTML header information is printed; for example, *Content-type: text/html*.
4 The *start_html* method produces the HTML tags to start HTML, the title *Forms and Textfields*, and the body tag.
5 The *h2* method produces an *<H2>*, heading level 2, tag.
6 This user-defined *print_form* function is called, with a reference to the CGI object passed as an argument.
7 The *do_work* function is called, with a reference to the CGI object passed as an argument. This is a user-defined function that will be called only if the *param* function returns true, and *param* returns true only if the form has been filled out.
8 The *print_form* function is defined.
9 The first argument is a reference to the CGI object.
10 The *startform* method produces the HTML *<FORM>* tag.
11 The *textfield* method produces a text box with one parameter, *name*. Whatever is assigned to the text box will be assigned to *name*.
12 The user is asked to provide input into the text box.
13 This *textfield* method is sent arguments as key/value hash pairs to further define the text field. The default will show in the box. See the output of this example in Figure 16.27.
14 The *submit* method creates a Submit button with the text *Enter* in the button.
15 The *reset* method creates a Reset button with the default text *Reset* in the button.
16 The *endform* method creates the HTML *</FORM>* tag.
17 This is the user's *do_work* function that is called after the user fills out the form and clicks the Submit (*Enter*) button. It processes the information supplied in the form with the *param* function.
18 The *param* function returns a key and a list of values associated with that key. The key is the name of the parameter for the input form, and the values are what were assigned to it either by the user or in the form. For example, the key named *occupation* was filled in by the user as *jack of all trades,* whereas the *action* key in the Submit button was assigned *Enter* within the form before it was processed.

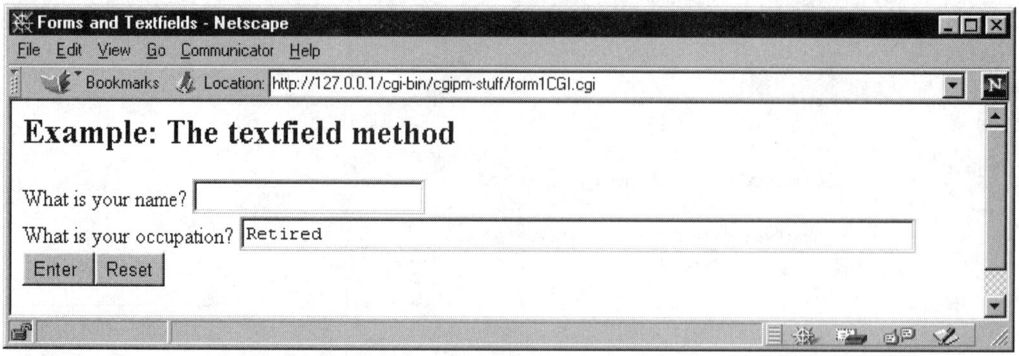

Figure 16.27 Output for text field form, Example 16.29.

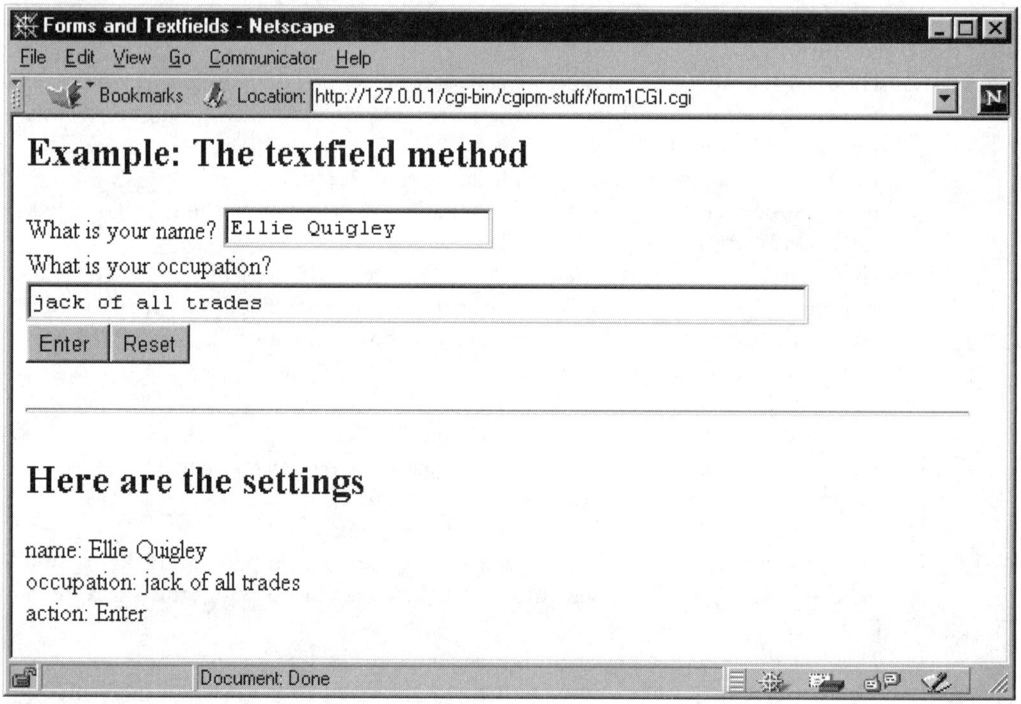

Figure 16.28 Output after the form was filled out and processed, Example 16.29.

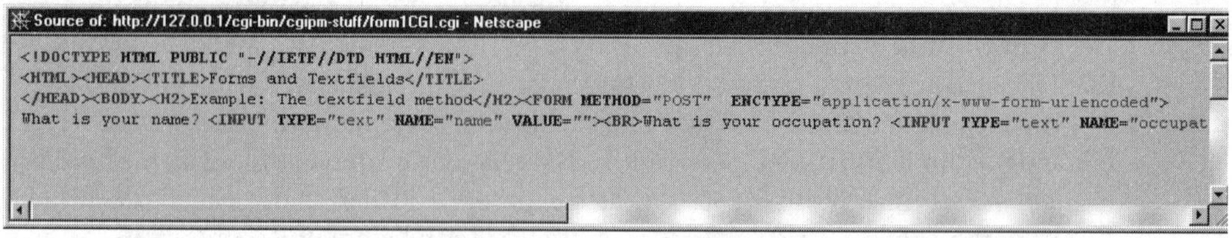

Figure 16.29 The HTML source that was produced by *CGI.pm*.

The *checkbox()* Method. The *checkbox()* method is used to create a simple check box for a *yes* or *no* (Boolean) response. The check box has *NAME* and *VALUE* attributes, where *-name* gives the CGI parameter a name, and *-value* contains one item or a reference to a list of items that can be selected. If the *-checked* is assigned *1*, the box will start as checked. If *-label is* assigned a value, it will be printed next to the check box; if not, the *-name* value of the check box will be printed. If not selected, the check box will contain an empty parameter.

The *checkbox_group()* method creates a set of check boxes all linked by a single name. The options are not mutually exclusive; that is, the user can check one or more items. If *-linebreak* is assigned a nonzero number, the options will be vertically aligned. Ordinarily, the options would be displayed in a horizontal row. (See Example 16.30.)

FORMAT

```
print $obj->checkbox(-name=>'name_of_checkbox',
                     -checked=>1,
                     -value=>'ON'
                     -label=>'Click on me'
                    );

%labels = ('choice1'=>'red',
           'choice2'=>'blue',
           'choice3'=>'yellow',
          );
print $obj->checkbox_group(-name=>'name_of_checkbox',
                           -values=>[ 'choice1', 'choice2',
                                      'choice3', 'green',...],
                           -default=>[ 'choice1', 'green' ],
                           -linebreak => 1,
                           -labels=>\%labels
                          );
```

EXAMPLE 16.30

```
#!/usr/bin/perl
use CGI;
$query = new CGI;
print $query->header;
print $query->start_html("The Object Oriented CGI and Forms");
print "<H2>Example using Forms with Checkboxes</H2>\n";

&print_formstuff($query);
&do_work($query) if ($query->param);
```

EXAMPLE 16.30 (CONTINUED)

```
    print $query->end_html;
    sub print_formstuff{
        my($query) = @_;
1       print $query->startform;

        print "What is your name? ";
        print $query->textfield('name');   # A simple text field
        print "<BR>";

        print "Are you married? <BR>";
2       print $query->checkbox(-name=>'Married',
                               -label=>'If not, click me' );
                               # Simple checkbox
        print "<BR><BR>";
        print "What age group(s) do you hang out with? <BR>";
3         print $query->checkbox_group(-name=>'age_group',
                                   -values=>[ '12-18', '19-38',
                                              '39-58','59-100' ],
                                   -default=>[ '19-38' ],
                                   -linebreak=>'true',
                                  );
4       print $query->submit('action', 'Select');
5       print $query->reset('Clear');
        print $query->endform;
        print "<HR>\n";
    }

6   sub do_work{
        my ($query) = @_;
        my (@values, $key);
        print "<H2>Here are the settings</H2>";
7       foreach $key ($query->param){
            print "$key: \n";
8           @values=$query->param($key);
            print join(", ",@values), "<BR>";
        }
    }
```

EXPLANATION

1. The *startform* method produces the HTML *<FORM>* tag.
2. This the simplest kind of check box. If the user is not married, he should click the box. The name of the check box is *Single*; the label *If not, click me* is displayed next to the check box. If *-checked* is assigned *1*, the box will be checked when it is first displayed.

EXPLANATION (CONTINUED)

3 This an example of a check box group where a set of related check boxes is linked by a common name, *age_group*. The *-values* argument is assigned a reference to a list of options that will appear to the right of each of the check boxes. If *-labels* were used, it would contain a hash consisting of key/value pairs that would be used as the labels on each of the check boxes. The *-default* argument determines which boxes will be checked when the check boxes are first displayed. The *-linebreak* argument is set to a nonzero value, true, which will cause the options to be displayed as a vertical list.

4 When the user clicks the Submit button, labeled *Select*, the form will be processed.

5 The Reset button clears the screen only if the user has not yet submitted the form. To override "stickiness," that is, to set the check boxes back to original default values, set the *-override* argument to a nonzero value.

6 The *do_work* function is called when the form is submitted. This is where all the reading and parsing of the form input is handled.

7 Each of the parameters that came in from the form (key/value pairs) is printed.

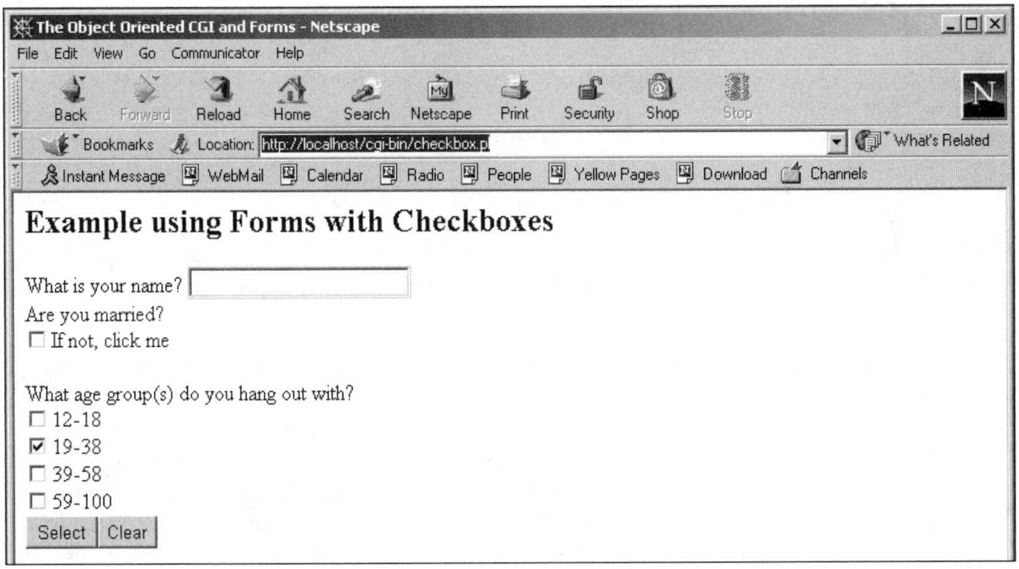

Figure 16.30 Output for check box form in Example 16.30.

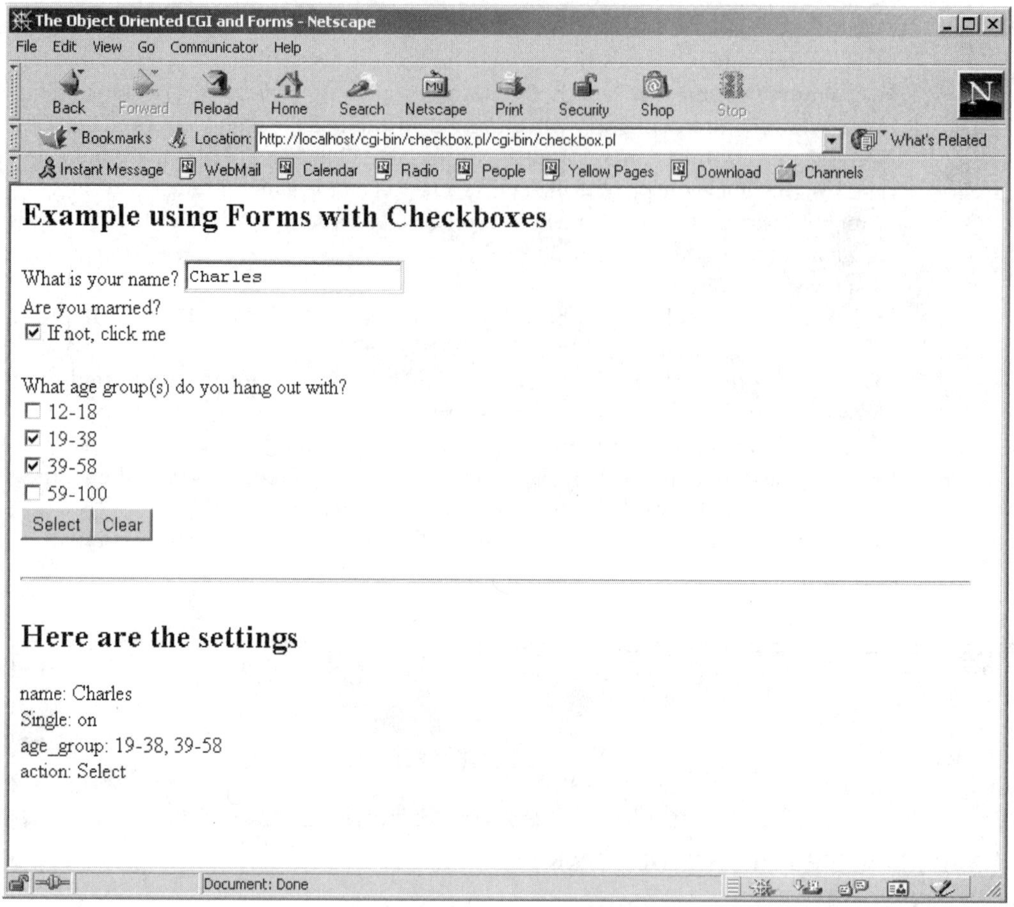

Figure 16.31 Output after the form was filled out and processed, Example 16.30.

The *radio_group()* and *popup_menu()* Methods. To select among a set of mutually exclusive choices, you can use radio buttons or pop-up menus. Radio button groups allow a small number of choices to be grouped together to fit in the form; for a large number of choices, the pop-up menu is better. They both have arguments consisting of name/value pairs. Since the *-value* argument consists of more than one selection, it takes a reference to an array. The *-default* argument is the value that is displayed when the menu first appears. The optional argument *-labels* is provided if you want to use different values for the user-visible label inside the radio group or pop-up menu and the value returned to your script. It's a pointer to an associative array relating menu values to corresponding user-visible labels. If a default isn't given, the first item is selected in the pop-up menu.

FORMAT

```
%labels = ('choice1'=>'red',
           'choice2'=>'blue',
           'choice3'=>'yellow',
          );
print $obj->radio_group(-name=>'name_of_radio_group',
                        -values=>['choice1','choice2',
                                  'choice3', 'green', ...],
                        -default=>[ 'choice1', 'green' ],
                        -linebreak => 1,
                        -labels=>\%labels
                       );

%labels = ('choice1'=>'red',
           'choice2'=>'blue',
           'choice3'=>'yellow',
          );
print $obj->popup_menu(-name=>'name_of_popup_menu',
                       -values=>['choice1','choice2','choice3',
                                 'green',...],
                       -default=>[ 'choice1', 'green' ],
                       -linebreak => 1,
                       -labels=>\%labels
                      );
```

EXAMPLE 16.31

```
    #!/bin/perl
1   use CGI;
    $query = new CGI;
    print $query->header;
    print $query->start_html("The Object-Oriented CGI and Forms");
    print "<H2>Example using Forms with Radio Buttons</H2>\n";
    &print_formstuff($query);
    &do_work($query) if ($query->param);
    print $query->end_html;

    sub print_formstuff{
    my($query) = @_;
    print $query->startform;
    print "What is your name? ";
    print $query->textfield('name');  # A simple text field
    print "<BR>";
    print "Select your favorite color? <BR>";
2   print $query->radio_group(-name=>'color',
                              -values=>[ 'red', 'green',
                                         'blue','yellow' ],
                              -default=>'green',
                              -linebreak=>'true',
                             );
```

EXAMPLE 16.31 (CONTINUED)

```
    print $query->submit('action', 'submit');
    print $query->reset('Clear');
    print $query->endform;
    print "<HR>\n";
    }
    sub do_work{
        my ($query) = @_;
        my (@values, $key);
        print "<H2>Here are the settings</H2>";
3       foreach $key ($query->param){
            print "$key: \n";
4           @values=$query->param($key);
            print join(", ",@values), "<BR>";
        }
    }
```

EXPLANATION

1. The *CGI.pm* module is loaded.
2. A radio group is created in the form by calling the CGI *radio_group* method with its arguments. The values of the individual radio buttons will be seen to the right of each button. The default button that will be checked when the form is first displayed is *green*. The *-linebreak* argument places the buttons in a vertical position rather than in a horizontal line across the screen. The user can select only **one** button.
3. After the user has filled out the form and clicked the Submit button, the *param* method will return the keys and values that were sent to the CGI script.
4. The key/value pairs are displayed.

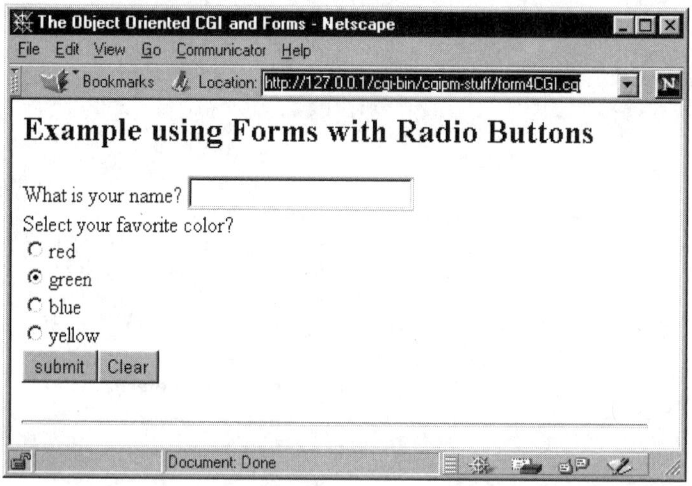

Figure 16.32 Output for radio button form, Example 16.31.

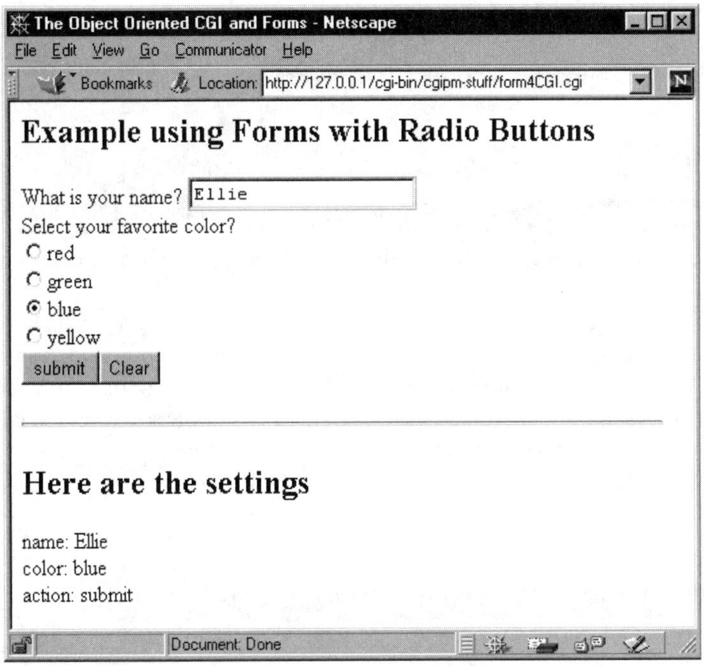

Figure 16.33 Output after form was filled out and processed, Example 16.31.

Labels. Labels allow the buttons to have user-friendly names that are associated with different corresponding values within the program. In the following example, the labels *stop*, *go*, and *warn* will appear beside radio buttons in the browser window. The values returned by the *param* method will be *red, green,* and *yellow,* respectively.

EXAMPLE 16.32

```
  ( The -labels Parameter -- Segment from CGI script)
    print $query->startform;
    print "What is your name? ";
    print $query->textfield('name');    # A simple text field
    print "<BR>";
    print "We're at a cross section. Pick your light.<BR>";
1   print $query->radio_group(-name=>'color',
2                             -values=>[ 'red', 'green', 'yellow' ],
                              -linebreak=>'true',
3                             -labels=>{red=>'stop',
                                        green=>'go',
                                        yellow=>'warn',
                                       },
4                             -default=>'green',
                             );
```

EXAMPLE 16.32 (CONTINUED)

```
print $query->submit('action', 'submit');
print $query->reset('Clear');
print $query->endform;
}
```

EXPLANATION

1 The *radio_group* method is called with its arguments. Only one value can be selected.
2 The values that the *params* function returns will be *red*, *green*, or *yellow*.
3 The labels are what actually appear next to each radio button. The user will see *stop*, *go*, and *warn* in the browser, but the CGI parameters associated with those labels are *red*, *green*, and *yellow*, respectively. If, for example, the user clicks on the *stop* button, the key/value pair passed to the script will be *color=>red*.
4 The default button is to have the button labeled *go* checked.

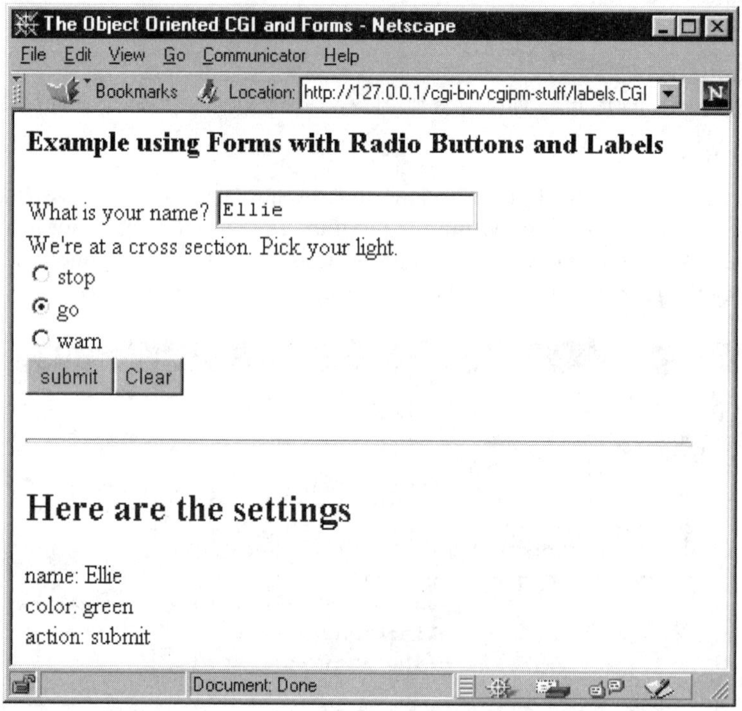

Figure 16.34 Output for labels form after being filled out and processed, Example 16.32.

The *popup_menu()* Method. The **pop-up menu** is also referred to as a **drop-down list**. It is a list of selections that will be displayed when the user clicks on the scrollbar icon to the right of the text. Only one selection can be made.

EXAMPLE 16.33

```
#!/usr/bin/perl
use CGI;
$query = new CGI;
print $query->header;
print $query->start_html("The Object-Oriented CGI and Forms");
print "<H2>Example using Forms with Pop-up Menus</H2>\n";
&print_formstuff($query);
&do_work($query) if ($query->param);
print $query->end_html;

sub print_formstuff{
my($query) = @_;
print $query->startform;
print "What is your name? ";
print $query->textfield('name');  # A simple text field
print "<BR>";
print "Select your favorite color? <BR>";
print $query->popup_menu(-name=>'color',
                         -values=>[ 'red', 'green', 'blue',
                                    'yellow' ],
                         -default=>'green',
                         -labels=>'\%labels',
                        );
print $query->submit('action', 'submit');
print $query->reset('Clear');
print $query->endform;
print "<HR>\n";
}

sub do_work{
   my ($query) = @_;
   my (@values, $key);
      print "<H2>Here are the settings</H2>";
      foreach $key ($query->param){
         print "$key: \n";
         @values=$query->param($key);
         print join(", ",@values), "<BR>";
   }
}
```

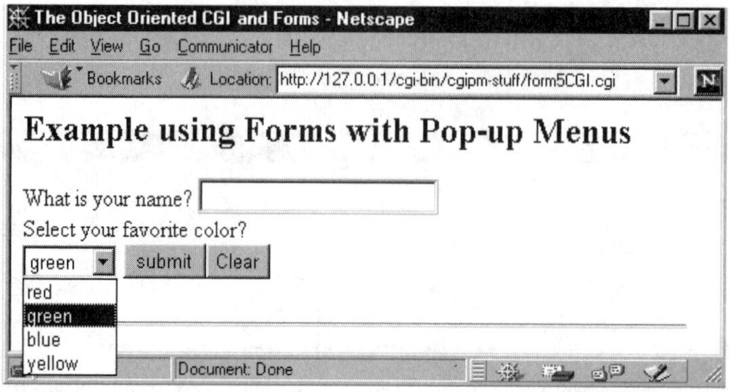

Figure 16.35 Output for pop-up menu form, Example 16.33.

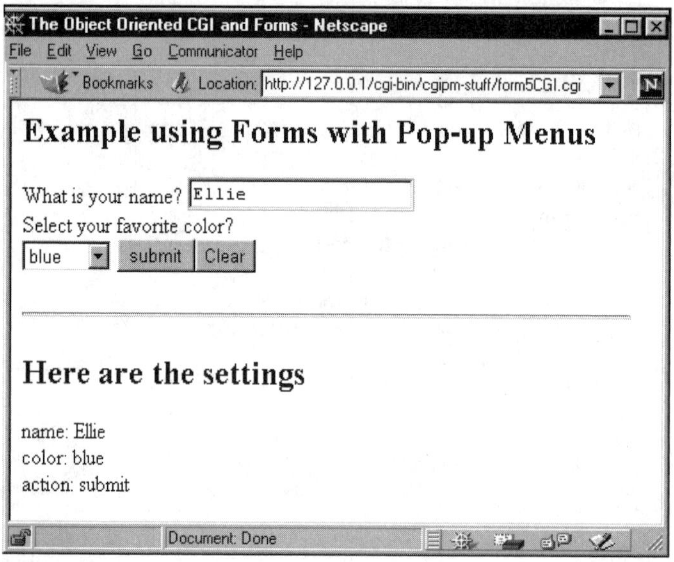

Figure 16.36 Output for pop-up menu form after being filled out and processed, Example 16.33.

The *submit()* and *reset()* Methods. The *submit()* method creates a button that, when clicked, sends form input to the CGI script. If given an argument, you can label the button, often for the purpose of distinguishing it from other buttons if several Submit buttons are used.

The *reset()* method is used to clear all the entries in a form. It restores the form to the state it was in when last loaded, not to its default state. (See "The *defaults* Method" in the following section.)

Clearing Fields

The *override* Argument

Note that if you click the Reset button or restart the same form, the previous information is sticky; in other words, the input box is not cleared. You can force the entry to be cleared by using the *-override* or *-force* argument with a nonzero value; for example:

```
textfield(-name=>'name', -override=>1);
```

The *defaults* Method

The *defaults()* method clears all entries in the form to the state of the form when it was first displayed in the browser window; that is, the parameter list is cleared. To create a user-readable button, call the *defaults* method; for example:

```
print defaults(-name=>'Clear All Entries');
```

16.7.9 Error Handling

When your *CGI.pm* script contains errors, the error messages are normally sent by the server to error log files configured under the server's root. If the program aborts, the browser will display "Document contains no data" or "Server Error." These messages are not very helpful.

The *carpout* and *fatalsToBrowser* Methods. *CGI.pm* provides methods not only to store errors in your own log file but also to see fatal error messages in the browser's window. The *carpout* function is provided for this purpose. Since it is not exported by default, you must import it explicitly by writing:

```
use CGI::Carp qw(carpout);
```

The *carpout* function requires one argument, a reference to a user-defined filehandle where errors will be sent. It should be called in a *BEGIN* block at the top of the CGI application so that compiler errors will be caught. To cause fatal errors from *die*, *croak*, and *confess* to also appear in the browser window, the *fatalsToBrowser* function must also be imported.

EXAMPLE 16.34

```
   #!/usr/bin/perl
1  use CGI;
2  BEGIN{ use CGI::Carp qw(fatalsToBrowser carpout);
3      open(LOG,">>errors.log") ||die "Couldn't open log file\n";
4      carpout(LOG);
   }
   $query = new CGI;
   <Program continues here>
```

EXPLANATION

1 The *CGI.pm* module is loaded.

2 The *CGI::Carp* module is also loaded. This *Carp* module takes two arguments: *fatalsToBrowser* and *carpout*. The first argument, *fatalsToBrowswer*, sends Perl errors to the browser, and *carpout* makes it all possible by redirecting the standard error from the screen to the browser and error log.

3 A file called *errors.log* is opened for creation/appending. This log file will contain the error messages that will also be seen in the browser.

4 The *carpout* function will send errors to the *errors.log* file. Here is a line from that file:

[Thu Feb 8 18:59:04 2001] C:\httpd\CGI-BIN\carpout.pl: Testing error messages from CGI script.

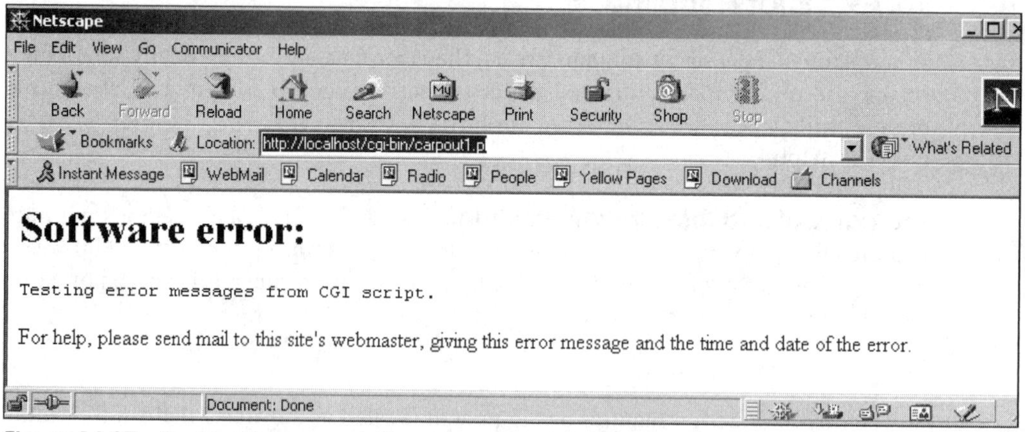

Figure 16.37 Redirecting errors with *carpout* and *fatalsToBrowser.*

Changing the Default Message. By default, the software error message is followed by a note to contact the Webmaster by e-mail with the time and date of the error. If you want to change the default message, you can use the *set_message* function, which must be imported into the program's namespace.

FORMAT

```
use CGI::Carp qw(fatalsToBrowser set_message);
set_message("Error message!");
set_message(\reference_to_subroutine);
```

EXAMPLE 16.35

```
1   #!c:/ActivePerl/bin/perl.exe

2   BEGIN{ use CGI::Carp qw(fatalsToBrowser carpout set_message);
3       open(LOG,">>errors.log") ||die "Couldn't open log file\n";
4       carpout(LOG);
5       sub handle_errors {
6           my $msg = shift;
7           print "<h1>Software Error Alert!!</h1>";
            print "<h2>Your program sent this error:<br><I>
                $msg</h2></I>";
        }

7       set_message(\&handle_errors);
    }
8   open(FH, "myfile" ) or
9   die("Can't open \"myfile\": $!\n");
```

EXPLANATION

1. The *shbang* line tells the server where your Perl interpreter is located.
2. The *CGI.pm* module is loaded within a BEGIN block to sure that any compiler errors are picked up immediately. See BEGIN. The *CGI::Carp* module is also loaded. The *Carp.pm* module imports three functions: *fatalsToBrowser*, *carpout*, and *set_message*. The first function, *fatalsToBrowser*, sends Perl errors to the browser and the server's error log. The *carpout* functon is used to redirect the standard error messages to your own error log. The *set_message* function is used to customize the default error message that will be sent to the browser. This function can take either a string to be printed or the address of a user-defined function.
3. A file called *errors.log* is opened for creation/appending. This log file will contain the error messages that will also be seen in the browser.
4. The *carpout* function will send errors to the *errors.log* file.
5. A user-defined subroutine called *handle_errors* is defined. It will produce a customized error message in the browser window. The first argument to the *handle_errors* function is the error message coming from a *die* or *croak*. In this example, the *die* message on line 9 will be be assigned to *$msg*, unless the *die* on line 3 happens first. This message will also be sent to the log file, *errors.log*.
6. The error message will be sent to the browser is shifted off the @_ array.
7. The *set_message* method is called with a reference to the user-defined subroutine *handle_errors*, which contains the customized error message.
8. The *die* function will cause the program to exit, sending its error message to the *handle_errors* subroutine via *set_message*.

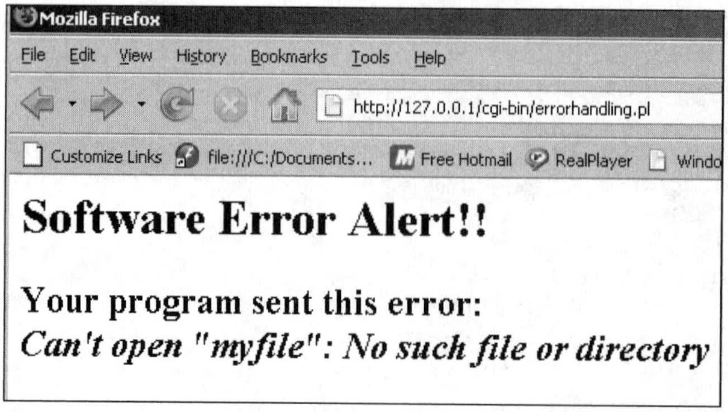

Figure 16.38 Output of error message from Example 16.35.

EXAMPLE 16.36

```
(The Apache log file)
[Thu May 24 14:12:00 2007] [error] [client 127.0.0.1] C:/wamp/A
pache2/cgi-bin/errorhandling.pl is not executable; ensure inter
preted scripts have "#!" first line
[Thu May 24 14:12:00 2007] [error] [client 127.0.0.1] (9)Bad fi
le descriptor: don't know how to spawn child process: C:/wamp/A
pache2/cgi-bin/errorhandling.pl
(The errors.log file created in the cgi-bin directory by the carpout
function)
[Thu May 24 14:21:16 2007] errorhandling.pl: Testing error mess
ages from CGI script.
[Thu May 24 14:22:16 2007] errorhandling.pl: Can't open myfile:
 No such file or directory
[Thu May 24 14:22:55 2007] errorhandling.pl: Can't open <em>myf
ile</em>: No such file or directory
[Thu May 24 14:23:12 2007] errorhandling.pl: Can't open "myfile
": No such file or directory
```

16.7.10 HTTP Header Methods

The cookie is assigned to an HTTP header as shown in the previous example. Table 16.14 lists other methods that can be used to create and retrieve information from HTTP headers.

Table 16.14 HTTP Header Methods

HTTP Header Method	***What It Does***
accept()	Lists MIME types or type
auth_type()	Returns authorization type for the current session
cookie()	Creates and retreives cookies
header()	Returns a valid HTTP header and MIME type
https()	Returns information about SSL for a session
path_info()	Sets and retrieves additional path information
path_translated()	Returns additional path information
query_string()	Returns the URL-encoded query string
raw_cookie()	Returns a list of unprocessed cookies sent from the browser
redirect()	Generates an HTTP header with a redirection request to the browser to load a page at that location
referer()	Returns the URL of the page the browser displayed before starting your script
remote_addr()	Returns the IP address of the remote host, possibly a proxy server
remote_host()	Returns the DNS name of the remote host
remote_ident()	Returns remote user's login name if the identity daemon is activiated
remote_user()	Returns the account name used to authenticate a password
request_method()	Returns the HTTP method *GET*, *POST*, or *HEAD*
script_name()	Returns the URL of this script relative to the server's root
self_url()	Returns the URL of the CGI script: protocol, host, port, path, additional path info, and parameter list; can be used to reinvoke the current script
server_name()	Returns the name of the Web server
server_port()	Returns the port number for the current session (usually 80)
server_software()	Returns the name and version of the Web server
url()	Returns the URL of the current script without additional path information and query string
user_agent()	Returns browser information
user_name()	Returns remote user's name if it can
virtual_host()	Returns the name of the virtual host being accessed by the browser

EXAMPLE 16.37

```
   #!/usr/bin/perl
   use CGI qw(:standard);
1  print header;
2  print start_html(-title=>'Using header Methods'),
   h1("Let's find out about this session!"),
   p,
3  h4 "Your server is called ", server_name(),
   p,
4  "Your server port number is ", server_port(),
   p,
5  "This script name is: ", script_name(),
   p,
6  "Your browser is ", user_agent(), "and it's out of date!",
   p,
7  "The query string looks like this: ", query_string(),
   p,
8  "Where am I? Your URL is: \n", url(),
   p,
9  "Cookies set: ", raw_cookie();

10 print end_html;
```

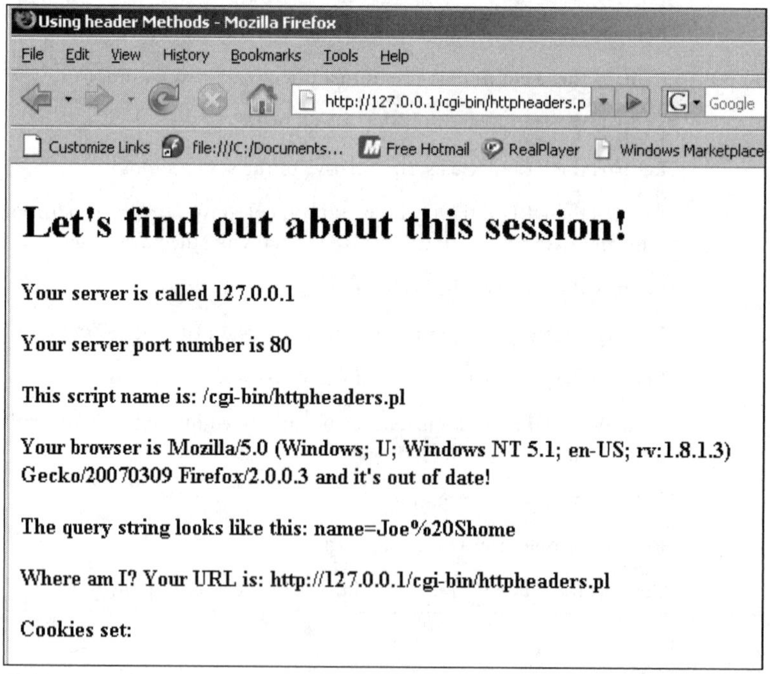

Figure 16.39 Output from Example 16.37.

EXERCISE 16
Surfing for Perls

Part 1.

1. **The Environment Variables and CGI**
   Create a CGI script that will print to the browser:
   The name of the server is: <Put the values here.>
   The gateway protocol is:
   The client machine's IP address:
   The client machine's name:
   The document root is:
   The CGI script name is:
   (Hint: Use the *%ENV* hash.)

2. **Creating a CGI Program**
   a. Write a CGI script called *town_crier* that will contain HTML text and Perl statements.
   b. The script will contain two subroutines: *&welcome* and *&countem*.
   c. The *welcome* subroutine will print *Welcome Sir Richard!!* Use a blue font that blinks the welcome. (Note: Internet Explorer ignores *blink*.) The subroutine will also print today's date. (Use the *ctime* library function.)
   d. The subroutine called *countem* will be written in a file called *countem.pl*. The *town_crier* script will call *countem*, passing its name (*town_crier*) as an argument to the subroutine. Remember, the name of the script is stored in the *$0* variable; e.g., *&countem ($0);*. The subroutine will return the number of times the page has been visited.
   e. See Figure 16.40 for an idea of how this script will display its output in the browser's window.
   f. The *countem* function should be designed to
      - Take an argument—the name of the file that called it. Unless there is a file called *town_crier.log* already in the directory, the file will be created. Either way, the file will be opened for reading and writing. (If the *countem* function were called from another Perl script, then the log file created would have the name of that script, followed by the *.log* extension.)
      - If the log file is empty, *countem* will write the value *1* into the file; otherwise, a line will be read from the file. The line will contain a number. The number will be read in and stored in a variable. Its value will be incremented by *1*. Each time *town_crier* is executed, this function is called.
      - The new number will sent back to the file, overwriting the number that was there.
      - The log file will be closed.
      - The *countem* subroutine will return the value of the number to the calling program. (In the example, I put the number in a cell of an HTML table and sent the whole string back to the *town_ crier.* Don't bother to try to create the table if you don't have time. Just send back the number.)

- If running on a UNIX system, use the *flock* function to put an exclusive lock on the log file while you are using it, and remove the lock when you are finished.

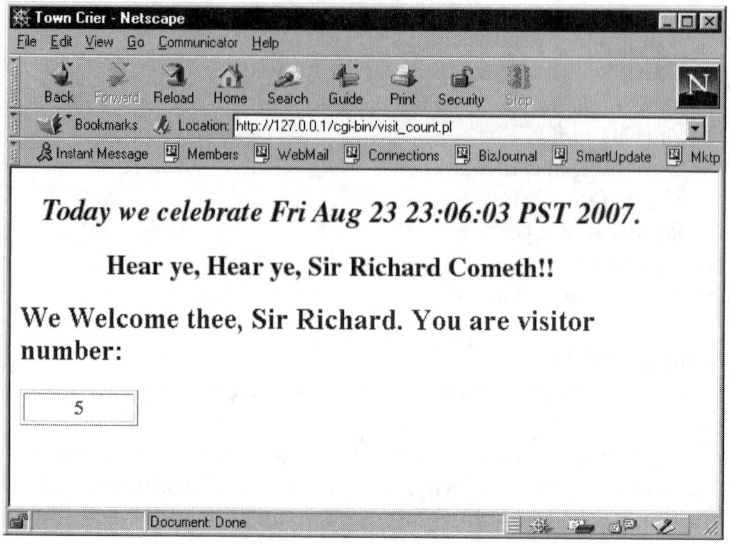

Figure 16.40 Output of the CGI program in Exercise 16.

Part 2.

1. **Creating Forms—HTML**
   a. Create a Web page called Stirbucks that contains a form to order coffee, similar to the order form in Figure 16.41.
   b. In the *action* attribute of the initial *<FORM>* tag, specify a URL that directs the server to a CGI script using the default *GET* method.
   c. Test your file in a browser.
   d. The CGI script will print the value of the *QUERY_STRING* environment variable.

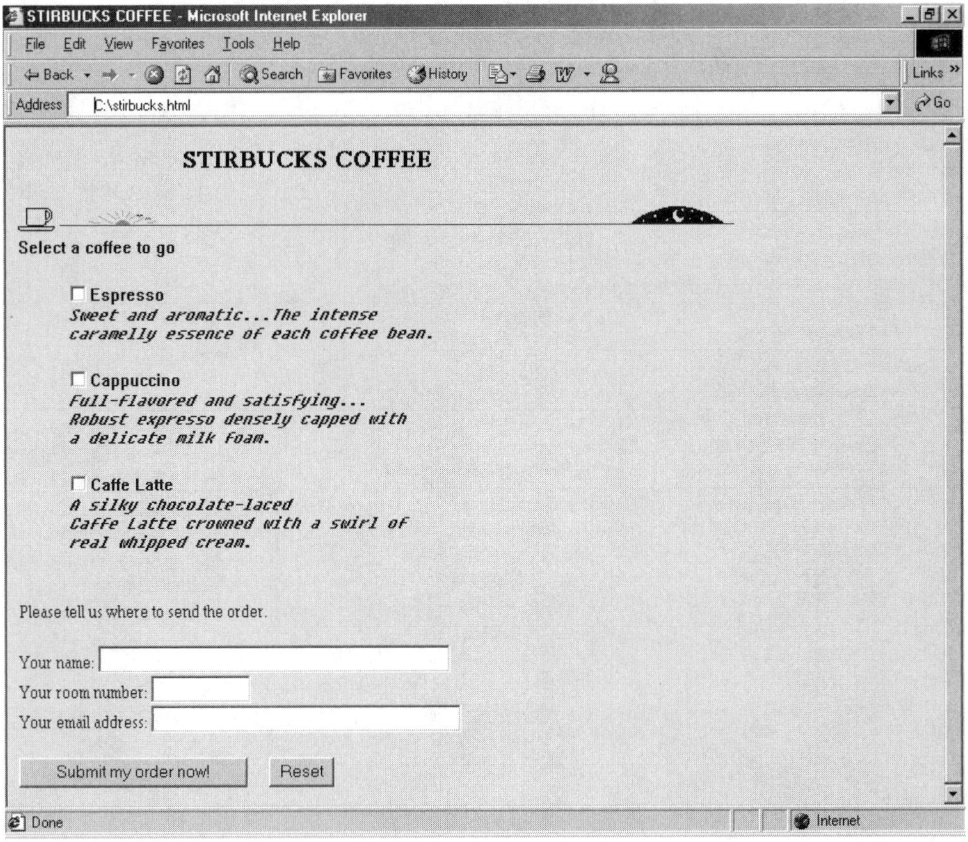

Figure 16.41 The Stirbucks Web page order form.

2. Processing Forms—CGI
   a. Write a CGI script that will send back to the user an HTML page that thanks him for his order and tells him the coffee he selected will be delivered to his shipping address. Use the *GET* method. After getting the information from the form, write your own fuction to parse the input.
   b. Redesign the form to include the *POST* method. The program will test which method was used and call the parse function.
   c. Create a DBM file that keeps a list of the e-mail addresses submitted. When a user submits an order, his e-mail address will be listed in the DBM file. Make sure there are no duplicates. Design a function to do this.
   d. The CGI script will handle e-mail. Send e-mail to yourself confirming the information that was submitted. Design another function to handle e-mail.

3. Rewrite the *Stirbucks* program so that the HTML form and the CGI script are in one CGI program created with the *CGI.pm* module. Use the function-oriented style.

chapter

17

Perl Meets MySQL—A Perfect Connection

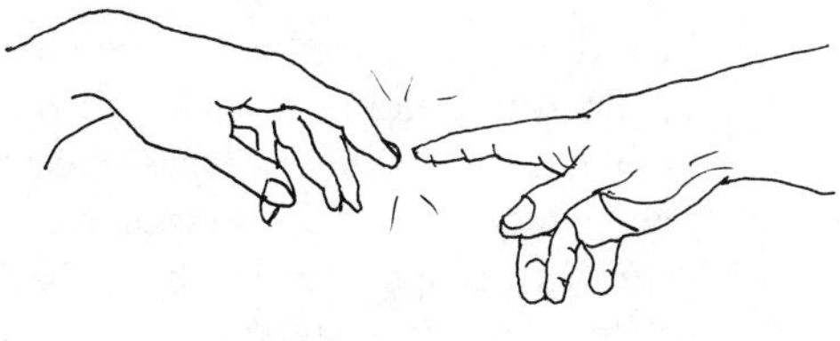

17.1 Introduction

The user has filled out a form and submitted it with a list of items he wants to purchase. Information for that user is stored in a database in a table called "customers." You want to open the database and add the new order directly from your Perl program. And you may want to retrieve all the previous orders and product information for that customer and format the data for a Web page, use it in an e-mail message, and send it to a spreadsheet, etc., also from a Perl program. This is all possible with Perl and the Perl DBI module, an object-oriented database interface that allows you to connect to any relational database and use Perl methods to perform all the necessary operations for opening and closing the database, for sending SQL queries to create tables, update and delete them, retrieve and modify records, manage transactions, and display results.

This chapter focuses on using Perl with the MySQL database, a very popular open source, fully functional, relational database. You will learn how to issue commands at the MySQL client and then use the DBI module to issue the same commands from a Perl script. Finally, we will tie all of this together by creating a dynamic Web page using both the DBI module and *CGI.pm*.

The subject of databases is huge. This chapter is not an attempt to teach you how to correctly design the structure of a database or the best practices for organizing the data. That would take another book or more, so if you are a complete novice, have never been exposed to databases and how they work, you might find *Databases Demystified* by Andy Oppel an excellent tutorial for getting started.[1] This chapter will cover the basic concepts and terminology you will need in order to work with the Perl DBI and MySQL.

1. Oppel, Andrew J. *Databases Demystified*. McGraw-Hill/Osbourne, Emeryville, CA, 2004.

17.2 What Is a Relational Database?

Until now, we have been storing data in ordinary text files with Perl by creating user-defined filehandles. We have also looked at Perl's DBM mechanism for storing data in binary files as simple hashes. But text files and DBM files are limited when you need to efficiently store and manage large amounts of data: for example, to maintain a business such as a hospital, research lab, bank, college, or Web site. A relational database system follows certain standards and has a number of features for storing large collections of data. The data is managed so that retrieving, updating, inserting, and deleting data is relatively easy and takes the least amount of time. The database management system must store the data so that it maintains its integrity; i.e., the data is accurate and is protected from being accessed by unauthorized users, the data is secure.

Introduced in the 1970s, the relational model made data manipulation easier and faster for the end users and easier to maintain by the administrator. At the core of this model is the concept of a relation, visually represented as a table in which all data is stored. The data is represented by different types, such as a string, number, date, etc. Each table is made up of records consisting of horizontal rows and vertical columns or fields, like a two-dimensional array. Tables in the database relate to each other; e.g., if you have a database called "school," it might consist of tables called "student," "teacher," "course," etc. The student takes a course from a teacher who teaches one or many courses. The data can be retrieved and manipulated for just the student, teacher, or course, but also joined together based on some common key field. The Structured Query Language (SQL) is used to "talk to" realtional databases, making it easy to retrieve, insert, update, and delete data from the tables in the database.

Due to the popularity of relational databases, known as relational database management systems (RDBMS), a number of relational databases are used today, among them Oracle, Sybase, PostgreSQL Informix, SQL server, and MySQL.

17.2.1 Client/Server Databases

Relational databases use a client/server model. Today, MySQL is one of the most popular client/server database systems in the open source community.

Figure 17.1 shows the model for a client/server architecture. The user goes to the command line and starts the MySQL client to issue MySQL commands. The client makes a request to the MySQL server, which in turn sends a query to the database. The database sends the results of the query back to the server, and the results are displayed in the client's window. In the second scenario, rather than using the command-line client, a Perl script makes a connection to the database server through a database interface that acts as an interpreter. If a Perl script contains an instruction to connect to a database, in this case MySQL, then once the connection is made and a database selected, the Perl program has access to the database through the MySQL server. The MySQL server receives requests, called queries, from the Perl program and sends back information collected from the database. In the third example, the user requests a page from the browser (the client); an HTTP connection is made to the Web server (Apache, ISS), where the request is received and handled. If the action is to start up a Perl program, the

Web server may use the Common Gateway Interface (CGI) to start up the Perl interpreter, and Perl starts processing the information that was sent from the HTTP server to format and send it back to the Web server, or if a request to the database server is made, then the steps to connect, query, and get results from the database are carried out. Figure 17.1 shows the client/server relationship between the MySQL client and the MySQL server, and the client/server realtionship between the Web browser, Web server Perl program, and the MySQL database server. By the end of this chapter, you will be able to get information sent from a Web browser (client) to a Web server and from the Web server to a Perl CGI program, which can connect to a database server to retrieve and store information from a MySQL database.

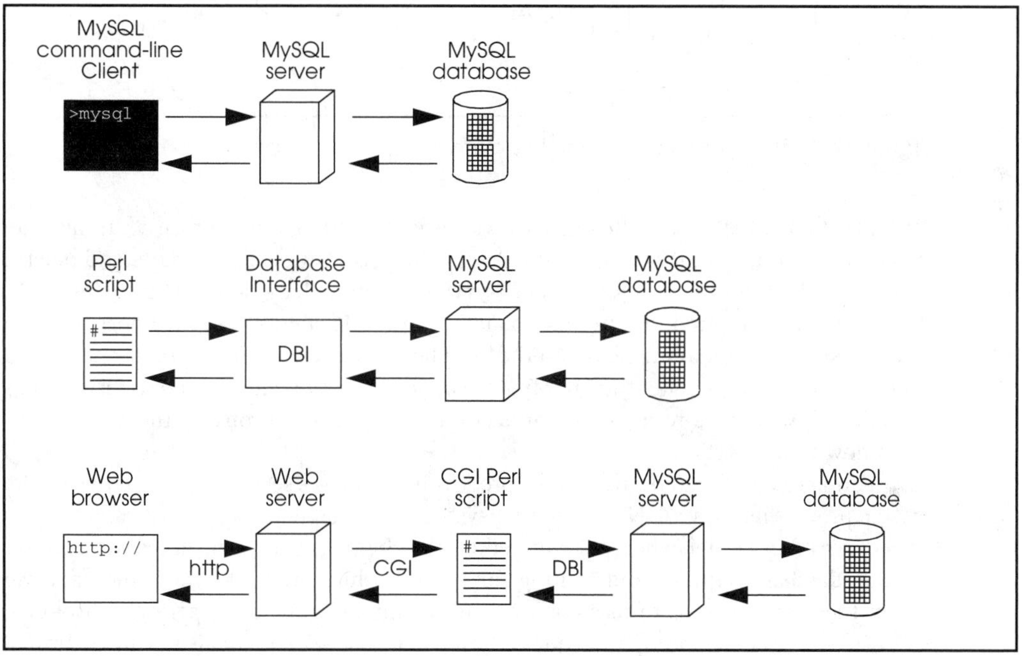

Figure 17.1 The client/server model.

17.2.2 Components of a Relational Database

What makes up a database? The main components of a relational database management system are:

- Database server
- Database
- Tables
- Fields
- Records
- Primary key
- Schema

We will discuss each of these concepts in the next sections of this chapter. Figure 17.2 illustrates their relationship to each other.

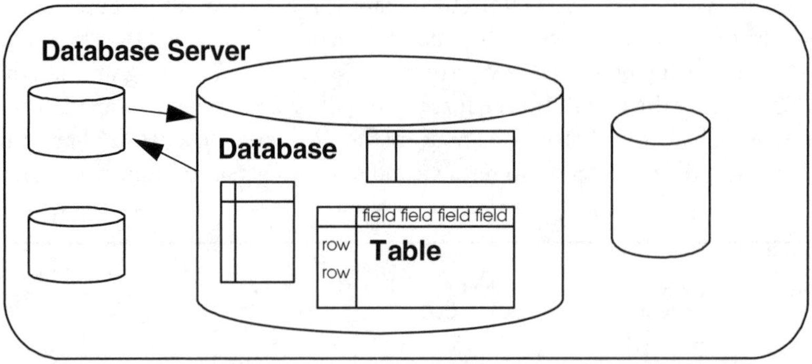

Figure 17.2 The database server, the database, and a table.

The Database Server. The database server is the actual server process running the databases. It controls the storage of the data, grants access to users, updates and deletes records, and communicates with other servers. The database server is normally on a dedicated host computer, serving and managing multiple clients over a network, but can also be used as a standalone server on the local host machine to serve a single client; e.g., you may be the single client using MySQL on your local machine, often referred to as "localhost," without any network connection at all. This is probably the best way to learn how to use MySQL.

If you are using MySQL, the server process is the *mysql* service on Windows or the *mysqld* process on Linux/UNIX operating systems. The database server typically follows the client/server model, where the front end is the client, a user sitting at his workstation making database requests and waiting for results, while the back end is the database server that grants access to users, stores and manipulates the data, performs backups, even talks to other servers. The requests to the database server can also be made from a program that acts on behalf of a user making requests from a Web page or a program. In the following chapters, you will learn how to make requests from the *MySQL* command line first and then to connect to the database server from a Perl program using Perl built-in functions to make requests to the MySQL database server, and finally how to make a request from a Web form and send the request to a Perl program and then onto MySQL.

The Database. A database is a collection of related data elements, usually corresponding to a specific application. A company may have one database for all its HR needs, perhaps another for its sales staff, and a third for e-commerce applications, etc. Figure 17.3 lists the databases installed on a particular version of MySQL. The databases are listed as "mysql", "northwind", "phpmyadmin", and "test".

```
+-------------+
| Database    |
+-------------+
| mysql       |
| northwind   |
| phpmyadmin  |
| test        |
+-------------+
```

Figure 17.3 MySQL databases.

Tables. Each database consists of two-dimensional tables identified by unique names. In fact, a relational database stores all of its data in tables, and nothing more. All operations are performed on the table, which can then produce other tables, etc.

One of the first decisions you will make when designing a database is what tables it will contain. A typical database for an organization might consist of tables for customers, orders, and products. All these tables are related to one another in some way. For example, customers have orders and orders have items. Although each table exists on its own, collectively the tables comprise a database. Figure 17.4 lists the tables in a database called "northwind",[2] a fictional database provided by Microsoft to serve as a model for learning how to manipulate a database. (This should be on the CD provided with this book.)

```
+----------------------+
| Tables_in_northwind  |
+----------------------+
| categories           |
| customercustomerdemo |
| customerdemographics |
| customers            |
| employees            |
| employeeterritories  |
| order_details        |
| orders               |
| products             |
| region               |
| shippers             |
| suppliers            |
| territories          |
| usstates             |
+----------------------+
```

Figure 17.4 Tables in the northwind database.

Records and Fields. A table has a name and consists of a set of rows and columns. It resembles a spreadsheet where each row, also called a record, is comprised of vertical columns, also called fields. All rows from the same table have the same set of columns. The "shippers" table from the "northwind" database has three columns and three rows.

2. The Northwind Traders sample database typically comes as a free sample with Microsoft Access but is available for MySQL at *http://www.flash-remoting.com/examples/*.

```
+-----------+------------------+----------------+
| ShipperID | CompanyName      | Phone          |
+-----------+------------------+----------------+
|         1 | Speedy Express   | (503) 555-9831 |
|         2 | United Package   | (503) 555-3199 |
|         3 | Federal Shipping | (503) 555-9931 |
+-----------+------------------+----------------+
```

Figure 17.5 The rows (records) and columns (fields) from the "shippers" table in the "northwind" database.

There are two basic operations you can perform on a relational table. You can retrieve a subset of its columns and you can retrieve a subset of its rows. Figures 17.6 and 17.7 are samples of the two operations.

```
mysql> select companyname from shippers;
+------------------+
| companyname      |
+------------------+
| Speedy Express   |
| United Package   |
| Federal Shipping |
+------------------+
```

Figure 17.6 Retrieving a subset of columns.

```
mysql> select * from shippers where companyname="Federal Shipping";
+-----------+------------------+----------------+
| ShipperID | CompanyName      | Phone          |
+-----------+------------------+----------------+
|         3 | Federal Shipping | (503) 555-9931 |
+-----------+------------------+----------------+
```

Figure 17.7 Retrieving a subset of rows.

Remember: a relational database manipulates only tables, and the results of all operations are also tables, called result sets. The tables are sets, which are themselves sets of rows and columns. The database itself is a set of tables.

You can also perform a number of other operations between two tables, treating them as sets: you can join information from two tables, make cartesian products of the tables, get the intersection between two tables, add one table to another, and so on. Later we'll show you how to perform operations on tables using the SQL language.

Columns/Fields

Columns are an integral part of a database table. Columns are also known as fields, or attributes. Fields describe the data. Each field has a name. For example, the "shippers" table has fields named "ShipperID", "CompanyName" and "Phone". The field also describes the type of data it contains. A data type can be a number, a character, a date, a time stamp, etc. In Figure 17.8 the ShipperID is the name of a field, the data type is an integer, and the shipper's ID will not exceed 11 numbers. There are many data types and sometimes they are specific to a particular database system; e.g., MySQL may have different data types available than Oracle. We will learn more about the MySQL data types in the next chapter.

Field	Type	Null	Key	Default	Extra
ShipperID	int(11)		PRI	NULL	auto_increment
CompanyName	varchar(40)				
Phone	varchar(24)	YES		NULL	

Figure 17.8 Each field has a name and a description of the data that can be stored there.

Rows/Records

A record is a row in the table. It could be a product in the product table, an employee record in the employee table, and so on. Each table is a database contains zero or more records. Figure 17.9 shows us that there are three records in the "shippers" table.

ShipperID	CompanyName	Phone
1	Speedy Express	(503) 555-9831
2	United Package	(503) 555-3199
3	Federal Shipping	(503) 555-9931

3 rows in set (0.00 sec)

Figure 17.9 There are three records in the "shippers" table.

Primary Key and Indexes

A primary key is a unique identifier for each record. For example, every employee in the United States has a Social Security Number, every driver has a driver's license, and every car has a license plate. These identifiers are unique. In the database world, the unique identifier is called a primary key. Although it is a good idea to have a primary key, not every table has one. The primary key is determined when the table is created and is more in keeping with a discussion on database design. In Figure 17.10 the "ShipperID" is the primary key for the "shippers" table in the "northwind" database. It is a unique ID that consists of a number that will automatically be incremented every time a new company (record) is added to the list of shippers.

Field	Type	Null	Key	Default	Extra
ShipperID	int(11)		PRI	NULL	auto_increment
CompanyName	varchar(40)				
Phone	varchar(24)	YES		NULL	

Figure 17.10 The "ShipperID" is the primary key in the "shippers" table.

When searching for a particular record in a table, MySQL must load all the records before it can execute the query. In addition to a primary key, one or more indexes are often used to enhance performance for finding rows in tables that are frequently accessed. Indexes are like the indexes in the back of a book that help you find a specific topic more quickly than searching through the entire book. An index, like the index of a book, is a reference to a particular record in a table.

The Database Schema. Designing a very small database isn't difficult, but designing a database for a large Web-based application can be daunting. Database design is both an art and a science and requires an understanding of how the relational model is implemented, a topic beyond the scope of this book. When discussing the design of the database, you will encounter the term "database schema," which refers to the structure of the database. It describes the design of the database similar to a template, or blueprint; it describes all the tables and how the data will be organized but does not contain the actual data. Figure 17.11 describes the schema for the tables in the "northwind" database.

Figure 17.11 Database schema.

17.2.3 Talking to the Database with SQL (the Structured Query Language)

When Perl output is sent to the browser, the browser understands markup languages, such as HTML or XHTML, and these language tags are embedded in Perl's *print* statements, output that could be displayed as forms, images, stylized text, colors, tables, etc. Likewise, in order to communicate with the MySQL server, your Perl scripts must speak a language the database will understand. That language is called SQL. SQL stands for Structured Query Language, the language of choice for most modern multiuser relational databases. It provides the syntax and language constructs needed to talk to relational databases in a standardized, cross-platform/structured way. Like the English language with a variety of dialects (British, American, Australian, etc.), there are many different versions of the SQL language. The version of SQL used by MySQL follows the ANSI (American National Standards Institute) standard, meaning that it must support the major keywords (such as SELECT, UPDATE, DELETE, INSERT, WHERE, etc.) as defined in the standard. As you can see by the names of these keywords, SQL is the language that makes it possible to manipulate the data in a database.

If you are not familiar with SQL, refer to Appendix B for a complete guide on how to use the SQL language. There are also a number of very well-written tutorials available on the Web, such as *http://www.w3schools.com/sql/default.asp*, *http://sqlcourse.com/select.html*, *http://www.1keydata.com/sql/sql.html*

English-like Grammar. When you create a SQL statement, it makes a request, or "queries" the database, in the form of a statement, similar to the structure of an English imperative sentence, such as "Select your partner," "Show your stuff," "Describe that bully." The first word in a SQL statement is an English verb, an action word called a command, such as **show**, **use**, **select**, **drop**, etc. The commands are followed by a list of noun-like words, such as *show databases*, *use datatabase*, or *create databases*. The statement may contain prepositions, such as "in" or "from"; e.g., show tables **in database** or select phones **from customer_table**. The language also lets you add conditional clauses to refine your query, such as select companyname from suppliers **where supplierid > 20**; .

When listing multiple items in a query, like English, the items are separated by commas; e.g., in the following SQL statement, each field in the list being selected is comma-separated: select **companyname**, **phone**, **address** from suppliers; .

If the queries get very long and involved, you might want to type them into your favorite editor, because once you have executed a query, it is lost. By saving the query in an editor, you can cut and paste it back into the MySQL browser or command line without retyping it. But most importantly, make sure your query makes sense and will not cause havoc on an important database. MySQL provides a "test" database for practice.

Semicolons Terminate SQL Statements. The semicolon is the standard way to terminate each query statement. Some database systems don't require the semicolon, but MySQL does (exceptions are the *USE* and *QUIT* commands), and if you forget it, you will see a secondary prompt, and execution will go on hold until you add the semicolon.

Naming Conventions. A database and its tables are easier to read when good naming conventions are used.

For example, it makes good sense to make table names plural and field/column names singular. Why? Because a table called Shippers normally holds more than one shipper, but the name of the field used to describe each shipper is a single value, such as his company_name, phone, etc. The first letter in a table or field name is usually capitalized.

Compound names, such as "company_name," are usually separated by the underscore, with the first letter of each word capitalized, "Company_Name".

Spaces and dashes are not allowed in any name in the database.

Reserved Words. All languages have a list of reserved words that have special meaning to the language. Most of these words will be used in this chapter. The SQL reserved words are listed in Table 17.1. (See MySQL documentation for a complete list of all reserved words.)

Table 17.1 SQL Reserved Words

CREATE	ALTER
INSERT	SELECT
FROM	ON
ORDER BY	JOIN
CROSS JOIN	RIGHT JOIN
DROP	DELETE
UPDATE	SET
INTO	WHERE
GROUP BY	LEFT JOIN
FULL JOIN	AND
LIMIT	LIKE
OR	AS

Case Sensitivity. Database and table names are case sensitive if you are using UNIX and not if you are using Windows. A convention is to always use lowercase names for databases and their tables.

SQL commands are not case sensitive. For example, the following SQL statements are equally valid:

```
show databases;
SHOW DATABASES;
```

Although SQL commands are not case sensitive, by convention, SQL keywords are capitalized for clarity, whereas only the first letter of the field, table, and database names is capitalized.

```
SELECT * FROM Persons WHERE FirstName='John'
```

For performing pattern matching with the *LIKE* and *NOT LIKE* commands, then the pattern being searched for is case sensitive when using MySQL.

The Result Set. A result set is just another table created to hold the results from a SQL query. Most database software systems even allow you to perform operations on the result set with functions, such as: *Move-To-First-Record*, *Get-Record-Content*, *Move-To-Next-Record*, etc. In the following example, the result set is the table created by asking MySQL to show all the fields in the table called "shippers".

```
mysql> show fields in shippers;
+-------------+-------------+------+-----+---------+----------------+
| Field       | Type        | Null | Key | Default | Extra          |
+-------------+-------------+------+-----+---------+----------------+
| ShipperID   | int(11)     |      | PRI | NULL    | auto_increment |
| CompanyName | varchar(40) |      |     |         |                |
| Phone       | varchar(24) | YES  |     | NULL    |                |
+-------------+-------------+------+-----+---------+----------------+
3 rows in set (0.00 sec)
```

Figure 17.12 The result set is just a table produced from a query.

17.3 Getting Started with MySQL

17.3.1 Why MySQL?

MySQL is an open source,[3] full-featured relational database management system and has been ported to most platforms, including Linux, Windows, OS/X, HP-UX, AIX, etc. MySQL is portable (runs on Linux, Windows, OS/X, HP-UX, etc.), fast, reliable, scalable,and easy to use.

It claims to be installed in more than 10 million computers all over the world, including Antarctica! There are two versions, one where you buy a commercial license and one that is free, free meaning you can use MySQL in any application as long as you don't copy, modify, or distribute the MySQL software. MySQL supports a number of APIs (application programming interfaces), including Perl, PHP, TCL, Python, C/C++, Java, etc.

When working with MySQL, a number of like-name terms are used. Table 17.2 is provided to help clarify the use of these terms.

Table 17.2 The Terms in MySQL, etc.

mySQL	The actual software for the database management system
mysqld	The MySQL daemon, or server process
mysql monitor	The monitor where MySQL commands are issued (command-line interpreter)
mysql	The name of the database MySQL uses to manage access privileges
mysqladmin	A MySQL utility program for administering the database

17.3.2 Installing MySQL

Here we assume you have installed a database server and it is running. Downloading and installing MySQL is usually a straightforward process. You can get MySQL from the mysql.com Web site or use integrated applications, such as XAMPP or WAMP.

3. MySQL is free use for those who are 100% GPL. See *http://www.mysql.com/company/legal/licensing/opensource-license.html* for details.

XAMPP (for Windows, Linux, Mac OS, and Solaris) is a free, easy-to-install Apache distribution containing MySQL, PHP, and Perl. All you have to do is download, extract, and start it up. For details, go to *http://www.apachefriends.org/en/xampp.html*.

For complete installation instructions, go to this Web page.

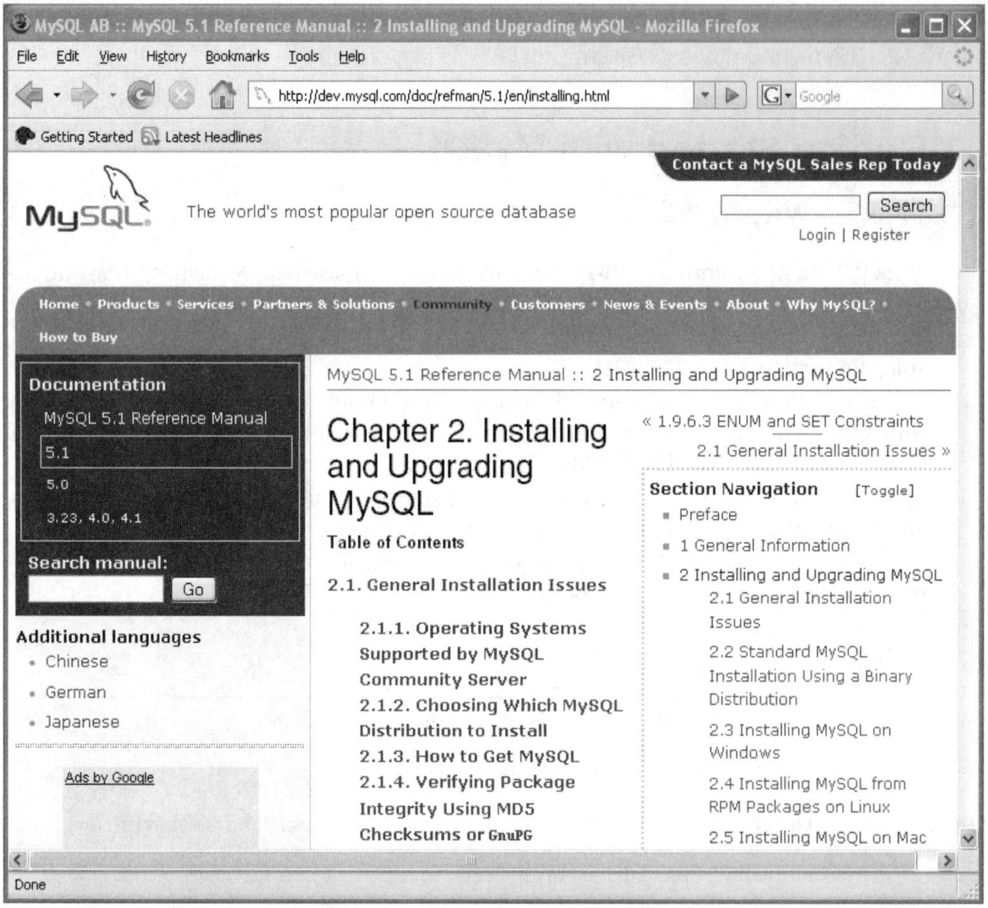

Figure 17.13 The MySQL installation documentation.

17.3.3 Connecting to MySQL

The MySQL database system uses the client/server model described in Section 17.2.1. You are the client connecting to the database from the command line, a graphical user interface, or from a program. Before connecting to the database from a Perl program, we will first use the the MySQL command-line client.

The MySQL command-line client comes with the MySQL installation and is universally available. It is a *mysql.exe* program located in the **bin** folder of your MySQL installation.

To run this command-line application, you must start the command-line prompt. On Windows, go to the *Start* menu, choose the *Run...* option, and then type *cmd* in the "run" window. On Mac OS X, go to the *Applications* folder in your *Finder* and then navigate to *Utilities*. You will find the *Terminal* application there. You should navigate to the location where you installed MySQL and find the *bin* folder. With UNIX, type commands at the shell prompt in a terminal window.

The MySQL client executable is normally located in the *bin* folder.

To connect to a database using this client, you will enter information similar to the following line:

```
mysql --user=root --password=my_password --host=localhost
```

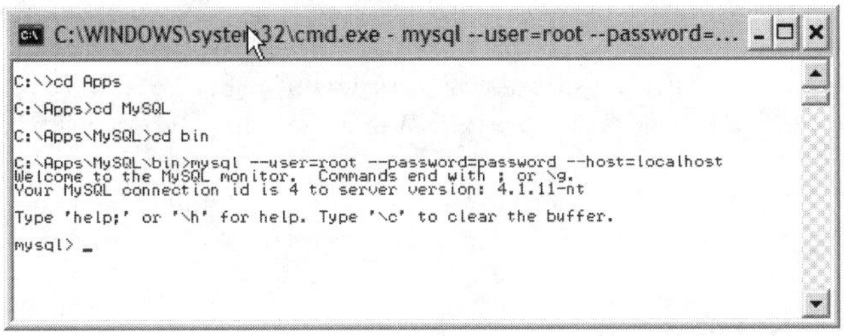

Figure 17.14 The MySQL client.

Regardless of the type of client you choose, you may be required to specify the user name and the host machine to which you are connecting. Most configurations expect you to have a password, although if just working by yourself, it is not required. You have the option to specify the default database as well.

Once you are successfully connected, you will get the **mysql>** prompt instead of your standard DOS/UNIX prompt. This means you are now sending commands to the MySQL database server and not to your local computer's operating system.

Editing Keys at the MySQL Console. MySQL supports input-line editing. The up-arrow and down-arrow keys allow you to move up and down through previous input lines, and the left-arrow and right-arrow keys to move back and forth within a line. The backspace and Delete keys are used to erase characters from the line and type in new characters at the cursor position. To submit an edited line, press Enter. For UNIX users, MySQL also supports tab completion, allowing you to enter part of a keyword or identifier and complete it using the Tab key.

Setting a Password. When you download MySQL, on some installations, you may be asked to enter a password for user "root." Even if you are not forced to create a password, it is a good idea to set one to protect the security of your database. To set a password, go to the MySQL console and type the following MySQL command. Replace 'MyNewPassword' with your password.

```
SET PASSWORD FOR 'root'@'localhost' = PASSWORD('MyNewPassword');
```

After setting the password, you can stop the MySQL server and then restart it in normal mode again. If you run the server as a service, start it from the Windows Services window. If you start the server manually, use whatever command you normally use. You should be able to connect using the new password.

Setting the Password at the MySQL Prompt

EXAMPLE 17.1

```
1 $ mysql -u root
ERROR 1045 (28000): Access denied for user 'root'@'localhost' (using
password: NO)
$
$ mysql -u root -p
Enter password: ********
Welcome to the MySQL monitor.  Commands end with ; or \g.
Your MySQL connection id is 91 to server version: 5.0.21-community-nt

Type 'help;' or '\h' for help. Type '\c' to clear the buffer.
```

17.3.4 Graphical User Tools

The MySQL Query Browser. The MySQL Query Browser is a graphical user interface (GUI) client available from mysql.com used to connect to the MySQL database server. Once you download it and follow the simple installation wizard, you can start the application from the *Start* menu under Windows.

The MySQL Query Browser then displays a connection dialog box. You must specify the MySQL server where you want to connect, the credentials needed for authorization on that server, which machine that server runs on (and which port it listens to), and the default database (called the "Schema") you will be using. There are also a number of additional options you can specify if necessary.

You must choose a default database in order to issue queries. Although it is possible to choose a default database after connecting to the server, setting the default from the connection dialog can save time on subsequent connections.

The information to enter is very similar to the command-line client: user name, password, and the server host where the database server is running. You can optionally enter the database name and port number (3306 is the default for MySQL) and save the connection information as a bookmark under the Stored Connection section.

By using the familiar tree-like navigation structure on the right-hand side of the application window, you can also navigate the various databases in the MySQL Query Browser.

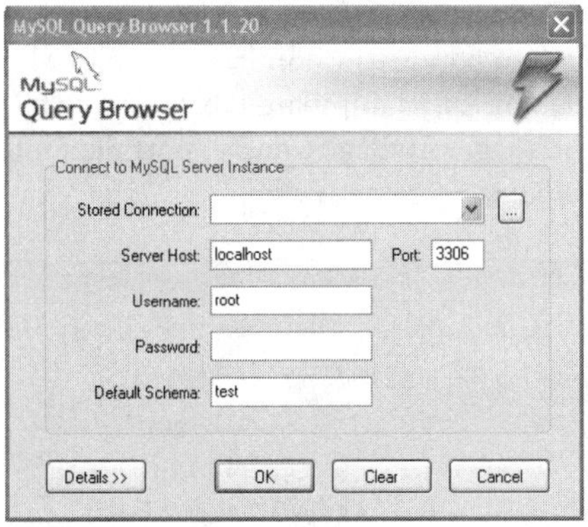

Figure 17.15 The MySQL Query Browser.

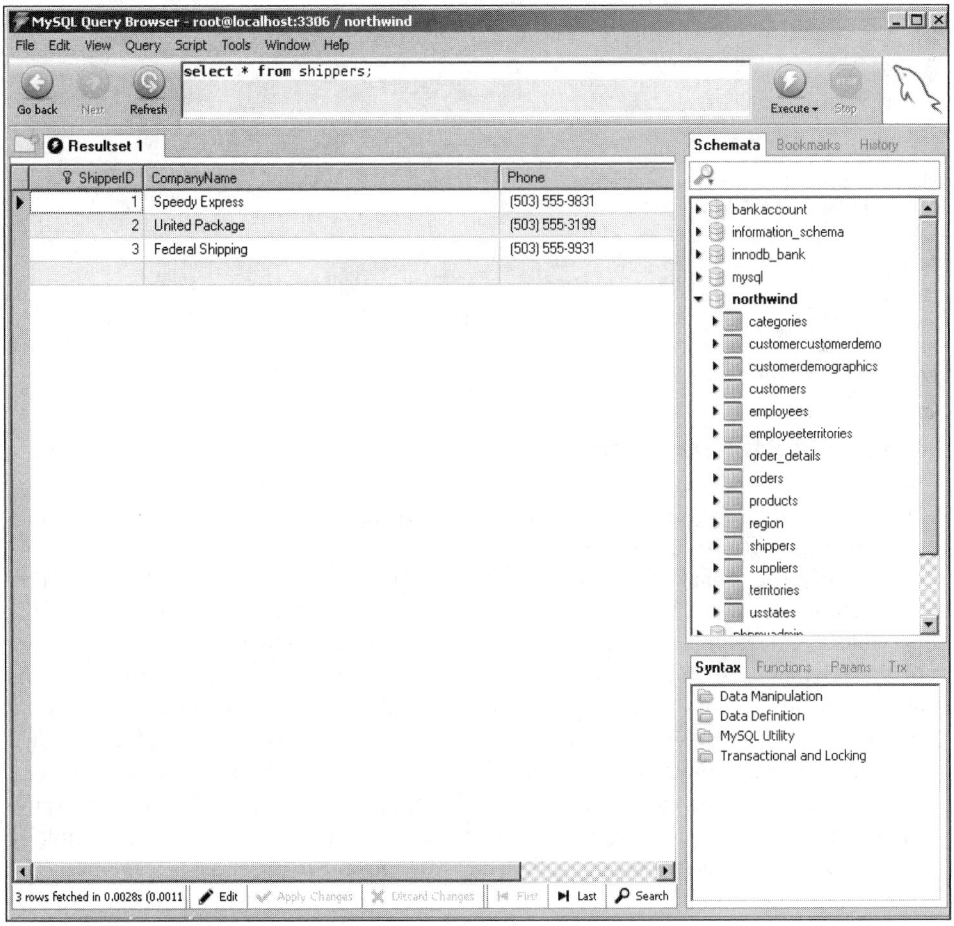

Figure 17.16 The MySQL Query Browser.

The *phpMyAdmin* Tool

The *phpMyAdmin* tool is written in PHP to handle the administration of MySQL over the Web. It is used to create and drop databases, manipulate tables and fields, execute SQL statements, manage keys on fields, manage privileges, and export data into various formats. See *http://www.phpmyadmin.net/home_page/index.php*.

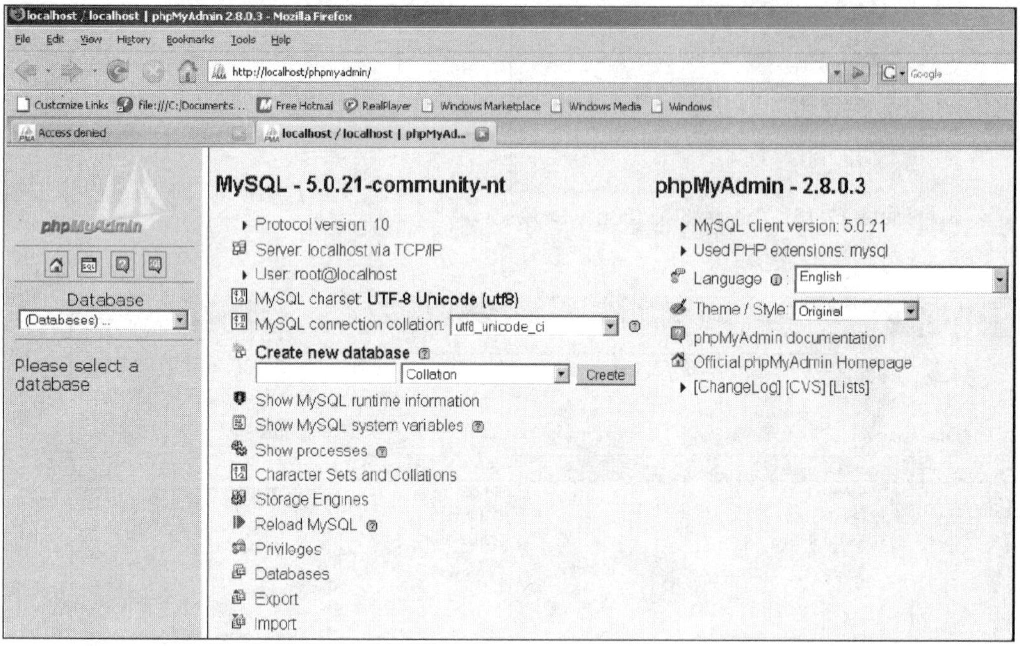

Figure 17.17 The *phpMyAdmin* tool.

The MySQL Privilege System. With a driver's license, "authentication" is verifying that it is really you who owns the license by checking your picture and expiration date, and "authorization" is validating what type of vehicle you are authorized to drive, such as a car, a large truck, or a school bus.

Similarly, the primary purpose of the MySQL privilege system is to authenticate that the user and password are valid to connect to the specified host, as demonstrated in the previous examples in both the command line and graphical client. The second purpose of the privilege system is to specify what the user, once connected to the database, is authorized to do. For example, some users may only be authorized to select and view the data from a specific table. When MySQL is installed, the MySQL database is created with tables called grant tables that define the initial user accounts and privileges. The first account is that of a user named "root," also called the superuser. The superuser can do anything, meaning anyone logging on to the database as root is granted all privileges. Initially, the root account has no password, making it easy for anyone to log on as the superuser. The other types of accounts created are anonymous-user accounts, also without a password. For both the root and anonymous accounts, Windows gets one each and UNIX gets two. Either way, to avoid security problems, the first thing you should do, once the MySQL server starts, is to set a password on the root account and the anonymous accounts.

For administration purposes, you should have root access rights to your server. The *mysqladmin* utility is useful for creating passwords and performing other MySQL administrative tasks. In the next example it is used to set the password for the user "root".

EXAMPLE 17.2

```
1   $ mysqladmin -u root -h localhost password quigley1

2   $ mysql -uroot -hlocalhost -pquigley1
    Welcome to the MySQL monitor.  Commands end with ; or \g.
    Your MySQL connection id is 29 to server version: 5.0.21
community-nt

    Type 'help;' or '\h' for help. Type '\c' to clear the buffer.
```

EXPLANATION

1 The *mysqladmin* program is used to set the password for user root on the localhost. The password is "quigley1".

2 The user root logs into the database server. The *-u* switch is followed by the user or login name (no spaces between *-u* and the user name). This user is logging in as "root". Similarly, the *-p* switch is followed by the actual password; in this case, "quigley1". If a password is not provided, you will prompted to enter one.

17.3.5 Finding the Databases

The database server keeps a list of available databases, which can be displayed as a table by issuing the *show* command at the mysql prompt, as shown in the following example. Typically when you install MySQL, it comes with two databases: *test* and *mysql*. *test* is an empty database used for practicing and testing various features. You normally don't need to have any special permissions to be able work in the *test* database. The *mysql* database is a special database where the MySQL server stores various access permissions. For now, you should not worry about this database unless you need to administer privileges. See the "GRANT" command in the MySQL manual.

EXAMPLE 17.3

```
1 mysql -uroot -pquigley1
  Welcome to the MySQL monitor.  Commands end with ; or \g.
  Your MySQL connection id is 5 to server version: 4.1.11-nt

  Type 'help;' or '\h' for help. Type '\c' to clear the buffer.
```

EXAMPLE 17.3 (CONTINUED)

```
2  mysql> show databases;
  mysql> show databases;
  +--------------------+
  | Database           |
  +--------------------+
  | information_schema |
  | mysql              |
  | phpmyadmin         |
  | test               |
  +--------------------+
  rows in set (0.00 sec)
 mysql>
```

EXPLANATION

2 The *show database* command lists all the databases on this server. Typically, when you install MySQL, you will be given the *mysql* database and the *test* database. The *test* database is just for testing purposes and is empty. The *mysql* database contains all the MySQL server privilege information.

Creating and Dropping a Database. Creating a database is simple. Designing it is another story and depends on your requirements and the model you will use to organize your data. With the smallest database, you will have to create a table. The next section will discuss how to create and drop both databases and tables. Assuming you have been granted permission to create a database, you can do it at the *mysql* command line or with the *mysqladmin* tool as follows:

EXAMPLE 17.4

```
1       mysql> create database my_sample_db;
        Query OK, 1 row affected (0.00 sec)

2       mysql> use my_sample_db;
        Database changed

3       mysql> show tables;
        Empty set (0.00 sec)

4       mysql> create table test(
        -> field1 INTEGER,
        -> field2 VARCHAR(50)
        -> );
        Query OK, 0 rows affected (0.36 sec)
```

EXAMPLE 17.4 (CONTINUED)

```
5       mysql> show tables;
        +------------------------+
        | Tables_in_my_sample_db |
        +------------------------+
        | test                   |
        +------------------------+
        1 row in set (0.00 sec)

6       mysql> drop table test;
        Query OK, 0 rows affected (0.11 sec)

7       mysql> drop database my_sample_db;
        Query OK, 0 rows affected (0.01 sec)
```

EXPLANATION

1. This command creates a database called *my_sample_db*.
2. Just because the database has been created doesn't mean you are in it. To enter the new database, the *use* command is executed.
3. The *show* command lists the tables in the database. This database is empty.
4. A table called *test* is created for the *my_sample_db* database. When a table is created, two columns, *field1* and *field2*, are defined. Each field is assigned the type of data that will be stored there; *field1* will store whole numbers, and *field2* will store a string of up to 50 characters.
5. The *show* command lists all the tables in the database.
6. The *drop table* command destroys a table and its contents.
7. The *drop database* command destroys a database and its contents.

17.3.6 Getting Started with Basic Commands

EXAMPLE 17.5

```
(At the MySQL Client Prompt)
1 mysql> select database();
+------------+
| database() |
+------------+
| northwind  |
+------------+
1 row in set (0.00 sec)
```

EXAMPLE 17.5 (CONTINUED)

```
2 mysql> select now();
+---------------------+
| now()               |
+---------------------+
| 2007-05-12 16:09:57 |
+---------------------+
1 row in set (0.00 sec)
```

The examples in this next section illustrate how to issue SQL commands from the MySQL client. These examples do not attempt to cover all the possible SQL statements supported by MySQL but are here to illustrate the basic syntax for creating and dropping databases and tables and how to insert, delete, edit, alter, and select data from the database tables. For a complete discription of all that you can do with MySQL, visit *http://dev.mysql.com/doc/*.

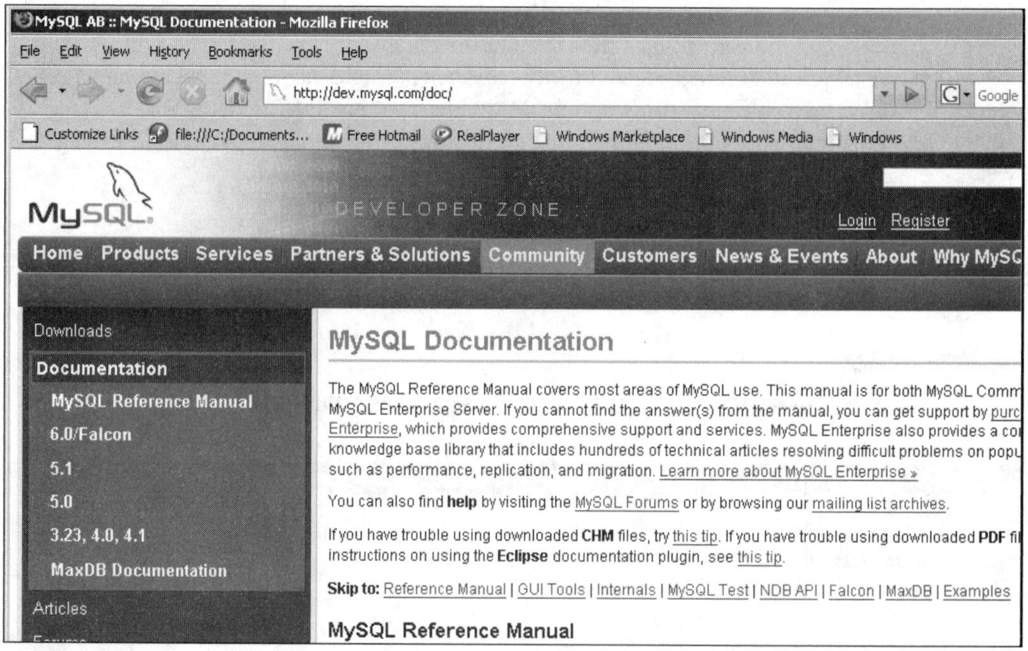

Figure 17.18 MySQL Documentation page.

Creating a Database with MySQL. Now we are ready to create a database. This database is called *sample_db*. The *CREATE DATABASE* command creates the database, and the *SHOW DATABASES* statement demonstrates that it is now listed with the other databases. (You can also use the *mysqladmin* command to create and drop databases.)

EXAMPLE 17.6

```
1  mysql> CREATE DATABASE sample_db;
Query OK, 1 row affected (0.03 sec)

2  mysql> SHOW DATABASES;
+--------------------+
| Database           |
+--------------------+
| information_schema |
| mysql              |
| northwind          |
| phpmyadmin         |
| sample_db          |
| test               |
+--------------------+
6 rows in set (0.00 sec)
```

EXPLANATION

1 The *CREATE DATABASE* statement allows you to create a database. Creating a database does not put you in that database. The *USE* statement will let you start working in the database, as shown in the next example.

2 The *SHOW DATABASES* statement lists all the MySQL databases currently available. The *sample_db* database was just created.

Selecting a Database with MySQL. After creating the database, we need to open it so we can use it. This is done with the *USE* statement. We now have a database to work in.

EXAMPLE 17.7

```
mysql> USE sample_db;
Database changed
```

Creating a Table in the Database. Once the database is created, it is time to create some tables. In a real situation, the relational database will be designed with rules that put logic in the structure of the tables, a process called "normalization" and a topic beyond the scope of this book. In our sample database, we will create one table and put some data in it, just to show you how it is done. The data types define the structure of each field in the table. The *CREATE TABLE* statement defines each field, its name, and its data type.

Data Types. First, we will have to decide what kind of data will be stored in the table: text, numbers, dates, photos, money, etc., and what to name the fields (columns) under which the data is stored. MySQL has specific data types to describe all the types of data that can be stored in the database. Most of the MySQL data types are listed in Table 17.3.

Table 17.3 MySQL Data Types

Data Type	***Description***
Numbers	
TINYINT	Very small numbers; suitable for ages. Can store numbers between 0 and 255 if UNSIGNED clause is applied; else the range is between –128 and 127.
SMALLINT	Suitable for numbers between 0 and 65535 (UNSIGNED) or –32768 and 32767.
MEDIUM INT	0 to 16777215 with UNSIGNED clause or -8388608 and 8388607.
INT	UNSIGNED integers fall between 0 and 4294967295 or –2147683648 and 2147683647.
BIGINT	Huge numbers (–9223372036854775808 to 9223372036854775807).
FLOAT	Floating point numbers (single precision).
DOUBLE	Floating point numbers (double precision).
DECIMAL	Floating point numbers represented as strings.
Text	
CHAR(*x*)	Where *x* can range from 1 to 255. Holds a fixed-length string (can contain letters, numbers, and special characters). The fixed size is specified in parentheses.
VARCHAR(*x*)	*x* ranges from 1 to 255. Holds a variable-length string (can contain letters, numbers, and special characters). The maximum size is specified in parentheses.
TINYTEXT	Small text, case insensitive.
TEXT	Slightly longer text, case insensitive.
MEDIUMTEXT	Medium-size text, case insensitive.
LONGTEXT	Really long text, case insensitive.
TINYBLOB	Blob means a Binary Large OBject. You should use blobs for case-sensitive searches.
Binary	
BLOB	Slightly larger blob, case sensitive.
MEDIUMBLOB	Medium-sized blobs, case sensitive.
LONGBLOB	Really huge blobs, case sensitive.
ENUM	Enumeration data type has fixed values, and the column can take only one value from the given set. The values are placed in parentheses following ENUM declaration. An example is a marital-status column—m_status ENUM("Y", "N").

Table 17.3 MySQL Data Types (continued)

Data Type	*Description*
Dates	
DATE: YYYY-MM-DD	Four-digit year followed by two-digit month and date; e.g., 20071030
TIME: hh:mm:ss	Hours:Minutes:Seconds
DATETIME	YYYY-MM-DD hh:mm:ss (Date and time separated by a space character)
TIMESTAMP	YYYYMMDDhhmmss
YEAR	YYYY (four-digit year); e.g., 2007

EXAMPLE 17.8

```
1  mysql> CREATE TABLE teams(
    -> name varchar(100) not null,
    -> wins int unsigned,
    -> losses int unsigned);
Query OK, 0 rows affected (0.09 sec)

2  mysql> SHOW TABLES;
+--------------------+
| Tables_in_sample_db |
+--------------------+
| teams              |
+--------------------+
1 row in set (0.00 sec);

3 mysql> DESCRIBE teams;
+--------+-----------------+------+-----+---------+-------+
| Field  | Type            | Null | Key | Default | Extra |
+--------+-----------------+------+-----+---------+-------+
| name   | varchar(100)    | NO   |     |         |       |
| wins   | int(10) unsigned | YES |     | NULL    |       |
| losses | int(10) unsigned | YES |     | NULL    |       |
+--------+-----------------+------+-----+---------+-------+
| teams              |
+--------------------+
1 row in set (0.00 sec)
```

EXPLANATION

1 The *CREATE TABLE* statement creates a table in the database. This table is named *teams*. It consists of three fields: *name*, *wins*, *losses*. The *name* field will consist of a varying string of up to 100 characters; the *wins* and *losses* fields will hold unsigned integers.
2 The *SHOW* command lists the table in a database.
3 The *DESCRIBE* command describes the structure of the table; i.e., the names of the fields and the type of data that can be stored in each field. Note that the *name* field cannot be "Null", and the default value for the *wins* and *losses* is NULL if a value isn't supplied; e.g., if a team hasn't played any games, the *wins* and *losses* will be assigned NULL.

Adding Another Table with a Primary Key. In the next example, we will create another table and add a primary key. A primary key is used to uniquely identify the records in the database. A user's login name, UID, account number, or license plate are examples of unique IDs. A primary key is a unique index where all key columns must be defined as NOT NULL. If they are not explicitly declared as NOT NULL, MySQL declares them so implicitly (and silently). A table can have only one PRIMARY KEY.

EXAMPLE 17.9

```
1  mysql> CREATE TABLE coaches(
     -> id INT NOT NULL AUTO_INCREMENT,
     -> name VARCHAR(75),
     -> team VARCHAR(100),
     -> title VARCHAR(50),
     -> start_date date,
     -> PRIMARY KEY(id));
   Query OK, 0 rows affected (0.38 sec)

2  mysql> DESCRIBE coaches;
   +------------+--------------+------+-----+---------+----------------
   | Field      | Type         | Null | Key | Default | Extra
   +------------+--------------+------+-----+---------+----------------
   | id         | int(11)      | NO   | PRI | NULL    |auto_increment
   | name       | varchar(75)  | YES  |     | NULL    |
   | team       | varchar(100) | YES  |     | NULL    |
   | title      | varchar(50)  | YES  |     | NULL    |
   | start_date | date         | YES  |     | NULL    |
   +------------+--------------+------+-----+---------+----------------
   5 rows in set (0.00 sec)
```

EXAMPLE 17.9 (CONTINUED)

```
3  mysql> SHOW TABLES;
   +----------------------+
   | Tables_in_sample_db |
   +----------------------+
   | coaches              |
   | teams                |
   +----------------------+
   2 rows in set (0.00 sec)
```

EXPLANATION

1 The *coach* table is created with the *id* field being assigned a primary key. This is the field that will used to uniquely identify a specific coach.

2 The structure of the new table shows that the *id* field has a primary key that will be automatically incremented by one by MySQL each time a new coach is added.

3 Now our database has two tables, one called *teams* and one called *coaches*.

Inserting Data into Tables. The SQL *INSERT* statement adds new records to a table. When you insert data, make sure you provide a value for each field name in the order the data is stored; otherwise, MySQL will send an error message. In the following example, data can be inserted with the *SET* clause where fields are assigned values, or the values can be specified with the *VALUES* list or by simply listing the values for each field in order. See the MySQL documentation for a complete list of ways to add new records to a table.

EXAMPLE 17.10

```
1  mysql> INSERT INTO teams
     -> set name='Fremont Tigers',
     -> wins=24,
     -> losses=26;
   Query OK, 1 row affected (0.00 sec)

2  mysql> INSERT INTO teams
     -> set name='Chico Hardhats',
     -> wins=19,
     -> losses=25;
   Query OK, 1 row affected (0.00 sec)

3  mysql> INSERT INTO teams values
     -> ('Bath Warships',32,3);
   Query OK, 1 row affected (0.00 sec)
```

EXAMPLE 17.10 (CONTINUED)

```
4  mysql> INSERT INTO teams values
    -> ('Bangor Rams', 22, 24);
   Query OK, 1 row affected (0.00 sec)

5 mysql> SELECT name FROM teams;
  +----------------+
  | name           |
  +----------------+
  | Fremont Tigers |
  | Chico Hardhats |
  | Bath Warships  |
  | Bangor Rams    |
  +----------------+
  4 rows in set (0.00 sec)

6  mysql> INSERT INTO coaches values
   -> (" ",'John Doe','Chico Hardhats','Head Coach', 20021210);
   Query OK, 1 row affected, 1 warning (0.05 sec)

7  mysql>  INSERT INTO coaches values
      -> (" ", 'Jack Mattsone','Chico Hardhats','Offensive Coach' ,
'20041005');
    Query OK, 1 row affected, 1 warning (0.00 sec)

8  mysql> INSERT INTO coaches(name,team, title,start_date)
       -> values( 'Bud Wilkins', 'Fremont Tigers', 'Head Coach',
'19990906');
    Query OK, 1 row affected (0.03 sec)

9  mysql>  INSERT INTO coaches(name, team, title,start_date)
       ->values( 'Joe Hayes', 'Fremont Tigers', 'Defensive Coach',
    '19980616');
    Query OK, 1 row affected (0.02 sec
```

EXPLANATION

1 The fields and values are assigned using the *SET* clause within the *INSERT* statement. For any field not named in the *SET*, MySQL assigns its default value.

2 Again the fields and values are inserted using the *SET* clause.

3 In this example, the *INSERT* statement contains a *VALUE* list where a value for each field is assigned in the order it was specified when the table was created. To see the order, if you are not sure, use the *DESCRIBE* statement as shown in the previous example.

4 The *VALUES* list is repeated in this example for a new record. Note that the date is inserted in the format `yyyy-mm-dd`

5 The *SELECT* statement displays the names of all the teams that have been inserted into the table.

6,7,8,9 More records are inserted with the *VALUES* list.

Selecting Data from Tables—The *SELECT* Command. One of the most commonly used SQL commands is *SELECT*, mandatory when performing a query. The *SELECT* command is used to retrieve data from a table based on some criteria. It specfies a comma-separated list of fields to be retrieved, and the *FROM* clause specifies the table(s) to be accessed. The results are stored in a result table known as the result set, just a little table itself. The * symbol can be used to represent all of the fields.

Selecting by Columns. In the following examples, data is retrieved for specific columns, each column (field) separated by a comma.

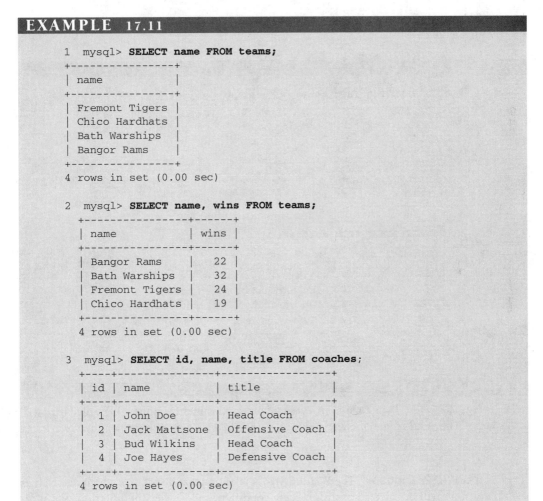

EXAMPLE 17.11

```
1  mysql> SELECT name FROM teams;
+-----------------+
| name            |
+-----------------+
| Fremont Tigers  |
| Chico Hardhats  |
| Bath Warships   |
| Bangor Rams     |
+-----------------+
4 rows in set (0.00 sec)

2  mysql> SELECT name, wins FROM teams;
   +----------------+------+
   | name           | wins |
   +----------------+------+
   | Bangor Rams    |   22 |
   | Bath Warships  |   32 |
   | Fremont Tigers |   24 |
   | Chico Hardhats |   19 |
   +----------------+------+
   4 rows in set (0.00 sec)

3  mysql> SELECT id, name, title FROM coaches;
   +----+---------------+-----------------+
   | id | name          | title           |
   +----+---------------+-----------------+
   |  1 | John Doe      | Head Coach      |
   |  2 | Jack Mattsone | Offensive Coach |
   |  3 | Bud Wilkins   | Head Coach      |
   |  4 | Joe Hayes     | Defensive Coach |
   +----+---------------+-----------------+
   4 rows in set (0.00 sec)
```

EXPLANATION

1 The *SELECT* statement retrieves all values in the *name* field from the table called *teams*.
2 The *SELECT* statement retrieves all values in the *name* field and the *wins* field from the table called *teams*. The list of field names are separated with a comma.
3 The *SELECT* statement retrieves all values in the *id* field, the *name* field, and the *title* field from the *coaches* table.

Select All Columns. The * is a wildcard that is used to represent all of the columns in a table.

EXAMPLE 17.12

```
1  mysql> SELECT * FROM teams;
+----------------+------+--------+
| name           | wins | losses |
+----------------+------+--------+
| Fremont Tigers |   24 |     26 |
| Chico Hardhats |   19 |     25 |
| Bath Warships  |   32 |      3 |
| Bangor Rams    |   22 |     24 |
+----------------+------+--------+

2  mysql> SELECT * FROM coaches;
+----+---------------+----------------+-----------------+-----------+
| id | name          | team           | title           | start_date|
+----+---------------+----------------+-----------------+-----------+
|  1 | John Doe      | Chico Hardhats | Head Coach      | 2002-12-10|
|  2 | Jack Mattsone | Chico Hardhats | Offensive Coach | 2004-10-05|
|  3 | Bud Wilkins   | Fremont Tigers | Head Coach      | 1999-09-06|
|  4 | Joe Hayes     | Fremont Tigers | Defensive Coach | 1998-06-16|
+----+---------------+----------------+-----------------+-----------+
4 rows in set (0.00 sec)
```

EXPLANATION

1 The *SELECT* statement retrieves all fields and values from the table called *teams*.
2 The *SELECT* statement retrieves all fields and values from the table called *coaches*.

The *WHERE* Clause. The *WHERE* clause is optional and specifies which data values or rows will be selected based on some condition, called selection criterion. SQL provides a set of operators to qualify the condition being set.

Table 17.4 SQL Operators

Operator	***Description***	***Example***
=	Equal to	where country = 'Sweden'
<>, !=	Not equal to[a]	where country <> 'Sweden'
>	Greater than	where salary > 50000
<	Less than	where salary < 50000
>=	Greater than or equal	
<=	Less than or equal	
IS [NOT] NULL	Is NULL (no value) or Not NULL	where birth = NULL
BETWEEN	Between an inclusive range	where last_name BETWEEN 'Doe' AND 'Hayes'
LIKE	Search for value like a pattern	where last_name LIKE 'D%'
NOT LIKE	Search for a value not like a pattern	where country NOT LIKE 'Sw%'
!, NOT	logical NOT for negation	where age ! 10;
||, OR	logical OR	where order_number > 10 || part_number = 80
&&, AND	logical AND	where age > 12 && age < 21
XOR	Exclusive OR	where status XOR

a. In some versions of SQL, the <> operator may be written as !=.

EXAMPLE 17.13

```
1  mysql> SELECT name, wins FROM teams WHERE wins > 25;
   +-------------------+------+
   | name              | wins |
   +-------------------+------+
   | Bath Destroyers   |   34 |
   | Portland Penguins |   28 |
   +-------------------+------+

2  mysql> SELECT name FROM teams WHERE losses < wins;
   +---------------+
   | name          |
   +---------------+
   | Bath Warships |
   +---------------+
   1 row in set (0.03 sec)
```

EXAMPLE 17.13 (CONTINUED)

```
3  mysql> SELECT name, title FROM coaches WHERE team = 'Chico
Hardhats';
   +--------------+-----------------+
   | name         | title           |
   +--------------+-----------------+
   | John Doe     | Head Coach      |
   | Jack Mattsone | Offensive Coach |
   +--------------+-----------------+
   2 rows in set (0.00 sec)

4 mysql> SELECT name FROM coaches WHERE name LIKE 'J%';
   +---------------+
   | name          |
   +---------------+
   | John Doe      |
   | Jack Mattsone |
   | Joe Hayes     |
   +---------------+
   3 rows in set (0.00 sec)

5  mysql> SELECT name FROM teams WHERE wins > 10 && losses < 10;
   +---------------+
   | name          |
   +---------------+
   | Bath Warships |
   +---------------+
   1 row in set (0.00 sec)

6  mysql> SELECT name FROM coaches WHERE id BETWEEN 1 AND 3;
   +---------------+
   | name          |
   +---------------+
   | John Doe      |
   | Jack Mattsone |
   | Bud Wilkins   |
   +---------------+
   3 rows in set (0.00 sec)
```

EXPLANATION

1 The *SELECT* statement retrieves the name of teams from the table called *teams* where the number of wins was greater than 25.

2 The *SELECT* statement retrieves the name of teams from the table called *teams* where the number of losses was less than the number of wins.

3 The *SELECT* statement retrieves the names of coaches and their titles from the table called *coaches* if their team is equal to the string 'Chico Hardhats'. The string must be quoted in either single or double quotes, and the match must be exact.

EXPLANATION (CONTINUED)

4 The *SELECT* statement retrieves the names of coaches from the table called *coaches* where the coachs name contains a string starting with a 'J'. The % sign is a wildcard representing any characters following the 'J'.

5 The *SELECT* statement retrieves the name of the team where the number of wins is greater than 10 and the number of losses less than 10. The && is called the logical AND. Both statements must be true or nothing will be selected.

6 The *SELECT* statement retrieves the names of coaches from the table called *coaches* where the coachs ID is between 1 and 3. The *BETWEEN* clause creates a range criteria from which to select.

Sorting Tables. You can display the output of a query in a particular order by using the *ORDER BY* clause. Rows can be sorted either in ascending (the default) or descending (DESC) order where the values being sorted are either strings or numbers. You can limit the output of any query with the *LIMIT* clause.

EXAMPLE 17.14

```
1  mysql> SELECT * FROM teams ORDER BY name;
   +----------------+------+--------+
   | name           | wins | losses |
   +----------------+------+--------+
   | Bangor Rams    |   22 |     24 |
   | Bath Warships  |   32 |      3 |
   | Chico Hardhats |   19 |     25 |
   | Fremont Tigers |   24 |     26 |
   +----------------+------+--------+
   4 rows in set (0.00 sec)

2  mysql> SELECT * FROM teams ORDER BY name DESC;
   +----------------+------+--------+
   | name           | wins | losses |
   +----------------+------+--------+
   | Fremont Tigers |   24 |     26 |
   | Chico Hardhats |   19 |     25 |
   | Bath Warships  |   32 |      3 |
   | Bangor Rams    |   22 |     24 |
   +----------------+------+--------+
   4 rows in set (0.00 sec)

3  mysql> SELECT name, wins FROM teams ORDER BY WINS LIMIT 2;
   +----------------+------+
   | name           | wins |
   +----------------+------+
   | Chico Hardhats |   19 |
   | Bangor Rams    |   22 |
   +----------------+------+
   2 rows in set (0.00 sec)
```

EXPLANATION

1 The *SELECT* statement retrieves all fields from the table called *teams* and sorts the result set by names in ascending order.
2 The *SELECT* statement retrieves all fields from the table called *teams* and sorts the result set by names in descending order.
3 The *SELECT* statement retrieves the names and wins of teams and sorts the number of wins in ascending order, limiting the result set to the top two winners.

Joining Tables. When a database is designed properly, the tables relate to one another based on some criteria; for example, in our database, every team has a name and every coach has a name and a team name. A join allows two or more tables to be combined and return a result set based on the relationships they share. There are different types of join statements (inner joins, cross joins, left, joins, etc.), but they all follow the basic syntax of a *SELECT* statement with the addition of a *JOIN* clause.

EXAMPLE 17.15

```
1  mysql> SELECT teams.name, coaches.name, teams.wins
 FROM teams, coaches WHERE
 teams.name = coaches.team && coaches.id = 4;
+----------------+-----------+------+
| name           | name      | wins |
+----------------+-----------+------+
| Fremont Tigers | Joe Hayes |   24 |
+----------------+-----------+------+
1 row in set (0.00 sec)

2  mysql> SELECT teams.name, coaches.name, teams.wins FROM teams,
    -> coaches  WHERE teams.name = coaches.team &&
-> coaches.title = "Head Coach";
+----------------+-------------+------+
| name           | name        | wins |
+----------------+-------------+------+
| Chico Hardhats | John Doe    |   21 |
| Fremont Tigers | Bud Wilkins |   24 |
+----------------+-------------+------+
2 rows in set (0.00 sec)


3  mysql> SELECT t.name, c.name, t.wins FROM teams t, coaches c
-> WHERE t.name = c.team && c.title LIKE "Head%";
+----------------+-------------+------+
| name           | name        | wins |
+----------------+-------------+------+
| Chico Hardhats | John Doe    |   21 |
| Fremont Tigers | Bud Wilkins |   24 |
+----------------+-------------+------+
2 rows in set (0.00 sec)
```

EXPLANATION

1 The *SELECT* statement will retrieve the team's name, the coach's name, and the number of wins for the team where the team and coach name are the same and the coach's ID is 4. The fields are prepended with the name of the table and a dot to identify the field and table. The join (inner join) means that all unmatched records are discarded. Only the rows that matched the criteria in the *WHERE* clause are displayed in the result set.

2 The *SELECT* statement will retrieve the team's name, the coach's name, and the number of wins for the team where the team and coach name are the same and the coach's title is "Head Coach." Like the last example, the join (inner join) means only the rows that matched the criteria in the *WHERE* clause are displayed in the result set.

3 The *SELECT* statement will retrieve the team name, the coach name, and the team wins from both the *teams* and *coaches* tables where the team name and the coach name are the same and the coach's title starts with "Head." The letters 't' and 'c' are called aliases for the respective tables, *teams* and *coaches*. Aliases save a lot of typing.

Deleting Rows. The *DELETE* command allows you to remove rows from a table. The only real difference between *DELETE* and *SELECT* is that the *DELETE* removes records based on some criteria, whereas the *SELECT* retrieves those records.

EXAMPLE 17.16

```
1  mysql> SELECT name FROM teams;
+----------------+
| name           |
+----------------+
| Fremont Tigers |
| Chico Hardhats |
| Bath Warships  |
| Bangor Rams    |
+----------------+
4 rows in set (0.00 sec)

2  mysql> DELETE FROM teams WHERE name = "Bath Warships";
Query OK, 1 row affected (0.20 sec)

3  mysql> SELECT name FROM teams;
+----------------+
| name           |
+----------------+
| Fremont Tigers
| Chico Hardhats |
| Bangor Rams    |
+----------------+
4 rows in set (0.00 sec)
```

EXPLANATION

1 The *SELECT* statement retrieves all values in the *name* field from the table called *teams*.
2 The *DELETE* statement removes all rows in the *name* field if the name of the team is "Bath Warships."
3 This *SELECT* statement retrieves all values in the name fields, showing us that the "Bath Warships" team was deleted in the previous *DELETE* statement.

Updating Data in a Table. The *UPDATE* command is used to edit a table; i.e., to modify or change the values in a table. This statement uses the *SET* clause to change the existing value to something else, as shown in Example 17.17.

EXAMPLE 17.17

```
1 mysql> SELECT * FROM teams;
+----------------+------+--------+
| name           | wins | losses |
+----------------+------+--------+
| Fremont Tigers |   24 |     26 |
| Chico Hardhats |   19 |     25 |
| Bath Warships  |   32 |      3 |
| Bangor Rams    |   22 |     24 |
+----------------+------+--------+
4 rows in set (0.00 sec)

1  mysql> UPDATE teams SET wins=wins + 2 WHERE name="Chico Hardhats";
   Query OK, 1 row affected (0.02 sec)
   Rows matched: 1  Changed: 1  Warnings: 0

2  mysql> UPDATE teams SET name="Bath Destroyers"
     ->  where name="Bath Warships";
      Query OK, 1 row affected (0.13 sec)
      Rows matched: 1  Changed: 1  Warnings: 0

3   mysql> SELECT * FROM teams;
+-----------------+------+--------+
| name            | wins | losses |
+-----------------+------+--------+
| Fremont Tigers  |   24 |     26 |
| Chico Hardhats  |   21 |     25 |
| Bath Destroyers |   32 |      3 |
| Bangor Rams     |   22 |     24 |
+-----------------+------+--------+
4 rows in set (0.00 sec)
```

EXPLANATION

1 The *SELECT* statement retrieves all rows from the table called *teams*. We will compare this result set with the one on line 3 after the the table is updated.
2 The *UPDATE* statement edits the name field. It causes the "Bath Warships" team to be renamed "Bath Destroyers".
3 This *SELECT* statement retrieves all values in the *name* field, showing us that the "Bath Warships" team's name was changed by the *UPDATE* statement.

Altering a Table. The *ALTER TABLE* command allows you to alter the structure of an existing table by adding and dropping columns. The *ALTER* statement has many possible clauses, such as *CHANGE*, *MODIFY*, *RENAME*, *DROP*, etc. Don't confuse *ALTER* with *UPDATE*. Altering a table changes the structure of how the table was described after it was created. You can use it to add primary keys, indexes, change the definition of a column or where it is positioned in the table, etc. Some of these alterations are demonstrated in the following examples.

Add a Column

EXAMPLE 17.18

```
1  mysql> ALTER TABLE teams ADD captain varchar(100);
Query OK, 11 rows affected (0.64 sec)
Records: 11  Duplicates: 0  Warnings:

2  mysql> select * from teams;
+-------------------------+------+--------+---------+
| name                    | wins | losses | captain |
+-------------------------+------+--------+---------+
| Fremont Tigers          |   24 |     26 | NULL    |
| Bath Destroyers         |   34 |      3 | NULL    |
| Chico Hardhats          |   21 |     25 | NULL    |
| Bangor Rams             |   23 |      5 | NULL    |
4 rows in set (0.01 sec)
```

EXPLANATION

1 The *ALTER* statement adds a new field called *captain* to the *teams* table. The values in the new field will consist of up to 100 characters.

Drop a Column

EXAMPLE 17.19

```
mysql> ALTER TABLE teams DROP captain;
Query OK, 11 rows affected (0.34 sec)
Records: 11  Duplicates: 0  Warnings: 0
```

Add a Primary Key

In Example 17.20, the *teams* table is altered by making the *name* field a primary key. This means that all new teams must have unique names.

EXAMPLE 17.20

```
1  mysql> ALTER TABLE teams MODIFY name VARCHAR(100) NOT NULL,
    -->  ADD PRIMARY KEY(name);
   Query OK, 10 rows affected (0.06 sec)
   Records: 10  Duplicates: 0  Warnings: 0

2  mysql> DESCRIBE teams;
  +--------+------------------+------+-----+---------+-------+
  | Field  | Type             | Null | Key | Default | Extra |
  +--------+------------------+------+-----+---------+-------+
  | name   | varchar(100)     | NO   | PRI | NULL    |       |
  | wins   | int(10) unsigned | YES  |     | NULL    |       |
  | losses | int(10) unsigned | YES  |     | NULL    |       |
  +--------+------------------+------+-----+---------+-------+
  3 rows in set (0.05 sec)
```

Dropping a Table. To drop a table is relatively simple. Just use the *DROP* command and the name of the table.

EXAMPLE 17.21

```
mysql> DROP TABLE teams;
Query OK, 5 rows affected (0.11 sec)
```

Dropping a Database. To drop a database, use the *DROP DATABASE* command.

EXAMPLE 17.22

```
mysql> DROP DATABASE sample_db;
Query OK, 1 row affected (0.45 sec)
```

17.4 What Is the Perl DBI?

> The DBI is a layer of "glue" between an application and one or more database driver modules.
>
> —Tim Bunce, author of DBI

DBI stands for the Database Independent Interface. DBI is an object-oriented module that allows your Perl application to talk to many different types of databases using the same method calls, variables, and conventions. It locates the database driver module (DBD) for a particular database system and dynamically loads the appropriate DBD module. The database driver contains the libraries necessary to talk to a specific database. For example, to connect to a MySQL database, you need to install the DBD-MySQL driver, and in order to talk to an Oracle database, you need the DBD-Oracle driver. DBI acts as the interface between your Perl script and the database driver modules; i.e., it translates Perl output to code that can be understood by a specific driver whether that driver is Oracle, Sybase, MySQL, etc. You set up the SQL query string and send it via a DBI method to the appropriate database driver, and you get back results that can be managed in your Perl program in the same way no matter what database you are using.

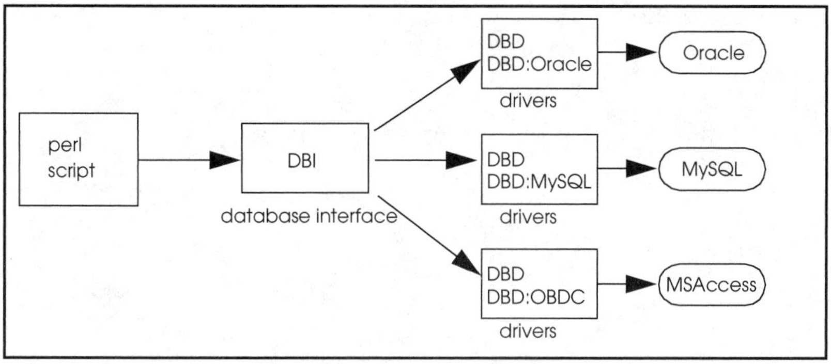

Figure 17.19 The DBI and drivers.

17.4.1 Installing the DBI

DBI-MySQL with PPM. Installation of the DBI is easy if you are using PPM (Perl Package Manager) from ActiveState. PPM is a package-management utility that simplifies finding, installing, upgrading, and removing Perl modules. Today the default version of PPM is a graphical user interface, but you can also use the command-line interface as shown in Example 17.23.

PPM Quickstart

The following example is taken from the PPM beginner's guide to help guide you through the steps for installing and removing modules from CPAN by using PPM at the command line.

EXAMPLE 17.23

```
(At the command line)
ppm help quickstart
quickstart -- a beginners' guide to PPM3
```

EXAMPLE 17.23 (CONTINUED)

```
Description
  PPM (Programmer's Package Manager) is a utility for managing
  software "packages". A package is a modular extension for a
  language or a software program. Packages reside in repositories.
  PPM can use three types of repositories:

   1) A directory on a CD-ROM or hard drive in your computer
   2) A website
   3) A remote Repository Server (such as ASPN)

  Common Commands:
  To view PPM help:
    help
    help <command>

 To view the name of the current repository:
    repository

 To search the current repository:
    search <keywords>

 To install a package:
    install <package_name>

  Most commands can be truncated; as long as the command is
  unambiguous, PPM will recognize it. For example, 'repository add
  foo' can be entered as 'rep add foo'.

  PPM features user profiles, which store information about
  installed packages. Profiles are stored as part of your ASPN
  account; thus, you can easily maintain package profiles for
  different languages, or configure one machine with your favorite
  packages, and then copy that installation to another machine by
  accessing your ASPN profile.

  For more information, type 'help profile' at the PPM prompt.
```

Steps to Install with PPM. The simple steps to install the necessary modules are listed here.

1. Make sure you are connected to the Internet.
2. At the shell command-line prompt (MS-DOS or UNIX), type: *ppm*
3. A PPM prompt will appear: *ppm>*
4. To see your options, at the PPM prompt type: *help*
5. To view available modules, first search for the one you want, and then use the *install* command.

EXAMPLE 17.24

```
1 $ ppm
 PPM - Programmer's Package Manager version 3.1.
 Copyright (c) 2001 ActiveState Corp. All Rights Reserved.
 ActiveState is a devision of Sophos.

Entering interactive shell. Using Term::ReadLine::Stub as readline
library.

Type 'help' to get started.

Setting 'target' set to 'ActivePerl 5.8.4.810'.
ppm>

2 ppm> query *
Querying target 1 (ActivePerl 5.8.7.813)
   1. ActivePerl-DocTools            [0.04] Perl extension for
Documentation TOC Generation
   2. ActiveState-RelocateTree       [0.03] Relocate a Perl installation
   3. ActiveState-Rx                 [0.60] Regular Expression Debugger
   4. Archive-Tar                    [1.07] Manipulates TAR archives
   5. Compress-Zlib                  [1.22] Interface to zlib compression
library
   6. Data-Dump                      [1.01] Pretty printing of data
structures
   7. DBD-mysql                  [2.9003] MySQL driver for the Perl5
                              Database Interface (DBI)
   8. DBI                  [1.47] Database independent interface for Perl
   9. Digest                          [1.0] Modules that calculate
message digests
  10. Digest-HMAC                    [1.01] Keyed-Hashing for Message
Authentication
  11. Digest-MD2                     [2.03] Perl interface to the MD2
Algorithm
  12. Digest-MD4                      [1.1] Perl interface to the MD4
Algorithm
  13. Digest-MD5               [2.20] Perl interface to the MD5 Algorithm
  14. Digest-SHA1                    [2.06] Perl interface to the SHA-1
Algorithm
  15. File-CounterFile               [1.01] Persistent counter class
  16. Font-AFM                       [1.18] Interface to Adobe Font
Metrics files
  17. HTML-Parser                    [3.34] HTML parser class
  18. HTML-Tagset                    [3.03] Data tables useful in parsing
HTML
  19. HTML-Tree                      [3.18] build and scan parse-trees of
HTML
  20. IO-Zlib                        [1.01] IO:: style interface to
Compress::Zlib
```

EXAMPLE 17.24 (CONTINUED)

```
  21. libwin32                        [0.21] A collection of extensions
that aims to provide comp~
  22. libwww-perl                     [5.75] Library for WWW access in
Perl
  23. Mail-Sendmail                   [0.79] Simple platform independent
mailer
  24. MD5                             [2.02] Perl interface to the MD5
Algorithm (obsolete)
  25. MIME-Base64                     [2.12] Encoding and decoding of
base64 strings
  26. PPM                           [2.1.6] Perl Package Manager: locate,
install, upgrade softw~
  27. PPM-Agent-Perl                 [3.0.4] PPM Installer Backend for
Perl
  28. PPM3                            [3.1] Perl Package Manager: locate,
install, upgrade softw~
  29. SOAP-Lite                       [0.55] Library for Simple Object
Access Protocol (SOAP) cli~
  30. Storable                      [1.0.12] persistency for perl data
structures
  31. Tk                           [800.024] A Graphical User Interface
Toolkit
  32. URI                             [1.27] Uniform Resource Identifiers
(absolute and relative)
  33. Win32-AuthenticateUser         [0.02] Win32 User authentication for
domains
  34. XML-Parser                     [2.34] A Perl module for parsing XML
documents
  35. XML-Simple                      [2.09] Easy API to read/write XML
(esp config files)
ppm>

3  ppm> describe DBI
   ====================
       Name: DBI
    Version: 1.50
     Author: Tim Bunce (dbi-users@perl.org)
      Title: DBI
   Abstract: Database independent interface for Perl
   Location: ActiveState PPM2 Repository
Available Platforms:
       1. MSWin32-x86-multi-thread-5.8
====================

4  ppm> describe DBD-mysql
    ====================
    Name: DBD-mysql
 Version: 3.0002
  Author: Patrick Galbraith (patg@mysql.com)
```

EXAMPLE 17.24 (CONTINUED)

```
   Title: DBD-mysql
Abstract: A MySQL driver for the Perl5 Database Interface (DBI)
Location: ActiveState PPM2 Repository
Prerequisites:
       1. DBI 0.0
Available Platforms:
       1. MSWin32-x86-multi-thread-5.8
====================
ppm>q

To install the DBI (Database Interface for Perl) and DBD-mysql (Driver
for MySQL) from CPAN, start PPM and execute the install command as
follows:

5       ppm> query *
6       ppm> install DBI
7       ppm> install DBD-mysql
```

The PPM GUI. When the Perl Package Manager is initially displayed, it will synchronize the ActiveState repository package list from its database. You can view all the currently installed packages or all the packages in the repository and use the search box to find a module you are looking for. If found, it will be highlighted.

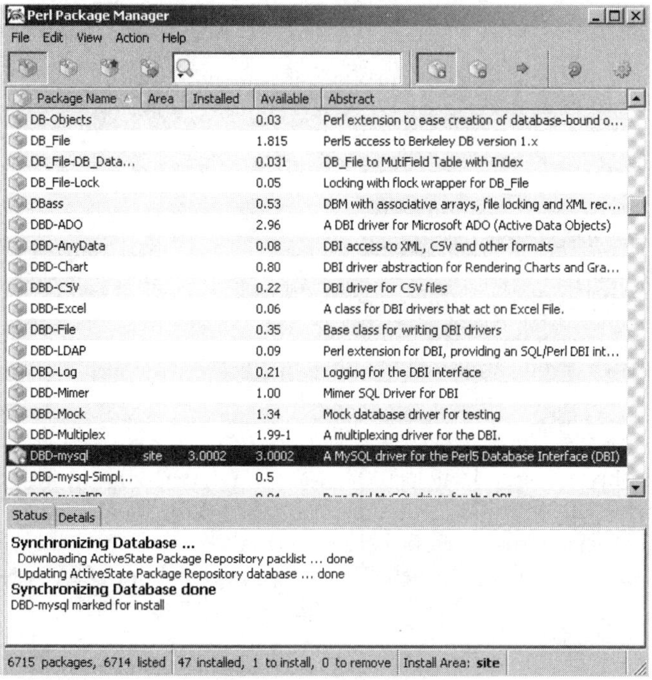

Figure 17.20 Package marked for install.

To install marked packages, click on the green arrow in the right-hand portion at the top of the screen.

Using PPM with Linux. If you are using Linux, you can download Perl 5.8.8 from ActiveState as an *rpm* (RedHat Package Manager) file or as a tarfile. The instructions for downloading ActivePerl are found at *http://aspn.activestate.com/ASPN/docs/ActivePerl/5.8/install.html*. Then run the *install.sh* shell script found in the *perl* directory. After you run the install script, set your *PATH* to the *perl* directory. Then you can use the PPM program to install modules from CPAN just as you would with Windows. This is by far easier than using CPAN with all its questions and issues.

You need to be connected to the Internet to install the required packages. To see the installed packages, type:

```
\rpm -i Active-State.....rpm
sh install.sh
```

Installing DBI Using CPAN. The primary tool used to maintain a local Perl distribution is the CPAN module, used to access the Comprehensive Perl Archive Network, aka CPAN. At the command-line prompt, type:

```
$ perl -MCPAN -e shell
```

At the CPAN prompt, type "help" and you will see a list of options. To get the latest version of CPAN, type at your CPAN prompt:

```
cpan >install Bundle::CPAN
```

After a barrage of questions, don't be surprised if you end up with:

Stop.
nmake -- NOT OK
Running make test
Can't test without successful make
Running make install
make had returned bad status, ***install seems impossible***

That's why it's easier if you can use PPM.

Try these steps for RedHat:

1. Install latest MySQL server/client RPM (the MySQL that comes with RedHat doesn't work well). MySQL-client-standard-5.0.24-0.rhel3.i386.rpm MySQL-server-standard-5.0.24-0.rhel3.i386.rpm
2. Install Perl-DBI and MySQL-devel. (RedHat Enterprise Linux ES release 3 (Taroon) comes with these RPMs.)
   perl-DBI-1.32-5.i386.rpm

mysql-devel-3.23.58-1.i386.rpm

3. Execute the following command to get DBD-MySQL from CPAN:

```
perl -MCPAN -e 'install Bundle::DBD::mysql'
```

EXAMPLE 17.25

```
cpan> h

Display Information
 command  argument          description
 a,b,d,m  WORD or /REGEXP/  about authors, bundles, distributions,
modules
 i        WORD or /REGEXP/  about anything of above
 r        NONE              reinstall recommendations
 ls       AUTHOR            about files in the author's directory

Download, Test, Make, Install...
 get                        download
 make                       make (implies get)
 test      MODULES,         make test (implies make)
 install   DISTS, BUNDLES   make install (implies test)
 clean                      make clean
 look                       open subshell in these dists' directories
 readme                     display these dists' README files

Other
 h,?          display this menu       ! perl-code   eval a perl
command
 o conf [opt] set and query options   q             quit the cpan
shell
 reload cpan  load CPAN.pm again      reload index  load newer
indices
 autobundle   Snapshot                force cmd     unconditionally
do cmd
cpan>
```

17.4.2 The DBI Class Methods

The DBI module is object oriented and comes with a number of methods and variables. The documentation for this module is listed next. The database objects are called handles. Database handles connect to a specific database, and statement handles are used to send SQL statements to the database. Notice that names such as *$dbi*, *$sth*, *$rc*, etc., are use to describe statement handles, return codes, rows of data, etc. (These names are conventions only in the documentation; e.g., *$dbh* represents a database handle, and *$sth* a statement handle.)

```
$ perldoc DBI
 Notation and Conventions
   The following conventions are used in this document:

     $dbh    Database handle object
     $sth    Statement handle object
     $drh    Driver handle object (rarely seen or used in applications)
     $h      Any of the handle types above ($dbh, $sth, or $drh)
     $rc     General Return Code  (boolean: true=ok, false=error)
     $rv     General Return Value (typically an integer)
     @ary    List of values returned from the database, typically a row
of dat

     $rows   Number of rows processed (if available, else -1)
     $fh     A filehandle
     undef   NULL values are represented by undefined values in Perl
     \%attr  Reference to a hash of attribute values passed to methods

   Note that Perl will automatically destroy database and statement
   handle objects if all references to them are deleted.

NAME
   DBI - Database independent interface for Perl

SYNOPSIS
     use DBI;
     @driver_names = DBI->available_drivers;
     @data_sources = DBI->data_sources($driver_name, \%attr);
     $dbh = DBI->connect($data_source, $username, $auth, \%attr);

     $rv  = $dbh->do($statement);
     $rv  = $dbh->do($statement, \%attr);
     $rv  = $dbh->do($statement, \%attr, @bind_values);

     $ary_ref  = $dbh->selectall_arrayref($statement);
     $hash_ref = $dbh->selectall_hashref($statement, $key_field);

     $ary_ref  = $dbh->selectcol_arrayref($statement);
     $ary_ref  = $dbh->selectcol_arrayref($statement, \%attr);

     @row_ary  = $dbh->selectrow_array($statement);
     $ary_ref  = $dbh->selectrow_arrayref($statement);
     $hash_ref = $dbh->selectrow_hashref($statement);

     $sth = $dbh->prepare($statement);
     $sth = $dbh->prepare_cached($statement);

     $rc = $sth->bind_param($p_num, $bind_value);
     $rc = $sth->bind_param($p_num, $bind_value, $bind_type);
     $rc = $sth->bind_param($p_num, $bind_value, \%attr);
```

```
$rv = $sth->execute;
$rv = $sth->execute(@bind_values);
$rv = $sth->execute_array(\%attr, ...);

$rc = $sth->bind_col($col_num, \$col_variable);
$rc = $sth->bind_columns(@list_of_refs_to_vars_to_bind);

@row_ary  = $sth->fetchrow_array;
$ary_ref  = $sth->fetchrow_arrayref;
$hash_ref = $sth->fetchrow_hashref;

$ary_ref  = $sth->fetchall_arrayref;
$ary_ref  = $sth->fetchall_arrayref( $slice, $max_rows );

$hash_ref = $sth->fetchall_hashref( $key_field );

$rv  = $sth->rows;

$rc  = $dbh->begin_work;
$rc  = $dbh->commit;
$rc  = $dbh->rollback;

$quoted_string = $dbh->quote($string);

$rc  = $h->err;
$str = $h->errstr;
$rv  = $h->state;

$rc  = $dbh->disconnect;

*The synopsis above only lists the major methods and parameters.*
```

17.4.3 How to Use DBI

Once you load the DBI module into your program with the *use DBI* statement, there are only five steps involved: connect to a database, prepare a query, execute the query, get the results, and disconnect.

To connect to MySQL, use the *connect()* method. This method specifies the type of database (MySQL, Oracle, Sybase, CSV files, Informix, etc.), the database name, host name, user and password with some additional, optional arguments to specify error and transaction handling, etc. It returns a database handle (*$dbh* is used in the manual page, but you can call it any valid scalar name).

Once connected to the MySQL database, you have a database handle (reference to the database object). Now you can send a query by preparing and executing a SQL statement. This can be done by calling the *prepare()* and *execute()* methods or by using the *do()* method. The *prepare()* and *execute()* methods are used for *SELECT* statements, whereas the *do()* method is normally used for SQL statements that don't return a result set, such as the *INSERT*, *UPDATE*, or *DELETE* statements. What is returned from these methods depends on what the query returns. For example, successful *SELECT* queries return a result set (represented as *$sth* in the DBI manual page); successful *INSERT/UPDATE/DELETE* queries with *do()* return the number of rows affected; and unsuccessful queries return an error or *undef*. Most data is returned to the Perl script as strings, and null values are returned as *undef*.

Once the query has been sent to the database and a result set returned (reference to the result object), you can extract the data with special methods, such as *fetchrow_array()* and *fetchrow_hashref()*. These methods retrieve each record as a Perl array or a Perl hash, respectively.

Finally, when you are done, the *finish()* method releases the result object returned from *prepare()* method, and the *disconnect()* method ends the session by disconnecting from the database.

Now we will go through each of these five steps in detail.

17.4.4 Connecting to and Disconnecting from the Database

Once loaded, the DBI module is responsible for loading the appropriate driver for a given database. Then you will work with the database by using the methods provided by the module listed in the output shown from *perldoc* DBI. The first method we will use is the *connect()* method to get a connection to the database, and the last method, *disconnect()*, to break the connection.

Checking Available Database Drivers for DBI

EXAMPLE 17.26

```
1 use DBI;
2 my @drivers = DBI->available_drivers;
3 print join(", ", @drivers),"\n";

(Output for Windows)
DBM, ExampleP, File, Gofer, Proxy, SQLite, Sponge, mysql
```

The *connect()* Method. The *connect()* method establishes a connection to the specified database and returns an object called a database handle. You can make multiple connections to the same database or even to different databases in a program by using multiple *connect* statements. The *connect()* method takes several arguments:

```
"dbi:$driver:$database,$port,$username,$password"
```

1. The first argument is the DSN string (Data Source Name), the logical name for the database. Any attributes that define the data source are assigned to the DSN for retrieval by the driver. The DSN contains the name of the DBI module, DBI, followed by a colon and the database driver (MySQL, Sybase, Oracle), another colon and the name of the actual database for which the connection will be made, and/or the hostname (default is "localhost"), port, etc., and terminated with a semicolon.

2. The next argument to connect is the name of the user.
3. Then the password of the user (optional, unless required).
4. And finally a reference to a hash (set of optional attributes for error handling, autocommiting, etc.).

EXAMPLE 17.27

```
1 $dbh=
DBI->connect("dbi:<RDMS>:<database>","<username>","<password>",
                  \%attributes) or die("Couldn't connect");

2 $dbh=DBI->connect('DBI:mysql:sample_db','root','quigley1') or
                                           die "Can't connect";

3 $dbh=DBI->connect('DBI:mysql:database=sample_db;user=root;
                                           password=quigley1');

4 $dsn = dbi:mysql:northwind; $username="root"; $password="letmein";
  $dbh = DBI->connect($dsn, $user, $password,
      { PrintError => 0, RaiseError => 1, AutoCommit => 0 });

-------------------Using Other Database Systems------------

5 $dbh = DBI->connect('dbi:Oracle:payroll','scott','tiger');
  $dbh = DBI->connect("dbi:Oracle:host=torch.cs.dal.ca;sid=TRCH",
$user, $passwd);
  (Oracle)

6 $dbh = DBI->connect('dbi:odbc:MSS_pubs','sa', '12mw_1');
  (MS SQL Server)
```

EXPLANATION

1 The *connect* method will return a database handle. This is the format you use to connect. At minimum, you must have the DSN string, which is the name of the module, *dbi*, the name of the database driver, and the name of the database represented as *<database>*. The username, hostname, password, and other attributes are optional.

2 The arguments to the *connect* method should be on one line with no spaces around the arguments.

3 DBI->errstr returns the reason why we couldn't connect—"Bad password," for example.

4 This connection will be made to a MySQL database named "northwind", with a user name "root" and password "letmein". The attributes are to turn on error.

5 This connection will be made to an Oracle database called "*payroll*", with a username of "*scott*" and a password "*tiger*".

6 The data source name of "*MSS_pubs*" uses the username "*sa*", password "*12mw_l*", and the ODBC driver.

17.4.5 The *disconnect()* Method

As you may remember from Chapter 10, after we opened a file with a user-defined filehandle, we closed it with the built-in *close* function when finished, and had we forgotten to close it, it would be left up to the operating system to do so when the Perl script exited. The same thing is true with closing a database. After you are finished using the database, it is always a good idea to close the connection with the *disconnect* method. Of course, because the database handle is an object, Perl will automatically remove the reference to it once the program exits or the object goes out of scope.

```
$dbh->disconnect();
```

17.4.6 Preparing a Statement Handle and Fetching Results

The SQL *select* statement is probably the statement used most when querying a database. When preparing a *select* statement for the database, the query is sent as a string argument to the DBI *prepare* method. The query is just as you would type it in the MySQL console **but minus the semicolon**. The database handle calls the *prepare* method. The database determines how it will execute the query (creates a "plan"), and DBI returns a statement handle containing the details on how the query will be executed. The statement handle (represented as *$sth*) encapsulates individual SQL statements to be executed within the database and calls the *execute* method.

This *execute* method tells the database to perform the SQL statement (execute its "plan") and to return the results back to the program. An *undef* is returned if an error occurs. A successful execute always returns true regardless of the number of rows affected, even if zero rows were affected. Once executed, the "plan" is discarded (see the *prepare_cache* method, on page 664). The number of statement handles that can be created and executed is basically unlimited.

Even though you have executed the plan, you can't see the results unless you use another DBI method to retrieve it, such as *dump_results()*, *fetchrow_array()*, or *fetch()*, etc.

Select, Execute, and Dump the Results. The DBI *dump_results* method gets all the rows from the statement handle object and prints the results in one simple statement.

Connect, Prepare, Execute, and Dump Results

EXAMPLE 17.28

```
   (The Script)
   use DBI;
1  $db=
DBI->connect('DBI:mysql:sample_db;user=root;password=quigley1');

2  $sth=$db->prepare("SELECT * FROM coaches")
   or die "Can't prepare sql statement" . DBI->errstr;
3  $sth->execute();
   print qq(\n\tContents of "coaches" table\n);
```

EXAMPLE 17.28 (CONTINUED)

```
4    $sth->dump_results();   # Display results of the execute

5    $sth->finish();
6    $dbh->disconnect();

(Output)
         Contents of "coaches" table
'1', 'John Doe', 'Chico Hardhats', 'Head Coach', '2002-12-10'
'2', 'Jack Mattsone', 'CHardhats', 'Offensive Coach', '2004-10-05'
'3', 'Bud Wilkins', 'Fremont Tigers', 'Head Coach', '1999-09-06'
'4', 'Joe Hayes', 'Fremont Tigers', 'Defensive Coach', '1998-06-16'
'5', 'George Jones', 'Bangor Rams', 'Offensive Coach', '2003-09-03'
'6', 'Jerry O'Connell','Portland Penguins','Head Coach', '2006-02-22'
6 rows
```

EXPLANATION

1. A connection is made to the MySQL database called *sample_db* and a database handle is returned called *$dbh*. It is the object that represents the connection. Now we have access to the database.
2. The *prepare* method is used to prepare the SQL query. It returns a statement handle, an object that encapsulates the query and prepares it for execution. (Note that the SQL statement does NOT end with a semicolon.)
3. The *execute* method causes the query to actually be excuted. Now we are ready to retrieve the results of the query.
4. The *dump_results* method is called by the statement handle and prints the results of the query.

Select, Execute, and Fetch a Row as an Array. When the *fetchrow_array()* method is called, the database will return the first row of results as an array, where each field is an element in the array. Each successive call to the *fetchrow_array()* method yields the next row of results, until there are no more results and the call yields a value of *undef*. A *while* or *for* loop can be used to fetch all of the rows as shown in Example 17.29. (An important point to remember is that when the fields are fetched, they are assigned in the order they were listed in the SQL query.)

Connnect, Prepare, Execute, and Fetch the Data with *fetchrow_array()*

EXAMPLE 17.29

```
(The Script)
   use DBI;
   my $dbh=DBI->connect(qq(DBI:mysql:database=sample_db;user=root;
        password=quigley1)) or die "Can't connect";
```

EXAMPLE 17.29 (CONTINUED)

```
2   my $sth=$dbh->prepare("SELECT name, wins, losses FROM teams");

3   $sth->execute();
    print "Contents of sample_db, the mysql database.\n\n";

4    while(my @row=$sth->fetchrow_array()){ # Get one row at a time
5        print "name=$row[0]\n";        # Field one
         print "wins=$row[1]\n";        # Field two
         print "losses=$row[2]\n\n";   # Field three
           }
6   print $sth->rows, " rows were retrieved.\n";

7   $sth->finish();
8   $dbh->disconnect();
```

```
(The Output)
Contents of sample_db, the mysql database.

name=Fremont Tigers
wins=24
losses=26

name=Chico Hardhats
wins=19
losses=25

name=Bath Warships
wins=32
losses=3

name=Bangor Rams
wins=22
losses=24

4 rows were retrieved.
```

EXPLANATION

1 The *connect()* method returns a database handle, *$dbh*, an object that references the MySQL database called *sample_db*.
2 A SQL *select* statement is prepared and a statement handle returned, called *$sth*.
3 The query is sent to the database for execution.
4 The *fetch_row_array()* method returns the first row from the database, where fields are elements of the array, called *@row*. To get subsequent rows, a *while* loop is used. The loop ends when there are no more rows.
5 Each field from a row is assigned to a variable and printed.
6 The *rows()* method returns the number of rows affected by the statement handle.

EXPLANATION (CONTINUED)

7 The *finish* method releases the statement handle.
8 The *disconnect* method releases the database handle.

Select, Execute, and Fetch a Row as a Hash. The *fetchrow_hashref()* method fetches a row from the database table as a hash reference where the keys are the names of the columns and the values are the data stored in that column. The following example is exactly like the previous one, except *fetchrow_arrayref()* is replaced with *fetchrow_hashref()*.

EXAMPLE 17.30

```
  use DBI;
1 $dbh=DBI->connect(qq(DBI:mysql:database=sample_db;user=root;
        password=quigley1)) or die "Can't connect";

2 $sth=$dbh->prepare("SELECT name, wins, losses FROM teams") ;

3 $sth->execute();
  $count=0;

  print "Contents of sample_db, the mysql database.\n\n";

4 while(  my $row = $sth->fetchrow_hashref()){
5    print "Name:    $row->{name}\n";
   print "Wins:    $row->{wins}\n";
   print "Losses: $row->{losses}\n\n";
   $count++;
 }

6 print "There are $count rows in the sample database.\n";
7 $sth->finish();
8 $dbh->disconnect();
```

EXPLANATION

1 The *connect()* method returns a database handle, *$dbh*, an object that references the MySQL database called *sample_db*.
2 A SQL *select* statement is prepared and a statement handle returned, called *$sth*.
3 The query is sent to the database for execution.
4 The *fetch_row_hashref()* method returns the first row from the database as a reference to an anonymous hash consisting of key/value pairs. The key is the name of the field in the table and the value is what is stored there. To get subsequent rows, a *while* loop is used. The loop ends when there are no more rows.
5 Each value from the field, specified as a key, is printed.

EXPLANATION (CONTINUED)

6 The *finish* method releases the statement handle.
7 The *disconnect* method releases the database handle.

17.4.7 Handling Quotes

When strings are sent to a database, they are enclosed in quotes. Strings themselves may also contain quotes as in the string "Mrs. O'Donnell", and these quotes must be properly escaped when sent to a database. To make things more complicated, different database systems have different rules for handling quotes. The DBI module handles quoting issues with its quote method. This method is used with a database handle to convert a string according to rules defined for a specific database and returns the string correctly escaped.

EXAMPLE 17.31

```
  use DBI;
  $dbh=DBI->connect(qq(DBI:mysql:database=sample_db;user=root;
        password=quigley1)) or die "Can't connect";
1 $namestring=qq(Jerry O'Connell);
2 $namestring=$dbi->quote($string);
3 print $namestring;
4 $sth=$dbi->prepare("SELECT * FROM coaches WHERE name=$namestring")
  or die "Can't prepare sql statement" . DBI->errstr;
  $sth->execute();
5 print qq(\nContents of "coaches" table\n);

6       while(my @val = $sth->fetchrow_array()){
          print "\tid=$val[0]\n";
          print "\tname=$val[1]\n";
          print "\tteam_name=$val[2]\n";
          print "\tteam_name=$val[3]\n";
          print "\tstart_date=$val[4]\n\n";
        }

  $sth->finish();
  $dbh->disconnect();

   (Output)
2 'Jerry O\'Connell'
5 Contents of "coaches" table
6       id=6
        name=Jerry O'Connell
        team_name=Portland Penguins
        team_name=Head Coach
        start_date=2006-02-22
```

EXPLANATION

1 A string variable, *$namestring*, is assigned a string of characters containing a single quote.
2 A DBI *quote* method is used to prepare the string for the *mysql* database by enclosing the string in quotes and escaping the single quote with a backslash.
3 This line shows you how the *quote* method prepared the string. Notice the apostrophe in O'Connell is escaped with a backslash.
4 In the *WHERE* clause the properly quoted string will be used to test whether its value matches the name of a coach in the *coaches* table. The following line illustrates how data is inserted at the MySQL client. You can see how quotes are managed in the string; i.e., single quote is embedded in double quotes:
mysql> insert into coaches values('',"Jerry O'Connell",'Portland Penguins', 'Head Coach','2006-2-22');
5, 6 The table is displayed.

17.4.8 Getting Error Messages

It is important to know what went wrong when working with DBI. Did the connection fail? Did you prepare the SQL statement correctly? DBI defines several ways to handle errors. You can use automatic error handling with the *PrintError* and *RaiseError* attributes for a specific handle, or you can use diagnostic methods and special DBI variables.

Automatic Error Handling. The DBI module provides automatic error handling when you connect to the database. You can either get warnings every time a DBI method fails or have the program send a message and abort. The two attributes most often used with the *connect* method are *PrintError* and *RaiseError*.

The *PrintError* Attribute

By default, the *connect()* method sets *PrintError* to "on" (set to 1) and automatically generates a warning message if any of the DBI methods fails.

The *RaiseError* Attribute

The *RaiseError* attribute can be used to force errors to raise exceptions. It is turned off by default. When set to "on," any DBI method that results in an error will cause DBI to die with an error, *$DBI::errstr*. If you turn *RaiseError* on, then you would normally turn *PrintError* off. If *PrintError* is also on, then the *PrintError* is done first. Typically, *RaiseError* is used in conjunction with an *eval* block so that you can catch the exception that's been thrown. If there is a "die," a compile, or runtime error in the *eval* block, the special variable $@ is set to the error message and set to null if there is not an error. If $@ has been set, then you can handle the error without exiting DBI. (See Example 17.32.)

Manual Error Handling. If you want to manually check for errors when a particular method fails, you can use either the error diagnostic methods or the error diagnostic variables provided by the DBI module. This gives you control over each method you call to trap the errors if they occur.

Error Diagnostic Methods

First we will look at two error diagnositc methods, *err()* and *errst()*. These methods can be invoked against any valid handle, driver, database, or statement. The *err()* method will return the error code associated with the problem that occurred. The error code is a number that differs depending on the database system being used. The *errstr()* method corresponds to the error code number but is a string that contains information as to why the last DBI method call failed. Before another method call, the error messages for a handle are reset, so they should be checked right after a specific handle has produced an error. The diagnosic methods are used as discussed next.

```
$rv  = $h->err();
$str = $h->errstr();
```

Error Diagnostic Variables

The DBI variables *$DBI::err* and *$DBI::errstr*, are class variables and behave similarly to the method described previously, except they have a shorter life span and always refer to the last handle that was used. The *$DBI::err* contains the error number associated with last method that was called, and *$DBI:errstr* contains a string describing the error message associated with the error number in *$DBI::err*. You should generally test the return status of connect and print *$DBI::errstr* if the *connect()* method failed.

EXAMPLE 17.32

```
   (The Script)
    use DBI;
    $driver="DBI:mysql";
    $database="sample_db";
    $user="root";
    $host="localhost";

    $dbh=DBI->connect('dbi:mysql:sample_db','root','quigley1',
                      {
1                           RaiseError => 1, # Die if there are errors
2                           PrintError => 0, # Warn if there are errors
                      }
3                   ) or die $DBI::errstr; # Report why connect failed

4   $sth=$dbh->prepare("SELECT name, wins, losses FROM teams") or die
"Can't prepare sql statement" . DBI->errstr;
    $sth->execute();
    print "Contents of sample_db, the mysql database.\n\n";
```

EXAMPLE 17.32 (CONTINUED)

```
    while(my @val = $sth->fetchrow_array()){
            print "name=$val[0]\n";
            print "wins=$val[1]\n";
            print "losses=$val[2]\n\n";
                }
5     print $sth->rows," rows were retrieved.\n";

      $sth->finish();
      $dbh->disconnect();
```

EXPLANATION

1. Here we turn on the *RaiseError* attribute, which will cause the program to die if there is an error from any DBI method call.
2. The *PrintError* attribute is turned on by default. It sends a warning message if a method fails. It is set to 0 here to turn it off, since *RaiseError* is turned on. You can have both *RaiseError* and *PrintError* turn on or off. If both are turned on, the *PrintError* sends a warning first, and then *RaiseError* prints a message, and the program dies.
3. The *$DBI::errstr* variable will print the reason the connection failed, if it did.
4. This time we use the *errstr* method to report an error that may have occurred if the *prepare* method failed; i.e., the SQL statement was incorrectly prepared.

Examples of Error Messsages

EXAMPLE 17.33

```
1 (Bad Database Name; connect failed)
    DBI connect('ample_db','root',...) failed: Unknown database
'ample_db'atfirst.dbi line 9

2   (Bad Password; connect failed)
   DBI connect('sample_db','root',...) failed: Access denied for user
'root'@'localhost' (using password: YES) at first.dbi line 9

3   (Bad SQL Query; execute failed)
DBD::mysql::st execute failed: Unknown column 'win' in 'field list' at
first.dbi line 23.
```

Binding Columns and Fetching Values. Binding columns is the most efficient way to fetch data. Binding allows you to associate a Perl variable with a field (column) value in the database. When values are fetched, the variables are automatically updated with the retrieved value, making fetching data fast. DBI provides the *bind_columns()* method to bind each column to a scalar reference. When the *fetch()* method is called, the values from the database are assigned to scalars of the same name rather than to arrays or hashes as seen in the previous examples.

Every time the *fetch()* method is called, the scalars will be updated with values from the current row.

(See *bind_col* in the DBI documentation for another way to bind columns.)

Binding Columns

EXAMPLE 17.34

```
     use DBI;
     my $driver="DBI:mysql";
     my $database="sample_db";
     my $user="root";
     my $host="localhost";

     my $dbh =
 DBI->connect("$driver:database=$database;host=$host;user=$user")
         or die "Can't connect: " . DBI->errstr;

1    my $sth=$dbh->prepare("SELECT name, wins, losses FROM teams")
         or die "Can't prepare sql statement" . DBI->errstr;

2    $sth->execute() or die "Can't prepare sql
         statement" . $sth->errstr;
;

3    my($name, $wins, $losses);# Scalars that will be bound to columns
4    $sth->bind_columns(\$name,\$wins,\$losses);
               # scalar references
         print "\nSelected data for teams.\n\n";
         printf"\t%-20s%-8s%-8s\n","Name","Wins", "Losses";
5        while( $sth->fetch()){
          # Fetch a row and return column values as scalars
             printf "   %-25s%3d%8d\n",$name, $wins, $losses;
         }

     $sth->finish();
     $dbh->disconnect();

     (Output)
     Selected data for teams.

         Name                    Wins     Losses
    Bath Warships                 34         3
    Berkeley Bombers              12        19
    Denver Daredevils             23         5
    Littleton's Tigers            14        18
    Middlefield Monsters           2        32
    Palo Alto Panthers            24        17
    Portland Penguins             28        14
    San Francisco Fogheads        24        12
    Sunnyvale Seniors             12        24
```

EXPLANATION

1 The SQL *SELECT* statement is prepared and a statement handle returned.
2 The DBI *execute()* method sends the query to the database for execution.
3 Three scalar variables are created that will be bound to each of the three fields (columns) listed in the *SELECT* statement.
4 The *bind_columns* method specifies the names of the scalar variables that will be bound to the individual fields when the result set is retrieved from the database with the *fetch* method. (In older versions of DBI, the first argument was specified as *undef*; e.g., `$sth->bind_columns(undef,\$name,\$wins,\$losses);`); *undef* is used to represent a null field.
5 The *fetch* method retrieves a row from the result set and assigns each value to the variables named as arguments in the *bind_columns()* method. The name of the team is automatically assigned to *$name*, the number of wins to *$wins*, and the number of losses to *$losses*. Each time through the loop, the next row of column values will be assigned to these variables, and so on, until there is no more data.

The ? Placeholder. Placeholders, represented by a ?, are used to optimize how queries are handled. Placeholders provide a template for a query and represent values that will be assigned to fields at a later time.They are used primarily with *SELECT*, *INSERT*, *UPDATE*, and *DELETE* statements.

When a query is prepared by DBI, the database has to plan how it can best handle the query. The statement handle is used to store the prepared plan for the query, called the "execution plan." Normally, once a query has been executed, the plan is discarded. When placeholders are used, instead of discarding the execution plan, the database accepts the placeholder in a template and makes a plan around it—making the template usable for future queries.

The ? represents values, such as: *name* = ?, where *name* is a field name in the database table and its value will be supplied a value later on. (Remember, the ? represents a value, not a field name: ? = *"John" is wrong!)* **The *execute()* method takes arguments representing the values of the placeholders**, and those values are replaced in the prepared plan each time the method is called. DBI has to figure out the data type of the value. (Not all databases and DBI drivers support placeholders.)

Using a Placeholder

EXAMPLE 17.35

```
    use DBI;
    my $driver="DBI:mysql";
    my $database="sample_db";
    my $user="root";
    my $host="localhost";

    my $dbh =
DBI->connect("$driver:$database:$host;user=$user;
  password=quigley1")or die "Can't connect: " . DBI->errstr;
```

EXAMPLE 17.35 (CONTINUED)

```
1   my $sth=$dbh->prepare("SELECT name, wins, losses FROM teams
       WHERE name = ?") or
     die "Can't prepare sql statement" . DBI->errstr;

    print "Enter the team name: ";
2   chomp($team_name=<STDIN>);
3   $sth->execute($team_name);
# The value of $team_name replaces the ?
    print "\nSelected data for team \"$name\".\n\n";

4    while(my @val = $sth->fetchrow_array()){
           print "name=$val[0]\n";
           print "wins=$val[1]\n";
           print "losses=$val[2]\n\n";
 }
    $sth->finish();
    $dbh->disconnect();

(Output)
Enter the team name: Chico Hardhats

Selected data for team "Chico Hardhats".

name=Chico Hardhats
wins=18
losses=6
```

EXPLANATION

1 The *SELECT* statement contains a *WHERE* clause with a placeholder ? for the value that will later be assigned to the *name* field. The statement is prepared and a statement handle returned.
2 The user is asked for a team name, assigned to *$team_name*, later to be used as an argument to the *execute* method.
3 The value of *$team_name* is plugged into the placeholder in the query.
4 The *fetchrow_array()* method retrieves the values for the team that was specified when the query was executed in line 3.

Using Multiple Placeholders

EXAMPLE 17.36

```
use DBI;
my $dbh=DBI->connect("DBI:mysql:host=localhost;user=root;
password=quigley1;database=sample_db");
```

EXAMPLE 17.36 (CONTINUED)

```
1    my $sth=$dbh->prepare("INSERT INTO teams(name, wins, losses)
                    VALUES(?,?,?)");

     # Preset the values in variables
2    my $team_name="Denver Daredevils";  # set values here
     my $wins=18;
     my $losses=5;
3    $sth->execute($team_name, $wins, $losses);
     print "\nData for team table. \n\n";
4    $sth=$dbh->prepare("SELECT * FROM teams");
     $sth->execute();
5     while(my @val = $sth->fetchrow_array()){
          print "name=$val[0]\n";
          print "wins=$val[1]\n";
          print "losses=$val[2]\n\n";
        }

     $sth->finish();
     $dbh->disconnect();
```

EXPLANATION

1. This time, three placeholders act as a template for values that will be filled in at some later time with the SQL *INSERT* statement. Each ? represents a value for the *name* field, the *wins* field, and the *losses* field, respectively.
2. The scalars are assigned the values that will be sent to the database when the SQL statement is executed.
3. The *execute()* method executes the SQL statement by plugging in the values of these variables where the placeholders are found in the *INSERT* statement.
4. Another SQL statement is prepared to select all the fields in the table so that we can see if the new data was actually inserted.
5. The result set from the previous query is fetched a row at a time and displayed.

Using Placeholders to Insert Multiple Records

EXAMPLE 17.37

```
     use DBI;
     my $dbh=DBI->connect("DBI:mysql:host=localhost;user=root;
     password=quigley1;database=sample_db");

     # Using a placeholder. Values will be assigned later

1   my $sth=$dbh->prepare("INSERT INTO teams(name, wins, losses)
                    VALUES(?,?,?)");
```

EXAMPLE 17.37 (CONTINUED)

```
    # Create a list of new entries
2   my @rows = (['Tampa Terrors', 4, 5],
                ['Arcata Angels', 3 , 4],
                ['Georgetown Giants', 1 ,6],
                ['Juno Juniors', 2, 7],
               );

3   foreach my $row (@rows ){
       $name = $row->[0];
       $wins = $row->[1];
       $losses=$row->[2];
4      $sth->execute($name, $wins, $losses);
    }
    print "\nData for team table. \n\n";
5   $sth=$dbh->prepare("SELECT * FROM teams");
    $sth->execute();
         while(my @row = $sth->fetchrow_array()){
           print "name=$row[0]\n";
           print "wins=$row[1]\n";
           print "losses=$row[2]\n\n";
         }

     $sth->finish();
     $dbh->disconnect();
```

EXPLANATION

1. Again, three placeholders act as a template for values that will be filled in at some later time with the SQL *INSERT* statement. Each ? represents a value for the *name* field, the *wins* field, and the *losses* field, respectively.
2. An array of rows is created to represent the new records that will later be inserted into the database.
3. Each row from *@row* is broken down into its individual fields and the values assigned to scalars representing the value for each field.
4. The *execute()* method executes the statement by plugging in the values of these variables where the placeholders are found in the *INSERT* statement. This is done for each row of new data until it is all entered. If any of the teams are duplicates, the *execute()* method will fail because the *name* field was earlier assigned to be the primary key.

Binding Parameters and the *bind_param()* Method. Another convenient and efficient way to use placeholders is with the *bind_param()* method. The placeholder tells the database that the value represented by the ? will be filled in later. The bound parameter is the value that will be filled in to replace the ? and eliminates sending arguments to the *execute()* method.

The *bind_param()* method takes up to three arguments. The first argument represents the position of the parameter in the placeholder; i.e., if the position is 1, then that would be represented by the first ? (placeholder) to be filled in with a value, and if the position is 2, that would be represented by the second ?, etc. The second argument to *bind_param()* is the actual value that will replace the ?, and last, an optional parameter that hints as to the data type of the replacement value, typically a number or string. The data type for a placeholder cannot be changed after the first *bind_param()* method call. However, it can be left unspecified, in which case it defaults to the previous value.

Two ways to handle the data type are either as an anonymous hash or as a DBI constant:

```
$sth->bind_param(1, $value, { TYPE => SQL_INTEGER }); # Hash
$sth->bind_param(1, $value, SQL_INTEGER);   # DBI Constant
```

See Example 17.44 for how to use this third optional argument.

EXAMPLE 17.38

```
   use DBI;
   my $driver="DBI:mysql";
   my $database="sample_db";
   my $user="root";
   my $password="quigley1";
   my $host="localhost";

   my $dbh = DBI->connect("$driver:$database:$host","$user",
   "$password") or die "Can't connect: " . DBI->errstr;

1  $sth=$dbh->prepare("SELECT name, wins,losses FROM teams
   where name LIKE ?") or die "Can't prepare sql statement" .
DBI->errstr;

2  $sth->bind_param(1, "Ch%");
3  $sth->execute();
4  $sth->dump_results();
   $sth->finish();
   $dbh->disconnect();

(Output)
'Cheyenne Chargers', '6', undef
'Chico Hardhats', '21', '25'
```

EXPLANATION

1. A SQL statement is prepared with a placeholder that will serve as a template for the query.
2. The *bind_param()* method takes two arguments: the position of the placeholder; i.e., the ? represents the first parameter that will be filled and the value that will be assigned to that position, "*Ch%*".

EXPLANATION

3 Since the parameters were bound to the statement with *bind_param()*, the *execute()* method does not require arguments.

4 The DBI function *dump_results()* method is used to quickly output the results returned from the database after the query was executed.

Cached Queries. A cache is a temporary storage area where data that is frequently used can be copied and accessed more quickly. Most database servers utilize a cache to improve the performance of recently seen queries. A SQL statement can be cached rather than destroyed after it is executed. If another query identical to the cached statement is executed, the cached query can be reused. The DBI *prepare_cached()* method is used to cache a query. It is just like the *prepare()*, except that it looks to see if the same SQL statement has been previously executed, and if so, gives you the cached statement handle rather than a brand new one. (If you are managing multiple connections, see Apache::DBI::Cache.)

EXAMPLE 17.39

```
   use DBI;
   my $driver="DBI:mysql";
   my $database="sample_db";
   my $host="localhost";
   my $user="root";
   my $password="quigley1";
   my$dbh=DBI->connect("$driver:database=$database;
   host=$host;user=$user;password=$password")or
        die "Can't connect: " . DBI->errstr;

1  sub get_wins{      # Subroutine to handle database query
2       my($dbh, $team) = @_;
3       my $sth=$dbh->prepare_cached("SELECT wins FROM teams
               WHERE name = ?") or
        die "Can't prepare sql statement" . DBI->errstr;

4       $sth->execute($team);

        $wins=$sth->fetchrow_array();
5       return $wins;
   }

     STARTOVER: {
6       print "To see how many wins, please enter the team's name. ";
        chomp($team_name=<STDIN>);
             # Call a function to process database query
```

EXAMPLE 17.39 (CONTINUED)

```
7       print "$team_name has won ", get_wins($db, $team_name),
             "   games.\n";
        print "Do you want to check wins for another team? ";
        chomp($ans = <STDIN>);
8       redo STARTOVER if $ans =~ /y|yes/i;
    }
    $sth->finish();
    $dbh->disconnect();

(Output)
5 To see how many wins, please enter the team's name. Tampa Terrors
  Tampa Terrors have won 3 games.
7 Do you want to check wins for another team? y
5 To see how many wins, please enter the team's name. San Francisco
Fogheads
 San Francisco Fogheads have won 24 games.
7 Do you want to check wins for another team? y
5  To see how many wins, please enter the team's name. Chico Hardhats
  Chico Hardhats have won 21 games.
7  Do you want to check wins for another team? n
```

EXPLANATION

1 A user-defined function called *get_wins* will be used to handle the database requests.

2 The @_ contains two values, the database handle and the field name of a team in the database.

3 A statement is prepared and for efficiency, it is cached, rather than being destroyed after it is executed. For repeating the same query many times, this is done to make the processing more efficient. Since this function may be called a number of times, the *prepare_cache()* method is used. Other than its name, this method is just like the *prepare* method.

4 The query is executed and the name of the team filled in where the ? appears in the SQL statement.

5 The number of wins for a specified team is retrieved and returned from this function.

6 In this main part of the program, a labeled block is entered and the user is asked to select a team.

7 Within the *print* statement, the user-defined function called *get_wins* is called. The database handle and the name of the team selected by the user are passed to the function.

8 If the user wants to see the number of wins for another team, program flow will go back to the beginning of the labeled block and start again.

17.5 Statements that Don't Return Anything

17.5.1 The *do()* method

The *do()* method is used to prepare and execute nonselect, nonrepeating statements in one step. Statements such as the *UPDATE*, *INSERT*, or *DELETE* are examples of SQL statements that would use the *do* method. These statements change the database but don't return data. Unlike the *prepare* method, *do* doesn't return a statement handle but instead returns a count of the number of rows that were affected and *undef* if the query failed. The *do()* method returns a count of the number of rows that were affected and *undef* if the query failed. (A return value of –1 means the number of rows is not known, not applicable, or not available.)

```
$rows_affected = $dbh->do("UPDATE your_table SET foo = foo + 1");
```

The only drawback is performance if you are repeating an operation a number of times with placeholders, as we did in Example 17.39, because then, for each query the steps of prepare and execute must also be repeated over and over again.

Adding Entries. To add entries to a table in the database, the SQL *INSERT* statement is used in the DBI *do* method. The *do* method will return the number of new entries or *undef* if it fails.

EXAMPLE 17.40

```
   use DBI;
   my $dbh=
        DBI->connect("DBI:mysql:host=localhost;user=root,
                     password=quigley1;
                      database=sample_db");
   # Add two new entries
1   $dbh->do("INSERT INTO teams(name,wins,losses)
                VALUES('San Francisco Fogheads', 24,12)");

2   $dbh->do(qq/INSERT INTO teams(name, wins, losses)
         VALUES(?,?,?)/, undef,"Middlefield Monsters", 2, 32);

    $dbh->do(qq/INSERT INTO teams(name, wins, losses)
         VALUES(?,?,?)/, undef,"Littleton's Tigers", 4, 18);

3   $dbh->do("INSERT INTO coaches
                VALUES('','Roger Outback','San Francisco Fogheads',
                       'Defensive Coach','2006-03-16'");

   my $dbh->disconnect();
```

EXPLANATION

1, 2, 3 The DBI *do* method is used to insert values into the *teams* table in the *sample_db* database. The *prepare* and *execute* methods are absent here, because *do* does it all. It returns the number of rows affected.

Deleting Entries. In the following example, a record is deleted if some condition is true. Since the *delete* method doesn't return a result set, it is called with the DBI *do* method.

EXAMPLE 17.41

```
    use DBI;
    my $driver="DBI:mysql";
    my $database="sample_db";
    my $user="root";
    my $host="localhost";

    my $dbh = DBI->connect("$driver:database=$database;
        host=$host;user=$user") or die "Can't connect: " . DBI->errstr;

    print "Enter the team name you want to delete: ";
    chomp($name=<STDIN>);
1   my $sth=$dbh->prepare('SELECT count(*) from teams WHERE name = ?');
2   $sth->execute($name);
3   print "Number of rows to be deleted: ", $sth->fetchrow_array(), "\n";
    print "Continue? ";
    chomp($ans = <STDIN>);
    $ans=lc($ans);
    if ( $ans =~ /y|yes/){
4       $num=$dbh->do(qq/DELETE from teams WHERE name = ?/, undef,
        $name);
5       print ($num > 1 ?"$num rows deleted.\n":"$num row deleted.\n");
    }
    else {
        die "You have not chosen to delete any entries. Good-bye.\n";
    }
    $sth->finish();
    $dbh->disconnect();

(Output)
Enter the team name you want to delete: Sunnyvale Seniors
Number of rows to be deleted: 1
Continue? y
1 row deleted.
```

EXPLANATION

1 The name of the team to be deleted is assigned to *$team* as input from the user. The SQL statement will query the database with the *count* function to find out how many rows were found matching the selected team name.
2 The *execute()* method will send the query to the database, and the number of rows that matched the name of the team found will be returned.
3 The results of the query are fetched. The user is given the opportunity to remove the entries found. If there aren't any matched teams, there is no point in continuing.
4 The DBI *do()* method is used to prepare and execute the SQL *DELETE* statement.
5 The number of rows deleted returned.

Updating Entries. To update or edit a database entry, we use the SQL *UPDATE* statement with the DBI *do()* method.

EXAMPLE 17.42

```
     use DBI;
     my $driver="DBI:mysql";
     my $database="sample_db";
     my $user="root";
     my $password="quigley1";
     my $host="localhost";

     my $dbi=
  DBI->connect("$driver:database=$database;host=$host;user=$user;
  password=$password")or die "Can't connect: " . DBI->errstr;

     my $num_of_wins;
     my $num_of_losses;
     my $count;
1    print "What is the name of the team to update? ";
     chomp($team_name=<STDIN>);

     # Show user the table before he tries to update it
2    my $sth=$dbi->prepare(qq/SELECT * FROM teams
        WHERE name="$team_name"/) or die "Select failed: ". $DBI::errstr;
     $sth->execute() or die "Execute failed:".$DBI::errstr;
3    while(($name, $wins, $losses) = $sth->fetchrow_array()){
4       $count++;
        print "\nData for $team_name before update:\n"if $count == 1;
        print "\t\twins=$wins\n";
     print "\t\tlosses=$losses\n\n";
     }
5    if ($count==0){ die "The team you entered doesn't exist.\n";}
6    print "How many games has $team_name won since the last update?";
     chomp($num_of_wins=<STDIN>);
```

EXAMPLE 17.42 (CONTINUED)

```
7  print "How many games has $team_name lost since the last update? ";
   chomp($num_of_losses=<STDIN>);

8  $dbi->do(qq/UPDATE teams SET wins=wins+$num_of_wins
      WHERE name = ? /, undef, "$team_name") or
      die "Can't update teams :". DBI->errstr;

9  $dbi->do(qq/UPDATE teams SET losses=losses+$num_of_losses
      WHERE name = ? /, undef, "$team_name") or
      die "Can't update teams :". DBI->errstr;

   # Show the user the table after it is updated
   print "\nData for $team_name after update:\n";
10 $sth=$dbi->prepare(qq/SELECT * FROM teams WHERE
   name="$team_name"/);
   $sth->execute();
   while(($name, $wins, $losses) = $sth->fetchrow_array()){
      print "\t\twins=$wins\n";
      print "\t\tlosses=$losses\n\n";
   }

   $sth->finish();
   $dbi->disconnect();
```

```
(Output)
What is the name of the team to update? Chico Hardhats
Data for Chico Hardhats before update:
                wins=15
                losses=3
How many games has Chico Hardhats won since the last update? 1
How many games has Chico Hardhats lost since the last update? 2
Data for Chico Hardhats after update:
                wins=16
                losses=5
```

EXPLANATION

1. The user is asked to enter the name of the team in the *teams* table that he will edit.
2. A *SELECT* statement is issued to retrieve all the data in the *teams* table.
3. Before performing the update, the table will be displayed to see it in its current state.
4. The counter will keep track of how many records were returned.
5. If the count is zero, nothing was returned from the *SELECT*, and the program will die with an error message.
6. The user is asked to enter the number of games that have been won since the last update occurred.
7. And the user is asked how many games have been lost since the last update.

EXPLANATION (CONTINUED)

8 The DBI *do* method is used to prepare and execute the SQL *UPDATE* statement. It returns the number of rows that were affected by the update. This statement will update the *wins* column in the *teams* table.

9 This update is the same as the last one, except it increases the number of losses.

10 After the database table has been updated, this *SELECT* statement is reissued to show the user the table after it was edited.

17.6 Transactions

In the simple example of the *teams* table, if when the data is inserted for two teams, and the number of wins and losses for the two teams is accidentally swapped, an update would require both teams be modified, not just one. Suppose you are updating more than one table and the update statements in one table succeed and those in the other fail. For example, a classic example is that you take money out of a savings account in one table and put it in a checking account in another table. The deposit succeeds but the withdrawal fails. The tables are then in an inconsistent state. A transaction is a set of SQL statements that succeed or fail all as a unit. For example, *INSERT*, *UPDATE*, and *DELETE* statements may be executed as a group. If one fails, then none of the statements is executed.

By default, MySQL runs with *autocommit* mode enabled. DBI also runs with *autocommit* mode on by default. This means that as soon as you execute any statement that modifies a table, as long as no errors are returned, MySQL immediately commits the statement to the database, and any changes to the affected tables are made permanent.

To use transactions with MySql, *autocommit* mode must be disabled. We can do that in a Perl script when connecting to the database by setting the hash value of *AutoCommit => 0* as shown in Example 17.43.

In the examples shown so far, when we connected to a database, the hash options available to the *connect()* method for error handling were used, *PrintError* and *RaiseError*. To use transactions, we need to turn off the *AutoCommit* attribute, turn *RaiseErrors* on, and optionally leave *PrintError* "on" or "off," "on" being the default.

EXAMPLE 17.43

```
1 my $dbh = DBI->connect( 'dbi:mysql:sample_db','root','quigley1',
                          {
                           PrintError => 0,
                           RaiseError => 1,
2                          AutoCommit => 0
                          }
```

RaiseError tells DBI to die with the $DBI::errstr message if there are errors, and *PrintError*, by default turned on, tells DBI to send a warning with the $DBI::errstr and the program will continue to execute.

Commit and Rollback. Commit means in a transaction that a set of statements will be executed and sent to the database as a group. If all of the statements are successful, the group is committed and the database is modified. If, however, there is an error in any one of the statements in the group, a rollback command is issued, which returns all the tables back to their previous state.

Transactions are often handled in Perl by using an *eval* block to trap errors, then using the *commit()* or *rollback()* methods to finish the transaction.

In the following example, a group of records will be inserted into a table. If an error occurs in the process of adding these entries, the entire process will be rolled back. The error could be because an entry already exists.

EXAMPLE 17.44

```
1   use DBI qw(:sql_types);

2   my $dbh = DBI->connect('dbi:mysql:sample_db','root','quigley1',
                       {
                          PrintError => 0,
3                         RaiseError => 1,
4                         AutoCommit => 0
                       }
             ) or die "Connection to sample_db failed:  $DBI::errstr";
5   my @rows = (  # New rows to be inserted
                  [ 'Tampa Terrors', 3, 5 ],
                  [ 'Los Alamos Lizzards', 12, 3 ],
                  [ 'Detroit Demons', 22, 0 ],
                  [ 'Cheyenne Chargers',6, 0 ],
             );
6   my $sql = qq{ INSERT INTO teams VALUES ( ?, ?, ? ) };
7   my $sth = $dbh->prepare( $sql );
8   foreach $param (@rows) {
9      eval { # The eval block is used to catch errors
10     $sth->bind_param( 1, $param->[0], SQL_VARCHAR );
       $sth->bind_param( 2, $param->[1], SQL_INTEGER );
       $sth->bind_param( 3, $param->[2], SQL_INTEGER);
       $sth->execute() or die;
       };
    }
11  if( $@ ) {  # If eval failed. $@ is set to the error that occurred
       warn "Database error: $DBI::errstr\n";
12     $dbh->rollback();     # Reverse all commit statements
    }
    else{
13     $dbh->commit();
       print "Success!\n";
    }
    $sth->finish();
    $dbh->disconnect();
```

EXPLANATION

1. Constants representing the values of the SQL standard types are included with the special DBI *:sql_types* tag. The constants are used by the *bind_param* method starting on line 10.
2. Connection to the MySQL database is made.
3. The *RaiseError* attribute is turned on to catch exceptions and die if there is one.
4. The *AutoCommit* attribute is turned off, so that SQL statements are not automatically sent to the database but must be manually committed.
5. A list of of anonymous arrays is created to represent the rows that will be inserted into the table.
6. A SQL statement is created to insert new teams later; the values to be substituted for the ? placeholders.
7. The SQL statement is prepared. A statement bundle is returned.
8. The *foreach* loop is used to iterate through each of the rows that will be added.
9. The *eval* block is entered. If an error occurred, it will be assigned to the special variable, $@. See line 11.
10. The *bind_param()* method binds the first parameter to the first (?) placeholder in line 6. The first parameter, *$param->[0]* is '*Tampa Terrors*', the first time in the loop. It is of type *SQL_VARCHAR*. Next, the second parameter, *param->[1]* is bound to the second placeholder (?); the first time through the loop, it represents the number of wins, i.e., three, etc.
11. If one of the statements in the *eval* block failed, this variable will be set to the error.
12. If there was an error in the execution of any of the statements in the *eval* block, all of them will be discarded. The database will be rolled back to its original state. In other words, if one transaction fails, nothing is done.
13. If there were no errors, this block is executed, and all of the inserts will happen.

17.7 Using CGI and the DBI to Select and Display Entries

Once you have learned how to connect to a database and submit queries, you may want to use DBI in your CGI scripts to store and retrieve data for dynamic Web pages. In the first example, a simple CGI program demonstrates how to fetch data from the database and then format it as a table to be sent to the user's browser.

EXAMPLE 17.45

```
1 #!c:/ActivePerl/bin/perl.exe
2 use DBI;
3 use CGI qw(:standard);

4 my $dbh =
DBI->connect("DBI:mysql:host=localhost;database=sample_db;
   user=root;password=quigley1")or die "Connection to sample_db
failed:  $DBI::errstr";
;

5 my $sth=$dbh->prepare("SELECT * FROM coaches");
  $sth->execute();

6  print header, start_html(-title=>"Sample Database",
                            -BGCOLOR=>"#66ff33");
   print "<div align='center'>";
   print h2("Contents of the \"coaches\" Table");

7  print qq/<table border="1" cellpadding="10" bgcolor="white">/;
8  while(my @val = $sth->fetchrow_array()){
        print <<EOF;
         <tr>
              <td>$val[0]</td>
              <td>$val[1]</td>
              <td>$val[2]</td>
              <td>$val[3]</td>
              <td>$val[4]</td>
         </tr>
EOF
  }
   print "</table>";
   print end_html();
   $sth->finish();
   $dbh->disconnect();
```

EXPLANATION

1. The *shbang* (pound sign, bang line) tells the Web server where Perl is installed so it can start up the Perl interpreter. This line is necessary for any operating system using the Apache server.
2. We are going to be using the DBI module in this program to talk to the MySQL database.
3. We will use the function-oriented version of the CGI module to use the standard CGI functions to talk to the Web browser.
4. A connection is make to the MySQL database.
5. A SQL *SELECT* statement is prepared. It will retrieve all of the records for the *coaches* table.
6. The CGI header function sets the "*Content-type: text/hmtl\n\n*" line, and the HTML startup line to set a title and color for the HTML page. This information will be sent through the Common Gateway to the server and onto the browser.
7. An HTML table is created to hold the data that will returned from the database.
8. As the data is fetched from the database, it is formatted and sent back to the server, then presented as a table in the browser window.

The second example takes us full circle.

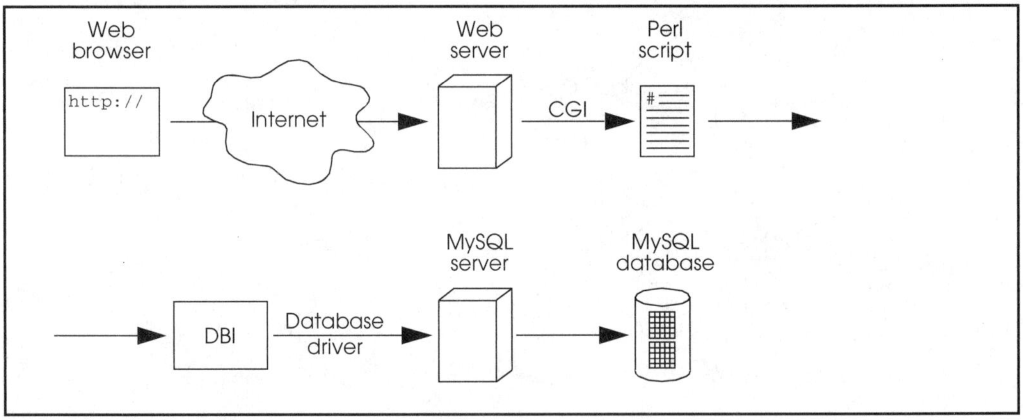

Figure 17.21 Client/server from browser to database.

CGI.pm creates a simple HTML form consisting of a text field. The user will select a team, type the team name into the form, and submit the form. The CGI program will process the form information, use the DBI module to connect to the MySQL database, retrieve the team's information, format it, and send it back to the browser as an HTML table.

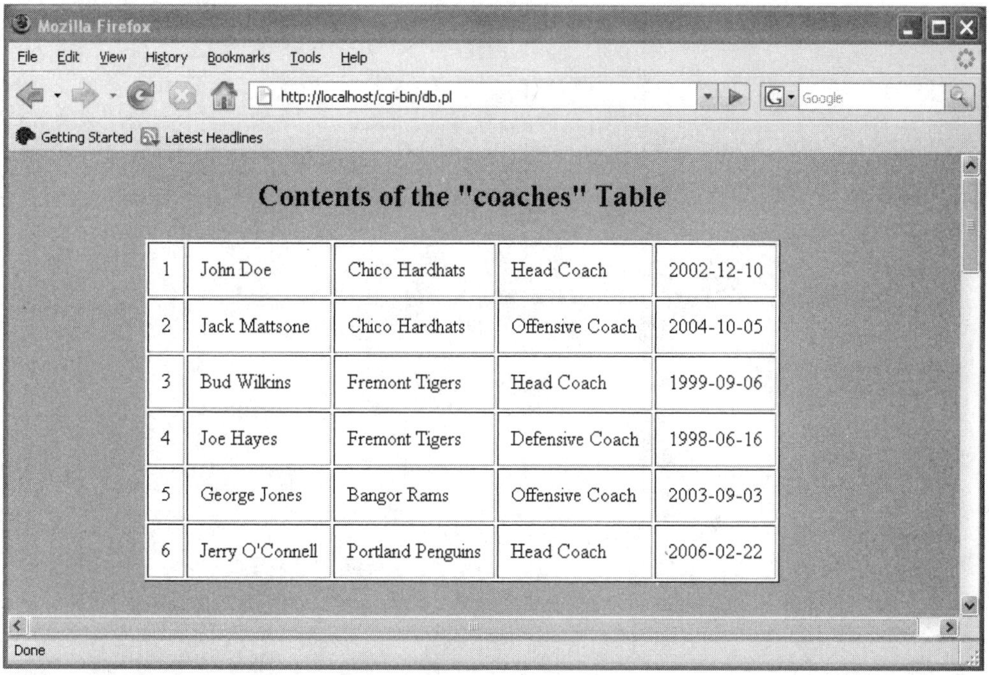

Figure 17.22 DBI and CGI output.

EXAMPLE 17.46

```
#!c:/ActivePerl/bin/perl.exe

use DBI;
use CGI qw(:standard);

print header, start_html(-title=>"Team Lookup",
                         -BGCOLOR=>"#66ff33"
                        );
print start_form,"<font face='arial' size='+1'>
Look up what team? ",textfield('name'),p;
print submit, end_form, hr;

if(param()) {
    $team = param('name');

    $dbh =
    DBI->connect("DBI:mysql:host=localhost;database=sample_db;
    user=root;password=quigley1") or
    print "Connection failed: ". $DBI::errstr;
```

EXAMPLE 17.46 (CONTINUED)

```
9        $sth=$dbh->prepare("SELECT name, wins, losses
                             FROM teams where name = ?"
                            );
         $sth->execute($team);
10       if ($sth->rows == 0){
            print "Your team isn't in the table.<br>";
            exit;
         }
         print h2("Data for \u$team");
         while(($name,$wins,$losses) = $sth->fetchrow_array()){
11          print <<EOF;
            <table border="1" bgcolor="yellow">
               <tr>
                  <th>Name</th>
                  <th>Wins</th>
                  <th>Losses</th>
               </tr>
               <tr>
                  <td>$name</td>
                  <td>$wins</td>
                  <td>$losses</td>
               </tr>
            </table>
12          EOF
            print end_html();
            $sth->finish();
            $dbh->disconnect();
         } # End while loop
      }  # End if block starting on line 6
```

EXPLANATION

1. The *shbang* (pound sign, bang line) tells the Web server where Perl is installed so that it can start up the Perl interpreter. This line is necessary for any operating system using the Apache server.
2. We are going to be using the DBI module in this program to talk to the MySQL database.
3. We will use the function-oriented version of the CGI module to use the standard CGI functions to talk to the Web browser.
4. This function starts an HTML form. This form is simple. It will consist of one HTML text field, where the user can enter data.
5. The CGI *submit* function creates the form's *Submit* button. Once the user clicks the *Submit* button, the form will be submitted, and the data that was entered into the text field will be sent to the CGI Perl script for processing.

EXPLANATION (CONTINUED)

6 Since the CGI module assigns this Perl script to the *ACTION* attribute in the HTML form, this Perl script will receive the form data and process it. The CGI module will check to see if there are any parameters, meaning, has the form returned any data? If the *params* function returns true, that means the form has been submitted and this part of the program will continue. If the params function returns false, then the form has not yet been submitted.

7 The name of the text field in the HTML form was "*name*". The CGI *params* function takes the name of the text field as an argument and sends back the value that was assigned to it; in this case, the name of a team.

8 We connect to the MySQL database to use the *sample_db* database.

9 A SQL statement is prepared with a placeholder that will later be assigned the name of a team from the *teams* table.

10 The query is executed and sent the name of the team the user selected when he filled out the form.

11 After the result-set is returned from the database, a *here doc* is started. An HTML table is created within the *here doc* to present the result set, returned from the database, in a nice structured format on the browser. CGI will send this table to the Web server (Apache) and then on to the broswer (Firefox).

12 This user-defined terminator marks the end of the *here doc*. Remember that this marker must be in the leftmost column of your Perl script and cannot have any trailing spaces; in fact, it must be terminated with a newline.

Figure 17.23 CGI, DBI, and a form.

17.8 What's Left?

This chapter was provided to introduce you to the MySQL relational database and how to issue SQL statements at the *mysql* client. After you learned the basic queries at the command line, the Perl DBI module was introduced so that you could perform the same *mysql* functions from your Perl scripts. We discussed the most commonly used DBI methods and how to use them for connecting to a database, selecting and retrieving data, updating and removing records, etc. Finally, we went to the next step and created a CGI/Perl program and used the DBI module to produce a dynamic Web page to interact with a user request from a fill-out form and respond with data retrieved from a database.

Although we have covered the DBI essentials, there is more to be learned. To find detailed documentaion of DBI, including methods, variables, constants, functions, etc., the best resource is found at the CPAN repository shown in Figure 17.24, written by Tim Bunce.

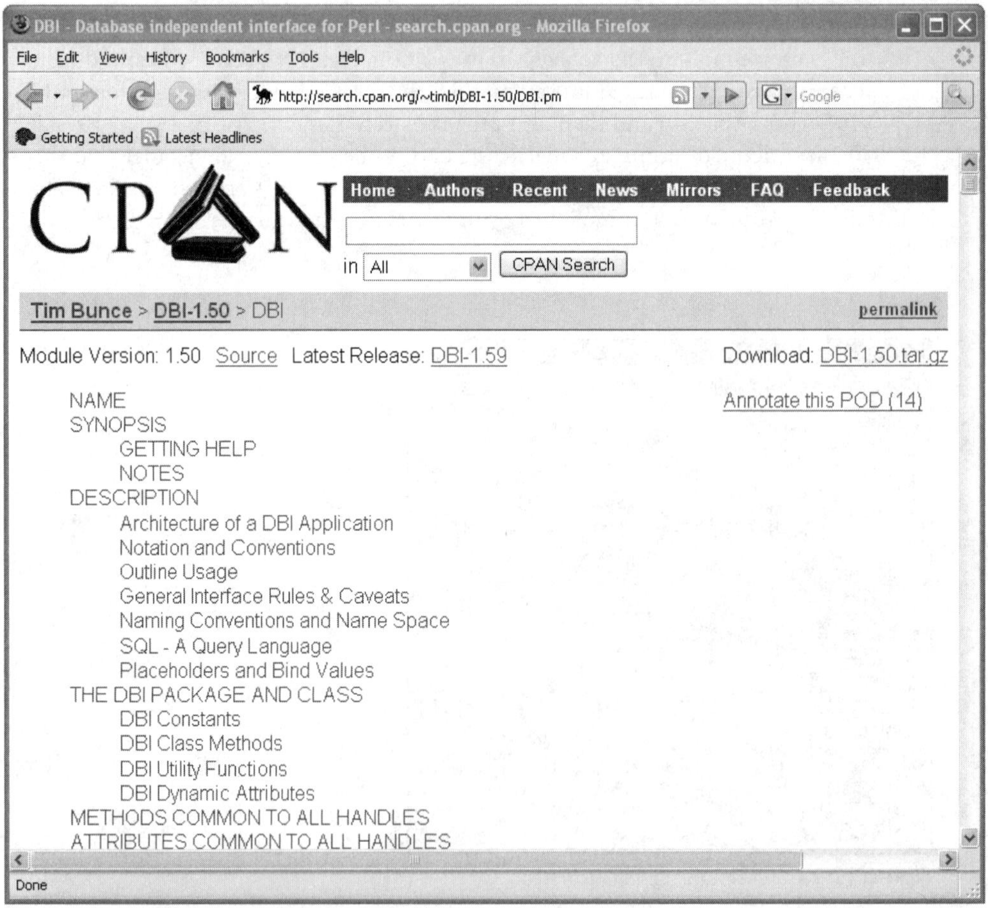

Figure 17.24 The CPAN repository.

17.9 What You Should Know

1. What is a relational database?
2. What is MySQL?
3. Where can you get MySQL?
4. What is the MySQL client?
5. How do you set a password for MySQL?
6. What is the *test* database for?
7. What is the *mysql* database for?
8. What is SQL?
9. What is DBI and how can you get it?
10. What is DBI-MySQL?
11. What is a database handle?
12. What is a statement handle?
13. How does Perl query a database, and where does the result set end up?
14. When you prepare a query for Perl's *prepare* method, is it the same as when you made the query in the MySQL client?
15. How do you retrieve the result-set from a Perl program?
16. What is a cached query?
17. What is the purpose of placeholders?
18. How do you know if your database connection was successful?
19. How do you close the database from a Perl script?
20. Who is Tim Bunce?
21. Where can you get a good tutorial on Perl DBI?
22. How does CGI fit in with DBI?

17.10 What's Next?

The next chapter discusses how Perl scripts can interface with the operating systems by issuing system calls and Perl functions to work with directories, permissions, ownerships, hard and soft links, renaming files, get file statistics, etc. You will learn how to use these functions on both UNIX- and Windows-based systems.

EXERCISE 17
Select * from Chapter

Part 1. SQL Lab—Using the "northwind" database:

1. Loading the "northwind" database from a script
2. The "northwind" database is a good sample database used with Microsoft's Access Database but tailored to work with MySQL as well.
3. You will be provided with the "northwind.sql" script for this exercise (on CD), a file containing SQL statements to create and populate the northwind database. The file must be located on the client host where you are running *mysql*.
4. To run the script, go to your MySQL console window and type:

    source c:\document\northwind.sql

   (Notice that there are no quotes around the name of the file and that absolute or relative pathnames can be used.)

   Ways to source the SQL script:
    mysql> SOURCE C:\path\northwind.sql;
    mysql> SOURCE ..\path\northwind.sql;
    shell> mysql db_name < input_file

   As the script executes, the results will be displayed on your screen, most of them SQL "*insert*" statements. If an error occurs, the process will be aborted, nothing done.

   See: *http://showroom.declarativa.com/northwind.htm*

Practice SQL Commands

1. After running the *northwind.sql* script, start by typing "*use northwind*".
2. Type the following SQL commands and explain what they do.
   a. *SHOW DATABASES;*
   b. *SHOW TABLES FROM NORTHWIND;*
   c. *SHOW FIELDS FROM SHIPPERS;*
   d. *DESCRIBE SHIPPERS;*

3. Use the SQL tutorial if you need it to:

   Select all rows from the *Shippers* table and display the fields.

   Select all rows from the *Employees* table and display only the *FirstName* and *Last-Name* fields.

Select the *CompanyName* and *Phone* from the *Customers* table only if the *Country* is Italy.

Print in sorted order the *ContactName*, and *Country* from the *Customers* table. Sort by *Country.*

Select the *ContactName*, *CompanyName*, and *Country* from the *Customers* table where the *Country* begins with either "*Po*" or "*Sw*".

The total number of products in the *Products* table.

Print only the first 10 products from the *Products* table.

Select countries from the *Customers* table in alphabetic order with no duplicates.

Find all the products between $10 and $20.

Insert a new product.

Update the products table by adding $5.25 to the unit price of Sir Rodney's Marmalade.

Select products below 10 units in stock.

Delete the oldest order in the database.

Use a SQL function to print the current date and time.

Part 2. Perl/MySQL Lab

Consult the MySQL documentation (mysql.com) to get the correct datatypes and functions to help you with this lab. The documentation is excellent.

1. Create a SQL script called "*school.sql*" that will:
   a. *DROP SCHOOL IF EXISTS SCHOOL;*
   b. *CREATE SCHOOL;*
   c. Create a table called "*student*". It will consist of the following fields:
      FirstName
      LastName
      Email
      CellPhone
      Major

GPA
StartDate
StudentID (primary key)

2. Use *school*
   a. Insert three rows of data into the student table.

3. At the MySQL prompt, execute the "*school.sql*" script.
   Use the SQL *describe* statement to see the structure of the *school* database.

4. Select all the rows in the *student* table. If the table has all the columns and data expected, then you are ready to go on to the next part of this lab.

5. In a Perl script use the DBI module to:
   a. Connect to MySQL and open the *school* database.
   b. Prepare a cached query to select all the rows in the *student* table, sorted by last names, and display all the columns with headings.

6.
   a. Create another Perl script so that the user can select options from a menu:
      1) Update a record
      2) Delete a record
      3) Insert a new record
      4) Display the table
      5) Exit

   For each of the options in the menu, create a subroutine that will perform the selected task, using MySQL functions. Can you create a CGI program to handle all of this?

   b. Create a loop so that the menu will be redisplayed until the user selects number 5.
   c. Rewrite the program by turning off *AutoCommit* and turning on *RaiseErrors*. Commit all changes to the database when the user chooses *exit*.

Part 3. Back to *Checking.pm*

1. Now you can redesign your original *Checking.pm* module to use the MySQL database rather than the text file you originally created to keep track of the balance.

   Create the database and the register table at the mysql prompt. This register should contain fields that match the text file called "*register*" you created in the first exercise.

   In the Perl module, *Checking.pm*, open the connection to the database. To get the balance, you will select it from the "*register*" table.

   When you call your *exit()* function, insert the last transaction into the database with the new information, using the SQL *INSERT* command.

   Create a Perl function that, when called, displays the contents of the register.

   You should know how to:
   Use PPM and CPAN to install MySQL, DBI, and the database driver.
   Issue basic MySQL commands.
   Connect to the database server from a Perl script.
   Use Perl MySQL functions to:
      Select a database
      Prepare and execute SQL statements
      Use DBI methods to iterate through the result set
      Use placeholders
      Bind columns and parameters
      Check for errors generated by the database server
      Keep track of the number of records retrieved
      Discard the planned query
      Disconnect from the database from a Perl script

chapter

18

Interfacing with the System

18.1 System Calls

Those migrating from shell (or batch) programming to Perl often expect that a Perl script is like a shell script—just a sequence of UNIX/Linux (or MS-DOS) commands. However, system utilities are not accessed directly in Perl programs as they are in shell scripts. Of course, to be effective there must be some way in which your Perl program can interface with the operating system. Perl has a set of functions, in fact, that specifically interface with the operating system and are directly related to the UNIX/Linux system calls so often found in *C* programs. Many of these system calls are supported by Windows. The ones that are generally not supported are found at the end of this chapter.

A **system call** requests some service from the operating system (kernel), such as getting the time of day, creating a new directory, removing a file, creating a new process, terminating a process, and so on. A major group of system calls deals with the creation and termination of processes, how memory is allocated and released, and sending information (e.g., signals) to processes. Another function of system calls is related to the file system: file creation, reading and writing files, creating and removing directories, creating links, etc.[1]

The UNIX[2] system calls are documented in Section 2 of the UNIX manual pages. Perl's system functions are almost identical in syntax and implementation. If a system call fails, it returns a –1 and sets the system's global variable *errno* to a value that contains the reason the error occurred. *C* programs use the *perror* function to obtain system errors stored in *errno*; Perl programs use the special *$!* variable. (See "Error Handling" on page 755.)

1. System calls are direct entries into the kernel, whereas library calls are functions that invoke system calls. Perl's system interface functions are named after their counterpart UNIX system calls in Section 2 of the UNIX manual pages.
2. From now on when referring to UNIX, assume that Linux also applies.

The following Perl functions allow you to perform a variety of calls to the system when you need to manipulate or obtain information about files or processes. If the system call you need is not provided by Perl, you can use Perl's *syscall* function, which takes a UNIX system call as an argument. (See"The *syscall* Function and the *h2ph* Script" on page 747.)

In addition to the built-in functions, the standard Perl library comes bundled with a variety of over 200 modules that can be used to perform portable operations on files, directories, processes, networks, etc. If you installed ActiveState, you will also find a collection of Win32 modules in the standard Perl library under *C:\perl\site\lib\Win32*.

To read the documentation for any of the modules (filenames with a *.pm* extension) from the standard Perl library, use the Perl built-in *perldoc* function or the UNIX *man* command. ActiveState (Win32) provides online documentation found by clicking the *Start* button, *Programs*, and then *ActiveState*.

EXAMPLE 18.1

```
(At the command line)
1   $ perldoc Copy.pm
```

EXPLANATION

The *perldoc* function takes a module name as its argument (with or without the *.pm* extension). The documentation for the module will then be displayed in a window (Notepad on Win32 platforms). This example displays part of the documentation for the *Copy.pm* module found in the standard Perl library.

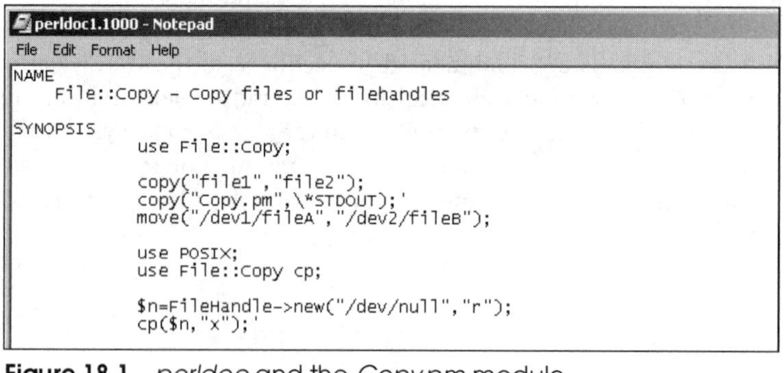

```
NAME
    File::Copy - Copy files or filehandles

SYNOPSIS
            use File::Copy;

            copy("file1","file2");
            copy("Copy.pm",\*STDOUT);'
            move("/dev1/fileA","/dev2/fileB");

            use POSIX;
            use File::Copy cp;

            $n=FileHandle->new("/dev/null","r");
            cp($n,"x");'
```

Figure 18.1 *perldoc* and the *Copy.pm* module.

18.1.1 Directories and Files

When walking through a file system, directories are separated by slashes. UNIX file systems indicate the root directory with a forward slash (/), followed by subdirectories separated by forward slashes where, if a filename is specified, it is the final component of the path. The names of the files and directories are case sensitive, and their names consist of alphanumeric characters and punctuation, excluding whitespace. A period in a filename has no special meaning but can be used to separate the base filename from its extension, such as in *program.c* or *file.bak*. The length of the filename varies from different operating systems, with a minimum of 1 character, and on most UNIX-type file systems, up to 255 characters are allowed. Only the root directory can be named / (slash).[3]

Win32 file systems, mainly FAT, FAT32, and NTFS, use a different convention for specifying a directory path. Basic FAT directories and files are separated by a backslash (\). Their names are case insensitive and start with a limit of 8 characters, followed by a period, and a suffix of no more than 3 characters. (Windows 2000/NT allow longer filenames.) The root of the file system is a drive number, such as *C:* or *D:*, rather than only a slash. In networked environments, the universal naming convention (UNC) uses a different convention for separating the components of a path; the drive letter is replaced with two backslashes, as in *\\myserver\dir\dir.*

Backslash Issues. The backslash in Perl scripts is used as an escape or quoting character (*\n, \t,\U, \$500*, etc.), so when specifying a Win32 path separator, two backslashes are often needed, unless a particular module allows a single backslash or the pathname is surrounded by single quote. For example, *C:\Perl\lib\File* should be written *C:\\Perl\\lib\\File*.

The *File::Spec* Module. The *File::Spec* module found in the standard Perl library was designed to portably support operations commonly performed on filenames, such as creating a single path out of a list of path components and applying the correct path delimiter for the appropriate operating system or splitting up the path into volume, directory, and filename, etc. A list of *File::Spec* functions is provided in Table 18.1.

Since these functions are different for most operating systems, each set of OS-specific routines is available in a separate module, including:

File::Spec::UNIX
File::Spec::Mac
File::Spec::OS2
File::Spec::Win32
File::Spec::VMS

3. The Mac OS file system (HFS) is also hierarchical and uses colons to separate path components.

Table 18.1 *File::Spec* Functions

Function	What It Does
abs2rel	Takes a destination path and an optional base path and returns a relative path from the base path to the destination path.
canonpath	No physical check on the file system but a logical cleanup of a path. On UNIX, eliminates successive slashes and successive "/.".
case_tolerant	Returns a true or false value indicating, respectively, that alphabetic case is or is not significant when comparing file specifications.
catdir	Concatenates two or more directory names to form a complete path ending with a directory and removes the trailing slash from the resulting string.
catfile	Concatenates one or more directory names and a filename to form a complete path ending with a filename.
catpath	Takes volume, directory, and file portions and returns an entire path. In UNIX, *$volume* is ignored, and directory and file are catenated. A "/" is inserted if necessary.
curdir	Returns a string representation of the current directory. "." on UNIX.
devnull	Returns a string representation of the null device. "*/dev/null*" on UNIX.
file_name_is_absolute	Takes as argument a path and returns true if it is an absolute path.
join	*join* is the same as *catfile.*
no_upwards	Given a list of filenames, strips out those that refer to a parent directory.
path	Takes no argument, returns the environment variable *PATH* as an array.
rel2abs	Converts a relative path to an absolute path.
rootdir	Returns a string representation of the root directory. "/" on UNIX.
splitpath	Splits a path into volume, directory, and filename portions. On systems with no concept of volume, returns *undef* for volume.
tmpdir	Returns a string representation of the first writable directory from the following list or "" if none is writable.
updir	Returns a string representation of the parent directory. ".." on UNIX.

EXAMPLE 18.2

```
1   use File::Spec;
2   $pathname=File::Spec->catfile("C:","Perl","lib","CGI");
3   print "$pathname\n";

(Output)
3   C:\Perl\lib\CGI
```

EXPLANATION

1. If the operating system is not specified, the *File::Spec* module is loaded for the current operating system, in this case *Windows 2000*. It is an object-oriented module but has a function-oriented syntax as well.
2. A scalar, *$pathname*, will contain a path consisting of the arguments passed to the *catfile* method. The *catfile* function will concatenate the list of path elements.
3. The new path is printed with backslashes separating the path components. On UNIX systems, the path would be printed */Perl/lib/CGI.*

18.1.2 Directory and File Attributes

UNIX. The most common type of file is a regular file. It contains data, an ordered sequence of bytes. The data can be text data or binary data. Information about the file is stored in a system data structure called an **inode**. The information in the inode consists of such attributes as the link count, the owner, the group, mode, size, last access time, last modification time, and type. The UNIX *ls* command lets you see the inode information for the files in your directory. This information is retrieved by the *stat* system call. Perl's *stat* function also gives you information about the file. It retrieves the device number, inode number, mode, link count, user ID, group ID, size in bytes, time of last access, and so on. (See "The *stat* and *lstat* Functions" on page 710.)

A directory is a specific file maintained by the UNIX kernel. It is composed of a list of filenames. Each filename has a corresponding number that points to the information about the file. The number, called an **inode number**, is a pointer to an inode. The inode contains information about the file as well as a pointer to the location of the file's data blocks on disk. The following functions allow you to manipulate directories, change permissions on files, create links, etc.

Directory Entry	
Inode #	Filename

Windows. Files and directories contain data as well as metainformation that describes attributes of a file or directory. The four basic attributes of Win32 files and directories are *ARCHIVE*, *HIDDEN*, *READONLY*, and *SYSTEM*. See Table 18.2.

Table 18.2 Basic File and Directory Attributes

Attribute	**Description**
ARCHIVE	Set when file content changes
HIDDEN	A file not shown in a directory listing
READONLY	A file that cannot be changed
SYSTEM	Special system files, such as *IO.SYS* and *MS-DOS.SYS*, normally invisible

To retrieve and set file attributes, use the standard Perl extension *Win32::File*. All of the functions return *FALSE* (*0*) if they fail, unless otherwise noted. The function names are exported into the caller's namespace by request. See Table 18.3.

Table 18.3 *Win32::File* Functions

Function	**What It Does**
GetAttributes(Filename, ReturnedAttributes)	Gets attributes of a file or directory. *ReturnedAttributes* will be set to the *or*ed combination of the filename attributes.
SetAttributes(Filename, NewAttributes)	Sets the attributes of a file or directory. *newAttributes* must be an *or*ed combination of the attributes.

To retrieve file attributes, use *Win32::File::GetAttributes($Path, $Attributes)*, and to set file attributes, use *Win32::File::SetAttributes($Path,$Attributes)*. See Table 18.4. The *Win32::File* also provides a number of constants; see Example 18.3.

Table 18.4 *Win32::File* Attributes

Attribute	**Description**
ARCHIVE	Set when file content changes. Used by backup programs.
COMPRESSED	Windows compressed file, not a zip file. Cannot be set by the user.
DIRECTORY	File is a directory. Cannot be set by the user.
HIDDEN	A file not shown in a directory listing.
NORMAL	A normal file. *ARCHIVE*, *HIDDEN*, *READONLY*, and *SYSTEM* are not set.
OFFLINE	Data is not available.
READONLY	A file that cannot be changed.
SYSTEM	Special system files, such as *IO.SYS* and *MS-DOS.SYS*, normally invisible.
TEMPORARY	File created by some program.

EXAMPLE 18.3

```
1   use Win32::File;
2   $File='C:\Drivers';
3   Win32::File::GetAttributes($File, $attr) or die;
4   print "The attribute value returned is: $attr.\n";
5   if ( $attr ){
6       if ($attr & READONLY){
            print "File is readonly.\n";
        }
        if ($attr & ARCHIVE){
            print "File is archive.\n";
        }
        if ($attr & HIDDEN){
            print "File is hidden.\n";
        }
        if ($attr & SYSTEM){
            print "File is a system file.\n";
        }
        if ($attr & COMPRESSED){
            print "File is compressed.\n";
        }
        if ($attr & DIRECTORY){
            print "File is a directory.\n";
        }
        if ($attrib & NORMAL){
            print "File is normal.\n";
        }
        if ($attrib & OFFLINE){
            print "File is normal.\n";
        }
        if ($attrib & TEMPORARY){
            print "File is temporary.\n";
        }
    }
    else{
7       print Win32::FormatMessage(Win32::GetLastError),"\n";
    }
```

```
(Output)
4   The attribute value returned is 18.
    File is hidden.
    File is a directory.
```

EXPLANATION

1 The *Win32::File* module is loaded.
2 The folder *Drivers* on the *C:* drive is assigned to *$File*.
3 The *GetAttributes* function is called with two arguments: the first is the name of the file, and the second is the bitwise *or*ed value of the attribute constants, *READONLY*, *HIDDEN*, etc. This value is filled in by the function *GetAttributes*. Note the *GetAttributes* function is called with a fully qualified package name. That is because it is listed in *@EXPORT_OK* in the *Win32::File* module and must be either specifically requested by the user or given a fully qualified name. If specifically requested, all of the constants would have to be listed as well or they will not be switched to the user's namespace.
4 The value of the *or*ed attributes is printed. If the value is *0*, something is wrong, and an error will be formatted and printed from line 7.
5 If one of the attributes for a file or directory is present, the following tests will show which ones were returned describing the file or directory.
6 By bitwise logically *and*ing the value of *$attr* with the value of a constant (in this case, *READONLY*), if the resulting value is true (nonzero), the file is read-only.
7 This function will produce a human-readable error message coming from the last error reported by Windows.

18.1.3 Finding Directories and Files

The *File::Find* module lets you traverse a file system tree for specified files or directories based on some criteria, like the UNIX *find* command or the Perl *find2perl* translator.

FORMAT

```
use File::Find;
find(\&wanted, '/dir1', '/dir2');
sub wanted { ... }
```

The first argument to *find()* is either a hash reference describing the operations to be performed for each file or a reference to a subroutine. Type *perldoc File::Find* for details. The *wanted()* function does whatever verification you want for the file. *$File::Find::dir* contains the current directory name, and *$_* is assigned the current filename within that directory. *$File::Find::name* contains the complete pathname to the file. You are *chdir()*ed to *$File::Find::dir* when the function is called, unless *no_chdir* was specified. The first argument to *find()* is either a hash reference describing the operations to be performed for each file or a code reference.

Table 18.5 Hash Reference Keys for *Find::File*

Key	Value
bydepth	Reports directory name after all entries have been reported.
follow	Follows symbolic links.
follow_fast	Similar to *follow* but may report files more than once.
follow_skip	Processes files (but not directories and symbolic links) only once.
no_chdir	Doesn't *chdir* to each directory as it recurses.
untaint	If -*T* (taint mode) is turned on, won't *cd* to directories that are tainted.
untaint_pattern	This should be set using the *qr* quoting operator. The default is set to *qr*|^([-+@\w./]+)$|.
untaint_skip	If set, directories (subtrees) that fail the **untaint_pattern** are skipped. The default is to *die* in such a case.
wanted	Used to call the *wanted* function.

EXAMPLE 18.4

```
(UNIX)
1   use File::Find;
2   find(\&wanted, '/httpd', '/ellie/testing' );

3   sub wanted{
        -d $_ && print "$File::Find::name\n";
    }

(Output)
/httpd
/httpd/php
/httpd/Icons
/httpd/Cgi-Win
/httpd/HtDocs
/httpd/HtDocs/docs
/httpd/HtDocs/docs/images
/httpd/Cgi-Bin
/httpd/Logs
/ellie/testing
/ellie/testing/Exten.dir
/ellie/testing/extension
/ellie/testing/mailstuff
/ellie/testing/mailstuff/mailstuff
/ellie/testing/OBJECTS
/ellie/testing/OBJECTS/polymorph
```

EXPLANATION

1. The *File::Find* module is loaded from the standard Perl library.
2. The first argument to *find()* is a reference to a subroutine called *wanted* followed by two directories to be found.
3. The *wanted* function will check that each name is a directory (*-d*) and list the full pathname of all subdirectories found. $_ is assigned the name of the current directory in the search.

EXAMPLE 18.5

```
   (Windows)
1  use File::Find;
2  use Win32::File;
   # Works on both FAT and NTFS file systems.
3  &File::Find::find(\&wanted,"C:\\httpd", "C:\\ellie\\testing");
4  sub wanted{
5      (Win32::File::GetAttributes($_,$attr)) &&
       ($attr & DIRECTORY) &&
       print "$File::Find::name\n";
   }

   (Output)
   C:\httpd
   C:\httpd/php
   C:\httpd/Icons
   C:\httpd/Cgi-Win
   C:\httpd/HtDocs
   C:\httpd/HtDocs/docs
   C:\httpd/HtDocs/docs/images
   C:\httpd/Cgi-Bin
   C:\httpd/Logs
   C:\ellie\testing
   C:\ellie\testing/Exten.dir
   C:\ellie\testing/extension
   C:\ellie\testing/mailstuff
   C:\ellie\testing/mailstuff/mailstuff
   C:\ellie\testing/OBJECTS
   C:\ellie\testing/OBJECTS/polymorph
```

EXPLANATION

1. The *File::Find* module is loaded from the standard Perl library.
2. The *Win32::File* module is loaded from the standard Perl library, from the site-specific directory for Win32 systems. It will be used to retrieve file or directory attributes.
3. The first argument to *find()* is a reference to a subroutine called *wanted* followed by two directories to be found.

EXPLANATION (CONTINUED)

4 The *wanted* function is defined.
5 The *wanted* function will check that each name is a directory by calling the *GetAttributes* function (*Win32::File::GetAttributes*) and will list the full pathname of all subdirectories found. $_ is assigned the name of the current directory in the search.

18.1.4 Creating a Directory—The *mkdir* Function

UNIX. The *mkdir* function creates a new, empty directory with the specified permissions (mode). The permissions are set as an octal number. The entries for the . and .. directories are automatically created. The *mkdir* function returns *1* if successful and *0* if not. If *mkdir* fails, the system error is stored in Perl's *$!* variable.

Windows. If creating a directory at the MS-DOS prompt, the permission mask has no effect. Permissions on Win32 don't use the same mechanism as UNIX. For files on FAT partitions (which means all files on Windows 95), you don't have to set permissions explicitly on a file. All files are available to all users, and the directory is created with all permissions turned on for everyone.

FORMAT

```
mkdir(FILENAME, MODE);   (UNIX)
mkdir(FILENAME);         (Windows)
```

EXAMPLE 18.6

```
(The Command Line)
1   $ perl -e 'mkdir("joker", 0755);'    # UNIX
2   $ ls -ld joker
    drwxr-xr-x  2 ellie         512 Mar  7 13:43 joker
3   $ perl -e "mkdir(joker);"            # Windows
```

EXPLANATION

1 The first argument to the *mkdir* function is the name of the directory. The second argument specifies the **mode**, or permissions, of the file. The permissions, *0755*, specify that the file will have read, write, and execute permission for the owner; read and execute for the group; and read and execute for the others. (Remember that without execute permission, you cannot access a directory.)
2 The *ls -ld* command prints a long listing of the directory file with information about the file, the inode information. The leading *d* is for directory, and the permissions are *rwxr-xr-x*.
3 On Win32 systems, the directory is created with all permissions turned on for everyone.

EXAMPLE 18.7

```
     # This script is called "makeit"
1    die "$0 <directory name>  " unless $#ARGV == 0;
2    mkdir ($ARGV[0], 0755 ) || die "mkdir:  $ARGV[0]:  $!\n";

(At The Command Line)
     $ makeit
1    makeit <directory name> at makeit line 3.
     $ makeit joker
2    makeit: joker: File exists
     $ makeit cabinet
     $ ls -d cabinet
     cabinet
```

EXPLANATION

1. If the user doesn't provide a directory name as an argument to the script, the *die* function prints an error message and the script exits.
2. Unless the directory already exists, it will be created.

18.1.5 Removing a Directory—The *rmdir* Function

The *rmdir* function removes a directory but only if it is empty.

FORMAT

```
rmdir(DIRECTORY);
rmdir DIRECTORY;
```

EXAMPLE 18.8

```
(At the Command Line)
1    $ perl -e 'rmdir("joke") || die qq(joke: $!\n)'      # UNIX
     joke: Directory not empty
2    $ perl -e 'rmdir("joker") || die qq(joker: $!\n)'
     joker: No such file or directory
3    $ perl -e "rmdir(joker) || die qq(joker: $!\n);"     # Windows
     joker: No such file or directory
```

EXPLANATION

1. The directory *joke* contains files. It cannot be removed unless it is empty. The *$!* variable contains the system error *Directory not empty.*
2. The directory *joker* does not exist; therefore, it cannot be removed. The system error is stored in *$!*.
3. On Win32 systems, *rmdir* works the same way. You just have watch the quotes if you are doing this at the MS-DOS prompt. The directory *joker* is not removed, because it doesn't exist.

18.1.6 Changing Directories—The *chdir* Function

Each process has its own present working directory. When resolving relative path references, this is the starting place for the search path. If the calling process (e.g., your Perl script) changes the directory, it is changed only for that process, not the process that invoked it, normally the shell. When the Perl program exits, the shell returns with the same working directory it started with.

The *chdir* function changes the current working directory. Without an argument, the directory is changed to the user's home directory. The function returns *1* if successful and *0* if not. The system error code is stored in Perl's *$!* variable.[4]

FORMAT

```
chdir (EXPR);
chdir EXPR;
chdir;
```

EXAMPLE 18.9

```
1  $ pwd          # UNIX
   /home/jody/ellie
2  $ perl -e 'chdir  "/home/jody/ellie/perl"; print `pwd`'
   /home/jody/ellie/perl
3  $ pwd
   /home/jody/ellie
4  $ perl -e  'chdir " fooler"  || die "Cannot cd to fooler: $!\n"'
   Cannot cd to fooler: No such file or directory
5  $ cd           # Windows
   C:\ellie\testing
6  $ perl -e "chdir fooler || die qq(Cannot to fooler: $!\n);"
   Cannot cd to fooler: No such file or directory
```

EXPLANATION

1. This is the present working directory for the shell.
2. The directory is changed to */home/jody/ellie/perl*. When the *pwd* command is enclosed in backquotes, command substitution is performed, and the present working directory for this process is printed.
3. Since the Perl program is a separate process invoked by the shell, when Perl changes the present working directory, the directory is changed only while the Perl process is in execution. When Perl exits, the shell returns and its directory is unchanged.
4. If the attempt to change the directory fails, the *die* function prints its message to the screen. The system error is stored in the *$!* variable and then printed.
5. The present working directory is printed at the MS-DOS prompt. *cd* prints the present working directory. (At the UNIX prompt, it is used to change directories.)
6. The attempt to change directory failed as in the preceding UNIX example. If the directory had existed, the present working directory would be changed.

---

4. *chdir* is a system call provided with Perl for changing directories. The *cd* command used at the command line is a shell built-in and cannot be used directly in a Perl script.

18.1.7 Accessing a Directory via the Directory Filehandle

The following Perl directory functions are modeled after the UNIX system calls sharing the same name. Although the traditional UNIX directory contained a 2-byte inode number and a 14-byte filename (Figure 18.2), not all UNIX systems have the same format. The directory functions allow you to access the directory regardless of its internal structure. The directory functions work the same way with Windows.

Inode	Filename
10	.
22	..
32	memo
45	mbox
23	notes
12	src

Figure 18.2 A UNIX directory.

The *opendir* Function. The *opendir* function opens a named directory and attaches it to the directory filehandle. This filehandle has its own namespace, separate from the other types of filehandles used for opening files and filters. The *opendir* function initializes the directory for processing by the related functions *readdir()*, *telldir()*, *seekdir()*, *rewinddir()*, and *closedir()*. The function returns *1* if successful.

FORMAT

```
opendir(DIRHANDLE, EXPR)
```

EXAMPLE 18.10

```
1   opendir(MYDIR, "joker");
```

EXPLANATION

1 The file *joker* is attached to the directory filehandle, *MYDIR*, and is opened for reading. The directory *joker* must exist and must be a directory.

The *readdir* Function. A directory can be read by anyone who has read permission on the directory. You can't write to the directory itself even if you have write permission. The write permission on a directory means that you can create and remove files from within the directory, not alter the directory data structure itself.

When we speak about reading a directory with the *readdir* function, we are talking about looking at the contents of the directory structure maintained by the system. If the *opendir* function opened the directory, in a scalar context, *readdir* returns the next directory entry. The *readdir* function returns the **next** directory entry. In an array context, it returns the rest of the entries in the directory.

FORMAT

```
readdir(DIRHANDLE);
readdir DIRHANDLE;
```

The *closedir* Function. The *closedir* function closes the directory that was opened by the *opendir* function.

FORMAT

```
closedir (DIRHANDLE);
closedir DIRHANDLE;
```

EXAMPLE 18.11

```
(The Script)
1   opendir(DIR, "..") || die "Can't open: $!\n";
                           # Open parent directory
2   @parentfiles=readdir(DIR);
                           # Gets a list of the directory contents
3   closedir(DIR);         # Closes the  filehandle
4   foreach $file ( @parentfiles )
                           # Prints each element of the array
        { print "$file\n";}

(Output)
.
..
filea
fileb
filec
.sh_history
stories
```

EXPLANATION

1. The *opendir* function opens the directory structure and assigns it to *DIR*, the directory filehandle. The .. (parent) directory is opened for reading.
2. The *readdir* function assigns all the rest of the entries in the directory to the array *@parentfiles*.
3. The *closedir* function closes the directory.
4. The files are printed in the order they are stored in the directory structure. This may not be the order that the *ls* command prints out the files.

The *telldir* Function. The *telldir* function returns the current position of the *readdir()* routines on the directory filehandle. The value returned by *telldir* may be given to *seekdir()* to access a particular location in a directory.

FORMAT

```
telldir(DIRHANDLE);
```

The *rewinddir* Function. The *rewinddir* function sets the position of *DIRHANDLE* back to the beginning of the directory opened by *opendir*. It is not supported on all machines.

FORMAT

```
rewinddir(DIRHANDLE);
rewinddir DIRHANDLE;
```

The *seekdir* Function. The *seekdir* sets the current position for *readdir()* on the directory filehandle. The position is set by the a value returned by *telldir()*.

FORMAT

```
seekdir(DIRHANDLE, POS);
```

EXAMPLE 18.12

```
(The Script)
1   opendir(DIR, "."); # Opens the current directory
2   while( $myfile=readdir(DIR) ){
3       $spot=telldir(DIR);
4       if ( "$myfile" eq ".login" ) {
            print "$myfile\n";
            last;
        }
    }
5   rewinddir(DIR);
6   seekdir(DIR, $spot);
7   $myfile=readdir(DIR);
    print "$myfile\n";

(Output)
.login
.cshrc
```

EXPLANATION

1 The *opendir* function opens the present working directory for reading.
2 The *while* statement is executed, and the *readdir* function returns the next directory entry from the directory filehandle and assigns the file to the scalar *$myfile*.
3 After the *readdir* function reads a filename, the *telldir* function marks the location of that read and stores the location in the scalar *$spot*.
4 When the *.login* file is read, the loop is exited.
5 The *rewinddir* function resets the position of the *DIR* filehandle to the beginning of the directory structure.
6 The *seekdir* function uses the results of the *telldir* function to set the current position for the *readdir* function on the *DIR* filehandle.
7 The **next** directory entry is read by the *readdir* function and assigned to the scalar *$myfile*.

18.1.8 Permissions and Ownership

UNIX. There is one owner for every UNIX file. The one benefit the owner has over everyone else is the ability to change the permissions on the file, thus controlling who can do what to the file. A group may have a number of members, and the owner of the file may change the group permissions on a file so that the group will enjoy special privileges.

Every UNIX file has a set of permissions associated with it to control who can read, write, or execute the file. There are a total of 9 bits that constitute the permissions on a file. The first 3 bits control the permissions of the owner of the file, the second set controls the permissions of the group, and the last set controls the rest of the world; that is, everyone else. The permissions are stored in the mode field of the file's inode.

Windows. Win32 systems do not handle file permissions the way UNIX does. Files are created with read and write turned on for everyone. Files and folders inherit attributes that you can set. By clicking the mouse on a file icon and selecting *Properties*, you can, in a limited way, select permission attributes, such as *Archive*, *Read-only*, and *Hidden*. See Figure 18.3.

If your platform is Windows NT, you can set file and folder permissions only on drives formatted to use NTFS.[5] To change permissions, you must be the owner or have been granted permission to do so by the owner. If you are using NTFS, go to Windows Explorer and then locate the file or folder for which you want to set permissions. Right-click the file or folder, click *Properties*, and then click the *Security* tab. You will be able to allow, deny, or remove permissions from the group or user.

See the *Win32::FileSecurity* module in the Perl Resource Kit for Win32 if you need to maintain file permissions. To retrieve file permissions from a file or directory, use the

5. NTFS is an advanced file system designed for Windows NT.

Win32::FileSecurity::Get($Path, \%Perms)* extension, where *$Path is the relative or absolute path to the file or directory for which you are seeking permissions, and *\%Perms* is a reference to a hash containing keys representing the user or group and corresponding values representing the permission mask.

Table 18.6 Win32 Extensions to Manage Files and Directories

Extension	***What It Does***
Win32::File	Standard module for retrieving and setting file attributes
Win32::File::GetAtributes(path,attribute)	Retrieves file attributes
Win32::File::SetAttributes(path,attribute)	Sets file attributes
Win32::AdminMisc::GetFileInfo	Retrieves file information fields: *CompanyName*, *FileVersion*, *InternalName*, *LegalCopyright*, *OriginalFileName*, *ProductName*, *ProductVersion*, *LangID*, and *Language*

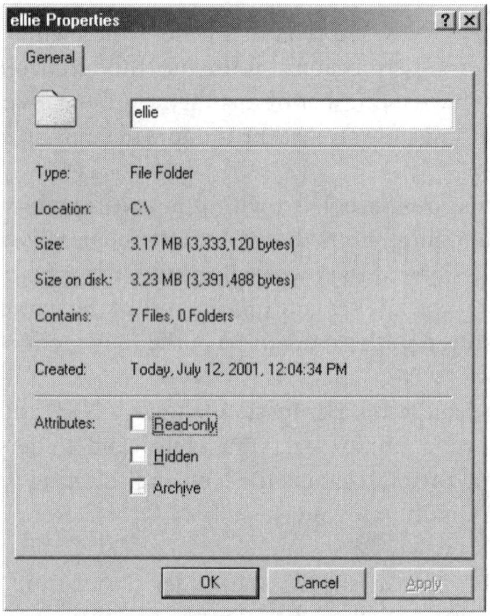

Figure 18.3 File attributes (Windows).

The *chmod* Function (UNIX). The *chmod* function changes permissions on a list of files. The user must own the files to change permissions on them. The files must be quoted strings. The first element of the list is the numeric octal value for the new mode. (Today, the binary/octal notation has been replaced by a more convenient mnemonic method for changing permissions. Perl does not use the new method.)

Table 18.7 illustrates the eight possible combinations of numbers used for changing permissions if you are not familiar with this method.

Table 18.7 Permission Modes

Octal	*Binary*	*Permissions*	*Meaning*
0	000	none	All turned off
1	001	--x	Execute
2	010	-w-	Write
3	011	-wx	Write, execute
4	100	r--	Read
5	101	r-x	Read, execute
6	110	rw-	Read, write
7	111	rwx	Read, write, execute

Make sure the first digit is a *0* to indicate an octal number. Do not use the mnemonic mode (e.g., +rx), because all the permissions will be turned off.

The *chmod* Function (Windows). ActivePerl supports a limited version of the *chmod* function. However, it can be used only for giving the owner read/write access. (The *group* and *other* bits are ignored.)

The *chmod* function returns the number of files that were changed.

FORMAT

```
chmod(LIST);
chmod LIST;
```

EXAMPLE 18.13

```
   (UNIX)
1  $ perl -e '$count=chmod 0755, "foo.p", "boo.p" ;print "$count
         files changed.\n"'
2  2 files changed.
3  $ ls -l foo.p boo.p
   -rwxr-xr-x  1 ellie    0 Mar  7 12:52 boo.p*
   -rwxr-xr-x  1 ellie    0 Mar  7 12:52 foo.p*
```

EXPLANATION

1. The first argument is the octal value *0755*. It turns on *rwx* for the user, *r* and *x* for the group and others. The next two arguments, *foo.p* and *boo.p*, are the files affected by the change. The scalar *$count* contains the number of files that were changed.
2. The value of *$count* is *2* because both files were changed to *0755*.
3. The output of the UNIX *ls -l* command is printed, demonstrating that the permissions on files *foo.p* and *boo.p* have been changed to *0755*.

The *chown* Function (UNIX). The *chown* function changes the owner and group of a list of files. Only the owner or superuser can invoke it.[6] The first two elements of the list must be a numerical *uid* and *gid*. Each authorized UNIX user is assigned a *uid* (user identification number) and a *gid* (group identification number) in the password file.[7] The function returns the number of files successfully changed.

FORMAT

```
chown(LIST);
chown LIST;
```

EXAMPLE 18.14

```
(The Script)
1   $ uid=9496;
2   $ gid=40;
3   $number=chown($uid, $gid, 'foo.p', 'boo.p');
4   print "The number of files changed is $number\.n";

(Output)
4   The number of files changed is 2.
```

EXPLANATION

1. The user identification number *9496* is assigned.
2. The group identification number *40* is assigned.
3. The *chown* function changes the ownership on files *foo.p* and *boo.p* and returns the number of files changed.

The *umask* Function (UNIX). When a file is created, it has a certain set of permissions by default. The permissions are determined by what is called the **system mask**. On

6. On BSD UNIX and some POSIX-based UNIX (Solaris), only the superuser can change ownership.
7. To get the *uid* or *gid* for a user, the *getpwnam* or *getpwuid* functions can be used.

most systems, this mask is *022* and is set by the login program.[8] A directory has *777* by default (rwxrwxrwx), and a file has *666* by default (rw-rw-rw). The *umask* function is used to remove or subtract permissions from the existing mask.

To take *write* permission away from the "others" permission set, the *umask* value is subtracted from the maximum permissions allowed per directory or file:

777 (directory)	666 (file)
– 002 (umask value)	– 002 (umask value)
775	664

The *umask* function sets the *umask* for this process and returns the old one. Without an argument, the *umask* function returns the current setting.

FORMAT

```
umask(EXPR)
umask EXPR
umask
```

EXAMPLE 18.15

```
1   $ perl -e 'printf("The umask is %o.\n", umask);'
    The umask is 22.
2   $ perl -e 'umask 027; printf("The new mask is %o.\n", umask);'
    The new mask is 27.
```

EXPLANATION

1. The *umask* function without an argument prints the current *umask* value.
2. The *umask* function resets the mask to octal *027*.

18.1.9 Hard and Soft Links

UNIX. When you create a file, it has one **hard** link; that is, one entry in the directory. You can create additional links to the file, which are really just different names for the same file. The kernel keeps track of how many links a file has in the file's inode. As long as there is a link to the file, its data blocks will not be released to the system. The advantage to having a file with multiple names is that there is only one set of data, or master file, and that file can be accessed by a number of different names. A hard link cannot span file systems and must exist at link-creation time.

A soft link is also called a **symbolic** link and sometimes a **symlink**. A symbolic link is really just a very small file (it has permissions, ownership, size, etc.). All it contains is the **name** of another file. When accessing a file that has a symbolic link, the kernel is pointed to the name of the file contained in the symbolic link. For example, a link

8. The user can also set the umask in the *.profile* (*sh* or *ksh*) or *.cshrc* (*csh*) initialization files.

from *thisfile* to */usr/bin/joking/otherfile* links the name *thisfile* to */usr/bin/joking/otherfile*. When *thisfile* is opened, *otherfile* is the file really accessed. Symbolic links can refer to files that do or don't exist and can span file systems and even different computers. They can also point to other symbolic links.[9]

Windows. The Win32 system introduced **shortcuts**, special binary files with a *.LNK* extension. A shortcut is similar to a UNIX link, but it is processed by a particular application rather than by the system and is an alias for a file or directory. Shortcuts are icons with a little arrow in a white box in the left corner. See the *Win32::Shortcut* module to create, load, retrieve, save, and modify shortcut properties from a Perl script. (See Figure 18.4.)

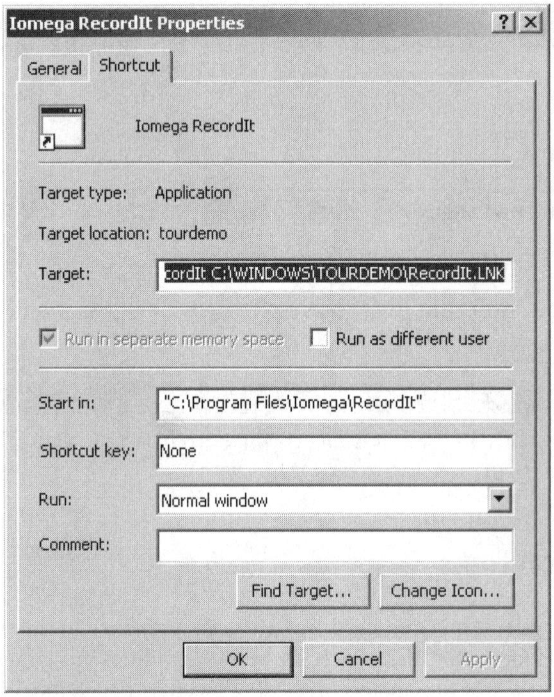

Figure 18.4 Shortcuts and the *.LNK* extension.

The *link* and *unlink* Functions (UNIX). The *link* function creates a hard link (i.e., two files that have the same name) on UNIX systems. The first argument to the *link* function is the name of an existing file; the second argument is the name of the new file, which cannot already exist. Only the superuser can create a link that points to a directory. Use *rmdir* when removing a directory.

9. Symbolic links originated in BSD and are supported under many ATT systems. They may not be supported on your system.

FORMAT

```
link(OLDFILENAME, NEWFILENAME);
```

EXAMPLE 18.16

```
   (UNIX)
1  $ perl -e 'link("dodo", "newdodo");'
2  $ ls -li dodo newdodo
   142726 -rw-r--r--  2 ellie        0 Mar  7 13:46 dodo
   142726 -rw-r--r--  2 ellie        0 Mar  7 13:46 newdodo
```

EXPLANATION

1 The old file *dodo* is given an alternative name, *newdodo*.
2 The *i* option to the *ls* command gives the inode number of the file. If the inode numbers are the same, the files are the same. The old file, *dodo*, started with one link. The link count is now two. Since *dodo* and *newdodo* are linked, they are the same file, and changing one will then change the other. If one link is removed, the other still exists. To remove a file, all hard links to it must be removed.

The *unlink* function deletes a list of files on both UNIX and Windows systems (like the UNIX *rm* command or the MS-DOS *del* command). If the file has more than one link, the link count is dropped by 1. The function returns the number of files successfully deleted. To remove a directory, use the *rmdir* function, since only the superuser can unlink a directory with the *unlink* function.

FORMAT

```
unlink (LIST);
unlink  LIST;
```

EXAMPLE 18.17

```
  (The Script)
1   unlink('a','b','c') || die "remove: $!\n";
2   $count=unlink <*.c>;
    print "The number of files removed was $count\n";
```

EXPLANATION

1 The files *a*, *b*, and *c* are removed.
2 Any files ending in *.c* (*C* source files) are removed. The number of files removed is stored in the scalar *$count*.

The *symlink* and *readlink* Functions (UNIX). The *symlink* function creates a symbolic link. The symbolic link file is the name of the file that is accessed if the old filename is referenced.

FORMAT

```
symlink(OLDFILE, NEWFILE)
```

EXAMPLE 18.18

```
1   $ perl -e 'symlink("/home/jody/test/old", "new");'
2   $ ls -ld new
    lrwxrwxrwx  1 ellie   8 Feb 21 17:32 new  -> /home/jody/test/old
```

EXPLANATION

1 The *symlink* function creates a new filename, *new*, linked to the old filename, */home/jody/test/old*.
2 The *ls-ld* command lists the symbolically linked file. The symbol –> points to the new filename. The *l* preceding the permissions also indicates a symbolic link file.

The *readlink* function returns the value of the symbolic link and is undefined if the file is not a symbolic link.

FORMAT

```
readlink(SYMBOLIC_LINK);
readlink SYMBOLIC_LINK;
```

EXAMPLE 18.19

```
1   $ perl -e 'readlink("new")';
    /home/jody/test/old
```

EXPLANATION

1 The file *new* is a symbolic link. It points to */home/jody/test/old*, the value returned by the *readlink* function.

18.1.10 Renaming Files

The *rename* Function (UNIX and Windows). The *rename* function changes the name of the file, like the UNIX *mv* command. The effect is to create a new link to an existing file and then delete the existing file. The *rename* function returns *1* for success and returns *0* for failure. This function does not work across file system boundaries. If a file with the new name already exists, its contents will be destroyed.

FORMAT

```
rename(OLDFILENAME, NEWFILENAME);
```

EXAMPLE 18.20

```
1   rename ("tmp", "datafile");
```

EXPLANATION

1 The file *tmp* is renamed *datafile*. If *datafile* already exists, its contents are destroyed.

18.1.11 Changing Access and Modification Times

The *utime* Function. The *utime* function changes the access and modification times on each file in a list of files, like the UNIX *touch* command. The first two elements of the list must be the numerical access and modification times, in that order. The *time* function feeds the current time to the *utime* function.The function returns the number of files successfully changed. The inode modification time of each file in the list is set to the current time.

FORMAT

```
utime (LIST);
utime LIST;
```

EXAMPLE 18.21

```
(The Script--UNIX)
1   print "What file will you touch (create or change time stamp)? ";
    chop($myfile=<STDIN>);
2   $now=time;   # This example makes the file if it doesn't exist
3   utime( $now, $now, $myfile) || open(TMP,">>$myfile");[a]

(The Command Line)
    $ ls -l brandnewfile
    brandnewfile: No such file or directory

    $ update.p
1   What file will you touch (create or update time stamp) ?
brandnewfile

    $ ls -l brandnewfile
2   -rw-r--r--   1  ellie    0 Mar    6  17:13 brandnewfile
```

a. Wall, L., Christianson, T., and Orwant, J., *Programming Perl*, 3rd ed., O'Reilly & Associates: Sebastopol, CA, 2000.

EXPLANATION

1 The user will enter the name of a file either to update the access and modification times or, if the file does not exist, to create it.
2 The variable *$now* is set to the return value of the *time* function, the number of nonleap seconds since January 1, 1970, UTC.

EXPLANATION (CONTINUED)

3 The first argument to *$now* is the access time, the second argument is the modification time, and the third argument is the file affected. If the *utime* function fails because the file does not exist, the *open* function will create the file, using *TMP* as the filehandle, emulating the UNIX *touch* command.

18.1.12 File Statistics

The information for a file is stored in a data structure called an **inode**, maintained by the kernel. For UNIX users, much of this information is retrieved with the *ls* command. In *C* and Perl programs, this information may be retrieved directly from the inode with the *stat* function. See the *File::stat* module, which creates a user interface for the *stat* function. Although the emphasis here is UNIX, the *stat* function also works with Win32 systems.

The *stat* and *lstat* Functions. The *stat* function returns a 13-element array containing statistics retrieved from the file's inode.The last two fields, dealing with blocks, are defined only on BSD UNIX systems.[10]

The *lstat* function is like the *stat* function, but if the file is a symbolic link, *lstat* returns information about the link itself rather than about the file it references. If your system does not support symbolic links, a normal *stat* is done.

The special *underscore* filehandle is used to provide *stat* information from the file most previously *stat*ed. The 13-element array returned contains the following elements stored in the *stat* structure. (The order is a little different from the UNIX system call *stat*.)

1. Device number
2. Inode number
3. Mode
4. Link count
5. User ID
6. Group ID
7. For a special file, the device number of the device it refers to
8. Size in bytes, for regular files
9. Time of last access
10. Time of the last modification
11. Time of last file status change
12. Preferred I/O block size for file system
13. Actual number of 512-byte blocks allocated

---

10. Wall, L., Christianson, T., and Orwant, J., *Programming Perl*, 3rd ed., O'Reilly & Associates: Sebastopol, CA, 2000, p. 188.

FORMAT

```
stat(FILEHANDLE);
stat FILEHANDLE;
stat(EXPR);
```

EXAMPLE 18.22

```
(UNIX)
1   open(MYFILE, "perl1") || die "Can't open: $!\n";
2   @statistics=stat(MYFILE);
3   print "@statistics\n";
    close MYFILE;

4   @stats=stat("perl1");
5   printf("The inode number is %d and the uid is %d.\n",
            $stats[1], $stats[4]);
6   print "The file has read and write permissions.\n",
            if -r _ && -w _;

(Output)
3   1819 142441 33261 1 9496 40 -21335 75 761965998 727296409 8192 2
5   The inode number is 142441 and the uid is 9496.
6   The file has read and write permissions.
```

EXPLANATION

1. The file *perl1* is opened via the filehandle *MYFILE.*
2. The *stat* function retrieves information from the file's inode and returns that information to a 13-element array, *@statistics*.
3. The 13-element array is printed. The last two elements of the array are the blockize and the number of blocks in 512-byte blocks. The size and number of blocks may differ because unallocated blocks are not counted in the number of blocks. The negative number is an NIS device number.
4. This time the *stat* function takes the filename as its argument, rather than the filehandle.
5. The second and fifth elements of the array are printed.
6. The special underscore (_) filehandle is used to retrieve the current file statistics from the previous *stat* call. The file *perl1* was *stat*ed last. The file test operators, *-r* and *-w,* use the current *stat* information of *perl1* to check for read and write access on the file.

EXAMPLE 18.23

```
(Windows)
    # Since UNIX and Windows treat files differently,
    # some of the fields here are
    # blank or values returned are not meaningful
    @stats = stat("C:\\ellie\\testing");
    print "Device: $stats[0]\n";
    print "Inode #: $stats[1]\n";
    print "File mode: $stats[2]\n";
    print "# Hard links: $stats[3]\n";
    print "Owner ID: $stats[4]\n";
    print "Group ID: $stats[5]\n";
    print "Device ID: $stats[6]\n";
    print "Total size: $stats[7]\n";
    print "Last access time: $stats[8]\n";
    print "Last modify time: $stats[9]\n";
    print "Last change inode time: $stats[10]\n";
    print "Block size: $stats[11]\n";
    print "Number of blocks: $stats[11]\n";

(Output)
    Device: 2
    Inode #: 0
    File mode: 16895
    # Hard links: 1
    Owner ID: 0
    Group ID: 0
    Device ID: 2
    Total size: 0
    Last access time: 981360000
    Last modify time: 977267374
    Last change inode time: 977267372
    Block size:
    Number of blocks:
```

18.1.13 Low-Level File I/O

The *read* Function (*fread*). The *read* function reads a specified number of bytes from a filehandle and puts the bytes in a scalar variable. If you are familiar with C's standard I/O *fread* function, Perl's *read* function handles I/O buffering in the same way. To improve efficiency, rather than reading a character at a time, a block of data is read and stored in a temporary storage area. C's *fread* function and Perl's *read* functions then transfer data, a byte at a time, from the temporary storage area to your program. (The *sysread* function is used to emulate C's low-level I/O *read* function.) The function returns the number of bytes read or an undefined value if an error occurred. If EOF (end of file) is reached, *0* is returned.

In Perl, the *print* function (**not** the *write* function) is used to output the actual bytes returned by the *read* function. Perl's *print* function emulates C's *fwrite* function.

FORMAT

```
read(FILEHANDLE, SCALAR, LENGTH, OFFSET);
read(FILEHANDLE, SCALAR, LENGTH);
```

EXAMPLE 18.24

```
(The Script)
1   open(PASSWD, "/etc/passwd") || die "Can't open: $!\n";
2   $bytes=read (PASSWD, $buffer, 50);
3   print "The number of bytes read is $bytes.\n";
4   print "The buffer contains: \n$buffer";

(Output)
3   The number of bytes is 50.
4   The buffer contains:
    root:YhTLR4heBdxfw:0:1:Operator:/:/bin/csh
    nobody:
```

EXPLANATION

1. The */etc/passwd* file is opened for reading via the *PASSWD* filehandle.
2. The *read* function attempts to read 50 bytes from the filehandle and returns the number of bytes *read* to the scalar *$bytes*.

The *sysread* and *syswrite* Functions. The *sysread* function is like C's *read* function. It bypasses the standard I/O buffering scheme and reads bytes directly from the filehandle to a scalar variable. Mixing *read* and *sysread* functions can cause problems, since the *read* function implements buffering, and the *sysread* function reads bytes directly from the filehandle.

The *syswrite* function writes bytes of data from a variable to a specified filehandle. It emulates C's *write* function.

FORMAT

```
sysread(FILEHANDLE, SCALAR, LENGTH, OFFSET);
sysread(FILEHANDLE, SCALAR, LENGTH);

syswrite(FILEHANDLE, SCALAR, LENGTH, OFFSET);
syswrite(FILEHANDLE, SCALAR, LENGTH);
```

The *seek* Function. Perl's *seek* function is the same as the *fseek* standard I/O function in C. It allows you to randomly access a file. It sets a position in a file, measured in bytes from the beginning of the file, where the first byte is byte *0*. The function returns *1* if successful, *0* if not.

FORMAT

```
seek(FILEHANDLE, OFFSET, POSITION);
```

POSITION = The absolute position in the file where
- 0 = Beginning of file
- 1 = Current position in file
- 2 = End of file

OFFSET = Number of bytes from *POSITION*. A positive offset advances the position forward in the file. A negative offset moves the position backward in the file. A negative *OFFSET* sets the file position for *POSITION* 1 or 2.

EXAMPLE 18.25

```
(The Script)
1   open(PASSWD, "/etc/passwd") || die "Can't open: $!\n";
2   while ( chomp($line = <PASSWD>) ){
3       print "---$line---\n" if $line =~ /root/;
    }
4   seek(PASSWD, 0, 0) || die "$!\n"; # Start back at the beginning
                                      # of the file at first byte
5   while(<PASSWD>){print if /ellie/;}
6   close(PASSWD);

(Output)
3   ---root:YhTLR4heBdxfw:0:1:Operator:/:/bin/csh---
5   ellie:aVD17JSsBMyGg:9496:40:Ellie Savage:/home/jodyellie:/bin/csh
```

EXPLANATION

1. The */etc/passwd* file is opened via the *PASSWD* filehandle.
2. The *while* statement loops through the *PASSWD* filehandle, reading a line at a time until end of file is reached.
3. The line is printed if it contains the regular expression *root*.
4. The *seek* function sets the file position at position *0*, the beginning of the file, byte offset *0*. Since the filehandle was not closed, it remains opened until closed with the *close* function.
5. The *while* statement loops through the file.
6. The *PASSWD* filehandle is officially closed.

The *tell* Function. The *tell* function returns the current byte position of a filehandle for a regular file. The position can be used as an argument to the *seek* function to move the file position to a particular location in the file.

FORMAT

```
tell (FILEHANDLE);
tell FILEHANDLE;
tell;
```

EXAMPLE 18.26

```
(The Script)
1   open(PASSWD, "/etc/passwd") || die "Can't open: $!\n";
    while ( chomp($line = <PASSWD>) ){
        if ( $line =~ /sync/){
2           $current = tell;
            print "---$line---\n";
        }
    }
3   printf "The position returned by tell is %d.\n", $current;
4   seek(PASSWD, $current, 0);
    while(<PASSWD>){
5       print;
    }

(Output)
2   --sync::1:1::/:/bin/sync--
3   The position returned by tell is 296.
5   sysdiag:*:0:1:Old System Diagnostic:/usr/diag/sysdiag/sysdiag
    sundiag:*:0:1:System Diagnostic:/usr/diag/sundiag/sundiag
    ellie:aVD17JSsBMyGg:9496:40:Ellie Savage:/home/jodyellie:/bin/csh
```

EXPLANATION

1. The */etc/passwd* file is opened via the *PASSWD* filehandle.
2. When the line containing the regular expression *sync* is reached, the *tell* function will return the current byte position to the scalar *$current*. The current position is the next byte after the last character read.
3. The byte position returned by the *tell* function is printed.
4. The *seek* function locates the current position starting from the beginning of the file to the offset position returned by the *tell* function.

18.1.14 Packing and Unpacking Data

Remember the *printf* and *sprintf* functions? They were used to format their arguments as floating point numbers, decimal numbers, strings, etc. But the *pack* and *unpack* functions take this formatting a step further. Both functions act on strings that can be represented as bits, bytes, integers, long integers, floating point numbers, etc. The format type tells both *pack* and *unpack* how to handle these strings.

The *pack* and *unpack* functions have a number of uses. These functions are used to pack a list into a binary structure and then expand the packed values back into a list. When working with files, you can use these functions to create uuencode files, relational databases, and binary files.

When working with files, not all files are text files. Some files, for example, may be packed into a binary format to save space, store images, or in a uuencoded format to facilitate sending a file through the mail. These files are not readable as is the text on this page. The *pack* and *unpack* functions can be used to convert the lines in a file from one format to another. The *pack* function converts a list into a scalar value that may be stored in machine memory. The template shown in Table 18.8 is used to specify the type of character and how many characters, will be formatted. For example, the string *c4*, or *cccc*, packs a list into four unsigned characters and *a14* packs a list into a 14-byte ASCII string, null padded. The *unpack* function converts a binary formatted string into a list. The opposite of *pack* puts a string back into Perl format.

Table 18.8 The Template *pack* and *unpack*—Types and Values

Template	Description
a	An ASCII string (null padded)
A	An ASCII string (space padded)
b	A bit string (low-to-high order, like *vec*)
B	A bit string (high-to-low order)
c	A signed *char* value
C	An unsigned *char* value
d	A double-precision float in the native format
f	A single-precision float in the native format
h	A hexadecimal string (low nybble first, to high)
H	A hexadecimal string (high nybble first)
i	A signed integer
I	An unsigned integer
l	A signed long value
L	An unsigned long value
n	A short in "network" (big-endian) order
N	A long in "network" (big-endian) order
p	A pointer to a null-terminated string
P	A pointer to a structure (fixed-length string)
q	A signed 64-bit value
Q	An unsigned 64-bit value
s	A signed short value (16-bit)
S	An unsigned short value (16-bit)
u	A uuencoded string

Table 18.8 The Template *pack* and *unpack*—Types and Values (continued)

Template	*Description*
v	A short in "VAX" (little-endian) order
V	A long in "VAX" (little-endian) order
w	A BER compressed unsigned integer in base 128, high bit first
x	A null byte
X	Back up a byte
@	Null fill to absolute position

FORMAT

```
$string=pack(Template, @list );
@list = unpack(Template, $string );
```

EXAMPLE 18.27

```
(The Script)
1   $bytes=pack("c5", 80,101,114, 108, 012);   # 5 ASCII characters
2   print "$bytes\n";

(Output)
Perl
```

EXPLANATION

1. The first element in the list, the template (see Table 18.8), is composed of the type and the number of values to be packed; in this example, four signed characters. The rest of the list consists of the decimal values for characters *P, e, r,* and *l* and the octal value for the newline. This list is packed into a binary structure. The string containing the packed structure is returned and stored in *$bytes.* (See your ASCII table.)
2. The 4-byte character string is printed.

EXAMPLE 18.28

```
(Script)
$string=pack("A15A3", "hey","you");   # ASCII string, space padded
print "$string";

(Output)
hey            you
```

EXPLANATION

1. Two strings, *hey* and *you*, are packed into a structure using the template *A15A3*. *A15* will convert the string *hey* into a space-padded ASCII string consisting of 15 characters. *A3* converts the string *you* into a 3-character space-padded string.
2. The strings are printed according to the *pack* formatting template. They are left justified.

EXAMPLE 18.29

```
(The Script)
    #!/bin/perl
    # Program to uuencode a file and then uudecode it
1   open(PW, "/etc/passwd") || die "Can't open: $!\n";
2   open(CODEDPW, ">codedpw") || die "Can't open: $!\n";

3   while(<PW>){
4       $uuline=pack("u*", $_);  # uuencoded string
5       print CODEDPW $uuline;
    }
    close PW;
    close CODEDPW;

6   open(UUPW, "codedpw") || die "Can't open: $!\n";
    while(<UUPW>){
7       print;
    }
    close UUPW;
    print "\n\n";

8   open(DECODED, "codedpw") || die;
9   while(<DECODED>){
10      @decodeline = unpack("u*", $_);
11      print "@decodeline";
    }

(Output)
7   E<F]O=#IX.C`Z,3I3=7!E<BU5<V5R.B\Z+W5S<B]B:6XO8W-H"@``
    19&%E;6]N.G@Z,3HQ.CHO.@H`
    58FEN.G@Z,CHR.CHO=7-R+V)I;CH*
    .<WES.G@Z,SHS.CHO.@H`
    :861M.G@Z-#HT.D%D;6EN.B]V87(O861M.@H`
    L;'`Z>#HW,3HX.DQI;F4@4')I;G1E<B!!9&UI;CHO=7-R+W-P;V]L+VQP.@H`
    ?<VUT<#IX.C`Z,#I-86EL($1A96UO;B!5<V5R.B\Z"@!R
    E=75C<#IX.C4Z-3IU=6-P($%D;6EN.B]U<W(O;&EB+W5U8W`Z"@!L
```

EXAMPLE 18.29 (CONTINUED)

```
    M;G5U8W`Z>#HY.CDZ=75C<"!!9&UI;CHO=F%R+W-
    P;V]L+W5U8W!P=6)L:6,Z
    5+W5S<B]L:6(O=75C<"]U=6-I8V\*
    J;&ES=&5N.G@Z,S<Z-#I.971W;W)K($%D;6EN.B]U<W(O;F5T+VYL<SH*
    ?;F]B;V1Y.G@Z-C`P,#$Z-C`P,#$Z3F]B;V1Y.B\Z"@`O
    I;F]A8V-E<W,Z>#HV,#`P,CHV,#`P,CI.;R!!8V-E<W,@57-E<CHO.@H`
    J;F]B;V1Y-#IX.C8U-3,T.C8U-3,T.E-U;D]3(#0N>"!.;V)O9'DZ+SH*
    M96QL:64Z>#HY-
    #DV.C0P.D5L;&EE(%%U:6=L97DZ+VAO;64O96QL:64Z+W5S
    *<B]B:6XO8W-H"@!C

11  root:x:0:1:Super-User:/:/usr/bin/csh
    daemon:x:1:1::/:
    bin:x:2:2::/usr/bin:
    sys:x:3:3::/:
    adm:x:4:4:Admin:/var/adm:
    lp:x:71:8:Line Printer Admin:/usr/spool/lp:
    smtp:x:0:0:Mail Daemon User:/:
    uucp:x:5:5:uucp Admin:/usr/lib/uucp:
    nuucp:x:9:9:uucp Admin:/var/spool/uucppublic:/usr/lib/uucp/uucico
    listen:x:37:4:Network Admin:/usr/net/nls:
    nobody:x:60001:60001:Nobody:/:
    noaccess:x:60002:60002:No Access User:/:
    nobody4:x:65534:65534:SunOS 4.x Nobody:/:
    ellie:x:9496:40:Ellie Quigley:/home/ellie:/usr/bin/csh
```

EXPLANATION

1. The local *passwd* file is opened for reading.
2. Another file, called *codepw*, is opened for writing.
3. Each line of the filehandle is read into $_ until the end of file is reached.
4. The *pack* function uuencodes the line ($_) and assigns the coded line to the scalar *$uuline*. uuencode is often used to convert a binary file into an encoded representation that can be sent using e-mail.
5. The uuencoded string is sent to the filehandle.
6. The file containing the uuencoded text is opened for reading and attached to the *UUPW* filehandle.
7. Each line of uuencoded text is printed.
8. The uuencoded file is opened for reading.
9. Each line of the file is read from the filehandle and stored in $_.
10. The *unpack* function converts the uuencoded string back into its original form and assigns it to *@decodeline*.
11. The uudecoded line is printed.

EXAMPLE 18.30

```
(The Script)
    #!/bin/perl
1   $ints=pack("i3", 5,-10,15);    # pack into binary structure
2   open(BINARY, "+>binary" ) || die;
3   print BINARY "$ints";
4   seek(BINARY, 0,0) || die;
    while(<BINARY>){
5       ($n1,$n2,$n3)=unpack("i3", $_);
6       print "$n1 $n2 $n3\n";
    }

(Output)
6   5 -10 15
```

EXPLANATION

1. The three integers *5* , *–10*, and *15* are packed into three signed integers. The value returned is a binary structure assigned to *$ints*.
2. The *BINARY* filehandle is opened for reading and writing.
3. The packed integers are sent to the file. This file is compressed and totally unreadable. To read it, it must be converted back into an ASCII format. This is done with *unpack*.
4. The *seek* function puts the file pointer back at the top of the file at byte position *0*.
5. We're reading from the file one line at a time. Each line, stored in $_, is unpacked and returned to its original list of values.
6. The original list values are printed.

EXAMPLE 18.31

```
(The Script)
    $str="0x123456789ABCDE ellie...";
1    print "$str\n";

    $bytes=unpack("H*",$str); # hex string (regular order)
2    print "$bytes\n";

    $str2 = pack("H*", $bytes);
3    print "$str2\n";

    $bytes = unpack("h*",$str); # hex string (reversed order)

4    print "$bytes\n";

    $str1 = pack("h*", $bytes);
5    print"$str1\n";
```

EXAMPLE 18.31 (CONTINUED)

```
(Output)
1  0x123456789ABCDE ellie...
2  3078313233343536373839414243444520656c6c69652e2e2e
3  0x123456789ABCDE ellie...
4  03871323334353637383931424344454025 6c6c69656e2e2e2
5  0x123456789ABCDE ellie...
```

EXPLANATION

1. The string contains a hexadecimal number and some text.
2. The "*h*" and "*H*" fields pack a string that many nybbles (4-bit groups, representable as hexadecimal digits, 0-9a-f) long. Each byte of the input field of *pack()* generates 4 bits of the result. The variable *$bytes* consists of a hexidecimal string in regular hex order, where each character in the original string is represented by two hexadecimal numbers. For example, "ellie" is represented as **65 6c 6c 69 65**, and the three dots are **e2 e2 e2**.

18.2 Processes

Your Perl script is a program that resides on disk. When the program is placed in memory and starts execution, it is called a **process**. Each process has a number of attributes that are inherited from its parent, the **calling process**. Perl has a number of functions that will allow you to retrieve the information about the process. Before examining these functions, a short discussion about processes may help you to understand (or recall) the purpose of some of Perl's system calls.

18.2.1 UNIX Processes

Every process has a unique process ID, a positive integer called the ***pid***. Every process has a **parent** except process 0, the swapper. The first process *init*, *pid* 1, is the ancestor of all future processes, called **descendants**, or more commonly, **child** processes.

In Figure 18.5, the Perl process is a descendant of the shell (*sh*).

Each process also belongs to a **process group**, a collection of one or more processes used for job control and signal handling. Each process group also has a unique *pid* and a process leader. When you log on, the process group leader may be your login shell. Any process created from your shell will be a member of this process group. The terminal opened by the process group leader is called the controlling terminal, and any processes it spawns inherit it. Any signals sent to the process will be sent to all processes in the group. That is why, when you press <Ctrl>-c, the process you are running and any of its children will terminate. Perl provides functions to obtain the process group ID and to set the process group.

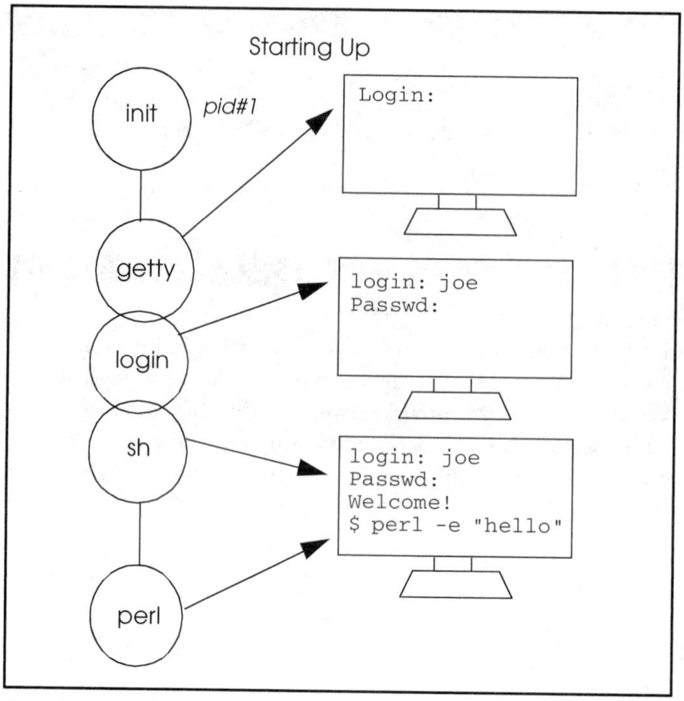

Figure 18.5 The Perl process as a descendant of the shell.

When a process is created, it is assigned four numbers indicating who owns the process. They are the real and effective user ID and the real and effective group ID. The user ID, called the real *uid*, is a positive integer that is associated with your login name. The real *uid* is the third field in the */etc/passwd* file. When you log on, the first process created is called the *login* shell, and it is assigned the user ID. Any processes spawned from the shell also inherit this *uid*. Any process running with the *uid* of zero is called a **root**, or **superuser**, process with special privileges.

There is also a group ID number, called the real *gid*, which associates a group with your login name. The default *gid* is the fourth field in the password file, and it is also inherited by any child process. The system administrator can allow users to become members of other groups by assigning entries in the */etc/group* file.

The following is an entry from the *passwd* file, illustrating how the *uid* and *gid* values are stored (fields are separated by colons).

EXAMPLE 18.32

```
(Entry from /etc/passwd)
    john:aYD17IsSjBMyGg:9495:41:John Doe:/home/dolphin/john:/bin/ksh
```

EXPLANATION

(The Fields)
1 login name
2 encrypted password
3 uid
4 gid
5 gcos
6 home directory
7 login shell

The **effective *uid* (*euid*)** and **effective *guid* (*guid*)** of a process are normally set to the same number as the real *uid* and real *gid* of the user who is running the process. UNIX determines what permissions are available to a process by the effective *uid* and *gid*. If the *euid* or *guid* of a file is changed to that of another owner, when you execute a program, you essentially become that owner and get his access permissions. Programs in which the effective *uid* or effective *gid* have been set are called **set user ID** programs, or *setuid* programs. When you change your password, the */bin/passwd* program has a *setuid* to *root*, giving you the privilege to change your password in the *passwd* file, which is owned by *root*.

18.2.2 Win32 Processes

The process model for Windows differs from UNIX systems, and since Perl was originally designed for UNIX, a number of library routines were added to the standard Perl library to accommodate the Windows world. The Win32 directory (*C:/Perl/lib/Win32*) is a Windows-specific directory that comes with Windows versions of Perl and contains a number of modules for creating, suspending, resuming, and killing processes. The *Win32::Process* module contains a number of functions to manipulate processes. Here is a listing from the Win32 directory:

```
AuthenticateUser.pm  Internet.pm       Registry.pm
ChangeNotify.pm      Mutex.pm          Semaphore.pm
Client.pl            NetAdmin.pm       Server.pl
Clipboard.pm         NetResource.pm    Service.pm
Console.pm           ODBC.pm           Shortcut.pm
Event.pm             OLE               Sound.pm
EventLog.pm          OLE.pm            Test.pl
File.pm              PerfLib.pm        TieRegistry.pm
FileSecurity.pm      Pipe.pm           WinError.pm
IPC.pm               Process.pm        test-async.pl
```

18.2.3 The Environment (UNIX and Windows)

When you log on, your shell program inherits a set of environment variables initialized by either the login program or one of shell's startup files (*.profile* or *.login*). These variables contain useful information about the process, such as the search path, the home directory, the user name, and the terminal type. The information in environment variables, once set and exported, is inherited by any child processes that are spawned from the process (parent) in which they were initialized. The shell process will pass the environment information on to your Perl program.

The special associative array *%ENV* contains the environment settings. If you change the value of an environment setting in your Perl script, it is set for this process and any of its children. The environment variables in the parent process, normally the shell, will remain untouched.

EXAMPLE 18.33

```
(The Script)
(UNIX)
1   foreach $key (keys(%ENV)){
2          print "$key\n";}
3   print "Your login name is $ENV{'LOGNAME'}\n";
4   $pwd=$ENV{'PWD'};
    print "/The present working directory is $pwd, "\n";

(Output)
2   OPENWINHOME
    MANPATH
    FONTPATH
    LOGNAME
    USER
    TERMCAP
    TERM
    SHELL
    PWD
    HOME
    PATH
    WINDOW_PARENT
    WMGR_ENV_PLACEHOLDER
3   Your login name is ellie
4   The present working directory is /home/jody/ellie
```

EXPLANATION

1. The *keys* function is used to get all the currently set environment variables from the *%ENV* array. These variables were inherited from the parent process, the shell.
2. Each environment variable is printed.
3. The value of *LOGNAME*, the user name, is printed.
4. The value of *PWD*, the present working directory, is assigned to *$pwd* and printed.

EXAMPLE 18.34

```
(Windows)
    while(($key,$value)=each(%ENV)){
        print "$key: $value\n" if $key =~ /^P/;
    }

(Output)
1   PROMPT: $p$g
    PROCESSOR_IDENTIFIER: x86 Family 6 Model 5 Stepping 2,
        GenuineIntel
    PATH: c:\Oracle\Ora81\bin;"C:\PROGRAM FILES
        \OCLE\JRE\1.1.7\BIN";C:\ORAWIN95\BIN;C:\PERL\BIN\;
        C:\MKSNT;C:\WINDOWS;C:\WINDOW
    PATHEXT: .pl;.COM;.EXE;.BAT;.CMD;.VBS;.VBE;.JS;.JSE;.WSF;.WSH
    PROGRAMFILES: C:\PROGRA~1
    PROCESSOR_ARCHITECTURE: x86
    PROCESSOR_REVISION: 0502
    PERL5LIB: C:\Perl\lib
    PROCESSOR_LEVEL: 6
```

EXPLANATION

1 The *each* function is used to get all the currently set environment variables from the *%ENV* array. These variables were inherited from the parent process, the MS-DOS shell.

18.2.4 Processes and Filehandles

As discussed in Chapter 10, "Getting a Handle on Files," processes can be opened in Perl via either an input or output filehandle. For example, if you want to see all the currently running processes on your machine, you could create a filehandle for the UNIX *ps* command. (See Chapter 10 for details. See also "The *system* Function" on page 750.)

EXAMPLE 18.35

```
(The Script)
    # UNIX ps command
1   open(PROC, "ps -aux  |" ) || die "$!\n";
                # If running System V, use ps -ef
2   print STDOUT <PROC>;

(Output)
2 ellie  3825  6.4  4.5  212  464 p5  R 12:18  0:00 ps -aux
  root      1  0.0  0.0   52    0 ?  IW Feb 5  0:02 /sbin/init
  root     51 10.0  0.0   52    0 ?  IW Feb 5  0:02 portmap
  root      2 10.0  0.0   52    0 ?   D Feb 5  0:02 pagedaemon
  root     90 10.0  0.0   52    0 ?  IW Feb 5  0:02 rpc.statd
```

EXAMPLE 18.35 (CONTINUED)

```
                    <more processes here>

ellie  1383  0.8  8.4   360   876 p4   S Dec 26 11:34 /usr/local/OW3/bin/xview
ellie   173  0.8 13.4 1932 1392 co    S Dec 20389:19 /usr/local/OW3/bin/xnews
ellie   164  0.0  0.0   100     0 co IW Dec 20  0:00 -c

              <some of the output was cut to save space>

ellie  3822  0.0  0.0     0     0 p5   Z Dec 20   0:00 <defunct>
ellie  3823  0.0  1.1    28   112 p5   S 12:18    0:00 sh -c ps -aux | grep '^'
ellie  3821  0.0  5.6   144   580 p5   S 12:18    0:00 /bin/perl checkon ellie
ellie  3824  0.0  1.8    32   192 p5   S 12:18    0:00 grep ^ellie
```

EXPLANATION

1 The *PROC* filehandle is opened for reading. It is called an **input filter**. The output from the *ps* command is piped to Perl via the *PROC* filehandle.
2 The contents of the filter are printed to *STDOUT*.

Login Information—The *getlogin* Function. The *getlogin* function returns the current login from */etc/utmp*. If *null* is returned from *getlogin*, use *getpwuid*. The *getpwuid* function takes the *uid* of the user as an argument and returns an entry from the password file associated with that *uid*.

The $< variable evaluates to the real *uid* of this process.

FORMAT

```
getlogin;
```

EXAMPLE 18.36

```
(The Script)
1   $loginname=getlogin || (getpwuid($<))[0]|| die "Not a user here!!";
2   print "Your loginname is $loginname.\n";

(Output)
2   Your loginname is john.
```

EXPLANATION

1 The *getlogin* function returns the login name from */etc/utmp* and, if that fails, retrieves it from the password file with the *getpwuid* function. The $< variable contains the real *uid* of this process.
2 The scalar *$loginname* contains the user's login name, the first entry of the password file.

Special Process Variables (*pid, uid, euid, gid, euid*). Perl provides some special variables that store information about the Perl process executing your script. If you want to make your program more readable, you can use the *English* module in the standard Perl library to represent these variables in English.

`$$`	The process ID of the Perl program running this script
`$<`	The real *uid* of this process
`$>`	The effective *uid* of this process
`$(`	The real *gid* of this process
`$)`	The effective *gid* of this process

The Parent Process ID—The *getppid* Function and the *$$* Variable. Each process on the system is identified by its process identification number (*pid*), a positive integer. The special variable $$ holds the value of the *pid* for this process. This variable is also used by the shell to hold the process ID number of the current process.

The *getppid* function returns the process ID of the parent process.

EXAMPLE 18.37

```
(The Script)
1   print "The pid of this process is $$\n";
2   print "The parent pid of this process is ", getppid,"\n";

(Output)
1   The pid of this process is 3304
2   The parent pid of this process is 2340

(At the Command Line)
3   $ echo $$
    2340
```

EXPLANATION

1 The process identification number (*pid*) for this process, this Perl script, is printed.
2 The process that spawned this process is ordinarily the shell, the parent process. The parent's *pid* is called the *ppid*.
3 After the Perl script exits, the $$ is used to print the *pid* of the shell. The *ppid* for the Perl script was *2340*; the value of its parent's *pid*, that of the shell.

The Process Group ID—The *pgrp* Function. The *pgrp* function returns the current group process for a specified *pid*. Without an argument or with an argument of *0*, the process group ID of the current process is returned.

FORMAT

```
getpgrp(PID);
getpgrp PID;
getpgrp;
```

EXAMPLE 18.38

```
(The Script)
print "The pid of the Perl program running this script is ", $$;
printf "The ppid, parent's pid (Shell) , is %d\n", getppid;
printf "The process group's pid is %d\n", getpgrp(0);

(Output)
The pid of the Perl program running this script is 6671
The ppid, parent's pid (Shell), is 6344
The process group's pid is 6671
```

18.2.5 Process Priorities and Niceness

The kernel maintains the scheduling priority selected for each process. Most interactive and short-running jobs are favored with a higher priority. The UNIX *nice* command allows you to modify the scheduling priority of processes (BSD, pre-System V). On moderately or heavily loaded systems, it may be to your advantage to make CPU-intensive jobs run slower so that jobs needing higher priority get faster access to the CPU. Those jobs that don't hog the processor are called *nice*.

The *nice* value is used in calculating the priority of a process. A process with a positive *nice* value runs at a low priority, meaning that it receives less than its share of the CPU time. A process with a negative *nice* value runs at a high priority, receiving more than its share of the processor. The *nice* values range from *–20* to *19*. Most processes run at priority zero, balancing their access to the CPU. (Only the superuser can set negative *nice* values.)

The following functions, *getpriority* and *setpriority*, are named for the corresponding system calls, found in Section 2 of the UNIX *man* pages.

The *getpriority* Function. The *getpriority* function returns the current priority (*nice* value) for a process, a process group, or a user. Not all systems support this function. If not implemented, *getpriority* produces a fatal error. *WHICH* is one of three values: *0* for the process priority, *1* for the process group priority, and 2 for the user priority. *WHO* is interpreted relative to the process identifier for the process priority, process group priority, or user priority. A value of zero represents the current process, process group, or user.

FORMAT

```
getpriority(WHICH, WHO);
```

EXAMPLE 18.39

```
(The Script)
1   $niceval = getpriority( 0,0);
2   print "The priority, nice value, for this process is $niceval\n";

(Output)
2   The priority, nice value, for this process is 0.
```

EXPLANATION

1. The *getpriority* function will return the *nice* value for the current process.
2. The *nice* value for this process is zero. This gives the process no special favor when taking its share of time from the CPU.

The *setpriority* Function (*nice*). The *setpriority* function sets the current priority (*nice* value) for a process, a process group, or a user. It modifies the scheduling priority for processes. If the *setpriority* system call is not implemented on your system, *setpriority* will return an error.

WHICH is one of three values: *0* for the process priority, *1* for the process group priority, and 2 for the user priority. *WHO* is interpreted relative to the process identifier for the process priority, process group priority, or user priority. A value of zero represents the current process, process group, or user. *NICEVALUE* is the *nice* value. A low *nice* value raises the priority of the process and a high *nice* value decreases the priority of the process. (Confusing!)

Unless you have superuser privileges, you cannot use a negative *nice* value. Doing so will not change the current *nice* value.

FORMAT

```
setpriority(WHICH, WHO, NICEVALUE);
```

EXAMPLE 18.40

```
(The Script)
1   $niceval = getpriority(0,0);
2   print "The nice value for this process is $niceval.\n";
3   setpriority(0,0, ( $niceval + 5 ));
4   print "The nice value for this process is now", getpriority(0,0);

(Output)
2   The nice value for this process is 0.
4   The nice value for this process is now 5.
```

EXPLANATION

1. The *getpriority* function will return the *nice* value for the current process.
2. The *nice* value is printed.
3. The *setpriority* function adds 5 to the *nice* value of the current process. The process will have a lower priority. It is being "nice."
4. The new *nice* value returned by the *getpriority* function is 5.

18.2.6 Password Information

UNIX. The following functions iterate through the */etc/passwd* file and retrieve information from that file into an array. These functions are named for the same functions found in the system library (Section 3 of the UNIX manual) and perform the same tasks. If you are interested in obtaining information about the */etc/group* file, the Perl functions *getgrent, getgrgid,* and *getgrnam* all return a four-element array with information about group entries. A description of these functions can be found in the UNIX manual pages. Here is an example of an */etc/passwd* file:

```
root:YhTLR4heBdxfw:0:1:Operator:/:/bin/csh
nobody:*:65534:65534::/:
sys:*:2:2::/:/bin/csh
bin:*:3:3::/bin
uucp:*:4:8::/var/spool/uucppublic:
news:*:6:6::/var/spool/news:/bin/csh
sync::1:1::/:/bin/sync
ellie:aVD17TSsBMfYg:9496:40:Ellie Shellie:/home/jody/ellie:/bin/ksh
```

Windows. Windows 2000 and NT store information about users in a binary database called *SAM* (Security Accounts Manager), part of the Registry. Because the data is stored in binary format, normal Perl read operations won't work. It is better to use the Win32 extensions to get user information. *Win32::NetAdmin* is bundled with ActiveState under *\perl\site\lib\win32*. (See Table 18.9.) A user account can be manipulated with two functions of this module: *UserGetAttributes()* and *UserSetAttributes*. Another good extension is David Roth's *Win32::AdminMisc* found at *www.roth.net*.

The Win 32 *net.exe* command also displays information about the user and the system.

EXAMPLE 18.41

```
1  C:\  net help
   The syntax of this command is:

   NET HELP command
      -or-
   NET command /HELP

   Commands available are:

   NET ACCOUNTS                NET HELP             NET SHARE
   NET COMPUTER                NET HC:\ELPMSG       NET START
   NET CONFIG                  NET LOCALGROUP       NET STATISTICS
   NET CONFIG SERVER           NET NAME             NET STOP
   NET CONFIG WORKSTATION      NET PAUSE            NET TIME
   NET CONTINUE                NET PRINT            NET USE
   NET FILE                    NET SEND             NET USER
   NET GROUP                   NET SESSION          NET VIEW
```

EXAMPLE 18.41 (CONTINUED)

```
NET HELP SERVICES lists the network services you can start.
NET HELP SYNTAX explains how to read NET HELP syntax lines.
NET HELP command | MORE displays Help one screen at a time.

C:\ net user

User accounts for \\HOMEBOUND

-------------------------------------------------------------------

Administrator            Ellie Quigley            Guest
SQLAgentCmdExec
The command completed successfully.
```

Table 18.9 *Win32::NetAdmin* Extensions

```
Win32::NetAdmin::UserGetAttributes($Machine,
                                   $UserName,
                                   $Password,
                                   $PasswordAge,
                                   $Privilege,
                                   $Homedir,
                                   $Comment,
                                   $Flags,
                                   $ScriptPath);

Win32::NetAdmin::UserSetAttributes( $Machine,
                                   $UserName,
                                   $Password,
                                   $PasswordAge,
                                   $Privilege,
                                   $Homedir,
                                   $Comment,
                                   $Flags,
                                   $ScriptPath);
```

EXAMPLE 18.42

```
use Win32::NetAdmin qw(GetUsers UserGetAttributes) ;
GetUsers("", FILTER_NORMAL_ACCOUNT,\%hash)or die;
foreach $key(sort keys %hash){
   print "$key\n";
}
```

EXAMPLE 18.42 (CONTINUED)

```
(Output)
Administrator
Ellie Quigley
Guest
SQLAgentCmdExec
```

Encrypted passwords cannot be transferred from UNIX to Win32 systems and vice versa. They are cryptologically incompatible. To manage passwords, use the *Win32::AdminMisc* or the *Win32::NetAdmin* module extension.

Table 18.10 Win32 Password Extensions

Win32::AdminMisc::UserCheckPassword($Machine, $User, $Password)
Win32::AdminMisc::SetPassword($Machine | $Domain), $User, $NewPassword);
Win32::AdminMisc::UserChangePassword($Machine | $Domain), $User, $OldPassword, $NewPassword);
Win32::NetAdmin::UserChangePassword(($Machine | $Domain), $User, $OldPassword, $NewPassword);

For Windows users, the following functions for obtaining group and user information have not been implemented by ActiveState as of this printing:

```
endgrent(), endpwent(), getgrent(), getgrgid(), getgrnam(),
getpwent(), getpwnam(), getpwuid(), setgrent(), setpwent()
```

Getting a Password Entry (UNIX)—The *getpwent* Function. The *getpwent* function retrieves information from the */etc/passwd* file. The return value from *getpwent* is a nine-element array consisting of:

1. Login name
2. Encrypted password
3. User ID
4. Group ID
5. Quota
6. Comment
7. Gcos (user information)
8. Home directory
9. Login shell

FORMAT

```
($name, $passwd, $uid, $gid, $quota, $comment, $gcos, $dir,
        $shell )=getpwent;
```

EXAMPLE 18.43

```
(The Script)
1   while( @info=getpwent) {
2       print "$info[0]\n" if $info[1]=~/\*+/;
    }

(Output)
2   nobody
    daemon
    sys
    bin
    uucp
```

EXPLANATION

1. The *getpwent* function gets a line from the */etc/passwd* file and stores it in the array *@info*. The loop continues until *getpwent* cannot read another entry from */etc/passwd.*
2. If the second element of the array contains at least one star (*), the first element, the user name, is printed.

Getting a Password Entry by Username—The *getpwnam* Function. The *getpwnam* function takes the user name as an argument and returns a nine-element array corresponding to that user's name field in the */etc/passwd* file.

FORMAT

```
getpwnam(loginname);
```

EXAMPLE 18.44

```
(The Script)
    #!/bin/perl
1   foreach $name ( "root", "bin", "ellie" ){
2       if (($login, $passwd, $uid)=getpwnam($name)){
3           print "$login--$uid\n";
        }
    }

(Output)
3   root--0
    ellie--9496
    bin--3
```

EXPLANATION

1. The *foreach* loop contains login names in its list, each to be processed in turn.
2. The *getpwnam* function retrieves information from */etc/passwd* and stores the first three fields of information in the array elements *$login, $passwd,* and *$uid*, respectively.
3. The *login* name and the *uid* are printed.

Getting a Password Entry by *uid*—The *getpwuid* Function. The *getpwuid* function takes a numeric user ID (*uid*) as an argument and returns a nine-element array corresponding to that user's *uid* entry in the */etc/passwd* file.

FORMAT

```
getpuid(UID)
```

EXAMPLE 18.45

```
(The Script)
1   foreach $num ( 1 .. 10 ){
2       if (($login, $passwd, $uid)=getpwuid($num)){
3       print "$login--$uid\n";}
    }

(Output)
3   daemon--1
    sys--2
    bin--3
    uucp--4
    news--6
    ingres--7
    audit--9
```

EXPLANATION

1. The *foreach* loop contains a range of *uid* numbers from *1* to *10* in its list, each to be processed in turn.
2. The *getpwuid* function retrieves information from */etc/passwd* and stores the first three fields of information in the array elements *$login, $passwd,* and *$uid*, respectively.
3. The *login* name and its corresponding *uid* are printed.

18.2.7 Time and Processes

When working in a computer environment, programs often need to obtain and manipulate the current date and time. UNIX systems maintain two types of time values: calendar time and process time.

The calendar time counts the number of seconds since 00:00:00 January 1, 1970, UTC (Coordinated Universal Time, which is a new name for Greenwich Mean Time).

The process time, also called CPU time, measures the resources a process utilizes in clock time, user CPU time, and system CPU time. The CPU time is measured in clock ticks per second.

Perl has a number of time functions that interface with the system to retrieve time information.

The *times* function. The *times* function returns a four-element array consisting of the CPU time for a process, measured in:

- User time—Time spent executing user's code
- System time—Time spent executing system calls
- Children's user time—Time spent executing all terminated child processes
- Children's system time—Time spent executing system calls for all terminated child processes

FORMAT

```
($user, $system, $cuser, $csystem) = times;
```

EXAMPLE 18.46

```
(The Script)
   #!/bin/perl
1  printf "User time in this program %2.3f seconds\n", (times)[0];
2  printf "System time in this program %2.3f seconds\n", (times)[1];

(Output)
3  User time in this program 0.217 seconds
4  System time in this program 0.600 seconds
```

EXPLANATION

1. The *times* function returns a four-element array and the first element is printed, the user time.
2. The *times* function returns a four-element array and the second element is printed, the system time.

The *time* Function (UNIX and Windows). The *time* function returns the number of nonleap seconds since January 1, 1970, UTC. Its return value is used with the *gmtime* and *localtime* functions to put the time in a human-readable format. The *stat* and *utime* functions also use the *time* functions when comparing file modification and access times.

The *gmtime* Function. The *gmtime* function converts the return value of the *time* function to a nine-element array consisting of the numeric values for the UTC. If you are a *C* programmer, you will recognize that these values are taken directly from the *tm structure* found in the header file */usr/include/time.h.* (See Table 18.11.)

FORMAT

```
gmtime(EXPR);
gmtime EXPR;
($sec, $min, $hour, $monthday, $month, $year, $weekday,
        $yearday, $isdaylight)=gmtime;
```

Table 18.11 Return Values for the *gmtime* Function

List Element	***Meaning***
$sec	Seconds after the minute: [0, 59]
$min	Minutes after the hour: [0, 59]
$hour	Hour since midnight: [0, 23]
$monthday	Day of the month: [1, 31]
$month	Months since January: [0, 11]
$year	Years since 1900
$weekday	Days since Sunday: [0, 6]
yearday	Days since January 1: [0, 365]
isdaylight	Flag for daylight savings time

EXAMPLE 18.47

```
(The Script)
   #!/bin/perl
1  ($sec, $min, $hour, $monthday, $month, $year, $weekday, $yearday,
       $isdaylight) = gmtime;
2  print "The weekday is $weekday and the month is $month.\n";
3  print "The time in California since midnight is ",
       `date "+%H:%M"`;
4  print "The Coordinated Univeral Time is $hour:$min
        since midnight\n";
5  print "Daylight saving is in effect.\n" if $isdaylight;
```

EXAMPLE 18.47 (CONTINUED)

```
(Output)
2   The weekday is 2 and the month is 6.
3   The time in California since midnight is 20:35.
4   The Coordinated Univeral Time is 3:35 since midnight.
5   <no output>
```

EXPLANATION

1. The *gmtime* function returns an array as defined in Table 18.11.
2. The weekday and the month are printed for Coordinated Universal Time.
3. The time in California is printed by utilizing the UNIX *date* command.
4. The Coordinated Universal Time is printed.
5. If daylight savings is in effect, the value of *$isdaylight* is set to nonzero. Daylight saving time is not in effect, so nothing prints.

The *localtime* Function. The *localtime* function converts the UTC to a nine-element array with the local time zone.

FORMAT

```
localtime(EXPR);
localtime EXPR;
($sec, $min, $hour, $mday, $mon, $year, $wday, $yday,
          $isdst)=localtime(time);
```

EXAMPLE 18.48

```
(At the Command Line)
1   $ perl -e "print scalar (localtime);"
    Wed May 30 15:26:16 2007

(In Script)
2   $localtime=localtime;
    print $localtime;
```

EXPLANATION

1. If the *localtime* function is use in scalar context, its return value is output similar to the UNIX/Win32 *date* command. The *scalar* function forces scalar context.
2. Assigning the return value of *localtime* to a scalar.

EXAMPLE 18.49

```
(The Script)
    #!/bin/perl
1   ($sec, $min, $hour, $mday, $mon, $year, $wday, $yday, $isdst)=
            localtime(time);
2       % weekday=(
        "0"=>"Sunday",
        "1"=>"Monday",
        "2"=>"Tuesday",
        "3"=>"Wednesday",
        "4"=>"Thursday",
        "5"=>"Friday",
        "6"=>"Saturday",
    );
     if ( $hour > 12 ){
3        print "The hour is ", $hour - 12 ," o'clock.\n";
     }
     else {
         print "The hour is $hour o'clock.\n";
     }
4   print qq/Today is $weekday{"$wday"}.\n/; # day starts at zero
5   print "It is ",$mon + 1, "/$mday/" , 1900+$year,".\n";
6   print "The isdst is $isdst.\n";

(Output)
3   The hour is 1 o'clock.
4   Today is Wednesday.
5   It is 5/30/2007.
6   The isdst is 1.
```

EXPLANATION

1. The *localtime* function converts the return of the time function to the local time.
2. An associative array, *%weekday,* associates a number of the weekday with the string for the day of the week.
3. The hour and the minutes are printed.
4. The scalar *$wday* returned from the *localtime* function represents the number of the weekday starting at 0. It is used to key into the associative array *%weekday* to get the value of the string *Wednesday.*
5. The month, day of the month, and year are printed.
6. The *$isdt* element of the array prints *1* if daylight savings is in effect, and 0 if not.

18.2.8 Process Creation UNIX

What happens when your Perl program starts executing? Here is a brief sketch of what goes on. Normally, the Perl program is executed from the shell command line. You type the name of your script (and its arguments) and then press the Enter key. At that point, the shell starts working. It first creates (*forks*) a new process called the **child process**. The child is essentially a copy of the shell that created it. There are now two processes running, the parent and child shells. After the child process is created, the parent shell normally sleeps (*waits*) while its child process gets everything ready for your Perl program; that is, handles redirection (if necessary) pipes, background processing, etc. When the child shell has completed its tasks, it then executes (*execs*) your Perl program in place of itself. When the Perl process completes, it exits (*exits*), and its exit status is returned to the waiting parent process, the shell. The shell wakes up, and a prompt appears on the screen. If you type in a UNIX command, this whole process is repeated.

It's conceivable that your Perl program may want to start up a child process to handle a specific task; for example, a database application or a client/server program.

The *fork* Function. The *fork* function is used to create processes on UNIX systems. The *fork* function is called once and returns twice. It creates a duplicate of the parent (calling) process. The new process is called the child process. The child process inherits its environment, open files, real and user IDs, masks, current working directory, signals, and so on. Both processes, parent and child, execute the same code, starting with the instruction right after the *fork* function call.

The *fork* function lets you differentiate between the parent and child because it returns a different value to each process. It returns *0* to the child process and the *pid* of the child to the parent process. It is not guaranteed which process will execute first after the call to the *fork* function.

Normally, the *wait, exec,* and *exit* functions work in conjunction with the *fork* function so that you can control what both the parent and the child are doing. The parent, for example, waits for the child to finish performing some task, and after the child exits, the parent resumes where it left off.

Figure 18.6 illustrates how the UNIX shell uses the *fork* system call to create a new process. After you type the name of your Perl program at the shell prompt, the shell forks, creating a copy of itself called the child process. The parent shell sleeps (*waits*). The child shell executes (*execs*) the Perl process in its place. The child never returns. Note that *ENV* variables, standard input, output, and standard error are inherited. When the Perl program completes, it exits and the parent shell wakes up. The shell prompt reappears on your screen. The Perl program could use the *fork* function to spawn off another application program.

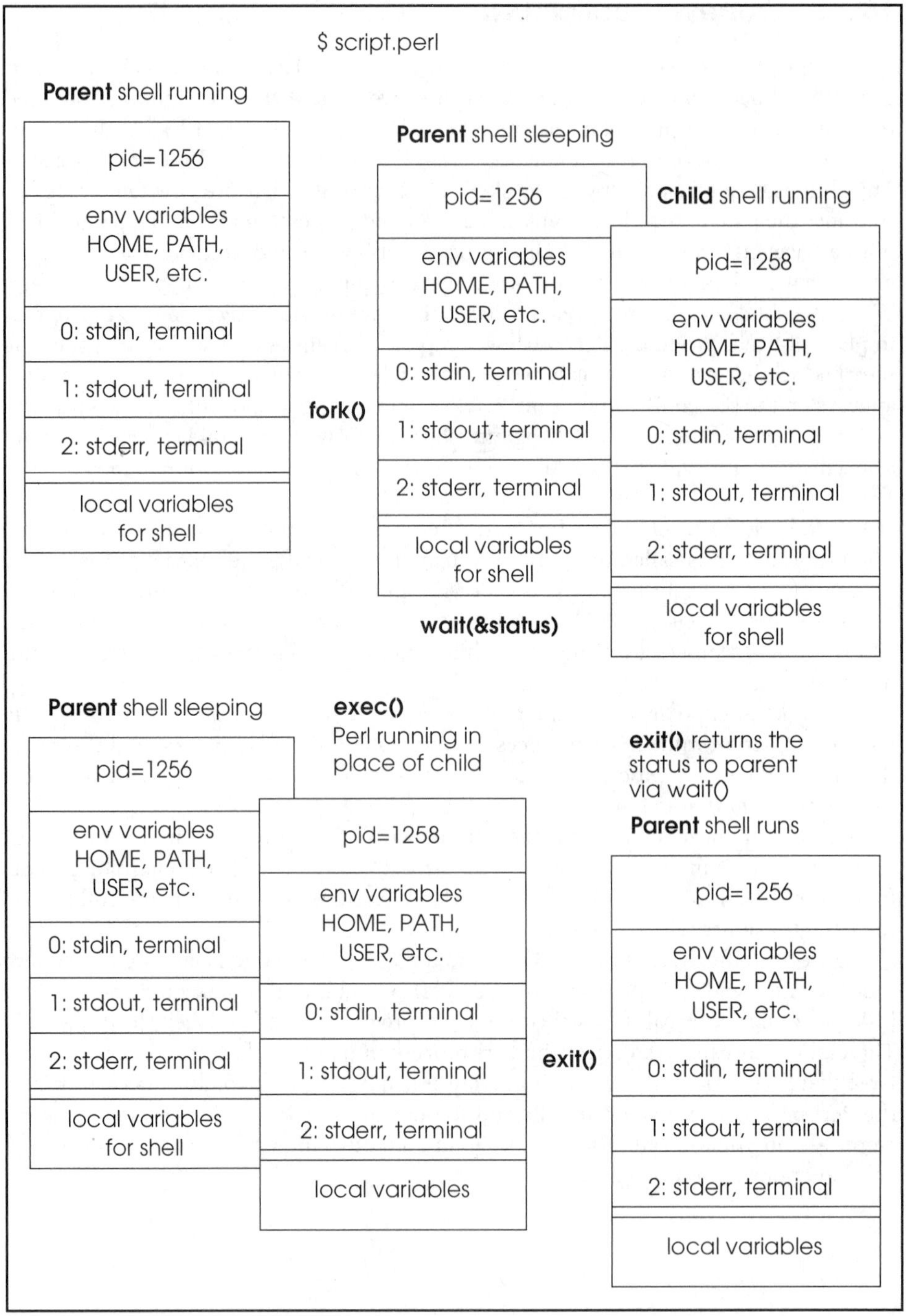

Figure 18.6 Perl process creation from the shell.

FORMAT

```
fork;
```

EXAMPLE 18.50

```
(The Script)
1   $return_val=fork;
2   if ( $return_val == 0 ){
        print "This is the child process; return value
               is $return_val.\n";
    }
3   elsif ( defined $return_val ){
        print "This is the parent process; return value
               is $return_val.\n";
    }
    else{
4       die "fork error: $!\n";
    }

(Output)
2   This is the child process; return value is 0.
3   This is the parent process; return value is 3512.
```

EXPLANATION

1. The *fork* function is called to create a copy of this process.
2. The return value is checked. If the return value is *0*, the child's code is in execution.
3. If the return value is nonzero, the parent process is executing.
4. This statement is executed if the *fork* function fails. It might fail if the process table is full; that is, if the system has reached its maximum number of allowed processes.

The *exec* Function. Whereas *fork* creates a brand new process, the *exec* function is used to initiate a new program in place of the currently running program. Normally, the *exec* function is called after *fork*. Perl inherits attributes from the shell, and a process that is executed from within Perl also inherits Perl's attributes, such as *pid*, *gid*, *uid*, signals, directories, etc. If, then, the *exec* function is called directly (no *fork*) from within a Perl script, the new program executes in place of the currently running Perl program. When that program completes, you do not return to your Perl program. Since *exec* does not flush the output buffer, the $| variable needs to be set to ensure command buffering.

The filehandles *STDIN*, *STDOUT*, and *STDERR* remain open following a call to the *exec* function.

At the system level there are six different *exec* functions used to initiate new programs. Perl calls the *C* library function *execvp* if more than one argument is passed to the *exec* function. The arguments are the name of the program to execute and any other arguments that will be passed to that program. If a single scalar is passed to the *exec* function and it contains any shell metacharacters, the shell command */bin/sh -c* is passed the command for interpretation.

FORMAT

```
exec(UNIX COMMAND);
exec UNIX COMMAND;
```

EXAMPLE 18.51

```
(The Script)
1   exec 'echo hi there you!';
2   print "hello";

(Output)
1   hi there you

(The Script)
1   exec 'ls *.c';
2   print "hello.";

(Output)
file1.c file2.c file3.c
```

EXPLANATION

1. In both examples, the *exec* function will execute the UNIX command.
2. In both examples, the *print* statement will not be executed, because *exec* never returns. The UNIX commands were executed **in place** of the Perl program.

The *wait* and *waitpid* Functions. The *wait* function waits for a child process to finish execution. After a *fork* call, both processes, parent and child, execute. The *wait* function forces the parent to wait until its child is finished and returns the *pid* of the child process to the parent. If there are no child processes, *wait* returns a *–1*.[11]

FORMAT

```
wait;
```

EXAMPLE 18.52

```
(The Script)
1   $return_val=fork;
2   if ( $return_val == 0 ){           # In child
        print "This is the child process; return value
            is $return_val.\n";
3       exec "/bin/date" || die "exec failed: $!\n";
    }
```

11. The *waitpid* function also waits for a child process to finish execution, but it can specify which child it will wait for, and it has special flags that control blocking.

EXAMPLE 18.52 (CONTINUED)

```
4   elsif ( defined $return_val ){    # In parent
        print "This is the parent process; return value is $pid.\n";
5       $pid = wait;
        print "Back in parent process.\n";
        print "The deceased child's pid is $pid.\n";
    }
    else{
6       die "fork error: $!\n";
    }

(Output)
4   This is the parent process; return value is 3530.
2   This is the child process; return value is 0.
3   Wed May 30 23:57:18 PST 2007.
5   Back in the parent process.
    The deceased child's pid is 3530.
```

EXPLANATION

1. The *fork* function creates a copy of the current process. Now there are two processes running, the parent Perl process and the child Perl process. They are both executing the code directly following the *fork* call. The return value is assigned *0* in the child and the *pid* of the child in the parent.
2. If in the child process, the *if* statement block is executed.
3. The *exec* function executes the UNIX *date* command and does not return.
4. If in the parent process, the *elsif* statement block is executed. The value of *$return_val* is the *pid* of the child process.
5. The *wait* function is called by the parent, which waits for the child to finish. The *pid* of the deceased child is returned.
6. If the *fork* failed (no more processes?), the *die* function will print the error message and the program will exit.

The *exit* Function. The *exit* function causes the program to exit. It can be given an integer argument ranging from values between zero and 255. The exit value is returned to the parent process via the *wait* function call. By convention, UNIX programs exiting with a zero status are successful, and those exiting with nonzero failed in some way. (Of course, the criteria for success for one programmer may not be the same as those for another.)

FORMAT

```
exit (Integer);
exit Integer;
```

EXAMPLE 18.53

```
(The Script)
    # The name of the script is args.p
1   exit 12 if $#ARGV == 0;

(Output)
1   $ args.p
2   $ echo $?
    12
```

EXPLANATION

1. The script is missing an argument.
2. The shell's *$?* variable contains the exit status of the Perl program. If using *C* shell, the exit status is stored in *$status*.

18.2.9 Process Creation Win32

You can use the *system* and *exec* functions and backquotes on Win32 systems just the same as you would with UNIX.

The *start* Command. The Perl *system* function is used by both Windows and UNIX to start an operating system command. The *system* function executes a program and doesn't return until that program finishes. If the Windows *start* command is given as an argument to the Perl *system* function, a new application will run, and your script will also continue to run.

EXAMPLE 18.54

```
    use warnings;
1   $return_value = system ("start /Program
Files/Netscape/Communicator/Program/netscape.exe");

2   print "Program continues; Netscape is running.\n";
3   print "The return_value from system is $return_value.\n";

(Output)
Program continues; Netscape is running.
The return_value from system is 0.
```

EXPLANATION

1. The Perl *system* function starts a new process. By using the Win32 *start* command, you can start a new process, and the Perl script will continue to run rather than waiting for the new process to complete. If the process starts up successfully, a return value of *0* is returned by the *system* function.

EXPLANATION (CONTINUED)

2 Netscape Communicator has started up and will continue to run until its window is closed.
3 The return value from the *system* function is printed.

The *Win32::Spawn* Module. The *Win32::Spawn* function behaves like the *system* function and the Windows *Start* menu.

FORMAT

```
use Win32;
Win32::Spawn($ProgramName, $CommandLine,$ProcessID);
```

EXAMPLE 18.55

```
1   use warnings;
2   use Win32;
3   $|=1;
4   $Application="C:/mksnt/date.exe";
5   $CommandLine="date +%D";
6   $status=Win32::Spawn($Application, $CommandLine, $ProcessID);
7   if ($status != 0){
8       print "pid is $ProcessID.\n";
    }
    else{
9       print "Didn't spawn $Application.\n";
10      print Win32::FormatMessage(Win32::GetLastError);
    }

(Output)
8 pid is 448.
11/01/00
```

EXPLANATION

1 The *warnings* pragma will send syntactic warnings, unitialized values, etc., to help with possible problems that may occur in the program.
2 The *Win32* module is loaded. This is a module that comes with ActiveState and is found in the standard Perl library under the *site/lib/Win32* directory. It contains a number of useful modules for Windows programmers to handle servers, clients, registries, events, network administration, processes, and more.
3 The special scalar $| is assigned the value *1*. It ensures that the output buffers will be flushed immediately when the *print* function is used.

EXPLANATION (CONTINUED)

4 The application is the MSK toolkit,[a] found on the C:\ drive. This toolkit contains *.exe* files that emulate UNIX commands. The *date.exe* file produces today's date.

5 The command line consists of any arguments that will be passed to the application.

6 The *Win32::Spawn* function is called with three arguments. Two of them have been given values, but *$ProcessID* is not known. It will be given a value after the application is started.

7 If the status returned from the *Win32::Spawn* function is not *0*, the process ID number will be printed.

8 The process ID number is *448*.

9 *Didn't spawn C:/mksnt/date.exe.* is displayed if the *.exe* file doesn't exist.

10 If the process couldn't be started because the application doesn't exist, the *GetLastError* function prints:

The system cannot find the file specified.
Program continues to run....

This is a Windows-generated error caused when the operating system failed to start the program. The *FormatMessage* function creates a readable printout of the error.

a. MSK Toolkit for Windows NT and Windows 95 Release 6.1, Mortice Kern Systems Inc.

The *Win32::Process* Module. Another extension you can use to launch Windows applications is the object-oriented *Win32::Process* module. It provides a number of methods for creating and managing processes. Processes can be suspended, resumed, and killed with this module.

Table 18.12 *Win32::Process* Methods

Method	*What It Does*
Create($Obj, $AppName, $CommandLine, $Inherit, $CreateFlags, $InitialDir);	Creates the process object
$Obj–>GetExitCode($ExitCode);	Gets the exit code of the process
$Obj–>GetPriorityClass($Class);	Gets the process priority class
$ProcessObj–>GetProcessID()	Returns the process ID
$Obj–>Kill($ExitCode);	Kills the process with exit code
$Obj–>Resume();	Resumes a suspended process
$Obj–>SetPriorityClass($Class);	Sets the process affinity mask (NT)
$Obj–>Suspend();	Suspends the process
$Obj–>Wait($Timeout);	Waits for the process to die

EXAMPLE 18.56

```
1   use Win32::Process;
2   use Win32;
3   sub ErrorReport{
        print Win32::FormatMessage( Win32::GetLastError() );
    }

4   Win32::Process::Create($ProcessObj,
        "C:\\windows\\notepad.exe", "notepad myfile.txt", 0,
        NORMAL_PRIORITY_CLASS, ".") || die ErrorReport();
    print "Notepad has started\n";
5   print "The exit code is:
        ",$ProcessObj->GetExitCode($ExitCode),"\n";

(Output)
Notepad has started
The exit code is: 1
```

EXPLANATION

1. The *Win32::Process* module is loaded. It is used to launch Windows applications.
2. The Win32 module is loaded.
3. The *ErrorReport* function will send a formatted error message for the last system error that occurred, if there was one.
4. The *Create* function creates a process. The first argument, *$ProcessObj,* is a container for the process object, followed by the full pathname of the application, command-line arguments, and required flags.
5. The exit code of the process is returned.

18.3 Other Ways to Interface with the Operating System

If the system functions are still not enough, Perl offers a number of alternative ways to deal with the operating system. You can use the *syscall* function, command substitution, the *system* function, and the *here document* to get system information.

18.3.1 The *syscall* Function and the *h2ph* Script

The *syscall* function calls a specified system call with its arguments. If the *C* system call is not implemented, a fatal error is returned. The first argument is the name of the system call, preceded by *&SYS_*. The remaining arguments are the actual parameters that are required by the real system call. If the argument is numeric, it is passed as a *C* integer. If not, the pointer to the string value is passed. You may have to coerce a number to an integer by adding *0* to it if it is not a literal and cannot be interpreted by context.

Before using the *syscall* function, you should run a script called *h2ph* (*h2ph.bat* on Windows) that comes with the Perl distribution. At the bottom of the *h2ph* script (after *_ _END_ _*) are the manual pages for *h2ph*, including an explanation on how to run the script. This script converts the proper *C* header files to the corresponding Perl header files. These files must be added to the Perl library if you are using functions that require them. All the files created have the *.ph* extension. After running the *h2ph* script, make sure that the *@INC* array in your program includes the path to these library functions.[12]

FORMAT

```
syscall (&SYS_NAME, LIST);
```

EXAMPLE 18.57

```
(UNIX: At the Command Line)
1   $ cd /usr/include; /usr/local/bin/perl/h2ph  *  sys/*

(In Script)
    #!/bin/perl
    # The name of the script is args.p
2   push(@INC, "/usr/local/lib");
3   require "syscall.ph";
4   $bytes=syscall(&SYS_getpagesize);
5   printf "The pagesize for this Sparc Sun Workstation is %d
            bytes \n",$bytes;

(Output)
5   The pagesize for this Sparc Sun Workstation is 4096 bytes.
```

EXPLANATION

1. *h2ph* is executed so that the necessary *C* header files are converted to Perl header files. The files created will be placed in */usr/local/lib* and end with a *.ph* extension.
2. The directory containing the *.ph* files is pushed onto the *@INC* array.
3. The file *syscall.ph* is required for using *C* system calls.
4. The Perl *syscall* function will call the *getpagesize* system call. The prefix *&SYS_* is necessary Perl syntax. It must be prepended to the real system call name.
5. The page size for this Sun4c is *4,096* bytes.

18.3.2 Command Substitution—The Backquotes

Although we have already discussed command substitution and backquotes in Chapter 5, "What's in a Name," a quick review might be in order here because command substitution is yet another way for Perl to interface with operating system commands.

---

12. See also the *h2xs* script that comes with Perl 5 distribution, for building a Perl extension from any *C* header file.

Backquotes are used by the UNIX/Linux shells (not Windows) to perform command substitution and are implemented in Perl scripts pretty much the same way. For example, the command line *echo The present working directory is `pwd`* will cause the command in backquotes to be executed and its results substituted into the string. **Like** the UNIX/Linux shell, enclosing a command in backquotes causes it to be executed. **Unlike** the shell, if double quotes surround the backquoted string, command substitution will **not** occur. The output resulting from executing the command is saved in a scalar variable.

EXAMPLE 18.58

```
(The Script)
   #!/bin/perl
1  print "The hour is ",`date`;

2  @d=`date`;
3  print $d[0]'

4  @d=split(/ /,`date`);
5  print "$d[0]\n"
6  $machine=`uname -n`;
7  print "$machine\n"'

(Output)
1  The hour is Thu May 31 20:47:17 PDT 2007
3  Thu May 31 20:59:11 PDT 2007
5  Thu
7  dolphin
```

EXPLANATION

1. The UNIX *date* command is enclosed in backquotes. It is executed and appended to the string *The hour is.*
2. The array *@d* is set to the output of the *date* command. The output is stored as a single string, unlike the shells, where the output is stored as a list.
3. Since the output of the command is stored as a single string, *$d[0]* is the entire string.
4. The *split* command creates a list from the output returned from the *date* command.
5. Now the first element of the array is the first word in the list, *Thu.*
6. The scalar *$machine* is assigned the value of the UNIX command, *uname -n*, which contains the name of the host machine (*hostname* on BSD).
7. The name of the host machine is printed.

18.3.3 The *Shell.pm* Module

This module lets you use UNIX commands that you normally type at the shell prompt in a Perl script. The commands are treated like Perl subroutines. Arguments and options are passed to the commands as a list of strings.

EXAMPLE 18.59

```
(The Script)
     #!/bin/perl
  1  use Shell qw(pwd ls date);     # Shell commands listed
  2  print "Today is ", date();
  3  print "The time is ", date("+%T");
  4  print "The present working directory is ", pwd;
  5  $list=ls( "-aF");
  6  print $list;

(Output)
  2  Today is Tue May 29 13:41:56 PDT 2007
  3  The time is 13:41:57
  4  The present working is /home/ellie/sockets
  6  ./
     ../
     sh.test*
     shellstuff
     timeclient*
     timeclient5*
     timeserver*
     timeserver5*
```

EXPLANATION

1. The *Shell.pm* module will be used in this program. The three UNIX shell commands *pwd, ls,* and *date* will be treated as ordinary Perl subroutines.
2. The *date* command is executed as a subroutine. This is an alternative to using backquotes.
3. Arguments passed to the *date* command are strings enclosed in quotes.
4. The *pwd* command is executed.
5. The output of the *ls* command is assigned to scalar *$list*. The argument is passed to the function as a single string.
6. The output of *ls -aF* is a list of files in the present working directory. The *-a* switch includes the dot files, and the *F* causes the executable scripts to be marked with an asterisk (*) and the directories with a /.

18.3.4 The *system* Function

Like its *C* counterpart, the *system* function takes a system command as its argument, sends the command to the system shell for interpretation, and returns control back to the calling program, your script. This is just like the *exec* functions, except that a *fork* is done first, so that control is returned to the Perl script. Because it does not flush the output buffer, the special Perl variable $| is set to *1* to force a flush of the buffer after *print* or *write* statements.[13]

---

13. A *fork* is done, the script waits for the command to be executed, and control is then returned to the script.

FORMAT

```
system("system command");
system "system command";
```

EXAMPLE 18.60

```
(UNIX: The Command Line)
1   system("cal 1 2007");
    print "Happy New  Year!\n";'

(Output)
    January 2007
Su  Mo  Tu  We  Th  Fr  Sa
 1   2   3   4   5  6
 7   8   9  10  11  12  13
14  15  16  17  18  19  20
21  22  23  24  25  26  27
28  29  30  31
    Happy New Year!

(Windows)
2   system("notepad.exe");
```

EXPLANATION

1. The *system* function executes the UNIX *cal* command to print out the calendar for the month of January 2007.
2. The *system* function executes the Windows *notebook.exe* command and starts up a session of Notepad.

EXAMPLE 18.61

```
    (The Script)
    1   print "Hello there\n";
    2   print "The name of this machine is ";
    3   system ("uname -n");        # Buffer is not flushed
    4   print "The time is ", `date`;

    (Output)
1       Hello there
3       jody
2,4     The name of this machine is The time is Tue May 29 13:39:35 PDT 2007
```

EXPLANATION

1. The first *print* statement is executed as expected.
2. Since Perl depends on the default I/O buffering mechanism, the buffer may not be flushed immediately after the *print* statement; the results of the *system* function, executed by the shell, are printed first.

EXPLANATION (CONTINUED)

3 The *system* function causes the shell to execute the UNIX command *uname -n*.
4 This *print* statement is printed directly after the *print* statement in line 2.

EXAMPLE 18.62

```
(The Script)
    #!/bin/perl
1   $|=1;        # Set special variable to flush the output buffer
2   print "Hello there\n";
3   print "The name of this machine is ";
    system ("uname -n");
4   print "The time is ", 'date';

(Output)
2   Hello there
3   The name of this machine is jody
4   The time is Tue Jan 26 13:43:54 PST 2001
```

EXPLANATION

1 The $| special variable, when set to nonzero, forces the output buffer to be flushed after every *write* or *print*.

18.3.5 here documents

The Perl *here document* is derived from the UNIX shell *here document*. As in the shell, the Perl *here document* is a line-oriented form of quoting, requiring the << operator followed by an initial terminating string. There can be no spaces after the <<. If the terminating string is not quoted or double quoted, variable expansion is performed. If the terminating string is single quoted, variable expansion is not performed. Each line of text is inserted between the first and last terminating strings. The final terminating string must be on a line by itself, with no surrounding whitespace.

Perl, unlike the UNIX shell, does not perform command substitution (backquotes) in the text of a *here document*. Perl, on the other hand, does allow you to execute commands in the *here document* if the terminator is enclosed in backquotes.

EXAMPLE 18.63

```
(The Script)
    #!/bin/perl
    $price=100;
1   print <<EOF;      # No quotes around terminator EOF are same
                      # as double quotes
2   The price of $price is right.     # Variables are expanded
3   EOF
```

EXAMPLE 18.63 (CONTINUED)

```
4   print <<'FINIS';
5   The price of $price is right.
                   # The variable is not expanded
                   # if terminator is enclosed in single quotes
6   FINIS

7   print << x 4;   # Prints the line 4 times
8   Christmas is coming!
        # Blank line is necessary here as terminating string

9   print <<`END`;  # If terminator is in backquotes,
                    # will execute UNIX commands
10  echo hi there
11  echo -n "The time is "
12  date
13  END

(Output)
2   The price of 100 is right.
5   The price of $price is right.
8   Christmas is coming!
    Christmas is coming!
    Christmas is coming!
    Christmas is coming!
10  hi there
    The time is Fri Nov  3 17:03:46 PST 2000
```

18.3.6 Globbing (Filename Expansion and Wildcards)

If you have worked at the UNIX or MS-DOS command line, you have been introduced to the shell metacharacters used to expand filenames. The asterisk (*) is used to match all characters in a filename, the question mark (?) to match one character in a filename, and brackets ([ ]) to match one of a set of characters in a filename. The process of expanding these shell metacharacters to a filename is called **globbing**.

Perl supports globbing if the filenames are placed within angle brackets, the read operators. There is also a Perl 5 function for globbing, as explained next.

EXAMPLE 18.64

```
(The Script)
    #!/bin/perl
1   @myfiles=<*.[1-5]>;
2   print "@myfiles\n";
3   foreach $file ( <p??l[1-5]*>){
4       print "$file\n" if -T $file;
    }
```

EXAMPLE 18.64 (CONTINUED)

```
(Output)
2   exer.3 exer.4 exer.5 fileter.1 format.1 format.2 format.3 perl.4
perl.4.1
4   perl1
    perl2
    perl3
    perl4
    perl4.1
    perl5
```

EXPLANATION

1. In an array context, after the globbing is performed, a list of all the matched files is returned and returned to the array *@myfiles*. The list consists of any files that start with zero or more of any character, followed by a period, and ending with a number between *1* and *5*.
2. The list of matched files is printed.
3. The *foreach* loop is entered. Each time through the loop, the scalar *$file* is set to the next file that is successfully globbed; that is, any file starting with a *p*, followed by any two characters, followed by an *l*, followed by a number between *1* and *5*, and ending in zero or more of any character.
4. If the file is a text file (*-T*), its name is printed.

The *glob* Function. The *glob* function does the same thing as the <*> operator. It expands the filename metacharacters just as the shell does and returns the expanded filenames.

EXAMPLE 18.65

```
(Command Line)
1   $ perl -e 'while(glob("p???[1-5]")) {print "$_\n";}'
    perl1
    perl2
    perl3
    perl4
    perl5

(In Script)
2   while ( glob("p???[1-5]")){
3      print "$_\n";
    }
```

EXAMPLE 18.65 (CONTINUED)

```
(Output)
3  perl1
   perl2
   perl3
   perl4
   perl5
```

EXPLANATION

1 At the command line, the *glob* function will "glob" onto any files in the current working directory whose name begins with a *p*, followed by any three characters (*???*), followed by any number between *1* and *5* (*[1–5]*). Each filename that matches the expression is assigned to $_ and then printed.
2 This time, *glob* is being used in a script. The behavior is exactly the same as in the first example.
3 The expanded filenames are printed.

18.4 Error Handling

There are a number of occasions when a system call can fail; for example, when you try to open a file that doesn't exist or remove a directory when it still contains files or when you try to read from a file for which you do not have read permission. Although we have used the *die* function in earlier examples, now we will go into more detail about error handling and functions you can use to handle errors. The functions are the *die* function, the *warn* function, and the *eval* function.

- The *die* function is used to quit the Perl script if a command or filehandle fails.
- The *warn* function is like the *die* function, but it does not exit the script.
- The *eval* function has multiple uses, but it is used primarily for exception handling.

You may remember that the *short-circuit* operators, *&&* and ||, evaluate the operands on the left and then evaluate the operands on the right. If the operand to the left of the *&&* is *true*, the right-hand side is evaluated. If the operand to the left of the || is *false*, the right-hand side is evaluated.

The *Carp.pm* Module. There are many ways to die. Perl 5's *Carp* module extends the functionality of *die* and *warn*. (See Example 12.10 on page 384.)

18.4.1 The *die* Function

If a system call fails, the *die* function prints a string to *STDERR* and exits with the current value of *$!*. The *$!* variable yields the current value of *errno*, the UNIX global variable containing a number indicating a system error. The only time that *errno* is updated is when a system call **fails**. When a system call fails, a code number is assigned to *errno* to indicate the type of error. If the newline is omitted in the string, the message is printed with its line number. (See */usr/include/sys* for a complete list.)

Here is an example from */usr/include/sys/errno.h*:

```
#define EPERM      1    /* Not owner */
#define ENOENT     2    /* No such file or directory */
#define ESRCH      3    /* No such process */
#define EINTR      4    /* Interrupted system call */
#define EIO        5    /* I/O error */
...
```

Win32 error codes differ from UNIX error codes, making it impossible to rely on the value returned in *$!*. There are a number of Win32 extensions that provide their own error functions to give more meaningful results. See the documentation for *Win32::GetLastError* in the standard Perl library included with ActiveState.

FORMAT

```
die(LIST)
die LIST
die
```

EXAMPLE 18.66

```
(In Script)
1   die "Can't cd to junk: $!\n" unless chdir "/usr/bin/junk";

(Output)
1   Can't cd to junk: No such file or directory
```

EXPLANATION

1 The *chdir* failed. The *$!* contains the error message from *errno*. The newline causes the string after the *die* function to be printed with the value of the *$!* variable.

EXAMPLE 18.67

```
(In Script)
1   die unless chdir '/plop' ;

(Output)
1   Died at croak.perl line 4.
```

EXPLANATION

1 The *chdir* function failed. This time the *$!* was not included in the *die* string. The line where the error took place is printed.

EXAMPLE 18.68

```
(In Script)
1   chdir '/plop' or die "Stopped";

(Output)
1   Stopped at croak.perl line 4.
```

EXPLANATION

1 This example produces the same output as the previous example but using a different syntax. If *chdir* fails, the *die* function to the right of *or* is executed.

18.4.2 The *warn* Function

The *warn* function (operator) is just like the *die* function except that the program continues to run. If the *die* function is called in an *eval* block, the argument string given to *die* will be assigned to the special variable $@. After a *die*, this variable can be passed as an argument to *warn* and the output sent to *STDERR*. (See "The *eval* Function".)

18.4.3 The *eval* Function

The *eval* function is used for exception handling; that is, catching errors. The block following *eval* is treated and parsed like a separate Perl program, except that all variable settings and subroutine and format definitions remain after *eval* is finished.

The value returned from the *eval* function is that of the last expression evaluated. If there is a compile or runtime error or the *die* statement is executed, an undefined value is returned, and a special variable, $@, is set to the error message. If there is no error, $@ is a null string.

Evaluating Perl Expressions with *eval*

EXAMPLE 18.69

```
(The Script)
    #!/bin/perl
    # The eval function will evaluate each line you type
    # and return the result. It's as though you are
    # running a little independent Perl script.
    # Script name: plsh

1   print "> ";            # Print the prompt
2   while(<STDIN>){
3       $result=eval ;   # eval evaluates the expression $_
4       warn $@ if $@;   # If an error occurs, it will be assigned to $@
5       print "$result\n if $result";
6       print "> ";      # Print the prompt
    }
```

EXAMPLE 18.69 (CONTINUED)

```
(Output)
(The Command line)
    $ plsh
2   > hello
5   hello
2   > bye
5   bye
2   > 5 + 4
5   9
2   > 8 / 3
5   2.66666666666667
2   > 5 / 0
4   Illegal division by zero at (eval 5) line 3, <STDIN> line 5.
    > "Oh I see
    Can't find string terminator '"' anywhere before EOF at (eval 6)
       line 1,   <STDIN> line
    > exit
```

EXPLANATION

1. This line prints a prompt for the user. This program is like a little Perl shell. It can help you in evaluating an expression before putting it in a program, especially if you're not sure how Perl will handle it.
2. The *while* loop is entered. Each time the loop is entered, it will read a line of input from the user and assign it to $_.
3. The *eval* function, without an argument, will evaluate the expression in $_ and assign the result of the evaluation to *$result*.
4. If the *eval* finds a syntax error or a system error results from the evaluation of the expression, the error message returned will be assigned to the $@ variable. If there is no error, the $@ variable is assigned a null string.
5. If the expression was successfully evaluated, the result will be printed.
6. The prompt is displayed and the loop reentered.

Using *eval* to Catch Errors in a Program

EXAMPLE 18.70

```
(In Script)
    #!/bin/perl
    print "Give me a number.";
    chop($a=<STDIN>);
    print "Give me a divisor.";
    chop($b=<STDIN>);
1   eval{ die unless $answer = $a/$b ; };
2   warn $@ if $@;
```

EXAMPLE 18.70 (CONTINUED)

```
3   printf "Division of %.2f by %.2f is %.2f.\n",$a,$b,
            $answer if $answer ;
4   print "I'm here now. Good-day!\n";

(Output)
    Give me a number.45
    Give me a divisor.6
3   Division of 45.00 by 6.00 is 7.50.
4   I'm here now. Good-day!

(Output)
    Give me a number.5
    Give me a divisor.0
2   Illegal division by zero at ./eval.p line 8, <STDIN> line 2.
4   I'm here now. Good-day!
```

EXPLANATION

1. The *eval* function will evaluate the division (*$a/$b*) and store the result in *$answer*. Note that *$answer* is first used inside the *eval* function. It remains after *eval* is finished.
2. If all went well, and the division was completed, this line is ignored. If there was an error (e.g., division by zero), the $@ variable is set to the system error. The *warn* function then prints the message to *STDERR*, and the program resumes. If the *die* function is called in an *eval* block, the program does not exit but continues execution after the *eval* block exits.
3. The result of the division is printed, if successful.
4. This line is printed just to show you that the program continued execution even after a failure, since the *warn* function does not cause the script to exit.

The *eval* Function and the *here document*

EXAMPLE 18.71

```
(The Script)
    #!/bin/perl
1   eval<<"EOF";
2       chdir "joker" || die "Can't cd: $!\n";
3   EOF
4   print "The error message from die: $@";
5   print "Program $0 still in progress.\n";

(Output)
4   The error message from die: Can't cd: no such file or directory
5   Program ./eval4.p still in progress.
```

EXPLANATION

1 The *here document* is like a special form of quoting. The *eval* function will get everything between the first EOF and the terminating EOF.
2 If the *chdir* function fails, the *die* function is called, and the program resumes after the last EOF of the *here document*.
3 EOF terminates the *here document*.
4 The error message from the *die* function is stored in the $@ variable.
5 The program continues.

18.5 Signals

A signal sends a message to a process and normally causes the process to terminate, usually due to some unexpected event, such as illegal division by zero, a segmentation violation, a bus error, or a power failure. The kernel also uses signals as timers, for example, to send an alarm signal to a process. The user sends signals when he hits the BREAK, DELETE, QUIT, or STOP keys.

The kernel recognizes 31 different signals, listed in */usr/include/signal.h*. You can get a list of signals by simply typing *kill -l* at the UNIX prompt. (See Table 18.13.)

Table 18.13 Signals (BSD)*

Name	***Number***	***Default***	***Description***
SIGHUP	1	Terminate	Hangup
SIGINT	2	Interrupt	Interrupt
SIGQUIT	3	Terminate	Quit/produces core file
SIGILL	4	Terminate	Terminate

*This is a partial listing of the signals.

Catching Signals. Signals are asynchronous events; that is, the process doesn't know when a signal will arrive. Programmatically you can ignore certain signals coming into your process or set up a signal handler to execute a subroutine when the signal arrives. In Perl scripts, any signals you specifically want to handle are set in the *%SIG* associative array. If a signal is ignored, it will be ignored after *fork* or *exec* function calls.

A signal may be ignored or handled for a segment of your program and then reset to its default behavior. See Example 18.72.

FORMAT

```
$SIG{'signal'};
```

EXAMPLE 18.72

```
(The Script)
     #!/bin/perl
1    sub handler{
2        local($sig) = @_;      # First argument is signal name
3        print "Caught SIG$sig--shutting down\n";
4        exit(1);
     }
5    $SIG{'INT'} = 'handler';   # Catch <Ctrl>-c
6    $SIG{'HUP'}='IGNORE';
7    print "Here I am!\n";
     sleep(10);
8    $SIG{'INT'}='DEFAULT';[a]

(Output)
7    Here I am
         < <Ctrl>-c is pressed while the process sleeps >
3    Caught SIGINT--shutting down
```

a. Wall, L., and Schwartz, R. L., *Programming Perl*, 2nd ed., O'Reilly & Associates:Sebastopol, CA, 1998.

EXPLANATION

1. The subroutine called *handler* is defined.
2. The *local* function sets the first argument, the signal name, to the scalar *$sig*.
3. If the signal arrives, the handler routine is executed and this statement is printed.
4. The program exits with a value of *1*, indicating that something went wrong.
5. A value for the *$SIG* associative array is set. The key is the name of the signal without the *SIG* prefix. The value is the name of the subroutine that will be called. If *<Ctrl>-c*, the interrupt key, is pressed during the run of the program, the handler routine is called.
6. *IGNORE* will ignore the hangup signal.
7. The *print* statement is executed and the process sleeps for 10 seconds. If the signal *<Ctrl>-c* arrives, the signal handler routine is called.
8. The *SIGINT* signal is reset to its default state, which is to terminate the process when *<Ctrl>-c* is pressed.

Sending Signals to Processes—The *kill* Function. If you want to send a signal to a process or list of processes, the *kill* function is used. The first element of the list is the signal. The signal is a numeric value or a signal name if quoted. The function returns the number of processes that received the signal successfully. A process group is killed if the signal number is negative. You must own a process to kill it; that is, the effective *uid* and real *uid* must be the same for the process sending the *kill* signal and the process receiving the *kill* signal.

For complex signal handling, see the *POSIX* module in the Perl standard library.

FORMAT

```
kill(LIST);
kill LIST;
```

EXAMPLE 18.73

```
1   $ sleep 100&
2   $ jobs -l
    [1] + 6505 Running    sleep 100&
3   $ perl -e 'kill 9, 6505'
    [1]      Killed       sleep 100
```

EXPLANATION

1. At the UNIX shell prompt, the *sleep* command is executed in the background. The *sleep* command causes the shell to pause for 100 seconds.
2. The *jobs* command lists the processes running in the background. The *sleep* process *pid* is *6505*.
3. Perl is executed at the command line. The *kill* function takes two arguments. The first, signal 9, guarantees that the process will be terminated. The second argument is the *pid* of the *sleep* process.

The *alarm* Function. The *alarm* function tells the kernel to send a *SIGALARM* signal to the calling process after some number of seconds. Only one alarm can be in effect at a time. If you call *alarm* and an alarm is already in effect, the previous value is overwritten.

FORMAT

```
alarm (SECONDS);
alarm SECONDS;
```

EXAMPLE 18.74

```
(The Script)
1   alarm(1);
2   print "In a Forever Loop!";
3   for (; ;){ printf "Counting...%d\n", $x++;}

(Output)
2   In a Forever Loop!
3   Counting...0
    Counting...1
    Counting...2
    Counting...3
    Counting...4
        ...
```

EXAMPLE 18.74 (CONTINUED)

```
    Counting...294
    Counting...295
4   Alarm Clock
```

EXPLANATION

1. A *SIGALARM* signal will be sent to this process after 1 second.
2. This statement is printed.
3. The loop starts. We wait for 1 second. The resolution on the actual second may be off. The *syscall* function can be used to call other functions, for example, *setitimer (2)* and *getitimer (2)*, with better timing resolution.
4. When the alarm goes off, the message *Alarm Clock* is printed by the function.

The *sleep* Function. The *sleep* function causes the process to pause for a number of seconds or forever if a number of seconds is not specified. It returns the number of seconds that the process slept. You can use the *alarm* function to interrupt the sleep.

FORMAT

```
sleep(SECONDS);
sleep SECONDS;
sleep;
```

EXAMPLE 18.75

```
(The Script)
    #!/bin/perl
1   $|=1          # flush output buffer
2   alarm(5);
    print "Taking a snooze...\n";
3   sleep 100;
4   print "\07 Wake up now.!\n";

(Output)
2   Taking a snooze...     # Program pauses now for 5 seconds
4   (Beep) Wake up now.
```

EXPLANATION

1. The $| variable forces the output buffer to be flushed after it writes and prints.
2. The *alarm* function tells the kernel to send a *SIGALARM* signal to the process in 5 seconds.
3. The process goes to sleep for 100 seconds or until a signal is sent to it.
4. The \07 causes a beep to sound before the statement *Wake up now!*

Attention, Windows Users! For those using ActivePerl on Win32 systems, the following functions have not been implemented. Primary among these is *alarm()*, which is used in a few Perl modules. Because they're missing in ActivePerl, you can't use those modules. Here is a complete list of unimplemented functions:

Functions for processes and process groups:
alarm(), fork(), getpgrp(), getppid(), getpriority(), setpgrp(), setpriority()

Functions for fetching user and group info:
endgrent(), endpwent(), getgrent(), getgrgid(), getgrnam(), getpwent(), getpwnam(), getpwuid(), setgrent(), setpwent()

System V interprocess communication functions:
msgctl(), msgget(), msgrcv(), msgsnd(), semctl(), semget(), semop(), shmctl(), shmget(), shmread(), shmwrite()

Functions for filehandles, files, or directories:
link(), symlink(), chroot()

Input and output functions:
syscall()

Functions for fetching network info:
getnetbyname(), getnetbyaddr(), getnetent(), getprotoent(), getservent(), sethostent(), setnetent(), setprotoent(), setservent(), endhostent(), endnetent(), endprotoent(), endservent(), socketpair()

See the *perlport* and *perlwin32* documentation pages for more information on the portability of built-in functions in ActivePerl.

18.6 What You Should Know

1. What are system calls?
2. How does Perl make calls to the system?
3. What module is used to traverse a file system?
4. How to create and remove directories.
5. What is meant by the environment?
6. What is a process?
7. What do *fork* and *exec* accomplish?

8. Where can you find modules for Windows processes?
9. How does the system function differ from using command substitution (backquotes) when executing system commands?
10. What is globbing?
11. How does *eval* work with *die*?
12. What are signals?
13. How does Perl deal with signals?
14. How do you rename a file with Perl?
15. How do you remove a file with Perl?

18.7 What's Next?

In the next chapter, you will learn how to format text with Perl pictures in order to nicely line up columns on a page. You will learn how to create templates to determine the field width and type of data that will be printed according to the rules of the template.

You will learn how to adjust the page size print headers, footers, and summaries and direct the formatted text to the screen or to another file.

chapter

19

Report Writing with Pictures

Perl is the Practical Extraction and Report Language. After you have practically extracted and manipulated all the data in your file, you may want to write a formatted report to categorize and summarize this information. If you have written reports with the *awk* programming language, you may find Perl's formatting a little peculiar at first.

19.1 The Template

In order to write a report, Perl requires that you define a template to describe visually how the report will be displayed; that is, how the report is to be formatted. Do you want left-justified, centered, or right-justified columns? Do you have numeric data that needs formatting? Do you want a title on the top of each page or column titles? Do you have some summary data you want to print at the end of the report?

We'll start with a simple template for a simple report and build on that until we have a complete example.

A format template is structured as follows:

FORMAT

```
format FILEHANDLE=

    picture line
    value line (text to be formatted)

write;
```

19.1.1 Steps in Defining the Template

The steps for defining a template are as follows.

1. Start the format with the keyword *format*, followed by the name of the output filehandle and an equal sign. The default filehandle is *STDOUT*, the screen. The template definition can be anywhere in your script.

```
format FILEHANDLE=
```

2. Although any text in the template will be printed as is, the template normally consists of a **picture line** to describe how the output will be displayed. The picture consists of symbols that describe the type of the fields (see Table 19.1). The fields are centered, left justified, or right justified (see Table 19.2). The picture line can also can be used to format numeric values.

Table 19.1 Field Designator Symbols

Field Designator	***Purpose***
@	Indicates the start of a field
@*	Used for multiline fields
^	Used for filling fields

Table 19.2 Field Display Symbols

Type of Field Symbol	***Type of Field Definition***
<	Left justified
>	Right justified
|	Centered
#	Numeric
.	Indicates placement of decimal point

3. After the field designator, the @ symbol, the *type* of field symbol is repeated as many times as there will be characters of that type. This determines the size of the field. If >>>>>> is placed directly after the @ symbol, it describes a seven-character right-justified field.[1] Strange, huh? Any real text is not placed directly after the @ symbol, or the field type is not interpreted.
4. After the picture line, which breaks the line into fields, comes the *value line*, text that will be formatted as described by the picture. Each text field is divided by a comma and corresponds, one to one, with the field symbol in the picture line. Any whitespace in the value line is ignored.

1. Even though there are only six > symbols, the @ field designator counts as one, making the total character width seven.

5. When you are finished creating the template, **a period (.) on a line by itself terminates** the template definition.
6. After the template has been defined, the *write* function invokes the format and sends the formatted records to the specified output filehandle. For now, the default filehandle is *STDOUT.*

EXAMPLE 19.1

```
(The Script)
    #!/bin/perl
1   $name="Tommy";
    $age=25;
    $salary=50000.00;
    $now="03/14/97";
    # Format Template
2   format STDOUT=
3   --------------------REPORT-----------------------
4   Name: @<<<<<< Age:@##Salary:@#####.## Date:@<<<<<<<<<<
5       $name,        $age,          $salary,         $now
6   .
         # End Template

7   write;
8   print "Thanks for coming. Bye.\n";

(Output)
    --------------------REPORT-----------------------
    Name: Tommy   Age: 25 Salary: 50000.00 Date:03/14/97
     Thanks for coming. Bye.
```

EXPLANATION

1 Variables are assigned.
2 The keyword *format* is followed by *STDOUT,* the default and currently selected filehandle, followed by an equal sign.
3 This line will be printed as is. Any text in the format that is not specifically formatted will print as is.
4 This line is called the **picture line**. It is a picture of how the output will be formatted. The @ defines the start of a field. There will be four fields. The first one is a left-justified seven-character field preceded by the string *Name:* and followed by the string *Age:*. The second field consists of two digits followed by *Salary:*. The third field consists of eight digits with a decimal point inserted after the sixth digit, followed by the string *Date.*
5 These are the variables that are formatted according to the picture. Each variable is separated by a comma and corresponds to the picture field above it.
6 The dot ends the template definition.
7 The *write* function will invoke the template to display the formatted output to *STDOUT.*

19.1.2 Changing the Filehandle

If you want to write the report to a file instead of to the screen, the file is assigned to a filehandle when it is opened. This same filehandle is used for the format filehandle when defining the template. To invoke the format, the *write* function is called with the name of the output filehandle as an argument.

EXAMPLE 19.2

```
     #!/bin/perl
1    $name="Tommy";
     $age=25;
     $salary=50000.00;
     $now="05/21/07";

2    open(REPORT, ">report" ) || die "report: $!\n";
     # REPORT filehandle is opened for writing
3    format REPORT=    # REPORT is also used for the format filehandle
     ------------------------
         | EMPLOYEE INFORMATION |
     ------------------------
4    Name: @<<<<<<
5        $name
     ------------------------
     Age:@###
         $age
     ------------------------
     Salary:@#####.##
         $salary
     ------------------------
     Date:@>>>>>>>>>>
         $now
     ------------------------
6    .
7    write REPORT;        # The write function sends output to the file
                          # associated with the REPORT filehandle
     ------------------------------------------------------------
```

```
(Output)
------------------------
| EMPLOYEE INFORMATION |
------------------------
Name: Tommy
------------------------
Age: 25
------------------------
Salary: 50000.00
------------------------
Date:    05/21/07
------------------------
```

EXPLANATION

1 Variables are defined.
2 The file *report* is opened and attached to the *REPORT* filehandle.
3 The *format* keyword is followed by the output filehandle *REPORT*.
4 The picture line describes the text string *Name:* , followed by a six-character left-justified field.
5 The scalar variable *$name* will be formatted as described in the picture line corresponding to it (see above).
6 The dot ends the format template definition.
7 The *write* function will invoke the format called *REPORT* and write formatted output to that filehandle. If the filehandle is not specified, the filehandle *REPORT* does not receive the formatted output, because the *write* function has not been told where the output should go.

19.1.3 Top-of-the-Page Formatting

In the following example, the title, *EMPLOYEE INFORMATION*, is printed each time the format is invoked. It might be preferable to print only the title at the top of each page. Perl allows you to define a **top-of-the-page format** that will be invoked only when a new page is started. The default length for a page is 60 lines. After 60 lines are printed, Perl will print the top-of-the-page format at the top of the next page. (The default length can be changed by setting the special variable $= to another value.) In the following example, the *write* function sends all output to *STDOUT* each time the *while* loop is entered.

The example is shown before top-of-the-page formatting is applied.

EXAMPLE 19.3

```
(The File)
    $ cat datafile
    Tommy Tucker:55:500000:5/19/66
    Jack Sprat:44:45000:5/6/77
    Peter Piper:32:35000:4/12/93

(The Script)
    #!/bin/perl
1   open(DB, "datafile" ) || die "datafile: $!\n";
2   format STDOUT=
    -----------------------
    | EMPLOYEE INFORMATION |
    -----------------------
    Name: @<<<<<<<<<<<<
        $name
    -----------------------
    Age: @##
        $age
    -----------------------
```

EXAMPLE 19.3 (CONTINUED)

```
    Salary: @#####.##
        $salary
    -----------------------
    Date: @>>>>>>>>>>
        $start
    .
3   while(<DB>){
4       ($name, $age, $salary, $start)=split(":");
5       write ;
    }
```

```
(Output)
-----------------------
| EMPLOYEE INFORMATION |
-----------------------
Name: Tommy Tucker
-----------------------
Age: 55
-----------------------
Salary: 50000.00
-----------------------
Date: 5/19/66

-----------------------
| EMPLOYEE INFORMATION |
-----------------------
Name: Jack Sprat
-----------------------
Age: 44
-----------------------
Salary: 45000.00
-----------------------
Date: 5/6/77
-----------------------
| EMPLOYEE INFORMATION |
-----------------------
Name: Peter Piper
-----------------------
Age: 32
-----------------------
Salary: 35000.00
-----------------------
Date: 4/12/54
```

EXPLANATION

1 The file *datafile* is opened for reading via the *DB* filehandle.
2 The format for *STDOUT* is created with picture lines and data.
3 The *while* loop reads one line at a time from the *DB* filehandle.

EXPLANATION (CONTINUED)

4 Each line is split by colons into an array of scalars.

5 The *write* function invokes the *STDOUT* format and sends the formatted line to *STDOUT*.

The format for top-of-the-page formatting follows.

FORMAT

```
format STDOUT_TOP=

    picture line
    value line (text to be formatted)

.(End of template)
```

The keyword *format* is followed by the name of the filehandle appended with an underscore and the word *TOP*. If a picture line is included, the value line consists of the formatted text. Any text not formatted by a picture is printed literally. The period (.) terminates the top-of-page format template.

The $% is a special Perl variable that holds the number of the current page.

The following example shows the results of top-of-the-page formatting.

EXAMPLE 19.4

```
(The Script)
    #!/bin/perl
1   open(DB, "datafile" ) || die "datafile: $!\n";
2   format STDOUT_TOP=
3       -@||-
4       $%
    -----------------------
5   | EMPLOYEE INFORMATION |
    -----------------------
6   .
7   format STDOUT=

    Name: @<<<<<<<<<<<<<
        $name
    -----------------------
    Age: @##
        $age
    -----------------------
    Salary: @#####.##
        $salary
   -----------------------
```

EXAMPLE 19.4 (CONTINUED)

```
Date: @>>>>>>>
    $start
.
while(<DB>){
    ($name, $age, $salary, $start)=split(":");
    write ;
}
```

```
(Output)
         -  1 -
-----------------------
| EMPLOYEE INFORMATION |
 -----------------------
Name: Tommy Tucker
-----------------------
Age: 55
-----------------------
Salary: 50000.00
-----------------------
Date: 5/19/66

Name: Jack Sprat
-----------------------
Age: 44
-----------------------
Salary: 45000.00
-----------------------
Date: 5/6/77

Name: Peter Piper
-----------------------
Age: 32
-----------------------
Salary: 35000.00
-----------------------
Date: 4/12/93
```

EXAMPLE 19.5

```
(The Script)
    #!/bin/perl
    open(DB, "datafile" ) || die "datafile: $!\n";
    open(OUT, ">outfile" )|| die "outfile: $!\n";
    format OUT_TOP=     # New filehandle
```

EXAMPLE 19.5 (CONTINUED)

```
4       -@||-
5       $%
    -----------------------
    | EMPLOYEE INFORMATION |
    -----------------------
    .
    format OUT=
    Name: @<<<<<<<<<<<<<
        $name
    -----------------------
    Age: @##
        $age
    -----------------------
    Salary: @#####.##
        $salary
     -----------------------
    Date: @>>>>>>>
          $start
    -----------------------
    .
    while(<DB>){
        ($name, $age, $salary, $start)=split(":");
6       write OUT;
    }
```

```
(Output)
$ cat outfile
        -  1 -
-----------------------
| EMPLOYEE INFORMATION |
-----------------------
Name: Tommy Tucker
-----------------------
Age: 55
-----------------------
Salary: 50000.00
-----------------------
Date: 5/19/66
-----------------------
Name: Jack Sprat
-----------------------
Age: 44
-----------------------
Salary: 45000.00
-----------------------
Date: 5/6/77
-----------------------
```

EXAMPLE 19.5 (CONTINUED)

```
Name: Peter Pumpkin
-----------------------
Age: 32
-----------------------
Salary: 35000.00
-----------------------
Date: 4/12/93
-----------------------
```

19.1.4 The *select* Function

The *select* function is used to set the default filehandle for the *print* and *write* functions. When you have **selected** a particular filehandle with the *select* function, the *write* or *print* functions do not require an argument. The selected filehandle becomes the default when a format is invoked or when the *print* function is called.

The *select* function returns the scalar value of the *previously* selected filehandle.

If you have a number of formats with different names, the $~ variable is used to hold the name of the report format for the currently selected output filehandle. The *write* and *print* functions will send their output to the currently selected output filehandle.

The $^ variable holds the name of the top-of-page format for the currently selected output filehandle.

The $. variable holds the record number (similar to the *NR* variable in *awk*).

EXAMPLE 19.6

```
(The Script)
    #!/usr/bin/perl
    # Write an awklike report
1   open(MYDB, "> mydb") || die "Can't open mydb: $!\n";
2   $oldfilehandle= select(MYDB);
                        # MYDB is selected as the filehandle for write
3   format MYDB_TOP =
                             DATEBOOK INFO

    Name               Phone             Birthday          Salary
    _________________________________________________________________
    .

4   format MYDB =
    @<<<@<<<<<<<<<<<<<<<<@<<<<<<<<<<<<<@||||||||@#######.##
    $.,       $name,            $phone,          $bd,        $sal
    .
```

EXAMPLE 19.6 (CONTINUED)

```
5   format SUMMARY =
    _____________________________________________________
6   The average salary for all employees is $@######.##.
                                             $total/$count
    The number of lines left on the page is @###.
                                             $-
    The default page length is @###.
                                $=
7   .
    open(DB,"datebook") || die "Can't open datebook: $!\n";
    while(<DB>){
        ( $name, $phone, $address, $bd, $sal )=split(/:/);
8       write ;
        $count++;
        $total+=$sal;
    }
    close DB;

9   $~=SUMMARY;     # New report format for MYDB filehandle
10  write;

11  select ($oldfilehandle); # STDOUT is now selected for further
                             # writes or prints
12  print "Report Submitted On" , `date`;

(Output)
16  Report Submitted On Sat Mar 26 11:52:04 PST 2001

(The Report)
    $ cat mydb
                         DATEBOOK INFO
    Name            Phone           Birthday        Salary
1   Betty Boop      245-836-8357    6/23/23         14500.00
2   Igor Chevsky    385-375-8395    6/18/68         23400.00
3   Norma Corder    397-857-2735    3/28/45         245700.00
          . . .
25  Paco Gutierrez  835-365-1284    2/28/53         123500.00
26  Ephram Hardy    293-259-5395    8/12/20         56700.00
27  James Ikeda     834-938-8376    12/1/38         45000.00
The average salary for all employees is $82572.50.
The number of lines left on the page is 32.
The default page length is 60.
```

EXPLANATION

1. The filehandle *MYDB* is opened for writing.
2. The *select* function sets the default filehandle for the *write* and *print* functions to the filehandle *MYDB*. The scalar *$oldfilehandle* is assigned the value of the **previously** assigned filehandle. The previously defined filehandle, in this example, is the default, *STDOUT*.

EXPLANATION (CONTINUED)

3 The top-of-the-page template is defined for filehandle *MYDB*.

4 The format for the body of the report is set for filehandle *MYDB*.

5 Another format template is defined with a new name, *SUMMARY*. This format can be invoked by assigning the format name *SUMMARY* to the special variable $~. (See line 9.)

6 The picture line is defined.

7 The format template is terminated.

8 The format is invoked and output is written to the currently selected filehandle, *MYDB*.

9 The $~ variable is assigned the new format name. This format will be used for the currently selected filehandle, *MYDB*.

10 The *write* function invokes the format *SUMMARY* for the currently selected filehandle, *MYDB*.

11 The *select* function sets the filehandle to the value of *$oldfilehandle*, *STDOUT*. Future *write* and *print* functions will send their output to *STDOUT* unless another output filehandle is selected.

12 This line is sent to the screen.

19.1.5 Multiline Fields

If the value line contains more than one newline, the @* variable is used to allow multiline fields. It is placed in a format template on a line by itself, followed by the multiline value.

EXAMPLE 19.7

```
(The Script)
    #!/bin/perl
1   $song="To market,\n
    to market, \nto buy a fat pig.\n";
2   format STDOUT=
3   @*
4   $song
5   @*
6   "\nHome again,\nHome again,\nJiggity, Jig!\n"
    .
    write;

(Output)
To market,
to market,
to buy a fat pig.
Home again,
Home again,
Jiggity, Jig!
```

EXPLANATION

1. The scalar *$song* contains newlines.
2. The format template is set for *STDOUT.*
3. The @* fieldholder denotes that a multiline field will follow.
4. The value line contains the scalar *$song*, which evaluates to a multiline string.
5. The @* fieldholder denotes that a multiline field will follow.
6. The value line contains a string embedded with newline characters.
7. End template definition.

19.1.6 Filling Fields

The caret (^) fieldholder allows you to create a filled paragraph containing text that will be placed according to the picture specification. If there is more text than will fit on a line, the text will wrap to the next line, etc., until all lines are printed in a paragraph block format. Each line of text is broken into words. Perl will place as many words as will fit on a specified line. The value line variable can be repeated over multiple lines. Only the remaining text for each line is printed rather than reprinting the entire value over again. If the number of value lines is more than the actual number of lines to be formatted, blank lines will appear.

Extra blank lines can be suppressed by using the special tilde (~) character, called the **suppression indicator**. If two consecutive tildes are placed on the value line, the field that is to be filled (preceded by a ^) will continue filling until all text has been blocked in the paragraph.

EXAMPLE 19.8

```
(The Script)
    #!/bin/perl
    $name="Hamlet";
    print "What is your favorite line from Hamlet? ";
1   $quote = <STDIN>;
2   format STDOUT=
3   Play: @<<<<<<<<<<   Quotation:    ^<<<<<<<<<<<<<<<<<<
4         $name,                      $quote
5                                     ^<<<<<<<<<<<<<<<<<<
                                      $quote
                                      ^<<<<<<<<<<<<<<<<<<
                                      $quote
6   ~                                 ^<<<<<<<<<<<<<<<<<<
                                      $quote
    .
    write;
```

EXAMPLE 19.8 (CONTINUED)

```
(Output)
What is your favorite line from Hamlet? To be or not to be, that is
the question:
Whether 'tis nobler in the mind to suffer the slings and arrows of
outrageous fortune...

Play: Hamlet        Quotation: To be or not to be, that is the
                               question: Whether 'tis nobler in the
                               mind to suffer the slings and arrows
                               of outrageous fortune...
```

EXPLANATION

1 The user is asked for input and should type a line from Shakespeare's *Hamlet*. (The line wraps.)
2 The format template for *STDOUT* is defined.
3 The picture line contains two fields, one for the name of the play, *$name,* or *Hamlet*, and one for the line of user input, *$quote*. The ^ fieldholder is used to create a filled paragraph. The quote will be broken up into words that will fit over four lines. If there are more words than value lines, they will not be formatted. If there are fewer words than lines, blank lines will be suppressed due to the ~ character preceding the last picture line.
4 The value line contains the variables to be formatted according to the picture above them.
5 The second line contained in *$quote* is placed here if all of it did not fit on the first line.
6 If we run out of text after formatting three lines, the blank line will be suppressed.

EXAMPLE 19.9

```
(The Script)
    #!/bin/perl
    $name="Hamlet";
    print "What is your favorite line from Hamlet? ";
    $quote = <STDIN>;
    format STDOUT=
    Play: @<<<<<<<<<<  Quotation:  ^<<<<<<<<<<<<<<<<<<
1          $name,                  $quote
2   ~~                             ^<<<<<<<<<<<<<<<<<<
                                   $quote
    .
3   write;
```

EXAMPLE 19.9 (CONTINUED)

```
(Output)
What is your favorite line from Hamlet? To be or not to be, that is
the question:
Whether 'tis nobler in the mind to suffer the slings and arrows of
outrageous fortune...

Play: Hamlet           Quotation: To be or not to be,
                                  that is the
                                  question: Whether
                                  'tis nobler in the
                                  mind to suffer the
                                  slings and arrows of
                                  outrageous fortune...
```

EXPLANATION

1 The value line is set. It will contain the name of the play and the quotation.
2 Using two tildes (suppression indicators) tells Perl to continue filling the paragraph until all of the text in *$quote* is printed or a blank line is encountered.
3 The *write* function invokes the format.

19.1.7 Dynamic Report Writing

Now that you know how to create a report, you can dynamically change the width of the fields in the template on demand. First, the designated field types are assigned to variables, and Perl's repeat string operator is used to designate the number of characters per field. This number can be assigned different values depending on how wide the field will be. The report template will be assigned to a string consisting of variables to represent the field type, number of characters, and field values. When needed, the format string can be interpreted by Perl's *eval* function. See Example 19.10.

EXAMPLE 19.10

```
(The Script)
1  open(FH, "datebook") or die;  # Open a file for reading
2  open(SORT, "|sort") or die;   # Open a pipe to sort output

3  $field1="<" x 18;  # Create format strings
   $field2="<" x 12;
   $field3="|" x 10;
   $field4="#" x 6 . ".##";
```

EXAMPLE 19.10 (CONTINUED)

```
   # Create the format template
4  $format=qq(
5  format SORT=
6    \@$field1\@$field2\@$field3\@$field4
7    \$name, \$phone, \$birth, \$sal
   .
   );

8  eval $format;
9  while(<FH>){
     ($name,$phone,$address,$birth,$sal)=split(":");
     ($first, $last)=split(" ", $name);
     $name=$last.", ". $first;
10   write SORT;
   }
   close(FH);
   close(SORT);
```

```
(Output)
Blenheim, Steve     238-923-7366  11/12/56     20300.00
Boop, Betty         245-836-8357   6/23/23     14500.00
Chevsky, Igor       385-375-8395   6/18/68     23400.00
Corder, Norma       397-857-2735   3/28/45    245700.00
Cowan, Jennifer     548-834-2348   10/1/35     58900.00
DeLoach, Jon        408-253-3122   7/25/53     85100.00
Evich, Karen        284-758-2857   7/25/53     85100.00
Evich, Karen        284-758-2867   11/3/35     58200.00
Evich, Karen        284-758-2867   11/3/35     58200.00
Fardbarkle, Fred    674-843-1385   4/12/23    780900.00
Fardbarkle, Fred    674-843-1385   4/12/23    780900.00
Gortz, Lori         327-832-5728   10/2/65     35200.00
```

EXPLANATION

1. The datebook file is opened for reading.
2. A pipe is created to send Perl's output to the system's "sort" utility. The sort will be ascending and by last name.
3. Variables are created to hold the strings to represent the "picture line." The "x" operator specifies the number of times the string on its left will be repeated. Doing this allows you to change the width of a field easily as you test the way the report looks when displayed.
4. The variable *$format* contains a string that will be used as the report format.
5. The template will send its output to the *SORT* filehandle, a pipe created on line 2.
6. These variables represent each field designator and its width. Note that the @ sign is preceded with a backslash to prevent Perl from trying to evaluate lines prematurely.

EXPLANATION (CONTINUED)

7 These variables represent the actual field values that will be displayed based on the picture line defined above. These fields are also backslashed so as not to be evaluated too soon.

8 The *eval* function evaluates the variable and replaces the results of the evaluation back into the program. When Perl interprets each line, it will see the current report format template as:

```
format SORT=
@<<<<<<<<<<<<<<<<<<<<<@<<<<<<<<<<<<<<@||||||||||@######.##
$name, $phone, $birth, $sal
.
```

9 Now we loop through the file one line at a time, splitting the name field to get the first and last names and then concatenating the first name to the last name in order to sort by last name.

10 To *write* function involves the *SORT* template to cause each line to be written to the screen according to the report template on lines 6 and 7.

19.2 What You Should Know

1. You should be able to define the steps necessary to create a template for generating formatted output.
2. Understand what is meant by the "picture line."
3. You should be able to format the top and bottom of a page.
4. You should know how to create multiline fields and filled fields.
5. Be able to change the format filehandle.
6. Be able to generate a picture line on the fly with the *eval* function.

19.3 What's Next?

In the next chapter, you will learn how Perl interacts with the network and the client/server model. You will learn about the networking protocols, network addressing, Perl's server and protocol functions, and how to obtain host information. There is also a discussion on how sockets are implemented and how to use them as communication end points on two Sun machines.

EXERCISE 19
Pretty as a Picture!

Generate a report from the following text and send it to a file.

supplierid	companyname	contactname	phone
1	Exotic Liquids	Charlotte Cooper	(171) 555-2222
2	New Orleans Cajun Delights	Shelley Burke	(100) 555-4822
3	Grandma Kelly's Homestead	Regina Murphy	(313) 555-5735
4	Tokyo Traders	Yoshi Nagase	(03) 3555-5011
5	Cooperativa de Quesos 'Las Cabras'	Antonio del Valle Saavedra	(98) 598 76 54
6	Mayumi's	Mayumi Ohno	(06) 431-7877
7	Pavlova, Ltd.	Ian Devling	(03) 444-2343
8	Specialty Biscuits, Ltd.	Peter Wilson	(161) 555-4448
9	PB KnSckebröd AB	Lars Peterson	031-987 65 43
10	Refrescos Americanas LTDA	Carlos Diaz	(11) 555 4640
11	Heli Snwaren GmbH & Co. KG	Petra Winkler	(010) 9984510
12	Plutzer LebensmittelgromSrkte AG	Martin Bein	(069) 992755
13	Nord-Ost-Fisch Handelsgesellschaft mbH	Sven Petersen	(04721) 8713
14	Formaggi Fortini s.r.l.	Elio Rossi	(0544) 60323
15	Norske Meierier	Beate Vileid	(0)2-953010
16	Bigfoot Breweries	Cheryl Saylor	(503) 555-9931
17	Svensk Sjöföda AB	Michael Björn	08-123 45 67
18	Aux joyeux ecclTsiastiques	GuylFne Nodier	(1) 03.83.00.68
19	New England Seafood Cannery	Robb Merchant	(617) 555-3267
20	Leka Trading	Chandra Leka	555-8787
21	Lyngbysild	Niels Petersen	43844108
22	Zaanse Snoepfabriek	Dirk Luchte	(12345) 1212
23	Karkki Oy	Anne Heikkonen	(953) 10956
24	G'day, Mate	Wendy Mackenzie	(02) 555-5914
25	Ma Maison	Jean-Guy Lauzon	(514) 555-9022
26	Pasta Buttini s.r.l.	Giovanni Giudici	(089) 6547665
27	Escargots Nouveaux	Marie Delamare	85.57.00.07
28	Gai pGturage	Eliane Noz	38.76.98.06
29	ForOts d'Trables	Chantal Goulet	(514) 555-2955

chapter

20

Send It Over the Net and Sock It to 'Em!

20.1 Networking and Perl

Because sharing information and transferring files among computers are so integral to everything we do, Perl offers a number of functions to obtain network information in your program. In order to write programs utilizing interprocess communication (sockets, message queues, etc.), it is essential to understand some of the basic terminology associated with the network. The following discussion is merely an introduction to some of the common networking vernacular, so that when you try to dissect or write Perl programs that require these functions, you will not have to search through all your *C* books or wade through the manual pages to figure out what is going on.

20.2 Client/Server Model

We have seen the client/server model in previous chapters when connecting to a database and a Web server. Most network applications use a client/server model. The server provides some service to one or more clients. The client may request a service from a server on the same machine or on a remote machine. Server programs provide such services as e-mail, Telnet, and FTP. In order for the client and server to talk to each other, a connection is made between the two processes, often by utilizing sockets. Today, one of the most well-known client/server models is the client (browser)/server (Web server) model used by the Web.

20.3 Network Protocols (TCP/IP)

When sending data over a network, there must be some reliable way to get the data from one machine to another. In order to facilitate this complicated process, networks are organized in a series of layers, each layer offering a specific networking service to the next layer. The layers are independent and have clearly defined interfaces for supplying functions to the next layer. A high layer passes data and information to the layer below it, until the bottom layer is reached. At the bottom layer, two machines can physically communicate with each other. The rules and procedures used for one network layer on a machine to communicate with its counterpart network layer on another machine are called **protocols**. The most popular software networking protocols in UNIX are Ethernet, IP, TCP, and UDP.

20.3.1 Ethernet Protocol (Hardware)

The Ethernet layer is the physical layer of the network. Any host connected to the Ethernet bus has physical access to data sent over the network. The Ethernet protocol prepares the data for transmission across a wire. It organizes the data in frames using 48-bit Ethernet source and destination addresses. The Ethernet layer, the lowest layer, represents the transfer of data on the physical network.

20.3.2 Internet Protocol (IP)

The IP layer is above the Ethernet layer; it prepares the data for routing on independent networks. IP uses a 4-byte Internet protocol address (IP address), and data is organized in pieces of information called **packets**. A packet contains an IP header with source and destination addresses, a protocol type, and a data portion. Although the IP protocol is more complicated than the Ethernet protocol, it is connectionless and unreliable in delivering packets. It doesn't guarantee how or even that the data will be received, but if the data being sent is too large, IP will break it down into smaller units. The IP protocol hides the underlying differences among the different networks from the user.

20.3.3 Transmission Control Protocol (TCP)

Although the IP layer provides some flow control, it is not guaranteed to be reliable; that is, the data may not be received in the same order it was sent or it may never get to its destination at all. The TCP protocol provides a reliable end-to-end service and flow of control analogous to making a phone call. Once the connection is made, both sides can communicate with each other, and even if they talk at the same time, the messages are received in the same order they were sent. Programs that use TCP are *rlogin*, *rsh*, *rcp*, and *telnet*.

20.3.4 User Datagram Protocol (UDP)

UDP is an alternative to TCP. It is used in applications that do not require a continuous connection and are sending short messages periodically with no concern whether some of the data is lost. A UDP datagram is similar to sending a letter in the mail: Each packet has an address, there is no guaranteed delivery time or sequencing, and duplicate packets may be sent.[1] This method prevents programs from hanging when a return is expected. Examples of programs that use this protocol are *rwho* and *ruptime*.

20.4 Network Addressing

Networks consist of a number of interconnected machines called **hosts**. The system administrator assigns the hostname when a new machine is added to the network. Each host on a TCP/IP/Ethernet network has a name and three types of addresses: an Ethernet address, an IP address, and a TCP service port number. When information is passed from one layer to another in a network, the packet contains header information, including the addresses needed to send the packet to its next destination.

Often, the addresses returned by the networking functions are in a binary format. In order to convert those addresses into an ASCII format, Perl's *pack* and *unpack* function can be used.

20.4.1 Ethernet Addresses

Since the Ethernet address is usually burned into the PROM when the machine is manufactured, it is not a number that is assigned by a system administrator. It is simply used to identify that particular piece of hardware. The */etc/ethers* (UCB) file contains the Ethernet addresses and hostnames for a particular network.

20.4.2 IP Addresses

The IP address is a 32-bit number assigned by the system administrator to a particular host on the network. If a host is connected to more than one network, it must have an IP address for each of the networks. It consists of a set of four decimal numbers (often called a four-octet address) separated by dots (e.g., 129.150.28.56). The first part of the address identifies the network to which the host is connected, and the rest of the address represents the host. The addresses are divided into classes (A through C). The classes determine exactly what part of the address belongs to the network and what part belongs to the host. The */etc/hosts* file contains the address of your host machine, the host's name, and any aliases associated with it. (See the *gethostent* and related functions on page 792.)

20.4.3 Port Numbers

When serving a number of user processes, a server may have a number of clients requesting a particular service that use either the TCP or UDP protocol. When delivering information to a particular application layer, these protocols use a 16-bit integer **port number** to identify a particular process on a given host. TCP and UDP port numbers

---

1. Rieken, B., and Weiman, L., *Adventures in Unix, Network Applications Programming*, John Wiley & Sons, Wiley Professional Computing: New York, 1992, p. 7.

between 0 and 255, called **well-known ports**, are reserved for common services. (Some operating systems reserve additional ports for privileged programs.)[2] The most common services are Telnet and FTP with TCP port numbers 23 and 21, respectively. If you write a server application that will use either the TCP or UDP protocols, the application must be assigned a unique port number. This port number should be some number outside the range of the special reserved port numbers. The */etc/services* file contains a list of the well-known port numbers.

20.4.4 Perl Protocol Functions

The following Perl functions allow you to retrieve information from the */etc/protocols* file. The functions are named after the system calls and library functions found in Sections 2 and 3 of the UNIX manual pages.

The *getprotoent* Function. The *getprotoent* function reads the next line from the network protocols database, */etc/protocol,* and returns a list. The entries are the official names of the protocols; a list of aliases, or alternative names, for the protocol; and the protocol number. The *setprotoent* function opens and rewinds the */etc/protocols* file. If *STAYOPEN* is nonzero, the database will not be closed after successive calls to the *getprotoent*. The *endprotoent* function closes the database.

FORMAT

```
getprotoent;
setprotoent (STAYOPEN);
endprotoent;
```

EXAMPLE 20.1

```
(The Script)
while (($name,  $aliases, $proto ) = getprotent){
printf "name=%-5s,aliases=%-6sproto=%-8s\n",
         $name, $aliases, $proto;
}

(Output)
2  name=ip,     aliases=IP    proto=0
   name=icmp,   aliases=ICMP  proto=1
   name=igmp,   aliases=OGMP  proto=2
   name=ggp,    aliases=GGP   proto=3
   name=tcp,    aliases=TCP   proto=6
   name=pup,    aliases=PUP   proto=12
   name=udp,    aliases=IDP   proto=17
```

2. Stevens, W. R., and Wright, G. R., *TCP/IP Illustrated, Volume 1: The Protocols*, Addison Wesley Longman, 1993, p. 13.

EXPLANATION

1 The *getprotoent* function gets an entry from the */etc/protocols* file. The loop will read through the entire file. The name of the protocol, any aliases associated with it, and the protocol number are retrieved.
2 Each entry and its values are printed.

The *getprotobyname* Function. The *getprotobyname* function is similar to *getprotoent* in that it gets an entry from the */etc/protocols* file. *getprotobyname* takes the protocol name as an argument and returns its name, any aliases, and its protocol number.

FORMAT

```
getprotobyname(NAME);
```

EXAMPLE 20.2

```
(The Script)
1   ($name,  $aliases, $proto ) = getprotobyname('tcp');
    print "name=$name\taliases=$aliases\t$protocol number=$proto\n";

(Output)
name=tcp     aliases=TCP     protocol number=6
```

EXPLANATION

1 The name of the protocol, any alias name, and the protocol number are retrieved from the */etc/protocols* function. The name of the protocol, *tcp*, is passed as the *NAME* argument.

The *getprotobynumber* Function. The *getprotobynumber* function is similar to the *getprotoent* function in that it gets an entry from the */etc/protocols* file. The *getprotobynumber* takes the protocol number as an argument and returns the name of the protocol, any aliases, and its protocol number.

FORMAT

```
getprotobynumber(NUMBER);
```

EXAMPLE 20.3

```
(The Script)
1   ($name,  $aliases, $proto) = getprotobynumber(0);
    print "name=$name\taliases=$aliases\t$protocol number=$proto\n";

(Output)
name=ip     aliases=IP     protocol number=0
```

EXPLANATION

1 *getprotobynumber* retrieves an entry from the */etc/protocols* file based on the protocol number passed as an argument. It returns the name of the protocol, any aliases, and the protocol number.

20.4.5 Perl's Server Functions

These functions let you look up information in the network services file, */etc/services*.

The *getservent* Function. The *getservent* function reads the next line from the */etc/services* file. If *STAYOPEN* is nonzero, the */etc/services* file will not be closed after each call.

FORMAT

```
getservent;
setservent (STAYOPEN);
endservent;
```

EXAMPLE 20.4

```
(The Script)
1   setservent(1 );
2   ($name, $aliases, $port, $proto) = getservent;
3   print
"Name=$name\nAliases=$aliases\nPort=$port\nProtocol=$protocol\n";
            < program continues here >

4   ($name, $aliases, $port, $proto) = getservent;
                  # Retrieves the next entry in /etc/services
5   print
"Name=$name\nAliases=$aliases\nPort=$port\nProtocol=$protocol\n";
6   endservent;

(Output)
3   Name=tcpmux
    Aliases=
    Port=1
    Protocol=tcp
5   Name=echo
    Aliases=
    Port=7
    Protocol=tcp
```

EXPLANATION

1. The *setservent* function guarantees that the */etc/services* file remains open after each call if the *STAYOPEN* flag is nonzero.
2. The *getservent* function returns the name of the service, any aliases associated with the services, the port number, and the network protocol.
3. The retrieved values are printed.
4. The second call to *getservent* retrieves the next line from the */etc/services* file.
5. The retrieved values are printed.
6. The *endservent* function closes the network file.

The *getservbyname* Function. The *getservbyname* function translates the service port name to its corresponding port number.

FORMAT

```
getservbyname(NAME, PROTOCOL);
```

EXAMPLE 20.5

```
($name,$aliases,$port,$protocol)=getservbyname('telnet', 'tcp');
```

EXPLANATION

The name of the service is *telnet* and the protocol is *tcp*. The service name, aliases, the port number, and the protocol are returned.

The *getservbyport* Function. The *getservbyport* function retrieves information from the */etc/services* file.

FORMAT

```
getservbyport(PORT, PROTOCOL);
```

EXAMPLE 20.6

```
(The Script)
    #!/bin/perl
    print "What is the port number? ";
    chomp($PORT=<>);

    print "What is the protocol? ";
    chomp($PROTOCOL=<>);
```

EXAMPLE 20.6 (CONTINUED)

```
1   ($name,  $aliases, $port, $proto ) = getservbyport(
                                         $PORT, $PROTOCOL);
    print "The getservbyport function returns:
        name=$name
        aliases=$aliases
        port number=$port
        prototype=$protocol \n";

(Output)
What is the port number?  517
What is the protocol?  udp
The getservbyport function returns:
    name=talk
    aliases=talk
    port number=517
    prototype=udp
```

EXPLANATION

1 The well-known port number *517* and the protocol name *udp* are passed to the *getservbyport* function. The name of the service, any aliases, the port number, and the protocol name are returned.

20.4.6 Perl's Host Information Functions

These functions allow you to retrieve information from the */etc/hosts* file. They are named after the system library routines found in Section 3 of the UNIX *man* pages.

The *gethostent* Function. The *gethostent* function returns a list consisting of the next line from the */etc/hosts* file. The entries are the official name of the host machine; a list of aliases, or alternative names for the host; the type of address being returned; the length, in bytes, of the address; and a list of network addresses, in byte order, for the named host.

FORMAT

```
gethostent;
sethostent(STAYOPEN);
endhostent;
```

EXAMPLE 20.7

```
(The Script)
    #!/bin/perl
```

EXAMPLE 20.7 (CONTINUED)

```
1  while ( ($name,  $aliases, $addrtype, $length, @addrs) =
           gethostent ){
2      ($a, $b, $c, $d) = unpack ( 'C4', $addrs[0]);
3      print "The name of the host is $name.\n";
4      print "Local host address (unpacked) $a.$b.$c.$d\n";
   }

(Output)
3  The name of the host is localhost.
4  Local host address (unpacked) 127.0.0.1
   The name of the host is jody.
   Local host address (unpacked) 129.150.28.56
```

EXPLANATION

1. The *gethostent* function retrieves the next entry from the */etc/hosts* file.
2. The raw address returned by the *gethostent* function is unpacked into 4 bytes (*C4*) so that it can be printed.
3. The name of the host, *jody*, is printed.
4. The local host's IP address is printed.

The *gethostbyaddr* Function. The *gethostbyaddr* function translates a network address to its corresponding names. It retrieves the information from the */etc/hosts* file for a host by passing a raw address as an argument. The entry consists of the official name of the host machine; a list of aliases, or alternative names for the host; the type of address being returned; the length, in bytes, of the address; and a list of network addresses, in byte order, for the named host.

FORMAT

```
gethostbyaddr(ADDRESS, DOMAIN_NUMBER);
```

EXAMPLE 20.8

```
(The Script)
   #!/bin/perl
1  $address=pack("C4", 127,0,0,1);
2  ($name,  $aliases, $addrtype, $length, @addrs) = gethostbyaddr
        ($address,2);
3  ($a, $b, $c, $d) = unpack ( 'C4', $addrs[0]);
4  print "Hostname Is $name and the Internet address Is
       $a.$b.$c.$d.\n";

(Output)
Hostname is localhost and the Internet address is 127.0.0.1.
```

EXPLANATION

1 The Internet address is *127.0.0.1*. It is packed into 4 bytes, and this address is used by the *gethostbyaddr* function.
2 The raw address and the value of *AF_INET* (found in */usr/lnclude/sys/socket.h*) are passed to the *gethostbyaddr* function.
3 The raw address is unpacked into 4 bytes.
4 The name of the host and Internet address are printed.

The *gethostbyname* Function. The *gethostbyname* function returns an entry from the */etc/hosts* file for the name of a specific host passed as an argument. The entry consists of the official name of the host machine; a list of aliases, or alternative names for the host; the type of address being returned; the length, in bytes, of the address; and a list of network addresses, in byte order, for the named host.

FORMAT

```
gethostbyname(NAME);
```

EXAMPLE 20.9

```
($name, $aliases, $addtrtype, $length,
        @addrs)=gethostbyname("dolphin");
```

EXPLANATION

(See the *gethostent* function for explanation.)

20.5 Sockets

Sockets were first developed at the University of California, Berkeley, in 1982 in order to support interprocess communication on networks. The client/server model is used for interprocess communication through sockets. Not all operating systems support sockets. If your system is one of these, the socket examples shown here will not work.

Sockets are a software abstraction representing the endpoints between two communicating processes, a server and a client; in other words, sockets allow processes to talk to each other. The communicating processes can be on the same machine or on different machines. The server process creates the socket. The client process knows the socket by name. In order to ensure where the data is coming from or going to on a network, the socket uses IP and port addresses. A program using a socket opens the socket (similar to opening a file), and once the socket is opened, I/O operations can be performed for reading and writing information to the communicating processes. When a file is opened, a file descriptor is returned. When a socket is opened, a socket descriptor is returned to the server and one is returned to the client. The socket interface, however, is much more complex than working with files, since communication is often done across networks.

Remote login and file transfer programs are common utilities that communicate across a network through the use of sockets.

20.5.1 Types of Sockets

Every socket has a type of communication path to identify how the data will be transferred through the socket. The two most common types of sockets, *SOCK_STREAM* and *SOCK_DGRAM*, utilize the TCP and UDP protocols, respectively.

There are other, less common types of sockets, such as *SOCK_SEQPACKET* and *SOCK_RAW*, but we will not discuss those here.

Stream Sockets. The *SOCK_STREAM* type of stream socket provides a reliable, connection-oriented, sequenced, two-way service. It provides for error detection and flow control, and it removes duplicate segments of data. The underlying protocol is TCP.

Datagram Sockets. The *SOCK_DGRAM* type of datagram socket provides a connectionless service. Packets sent may be received in any order or may not be received on the other end at all. There is no guarantee of delivery and packets may be duplicated. The underlying protocol is UDP.

20.5.2 Socket Domains

When a socket is opened, a number of system calls are issued describing how the socket is to be used. The process must specify a communication domain, also called an **address family**, to identify the way the socket is named and what protocols and addresses are needed in order to send or receive data. The domain of a socket identifies where the server and client reside—on the same machine, on the Internet, or on a Xerox network.

The two standard domains are the **UNIX domain** and the **Internet domain**. When using sockets for interprocess communication, the UNIX domain is used for processes communicating on the same machine, whereas the Internet domain is used for processes communicating on remote machines using the TCP/IP protocols. (The ***AF_NS* domain** is used for processes on a Xerox network.)

The UNIX Domain and the *AF_UNIX* Family. If the communication is between two processes on a local machine, the address family (AF) is called *AF_UNIX*. The UNIX domain supports the *SOCK_STREAM* socket type and the *SOCK_DGRAM* socket type. The *SOCK_STREAM* type in the UNIX domain provides a bidirectional communication between processes, similar to the *pipe* facility. *SOCK_STREAM* is a reliable byte-stream transfer between processes. The datagram sockets are unreliable, not often used, and cause the socket to behave like message queues or telegrams.

Sockets in the UNIX domain have pathnames in the UNIX file system. The *ls -l* command lists the file as a socket if the first character is an *s* (see Example 20.10). In the system file */usr/include/sys/socket.h*, the *AF_UNIX* family is assigned the constant value *1*.

EXAMPLE 20.10

```
$ ls -lF greetings
srwxrwxrwx            1  ellie     0 Apr 26 09:31  greetings=
```

The Internet Domain and the *AF_INET* Family. The Internet domain sockets, identified as *AF_INET*, are used for interprocess communication between processes on different computers. The Internet domain also supports the socket types *SOCK_STREAM* and *SOCK_DGRAM*.

The Internet socket is defined by its IP address to identify the Internet host and its port number to identify the port on the host machine.

The underlying protocol for *SOCK_STREAM* is TCP. The underlying protocol for *SOCK_DGRAM* is UDP. In the system file */usr/include/sys/socket.h*, the *AF_INET* family is defined as the constant 2.

Socket Addresses. A socket, once created, needs an address so that data can be sent to it. In the *AF_UNIX* domain, the address is a filename, but in the *AF_INET* domain, it is an IP address and a port number.

20.5.3 Creating a Socket

The *socket* function creates the socket and returns a filehandle for the socket. In the server this socket is called the rendezvous socket.

FORMAT

```
socket(SOCKET_FILEHANDLE, DOMAIN, TYPE, PROTOCOL);
```

EXAMPLE 20.11

```
    $AF_UNIX=1;
    $SOCK_STREAM=1;
    $PROTOCOL=0;

1   socket(COMM_SOCKET, $AF_UNIX, $SOCK_STREAM, $PROTOCOL);
```

EXPLANATION

1 In this example, the *socket* function creates a filehandle called *COMM_SOCKET*. The domain or family is UNIX, the socket type is *STREAM*, and the protocol is assigned *0*, which allows the system to choose the correct protocol for this socket type.

20.5.4 Binding an Address to a Socket Name

The *bind* Function. The *bind* function attaches an address or a name to a *SOCKET* filehandle. (See Example programs at the end of this chapter.)

FORMAT

```
bind(SOCKET_FILEHANDLE, NAME);
```

EXAMPLE 20.12

```
1   bind(COMM_SOCKET, "/home/jody/ellie/perl/tserv");
2   bind(COMM_SOCKET, $socket_address);
```

EXPLANATION

1 When using the UNIX domain, the socket filehandle *COMM_SOCKET* is bound to a UNIX pathname.
2 When using the Internet domain, the socket filehandle *COMM_SOCKET* is bound to the packed address for the socket type.

20.5.5 Creating a Socket Queue

The *listen* Function. The *listen* function waits for *accepts* on the socket and specifies the number of connection requests to be queued before rejecting further requests. Imagine having call waiting on your phone with up to five callers queued.[3] If the number of client requests exceeds the queue size, an error is returned. The function returns true if successful, false otherwise. The error code is stored as *$!*.

FORMAT

```
listen(SOCKET_FILEHANDLE, QUEUE_SIZE);
```

EXAMPLE 20.13

```
listen(SERVERSOCKET, 5);
```

EXPLANATION

The number of waiting connections in the queue is set to 5. The *listen* function queues the incoming client requests for the *accept* function (see following).

3. Wall, L., and Schwartz, R. L., *Programming Perl*, 2nd ed., O'Reilly & Associates: Sebastopol, CA, 1998, p. 158.

20.5.6 Waiting for a Client Request

The *accept* Function. The *accept* function in the server process waits for a request from the client to arrive. If there is a queue of requests, the first request is removed from the queue when a connection is made. The *accept* function then opens a new socket filehandle with the same attributes as the original, or **generic**, socket, also called the **rendezvous socket**, and attaches it to the client's socket. The new socket is ready to communicate with the client socket. The generic socket is now available to accept additional connections. The *accept* function returns true if successful, false otherwise. The error code is stored as *$!*.

FORMAT

```
accept(NEWSOCKET, GENERICSOCKET);
```

EXAMPLE 20.14

```
accept (NEWSOCK, RENDEZ_SOCK );
```

EXPLANATION

The server process uses the *accept* function to accept requests from clients. It takes the first pending request from the queue and creates a new socket filehandle, *NEWSOCK*, with the same properties as *RENDEZ_SOCK* filehandle, also called the generic or rendezvous socket.

20.5.7 Establishing a Socket Connection

The *connect* Function. The *connect* function uses the socket filehandle and the address of the server socket to which it will connect. It makes a rendezvous with the *accept* function in the server. After the connection is made, data can be transferred. If the UNIX domain is used, the pathname of the UNIX file is provided. If the Internet domain is used, the address is a packed network address of the proper type for the server. It returns true if successful, false otherwise. An error code is stored as *$!*.

FORMAT

```
connect(SOCKET, ADDRESS);
```

EXAMPLE 20.15

```
1   connect(CLIENTSOCKET, "/home/joe/sock" );
2   connect(CLIENTSOCKET, $packed_address);
```

EXPLANATION

1 In the UNIX domain, a UNIX pathname is attached to the filehandle *CLIENTSOCKET.*
2 In the Internet domain, a packed network address is attached to the filehandle *CLIENTSOCKET*. The address is obtained from the *gethostbyname* function and is packed with the Perl *pack* function. For example:
    $hostname="houston";
    $port=9876;
    $AF_INET=2;
    $SOCK_STREAM=1;
    ($name, $aliases, $type, $len, $address)=gethostbyname($hostname);
    $packed_address=pack(S n a4 x8, $AF_INET, $port, $address);

20.5.8 Socket Shutdown

The *shutdown* Function. The *shutdown* function shuts down a socket connection as specified. If the *HOW* argument is *0*, further *receives* on the socket will be refused. If the *HOW* argument is *1*, further *sends* on the socket will be refused, and if the argument is *2*, all *sends* and *receives* are stopped.

FORMAT

```
shutdown(SOCKET, HOW);
```

EXAMPLE 20.16

```
shutdown(COMM_SOCK, 2);
```

EXPLANATION

The socket filehandle *COMM_SOCK* will disallow further *sends* or *receives*. It is shut down.

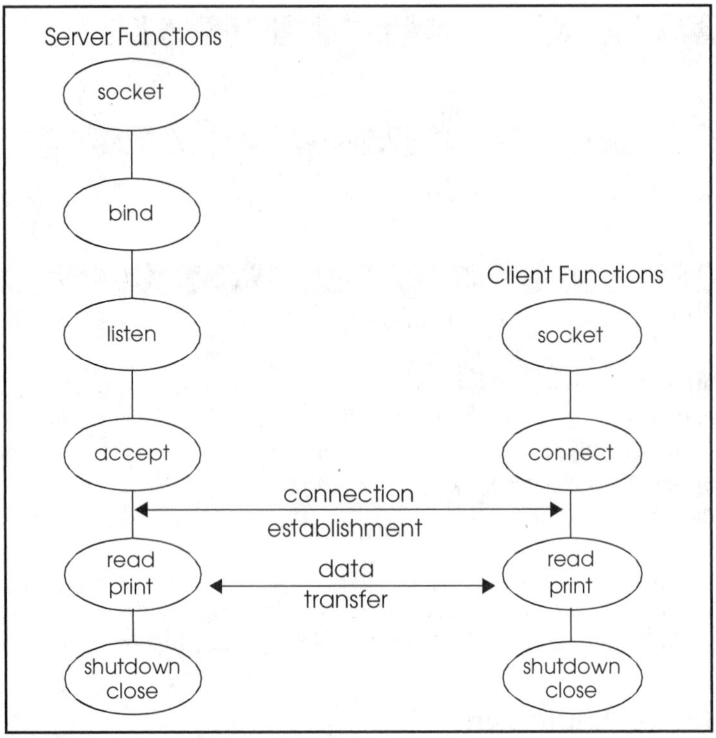

Figure 20.1 Sockets for a server and client connection-oriented communication.

20.6 Client/Server Programs

The sample programs shown here were tested on Sun workstations running SunOS 4.1.3 and SunOS 5.3. These programs are examples of stream sockets for the UNIX and Internet domains. Although datagrams (UDP) are supported, they are unreliable and delivery of packets is not guaranteed. They are used in the Internet domain by programs such as *rwho* and *ruptime* but are rarely used in the UNIX domain.

20.6.1 Connection-Oriented Sockets on the Same Machine

The following scripts are very simple examples of the client/server model utilizing stream sockets for communication endpoints. Both client and server reside on the same machine, and the client simply reads a greetings message from the server and prints the message on the screen. There is little error checking or signal handling. The programs are simple demonstrations of how those socket functions are used. (For socket functions not included in this chapter, see Table A.1 in Appendix A.)

The Server Program

EXAMPLE 20.17

```
(The Script)
    #!/bin/perl

    # The server and the client are on the same machine.
    print "Server Started.\n";
    $AF_UNIX=1;       # The domain is AF_UNIX
    $SOCK_STREAM=1; # The type is SOCK_STREAM
    $PROTOCOL=0;      # Protocol 0 is accepted as the "correct
                      # protocol" by most systems.

    socket(SERVERSOCKET, $AF_UNIX, $SOCK_STREAM, $PROTOCOL) ||
        die " Socket $!\n";
    print "socket OK\n";
    $name="./greetings";  # The name of the socket is associated
                          # within the file system
    unlink "./greetings" || warn "$name: $!\n";

    bind(SERVERSOCKET, $name) || die "Bind $!\n";
    print "bind OK\n";

    listen(SERVERSOCKET, 5) || die "Listen $!\n";
    print "listen OK\n";

    while(1){

        accept(NEWSOCKET, SERVERSOCKET ) || die "Accept $!\n";
        # Accept client connection

        $pid=fork || die "Fork: $!\n";
        if ($pid == 0 ){
            print (NEWSOCKET "Greetings from your server!!\n";

            close(NEWSOCKET);
            exit(0);
        }
        else{
            close (NEWSOCKET);
        }
    }
```

EXPLANATION

1. The domain is set to UNIX. The client and server are on the same machine.
2. The socket type is *SOCK_STREAM*, a connection-oriented, byte-stream type of communication.
3. The *protocol* is set to *0*. This value is handled by the system if set to *0*.
4. The *socket* function is called. The filehandle *SERVERSOCKET* is created in the server.
5. The pathname of the file *greetings* is the name in the file system the socket *SERVERSOCKET* will be associated with. It will be the real name to which the socket filehandle is attached. If the file already exists, it will be removed with the *unlink* function.
6. The socket filehandle is bound to the UNIX file *greetings*.
7. The *listen* function allows the process to specify how many pending connections it will accept from the client. The requests are queued and the maximum number that can be queued is 5.
8. The *accept* function waits for a client request and creates a new socket filehandle, *NEWSOCKET*, with the same attributes as the original filehandle, *SERVERSOCKET* (also called the rendezvous socket). *NEWSOCKET* is the socket that actually communicates with the client. The rendezvous socket remains available to accept future connections.
9. A child process is created with the *fork* function. Now both parent and child are in execution.
10. If the *pid* returned is zero, the child is in execution. If the *pid* is nonzero, the parent is in execution.
11. If the child process is in execution (*pid* is zero), the *greetings* message is written to the socket *NEWSOCKET*. The server is communicating with its client.
12. The *NEWSOCKET* filehandle is closed by the child and the child exits.
13. The *NEWSOCKET* filehandle is closed by the parent so that it can receive more client requests.

The Client Program

EXAMPLE 20.18

```
(The Script)
    #!/usr/bin/perl
    print "Hi I'm the client\n";

    $AF_UNIX=1;
    $SOCK_STREAM=1;
    $PROTOCOL=0;

    socket(CLIENTSOCKET, $AF_UNIX, $SOCK_STREAM, $PROTOCOL);
    $name="./greetings";
```

EXAMPLE 20.18 (CONTINUED)

```
     do{
          # Client connects  with server
6         $result = connect(CLIENTSOCKET, "$name" );
          if ($result != 1 ){
               sleep(1);
          }
7    }while($result !=  1 );  # Loop until a connection is made

8    read(CLIENTSOCKET, $buf, 500);
9    print STDOUT "$buf\n";
10   close (CLIENTSOCKET);
     exit(0);
```

EXPLANATION

1 The domain is *AF_UNIX*. The client and server reside on the same machine. The value assigned to the scalar is the value that is assigned to the *AF_UNIX* macro in the system file */usr/include/sys/socket.h*. The *socket* function requires these values as arguments in order to create a socket.

2 The type of socket is *SOCK_STREAM*, a sequenced, reliable, bidirectional method of communication between the client and server. The value assigned to the scalar is the value that is assigned to the *SOCK_STREAM* macro in the system file */usr/include/sys/socket.h*. The *socket* function requires these values as arguments in order to create a socket.

3 The protocol value is handled by the system calls involved in creating the socket. It determines how the socket is implemented at a low level. By assigning *0* as the protocol value, the *socket* function considers this the "correct protocol"; that is, you don't have to worry about the details.

4 The *socket* function creates a socket filehandle called *CLIENTSOCKET*.

5 The socket filehandle *CLIENTSOCKET* will be associated with the UNIX file *greetings*.

6 The *connect* function connects the *CLIENTSOCKET* filehandle to the UNIX file *greetings* so that the client can communicate with the server. The return from the function is true if it succeeded and false otherwise.

7 Until the connection is made, the program loops.

8 Now that the connection has been made, the client reads as many as 500 bytes from the server socket and stores the bytes in the scalar *$buf*.

9 The contents of *$buf* are printed to *STDOUT*.

10 The *CLIENTSOCKET* filehandle is closed. For more control, the *shutdown* function should be used.

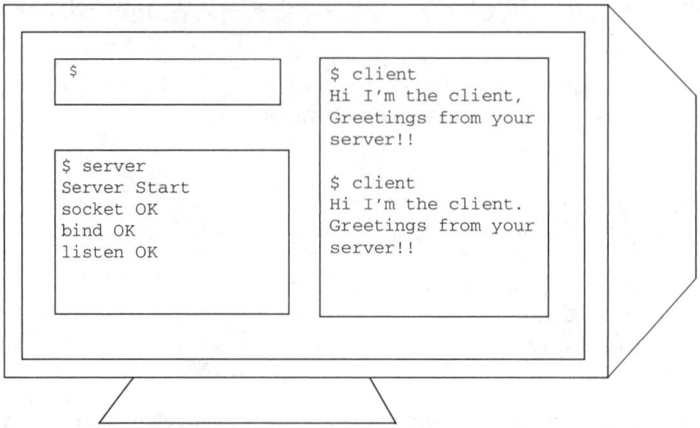

Figure 20.2 The output.

20.6.2 Connection-Oriented Sockets on Remote Machines (Internet Clients and Servers)

The following program was executed on two Sun workstations. The server's hostname is *scarecrow*, running SunOS 5.3, and the client's hostname is *houston*, running SunOS 4.1.3. In this program, the client on one machine asks the server on another machine for the time. The server sends the time to the client socket, and the client prints the time in readable format to the screen. These examples do not take advantage of Perl 5's *Socket.pm* module in the standard library. All values are hardcoded and therefore are not necessarily portable from one machine to another. (See "The *Socket.pm* Module" on page 808.)

EXAMPLE 20.19

```
#!/usr/bin/perl  -T
# timeserver -- a Time Server program,
# opens a Rendezvous Socket on port 9876
# and waits for a client to connect.
# When each client connects, this server determines the machine
# time on its host and writes the value on the communication
# socket to the client.
#
#                      Usage: timeserver [port number]
#
use strict;
use warnings;
($port)=@ARGV;
$port=9876 unless $port;
$AF_INET=2;
$SOCK_STREAM = 1;
```

EXAMPLE 20.19 (CONTINUED)

```
5   $sockaddr = 'S n a4 x8';
6   ($name,$aliases,$proto)=getprotobyname('tcp');
7   if($port !~ /^\d+$/){
8       ($name, $aliases, $port)=getservbyport($port,'tcp');
    }
    print "Port = $port\n";
9   $this = pack($sockaddr, $AF_INET, $port, "\0\0\0\0");
10  select(COMM_SOCK); $| = 1; select (STDOUT);
        # Create R_SOCKET, the rendezvous socket descriptor
11  socket(R_SOCKET, $AF_INET, $SOCK_STREAM, $proto ) ||
            die "socket: $!\n";
        # Bind R_SOCKET to my address, $this
12  bind(R_SOCKET, $this) || die "bind: $!\n";
13  listen(R_SOCKET, 5) || die "connect: $!\n";
        # Infinite loop - wait until client connects,
        # then serve the client
    while(1){
14      accept(COMM_SOCK, R_SOCKET) || die "$!\n";
15      $now = time;
16      print COMM_SOCK $now;
    }
```

EXPLANATION

1. A hostname may be passed as a command-line argument (see line 7).
2. If the *ARGV* array is empty, the scalar *$port* is assigned the value *9876*. This port number is assigned by the programmer to a number outside the reserved port numbers. On a Sun system, port numbers through *1024* are reserved. The port number *9876* is also called an *ephemeral port*; i.e., it is short-lived.
3. The scalar *$AF_INET* is assigned the value 2, the constant value assigned to the macro *AF_INET* in */usr/include/sys/socket.h*. This number represents the Internet domain, *AF_INET*.
4. The type of socket is *SOCK_STREAM*, assigned the value of *1* in */usr/include/sys/socket.h*.
5. The *pack* function will use this format for the socket address.
6. The *getprotobyname* function returns the official protocol name, any aliases, and the protocol number, using the *tcp* protocol as the name.
7. If the scalar *$port* is not an assigned number, but the name of the server machine was passed in at the command line, the *getservbyport* function will return the correct port number for the server, using the *tcp* protocol.
8. The *port number* is printed.
9. The address for this Internet domain and port number is packed into a binary structure consisting of an unsigned short, a short in "network" order, four ASCII characters, and 8 null bytes. In comparable *C* programs, you will note that the method for getting addresses is by using a *sockaddr* (see line 5) structure (see */usr/include/ sys/socket.h*). Perl handles most of this for you.

EXPLANATION (CONTINUED)

10 The *socket* filehandle is selected as the current default handle for output. The $| special variable is set to *1*, forcing buffers to be flushed on every *write* or *print*. The *stdout* filehandle is normally line buffered when sending output to a terminal and block buffered otherwise. When output is going to a pipe or socket, the buffers will be flushed.

11 The *socket* function creates the rendezvous socket filehandle *R_SOCKET*.

12 The *bind* function binds the socket filehandle to the correct address for the server.

13 The *listen* function sets the queue limit to 5, the maximum for pending requests from the client.

14 The *accept* function waits for a client request, and when it gets one, accepts it by creating a new socket filehandle called *COMM_SOCK* with all the same attributes as *R_SOCKET. COMM_SOCK* is the server socket that will communicate with the client.

15 The *time* function returns the number of non-leap-year seconds since Jan. 1, 1970, UTC.

16 The *time* is sent to the socket filehandle *COMM_SOCK*.

EXAMPLE 20.20

```
   #!/usr/local/bin/perl
   # timeclient--a client for the Time Server program,
   # creates a socket and connects it to the server on port 9876.
   # The client then expects the server to write the server's
   # host time onto the socket. The client simply does
   # a read on its socket, SOCK, to get the server's time.
   #
   #          Usage:  timeclient [server_host_name]
   #
   print "Hi, I'm in Perl program \'client\' \n";
1  ($them) = @ARGV;
2  $them = 'localhost' unless $them;
3  $port = 9876 ;        # timeserver is at this port number
4  $AF_INET = 2;
5  $SOCK_STREAM = 1;
6  $sockaddr = 'S n a4 x8';
7  ($name, $aliases, $proto) = getprotobyname('tcp');
8  ($name,$aliases, $port, $proto)=getservbyname($port, 'tcp')
       unless $port =~ /^\d+$/;

9  ($name,$aliases, $type, $len, $thataddr)=gethostbyname($them);
10 $that = pack($sockaddr, $AF_INET, $port, $thataddr);
```

EXAMPLE 20.20 (CONTINUED)

```
   # Make the socket filehandle
11 if ( socket(SOCK, $AF_INET, $SOCK_STREAM, $proto ) ){
       print "Socket ok.\n";
   }
   else { die $!; }
   # Call up the server
12 if(connect(SOCK, $that)){
       print "Connect ok.\n";
   }
   else { die $!;}
   # Set socket to be command buffered
13 select(SOCK); $| = 1; select (STDOUT);
   # Now we're connected to the server, let's read her host time
14 $hertime = <SOCK>;
   close(SOCK);
   print "Server machine time is: $hertime\n";
15 @now = localtime($hertime);
   print "\t$now[2]:$now[1] ", $now[4]+1,"/$now[3]/$now[5]\n";
```

EXPLANATION

1. The server's hostname may be passed as a command-line argument.
2. If the *ARGV* array is empty, the hostname is set to *localhost*.
3. To identify the server process, the client needs to know the server's port number.
4. The domain is *Internet*.
5. The type of socket is *SOCK_STREAM*, assigned the value of *1* in */usr/include/sys/socket.h*.
6. The *pack* function will use this format for the socket address.
7. The *getprotobyname* function returns the official protocol name, any aliases, and the protocol number, using the *tcp* protocol as the name.
8. The *getservbyname* function returns the name of the official name of the server, any aliases, the port number, and the protocol name, unless *$port* contains already assigned digits.
9. The raw network address information is obtained from the host by *gethostbyname*.
10. The address for the server's Internet domain and port number is packed into a binary structure consisting of an unsigned short, a short in "network" order, four ASCII characters, and 8 null bytes. In comparable *C* programs, you will note that the method for getting addresses is by using a *sockaddr* structure (see */usr/include/sys/socket.h*).
11. The *socket* function creates an Internet domain, connection-oriented socket filehandle, *SOCK*.
12. The *connect* function connects the client's socket to the server's address.
13. The *SOCK* filehandle is selected. Buffers will be flushed after prints and writes.
14. Perl reads from the *SOCK* filehandle. The server's time is retrieved.
15. The time is converted to local time and printed.

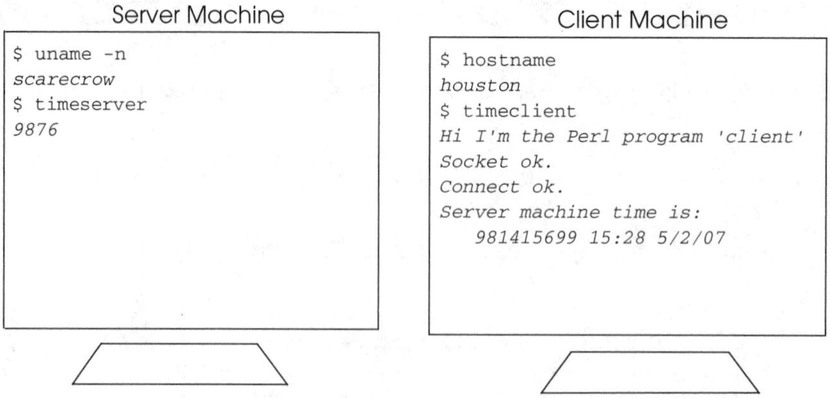

Figure 20.3 Connection-oriented sockets on remote machines.

20.7 The *Socket.pm* Module

Although sockets were originally an idea started at Berkeley for UNIX systems, they are now supported on many other operating systems. Perl 5 introduced a special module, called *Socket.pm,* to deal with sockets. This makes it much easier to port programs from one machine to another, because the necessary functions and constants needed for your machine are handled in the module, thus allowing you to get away from hardcoding values into the program as seen in the previousl examples. However, a caveat: You must understand the way the *Socket* module works before using it. The names of constants are not intuitive, and the later versions of Perl 5 have introduced more functionality to the module.

The following examples demonstrate how to write the previous TCP/IP server and client programs by taking advantage of *Socket.pm* and some of the other pragmas offered in Perl 5 to better secure the programs when used on a network.

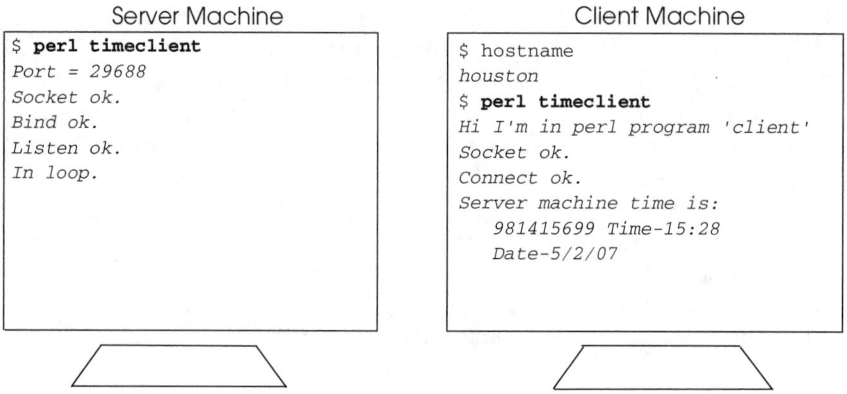

Figure 20.4 Server/client and *Socket.pm,* discussed in the following examples.

The Server

EXAMPLE 20.21

```
(The Server Script)
#!/bin/perl  -Tw
require 5.6;
use strict;
use Socket;
use FileHandle;

# timeserver --  a Time Server program, opens a rendezvous
# socket on port 29688 and waits for a client to connect.
# When each client connects, this server determines the machine
# time on its host and writes the value on the communication
# socket to the client.
#
#                        Usage: timeserver
#
my($this, $now);
my $port = shift || 29688;

$this = pack('Sna4x8', AF_INET, $port, "\0\0\0\0");
print "Port = $port\n";
my $prototype = getprotobyname('tcp');
socket(SOCKET, PF_INET, SOCK_STREAM, $prototype) ||
                         die "socket: $!\n";
print "Socket ok.\n";

bind(SOCKET, $this) || die "bind: $!\n";
print "Bind ok.\n";

listen(SOCKET, SOMAXCONN) || die "connect: $!\n";
print "Listen ok.\n";

COMM_SOCKET->autoflush;
SOCKET->autoflush;

# Infinite loop -- wait until client connects,
# then serve the client
while(1){
    print "In loop.\n";
    accept(COMM_SOCKET, SOCKET) || die "$!\n";
    print "Accept ok.\n";
    $now = time;
    print COMM_SOCKET $now;
}
```

EXPLANATION

1 The *-w* switch sends diagnostics to *STDERR* if an identifier is mentioned only once, a scalar is used before being set, a non-number is used as a number, etc. The *-T* switch turns on taint checking to prevent data coming into your program from affecting something inside your program. If using a directory path, the taint mode checks to see if the directory is writeable by others, and it checks arguments coming into the program. Once tainted, the data (or any variable that references the tainted data) cannot be used in any command that invokes a subshell. It is suggested that taint checking be turned on for server programs and CGI scripts; that is, programs that are run by someone else.

2 The *require* function uses the version number as an argument. This ensures that Perl versions prior to 5.6 will abort.

3 The *strict* pragma ensures that your program does not use unsafe constructs. It disallows symbolic references and barewords, and variables must be declared using the *my* function.

4 The *Socket* module will be used in this program. The module is designed to make the use of sockets more portable.

5 The *FileHandle* module is used here to take advantage of its method *autoflush,* which will force the proper flushing of buffers when writing to the socket.

6 These variables will be used later in the program. They must be declared with *my* because the *strict* pragma enforces this as a safety feature.

7 A hostname may be passed as a command-line argument and shifted into the *$port* variable. If the *ARGV* array is empty, the scalar *$port* is assigned the value *9688*, a number well outside the range of reserved port numbers.

8 *AF_INET* is a constant defined in the *Socket* module to represent the Internet domain. The *pack* function packs the IP address and port number for the server socket into *$this*.

9 The *getprotobyname* function returns the official protocol name, any aliases, and the protocol number, using the *tcp* protocol as the name.

10 The *socket* function creates the rendezvous socket filehandle, *SOCKET*.

11 The *bind* function binds the socket filehandle to the correct address for the server.

12 The *listen* function sets the queue limit to *SOMAXCONN*, the maximum for pending requests from the client (usually 5).

13 The *autoflush* method from the *FileHandle* class forces buffers to be flushed as soon as something is written to the socket.

14 An infinite loop is started. The server is now waiting for a client request.

15 The *accept* function waits for a client request, and when it gets one, accepts it by creating a new socket filehandle called *COMM_SOCK*, with all the same attributes as *SOCKET*.

16 The server calls the *time* function to get the current time and assigns that value to *$now*.

17 The server sends the time to *COMM_SOCK*. The client will get it at its end.

The Client

EXAMPLE 20.22

```
   #!/usr/local/bin/perl -Tw
   require 5.6.0;
1  use Socket;
   use FileHandle;
2  use strict;
3  my($remote, $port, @thataddr, $that,$them, $proto,@now,
       $hertime);

   #  timeclient --  a client for the Time Server program,
   #  creates a socket and connects it to the server on
   #  port 29688.
   #  The client then expects the server to write server's
   #  host time onto the socket, so the client simply does
   #  a read on its socket, SOCK, to get the server's time
   #
   #
   #                   Usage:  timeclient [server_host_name]
   #
   print "Hi, I'm in perl program \'client\' \n";
4  $remote = shift || 'localhost' ;
5  $port =  29688 ;     # timeserver is at this port number
6  @thataddr=gethostbyname($remote);

7  $that = pack('Sna4x8', AF_INET, $port, $thataddr[4]);

8  $proto = getprotobyname('tcp');

   # Make the socket filehandle

9  if ( socket(SOCK, PF_INET, SOCK_STREAM, $proto ) ){
       print "Socket ok.\n";
   }
   else { die $!; }

   # Call up the server
10 if (connect(SOCK, $that)) {
       print "Connect ok.\n";
   }
   else { die $!;}

   # Set socket to be command buffered
11 SOCK->autoflush;

   # Now we're connected to the server, let's read her host time
12 $hertime = <SOCK>;
13 close(SOCK);
```

EXAMPLE 20.22 (CONTINUED)

```
14 print "Server machine time is: $hertime\n";
15 @now = localtime($hertime);
16 print "\tTime-$now[2]:$now[1] ",
        "Date-",$now[4]+1,"/$now[3]/$now[5]\n";

(Output)
$ perl timeserver
Port = 29688
Socket ok.
Bind ok.
Listen ok.
In loop.

$ perl timeclient
Hi, I'm in perl program 'client'
Socket ok.
Connect ok.
Server machine time is: 981415699
        Time-15:28 Date-2/5/07
```

EXPLANATION

1. The *Socket* module will be used in this program.
2. The *strict* pragma is used to ensure that variables used in this program are "safe."
3. These variables will be used later in the program. They must be declared with *my* because the *strict* pragma enforces this as a safety feature.
4. A server's hostname may be passed as a command-line argument and shifted into the *$port* variable. If the *ARGV* array is empty, the scalar *$port* is assigned *localhost*.
5. The client gets the server's port number if it was assigned a value.
6. Now the client gets the server's official address.The raw network address information is obtained by *gethostbyname*.
7. The address for the server's Internet domain and port number is packed into a binary structure consisting of an unsigned short, a short in "network" order, four ASCII characters, and 8 null bytes.
8. The *tcp* protocol information is returned.
9. The *socket* function creates an Internet domain, connection-oriented socket filehandle, *SOCK*.
10. The *connect* function connects the client's socket to the server's address.
11. The *autoflush* method forces the socket's buffers to be flushed after prints and writes.
12. Perl reads from the *SOCK* filehandle. The server's time is retrieved via the socket.
13. The socket is closed.
14. The time value (number of non-leap-year seconds since 1/1/1970, UTC) retrieved from the server is printed.
15. The time is converted to local time and assigned to array *@now*.
16. The converted time is printed.

20.8 What You Should Know

1. What is TCP?
2. What are the Perl protocol functions?
3. What is the purpose of a port number?
4. What service uses port number 21?
5. What is the Ethernet address used for?
6. What is the socket?
7. What is the difference between a stream socket and a datagram socket?
8. What is the domain of a socket?
9. What does the *accept* function do? Is it on the server or client side of the socket?
10. What are advantages of using *Socket.pm*?

appendix

A

Perl Built-ins, Pragmas, Modules, and the Debugger

A.1 Perl Functions

The following is a complete list of Perl functions and a short description of what they do. Note: The text in parentheses is a reference to the like-named UNIX system call found in Section 2 of the UNIX manual pages. The like-named UNIX library functions are found in Section 3 of the UNIX manual pages.

Table A.1 Perl Functions

Function	***Description***
abs	*abs VALUE* Returns the absolute value of its argument ($_ is the default). Ignores signs.
accept	*accept(NEWSOCKET, GENERICSOCKET)* Accepts a socket connection from clients waiting for a connection. *GENERICSOCKET*, a filehandle, has been previously opened by the *socket* function, is bound to an address, and is listening for a connection. *NEWSOCKET* is a filehandle with the same properties as *GENERICSOCKET*. The *accept* function attaches *GENERICSOCKET* to the newly made connection. See accept(2).
alarm	*alarm(SECONDS)* *alarm SECONDS* Sends a *SIGALARM* signal to the process after a number of *SECONDS*. See alarm(3).
atan2	*atan2(X,Y)* Returns the arctangent of X/Y in the range <pi>.

Table A.1 Perl Functions (continued)

Function	*Description*
bind	*bind(SOCKET, NAME)* Binds an address, *NAME*, to an already opened unnamed socket, *SOCKET*. See bind(2).
binmode	*binmode(FILEHANDLE)* *binmode FILEHANDLE* For operating systems that distinguish between text and "binary" mode (not UNIX). Prepares the *FILEHANDLE* for reading in binary mode.
bless	*bless(REFERENCE, CLASS)* *bless REFERENCE* Tells the object referenced by *REFERENCE* that it is an object in a package (*CLASS*) in the current package if no *CLASS* is specified. Returns the reference.
caller	*caller(EXPR)* *caller EXPR* *caller* Returns an array with information about the subroutine call stack, including the package, filename, and line number. With *EXPR*, a number, the function seeks backward *EXPR* stack frames before the current one.
chdir	*chdir(EXPR)* *chdir EXPR* *chdir* Changes the present working directory to *EXPR*. If *EXPR* is omitted, changes directory to home directory. See chdir(2).
chmod	*chmod(MODE, LIST)* *chmod MODE, LIST* Changes permissions of a list of files; first argument is the permission *MODE* number (octal); the remaining arguments are a list of filenames. Returns the number of files changed. See chmod(2).
chomp	*chomp(LIST)* *chomp(VARIABLE)* *chomp VARIABLE* *chomp* Chops off the last character of a string, *VARIABLE*, or the last character of each item in a *LIST* if that character corresponds to the current value of $/, which is by default set to the newline. Unlike *chop* (see following), it returns the number of characters deleted.

Table A.1 Perl Functions (continued)

Function	*Description*
chop	*chop(LIST)* *chop(VARIABLE)* *chop VARIABLE* *chop* Chops off the last character of a string, *VARIABLE*, or the last character of each item in a *LIST* and returns the chopped value. Without an argument, chops the last character off $_.
chown	*chown(LIST)* *chown LIST* Changes the owner and group IDs of a list of files. First two elements in the list are the numerical *uid* and *gid*, respectively. The rest of the list are the names of files. Returns the number of files changed. See chown(2).
chr	*chr NUMBER* Returns the ASCII value for *NUMBER*; e.g., *chr(66)* returns *B*.
chroot	*chroot(FILENAME)* *chroot FILENAME* Changes root directory for the current process to *FILENAME*, which is the starting point for pathnames starting with /. Must be superuser to do this. See chroot(2).
close	*close(FILEHANDLE)* *close FILEHANDLE* Closes the file, socket, or pipe associated with *FILEHANDLE*.
closedir	*closedir(DIRHANDLE)* *closedir DIRHANDLE* Closes a directory structure opened by *opendir*. See directory(3).
connect	*connect(SOCKET, NAME)* Connects a process with one that is waiting for an *accept* call. *NAME* is a packed network address. See connect(2).
cos	*cos(EXPR)* *cos EXPR* Returns the cosine of *EXPR* (in radians).
crypt	*crypt(PLAINTEXT, SALT)* The password encryption function, where *PLAINTEXT* is the user's password and *SALT* is a two-character string consisting of characters in the set [*a–zA–Z./*]. See crypt(3).

Table A.1 Perl Functions (continued)

Function	***Description***
dbmclose	*dbmclose(%ASSOC_ARRAY)* *dbmclose %ASSOC_ARRAY* Breaks the binding between a DBM file and an associative array. Useful only with NDBM, a newer version of DBM, if supported. See *untie*. See dbm(3).
dbmopen	*dbmopen(%ASSOC_ARRAY, DBNAME, MODE)* Binds a DBM or NDBM file to an associative array. Before a database can be accessed, it must be opened by *dbmopen*. The files *file.dir* and *file.pag* must exist. *DBNAME* is the name of the file without the *.dir* and *.pag* extension. If the database does not exist and permission *MODE* is specified, the database is created. See *tie*. See dbminit(3).
defined	*defined(EXPR)* *defined EXPR* Returns a Boolean value *1* if *EXPR* has a real value. Returns a Boolean value *0* if *EXPR* does not have a real value. *EXPR* may be a scalar, array, hash, or subroutine. For a hash, checks only whether the value (not key) is defined.
delete	*delete $ASSOC{KEY}* Deletes a value from an associative array. If successful, returns the deleted value; otherwise, returns an undefined value. If a value in *%ENV* is deleted, the environment will be modified. The *undef* function can also be used and is faster.
die	*die(LIST)* *die LIST* *die* Prints the *LIST* to *STDERR* and exits with the value of *$!*, the system error message (*errno*). When in an *eval* function, sets the $@ value to the error message, and aborts *eval*. If the value of *LIST* does not end in a newline, the name of the current script, the line number, and a newline are appended to the message.
do	*do BLOCK* *do SUBROUTINE(LIST)* *do EXPR* *do BLOCK* returns the value of the last command in the *BLOCK*. *do SUBROUTINE(LIST)* calls a *SUBROUTINE* that has been defined. *do EXPR* uses *EXPR* as a filename and executes the contents of the file as a Perl script. Used primarily to include subroutines from the Perl subroutine library.

Table A.1 Perl Functions (continued)

Function	***Description***
dump	*dump LABEL* Causes an immediate binary image core dump. The *undump* command, used for undumping a core file, is not part of the Perl 5.6.0 distribution.
each	*each(%ASSOC_ARRAY)* *each %ASSOC_ARRAY* Returns a two-element array, the key and value for the next value of an associative array, in random order.
eof	*eof(FILEHANDLE)* *eof()* *eof* Returns *1* if the next read on *FILEHANDLE* indicates the end of file. If *FILEHANDLE* is omitted, it returns the end of file for the last file read.
eval	*eval(EXPR)* *eval EXPR* Evaluates *EXPR* as a Perl program in the context of the current Perl script. Often used for trapping otherwise fatal errors. Syntax errors or runtime errors or those coming from the *die* function are returned to the $@ variable. The $@ variable is set to NULL if there are no errors. The value returned is the value of the last expression evaluated.
exec	*exec(LIST)* *exec LIST* Executes a system command *LIST* in context of the current program. Never returns. If *LIST* is scalar, checks for *shell* metacharacters and *passes* them to */bin/sh*. Otherwise, arguments are passed to the *C* function call *execvp*. Does not flush output buffer.
exists	*exists EXPR* Returns TRUE if a specified key from an associative array exists, even if its corresponding value is undefined.
exit	*exit(INTEGER)* *exit INTEGER* Exits with script with status value of *INTEGER*. If *INTEGER* is omitted, exits with *0*, meaning the program exits with successful status. A nonzero status implies that something went wrong in the program.
exp	*exp(EXPR)* *exp EXPR* The exponential function. Returns *e* to the power of *EXPR*.

Table A.1 Perl Functions (continued)

Function	*Description*
fcntl	*fcntl(FILEHANDLE, FUNCTION, SCALAR)* Changes properties on an open file. Requires *sys/fcntl.ph*. The *FUNCTION* can duplicate an existing file descriptor, get or set file descriptor flags, get or set file status flags, get or set asynchronous I/O ownership, and get or set record locks. *SCALAR* is an integer for flags. See fcntl(2).
fileno	*fileno(FILEHANDLE)* *fileno FILEHANDLE* Returns the integer file descriptor for *FILEHANDLE*. Descriptors start with *STDIN, STDOUT, STDERR, 0, 1*, and 2, respectively. May not be reliable in Perl scripts if a file is closed and reopened. See ferror(3).
flock	*flock(FILEHANDLE, OPERATION)* Applies or removes advisory locks on files. *OPERATION* specifies an operation on a lock for a file, shared locks, exclusive locks, or nonblocking locks. The *OPERATION* to remove a file is *unlock*. See flock(2).
fork	*fork* Creates a new (child) process. The child is a copy of the parent process. Both child and parent continue execution with the instruction immediately following the *fork*. Returns *0* to the child process and the *pid* of the child to the parent.

format	*format NAME =*
	  picture line
	  value list
	    ...
	.
	Declares a set of picture lines to describe the layout of corresponding values. The *write* function uses the specified format to send output to a named filehandle represented by *NAME*. If *NAME* is omitted, the default is *STDOUT*.

formline	*formline PICTURE, LIST* An internal function used by *format* to format a list of values according to the picture line. Can also be called directly in a program.
getc	*getc(FILEHANDLE)* *getc FILEHANDLE* *getc* Returns the next character from the input file associated with *FILEHANDLE*. Returns a NULL string at EOF. If *FILEHANDLE* is omitted, reads from *STDIN*.

Table A.1 Perl Functions (continued)

Function	***Description***
getgrent	*getgrent* *setgrent* *endgrent* Iterates through */etc/group* and returns an entry from */etc/group* as a list, including group name, password, group ID (*gid*), and members. See getgrent(3).
getgrgid	*getgrgid(GID)* Returns a group entry file by group number. See getgrgid(3).
getgrnam	*getgrnam(NAME)* Returns a group file entry by group name. See getgrent(3).
gethostbyaddr	*gethostbyaddr(ADDRESS, AF_INET)* Translates a network address to its corresponding names and alternative addresses. Returns the hostname, aliases, address type, length, and unpacked raw addresses. *AF_INET* is always 2. See gethostbyaddr(3).
gethostbyname	*gethostbyname(HOSTNAME)* Translates a hostname to an entry from the */etc/hosts* file as a list, including the hostname, aliases, addresses. In scalar context, returns only the host address. See gethostbyname(3).
gethostent	*gethostent* *sethostent(STAYOPEN)* *endhostent* Iterates through */etc/hosts* file and returns the entry as a list, including name, aliases, addresss type, length, and alternative addresses. Returns a list from the network host database, */etc/hosts*. See gethostent(3).
getlogin	*getlogin* Returns the current login from */etc/utmp*, if there is such a file. If *getlogin* does not work, try *$loginname = getlogin \|\| (getpwuid($<))[0] || die "Not a user here"* See getlogin(3).
getnetbyaddr	*getnetbyaddr(ADDR, ADDRESSTYPE)* Translates a network address to its corresponding network name or names. Returns a list from the network database, */etc/networks*. In scalar context, returns only the network name. See getnetent(3).

Table A.1 Perl Functions (continued)

Function	***Description***
getnetbyname	*getnetbyname(NAME)* Translates a network name to its corresponding network address. Returns a list from the network database, */etc/networks*. In scalar context, returns only the network address. See getnetent(3).
getnetent	*getnetent* *setnetent(STAYOPEN)* *endnetent* Iterates through the */etc/networks* file and returns the entry as a list. Returns a list from the network database, */etc/networks*. In scalar context, returns only the network name. See getnetent(3).
getpeername	*getpeername(SOCKET)* Returns the packed *sockaddr* address of other end of the *SOCKET* connection. See getpeername(2).
getpgrp	*getpgrp(PID)* *getpgrp PID* Returns the current process group for the specified *PID* (*PID 0* is the current process). Without *EXPR*, returns the process group of the current process. See getpgrp(2).
getppid	*getppid* Returns the *pid* of the parent process. If *1* is returned, that is the *pid* for *init*. *Init* adopts a process whose parent has died. See getpid(2).
getpriority	*getpriority(WHICH, WHO)* Returns the current priority, *nice* value, for *WHICH*—a process, a process group, or a user. *WHO* is relative to *WHICH* group. A *WHO* value of zero denotes the current process, process group, or user. See getpriority(2).
getprotobyname	*getprotobyname(NAME)* Translates a protocol *NAME* to its corresponding number and returns a list including the protocol name, aliases, and the protocol number. Returns a line from the network protocol database, */etc/protocols*. See getprotoent(3).

Table A.1 Perl Functions (continued)

Function	Description
getprotobynumber	*getprotobynumber(NUMBER)* Translates a protocol *NUMBER* to its corresponding name and returns a list including the protocol name, aliases, and the protocol number. Returns a line from the network protocol database, */etc/protocols*. See getprotoent(3).
getprotoent	*getprotoent* *setprotent(STAYOPEN)* *endprotoent* Returns a list from the */etc/protocols* database, including the protocol name, aliases, and the protocol number. If the *STAYOPEN* flag is nonzero, the database will not be closed during subsequent calls. The *endprotoent* function closes the file. In scalar context, returns the protocol name. See getprotoent(3).
getpwent	*getpwent* *setpwent* *endpwent* Iterates through the */etc/passwd* file and returns the entry as a list, username, password, *uid*, *gid*, quotas, comment, *gcos* field, home directory, and startup *shell*. The *endpwent* function closes the file. In scalar context, returns the username. See getpwent(3).
getpwnam	*getpwnam(NAME)* Translates a username to the corresponding entry in */etc/passwd* file. Returns a list, including the username, password, *uid*, *gid*, quotas, comment, *gcos* field, home directory, and startup *shell*. In scalar context, returns the numeric user ID. See getpwent(3).
getpwuid	*getpwuid(UID)* Translates the numeric user ID to the corresponding entry from the */etc/passwd* file. Returns a list, including the username, password, *uid*, *gid*, quotas, comment, *gcos* field, home directory, and startup shell. In scalar context, returns the username. See getpwent(3).
getservbyname	*getservbyname(NAME, PROTOCOL)* From */etc/services* database, translates a port name to its corresponding port number as a scalar and, returns as an array, the service name, aliases, port where service resides and protocol needed from the */etc/services* database. In scalar context, returns only the service port number. See getservent(3).

Table A.1 Perl Functions (continued)

Function	Description
getservbyport	*getservbyport(PORT_NUMBER, PROTOCOL)* From */etc/services* database, translates a port number to its corresponding port name as a scalar and returns as an array the service name, aliases, port where service resides, and protocol needed, from the */etc/services* database. In scalar context, returns only the service port number. See getservent(3).
getservent	*getservent* *setservent(STAYOPEN)* *endservent* Iterates through the */etc/services* database, returning the service name, aliases, port where service resides, and protocol needed. If *STAYOPEN* flag is nonzero, the database will not be closed during subsequent calls and *endservent* closes the file. In scalar context, returns only the service port name. See getservent(3).
getsockname	*getsockname(SOCKET)* Returns the packed sockaddr address of the local end of the *SOCKET* connection. See getsockname(2).
getsockopt	*getsockopt(SOCKET, LEVEL, OPTNAME)* Returns the requested options, *OPTNAME*, associated with *SOCKET* at the specified protocol *LEVEL*. See getsockopt(2).
glob	*glob EXPR* Performs filename expansion on *EXPR* as the *shell* does. Without *EXPR*, $_ is used. Uses the internal <*> operator.
gmtime	*gmtime(EXPR)* *gmtime EXPR* Converts the results of the *time* function to a 9-element array with the Greenwich Mean Time zone, including the second, minute, hour, day of the month, month, year, day of the week, day of the year, and *1* if daylight saving time is in effect. See ctime(3) and *timegm()* in the Perl library module *Time::Local*.
goto	*goto LABEL* *goto EXPR* *goto &NAME* Program branches to the LABEL and resumes execution. Cannot *goto* any construct that requires intialization, such as a subroutine or *foreach* loop. *Goto* never returns a value. The form *goto &NAME* substitutes the currently running subroutine with a call to *NAME* (used by the *AUTOLOAD* subroutine).

Table A.1 Perl Functions (continued)

Function	***Description***
grep	*grep(EXPR, LIST)* *grep BLOCK LIST* Returns to a new array any element in *LIST* where *EXPR* matches that element. Returns a scalar, the number of matches.
hex	*hex(EXPR)* *hex EXPR* Returns the decimal value of *EXPR* interpreted as a hexadecimal string. Without *EXPR*, uses $_.
import	*import CLASSNAME LIST* *import CLASSNAME* Not a built-in function but a class method defined by modules that will export names to other modules through the *use* function.
index	*index(STR, SUBSTR, POSITION)* *index(STR, SUBSTR)* Returns the position of the first occurrence of *SUBSTR* in *STR*. *POSITION* specifies a starting position for the substring in the string starting with base 0.
int	*int(EXPR)* *int EXPR* Returns the integer portion of *EXPR*. Without *EXPR*, $_ is used.
ioctl	*ioctl(FILEHANDLE, FUNCTION, SCALAR)* Used to control I/O operations, mainly terminal I/O. Requires *sys/ioctl.ph*. *FUNCTION* is an I/O request. *SCALAR* will be read or written depending on the request. See ioctl(2).
join	*join(EXPR, LIST)* Returns a single string by joining the separate strings of *LIST* into a single string where the field separator is specified by *EXPR*, a delimiter.
keys	*keys(%ASSOC_ARRAY)* *keys %ASSOC_ARRAY* Returns a normal array consisting of all the keys in the associative array.
kill	*kill(SIGNAL, PROCESS_LIST)* *kill PROCESS_LIST* Sends a *SIGNAL* to a list of processes. The *SIGNAL* can be either a number or a signal name (signal name must be quoted). (Negative *SIGNAL* number kills process group.) See kill(2).

Table A.1 Perl Functions (continued)

Function	***Description***
last	*last LABEL* *last* The last command is comparable to C's *break* command. It exits the innermost loop or, if the loop is labeled *last LABEL*, exits that loop.
lc	*lc EXPR* Returns *EXPR* in lowercase. Same as \L \E escape sequence.
lcfirst	*lcfirst EXPR* Returns *EXPR* with the first character in lowercase. Same as \l \E sequence.
length	*length(EXPR)* *length EXPR* Returns the length in characters of scalar *EXPR* or, if *EXPR* is omitted, returns length of $_. Not used to find the size of an array or associative array.
link	*link(OLDFILE, NEWFILE)* Creates a hard link. *NEWFILE* is another name for *OLDFILE*. See link(2).
listen	*listen(SOCKET, QUEUESIZE)* Listens for connections on a *SOCKET* with a *QUEUESIZE* specifying the number of processes waiting for connections. See listen(2).
local	*local(LIST)* Makes variables in *LIST* local for this block, subroutine, or *eval*.
localtime	*localtime(EXPR)* *localtime EXPR* Converts the time returned by the *time* function to a 9-element array for the local time zone. The array consists of seconds minutes hours day of the month number of the month (0 is January) years since 1990 day of the week (0 is Sunday) day of the year (0 is January 1) *isdst* (true if daylight savings is on) See ctime(3).
lock	*lock THING* Places a lock on a variable, subroutine, or object referenced by *THING* until the lock goes out of scope. Used only with threads if they are enabled.

Table A.1 Perl Functions (continued)

Function	*Description*
log	*log(EXPR)* *log EXPR* Returns the logarithm (base *e*) of *EXPR*. If *EXPR* is omitted, returns *log($_)*.
lstat	*lstat(FILEHANDLE)* *lstat FILEHANDLE* *lstat(EXPR)* Returns a 14-element array consisting of file statistics on a symbolic link, rather than the file the symbolic link points to. The array consists of device file inode number file mode number of hard links to the file user ID of owner group ID of owner raw device size of file file last access time file last modify time file last status change time preferred block size for filesystem I/O actual number of blocks allocated See stat(2).
m	*/PATTERN/* *m/PATTERN/* *m* is the match operator that interprets *PATTERN* as a regular expression and is used when alternative delimeters are needed, such as *m!PATTERN!*.
map	*map(BLOCK LIST)* *map(EXPR, LIST)* Evaluates *BLOCK* or *EXPR* for each element of *LIST* and returns the list value containing the results of the evaluation. The following example translates a list of numbers to characters: *@chars = map chr, @numbers*
mkdir	*mkdir(NAME, MODE)* Creates a directory, *NAME*, with *MODE* permissions (octal). See mkdir(2).
msgctl	*msgctl(MSGID, CMD, FLAGS)* Calls the *msgctl* system call, allowing control operations on a message queue. Has weird return codes. Requires library files *ipc.ph* and *msg.ph*. See System V IPC. See also msgctl(2).

Table A.1 Perl Functions (continued)

Function	***Description***
msgget	*msgget(KEY, FLAGS)* Calls *msgget* system call. Returns the message queue ID number or, if undefined, an error. See System V IPC. See also msgget(2).
msgrcv	*msgrcv(MSGID, VAR, MSG_SIZE, TYPE, FLAGS)* Calls the *msgrv* system call. Receives a message from the message queue, stores the message in *VAR*. *MSG_SIZE* is the maximum message size, and *TYPE* is the message type. See System V IPC. See also msgrcv(2).
msgsnd	*msgsnd(ID, MSG, FLAGS)* Calls the *msgsnd* system call. Sends the message *MSG* to the message queue. *MSG* must begin with the message type. The *pack* function is used to create the message. See System V IPC. See also msgsnd(2).
my	*my TYPE EXPR : ATTRIBUTES* *my EXPR : ATTRIBUTES* *my TYPE EXPR* *my EXPR* Variables declared with the *my* function are made private; i.e., they exist only within the innermost enclosing block, subroutine, *eval*, or file. Only simple scalars, complete arrays, and hashes can be declared with *my*. *TYPE* and *ATTRIBUTES* optional and experimental at this time.
new	*new CLASSNAME LIST* *new CLASSNAME* Not a built-in function but a constructor method defined by the *CLASSNAME* module for creating *CLASSNAME*-type objects. Convention taken from *C++*.
next	*next LABEL* *next* Starts the next iteration of the innermost or loop labeled with *LABEL*. Like the *C continue* function.
no	*no Module LIST* If a pragma or module has been imported with *use*, the *no* function says you don't want to use it anymore.
not	*not EXPR* Logically negates the truth value of *EXPR*.

Table A.1 Perl Functions (continued)

Function	**Description**
oct	*oct(EXPR)* *oct EXPR* *oct* Returns the decimal value of *EXPR*, an octal string. If *EXPR* contains a leading *0x*, *EXPR* is interpreted as hex. With no *EXPR*, $_ is converted.
open	*open(FILEHANDLE, EXPR)* *open(FILEHANDLE)* *open FILEHANDLE* Opens a real file, *EXPR*, and attaches it to *FILEHANDLE*. Without *EXPR*, a scalar with the same name as *FILEHANDLE* must have been assigned that filename. read "FILEHANDLE" write ">FILEHANDLE" read/write "+>FILEHANDLE" append ">>FILEHANDLE" pipe out "| UNIX Command" pipe in "UNIX Command |"
opendir	*opendir(DIRHANDLE, EXPR)* Opens a directory structure named *EXPR* and attaches it to *DIRHANDLE* for functions that examine the structure. See directory(3).
ord	*ord(EXPR)* *ord* Returns the unsigned numeric ASCII values of the first character of *EXPR*. If *EXPR* is omitted, $_ is used.
our	*our TYPE EXPR : ATTRIBUTES* *our EXPR : ATTRIBUTES* *our TYPE EXPR* *our EXPR* Declares one or more variables to be valid globals within the enclosing block, file, or *eval*. Like *my* for globals but does not create a new private variable. Useful when the *strict* pragma is turned on and a global variable is wanted.

Table A.1 Perl Functions (continued)

Function	Description
pack	*$packed=pack(TEMPLATE, LIST)* Packs a list of values into a binary structure and returns the structure. *TEMPLATE* is a quoted string containing the number and type of value. *TEMPLATE* is a An ASCII string, null padded A An ASCII string, space padded b A bit string, low-to-high order B A bit string, high-to-low order h A hexadecimal string, low nybble first H A hexadecimal string, high nybble first c A signed char value C An unsigned char value
pack (cont.)	s A signed short value S An unsigned short value i A signed integer value I An unsigned integer value l A signed long value L An unsigned long value n A short in "network" order N A long in "network" order f A single-precision float in native format d A double-precision float in native format p A pointer to a string x A null byte X Back up a byte @ Null-fill to absolute precision u A uuencoded string
package	*package NAMESPACE* A package declaration creates a separate namespace (symbol table) for *NAMESPACE*, the Perl way of creating a class. The *NAMESPACE* belongs to the rest of the innermost enclosing block, subroutine, *eval*, or file. If the package declaration is at the same level, the new one overrides the old one.
pipe	*pipe(READHANDLE, WRITEHANDLE)* Opens a pipe for reading and writing, normally after a *fork*. See pipe(2).
pop	*pop(ARRAY)* *pop ARRAY* Pops and returns the last element of the array. The array will have one less element.

Table A.1 Perl Functions (continued)

Function	Description
pos	*pos(SCALAR)* *pos SCALAR* Returns the offset of the character after the last matched search in *SCALAR* left off; i.e., the position where the next search will start. Offsets start at 0. If the *$scalar* is a signed *"hello"* and the search is *$scalar =~ m/l/g*, the *pos* function would return the position of the character after the first *l*, position 3.
print	*print(FILEHANDLE LIST)* *print(LIST)* *print FILEHANDLE LIST* *print LIST* *print* Prints a string or a comma-separated list of strings to *FILEHANDLE* or to the currently selected *FILEHANDLE* or to *STDOUT*, the default. Retuns *1* if successful, *0* if not.
printf	*printf(FILEHANDLE FORMAT, LIST)* *printf(FORMAT, LIST)* Prints a formatted string to *FILEHANDLE* or, if *FILEHANDLE* is omitted, to the currently selected output filehandle. *STDOUT* is the default. Similar to *C's printf*, except * is not supported. See printf(3).
prototype	*prototype FUNCTION* Returns the prototype of a function as a string, where *FUNCTION* is the name of the function. Returns *undef* if there is no prototype.
push	*push(ARRAY, LIST)* Pushes the values in *LIST* onto the end of the *ARRAY*. The array will be increased. Returns the new length of *ARRAY*.
q, qq, qw, qx	*q/STRING/* *qq/STRING/* *qw/LIST/* *qx/COMMAND/* An alternative form of quoting. The *q* construct treats *STRING* as if enclosed in single quotes. The *qq* construct treats *STRING* as if enclosed in double quotes. The *qw* construct treats each element of *LIST* as if enclosed in single quotes, and the *qx* treats *COMMAND* as if in backquotes.
quotemeta	*quotemeta EXPR* Returns the scalar value of *EXPR* with all regular expression metacharacters backslashed.

Table A.1 Perl Functions (continued)

Function	***Description***
rand	*rand(EXPR)* *rand EXPR* *rand* Returns a random fractional number (scalar) between 0 and *EXPR*, where *EXPR* is a positive number. Without *srand* generates the same sequence of numbers. If *EXPR* is omitted, returns a value between 0 and 1. See rand(3).
read	*read(FILEHANDLE, SCALAR, LENGTH, OFFSET)* *read(FILEHANDLE, SCALAR, LENGTH)* Reads *LENGTH* number of bytes from *FILEHANDLE*, starting at position *OFFSET*, into *SCALAR* and returns the number of bytes read, or *0* if EOF. (Similar to *fread* system call.) See fread(3).
readdir	*readdir(DIRHANDLE)* *readdir DIRHANDLE* Reads the next entry of the directory structure, *DIRHANDLE*, opened by *opendir*. See directory(3).
readline	*readline FILEHANDLE* Reads and returns a line from selected *FILEHANDLE;* e.g., *$line = readline(STDIN)*.
readlink	*readlink(EXPR)* *readlink EXPR* Returns the value of a symbolic link. *EXPR* is the pathname of the symbolic link, and if omitted, $_ is used. See readlink(2).
readpipe	*readpipe scalar EXPR* *readpipe LIST(proposed)* An internal function that implements the *qw//* quote construct or backquotes for command subsitution; e.g., to print the output of the UNIX *ls* command, type *print reapipe(ls)*.
recv	*recv(SOCKET, SCALAR, LEN, FLAGS)* Receives a message of *LEN* bytes on a socket into *SCALAR* variable. Returns the address of the sender. See recv(2).
redo	*redo LABEL* *redo* Restarts a loop block without reevaluting the condition. If there is a *continue* block, it is not executed. Without *LABEL*, restarts at the innermost enclosing loop.

Table A.1 Perl Functions (continued)

Function	Description
ref	*ref EXPR* Returns a scalar TRUE value, the data type of *EXPR*, if *EXPR* is a reference, else the NULL string. The returned value depends on what is being referenced, a *REF*, *SCALAR*, *ARRAY*, *HASH*, *CODE*, or *GLOB*. If *EXPR* is an object that has been blessed into a package, the return value is the package (class) name.
rename	*rename(OLDNAME, NEWNAME)* Renames a file *OLDNAME* to *NEWNAME*. Does not work across filesystem boundaries. If *NEWNAME* already exists, it is destroyed. See rename(2).
require	*require(EXPR)* *require EXPR* *require* Includes file *EXPR* from the Perl library by searching the *@INC* array for the specified file. Also checks that the library has not already been included. $_ is used if *EXPR* is omitted.
reset	*reset(EXPR)* *reset EXPR* *reset* Clears variables and arrays or, if *EXPR* is omitted, resets ?? searches.
return	*return LIST* Returns a value from a subroutine. Cannot be used outside of a subroutine.
reverse	*reverse(LIST)* Reverses the order of *LIST* and returns an array.
rewinddir	*rewinddir(DIRHANDLE)* *rewinddir DIRHANDLE* Rewinds the position in *DIRHANDLE* to the beginning of the directory structure. See directory(3).
rindex	*rindex(STRING, SUBSTR, OFFSET)* *rindex(STRING, SUBSTR)* Returns the last position of *SUBSTR* in *STRING* starting at *OFFSET*, if *OFFSET* is specified like *index* but returns the last position of the substring rather than the first.
rmdir	*rmdir(FILENAME)* *rmdir FILENAME* Removes a directory, *FILENAME*, if empty.

Table A.1 Perl Functions (continued)

Function	***Description***
s	*s/SEARCH_PATTERN/REPLACEMENT/[g] [i] [e] [o]* Searches for *SEARCH_PATTERN* and, if found, replaces the pattern with some text. Returns the number of substitutions made. The g option is global across a line. The *i* option turns off case sensitivity. The *e* option evaluates the replacement string as an expression; e.g., *s/\d+/$&+5/e*
scalar	*scalar(EXPR)* Forces *EXPR* to be evaluated in a scalar context.
seek	*seek(FILEHANDLE, POSITION, WHENCE)* Positions a file pointer in a file, *FILEHANDLE*, from some position, relative to its postition in the file *WHENCE*. If *WHENCE* is *0*, starts at the beginning of the file; if WHENCE is *1*, starts at the current position of the file, and if *WHENCE* is 2, starts at the end of the file. *POSITION* cannot be negative if *WHENCE* is *0*.
seekdir	*seekdir(DIRHANDLE, POSITION)* Sets the *POSITION* for the *readdir* function on the directory structure associated with *DIRHANDLE*. See directory(3).
select	*select(FILEHANDLE)* *select* Returns the currently selected filehandle if *FILEHANDLE* is omitted. With *FILEHANDLE*, sets the current default filehandle for *write* and *print*. See Formatting.
select	*select(RBITS, WBITS, EBITS, TIMEOUT)* Examines the I/O file descriptors to see if descriptors are ready for reading or writing or have exceptional conditions pending. Bitmasks are specified, and *TIMEOUT* is in seconds. See select(2).
semctl	*semctl(ID, SEMNUM, CMD, ARG)* Calls the *semctl* system call, allowing control operations on semaphores. Has weird return codes. Requires library files *ipc.ph* and *sem.ph*. See System V IPC. See also semctl(2).
semget	*semget(KEY, NSEMS, SIZE, FLAGS)* Returns the semaphore ID associated with *KEY*, or undefined if an error. Requires library files *ipc.ph* and *sem.ph*. See System V IPC. See also semget(2).

Table A.1 Perl Functions (continued)

Function	Description
semop	*semop(KEY, OPSTRING)* Calls the *semop* system call to perform operations on a semaphore identified by *KEY*. *OPSTRING* must be a packed array of *semop* structures. Requires library files *ipc.ph* and *sem.ph*. See System V IPC. See also semop(2).
send	*send(SOCKET, MSG, FLAGS,TO)* *send(SOCKET, MSG, FLAGS)* Sends a message on a *SOCKET*. See send(2).
setpgrp	*setpgrp(PID, PGRP)* Sets the current process group for the specified process, process group, or user. See getpgrp(2).
setpriority	*setpriority(WHICH,WHO, PRIORITY)* Sets the current priority, *nice* value, for a process, process group, or user. See getpriority(2).
setsockopt	*setsockopt(SOCKET, LEVEL, OPTNAME, OPTVAL)* Sets the requested socket option on *SOCKET*. See getsockopt(2).
shift	*shift(ARRAY)* *shift ARRAY* *shift* Shifts off the first value of the *ARRAY* and returns it, shortening the array. If *ARRAY* is omitted, the *@ARGV* array is shifted, and if in subroutines, the @_ array is shifted.
shmctl	*shmctl(ID, CMD, ARG)* Calls the *shmctl* system call, allowing control operations on shared memory. Has weird return codes. Requires library file *ipc.ph* and *shm.ph*. See System V IPC. See also shmctl(2).
shmget	*shmget(KEY, SIZE, FLAGS)* Returns the shared memory segment ID associated with the *KEY*, or undefined if an error. The shared memory segment created is of at least *SIZE* bytes. Requires *ipc.ph* and *shm.ph*. See System V IPC. See also shmget(2).

Table A.1 Perl Functions (continued)

Function	***Description***
shmread	*shmread(ID, VAR, POS, SIZE)* Reads from the shared memory *ID* starting at position *POS* for *SIZE*. *VAR* is a variable used to store what is read. The segment is attached, data is read from, and the segment is detached. Requires *ipc.ph* and *shm.ph*. See System V IPC. See also shmat(2).
shmwrite	*shmwrite(ID, VAR, POS, SIZE)* Writes to the shared memory *ID* starting at position *POS* for *SIZE*. *VAR* is a variable used to store what is written. The segment is attached, data is written to, and the segment is detached. Requires *ipc.ph* and *shm.ph*. See System V IPC. See also shmat(2).
shutdown	*shutdown(SOCKET, HOW)* Shuts down a *SOCKET* connection. If *HOW* is 0, further *receives* will be disallowed. If *HOW* is *1*, further *sends* will be disallowed. If *HOW* is 2, then further *sends* and *receives* will be disallowed. See shutdown(2).
sin	*sin(EXPR)* *sin* Returns the sine of *EXPR* (expressed in radians). If *EXPR* is omitted, returns sine of $_.
sleep	*sleep(EXPR)* *sleep EXPR* *sleep* Causes program to sleep for *EXPR* seconds. If *EXPR* is omitted, program sleeps forever. See sleep(3).
socket	*socket(SOCKET, DOMAIN, TYPE, PROTOCOL)* Opens a socket of a specified type and attaches it to filehandle, *SOCKET*. See socket(2).
socketpair	*socketpair(SOCKET, SOCKET2, DOMAIN, TYPE, PROTOCOL)* Creates an unnamed pair of *connect* sockets in the specified domain of the specified type. See socketpair(2).

Table A.1 Perl Functions (continued)

Function	***Description***
sort	*sort(SUBROUTINE LIST)* *sort(LIST)* *sort SUBROUTINE LIST* *sort LIST* Sorts the *LIST* and returns a sorted array. If *SUBROUTINE* is omitted, sorts in string comparison order. If *SUBROUTINE* is specified, gives the name of a subroutine that returns an integer less than, equal to, or greater than 0, depending on how the elements of the array are to be ordered. The two elements compared are passed (by reference) to the subroutine as *$a* and *$b*, rather than @_. *SUBROUTINE* cannot be recursive. See Array Functions.
splice	*splice(ARRAY, OFFSET, LENGTH,LIST)* *splice(ARRAY, OFFSET, LENGTH)* *splice(ARRAY, OFFSET)* Removes elements designated starting with *OFFSET* and ending in *LENGTH* from an array and, if *LIST* is specified, replaces those elements removed with *LIST*. Returns the elements removed from the list. If *LENGTH* is not specified, everything from *OFFSET* to the end of *ARRAY* is removed.
split	*split(/PATTERN/, EXPR, LIMIT)* *split(/PATTERN/, EXPR)* *split(/PATTERN/)* *split* Splits *EXPR* into an array of strings and returns them to an array. The *PATTERN* is the delimiter by which *EXPR* is separated. If *PATTERN* is omitted, whitespace is used as the delimiter. *LIMIT* specifies the number of fields to be split.
sprintf	*$string=sprintf(FORMAT, LIST)* Returns a string rather than sending output to *STDOUT* with the same formatting conventions as the *printf* function. See printf(3).
sqrt	*sqrt(EXPR)* *sqrt EXPR* Returns the square root of *EXPR*. If *EXPR* is omitted, the square root of $_ is returned.
srand	*srand(EXPR)* *srand EXPR* *srand* Sets the random seed for the *rand* function. If *EXPR* is omitted, the seed is the *time* function. See rand(3).

Table A.1 Perl Functions (continued)

Function	*Description*
stat	*stat(FILEHANDLE)* *stat FILEHANDLE* *stat(EXPR)* Returns a 13-element array consisting of file statistics for *FILEHANDLE* or file named as *EXPR*. The array consists of the device the file inode number file mode number of hard links to the file user ID of owner group ID of owner raw device size of file file last access time file last modify time file last status change time preferred block size for filesystem I/O actual number of blocks allocated See stat(2).
study	*study(SCALAR)* *study SCALAR* *study* Uses a linked-list mechanism to increase efficiency in searching for pattern matches that are to be repeated many times. Can study only one *SCALAR* at a time. If *SCALAR* is omitted, $_ is used. Most beneficial in loops where many short constant strings are being scanned.
sub	*sub NAME BLOCK* *sub NAME* *sub BLOCK* *sub NAME PROTO BLOCK* *sub NAME PROTO* *sub PROTO BLOCK* The first two declare the existence of named subroutines and return no value. Without a block, *sub NAME* is a forward declaration. The *sub BLOCK* is used to create an anonymous subroutine. The last three are like the first three, except they allow prototypes to describe how the subroutine will be called. A prototype will notify the compiler that a subroutine definition will appear at some later time and can tell the compiler what type and how many arguments the subroutine expects. For example, *sub foo ($$@)* declares that the subroutine *foo* will take three arguments, two scalars and an array. An error will occur if, for example, fewer than three arguments are passed.

Table A.1 Perl Functions (continued)

Function	***Description***
substr	*substr(EXPR, OFFSET, LENGTH)* *substr(EXPR, OFFSET)* Returns a substring after extracting the substring from *EXPR* starting at position *OFFSET* and, if *LENGTH* is specified, for that many characters from *OFFSET*. If *OFFSET* is negative, starts from the far end of the string.
symlink	*symlink(OLDFILE, NEWFILE)* Creates a symbolic link. *NEWFILE* is symbolically linked to *OLDFILE*. The files can reside on different partitions. See symlink(2).
syscall	*syscall(LIST)* *syscall LIST* Calls the system call specified as the first element in *LIST*, where the system call is preceded with *&SYS_* as in *&SYS_system* call. The remaining items in *LIST* are passed as arguments to the system call. Requires *syscall.ph*.
sysopen	*sysopen(FILEHANDLE, FILENAME, MODE)* *sysopen(FILEHANDLE, FILENAME, MODE, PERMS)* Opens *FILENAME*, using the underlying operating system's version of the *open* call, and assigns it to *FILEHANDLE*. The file modes are system dependent and can be found in the *Fcntl* library module. 0 means read-only, 1 means write-only, and 2 means read/write. If *PERMS* is omitted, the default is 0666. See open(2).
sysread	*sysread(FILEHANDLE, SCALAR, LENGTH, OFFSET)* *sysread(FILEHANDLE, SCALAR, LENGTH)* Reads *LENGTH* bytes into variable *SCALAR* from *FILEHANDLE*. Uses the *read* system call. See read(2).
sysseek	*sysseek(FILEHANDLE, POSITION, WHENCE)* Sets *FILEHANDLE*'s system position, using the syscall *lseek* function, bypassing standard I/O. The values of *WHENCE* are *0* to set the new position to *POSITION*, *1* to set it to the current position plus *POSITION*, and 2 to set it to EOF plus *POSITION* (often negative). See *lseek*(2).

Table A.1 Perl Functions (continued)

Function	***Description***
system	*system(LIST)* *system LIST* Executes a shell command from a Perl script and returns. Like the *exec* function, except *forks* first, and the script waits until the command has been executed. Control then returns to script. The return value is the exit status of the program and can be obtained by dividing by 256 or right-shifting the lower 8 bits. See system(3).
syswrite	*syswrite(FILEHANDLE, SCALAR, LENGTH, OFFSET)* *syswrite(FILEHANDLE, SCALAR, LENGTH)* *syswrite(FILEHANDLE, SCALAR)* Returns the number of bytes written to *FILEHANDLE*. Writes *LENGTH* bytes from variable *SCALAR* to *FILEHANDLE*, starting at position *OFFSET*, if *OFFSET* is specified. Uses the *write* system call. See write(2).
tell	*tell(FILEHANDLE)* *tell FILEHANDLE* *tell* Returns the current file position, in bytes (starting at byte 0), for *FILEHANDLE*. Normally the returned value is given to the *seek* function in order to return to some position within the file. See lseek(2).
telldir	*telldir(DIRHANDLE)* *telldir DIRHANDLE* Returns the current position of the *readdir* function for the directory structure, *DIRHANDLE*. See directory(3).

Table A.1 Perl Functions (continued)

Function	Description

tie	*tie(VARIABLE, CLASSNAME, LIST)*
	Binds a *VARIABLE* to a package (*CLASSNAME*) that will use methods to provide the implementation for the variable. *LIST* consists of any additional arguments to be passed to the new method when constructing the object. Most commonly used with associative arrays to bind them to databases. The methods have predefined names to be placed within a package. The predefined methods will be called automatically when the tied variables are fetched, stored, destroyed, etc.
	The package implementing an associative array provides the following methods:
	TIEHASH $classname, LIST
	DESTROY $self
	FETCH $self, $key
	STORE $self, $key
	DELETE $self, $key
	EXISTS $self, $key
	FIRSTKEY $self
	NEXTKEY $self, $lastkey
	Methods provided for an array are:
	TIEARRAY $classname, LIST
	DESTROY $self
	FETCH $self, $subscript
	STORE $self, $subscript, $value
	Methods provided for a scalar are:
	TIESCALAR $classname, LIST
	DESTROY $self
	FETCH $self
	STORE $self, $value
	
	Example:
	`$object = tie %hash, Myhashclass`
	`   while($key, $value)=each (%hash){`
	`   print "$key, $value\n" # invokes the FETCH method`
	`$object = tie @array, Myarrayclass`
	`   $array[0]=5            # invokes the STORE method`
	`$object = tie $scalar, Myscalarclass`
	`   untie $scalar          # invokes the DESTROY method`

tied	*tied VARIABLE* Returns a reference to the object that was previously bound with the *tie* function or undefined if *VARIABLE* is not tied to a package.

Table A.1 Perl Functions (continued)

Function	Description
time	*time* Returns a 4-element array of non-leap-year seconds since January 1, 1970, UTC. Used with *gmtime* and *localtime* functions. See ctime(3).
times	*times* Returns a 4-element array giving the user and system CPU times, in seconds, for the process and its children. See times(3).
tr	*tr/SEARCHPATTERN/REPLACEMENT/[c] [d] [e]* *y/SEARCHPATTERN/REPLACEMENT/[c] [d] [e]* Translates characters in *SEARCHPATTERN* to corresponding character in *REPLACEMENT*. Similar to UNIX *tr* command.
truncate	*truncate(FILEHANDLE, LENGTH)* *truncate(EXPR, LENGTH)* Truncate *FILEHANDLE* or *EXPR* to a specified *LENGTH*. See truncate(2).
uc	*uc EXPR* Returns *EXPR* (or $_ if no *EXPR*) in uppercase letters. Same as *U* *E* escape sequences.
ucfirst	*ucfirst EXPR* Returns the first character of *EXPR* (or $_ if no *EXPR*) in uppercase. Same as *u* escape sequence.
umask	*umask(EXPR)* *umask EXPR* *umask* Sets the *umask* (file creation mask) for the process and returns the old *umask*. With *EXPR* omitted, returns the current *umask* value. See umask(2).
undef	*undef(EXPR)* *undef EXPR* *undef* Undefines *EXPR*, an *lvalue*. Used on scalars, arrays, hashes, or subroutine names (*&subroutine*) to recover any storage associated with it. Always returns the undefined value. Can be used by itself when returning from a subroutine to determine if an error was made.

Table A.1 Perl Functions (continued)

Function	***Description***
unlink	*unlink(LIST)* *unlink LIST* *unlink* Removes a *LIST* of files. Returns the number of files deleted. Without an argument, unlinks the value stored in $_. See unlink(2).
unpack	*unpack(TEMPLATE, EXPR)* Unpacks a string representing a structure and expands it to an array value, returning the array value, using *TEMPLATE* to get the order and type of values. Reverse of *pack*. See *pack*.
unshift	*unshift(LIST)* *unshift* Prepends *LIST* to the beginning of an array. Returns the number of elements in the new array.
untie	*untie VARIABLE* Breaks the binding (unties) between a variable and the package it is tied to. Opposite of *tie*.
use	*use MODULE VERSION LIST* *use MODULE LIST* *use MODULE* *use MODULE()* *use pragma* A compiler directive that imports subroutines and variables from *MODULE* into the current package. *VERSION* is the current version number of Perl. *LIST* consists of specific names of the variables and subroutines the current package will import. Use empty parameters if you don't want to import anything into your namespace. The *-m* and *-M* flags can be used at the command line instead of *use*. Pragmas are a special kind of module that can affect the behavior for a block of statements at compile time. Three common pragmas are *integer, subs*, and *strict*.
utime	*utime(LIST)* *utime LIST* Changes the access and modification times on a list of files.The first two elements of *LIST* are the numerical access and modification times.
values	*values(%ASSOC_ARRAY)* *values ASSOC_ARRAY* Returns an array consisting of all the values in an associative array, *ASSOC_ARRAY*, in random order.

Table A.1 Perl Functions (continued)

Function	***Description***
vec	*vec(EXPR, OFFSET, BITS)* Treats a string, *EXPR*, as a vector of unsigned integers. Returns the value of the element specified. *OFFSET* is the number of elements to skip over in order to find the one wanted, and *BITS* is the number of bits per element in the vector. *BITS* must be one of a power of 2 from 1 to 32; e.g., 1, 2, 4, 8, 16, or 32.
wait	*wait* Waits for the child process to terminate. Returns the *pid* of the deceased process and *–1* if there are no child processes. The status value is returned in the *$?* variable. See wait(2).
waitpid	*waitpid(PID, FLAGS)* Waits for a child process to terminate and returns true when the process dies or *–1* if there are no child processes or if *FLAGS* specify nonblocking and the process hasn't died. *$?* gets the status of the dead process. Requires *sys/wait.ph*. See wait(2).
wantarray	*wantarray* Returns true if the context of the currently running subroutine wants an array value; i.e., the returned value from the subroutine will be assigned to an array. Returns false if looking for a scalar. Example: *return wantarray ? () : undef*
warn	*warn(LIST)* *warn LIST* Sends a message to *STDERR*, like the *die* function, but doesn't exit the program.
write	*write(FILEHANDLE)* *write FILEHANDLE* *write* Writes a formatted record to *FILEHANDLE* or currently selected *FILEHANDLE* (see *select*); i.e., when called, invokes the format (picture line) for the *FILEHANDLE*, with no arguments. Goes either to *STDOUT* or to the *FILEHANDLE* currently selected by the *select* call. Has nothing to do with the *write*(2) system call. See *syswrite*.
y	*y/SEARCHPATTERN/REPLACEMENT/[c][d][e]* Translates characters in *SEARCHPATTERN* to corresponding characters in *REPLACEMENT*. Also known as *tr* and similar to UNIX *tr* command or *sed y* command.

A.2 Special Variables

Table A.2 Filehandles

Variable	*What It Does*
$|	If nonzero, forces buffer flush after every write and print on the currently selected filehandle
$%	Current page number of currently selected filehandle
$=	Current page length of currently selected filehandle
$–	Number of lines left on the page for currently selected filehandle
$~	Name of current report format for currently selected filehandle
$^	Name of current top-of-page format for currently selected filehandle

Table A.3 Local to Block

Variable	*What It Does*
$*1*.. $*9*	Contains remembered subpatterns that reference a corresponding set of parentheses (same as *1*..*9*)
$&	The string matched by the last pattern match (like *sed* editor)
$'	The string preceding what was matched in the last pattern match
$'	The string that follows whatever was matched by the last pattern match
$+	The last pattern matched by the last search pattern

EXAMPLE A.1

```
$str="old and restless";

print "$&\n" if $str =~ /and/;
print "$`\n" if $str =~ /and/;
print "$'\n" if $str =~ /and/;
print "\nold string is: $str\n";
$str=~s/(old) and (restless)/$2 and $1/;
print "new string is: $str\n";
print "\nlast pattern matched: $+\n";

(Output)
and
old
restless
old string is: old and restless
new string is: restless and old
last pattern matched is: restless
```

Table A.4 Global

Variable	What It Does
$_	Default input and pattern-searching space.
$.	Current input line number of last filehandle that was read; must close the filehandle to reset line numbers for next filehandle.
$/	Input record separator, newline by default. (Like RS in *awk.*)
$\	Output record separator for the print function. Does not print a newline unless set: $\="\n"
$,	Output field separator for the print function. Normally delimiter is not printed between comma-separated strings unless set: *S*,=" ".
$"	Same as $ but applies to printing arrays when in double quotes. Default is space.
$#	Output format for numbers printed with the *print* function. (Like OMFT in *awk.*)
$$	The process ID number of the Perl program running this script.
$?	Status returned by last pipe closed, command in backquotes, or system function.
$*	Default is *0*. If set to *1*, does a multiline match within a string; *0* for a match within a single line.
$0	Name of this Perl script.
$[	Index of first element of an array, and first character in a substring. Default is *0*.
$]	The first part of the string is printed out when using *perl -v* for version information.
$;	The subscript separator for multidimensional array emulation. Default is \034. (Like *SUBSEP* in *awk.*)
$!	Yields the current value of *errno* (system error number) if numeric, and the corresponding system error string.
$@	Error message from the last *eval*, *do*, or *require* function.
$<	The real *uid* of this process.
$>	The effective *uid* of this process.
$(	The real *gid* of this process.
$)	The effective *gid* of this process.

Table A.4 Global (continued)

Variable	*What It Does*
$:	The set of characters after which a string may be broken to fill continuation lines (starting with ^) in a format. Default is \n- to break on whitespace, newline, or colon.
$^A	The accumulator for *formline* and *write* operations.
$^C	TRUE if Perl is run in compile-only mode using command-line option *-c*.
$^D	Perl's debug flags when *-D* switch is used.
$^E	Operating-system-dependent error information.
$^F	Maximum file descriptor passed to subprocess, usually 2.
$^H	The current state of syntax checks.
$^I	Current value of inplace-edit extension when *-i* switch is used. Use *undef* to disable inplace editing.
$^L	Form feed character used in formats.
$^M	Emergency memory pool.
$^O	Name of the operating system.
$^P	Internal Perl debugging flag.
$^S	State of the Perl interpreter.
$^T	Time of day when script started execution. Used by *-A*, *-C*, and *-M* test operators and can be set to any number value returned by *time* to perform file tests relative to the current time.
$^V	The Perl version.
$^W	The current value of the warning switch.
$^X	The full pathname by which this Perl was invoked.
_	An underscore. The special designator for file testing when stating files.
ARGV	The special filehandle array for looping over line arguments.
$ARGV	The variable containing the name of the current file when reading from *<ARGV>*.
@ARGV	The array containing command-line arguments.
DATA	Special filehandle referring to anything following *_ _END_ _*.

Table A.4 Global (continued)

Variable	What It Does
@F	The array into which input lines are autosplit when the *-a* switch is used.
@INC	Array containing pathnames where *require* and *do* functions look for files that are to be included in this script.
%INC	Associative array containing entries for files that have been included by calling *do* or *require*. The key is the filename and the value is its location.
%ENV	Associative array containing the current environment.
@EXPORT	Default symbols to be exported.
@EXPORT_OK	Symbols to be exported upon request by the user.
%EXPORT_TAGS	Used by *Exporter.pm* to collectively name sets of symbols.
%SIG	Associative array used to set signal handlers.
STDERR	Special filehandle for standard error.
STDIN	Special filehandle for standard input.
STDOUT	Special filehandle for standard output.

A.3 Perl Pragmas

A pragma is a special "pseudo" module that hints how the compiler should behave. The *use declaration* allows the importation of compiler directives called pragmas into your Perl program. Pragmas determine how a block of statements will be compiled. They are lexically scoped; the scope is limited to the current enclosing block and can be turned off with the *no* directive. Pragma names are conventionally lowercase. Table A.5 is a partial list.

Table A.5 Perl Pragmas

Pragma	What It Does
use autouse	Provides a mechanism for runtime demand loading of a module only when a function from that module gets called.
use base	Lets a programmer declare a derived class based on listed parent classes at compile time and eliminates the need for *require*; e.g., *use base qw(A B);* is equivalent to *BEGIN{ require A; require B;; push(@ISA, qw(A B));}*

Table A.5 Perl Pragmas (continued)

Pragma	*What It Does*
use bytes	Prior to Perl 5.6, all strings were treated as a sequence of bytes. Now strings can contain characters wider than a byte that are represented as numbers. The *bytes* pragma allows you to specify that the code is using the older, byte-oriented semantics.
use constant	Declares the named symbol to be a constant with a given scalar or list; For example: *use constant BUFFER_SIZE => 4096;* *use constant OS=> 'Solaris';*
use diagnostics	Forces verbose warning messages beyond the normal diagnostics issued by the Perl compiler and interpreter. Since it affects only the innermost block, the pragma is normally placed at the beginning of the program. Cannot use *no diagnostics*.
use integer	A lexically scoped pragma that tells the compiler to handle all mathematical operations as integer math and truncates the fractional part of floating point numbers when performing such operations.
use locale	A lexically scoped pragma that tells the compiler to enable or disable the use of POSIX locales when dealing with regular expressions, built-in operations, character conversions, etc.
use open	Declares one or more default disciplines for I/O operations; the two disciplines currently supported are *:raw* and *:crlf.*
use overload	Used to redefine the meanings of built-in operations when using objects. See *Math::BigFloat* in the standard Perl library for examples of overloaded operators.
use strict 'vars'	With *'vars'* as an argument, must use lexical (*my*) variables or fully qualified variable names with the package name and the scope operator or imported variables. If not adhered to, will cause a compilation error.
use strict 'ref'	Generates a runtime error if symbolic references are used, such as typeglobs.
use strict 'subs'	Generates a compile-time error if a bareword is used and it is not a predeclared subroutine or filehandle.
use strict	Generates compile-time errors if symbolic references are used, if non-lexical variables are declared, or if barewords that are not subroutines or filehandles are used.
use vars qw(list)	Used to declare global variables before *our* was introduced.
use warnings	A lexically scoped pragma that permits flexible control over Perl's built-in warnings like the *-w* switch or $^W variable.

Table A.5 Perl Pragmas (continued)

Pragma	What It Does
use lib 'library path'	Loads in the library at compile time, not runtime.
use sigtrap 'signal names'	Initializes a set of signal handlers for the listed signals. Without an argument for a set of default signals. Prints a stack dump of the program and issues an *ABRT* signal.
use subs qw(subroutine list)	Predeclares a list of subroutines allowing the subroutines listed to be called without parentheses and overrides built-in functions.
no integer	To turn off or unimport the pragma, the pragma name is preceded with *no*.

A.4 Perl Modules

Table A.6 General Programming

Module	Description
Benchmark	Checks and compares the speed of running code in CPU time.
Config	Accesses Perl configuration options from the *%Config* hash.
Env	Converts the *%ENV* hash to scalars containing environment variables; e.g., *$ENV{HOME}* becomes *$HOME*.
English	Provides scalars in English or *awk* names for special variables; e.g., *$0* can be represented as *$PROGRAM_NAME*.
Getopt	Provides for processing of command-line options and switches with arguments.
Shell	Used to run shell commands within Perl scripts by treating the commands as subroutines; e.g., *$today=date();*
Symbol	Generates anonymous globs with *gensym()* and qualifies variable names with *qualify()*.

Table A.7 CGI

Module	Description
CGI	CGI (Common Gateway Interface) class.
CGI::Apache	Used with *CGI.pm* and the Perl-Apache API.
CGI::Carp	Handles HTTP error messages and creates error log files.
CGI::Cookie	Interfaces with Netscape cookies.
CGI::Fast	Interfaces with Fast CGI.
CGI::Pretty	Produces pretty formatted HTML code.
CGI::Push	Simple interface to server push.

Table A.8 Error Handling

Module	Description
Carp	Generates *die*-like error messages to report line numbers of the calling routine where the error occurred. The subroutines that can be called from this module are *carp()*, *croak()*, and *confess()*.
Errno	Loads the *libc errno.h* defines.
Sys::Syslog	Provides a Perl interface to the UNIX *syslog(3)* library calls.

Table A.9 File Handling

Module	Description
Cwd	Gets the pathname of the current working directory. Produces an error message if used with the *-w* switch.
DirHandle	Provides an object-oriented interface for directory handles.
Fcntl	Loads the *libc fcntl.h* (file control) defines.
File::Basename	Splits a filename into components or extracts a filename or a directory from full directory path.
File::CheckTree	Runs file tests on a collection of files in a directory tree.
File::Copy	Used to copy files or filehandles.
File::DosGlob	Does DOS-like globbing.
File::Find	Used to traverse a UNIX file tree.
File::Finddepth	Searches depth-first through a file system.

Table A.9 File Handling (continued)

Module	Description
File::Glob	Does UNIX filename globbing.
File::Path	Creates and removes a list of directories.
File::Spec	Performs portable operations on filenames.
FileCache	Allows more files to be opened than permitted by the system.
FileHandle	Provides an object-oriented interface to filehandle access methods.
SelectServer	Saves and restores a selected filehandle.
flush.pl	Writes any data remaining in the filehandle's buffer or prints an expression and then flushes the buffer.
pwd.pl	Sets the *PWD* environment variable to the present working directory after using *chdir*.
stat.pl	Puts the values returned by the *stat* function into scalars—*$st_dev, $st_ino, $st_mode, $st_nlink, $st_uid, $st_rdev, $st_atime, $st_mtime, $st_ctime, $st_blksize, $st_blocks*.

Table A.10 Text Processing

Module	Description
Pod::Text	Converts *pod* documentation to ASCII-formatted text.
Search::Dict	Searches for a string in a dictionary (alphabetically ordered) file and sets the file pointer to the next line.
Term::Complete	Provides a filename-completion-like interface for prompting a user for partial input that can be completed by pressing a Tab key or a complete list of choices by pressing <Ctrl>-d.
Text::Abbrev	Creates an abbreviation table, a hash consisting of key/value pairs from a list. The key is the abbreviation and the value is the string that was abbbreviated; e.g., *ma/mail, mo/more*.
Text::ParseWords	Parses a line of text into a list of words like the *shell* does, stripping leading whitespace.
Text::Soundex	Maps words to four character-length codes that roughly correspond to how the word is pronounced or sounds.
Text::Tabs	Expands tabs into spaces and unexpands tabs to spaces.
Text::Warp	Wraps text into a paragraph.

Table A.11 Database Interfaces

Module	**Description**
AnyDBM_File	A UNIX-based module providing framework for multiple DBMs.
DB_File	Provides access to Berkeley DB manager. See *ftp//ftp.cs.berkeley.edu/ucb/4bsd*.
DBI	Returns a list of DBs and drivers on the system, and functions to interact with the database.
GDBM_File	Provides access to the GNU database manager. See *ftp://prep.ai.mit.edu/pub/gnu*.
NDBM_File	A UNIX-based module providing an interface to NDBM files.
ODBM_File	A UNIX-based module providing an interface to ODBM files.
SDBM_File	A UNIX-based module providing an interface to SDBM files.

Table A.12 Math

Module	**Description**
bigrat.pl	Enables infinite precision arithmetic on fractions.
Math::BigFloat	Supports arbitary-sized floating point arithmetic.
Math::BigInt	Supports arbitrary-sized integer arithmetic.
Math::Complex	Supports complex numbers to demonstrate overloading.
Math::Trig	Supports trigonometric functions.

Table A.13 Networking

Module	**Description**
chat2.pl	Allows Perl to manipulate interactive network services such as FTP.
comm.pl	Newer than *chat2.pl*. Allows Perl to manipulate interactive services.
IPC::Open2	Opens a process for reading and writing to allow data to be piped to and from an external program.
IPC::Open3	Opens a process for reading, writing, and error handling so that data can be piped to and from an external program.
Net::Ping	Checks whether a remote machine is up.

Table A.13 Networking (continued)

Module	Description
Socket	Creates sockets and imports socket methods for interprocess communication and loads *socket.h* header file.
Sys::Hostname	Gets the hostname for the system.

Table A.14 Time and Locale

Module	Description
I18N::Collate	Compares 8-bit scalar data according to the current locale.
Time::gmtime	An interface to Perl's built-in *gmtime()* function.
Time::Local	Computes the UNIX time (the number of non-leap-year seconds since January 1, 1970) from local and GMT (UTC) time.
Time::localtime	An interface to Perl's built-in *localtime()* function.

Table A.15 Terminals

Module	Description
Term::Cap	Provides low-level functions to manipulate terminal configurations as a terminal interface to the *termcap* database.

Table A.16 Object-Oriented Module Functions

Module	Description
Autoloader	For large modules, loads in only needed sections of a module.
AutoSplit	Splits module into bite-sized chunks for autoloading.
Devel::SelfStubber	Generates stubs for self-loading modules to ensure that if a method is called, it will get loaded.
DynaLoader	Used to automatically and dynamically load modules.
Exporter	Used by other modules to make methods and variables available through importation.
overload	Used to overload mathmatical operations.
Tie::Hash	Provides methods for tying a hash to a package.

Table A.16 Object-Oriented Module Functions (continued)

Module	Description
Tie::Scalar	Provides methods for tying a scalar to a package.
Tie::SubstrHash	Provides a hash-table-like interface to an array with constant key and record size.

Table A.17 Language Extension

Module	Description
ExtUtils::Install	For installing and deinstalling platform-dependent Perl extensions.
ExtUtils::Liblist	Determines what libraries to use and how to use them.
ExtUtils::MakeMaker	Creates a *Makefile* for a Perl extension in the extension's library.
ExtUtils::Manifest	Automates the maintenance of *MANIFEST* files, consisting of a list of filenames.
ExtUtils::Miniperl	Writes *C* code for *perlmain.c*, which contains the bootstrap code for making archive libraries needed by modules available from within Perl.
ExtUtils::Mkbootstrap	Is called from the extension's *Makefile* to create a bootstrap file needed to do dynamic loading on some systems.
ExtUtils::Mksysmlists	Writes *linker* option files used by some linkers during the creation of shared libraries for dynamic extensions.
ExtUtils::MM_OS2	Overrides the implementation of methods, causing UNIX behavior.
ExtUtils::MM_Unix	To be used with *MakeMaker* to provide methods for both UNIX and non-UNIX systems.
ExtUtils::MM_VMS	Overrides the implementation of methods, causing UNIX behavior.
Fcntl	Translates the *C fcntl* header file.
POSIX	Provides the Perl interface to IEEE std 1003.1 identifiers.
Safe	Provides private compartments where unsafe Perl code can be evaluated.
Test::Harness	Used by *MakeMaker* to run test scripts for Perl extensions and produce diagnostics.

A.5 Command-Line Switches

Table A.18 Command-Line Switches

<table>
<tr><th>Switch</th><th>Description</th></tr>
<tr><td>-0</td><td>Specify a record separator.</td></tr>
<tr><td>-a</td><td>Turns on autosplit mode when used with -n or -p, performing implicit split on whitespace. Fields are put in @F array.
<code>date | perl -ane 'print "$F[0]\n";</code></td></tr>
<tr><td>-c</td><td>Checks Perl syntax without executing script.</td></tr>
<tr><td>-d</td><td>Turns on Perl debugger for script.</td></tr>
<tr><td>-D</td><td>Sets Perl debugging flags. (Check your Perl installation to make sure debugging was installed.) To watch how Perl executes a script, use -D14.</td></tr>
<tr><td>-e command</td><td>Used to execute Perl commands at the command line rather than in a script.</td></tr>
<tr><td>-Fpattern</td><td>Specifies a pattern to use when splitting the input line. The pattern is just a regular expression enclosed in slashes or single or double quotes. For example, -F/:+/ splits the input line on one or more colons. Turned on if -a is also in effect.</td></tr>
<tr><td>-h</td><td>Prints a summary of Perl's command-line options.</td></tr>
<tr><td>-iextension</td><td>Enables in-place editing when using <> to loop through a file. If extension is not specified, modifies the file in place. Otherwise, renames the input file with the extension (used as a backup) and creates an output file with the original filename, which is edited in place. This is the selected filehandle for all print statements.</td></tr>
<tr><td>-Idirectory</td><td>Used with -P to tell the C preprocessor where to look for included files, by default /usr/include and /usr/lib/perl and the current directory.</td></tr>
<tr><td>-ldigits</td><td>Enables automatic line-ending processing. Chops the line terminator if -n or -p are used. Assigns $\ the value of digits (octal) to add the line terminator back on to print statements. Without digits specified, sets $\ to the current value of $/. (See Table A.2, "Filehandles.")</td></tr>
<tr><td>-m[-]module</td><td></td></tr>
<tr><td>-M[-]module</td><td></td></tr>
<tr><td>-M[-]'module'</td><td></td></tr>
<tr><td>-[mM]module=arg[,arg]...</td><td></td></tr>
</table>

Table A.18 Command-Line Switches (continued)

Switch	***Description***
-mmodule	Executes the *use* module before executing the Perl script.
-Mmodule	Executes the *use* module before executing the Perl script. Quotes are used if extra text is added. The dash shown in square brackets means that the *use* directive will be replaced with *no*.
-n	Causes Perl to implicitly loop over a named file, printing only lines specified.
-p	Causes Perl to implicitly loop over a named file, printing all lines in addition to those specified.
-P	Causes script to be run through the C preprocessor before being compiled by Perl.
-s	Enables switch parsing after the script name but before filename arguments, removing any switches found there from the *@ARGV* array. Sets the switch names to a scalar variable of the same name and assigns *1* to the scalar; e.g., *-abc* becomes *$abc* in the script.
-S	Makes Perl use the *PATH* environment variable to search for the script if the *#!/usr/bin/perl* line is not supported.
-T	Forces "taint" checks to be turned on for testing a script, which is ordinarily done only on *setuid* or *setgid* programs. Recommended for testing CGI scripts.
-u	Causes a core dump of script after compilation (UNIX based).
-U	Allows Perl to do unsafe operations; e.g., unlinking directories if superuser.
-v	Prints Perl version information (UNIX based).
-V	Prints a summary of the most important Perl configuration values and the current value of the *@INC* array.
-V:NAME	Prints the value of *NAME*, where *NAME* is a configuration variable.
-w	Prints warnings about possible misuse of reserved words, filehandles, subroutines, etc.
-W	Enables all warnings even if disabled locally using *no warnings*.
-xdirectory	Any text preceding the *#!/usr/bin/perl* line will be ignored. If a directory name is provided as an argument to the *-x* switch, Perl will change to that directory before execution of the script starts.
-X	Disables all warnings.

A.6 Debugger

A.6.1 Getting Information about the Debugger

Information on how to use the debugger is found by typing at your command line:

```
perldoc perldebug
```

Here is a sample of the output:

NAME
 perldebug - Perl debugging

DESCRIPTION
 First of all, have you tried using the *-w* switch?

A.6.2 The Perl Debugger

If you invoke Perl with the *-d* switch, your script runs under the Perl source debugger. This works like an interactive Perl environment, prompting for debugger commands that let you examine source code, set breakpoints, get stack backtraces, change the values of variables, etc. This is so convenient that you often fire up the debugger all by itself just to test out Perl constructs interactively to see what they do. For example:

```
$ perl -d -e 42
```

In Perl, the debugger is not a separate program the way it usually is in the typical compiled environment. Instead, the *-d* flag tells the compiler to insert source information into the parse trees it's about to hand off to the interpreter. That means your code must first compile correctly for the debugger to work on it. Then when the interpreter starts up, it preloads a special Perl library file containing the debugger.

The program will halt **right before** the first runtime executable statement (but see following regarding compile-time statements) and ask you to enter a debugger command. Contrary to popular expectations, whenever the debugger halts and shows you a line of code, it always displays the line it's **about** to execute rather than the one it has just executed.

Any command not recognized by the debugger is directly executed (*eval*'d) as Perl code in the current package. (The debugger uses the DB package for keeping its own state information.)

For any text entered at the debugger prompt, leading and trailing whitespace is first stripped before further processing. If a debugger command coincides with some function in your own program, merely precede the function with something that doesn't look like a debugger command, such as a leading ; or perhaps a +, or by wrapping it with parentheses or braces.

<continues here>

A.6.3 Entering and Exiting the Debugger

To invoke the Perl debugger, use the *-d* switch. It allows you to examine your program in an interactive-type environment after it has successfully compiled. After each line, the script will stop and ask for a command. The line you will be looking at is the next line that will be executed, not the previous one. The prompt contains the current package, function, file and line number, and the current line. Following is a list of the debug commands.

Once you start the debugger, all the debugging commands are listed by typing *h* at the debug prompt, or *h h* if you can't read what is displayed.

To exit the debugger, type *q* for quit or *R* for restart.

```
$ perl -d exer.1

Loading DB routines from $RCSfile: perldb.pl,v $$Revision: 4.0.1.2
$$Date: 91/11/05 17:55:58 $
Emacs support available.
Enter h for help.
main'(exer.1:3):          print "Today is ", `date`;
  DB<1> h
T                     Stack trace.
s                     Single step.
n                     Next, steps over subroutine calls.
r                     Return from current subroutine.
c [line]              Continue; optionally inserts a one-time-only
                      breakpoint at the specified line.
<CR>                  Repeat last n or s.
l min+incr            List incr+1 lines starting at min.
l min-max             List lines.
l line                List line.
l                     List next window.
-                     List previous window.
w line                List window around line.
l subname             List subroutine.
f filename            Switch to filename.
/pattern/             Search forwards for pattern; final / is optional.
?pattern?             Search backwards for pattern.
L                     List breakpoints and actions.
S                     List subroutine names.
```

```
t                         Toggle trace mode.
b [line] [condition]      Set breakpoint; line defaults to the current
                          execution line; condition breaks if it evaluates
                          to true, defaults to 1.
b subname [condition]     Set breakpoint at first line of subroutine.
d [line]                  Delete breakpoint.
D                         Delete all breakpoints.
a [line] command          Set an action to be done before the line is
                          executed. Sequence is: check for breakpoint, print
                          line if necessary, do action, prompt user if
                          breakpoint or step, evaluate line.
A                         Delete all actions.
V [pkg [vars]]            List some (default all) variables in package
                          (default current).
X [vars]                  Same as "V currentpackage [vars]".
< command                 Define command before prompt.
> command                 Define command after prompt.
! number                  Redo command (default previous command).
! -number                 Redo numberth-to-last command.
H -number                 Display last number commands (default all).
q or ^D                   Quit.
p expr                    Same as "print DB'OUT expr" in current package.
= [alias value]           Define a command alias, or list current aliases.
command                   Execute as a Perl statement in current package.
   DB<1> l
3:      print "Today is ", `date`;
4:      print "The name of this \uperl script\e is $0.\n";
5:      print "Hello. The number we will examine is 125.5.\n";
6:      printf "The \unumber\e  is %d.\n", 125.5;
7:      printf "The \unumber\e  is %d.\n", 125.5;
8:      printf "The following number is taking up 20 spaces and is
        right-justified.\n";
9:      printf "|%-20s|\n", 125;
10:     printf "\t\tThe number in hex is %x\n", 125.5;
11:     printf "\t\tThe number in octal is %o\n", 125.5;
12:     printf "The number in scientific notation is %e\n", 125.5;
  DB<1> q      (quit)
```

A.6.4 Debugger Commands

Getting help:

h	Lists help messages for all debugger commands.
h p	Lists a help message for debugger command *p*.

Listing parts of a script:

l	Lists 10 lines of the program.
l 8	Lists line 8.
l 5–10	Lists lines 5 through 10.
l greetme	Lists statements in subroutine *greetme*.

L	Lists the next line to execute.
w7	Lists a window of lines containing specified line 7. Lists three lines before the specified lines and fills the window with lines after it.
/^abc/	Searches forward for regular expression *abc*, where *abc* is at the beginning of the line.
?abc?	Searches backward for regular expression *abc*.
S	Lists all subroutines in the program by package name, two colons, and the name of the subroutine.
r	Executes the remainder of statements in the current subroutine and then displays the line immediately after the subroutine call.

Stepping line by line:

s	Single step a line at a time through the script.
n	Like *s* but executes subroutine calls without stepping through them.
Enter	Pressing the Enter key causes the previous *s* or *n* command to be repeated.
.	Repeats the last line executed.
–	Repeats all lines preceding the current one.
r	Continues until the currently executing subroutine returns and displays the return value and type after returning.

Getting out of the debugger:

q	Quit the debugger.
<Ctrl>-d	Quit the debugger.
R	Restart the debugger and a new session.

Breakpoints:

Breakpoints allow you to set a place where the program will stop so you can examine what's going on. They must be set on lines that start an executable statement.

b 45	Sets breakpoint to line 45. Type *c* to continue and the program will stop execution at line 45.
c	Continue execution.
b greetme	Sets breakpoint to subroutine *greetme*.
b $x > 10	Triggers a breakpoint only if the condition is true.
w	Creates a window around the breakpoint and marks the line where the breakpoint is found; e.g., *10==>b* (breakpoint is at line 10).
d	Deletes the breakpoint on the line about to execute.
d 12	Deletes the breakpoint at line 12.
D	Deletes all breakpoints.

Printing variable values:

X name	Displays the value of any variables called *name*. Variable names are NOT preceded by their identifying funny character; e.g., use *x* rather than *$x* or *@x*.
V package	Displays all variables within a package.
p $x + 3	Evaluates and prints the expression.

Tracing:

T	Produces a stack backtrace listing of what subroutines were called.
t	Toggles trace mode.

Aliases:

= Lists all aliases.	
= *ph print "$hashref->{Science}->{Lou}"*	*ph* is an alias for printing a hash value.

appendix

B

SQL Language Tutorial

```
> SELECT * FROM geeks WHERE
   style LIKE '%kewl%';
0 rows selected
```

B.1 What Is SQL?

When you go to Google and request information, that request is called a *query*, and the search engine will collect any Web pages that match your query. To narrow the search, you might have to refine your request with more descriptive keywords. The same process applies to database lookups. When you make requests to a database, the request follows a certain format, and the database server will try to locate the information and return a result. The way in which you query the database is defined by the query language you are using. The standard language for communicating with relational databases is SQL, the Structured Query Language. SQL is an ANSI (American National Standards Institute) standard computer language, designed to be as close to the English language as possible, making it an easy language to learn. Popular database management systems, such as Oracle, Sybase, and Microsoft SQL Server, all use SQL, and, although some create their own proprietary extensions to the language, the standard basic commands for querying a database, such as `SELECT`, `INSERT`, `DELETE`, `UPDATE`, `CREATE`, and `DROP`, will handle most of the essential tasks you will need to perform database operations.

The SQL language can be traced back to E. F. "Ted" Cobb, an IBM researcher who first published an article in June 1970 that laid the foundations for the theory of relational databases, an English-like language used to communicate with these databases. Cobb's article triggered a major research project at IBM to design a relational database system called System/R and a database language called SEQUEL (Structured English Query Language), which is known today as SQL (often pronounced "see-quell"). In the late 1970s, two other companies were started to develop similar products, which became Oracle and Ingres. By 1985, Oracle claimed to have more than 1,000 installations, and by the early 1990s, SQL had become the standard for database management in medium to large organizations, especially on UNIX and mainframes.

B.1.1 Standarizing SQL

Like the English language, with all its dialects, many flavors of SQL evolved. Today's SQL is based on IBM's original implementation, with a considerable number of additions. Standards are created to help specify what should be supported in a language. In 1986, the ANSI designated the SQL standard. It was then revised in 1989, 1992, and 1999. The most commonly used standard today is SQL92, representing the second revision of the original specification (SQL2). Most commercial databases (MySQL, Oracle, Sybase, Microsoft Access, and Microsoft SQL Server) support the full SQL and claim to be 100 percent compliant with the standard. However, the standard is quite complex, and as with different dialects of the English language, various vendors have added extensions to their version of SQL, making it difficult to guarantee that an application will run on all SQL server databases.

In this appendix, we focus on the basic SQL language and examine such concepts as table creation, insertion, deletion, and selection of data.

B.1.2 Executing SQL Statements

Because the database management system discussed in this book is MySQL, the server being used in the following examples is the MySQL database server, and most of the SQL commands will be executed at the `mysql` command-line client, although you might prefer to use the MySQL Query Browser. Once connected to the database, you simply type the commands in the `mysql` console (command-line window, see Figure B.1) as explained in Chapter 17.

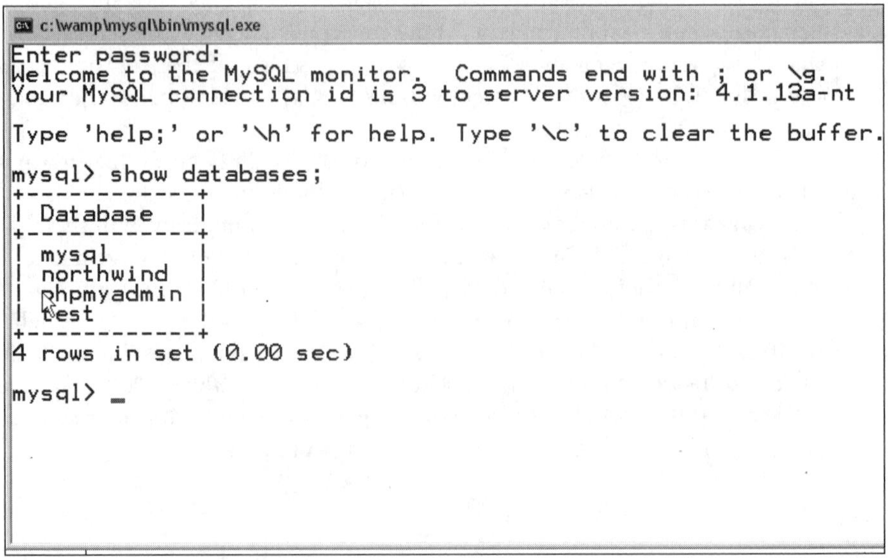
c:\wamp\mysql\bin\mysql.exe
Enter password:
Welcome to the MySQL monitor. Commands end with ; or \g.
Your MySQL connection id is 3 to server version: 4.1.13a-nt
Type 'help;' or '\h' for help. Type '\c' to clear the buffer.
mysql> show databases;
+------------+
| Database |
+------------+
| mysql |
| northwind |
| phpmyadmin |
| test |
+------------+
4 rows in set (0.00 sec)
mysql>

Figure B.1 The `mysql` console.

The MySQL Query Browser. To run SQL commands in the MySQL Query Browser, type them in the box in the top of the application window and click the Execute button.

Once you click the Execute button (the green button to the right of the query window), the result will be displayed in the center of the application as a Resultset tab (see Figure B.2).

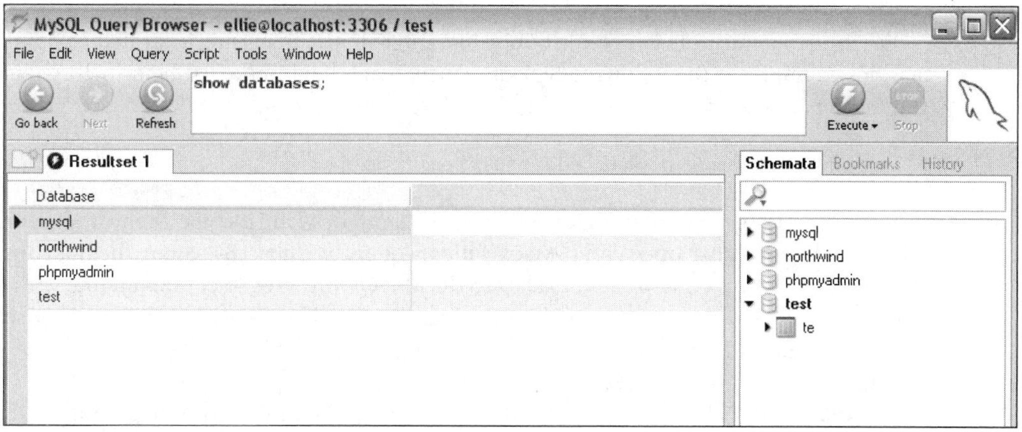

Figure B.2 The MySQL Query Browser GUI.

B.1.3 About SQL Commands/Queries

SQL is a computer language, and like languages in general, SQL has its rules, grammar, and a set of special or reserved words. Different variants of the language have evolved over the years because different relational database vendors offer additional features to manipulate data in the name of competition. This section covers the basic SQL commands and syntax.

Because SQL has so many commands, they are divided into two major categories: the commands to manipulate data in tables and the commands to manipulate the database itself. There are many excellent tutorials on the Web that cover all the SQL commands and how to use them. See *http://www.w3schools.com/sql/default.asp*.

English-like Grammar. When you create a SQL statement, it makes a request, or "queries" the database, in the form of a statement, similar to the structure of an English imperative sentence, such as "Select your partner," "Show your stuff," or "Describe that bully." The first word in a SQL statement is an English verb, an action word called a command, such as `show`, `use`, `select`, `drop`, and so on. The commands are followed by a list of noun-like words, such as `show databases`, `use database`, or `create databases`. The statement might contain prepositions, such as `in` or `from`. For example:

```
show tables in database
```

or

```
select phones from customer_table
```

The language also lets you add conditional clauses to refine your query, such as:

```
select companyname from suppliers where supplierid > 20;
```

When listing multiple items in a query, like English, the items are separated by commas; for example, in the following SQL statement, each field in the list being selected is comma-separated:

```
select companyname, phone, address from suppliers;
```

If the queries get very long and involved, you might want to type them into your favorite editor, because once you have executed a query, it is lost. By saving the query in an editor, you can cut and paste it back into the MySQL browser or command line without retyping it. Most important, make sure your query makes sense and will not cause havoc on an important database. MySQL provides a "test" database for practice.

Semicolons Terminate SQL Statements. When searching with Google for "SQL query," one of the top results is a Web site called *thinkgeek.com*, which sells T-shirts and apparel, electronics, gadgets, and home office and computing items. Its ad for the "SQL query" T-shirt reads:

> Black tshirt with the following SQL query written in white on front "SELECT * FROM users WHERE clue > 0". Unfortunately, zero rows are then returned....uh oh. And hey! there is no freakin semi-colon at the end of this query because not everybody under the sun uses the same database with the same console/shell—and there is more than one way to skin a cat. Umkay? Umkay.

The semicolon is the standard way to terminate each query statement. Some database systems do not require the semicolon, but MySQL does (exceptions are the `USE` and `QUIT` commands), and if you forget it, you will see a secondary prompt, and execution will go on hold until you add the semicolon, as shown in Figure B.3.

```
mysql> show databases
    ->
    -> ;
+------------+
| Database   |
+------------+
| mysql      |
| northwind  |
| phpmyadmin |
| test       |
+------------+
4 rows in set (0.00 sec)
```

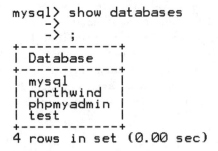

Figure B.3 Missing semicolon and the secondary prompt.

Naming Conventions. A database and its tables are easier to read when good naming conventions are used.

For example, it makes good sense to make table names plural and field/column names singular. Why? Because a table called "Shippers" normally holds more than one shipper, but the name of the field used to describe each shipper is a single value, such as "Company_Name", "Phone", and so on. The first letter in a table or field name is usually capitalized.

Compound names, such as "Company_Name", are usually separated by the underscore, with the first letter of each word capitalized.

Spaces and dashes are not allowed in any name in the database.

Reserved Words. All languages have a list of reserved words that have special meaning to the language. Most of these words will be used in this chapter. The SQL reserved words are listed in Table B.1. (See the MySQL documentation for a complete list of all reserved words.)

Table B.1 SQL Reserved Words

ALTER	JOIN
AND	LEFT JOIN
AS	LIKE
CREATE	LIMIT
CROSS JOIN	ON
DELETE	OR
DROP	ORDER BY
FROM	RIGHT JOIN
FULL JOIN	SELECT
GROUP BY	SET
INSERT	UPDATE
INTO	WHERE

Case Senstivity. Database and table names are case sensitive if you are using UNIX but not if you are using Windows. A convention is to always use lowercase names for databases and their tables.

SQL commands are not case sensitive. For example, the following SQL statements are equally valid:

```
show databases;
SHOW DATABASES;
```

Although SQL commands are not case sensitive, by convention, SQL keywords are capitalized for clarity, whereas only the first letter of the field, table, and database names is capitalized.

```
SELECT * FROM Persons WHERE FirstName='John'
```

If performing pattern matching with the `LIKE` and `NOT LIKE` commands, then the pattern being searched for is case sensitive when using MySQL.

The Result Set. A result set is just another table created to hold the results from a SQL query. Most database software systems even allow you to perform operations on the result set with functions, such as `Move-To-First-Record`, `Get-Record-Content`, `Move-To-Next-Record`, and so on. In Figure B.4, the result set is the table created by asking `mysql` to show all the fields in the table called "shippers".

```
mysql> show fields in shippers;
+-------------+-------------+------+-----+---------+----------------+
| Field       | Type        | Null | Key | Default | Extra          |
+-------------+-------------+------+-----+---------+----------------+
| ShipperID   | int(11)     |      | PRI | NULL    | auto_increment |
| CompanyName | varchar(40) |      |     |         |                |
| Phone       | varchar(24) | YES  |     | NULL    |                |
+-------------+-------------+------+-----+---------+----------------+
3 rows in set (0.00 sec)
```

Figure B.4 The result set is just a table produced from a query.

B.1.4 SQL and the Database

A database server can support multiple databases. For example, an Oracle or MySQL database server might serve one database for accounting, a second for human resources, a third for an e-commerce application, and so on. To see the available databases, SQL provides the `show` command.

The *show databases* Command. To see what databases are available on your database server, use the `show databases` command. The list of databases might be different on your machine, but the *mysql* and *test* databases are provided when you install MySQL. The *mysql* database is required because it describes user access privileges, and the *test* database, as the name suggests, is provided as a practice database for testing how things work.

FORMAT

```
SHOW DATABASES;
```

EXAMPLE B.1

```
1   mysql> SHOW databases;
    +------------+
    | Database   |
    +------------+
    | mysql      |
    | northwind  |
    | phpmyadmin |
    | test       |
    +------------+
    4 rows in set (0.03 sec)show databases;
```

The *USE* Command. The `USE` command makes the specified database your default database. From that point on, all SQL commands will be performed on the default database. This is one of the few commands that does not require a semicolon to terminate it.

FORMAT

```
USE database_name;
```

EXAMPLE B.2

```
1   mysql> USE northwind;
    Database changed
```

EXPLANATION

1 The `USE` command changes the database to "northwind".[a] The command-line client will report that the database has been changed.

a. The "northwind" database is available for downoad from *http://www.microsoft.com/downloads/details.aspx?FamilyID=C6661372-8DBE-422B-8676-C632D66C529C&displaylang=EN.*

B.1.5 SQL Database Tables

A database usually contains one or more tables. Each table is identified by a name, such as "Customers" or "Orders." The `SHOW TABLES IN` command displays all the tables within a database, as shown in Figure B.5. The `SELECT * FROM` command lists all the fields and rows in a specified table. Tables contain rows, called records, and columns, called fields. The table in Figure B.6 contains three records (one for each shipper) and three columns ("ShipperID," "CompanyName," and "Phone").

```
mysql> show tables in northwind;
+-----------------------+
| Tables_in_northwind   |
+-----------------------+
| categories            |
| customercustomerdemo  |
| customerdemographics  |
| customers             |
| employees             |
| employeeterritories   |
| order_details         |
| orders                |
| products              |
| region                |
| shippers              |
| suppliers             |
| territories           |
| usstates              |
+-----------------------+
14 rows in set (0.03 sec)
```

Figure B.5 Show all the tables in the "northwind" database.

```
mysql> select * from shippers;
+-----------+------------------+----------------+
| ShipperID | CompanyName      | Phone          |
+-----------+------------------+----------------+
|         1 | Speedy Express   | (503) 555-9831 |
|         2 | United Package   | (503) 555-3199 |
|         3 | Federal Shipping | (503) 555-9931 |
+-----------+------------------+----------------+
3 rows in set (0.00 sec)
```

Figure B.6 Display the contents of a particular table.

The *SHOW* and *DESCRIBE* Commands. To see what type of data can be assigned to a table, use the `DESCRIBE` command, specific to MySQL, and `SHOW FIELDS IN` command, a standard SQL command. The output displayed is the name of each field and the data types of the values that correspond to each field, as shown in Figure B.7. The data type can be a variable string of characters, a date, a number, and so on. For example, the type `varchar(40)` means a field with up to 40 characters. Also displayed is the primary key that is used to uniquely identify the record.

FORMAT

```
SHOW FIELDS IN table_name;
```

or

```
DESCRIBE table_name;
```

```
mysql> show fields in customers;
+--------------+-------------+------+-----+---------+-------+
| Field        | Type        | Null | Key | Default | Extra |
+--------------+-------------+------+-----+---------+-------+
| CustomerID   | varchar(5)  |      | PRI |         |       |
| CompanyName  | varchar(40) |      | MUL |         |       |
| ContactName  | varchar(30) | YES  |     | NULL    |       |
| ContactTitle | varchar(30) | YES  |     | NULL    |       |
| Address      | varchar(60) | YES  |     | NULL    |       |
| City         | varchar(15) | YES  | MUL | NULL    |       |
| Region       | varchar(15) | YES  | MUL | NULL    |       |
| PostalCode   | varchar(10) | YES  | MUL | NULL    |       |
| Country      | varchar(15) | YES  |     | NULL    |       |
| Phone        | varchar(24) | YES  |     | NULL    |       |
| Fax          | varchar(24) | YES  |     | NULL    |       |
+--------------+-------------+------+-----+---------+-------+
11 rows in set (0.05 sec)
```

Figure B.7 The SQL `SHOW FIELDS IN` command.

The shorter `DESCRIBE` version is shown in Figure B.8.

```
mysql> describe shippers;
+-------------+-------------+------+-----+---------+----------------+
| Field       | Type        | Null | Key | Default | Extra          |
+-------------+-------------+------+-----+---------+----------------+
| ShipperID   | int(11)     |      | PRI | NULL    | auto_increment |
| CompanyName | varchar(40) |      |     |         |                |
| Phone       | varchar(24) | YES  |     | NULL    |                |
+-------------+-------------+------+-----+---------+----------------+
3 rows in set (0.00 sec)
```

Figure B.8 The MySQL `DESCRIBE` command.

B.2 SQL Data Manipulation Language (DML)

SQL is a nonprocedural language providing a syntax for extracting data, including a syntax to update, insert, and delete records.

These query and update commands together form the Data Manipulation Language (DML) part of SQL. We cover the following SQL commands in this section:

- `SELECT`—Extracts data from a database table.
- `UPDATE`—Updates data in a database table.
- `DELETE`—Deletes data from a database table.
- `INSERT INTO`—Inserts new data into a database table.

B.2.1 The *SELECT* Command

One of the most commonly used SQL commands is `SELECT`, mandatory when performing a query. The `SELECT` command is used to retrieve data from a table based on some criteria. It specifies a comma-separated list of fields to be retrieved, and the `FROM` clause specifies the table(s) to be accessed. The results are stored in a result table known as the result set. The * symbol can be used to represent all of the fields.

FORMAT

```
SELECT column_name(s) FROM table_name
```

Example:

```
SELECT LastName, FirstName, Address FROM Students;
```

EXAMPLE B.3

```
mysql> SELECT CompanyName FROM Shippers;
+------------------+
| CompanyName      |
+------------------+
| Speedy Express   |
| United Package   |
| Federal Shipping |
+------------------+
3 rows in set (0.05 sec)
```

EXPLANATION

The `SELECT` command will retrieve all items in the field *CompanyName* `FROM` the *Shippers* table. The result-set table is displayed in response to the query.

Select Specified Columns. To select the columns named *CompanyName* and *Phone* from the *Shippers* table, `SELECT` is followed by a comma-separated list of fields to be selected `FROM` the *Shippers* table. The resulting table is called the result set, as shown in Example B.4.

EXAMPLE B.4

```
mysql> SELECT CompanyName, Phone FROM Shippers;
+------------------+----------------+
| CompanyName      | Phone          |
+------------------+----------------+
| Speedy Express   | (503) 555-9831 |
| United Package   | (503) 555-3199 |
| Federal Shipping | (503) 555-9931 |
+------------------+----------------+
3 rows in set (0.09 sec)
```

Select All Columns. To select all columns from the *Shippers* table, use a * symbol instead of column names, as shown in Example B.5. The * is a wildcard character used to represent all of the fields (columns).

EXAMPLE B.5

```
mysql> SELECT * FROM Shippers;
+-----------+------------------+----------------+
| ShipperID | CompanyName      | Phone          |
+-----------+------------------+----------------+
|         1 | Speedy Express   | (503) 555-9831 |
|         2 | United Package   | (503) 555-3199 |
|         3 | Federal Shipping | (503) 555-9931 |
+-----------+------------------+----------------+
3 rows in set (0.06 sec)
```

The *SELECT DISTINCT* Statement. The `DISTINCT` keyword is used to return only distinct (unique) values from the table. If there are multiple values of a specified field, the `DISTINCT` result set will display only one.

In the next example, ALL values from the column named *ShipName* are first selected, and more than 800 records are displayed, but notice that with the `DISTINCT` keyword, fewer than 90 records are retrieved.

FORMAT

```
SELECT DISTINCT column_name(s) FROM table_name
```

EXAMPLE B.6

```
SELECT ShipName from Orders
(Partial Output)
| North/South                        |
| Blauer See Delikatessen            |
| Ricardo Adocicados                 |
| Franchi S.p.A.                     |
| Great Lakes Food Market            |
| Reggiani Caseifici                 |
| Hungry Owl All-Night Grocers       |
| Save-a-lot Markets                 |
| LILA-Supermercado                  |
| White Clover Markets               |
| Drachenblut Delikatessen           |
| Queen Cozinha                      |
| Tortuga Restaurante                |
| Lehmanns Marktstand                |
| LILA-Supermercado                  |
| Ernst Handel                       |
| Pericles Comidas clásicas          |
```

EXAMPLE B.6 (CONTINUED)

```
| Simons bistro                         |
| Richter Supermarkt                    |
| Bon app'                              |
| Rattlesnake Canyon Grocery            |
+---------------------------------------+
830 rows in set (0.00 sec)
```

With the `DISTINCT` keyword, fewer than 90 records are retrieved:

```
SELECT DISTINCT ShipName FROM Orders;
| Océano Atlántico Ltda.                |
| Franchi S.p.A.                        |
| Gourmet Lanchonetes                   |
| Consolidated Holdings                 |
| Rancho grande                         |
| Lazy K Kountry Store                  |
| Laughing Bacchus Wine Cellars         |
| Blauer See Delikatessen               |
| North/South                           |
| Cactus Comidas para llevar            |
| Great Lakes Food Market               |
| Maison Dewey                          |
| Trail's Head Gourmet Provisioners     |
| Let's Stop N Shop                     |
```

Limiting the Number of Lines in the Result Set with *LIMIT*. If you do not want to display a huge database, you can limit the number of lines to print by using `LIMIT`; for example, the tables in the *northwind* database contain thousands of records. In the previous examples, it would have been better to display a few lines to demonstrate that the query was successful. Because you are getting only a partial list, you might want to know the total number in the table. This can be done by using the `SQL_CALC_FOUND_ROWS` option and the SQL `FOUND_ROWS()` function. SQL will calculate the total number of records, and the `FOUND_ROWS()` function will let you display the results of that calculation.

EXAMPLE B.7

```
mysql> select ShipName from Orders LIMIT 10;
+---------------------------+
| ShipName                  |
+---------------------------+
| Vins et alcools Chevalier |
| Toms Spezialitaten        |
| Hanari Carnes             |
| Victuailles en stock      |
| Suprêmes délices          |
| Hanari Carnes             |
| Chop-suey Chinese         |
| Richter Supermarkt        |
| Wellington Importadora    |
| HILARION-Abastos          |
+---------------------------+
10 rows in set (0.00 sec)
```

EXPLANATION

With one argument, in this case `10`, `LIMIT` specifies the number of rows to return from the beginning of the result set.

EXAMPLE B.8

```
mysql> SELECT SQL_CALC_FOUND_ROWS ShipName from Orders
    -> LIMIT 5;
+---------------------------+
| ShipName                  |
+---------------------------+
| Vins et alcools Chevalier |
| Toms Spezialitaten        |
| Hanari Carnes             |
| Victuailles en stock      |
| Suprêmes délices          |
+---------------------------+
5 rows in set (0.03 sec)

mysql> SELECT FOUND_ROWS();
+--------------+
| FOUND_ROWS() |
+--------------+
|          830 |
+--------------+
1 row in set (0.03 sec)
```

EXPLANATION

SQL will calculate the total number of records, limited to `5`, and the `FOUND_ROWS()` function will let you display the results of that calculation.

The *WHERE* Clause. What if you want to select fields only when a certain set of conditions is true? For example, you might want to list all the customers who come from Sweden and were paid more than $50,000 last year. The `WHERE` clause is optional and specifies which data values or rows will be selected, based on a condition described after the keyword `WHERE`. To create the conditions, called the selection criteria, SQL provides a set of operators to further qualify what criteria should be specified in the `WHERE` clause. See Table B.2.

FORMAT

```
SELECT column FROM table WHERE column operator value
```

Example:

```
SELECT phone FROM shippers WHERE country like "Sw";
```

Table B.2 SQL Operators

Operator	*Description*	*Example*
`=`	Equal to	`where country = 'Sweden'`
`<>, !=`	Not equal to[a]	`where country <> 'Sweden'`
`>`	Greater than	`where salary > 50000`
`<`	Less than	`where salary < 50000`
`>=`	Greater than or equal	`where salary >= 50000`
`<=`	Less than or equal	`where salary <= 50000`
`IS [NOT] NULL`	Is NULL (no value) or Not NULL	`where birth = NULL`
`BETWEEN`	Between an inclusive range	`where last_name BETWEEN 'Dobbins' AND 'Main'`
`LIKE`	Search for a value like a pattern	`where last_name LIKE 'D%'`
`NOT LIKE`	Search for a value not like a pattern	`where country NOT LIKE 'Sw%'`
`!, NOT`	Logical not for negation	`where age ! 10;`
`||, OR`	Logical OR	`where order_number > 10 || part_number = 80`
`&&, AND`	Logical AND	`where age > 12 && age < 21`
`XOR`	Exclusive OR	`where status XOR`

a. In some versions of SQL, the <> operator can be written as `!=`.

Using Quotes. Quotes are always an issue in programming languages. Should you use a set of single quotes or double quotes, and when should you use them?

SQL uses single quotes around text values (most database systems, including MySQL, also accept double quotes). Numeric values should not be enclosed in quotes.

For text values, this example is correct:

```
SELECT * FROM Students WHERE FirstName='Marco'
```

and this example is wrong:

```
SELECT * FROM Students WHERE FirstName=Marco     Marco should be
"Marco"
```

For numeric values, this example is correct:

```
SELECT * FROM Students WHERE Year>2004
```

and this example is wrong:

```
SELECT * FROM Students WHERE Year>'2004'     '2004' should be 2004
```

Using the = and <> Operators. In Figure B.9, the *CompanyName* and *Phone* fields are retrieved from the *Customers* table if the condition following the `WHERE` clause is true; that is, if the string values in the *Country* field are exactly equal to the string *Italy* (they must contain the same number and type of characters). The <> operator can be used to test for "not equal to."

```
mysql> select CompanyName, Phone FROM Customers
    -> WHERE Country='Italy';
+------------------------------+-------------+
| CompanyName                  | Phone       |
+------------------------------+-------------+
| Franchi S.p.A.               | 011-4988260 |
| Magazzini Alimentari Riuniti | 035-640230  |
| Reggiani Caseifici           | 0522-556721 |
+------------------------------+-------------+
3 rows in set (0.00 sec)
```

Figure B.9 The `WHERE` clause with the = operator.

What Is *NULL*? Null means that there is not a value in a field, or it is unknown, but does not mean a value of zero. If a field is `NULL`, it is empty, and if it is `NOT NULL`, it has data. Fields have `NULL` as a default unless they are specified by `NOT NULL` in the definition of the table.

EXAMPLE B.9

```
mysql> SELECT region, country FROM suppliers
    -> WHERE region IS NULL;
+--------+-------------+
| region | country     |
+--------+-------------+
| NULL   | UK          |
| NULL   | Japan       |
| NULL   | Japan       |
| NULL   | UK          |
| NULL   | Sweden      |
| NULL   | Brazil      |
| NULL   | Germany     |
| NULL   | Germany     |
| NULL   | Germany     |
| NULL   | Italy       |
| NULL   | Norway      |
| NULL   | Sweden      |
| NULL   | France      |
| NULL   | Singapore   |
| NULL   | Denmark     |
| NULL   | Netherlands |
| NULL   | Finland     |
| NULL   | Italy       |
| NULL   | France      |
| NULL   | France      |
+--------+-------------+
20 rows in set (0.00 sec)
```

EXPLANATION

Displays the region and country from the *suppliers* database where the region `IS NULL`; that is, has no value.

EXAMPLE B.10

```
mysql> SELECT region, country FROM suppliers
    -> WHERE region NOT NULL;
+----------+-----------+
| region   | country   |
+----------+-----------+
| LA       | USA       |
| MI       | USA       |
| Asturias | Spain     |
| Victoria | Australia |
```

EXAMPLE B.10 (CONTINUED)

```
| OR         | USA       |
| MA         | USA       |
| NSW        | Australia |
| Québec     | Canada    |
| Québec     | Canada    |
+------------+-----------+
9 rows in set (0.00 sec)
```

EXPLANATION

Displays the *region* and *country* from the *suppliers* database where the region is NOT NULL; that is, has a value.

The > and < Operators. The > and < operators are used to select rows where the value of a field is greater or less than some value, such as:

```
SELECT product, price FROM table WHERE price > 50;

SELECT product, price FROM table
WHERE price > 50 && price < 100;
```

You can also use the >= and <= operators to select rows that are greater than or equal to or less than or equal to some value:

```
SELECT product, price FROM table
WHERE price >=50;
```

EXAMPLE B.11

```
mysql> SELECT UnitPrice, Quantity FROM Order_Details
    -> WHERE UnitPrice > 1 && UnitPrice < 3;
+-----------+----------+
| UnitPrice | Quantity |
+-----------+----------+
|    2.0000 |       25 |
|    2.0000 |       60 |
|    2.0000 |       24 |
|    2.0000 |       20 |
|    2.0000 |        8 |
|    2.0000 |       60 |
|    2.0000 |       49 |
|    2.0000 |       50 |
|    2.0000 |       20 |
```

EXAMPLE B.12

```
mysql> SELECT CategoryName from categories WHERE CategoryName < 'D';
+---------------+
| CategoryName |
+---------------+
| Beverages     |
| Condiments    |
| Confections   |
+---------------+
3 rows in set (0.00 sec)
```

The *AND* and *OR* Operators. AND and OR operators are used in a WHERE clause to further qualify what data you want to select from a table. The AND operator tests one or more conditions to see if all the conditions are true; if so, SELECT displays the rows. The OR operator displays a row if only one of the conditions listed is true. The AND operator can be designated by the && symbol, and the OR operator can be designated as ||.

EXAMPLE B.13

```
mysql> SELECT ContactName FROM Suppliers
        -> WHERE City = 'Montreal' AND Region = 'Quebec';
+------------------+
| contactname      |
+------------------+
| Jean-Guy Lauzon |
+------------------+
1 row in set (0.03 sec)
```

EXPLANATION

When using the && (AND) operator, both of the conditions being tested in the WHERE clause must be true; that is, both the *City* must be *Montreal* and the *Region* must be *Quebec*. If both conditions are true, then SELECT will print the *ContactName* from the *Suppliers* database.

EXAMPLE B.14

```
mysql> SELECT CompanyName, City FROM Suppliers WHERE
    -> City = 'Montreal' OR City = 'Boston';
+------------------------------+----------+
| CompanyName                  | City     |
+------------------------------+----------+
| New England Seafood Cannery  | Boston   |
| Ma Maison                    | Montreal |
+------------------------------+----------+
2 rows in set (0.00 sec)
```

EXPLANATION

When using the || (OR) operator, only one of the conditions being tested must be true; that is, if either the *City* is *Montreal* or the *City* is *Boston*, then SELECT will print the *CompanyName* and *City* from the *Suppliers* database.

The *LIKE* and *NOT LIKE* Condition. The LIKE pattern-matching operator is a powerful operator that can be used as a condition in the WHERE clause, allowing you to select only rows that are "like" or match a pattern.

A percent sign (%) can be used as a wildcard to match any possible character that might appear before and/or after the characters specified.

A _ is used to match a single character.

The LIKE condition can be used in any valid SQL statement, including SELECT, INSERT, UPDATE, or DELETE.

FORMAT

```
SELECT column FROM table WHERE column LIKE pattern
SELECT column FROM table WHERE column NOT LIKE pattern
```

Example:

```
SELECT column FROM customer WHERE last_name LIKE 'Mc%';
```

The next examples will demonstrate how the % and _ are used with LIKE and NOT LIKE as a wildcard in pattern matching.

Pattern Matching and the % Wildcard. The % wildcard is used to represent one or more of any character when performing pattern matching. For example, if you are looking for all phone numbers in the 408 area code, you could say 408%, and the % will be replaced by any characters after 408.

EXAMPLE B.15

```
mysql> SELECT CompanyName, Country FROM Customers
    -> WHERE country like 'Sw%';
+--------------------+-------------+
| CompanyName        | Country     |
+--------------------+-------------+
| Berglunds snabbköp | Sweden      |
| Chop-suey Chinese  | Switzerland |
| Folk och fä HB     | Sweden      |
| Richter Supermarkt | Switzerland |
+--------------------+-------------+
4 rows in set (0.00 sec)
```

EXPLANATION

The `SELECT` returns all the customers who are from countries that start with `Sw`.

EXAMPLE B.16

```
mysql> SELECT City, Country FROM Suppliers WHERE City LIKE '%o';
+-----------+---------+
| City      | Country |
+-----------+---------+
| Tokyo     | Japan   |
| Oviedo    | Spain   |
| Sao Paulo | Brazil  |
| Salerno   | Italy   |
+-----------+---------+
4 rows in set (0.00 sec)
```

EXPLANATION

The `SELECT` returns all cities and countries where the `%` matches any city that ends with a letter `o`.

EXAMPLE B.17

```
mysql> SELECT Companyname FROM customers
    ->     WHERE CompanyName LIKE '%Super%';
+--------------------+
| Companyname        |
+--------------------+
| LILA-Supermercado  |
| Richter Supermarkt |
+--------------------+
2 rows in set (0.00 sec)
```

EXPLANATION

The `SELECT` returns all company names where the `%` matches any company name that contains the pattern `Super`.

The _ Wildcard. The next example shows how the underscore (_) wildcard character works. Remember that the _ matches only one character.

EXAMPLE B.18

```
mysql> SELECT extension, firstname FROM employees
    -> WHERE extension LIKE '4_ _';
+-----------+-----------+
| extension | firstname |
+-----------+-----------+
| 428       | Michael   |
| 465       | Robert    |
| 452       | Anne      |
+-----------+-----------+
3 rows in set (0.00 sec)
```

EXPLANATION

This SELECT returns all extensions and first names where the extension has three characters and the first character is a 4. The _ symbol is used to match a single character.

The *BETWEEN* Statement. The BETWEEN keyword allows you select a field based on criteria that represent a range of values. The syntax for the BETWEEN clause is as follows:

FORMAT

```
SELECT column  FROM table
WHERE column BETWEEN 'value1' AND 'value2'
```

Example:

```
select age from person where age BETWEEN 10 && 20;
```

EXAMPLE B.19

```
mysql> SELECT ProductName, ProductId
    -> FROM Products WHERE ProductId BETWEEN 30 AND 33;
+-----------------------+-----------+
| ProductName           | ProductId |
+-----------------------+-----------+
| Nord-Ost Matjeshering |        30 |
| Gorgonzola Telino     |        31 |
| Mascarpone Fabioli    |        32 |
| Geitost               |        33 |
+-----------------------+-----------+
4 rows in set (0.06 sec)
```

EXPLANATION

The SELECT returns product names and product IDs if the *ProductId* value is in the range between 30 and 33.

Sorting Results with *ORDER BY*. You can display the output of a query in a particular order by using the `ORDER BY` clause. Rows can be sorted in either ascending (`ASC`, the default) or descending (`DESC`) order where the values being sorted are either strings or numbers.

FORMAT

```
SELECT column FROM table
[WHERE condition]
ORDER BY column [ASC, DESC]
```

Example:

```
SELECT Company, OrderNumber FROM Orders
ORDER BY Company
```

EXAMPLE B.20

```
mysql> SELECT CompanyName, ContactName FROM suppliers
    -> ORDER BY CompanyName LIMIT 10;
+---------------------------------+--------------------------+
| CompanyName                     | ContactName              |
+---------------------------------+--------------------------+
| Aux joyeux ecclésiastiques      | Guylène Nodier           |
| Bigfoot Breweries               | Cheryl Saylor            |
| Cooperativa de Quesos 'Las Cabras' | Antonio del Valle Saavedra |
| Escargots Nouveaux              | Marie Delamare           |
| Exotic Liquids                  | Charlotte Cooper         |
| Forêts d'Trables                | Chantal Goulet           |
| Formaggi Fortini s.r.l.         | Elio Rossi               |
| G'day, Mate                     | Wendy Mackenzie          |
| Gai pâturage                    | Eliane Noz               |
| Grandma Kelly's Homestead       | Regina Murphy            |
+---------------------------------+--------------------------+
10 rows in set (0.06 sec)
```

EXPLANATION

The *CompanyName* is sorted in ascending order, limited to 10 records.

EXAMPLE B.21

```
mysql> SELECT CompanyName, ContactName FROM suppliers
    -> ORDER BY CompanyName DESC LIMIT 10;
+----------------------------------------+-----------------------------+
| CompanyName                            | ContactName                 |
+----------------------------------------+-----------------------------+
| Zaanse Snoepfabriek                    | Dirk Luchte                 |
| Tokyo Traders                          | Yoshi Nagase                |
| Svensk Sjöföda AB                      | Michael Björn               |
| Specialty Biscuits, Ltd.               | Peter Wilson                |
| Refrescos Americanas LTDA              | Carlos Diaz                 |
| Plutzer Lebensmittelgro-markte AG      | Martin Bein                 |
| PB Knackebröd AB                       | Lars Peterson               |
| Pavlova, Ltd.                          | Ian Devling                 |
| Pasta Buttini s.r.l.                   | Giovanni Giudici            |
| Norske Meierier                        | Beate Vileid                |
29 rows in set (0.00 sec)
```

EXPLANATION

The *CompanyName* is sorted in descending order, limited to 10 records.

B.2.2 The *INSERT* Command

The `INSERT INTO` statement is used to insert new rows into a table. After the `VALUES` keyword, a comma-separated list of column names follows.

FORMAT

```
INSERT INTO table_name VALUES (value1, value2,....)
```

You can also specify the columns for which you want to insert data:

```
INSERT INTO table_name (column1, column2,...)
VALUES (value1, value2,....)
```

EXAMPLE B.22

```
INSERT INTO Shippers (CompanyName, Phone)
VALUES ('Canada Post', '416-555-1221');
+-----------+------------------+----------------+
| ShipperID | CompanyName      | Phone          |
+-----------+------------------+----------------+
|         1 | Speedy Express   | (503) 555-9831 |
|         2 | United Package   | (503) 555-3199 |
|         3 | Federal Shipping | (503) 555-9931 |
|         4 | Canada Post      | 416-555-1221   |
+-----------+------------------+----------------+
```

EXPLANATION

The INSERT INTO statement is inserting a new row into the *Shippers* table, first by listing the field name, and then the corresponding values after the VALUES keyword. The *ShipperID* value is not included, because when the table was created, *ShipperID* was set as a PRIMARY KEY to be autoincremented by the database every time a new shipper record is added. (Letting the database increment the PRIMARY KEY ensures that the value is always unique.) To see how the table was originally set up, see the output from the DESCRIBE command here:

```
mysql> DESCRIBE shippers;
+-------------+-------------+------+-----+---------+----------------+
| Field       | Type        | Null | Key | Default | Extra          |
+-------------+-------------+------+-----+---------+----------------+
| ShipperID   | int(11)     |      | PRI | NULL    | auto_increment |
| CompanyName | varchar(40) |      |     |         |                |
| Phone       | varchar(24) | YES  |     | NULL    |                |
+-------------+-------------+------+-----+---------+----------------+
```

B.2.3 The *UPDATE* Command

The UPDATE statement is used to modify the data in a table. After the UPDATE command, you list the name of the table where the data will be changed, followed by the SET statement to indicate what field will be changed, and then the new value that will be assigned to the field. The WHERE clause further qualifies what data is to be modified, thereby limiting the scope of the update.

In Example B.23, the key is the use of the WHERE statement to limit the scope of the update.

FORMAT

```
UPDATE table_name
SET column_name = new_value
WHERE column_name = some_value
```

Example:

```
UPDATE orders SET ShipCountry="Luxembourg" WHERE CustomerId='whitc';
```

EXAMPLE B.23

```
1   mysql> select * from shippers;
    +-----------+------------------+----------------+
    | ShipperID | CompanyName      | Phone          |
    +-----------+------------------+----------------+
    |         1 | Speedy Express   | (503) 555-9831 |
    |         2 | United Package   | (503) 555-3199 |
    |         3 | Federal Shipping | (503) 555-9931 |
    +-----------+------------------+----------------+
    3 rows in set (0.00 sec)

2   mysql> UPDATE shippers SET PHONE='(777) 444-1234'
     -> WHERE companyname = 'Federal Shipping';
    Query OK, 1 row affected (0.08 sec)
    Rows matched: 1  Changed: 1  Warnings: 0

3   mysql> select * from shippers;
    +-----------+------------------+----------------+
    | ShipperID | CompanyName      | Phone          |
    +-----------+------------------+----------------+
    |         1 | Speedy Express   | (503) 555-9831 |
    |         2 | United Package   | (503) 555-3199 |
    |         3 | Federal Shipping | (777) 444-1234 |
    +-----------+------------------+----------------+
    3 rows in set (0.00 sec)
```

EXPLANATION

1. The `SELECT` command shows all the fields in the *Shippers* table.
2. The `UPDATE` command allows you to change an existing record. The phone number for Federal Shipping is being changed.
3. This `SELECT` command shows that the phone number for Federal Shipping was changed by the previous `UPDATE` command.

B.2.4 The *DELETE* Statement

The `DELETE` statement is used to delete rows in a table and returns the number of rows that were deleted. `DELETE` uses the `FROM` clause to specify the name of the table that contains the data you want to delete, and the `WHERE` clause specifies the criteria to identify what data should be removed.

Be careful! Without a `WHERE` clause, all rows are deleted.[1]

If the `ORDER BY` clause is specified, the rows are deleted in the order that is specified. The `LIMIT` clause places a limit on the number of rows that can be deleted.

1. You can set up MySQL so that if you use `DELETE` without a `WHERE` clause, the rows will not be deleted.

FORMAT

```
DELETE FROM table_name
WHERE column_name = some_value
```

The `DELETE` statement is very similar to the `UPDATE` statement. To delete the previous record, you would enter this query:

```
DELETE FROM Shippers WHERE CompanyName='Canada Post';
```

B.3 SQL Data Definition Language

The Data Definition Language (DDL) part of SQL permits database objects to be created or destroyed. You can also define indexes (keys), specify links between tables, and impose constraints between database tables. Often, decisions to create and remove databases are handled by a database administrator, and having permission to create and drop tables depends on what access rights are granted.

The most important data definition statements in SQL are:

- `CREATE TABLE`—Creates a new database table.
- `ALTER TABLE`—Alters (changes) a database table.
- `DROP TABLE`—Deletes a database table.
- `CREATE INDEX`—Creates an index (search key).
- `DROP INDEX`—Deletes an index.

B.3.1 Creating the Database

Creating the database is very simple. All you have to do is issue one command, and the only parameter is the database name.

FORMAT

```
CREATE DATABASE database_name
```

In the earlier examples, we used the *northwind* database. Because we will be working on a complete Web application for an art gallery in Appendix A, now we will create the database for that application.

EXAMPLE B.24

```
mysql> CREATE DATABASE gallerydb;
Query OK, 1 row affected (0.03 sec)

mysql> show databases;
+------------+
| Database   |
+------------+
| gallerydb  |
| mysql      |
| northwind  |
| phpmyadmin |
| test       |
+------------+
5 rows in set (0.00 sec)
```

EXPLANATION

That's it. The database is now created. Note that just because we created the database, we are still not in that database. The `USE` command in the next example will make the new database the current default database.

EXAMPLE B.25

```
mysql> USE gallerydb;
Database changed
```

EXPLANATION

We are now in the *gallerydb* database, and all the SQL commands will be executed on that database.

B.3.2 SQL Data Types

After creating a database, you will add the tables that make up the database. Before creating a table, you have to decide what kind of data will be stored in it; for example, will you have rows of names, dates, part numbers, Social Security numbers, prices, and so on? The data type specifies what type of data the column can hold. The basic types are string, numeric, and date and time types. For a fully documented list, see *http://dev.mysql.com/doc/refman/5.0/en/data-types.html.*

Table B.3 contains the most common data types in SQL.

Table B.3 Most Common SQL Data Types

Data Type	*Description*
Numbers	
`INTEGER`	Holds a 4-byte whole number.
`INT UNSIGNED`	Holds a 4-byte non-negative whole number.
`SMALLINT`	Holds a 2-byte whole number.
`TINYINT`	Holds a 1-byte whole number.
`FLOAT(m,d)`	A 4-byte fractional number. `FLOAT(7,4)` for value `999.00009` results in `999.0001`. The maximum number of digits is specified in `m`. The maximum number of digits to the right of the decimal is specified in `d`.
`DOUBLE(m,d)`	An 8-byte fractional double-precision number.
`DECIMAL(m,d)`	A real or fractional 8-byte number. The maximum number of digits is specified in `m`. The maximum number of digits to the right of the decimal is specified in `d`.
`NUMERIC(m,d)`	The `DECIMAL` and `NUMERIC` data types are used to store exact numeric data values with exact precision; e.g., monetary data. Hold numbers with fractions.
Strings	
`CHAR(SIZE)`	Holds a fixed-length string (can contain letters, numbers, and special characters) from 0 to 255 characters long. The fixed size is specified in the parentheses.
`VARCHAR(SIZE)`	A variable-length string (can contain letters, numbers, and special characters) from 0 to 65,535 in MySQL 5.0.3 and later versions. The maximum size is specified in the parentheses.
`TINYTEXT`	A string with a maximum length of 255 characters.
`TEXT`	A variable-length text string with a maximum length of 65,535 characters, used for storing large text files, documents, text areas, etc.
`BLOB`	Binary large object. A binary string with a maximum length of 65,535 characters, used for storing binary files, images, sounds, etc.
Date and Time	
`DATE`	(yyyy-mm-dd) year, month, day; e.g., `2006-10-30` (Note: MySQL also allows you to store `0000-00-00` as a "dummy date.")
`DATETIME`	(`yyyy-mm-dd hh:mm:ss`) date and time; e.g., `2006-10-30 22:59:59`
`TIMESTAMP`	(`yyyy-mm-dd hh:mm:ss`) date and time; e.g., `1970-01-01` (date and time of last transaction on a row)
`TIME`	(`hh:mm:ss`) time; e.g., `10:30:58`
`YEAR`	(`yyyy | yy`) year in four or two digits; e.g., `1978` or `78`

B.3.3 Creating a Table

Creating a table is a little more complicated than creating the database. The `CREATE TABLE` statement is used to create a new table in the database. First, you must name the new table and then specify all the fields that will be included in the table as well as the data types and any other attributes. A data type can be an integer, a floating point (real) number such as 5.4, a string of characters, a date, a time, and so on. Not all databases will specify data types in the same way. To see what data types and attributes are available for MySQL, see Table B.3 or the MySQL documentation.

Designing your tables correctly is important and a subject that merits further research if you have not worked with databases before. See *http://databases.about.com/od/specificproducts/a/normalization.htm* for an excellent beginner's tutorial on database design. For now, here are some rules to keep in mind when designing the table.

1. Choose the right data type for your fields; for example, use integer types for primary keys, use float and double types for large numbers, use decimal or numeric types for currency, use the correct date format for times and dates, and give yourself ample field width for strings containing variable numbers of characters, such as names and addresses. If you are saving binary data, such as images and sounds, use a data type that supports large amounts of data, such as blob and text types. See Table B.3.

2. Give columns sensible and concise names. Make them unique within the table. Do not have duplicate columns in the same table, as shown here. These should not be three columns all headed with phone.

First_Name	Last_Name	Phone1	Phone2	Phone3
Joe	Blow	415-444-3333	333-111-1233	652-345-1123

3. Store only one value under each column heading in each row; for example, if you have a *Phone* field, you should not have "cell, home, business" all in one table cell, as shown here:

First_Name	Last_Name	Phone
Joe	Blow	415-444-3333, 333-111-1233, 652-345-1123

4. Create separate tables for each group of related items, and give each row a unique column or primary key, as shown here:

User Table:

Customer_Id	First_Name	Last_Name
1	Joe	Blow

Phone Table:

Customer_Id	Cell	Business	Home
1	415-444-3333	333-111-1233	652-345-1123

5. If you still have redundant data, put it in its own table and establish a relation between the tables with foreign keys.

FORMAT

```
CREATE TABLE table_name
(
column_name1 data_type,
column_name2 data_type,
column_name3 data_type    <-- no comma on the last entry
)
```

EXAMPLE B.26

```
1   mysql> CREATE DATABASE pets;
    Query OK, 1 row affected (0.24 sec)
2   mysql> USE pets;
3   mysql> CREATE TABLE dog
    -> ( name varchar(20),
    ->   owner varchar(20),
    ->   breed varchar(20),
    ->   sex char(1),
    ->   birth date,
    ->   death date
    -> );
    Query OK, 0 rows affected (0.16 sec)
4   mysql> describe dog;
    +-------+-------------+------+-----+---------+-------+
    | Field | Type        | Null | Key | Default | Extra |
    +-------+-------------+------+-----+---------+-------+
    | name  | varchar(20) | YES  |     | NULL    |       |
    | owner | varchar(20) | YES  |     | NULL    |       |
    | breed | varchar(20) | YES  |     | NULL    |       |
    | sex   | char(1)     | YES  |     | NULL    |       |
    | birth | date        | YES  |     | NULL    |       |
    | death | date        | YES  |     | NULL    |       |
    +-------+-------------+------+-----+---------+-------+
    6 rows in set (0.00 sec)
```

EXPLANATION

1. A database called *pets* is created.
2. The *pets* database is selected and entered.
3. A table called *dogs* is created with fields and their data types. The *name*, *owner*, and *breed* will consist of a varying number of up to 20 characters. The *sex* is one character, either *f* or *m* for female or male. The *birth* and *death* columns are assigned `date` type.
4. The `DESCRIBE` command is like the `SHOW` command. It displays the layout of the new table.

Now we can insert some data into the new table.

EXAMPLE B.27

```
mysql> INSERT INTO dog(name,owner,breed, sex, birth, death)
    -> VALUES('Fido','Mr. Jones', 'Mutt', 'M', '2004-11-12',
       '2006-04-02');
Query OK, 1 row affected (0.09 sec)
```

B.3.4 Creating a Key

In real life, people can be identified by Social Security numbers, driver's license numbers, and employee numbers; books can be identified by ISBN numbers; and a Web store order can be identified by a purchase order number. These identification numbers must be unique so that no two people have the same Social Security number, no two books have the same ISBN number, and so on. Keys are used to uniquely identify a record in a table. There are two types of keys: *primary* keys and *foreign* keys.

Primary Keys. Each table typically has a primary key. Primary keys are used to uniquely identify a record in the database. They must be unique, never change, occur only once per table, and are normally numeric types.

You can choose to manually generate this unique number for each record or let the database do it for you. If you let the database generate the primary key, it will generate a unique number, given a starting value (e.g., 1) and then for each new record, increment that number by 1. Even if a record is deleted, that number is never recycled. The database increments its internal counter, guaranteeing that each record will be given a unique "key."

To set a field as a primay key, use the attribute `PRIMARY KEY (field_name)`, and to tell the database to automatically create the unique number, use the `AUTO_INCREMENT` attribute following the field definition. The primary key cannot be null.

The following two examples describe a table called *categories* where the primary key is called *CategoryID*. It will automatically be incremented each time a new category is added to the table.

EXAMPLE B.28

```
mysql> USE northwind;
Database changed
mysql> DESCRIBE categories;
+--------------+-------------+------+-----+---------+----------------+
| Field        | Type        | Null | Key | Default | Extra          |
+--------------+-------------+------+-----+---------+----------------+
| CategoryID   | int(11)     |      | PRI | NULL    | auto_increment |
| CategoryName | varchar(15) |      | MUL |         |                |
| Description  | longtext    | YES  |     | NULL    |                |
| Picture      | longblob    | YES  |     | NULL    |                |
+--------------+-------------+------+-----+---------+----------------+
4 rows in set (0.09 sec)
```

EXPLANATION

The *CategoryID* is the primary key, an integer of up to 11 digits, which will be incremented by 1, initially set to `NULL` (no value). The first time a record is inserted into the database, the value will be 1.

EXAMPLE B.29

```
mysql> SELECT CategoryID, CategoryName FROM categories;
+------------+----------------+
| CategoryID | CategoryName   |
+------------+----------------+
|          1 | Beverages      |
|          2 | Condiments     |
|          3 | Confections    |
|          4 | Dairy Products |
|          5 | Grains/Cereals |
|          6 | Meat/Poultry   |
|          7 | Produce        |
|          8 | Seafood        |
+------------+----------------+
8 rows in set (0.16 sec)
```

EXPLANATION

The primary key is called *CategoryID*. It is used to uniquely identify the different categories in this table from the *northwind* database. When a new category is added to the table, the *CategoryID* will be automatically incremented by 1.

Foreign Keys. If a primary key is referenced in another table, it is called a foreign key. Foreign keys are used to create relation between tables. In the following example, two tables are described that both reference the *CategoryID* key, although it is primary in one and foreign in the other.

EXAMPLE B.30

```
    mysql> DESCRIBE categories;
    +--------------+------------+------+-----+---------+----------------+
    | Field        | Type       | Null | Key | Default | Extra          |
    +--------------+------------+------+-----+---------+----------------+
1   | CategoryID   | int(11)    |      | PRI | NULL    | auto_increment |
    | CategoryName | varchar(15)|      | MUL |         |                |
    | Description  | longtext   | YES  |     | NULL    |                |
    | Picture      | longblob   | YES  |     | NULL    |                |
    +--------------+------------+------+-----+---------+----------------+
    4 rows in set (0.00 sec)

    mysql> DESCRIBE products;
    +---------------+--------------+-----+-----+--------+---------------+
    | Field         | Type         | Null| Key | Default| Extra         |
    +---------------+--------------+-----+-----+--------+---------------
    | ProductID     | int(11)      |     | PRI | NULL   | auto_increment|
    | ProductName   | varchar(40)  |     | MUL |        |               |
    | SupplierID    | int(11)      | YES | MUL | NULL   |               |
2   | CategoryID    | int(11)      | YES | MUL | NULL   |               |
    | QuantityPerUnit| varchar(20) | YES |     | NULL   |               |
    | UnitPrice     | decimal(19,4)| YES |     | NULL   |               |
    | UnitsInStock  | smallint(6)  | YES |     | NULL   |               |
    | UnitsOnOrder  | smallint(6)  | YES |     | NULL   |               |
    | ReorderLevel  | smallint(6)  | YES |     | NULL   |               |
    | Discontinued  | tinyint(4)   |     |     | 0      |               |
    +---------------+--------------+-----+-----+--------+---------------+
       10 rows in set (0.00 sec)
```

EXPLANATION

1. The *categories* table has a primary key field called *CategoryID*.
2. The *products* table has its own primary key (*ProductID*) in addition to a foreign key called *CategoryID*. If a primary key is referenced in another table, it is called a foreign key.

B.3.5 Relations

A major advantage of the relational database system is the ability to create relations between tables. Simply put, a relation is a connection between a field of one table and a field of another. This relation allows you to look up related records in the database.

The operation of matching rows from one table to another using one or more column values is called a *join*. There are several types of join statements, such as *full joins*, *cross joins*, *left joins*, and so on, but let's start with a simple joining of two tables, called an *inner join*.

Tables can be related to each other with keys. As we discussed earlier, a primary key is a column with a unique value for each row. A matching key in a second table is called a foreign key. With these keys, you can bind data together across tables without repeating all of the data in every table where a certain condition is met.

Consider the previous Example B.30, in which two tables from the *northwind* database are described. One table is called *categories* and the other called *products*. *CategoryID* is a primary key field in the *categories* table, and it is a foreign key in the *products* table. The *CategoryID* key is used to create a relationship between the two tables.

Two Tables with a Common Key. As discussed previously, both the *categories* table and the *products* table have a *CategoryID* key with the same values, making it possible to create a relation between the two tables.

Let's create a relation in which all the product names are listed if they are in the *Seafood* category. Because every product in the *products* table falls into one of the eight categories in the *categories* table, the two tables can be bound by their common *CategoryID*.

EXAMPLE B.31

```
mysql> SELECT CategoryID, CategoryName FROM categories;
+------------+----------------+
| categoryID | categoryName   |
+------------+----------------+
|          1 | Beverages      |
|          2 | Condiments     |
|          3 | Confections    |
|          4 | Dairy Products |
|          5 | Grains/Cereals |
|          6 | Meat/Poultry   |
|          7 | Produce        |
|          8 | Seafood        |
+------------+----------------+
8 rows in set (0.00 sec)
```

EXAMPLE B.31 (CONTINUED)

```
mysql> SELECT CategoryID, ProductName FROM products;
(Partial Output)
+------------+----------------------------------+
| CategoryID | ProductName                      |
+------------+----------------------------------+
|          1 | Chai                             |
|          1 | Chang                            |
|          2 | Aniseed Syrup                    |
|          2 | Chef Anton's Cajun Seasoning     |
|          2 | Chef Anton's Gumbo Mix           |
|          2 | Grandma's Boysenberry Spread     |
|          7 | Uncle Bob's Organic Dried Pears  |
|          2 | Northwoods Cranberry Sauce       |
|          6 | Mishi Kobe Niku                  |
|          8 | Ikura                            |
|          4 | Queso Cabrales                   |
|          4 | Queso Manchego La Pastora        |
|          8 | Konbu                            |
|          7 | Tofu                             |
|          2 | Genen Shouyu                     |
```

EXPLANATION

This example displays columns from both the *categories* table and the *products* table. In the *categories* table, the *CategoryID* is the primary field and uniquely identifies all other fields in the table. In the *products* table, the *CategoryID* is a foreign key and is repeated many times for all the products.

Using a Fully Qualified Name and a Dot to Join the Tables. When querying more than one table, a dot is used to fully qualify the columns by their table name to avoid potential ambiguity if two tables have a field with the same name, as shown in Example B.32.

EXAMPLE B.32

```
mysql> SELECT CategoryName, ProductName FROM categories, products
    -> WHERE products.CategoryID = 8 AND categories.CategoryID = 8;
+--------------+---------------------------------+
| CategoryName | ProductName                     |
+--------------+---------------------------------+
| Seafood      | Ikura                           |
| Seafood      | Konbu                           |
| Seafood      | Carnarvon Tigers                |
| Seafood      | Nord-Ost Matjeshering           |
| Seafood      | Inlagd Sill                     |
| Seafood      | Gravad lax                      |
| Seafood      | Boston Crab Meat                |
```

EXAMPLE B.32 (CONTINUED)

```
| Seafood       | Jack's New England Clam Chowder |
| Seafood       | Rogede sild                     |
| Seafood       | Spegesild                       |
| Seafood       | Escargots de Bourgogne          |
| Seafood       | Röd Kaviar                      |
+---------------+---------------------------------+
12 rows in set (0.00 sec)
```

EXPLANATION

In the `SELECT`, two tables (separated by commas) will be joined by the *CategoryID* field. Because the field name is the same in both tables, the table name is prepended to the field name with a dot, as `products.CategoryId` and `categories.CategoryId`. In the `WHERE` clause, the two tables are connected if both tables have a *CategoryID* equal to 8.

Aliases. To make things a little easier by typing less with complicated queries, SQL provides an aliasing mechanism that allows you to use symbolic names for columns and tables. The alias is defined with the `AS` keyword and consists of a single character or an abbreviated string. When the alias is used in the `WHERE` clause to represent a table name, it is appended with a dot and the name of the field being selected from that table.

FORMAT

(Column Alias)

```
SELECT column_name AS column_alias_name
FROM table_name
```

(Table Alias)

```
SELECT column_name
FROM table_name AS table_alias_name
```

EXAMPLE B.33

```
mysql> SELECT CategoryName as Foods FROM categories;
+----------------+
| Foods          |
+----------------+
| Beverages      |
| Condiments     |
| Confections    |
| Dairy Products |
| Grains/Cereals |
| Meat/Poultry   |
| Produce        |
| Seafood        |
+----------------+
8 rows in set (0.00 sec)
```

EXPLANATION

The column name from table *categories* was named *CategoryName*. An alias called *Foods* is created by using the `AS` keyword after *CategoryName*. Now when the `SELECT` returns a result-set, the output will show *Foods* as the name of the column.

EXAMPLE B.34

```
mysql> SELECT ProductName FROM products AS p, categories AS c WHERE
    -> p.CategoryID = c.CategoryID AND c.CategoryName="SeaFood";
+----------------------------------+
| ProductName                      |
+----------------------------------+
| Ikura                            |
| Konbu                            |
| Carnarvon Tigers                 |
| Nord-Ost Matjeshering            |
| Inlagd Sill                      |
| Gravad lax                       |
| Boston Crab Meat                 |
| Jack's New England Clam Chowder  |
| Rogede sild                      |
| Spegesild                        |
| Escargots de Bourgogne           |
| Röd Kaviar                       |
+----------------------------------+
12 rows in set (0.00 sec)
```

EXPLANATION

This example might look a little tricky at first. The table named *products* is given an alias called *p*, and the table name *categories* is given the alias *c*. These aliases are short names, making it easier to type the query when more than one table is involved; for example, instead of typing `products.CategoryID`, we can type `p.CategoryID`, and `categories.CategoryName` can be referenced as `c.CategoryName`.

B.3.6 Altering a Table

When you alter a table, you redefine its structure by adding or dropping new columns, keys, indexes, and tables. You can also use the `ALTER` command to change column names, types, and the table name.

FORMAT

```
ALTER TABLE tablename
ADD column datatype
```

Example:

```
alter table artist add column ArtDate date;
alter table artist drop column "Address";
```

EXAMPLE B.35

```
    use pets;
1   mysql> ALTER TABLE dog ADD pet_id int(11);
    Query OK, 0 rows affected (0.13 sec)
    Records: 0  Duplicates: 0  Warnings: 0
2   mysql> ALTER TABLE dog MODIFY column pet_id int(11)
    --> auto_increment primary key;
    Query OK, 1 row affected (0.11 sec)
    Records: 1  Duplicates: 0  Warnings: 0
3   mysql> describe dog;
    +--------+-------------+------+-----+---------+----------------+
    | Field  | Type        | Null | Key | Default | Extra          |
    +--------+-------------+------+-----+---------+----------------+
    | name   | varchar(20) | YES  |     | NULL    |                |
    | owner  | varchar(20) | YES  |     | NULL    |                |
    | breed  | varchar(20) | YES  |     | NULL    |                |
    | sex    | char(1)     | YES  |     | NULL    |                |
    | birth  | date        | YES  |     | NULL    |                |
    | death  | date        | YES  |     | NULL    |                |
    | pet_id | int(11)     |      | PRI | NULL    | auto_increment |
    +--------+-------------+------+-----+---------+----------------+
    7 rows in set (0.00 sec)
    mysql> select * from dog;
+-------+-------------+-------+-----+----------+----------+--------+
| name  | owner       | breed | sex | birth    | death    | pet_id |
+-------+-------------+-------+-----+----------+----------+--------
| Fido  | Mr. Jones   | Mutt  | M   | 2004-11-12| 2006-04-02|     1 |
| Lassie| Tommy Rettig| Collie| F   | 2006-01-10| NULL     |      2 |
+-------+-------------+-------+-----+----------+----------+--------+
2 rows in set (0.00 sec)
```

EXPLANATION

1 The `ALTER` command will change the table by adding a new field, called *pet_id*, an integer of 11 digits.

2 Once the *pet_id* field has been created, the `ALTER` command is used again to make this a primary key that will automatically be incremented each time a record is added.

3 The `DESCRIBE` command shows the structure of the table after it was changed. A primary key has been added.

B.3.7 Dropping a Table

To drop a table is relatively simple. Just use the `drop` command and the name of the table:

```
mysql> drop table dog;
Query OK, 20 rows affected (0.11 sec)
```

B.3.8 Dropping a Database

To drop a database, use the `drop database` command:

```
mysql> drop database pets;
Query OK, 1 row affected (0.45 sec)
```

B.4 SQL Functions

The following functions are used to alter or format the output of a SQL query. Functions are provided for strings, numbers, dates, server and information, and so on. They return a result set. Functions are vendor specific, meaning functions supported by MySQL might not be supported by Microsoft SQL Server. See the MySQL documenation for a list of all functions supported.

When using `SELECT` with a function, the function, as it was called, is displayed as the name of the column in the result set as shown in Example B.36.

EXAMPLE B.36

```
1   mysql> SELECT avg(UnitPrice)
    FROM order_details;
    +----------------+
    | avg(UnitPrice) |
    +----------------+
    |    26.21851972 |
    +----------------+
    1 row in set (0.01 sec)

2   mysql> SELECT avg(UnitPrice) as 'Average Price'
    FROM order_details;
    +---------------+
    | Average Price |
    +---------------+
    |   26.21851972 |
    +---------------+
    1 row in set (0.00 sec)
```

EXPLANATION

1 The function is displayed as the name of the column.
2 You can use the AS keyword to create an alias or another name for the column where the function displays the result set.

B.4.1 Numeric Functions

Suppose you want to get the sum of all the orders or the average cost of a set of items or to count all the rows in a table based on a certain condition. The aggregate functions will return a single value based on a set of other values. If used among many other expressions in the item list of a SELECT statement, the SELECT must have a GROUP BY clause. No GROUP BY clause is required if the aggregate function is the only value retrieved by the SELECT statement. The functions and their syntax are listed in Table B.4.

Table B.4 Aggregate Functions

Function	*What It Does*
AVG()	Computes and returns the average value of a column.
COUNT(*expression*)	Counts the rows defined by the expression.
COUNT()	Counts all rows in a table.
MIN()	Returns the minimum value in a column.
MAX()	Returns the maximum value in a column by the expression.
SUM()	Returns the sum of all the values in a column.

EXAMPLE B.37

```
1  mysql> select count(*) from products;
   +----------+
   | count(*) |
   +----------+
   |       81 |
   +----------+
   1 row in set (0.00 sec)

   mysql> SELECT count(*) as 'Number of Rows' FROM products;
   +----------------+
   | Number of Rows |
   +----------------+
   |             81 |
   +----------------+
   1 row in set (0.00 sec)
```

EXPLANATION

1 The `COUNT()` function counts all rows in a table.

EXAMPLE B.38

```
1   mysql> SELECT avg(UnitPrice)
    FROM order_details;
    +----------------+
    | avg(UnitPrice) |
    +----------------+
    |    26.21851972 |
    +----------------+
    1 row in set (0.01 sec)

2   mysql> SELECT FORMAT(avg(UnitPrice),2) as 'Average Price'
    FROM  order_details;
    +---------------+
    | Average Price |
    +---------------+
    | 26.22         |
    +---------------+
    1 row in set (0.00 sec)
```

EXPLANATION

1 The `AVG()` function computes and returns the average value of a column, called *UnitPrice*.

2 The `FORMAT` function returns the result of the `AVG()` function with a precision of two decimal places.

Using *GROUP BY*. The `GROUP BY` clause can be used with a `SELECT` to collect all the data across multiple records and group the results by one or more columns. This is useful with the aggregate functions, such as `SUM`, `COUNT`, `MIN`, or `MAX`. See the following two examples.

EXAMPLE B.39

```
mysql> select CategoryID, SUM(UnitsInStock) as 'Total Units in Stock'
    -> FROM products
    -> GROUP BY CategoryID;
+------------+----------------------+
| CategoryID | Total Units in Stock |
+------------+----------------------+
|       NULL |                    0 |
|          1 |                  559 |
|          2 |                  507 |
|          3 |                  386 |
|          4 |                  393 |
|          5 |                  308 |
|          6 |                  165 |
|          7 |                  100 |
|          8 |                  701 |
+------------+----------------------+
9 rows in set (0.00 sec)
```

EXAMPLE B.40

```
mysql> select C.CategoryName,
    -> SUM(P.unitsInsStock) AS Units
    -> FROM products as P
    -> join categories AS C ON C.CategoryID=
    -> P.CategoryID Group By C.CategoryName;
+----------------+-------+
| CategoryName   | Units |
+----------------+-------+
| Beverages      |   559 |
| Condiments     |   507 |
| Confections    |   386 |
| Dairy Products |   393 |
| Grains/Cereals |   308 |
| Meat/Poultry   |   165 |
| Produce        |   100 |
| Seafood        |   701 |
+----------------+-------+
8 rows in set (0.00 sec)
```

B.4.2 String Functions

SQL provides a number of basic string functions, as listed in Table B.5.

Table B.5 MySQL String Functions

Function	*What It Does*
`CONCAT(string1,string2,...)`[a]	Combines column values, or variables, together into one string.
`LOWER(string)`	Converts a string to all lowercase characters.
`SUBSTRING(string, position)`	Extracts a portion of a string (see Example B.41).
`TRANSLATE`	Converts a string from one character set to another.
`TRIM(' string ');`	Removes leading characters, trailing characters, or both from a character string.
`UPPER(string)`	Converts a string to all uppercase characters (see Example B.41).

a. SQL99 defines a concatenation operator (| |) to use with the `CONCATENATE()` function. MySQL uses the `concat()` function shown in Table B.5.

EXAMPLE B.41

```
mysql> select upper(CompanyName) as 'Company' from shippers;
+------------------+
| Company          |
+------------------+
| SPEEDY EXPRESS   |
| UNITED PACKAGE   |
| FEDERAL SHIPPING |
+------------------+
3 rows in set (0.00 sec)

mysql> select lower(CompanyName) as 'Company' FROM shippers;
+------------------+
| Company          |
+------------------+
| speedy express   |
| united package   |
| federal shipping |
+------------------+
3 rows in set (0.00 sec)
```

B.4.3 Date and Time Functions

To get the date and time, MySQL provides the functions shown in Table B.6.

Table B.6 MySQL Date and Time Functions

Function	***Example***

`NOW()`	`select NOW()`
	`--> 2006-03-23 20:52:58`
	(See Example B.42.)

`CURDATE()`	`select CURDATE();`
	`--> '2006-12-15'`
	(See Example B.42.)

`CURTIME()`	`select CURTIME();`
	`--> '23:50:26'`
	(See Example B.42.)

`DAYOFYEAR(date)`	`select DAYOFYEAR('2006-12-15');` `--> 349`
`DAYOFMONTH(date)`	`select DAYOFMONTH('2006-12-15');` `--> 15`
`DAYOFWEEK(date)`	`select DAYOFWEEK('2006-12-15');` `--> 6`
`WEEKDAY(date)`	`select WEEKDAY('2006-12-15');` `--> 4`
`MONTHNAME(date)`	`select MONTHNAME('2006-12-15');` `--> December`
`DAYNAME(date)`	`select DAYNAME('2006-12-15');` `--> Friday`
`YEAR(date)`	`select YEAR('2006-12-15');` `--> 2006`
`QUARTER(date)`	`select QUARTER('2006-12-15');` `--> 4`

EXAMPLE B.42

```
mysql> select NOW();
+---------------------+
| NOW()               |
+---------------------+
| 2006-03-21 00:32:37 |
+---------------------+
1 row in set (0.00 sec)

mysql> select CURDATE();
+----------------+
|    CURDATE()   |
+----------------+
| 2006-03-21     |
+----------------+
1 row in set (0.03 sec)

mysql> select CURTIME();
+----------------+
|    CURTIME()   |
+----------------+
| 00:12:46       |
+----------------+
1 row in set (0.01 sec)
```

Formatting the Date and Time. When retrieving dates and times from a table, you might find you want to format the output. For example, when selecting the dates of the orders from the orders table in the *northwind* database, the result set is not user friendly. Date values in SQL are always saved in `MM/DD/YY(YY)` format. The `DATE_FORMAT()` and `TIME_FORMAT()` functions (see Example B.43) are provided with a list of parameters (see Table B.7) used to specify how the output should be displayed.

EXAMPLE B.43

```
mysql> select DATE_FORMAT('2006-03-23', '%W %M %d, %Y') as Today;
+-------------------------+
| Today                   |
+-------------------------+
| Thursday March 23, 2006 |
+-------------------------+
1 row in set (0.00 sec)
```

EXAMPLE B.43 (CONTINUED)

```
mysql> select DATE_FORMAT(OrderDate,'%M %e, %Y - %l:%i %p')
              FROM orders LIMIT 5;

+---------------------------------------------+
| DATE_FORMAT(OrderDate,'%M %e, %Y - %l:%i %p') |
+---------------------------------------------+
| July 4, 1996 - 12:00 AM                     |
| July 5, 1996 - 12:00 AM                     |
| July 8, 1996 - 12:00 AM                     |
| July 8, 1996 - 12:00 AM                     |
| July 9, 1996 - 12:00 AM                     |
+---------------------------------------------+
5 rows in set (0.00 sec)
```

Table B.7 `DATE_FORMAT()` and `TIME_FORMAT()`

Parameter	*What It Means*
`%a`	Weekday abbreviation (Sun, Mon, Tues, etc.)
`%b`	Month name abbreviation (Jan, Feb, Mar, etc.)
`%c`	Month (1–12)
`%d`	Two-digit day of the month (01–31)
`%D`	Day with a suffix (30th, 31st)
`%e`	Day of the month (1–31)
`%f`	Microseconds (000000..999999)
`%H`	Hour (00..23)
`%h`	Hour (01..12)
`%i`	Minutes, numeric (00..59)
`%I`	Hour (01–12)
`%j`	Day of year (001–366)
`%k`	Hour (0..23)
`%l`	Hour (1–12)
`%m`	Month with a leading 0 (01, 06, etc.)
`%M`	Month name (March, April, May, etc.)
`%p`	AM/PM

Table B.7 `DATE_FORMAT()` and `TIME_FORMAT()` (continued)

Parameter	***What It Means***
`%r`	Time, 12-hour (hh:mm:ss followed by AM or PM)
`%S`	Seconds (00..59)
`%s`	Seconds (00..59)
`%T`	Time, 24-hour (hh:mm:ss)
`%U`	Week (00..53) starting with Sunday
`%u`	Week (00..53) starting with Monday
`%v`	Week (01..53) starting with Monday
`%V`	Week (01..53) starting with Sunday
`%W`	Weekday (Sunday, Monday, etc.)
`%w`	Day of the week (0 = Sunday..6 = Saturday)
`%Y`	Year (1999, 2007)
`%y`	Two-digit year (99, 07)
`%%`	A literal % character

The MySQL *EXTRACT* Command. The `EXTRACT` command is an example of a MySQL extension, not described in the SQL standard. It allows you to extract different parts of a date or time, as shown in Table B.8.

Table B.8 Date and Time Parts

Type	***Format***
`SECOND`	SECONDS
`MINUTE`	MINUTES
`HOUR`	HOURS
`DAY`	DAYS
`MONTH`	MONTHS
`YEAR`	YEARS (see Example B.44)
`MINUTE SECOND`	"MINUTES:SECONDS"
`HOUR_MINUTE`	"HOURS:MINUTES"

Table B.8 Date and Time Parts (continued)

Type	*Format*
DAY_HOUR	"DAYS HOURS"
YEAR_MONTH	"YEARS-MONTHS"
HOUR_SECOND	"HOURS:MINUTES:SECONDS"
DAY_MINUTE	"DAYS HOURS:MINUTES"
DAY_SECOND	"DAYS HOURS:MINUTES:SECONDS"

EXAMPLE B.44

```
mysql> select EXTRACT(YEAR FROM NOW());
+--------------------------+
| EXTRACT(YEAR FROM NOW()) |
+--------------------------+
|                     2006 |
+--------------------------+
1 row in set (0.03 sec)
```

B.5 Appendix Summary

In this appendix, you learned how to use the SQL language to create database schemas and how to insert, update, retrieve, alter, and delete records from a database.

B.6 What You Should Know

Now that you have finished this appendix, you should be able to answer the following questions:

1. How do you retrieve all the records from a database table?
2. How do you retrieve a select set of records or a single record from a table based on specific criteria?
3. How do you select and sort records in a database?
4. How do you select a range of rows from a database?
5. How do you create a database?
6. How do you create database tables?

7. How do you assign a primary key to a field?

8. How are records inserted into the database table?

9. How are records updated in a table?

10. How do you delete a record?

EXERCISE B

1. Go to the MySQL console and use the `show` command to list all the databases. Use the `mysql` database. Now display all of its tables.

2. Create a new database called `school`. Once you create the database, you need to be able to use it:

   ```
   use school;
   ```

3. Create a table called `student`. The table will consist of the following fields:

   ```
   FirstName
   LastName
   Email
   CellPhone
   Major
   GPA
   StartDate
   ```
   `StudentId` (the primary key)

   The following information is the type of data you will use to define your table. Go to the Web and look for a table similar to this to use as your guide.

Data Type	Description

`integer(size)`
`int(size)`
`smallint(size)`
`tinyint(size)`
	Holds integers only

   The maximum number of digits is specified by *`size`* in parentheses.

`decimal(size,d)` `numeric(size,d)`	Holds numbers with fractions.

   The maximum number of digits is specified in *`size`*. The maximum number of digits to the right of the decimal is specified in *`d`*.

`char(size)`	Holds a fixed-length string (can contain letters, numbers, and special characters). The fixed size is specified by *`size`* in parentheses.

`varchar(size)`	Holds a variable-length string (can contain letters, numbers, and special characters). The maximum size is specified by *`size`* in parentheses.
`date(yyyymmdd)`	Holds a date.

4. Use the SQL `describe` statement to display the information you used to create the `school` database.

5. Insert three rows into the table:

Row 1:
FirstName: John
LastName: Doe
Email: johndoe@smileyface.edu
CellPhone: 408-333-3456
Major: CIS
GPA: 2.8
StartDate: 09/22/2004 (use the correct date format!)
StudentId: 1

Row 2:
FirstName: Mary
LastName: Chin
Email: mchin@qmail.com
CellPhone: 408-204-1234
Major: Biology
GPA: 3.3
StartDate: 06/22/2003
StudentId: 2

Row 3:
FirstName: Sadish
LastName: Pamel
Email: sadi@univ_ab.edu
CellPhone: 415-204-1234
Major: CIS
GPA: 3.9
StartDate: 06/22/2003
StudentId: 2

6. Use the `show` commands to display all the fields.

7. Use `select` statements to display the following (write your query in the blank line):
   a. The data in all of the columns
   b. The first and last names of the students
   c. The student's first and last names and major
   d. The student's cellphone and e-mail addresses
   e. Any distinct majors
   f. Only 2 rows

8. a. Select all students who have a GPA over 3.0.
   b. Select all students who have a GPA between 3.0 and 4.0.
   c. Select students whose cellphones are in the 408 area code.
   d. Display rows for students who started in 2003.
   e. Select student first and last names who are majoring in CIS and have a GPA over 3.5.
   f. Select student first name and e-mail address if the e-mail address ends in `.com`.

9. a. Insert a new entry into the table.
   b. Sort the student table by last names.
   c. Sort the student table by GPA in descending order.

10. Change Mary's phone number to 650-123-4563.

The next three questions deal with SQL functions:

11. Find the average GPA for all the students.

12. Find the number of rows in the table.

13. Print today's date using a SQL function.

appendix

C

Perl and Biology

C.1 What Is Bioinformatics?

"The avalanche of genome data grows daily. The new challenge will be to use this vast reservoir of data to explore how DNA and proteins work with each other and the environment to create complex, dynamic, living systems. Systematic studies of function on a grand scale—functional genomics—will be the focus of biological explorations in this century and beyond..." *http://www.ornl.gov/sci/techresources/Human_Genome/project/*. Bioinformatics refers to the processing of these vast amounts of biological data on a computer.

In the past decade, computers have become more and more important in biological research, especially since 2003 when the Human Genome Project completed its goal to identify all the genes in human DNA. (See the goals of the project at *http://www.ornl.gov/sci/techresources/Human_Genome/home.shtml*.) Programs can now analyze large amounts of data quickly, and Perl has become one of the most, if not the most, popular language used in the field of bioinformatics for tasks such as accessing sequence data from local and remote databases, transforming sequence files, manipulating sequence data, obtaining statistics, modeling biological systems, etc.

Many biologists may prefer to write their own functions to handle the massive amounts of data and may find that downloading and using the *BioPerl* modules will provide tools to speed the development of their programs. Not all Perl programmers have a strong background in biology any more than all biolgists understand Perl. Therefore, the following overview briefly describes some of the biology and some of the ways Perl is used to manipulate symbols that represent DNA sequences and proteins with and without the BioPerl modules.

C.2 A Little Background on DNA

DNA is the stuff of which every living thing is made. It contains the genetic instructions to make me and you who we are. It is also reponsible for creating proteins. Proteins are of great interest because they control cell activity and how the cell functions; i.e., how you digest your food, fight off infection, get oxygen to your muscles, organs, etc.

In order to use Perl to work with DNA, here are some of the terms you will encounter:

1. Nucleotides, or bases
2. Base pairing
3. Reverse complement
4. Sequencing
5. Proteins and amino acids
6. RNA molecues and transcription
7. BLAST and FASTA

DNA is found in the nucleus of our cells, called a double helix because it is shaped like a spiral ladder, and consists of thousands of genes. The rungs of the ladder are made up of four chemicals, called **nucleotides, or bases**, that carry the information used to make a body and to keep it running. Each of the four bases is named with a letter, G (guanine), A (adenine), T (thymine), or C (cytosene). All of the letters in one cell make up the human genome, joined end to end, to hold a complete set of instructions for coding all life on Earth.

In a complete DNA helix, hydrogen bonds always link the As with the Ts and the Gs with the Cs. When new cells are made, different letters of the DNA alphabet are combined, but even with just four letters, the DNA alphabet spells out all the information you need to create new cells. (If you have one strand of DNA, the opposite strand is the reverse complement of the other strand.) The order of the DNA bases is called the **sequence**. The sequence of the four bases in DNA can spell all the instructions to create cells for your whole body and determine individual hereditary characteristics. "If you wrote down all of the bases in one cell, you would fill a stack of 1,000 phone books with As, Ts, Gs and Cs. Scientists trying to locate small sections of DNA out of the whole genome have to flip through billions of bases to find what they want! Sometimes this takes years." (From *http://www.thetech.or/exhitits/online/genome.*) Genbank, the Genetic Sequence Data Bank (*http://www.ncbi.nlm.nih.gov/Genbank*), holds most of the known sequence data.

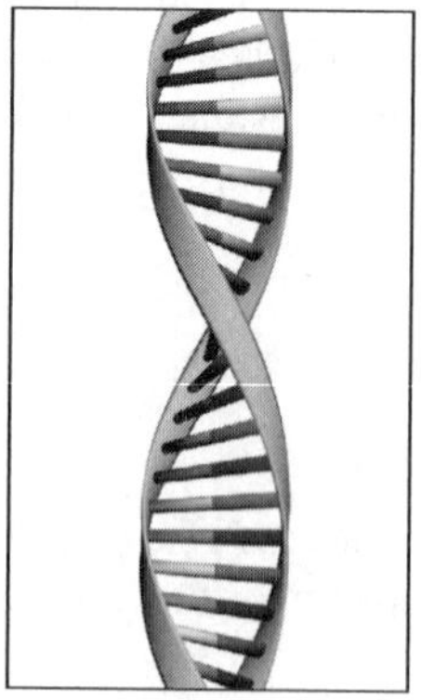

Figure C.1 The double helix and nucleotides, or bases.

What is RNA? RNA is like DNA but is only one strand rather than two and isn't confined to the nucleus. RNA has the same pairing scheme as DNA, except the T (thiamine) is replaced with a U (uracil). There are different types of RNA; one type is the messenger that transports DNA coded instructions from outside the nucleus of the cell to message centers, areas of the cell where the information is needed to create proteins. Proteins are long chains of differently shaped molecules called amino acids. When you eat food, the body digests the food and breaks it down into amino acids, which can then be reused by the cells. The transfer RNA helps translate the coded instructions into amino acids. The term "transcription" is used to describe the process where DNA makes RNA (ribonucleic acid), and "translation" is when the RNA translates the code into proteins.

BLAST (Basic Local Alignment Search Tool) is one of the most popular biological search tools today. It is used to test a sequence by issuing a query and testing it against a library of known sequences. It provides a file with scores showing how the sequence measures up statistically. FASTA files are simple text files with one header line starting with a ">" character and the name of the DNA or gene from which it is produced, followed by lines of nucleotide or amino-acid sequence data.

Understanding some of these terms will be helpful when looking at examples in this appendix and on the Web.

C.3 Some Perl Examples

The following examples are very basic. They demonstrate how basic Perl can be used to perform a reversed complement of a sequence using the *tr* function, how to search for a pattern or motif from a file using regular expressions, and a third example to filter the bases from a sequence using regular expressions in a loop.

EXAMPLE C.1

```
# Sequence--Reverse Complement
$dna_strand='GGGGaaaaaaaattAtAtat';
$dna_strand=reverse($dna_strand);
print "The original DNA strand is $dna_strand\n";
$dna_strand =~ tr/ACGTacgt/TGCAtgca/;

print "The reversed complement is ",$dna_strand,"\n";

(Output)
The original DNA strand is tatAtAttaaaaaaaaGGGG
The reversed complement is ataTaTaattttttttCCCC
```

EXAMPLE C.2

```
File name: fasta
>testsrings
MTKKIGLFYGTQTGKTESVAEIIRDEFGNDVVTLHDVSQAEVTDLNDYQYLIIGCPTWNI
GELQSDWEGLYSELDDVDFNGKLVAYFGTGDQIGYADNFQDAIGILEEKISQRGGKTVGY
WSTDGYDFNDSKALRNGKFVGLALDEDNQSDLTDDRIKSWVAQLKSEFG

(Perl script)
 # Finding a pattern/motif in a protein file
open(PFH, "fasta") or die "Can't open file: $!\n";
$pattern="QTGK";
while($string=<PFH>){
   print "$pattern found on line $..\n"
            if $string =~/$pattern/i;
}
close(PFH);

(Output)
QTGK found on line 1.
```

EXAMPLE C.3

```
# Filter sequence from any unwanted characters
# Prints just nucleotides
open(JF, "junkseq") or die;

@line=<JF>;
@chars =  split(//,$line[0]);
print "Original sequence with junk\n";
print @chars,"\n\n";
print "Cleaned up sequence\n";
 for($i=0; $i <= $#chars; $i++){
        if($chars[$i] =~ /[Aa]|[Tt]|[Gg]|[Cc]/){
               print uc "$chars[$i]";
        }
}
print "\n";

(Output)
Original sequence with junk
tg^c*ttcgh#ittgcatgggttc'tt:igg!tt~8$gttcggsstt$$@^ucgte+2%%&tagc

Cleaned up sequence


TGCTTCGTTGCATGGGTTCTTGGTTGTTCGGTTCGTTAGC
```

C.4 What Is BioPerl?

BioPerl is an open source (essentially free) toolkit of over 500 Perl modules that enable scripts to analyze large quatities of data for Web-based systems. "Bioperl provides reusable Perl modules that facilitate writing Perl scripts for sequence manipulation, accessing of databases using a range of data formats, and execution and parsing of the results of various molecular biology programs including Blast, clustalw, TCoffee, genscan, ESTscan, and HMMER." BioPerl also supports accessing remote databases as well as creating indices for accessing local databases. BioPerl lets you build programs that can analyze huge quantities of sequence data. It does require familiarity with object-oriented Perl and does not provide complete ready-made programs; it provides a set of tools to simplify common bioinformatic tasks. BioPerl is always being developed and maintained by a large number of programmers.

For complete installation instructions, see the BioPerl home page at *www.bioperl.org*. The easiest way to install BioPerl is to use the PPM manager provided by ActiveState for all major operating systems or by upacking the *tar* file and entering the following commands:

```
>gunzip bioperl-1.2.tar.gz
>tar xvf bioperl-1.2.tar
>cd bioperl-1.2
```

Now issue the *make* commands:

```
>perl Makefile.PL
>make
>make test
```

For downloads and information, go to the BioPerl Web site shown in Figure C.2.

Figure C.2 Installing bioperl with PPM (ActiveState).

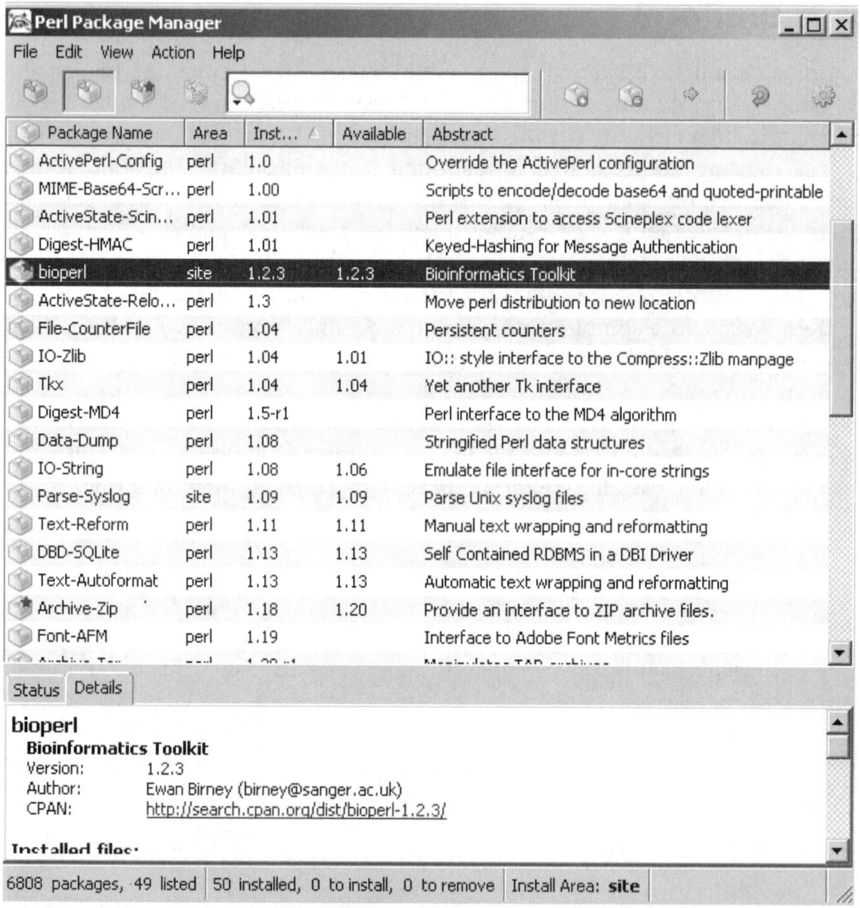

Figure C.3 `bioperl` is a large set of modules as shown here from a Windows32 system.

```
Directory of C:\ActivePerl\site\lib\Bio

07/03/2007  07:14 PM    <DIR>          .
07/03/2007  07:14 PM    <DIR>          ..
07/03/2007  07:14 PM    <DIR>          Align
07/03/2007  07:14 PM    <DIR>          AlignIO
07/03/2007  07:14 PM            14,301 AlignIO.pm
07/03/2007  07:14 PM            23,350 AnalysisI.pm
07/03/2007  07:14 PM             6,042 AnalysisParserI.pm
07/03/2007  07:14 PM             6,422 AnalysisResultI.pm
07/03/2007  07:14 PM             2,798 AnnotatableI.pm
07/03/2007  07:14 PM    <DIR>          Annotation
07/03/2007  07:14 PM             5,004 AnnotationCollectionI.pm
07/03/2007  07:14 PM             4,654 AnnotationI.pm
07/03/2007  07:14 PM    <DIR>          Assembly
```

```
07/03/2007  07:14 PM    <DIR>          Biblio
07/03/2007  07:14 PM            11,153 Biblio.pm
07/03/2007  07:14 PM    <DIR>          Cluster
07/03/2007  07:14 PM             4,100 ClusterI.pm
07/03/2007  07:14 PM    <DIR>          ClusterIO
07/03/2007  07:14 PM             7,792 ClusterIO.pm
07/03/2007  07:14 PM    <DIR>          Coordinate
07/03/2007  07:14 PM    <DIR>          Das
07/03/2007  07:14 PM            13,084 DasI.pm
07/03/2007  07:14 PM    <DIR>          DB
07/03/2007  07:14 PM             2,738 DBLinkContainerI.pm
07/03/2007  07:14 PM             2,882 DescribableI.pm
07/03/2007  07:14 PM    <DIR>          Event
07/03/2007  07:14 PM    <DIR>          Expression
07/03/2007  07:14 PM    <DIR>          Factory
07/03/2007  07:14 PM             5,327 FeatureHolderI.pm
07/03/2007  07:14 PM    <DIR>          Graphics
07/03/2007  07:14 PM             2,793 Graphics.pm
07/03/2007  07:14 PM             2,530 IdCollectionI.pm
07/03/2007  07:14 PM             5,146 IdentifiableI.pm
07/03/2007  07:14 PM    <DIR>          Index
07/03/2007  07:14 PM    <DIR>          LiveSeq
07/03/2007  07:14 PM            10,986 LocatableSeq.pm
07/03/2007  07:14 PM    <DIR>          Location
07/03/2007  07:14 PM            12,304 LocationI.pm
07/03/2007  07:14 PM    <DIR>          Map
07/03/2007  07:14 PM    <DIR>          MapIO
07/03/2007  07:14 PM             5,329 MapIO.pm
07/03/2007  07:14 PM    <DIR>          Matrix
07/03/2007  07:14 PM    <DIR>          Ontology
07/03/2007  07:14 PM    <DIR>          OntologyIO
07/03/2007  07:14 PM             8,235 OntologyIO.pm
07/03/2007  07:14 PM            17,252 Perl.pm
07/03/2007  07:14 PM    <DIR>          Phenotype
07/03/2007  07:14 PM            24,568 PrimarySeq.pm
07/03/2007  07:14 PM            20,679 PrimarySeqI.pm
07/03/2007  07:14 PM             7,472 Range.pm
07/03/2007  07:14 PM            11,972 RangeI.pm
07/03/2007  07:14 PM    <DIR>          Root
07/03/2007  07:14 PM    <DIR>          Search
07/03/2007  07:14 PM             5,435 SearchDist.pm
07/03/2007  07:14 PM    <DIR>          SearchIO
07/03/2007  07:14 PM            15,069 SearchIO.pm
07/03/2007  07:14 PM    <DIR>          Seq
07/03/2007  07:14 PM            37,739 Seq.pm
07/03/2007  07:14 PM             3,299 SeqAnalysisParserI.pm
07/03/2007  07:14 PM    <DIR>          SeqFeature
07/03/2007  07:14 PM            17,041 SeqFeatureI.pm
07/03/2007  07:14 PM             6,484 SeqI.pm
07/03/2007  07:14 PM    <DIR>          SeqIO
07/03/2007  07:14 PM            21,805 SeqIO.pm
```

```
07/03/2007  07:14 PM             9,799 SeqUtils.pm
07/03/2007  07:14 PM            50,828 SimpleAlign.pm
07/03/2007  07:14 PM             8,380 Species.pm
07/03/2007  07:14 PM    <DIR>          Structure
07/03/2007  07:14 PM    <DIR>          Symbol
07/03/2007  07:14 PM    <DIR>          Taxonomy
07/03/2007  07:14 PM             6,372 Taxonomy.pm
07/03/2007  07:14 PM    <DIR>          Tools
07/03/2007  07:14 PM    <DIR>          Tree
07/03/2007  07:14 PM    <DIR>          TreeIO
07/03/2007  07:14 PM             6,223 TreeIO.pm
07/03/2007  07:14 PM             3,251 UpdateableSeqI.pm
07/03/2007  07:14 PM    <DIR>          Variation
              39 File(s)        430,638 bytes
              38 Dir(s)  62,847,074,304 bytes free
```

EXAMPLE C.4

```
(Perl Script using bioperl modules from the bioperl Web site)
use Bio::Seq;
use Bio::SeqIO;

# create a sequence object of some DNA
my $seq = Bio::Seq->new(-id => 'testseq', -seq => 'CATGTAGATAG'
);

# print out some details about it
print "seq is ", $seq->length, " bases long\n";
print "reversed complement seq is ", $seq->revcom->seq, "\n";

# write it to a file in Fasta format
my $out = Bio::SeqIO->new(-file => '>testseq.fsa', -format => '
Fasta');
$out->write_seq($seq);

(Output)
seq is 11 bases long
reversed complement seq is CTATCTACATG

$ more testseq.fsa    <-- The FASTA file
>testseq
CATGTAGATAG
```

For more examples using BioPerl go to:
http://www.bioperl.org/wiki/Bptutorial#Quick_getting_started_scripts

BioPerl comes with a set of production-quality scripts that are kept in the *scripts/* directory. You can install these scripts by answering the questions on *make install*. The default location directory is */usr/bin*. Installation will copy the scripts to the specified directory, change the *PLS* suffix to *pl*, and prepend *bp_* to all the script names if they aren't so named already.

C.5 Resources

There a number of excellent Web sites to find out information about the topics covered here as well as some excellent text books. For starters, you might try:

1. Walker, Sharon. *Biotechnology DeMystified*. McGraw-Hill 2007.
2. Tisdall, James. *Beginning Perl for Bioinformatics*. O'Reilly & Associates, 2001.
3. Tisdall, James. *Mastering Perl for Bioinformatics*. O'Reilly & Associates, 2003.

appendix

D

Power and Speed: CGI and *mod_perl*

D.1 What Is *mod_perl*?

Some people may tell you that CGI scripts are a thing of the past. You should be using PHP, ASP.NET, etc. Not true. The *mod_perl* module (originally written by Doug MacEachern and licensed under the Apache Software license) gives you a whole new way to create dynamic content by integrating the Apache server and Perl. *mod_perl* is described as the marriage between Apache and Perl. It is an open source module implemented as a Perl interface to the Apache API and allows existing CGI scripts to run much faster.

By embedding the Perl interpreter right in the Apache server, there is no need to start up (*fork*) a separate, external interpreter to run CGI programs. In addition, modules and scripts are loaded and compiled only once, and for the rest of the server's life they are served from the cache. Thus, the server spends its time running already loaded and compiled code, which is very fast.

Lincoln Stein, author of *CGI.pm*, describes *mod_perl* as follows:

> "*mod_perl* is more than CGI scripting on steroids. It is a whole new way to create dynamic content by utilizing the full power of the Apache web server to create stateful sessions, customized user authentication systems, smart proxies and much more. Yet, magically, your old CGI scripts will continue to work and work very fast indeed."

Today, Apache is the most popular Web server on the Internet, and *mod_perl* is one of the most popular modules for extending it. With the *mod_perl* API, it is possible to write customized Apache modules in Perl rather than in C and to dynamically configure the server itself, making the administration of servers with complex configurations easier to manage. You can write authentication and authoriztion handlers to allow or restrict usage of certain pages, perform database lookups, rewrite HTTP requests and URLs, log requests, etc.

Bundled with *mod_perl* are two general-purpose modules that make it possible to run existing Perl CGI scripts without modification (as long as they are well written, not "sloppy"). These Perl modules are found in the Perl *site/lib* library; they are called *Apache::Registry.pm* (or *ModPerl::Registry.pm*) and *Apache::PerlRun.pm* or (*ModPerl::PerlRun.pm*). The difference between these two modules is that the Registry.pm module caches all scripts, and the *PerRun.pm* module doesn't. The advantage of caching (i.e., compiling the script once and keeping it in memory) is speed and persistence. This is all fine as long as the script is well-written, has initialized variables, closed filehandles, sets warnings and diagonostics, and generally follows rules of good Perl programming. If the script is written in a sloppy way, then the *PerlRun.pm* module is a safer choice. Each time a request is made for the script, everything starts fresh because the code was not cached. Either way, the big advantage is that the Perl interpreter is loaded only once, thereby increasing the performance of your scripts. The *mod_perl* site (*http://perl.apache.org/download/index.html*) says that "the standard Apache::Registry module can provide 100x speedups for your existing CGI scripts and reduce the load on your server at the same time."

Check this site for statistics on *mod_perl* and Apache usage worldwide.

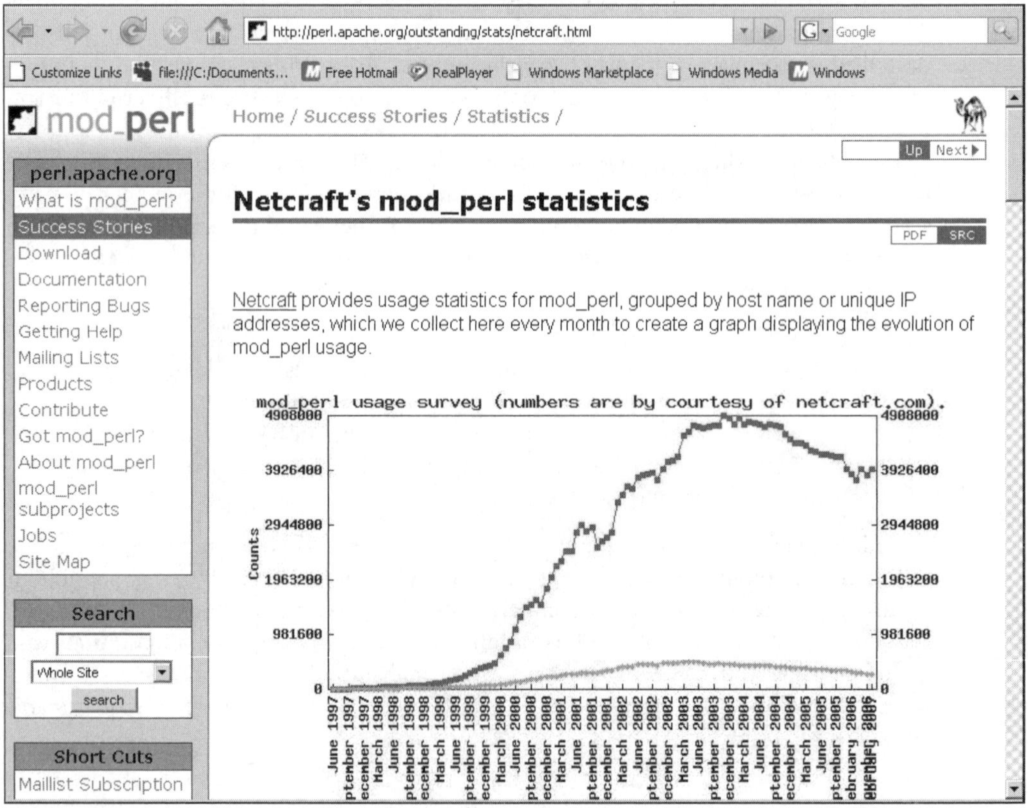

Figure D.1

D.2 The *mod_perl* Web Site

The following topics are discussed at the *mod_perl* home page and will give you everything you need to know about *mod_perl*, including installation, downloads, documentation, help, bugs, etc. A synopsis of this site is shown here.

What Is *mod_perl*?

mod_perl is the marriage of Apache and Perl.
mod_perl brings together two of the most powerful and mature technologies available to the Web professional today.

mp2 is *mod_perl* for the 2.x.x branch of the Apache HTTPD Server.
mp1 is *mod_perl* for the 1.3 branch of the Apache HTTPD Server.

mp2 is fully compatible with HTTPD 2.0.x and supports most of the 2.2.x feature set.

mod_perl's future plans are to keep on supporting HTTPD as it evolves—that has always been the goal and will always be so.

Simply install *mod_perl* and you have the full power of the Apache Web Server at your fingertips.

Success Stories

mod_perl is the power behind many of the Internet's busiest and most advanced Web sites. Listed here are success stories from people using *mod_perl*; also, worldwide statistics of *mod_perl* usage.

Download

Get source and binary *mod_perl* distributions and download the documentation.

Documentation

The *mod_perl* project features a lot of documentation, for both *mod_perl* 1.0 and 2.0. If there is anything you need to learn about *mod_perl*, you'll learn it here.

Reporting Bugs

Before a bug can be solved, developers need to be able to reproduce it. Users need to provide all the relevant information that may assist in reproducing the bug. However, it's hard to know what information needs to be supplied in the bug report. In order to speed up the information retrieval process, we wrote the guidelines explaining exactly what information is expected. Usually, the better the bug report is, the sooner it's going to be reproduced and therefore fixed.

Getting Help

Solve your *mod_perl* problems: with the help of the *mod_perl* mailing lists, a *mod_perl* training company, or a commercial support company. Find an ISP providing *mod_perl* services.

Mailing Lists

mod_perl and related projects' mailing lists.

Products

There is a lot of software out there ready to run with *mod_perl* and/or help you with your programming project.

Contribute

How to contribute to the *mod_perl* community.

Got *mod_perl*?

Advocacy documents and resources for *mod_perl*.

About *mod_perl*

General information regarding *mod_perl* of historical interest.

mod_perl Subprojects

Other projects maintained under the *mod_perl* umbrella.

Jobs

Find the *mod_perl* job of your dreams!

Site Map

You can reach any document on this site from this sitemap.

D.3 Installing *mod_perl*

This section describes the general series of steps used to install *mod_perl* and configure Apache to use it for executing fast CGI scripts. You should already have a current version of Perl and Apache up and running and have some familiarity with how CGI works (see Chapter 16).

The examples demonstrate how to install and run *mod_perl* scripts on a Windows system using Apache2.x and ActivePerl5.8.8.

For documentation, go to the *mod_perl* site, *http://perl.apache.org/docs/index.html*. To get source and binary *mod_perl* distributions, go to the download page at *http://perl.apache.org/download/index.html*. Configuring the Apache *httpd.conf* file may have some differences due to the fact that the Perl modules required are not necessarily located in the same library. It took some time to figure out how to adapt this to the current versions of Apache and Perl being used here.

There are two versions of *mod_perl*:

mp2—*mod_perl* for the 2.x.x branch of the Apache HTTPD Server.
mp1—*mod_perl* for the 1.3 branch of the Apache HTTPD Server.

For this example, we will be using *mp2* is fully compatible with HTTPD 2.0.x, and supports most of the 2.2.x feature set.

Installing *mod_perl* for ActiveState with PPM. Installation of modules has become increasingly simplified with ActiveState's PPM tool. It is included now with every ActivePerl release for not only Windows but also UNIX/Linux versons of ActivePerl. This tool allows you to install, remove, upgrade, and otherwise manage the use of common Perl pre-compiled CPAN modules.

The following examples use PPM on a Windows system.

EXAMPLE D.1

```
C:\>ppm install mod_perl
Downloading ActiveState Package Repository packlist...done
Updating ActiveState Package Repository database...done
ppm install failed: Can't find any package that provide mod_perl

C:\>ppm install http://theoryx5.uwinnipeg
/ppms/mod_perl-2.0.ppd
Downloading mod_perl-2.0-2.0.3...done
Unpacking mod_perl-2.0-2.0.3...done
Generating HTML for mod_perl-2.0-2.0.3...done
Updating files in site area...done
Downloading mod_perl-2.0-2.0.3 install script...done
Running mod_perl-2.0-2.0.3 install script...
The Apache module mod_perl.so is needed to complete the installation,
and should be placed in your Apache2 modules directory. I will
now fetch and install this for you.

Fetching http://theoryx5.uwinnipeg.ca/ppms/x86/mod_perl-2.0.so ...
done!
Where should mod_perl.so be placed? [C:/Apache2/modules]
c:/wamp/Apache2/modu

mod_perl.so has been successfully installed to c:/wamp/Apache2/modules
done
 465 files installed
```

Apache's *conf* Directory (Configuration Files)

EXAMPLE D.2

```
cd c:\wamp\Apache2\conf
C:\wamp\Apache2\conf>dir /b
alias
httpd.conf
httpd.default.conf
magic
magic.default
mime.types
mime.types.default
```

Editing Apache's *httpd.conf* File

The Apache *httpd.conf* file then must be modified by adding the following line:

EXAMPLE D.3

```
#LoadModule mime_magic_module modules/mod_mime_magic.so
#LoadModule proxy_module modules/mod_proxy.so
#LoadModule proxy_connect_module modules/mod_proxy_connect.so
#LoadModule proxy_http_module modules/mod_proxy_http.so
#LoadModule proxy_ftp_module modules/mod_proxy_ftp.so
LoadModule negotiation_module modules/mod_negotiation.so
#LoadModule rewrite_module modules/mod_rewrite.so
LoadModule setenvif_module modules/mod_setenvif.so
#LoadModule speling_module modules/mod_speling.so
#LoadModule status_module modules/mod_status.so
#LoadModule unique_id_module modules/mod_unique_id.so
LoadModule userdir_module modules/mod_userdir.so
#LoadModule usertrack_module modules/mod_usertrack.so
#LoadModule vhost_alias_module modules/mod_vhost_alias.so
LoadModule php5_module "c:/wamp/php/php5apache2.dll"
LoadModule perl_module modules/mod_perl.so
#
# ExtendedStatus controls whether Apache will generate "full" s
tatus
# information (ExtendedStatus On) or just basic information (Ex
tendedStatus
# Off) when the "server-status" handler is called. The default
is Off.
===================================
```

Create the Locations for *mod_perl* Scripts. We will now create the directory/folder where the *mod_script* programs will be stored. Instead of storing CGI scripts in this normal *cgi-bin* directory, they will be moved to this new directory, called *c:/home/stas/modperl*.

In this example, we will store Perl scripts in:

```
c:/home/stas/modperl
```

Where Are the Apache Perl Modules Stored?

Depending on your version of Perl, the Apache modules we will use to run existing Perl CGI scripts are located in the standard libraries found in the *@INC* array.

EXAMPLE D.4

```
cd /c/ActivePerl/site/lib/ModPerl
$ ls
BuildMM.pm          Manifest.pm           RegistryLoader.pm
BuildOptions.pm     MapUtil.pm            RegistryPrefork.pm
CScan.pm            MethodLookup.pm       StructureMap.pm
Code.pm             ParseSource.pm        TestReport.pm
Config.pm           PerlRun.pm            TestRun.pm
Const.pm            PerlRunPrefork.pm     TypeMap.pm
FunctionMap.pm      Registry.pm           Util.pm
Global.pm           RegistryBB.pm         WrapXS.pm
MM.pm               RegistryCooker.pm
```

The *PerlRequire* Directive

Next, we will create a file in Apache's *conf* directory for the most commonly used Perl modules. This file is called *extras.pl* and contains the modules that are most commonly used with *mod_perl*. By assigning this filename to the *PerlRequire* directive in the Apache configuration file, every time the Apache server starts, these modules will be loaded. (Note in most documentation for adding modules, the *Registry.pm* module is called *Apache::Registry*, but this module, under the current version of ActiveStatePerl, is now *ModPerl::Registry*.)

EXAMPLE D.5

```
C:\wamp\Apache2\conf>more extras.pl
use ModPerl::Util ();
  use Apache2::RequestRec ();
  use Apache2::RequestIO ();
  use Apache2::RequestUtil ();
  use Apache2::ServerRec ();
  use Apache2::ServerUtil ();
  use Apache2::Connection ();
  use Apache2::Log ();
  use Apache2::Const -compile => ':common';
  use APR::Const -compile => ':common';
  use APR::Table ();
  use Apache2::compat ();
  use ModPerl::Registry ();
  use CGI ();
  1;
```

Editing Apache's *httpd.conf* File

Now we will edit the *httpd.conf* file, found under the Apache directory. For the version of Apache on this Windows system, the *conf* directory/folder is under the *Apache2* folder.

Apache's *conf* Directory

EXAMPLE D.6

```
C:\wamp\Apache2>dir /b
ABOUT_APACHE.txt
bin
cgi-bin
CHANGES.txt
conf
error
icons
include
INSTALL.txt
lib
LICENSE.txt
logs
modules
NOTICE.txt
README.txt
```

Now we will *cd* into the *conf* directory and find the *httpd.conf* file.

Apache's Configuration file, *http.conf*

EXAMPLE D.7

```
C:\wamp\Apache2>cd conf

C:\wamp\Apache2\conf>dir /b
alias
extra.pl
httpd.conf
httpd.default.conf
magic
magic.default
mime.types
mime.types.default
```

Next, we edit the *httpd.conf* file by adding the lines in Example D.8 to the bottom of the file. (The numbers preceding each line are here only to explain each line in the Explanation section following the example.)

Editing Apche's Configuration File

EXAMPLE D.8

```
1  Alias /perl/ c:/home/stas/modperl/

2  LoadFile "c:/ActivePerl/bin/perl58.dll"

3  PerlRequire "c:/wamp/Apache2/conf/extras.pl"

4  PerlModule ModPerl::Registry

5  <Location /perl/>
6      SetHandler perl-script
7      PerlHandler ModPerl::Registry
8      Options +ExecCGI
9      PerlSendHeader On
10   Allow from All
   </Location>
```

EXPLANATION

1 This line is the alias for the place where *mod_perl* scripts will be stored. */perl/* is the name of the alias, and *c:/home/stas/modperl/* is the real location. In the browser window's location box, you would type *http://localhost/perl/mod_script_filename* if the server is the local server.

2 The *LoadFile* directive ensures that the correct version of the Perl interpreter is installed.

3 The *extras.pl* file contains commonly used *mod_perl* modules. The *PerlRequire* directive tells Apache to load these files every time the server starts.

4 The *PerlModule* directive is used to load the *Registry.pm* module. (Much of the documentation for *mod_perl* tells you to use *Apache::Registry*. The module being used here is *ModPerl::Registry*. Check your *@INC* array and go to the library where the *Registry* module is installed. Make sure it is named correctly when using this directive and any others that require using the *Registry* module. If you don't want the scripts cached, simply change *Registry* to *PerlRun* where *Registry* is found.)

5 The *Location* section defines the rules Apache follows when handling requests at the URI listed in the alias we created earlier, called */perl/*.
The module we will use to execute CGI scripts is called *Register.pm* and, on this installation of ActivePerl, is found in the site library, listed in the *@INC* array.

6 When content is generated, this directive assigns the *mod_perl* module to handle it.

7 This directive tells Apache what module to use to generate the content. The module determines how the content is loaded each time a request is made.

8 This option tells Apache that CGI scripts are acceptable and that they have execute permissions.

9 When this directive is turned on, *mod_perl* will create correctly formatted HTTP headers.

10 When *Allow from All* is set, any client can run the script at that IP address and domain.

Next, restart Apache.

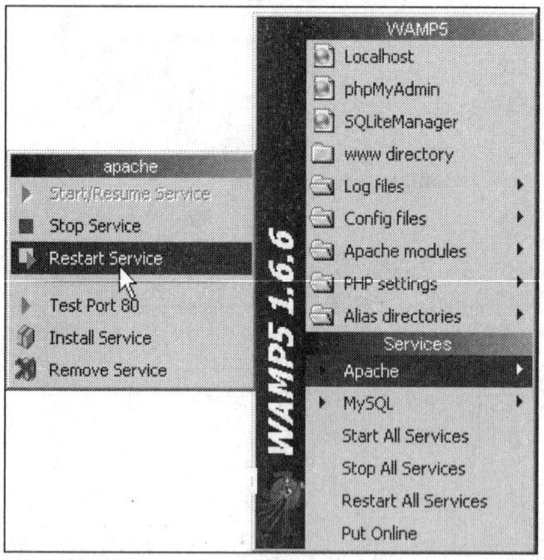

Figure D.2 Using WAMP5 to manage Apache.

Is *mod_perl* Installed?

There are a number of ways to check to see if *mod_perl* is actually working. You can look in the Apache error log after restarting the server, as shown here.

```
cd c:\wamp\logs
C:\wamp\logs>dir /b
access.log
apache_error.log
log_dir
mysql_error.log
php_error.log
```

Check the Apache error log after restarting the server. You should see something like the following:

```
[Mon Jul 02 14:08:11 2007] [notice] Apache/2.0.55 (Win32) PHP/5.1.4
mod_perl/2.
0.3 Perl/v5.8.8 configured -- resuming normal operations
[Mon Jul 02 14:08:11 2007] [notice] Server built: Oct  9 2005 19:16:56
[Mon Jul 02 14:08:11 2007] [notice] Parent: Created child process 5008
```

Testing *mod_perl* with a CGI Script

In the traditional *cgi-bin* directory under Apache's root directory, you will find a standard test file that is normally distributed with Apache. It is called *printenv.pl*. Copy this script to the new *mod_perl* directory you created, in this case *c:/home/stas/modperl* (see page 931), aliased as */perl/* in the *http.conf* file. Make sure permissions are set properly. This server should have execute permission for your script. If not, the following error will be sent to the browser (see Figure D.3).

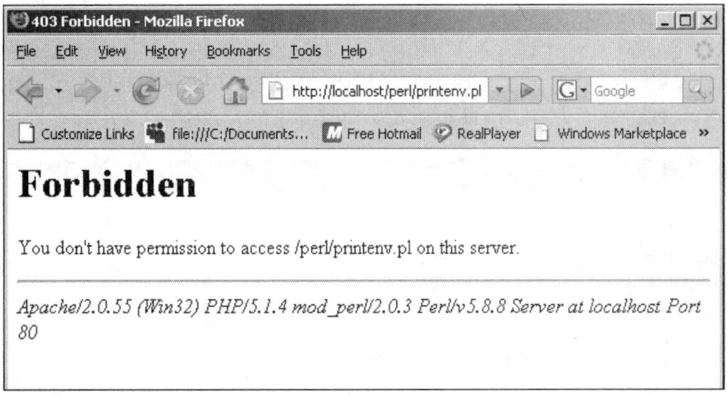

Figure D.3 Permission error from Apache.

Now go to the URL in your browser and execute the *printenv.pl* file as shown in Figure D.4. This file displays environment variables, including the *MOD_PERL* and *MOD_PERL_API_VERSION* variables.

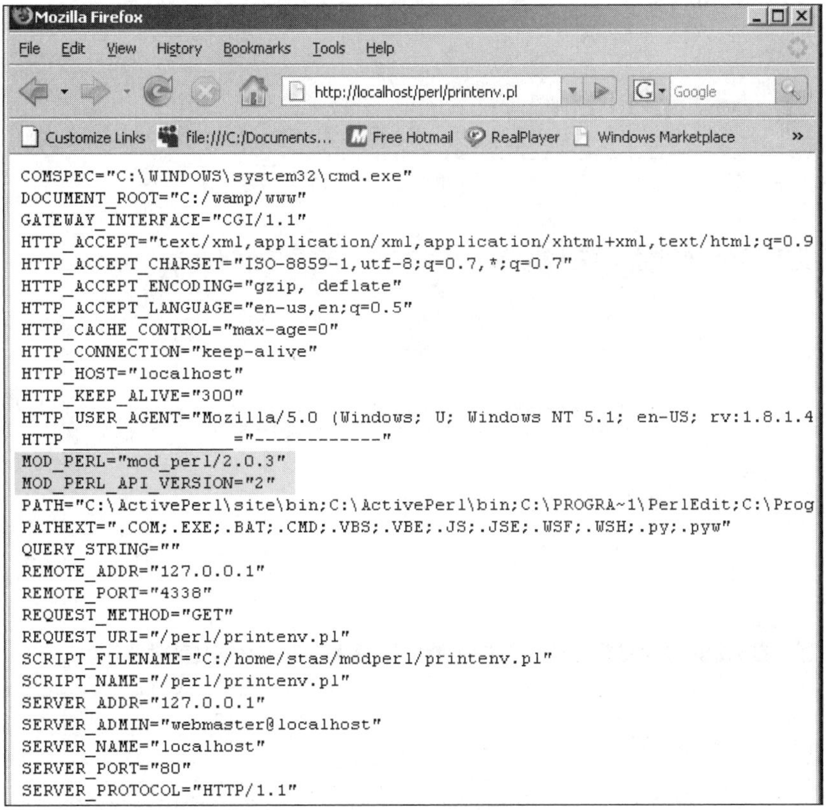

Figure D.4 Executing the *printenv.pl* Perl script.

Try another CGI script:
Put the following CGI script in your *mod_perl* directory. This script uses *CGI.pm*, the object-oriented style. CGI Perl scripts should be executable from this directory once *mod_perl* is installed. (See: *http://perl.apache.org/start/tips/registry.html*.)

EXAMPLE D.9

```
#!c:/ActivePerl/bin/perl.exe
use strict;
use CGI;
my $q = CGI->new;
print $q->header, $q->start_html(-title=>'First mod_perl Try',
                                    -BGCOLOR=>'lightgreen'),
        $q->h1('Hi, mod_perl is working!!'),
        $q->end_html;
```

Figure D.5 Running a CGI script with *mod_perl*.

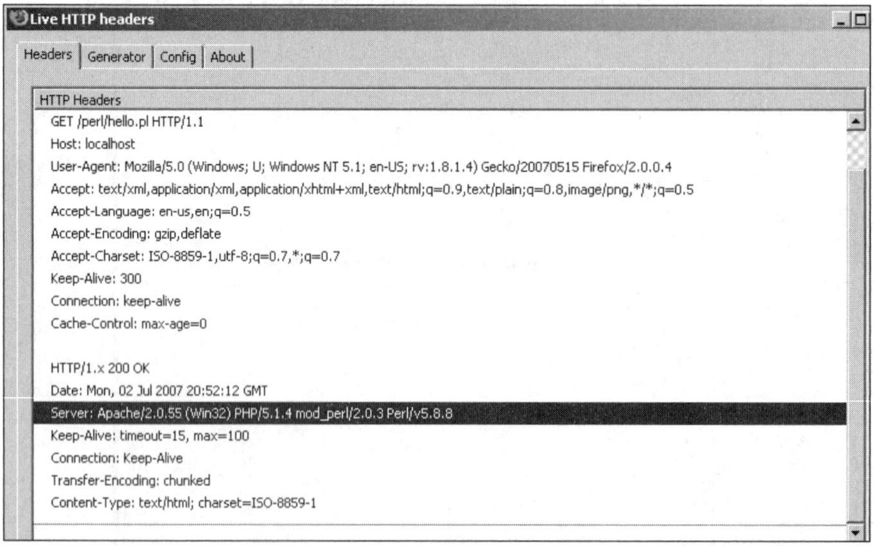

Figure D.6 Live HTTP Headers, a Firefox browser add-on, displays HTTP requests/responses.

UNIX/Linux Installation

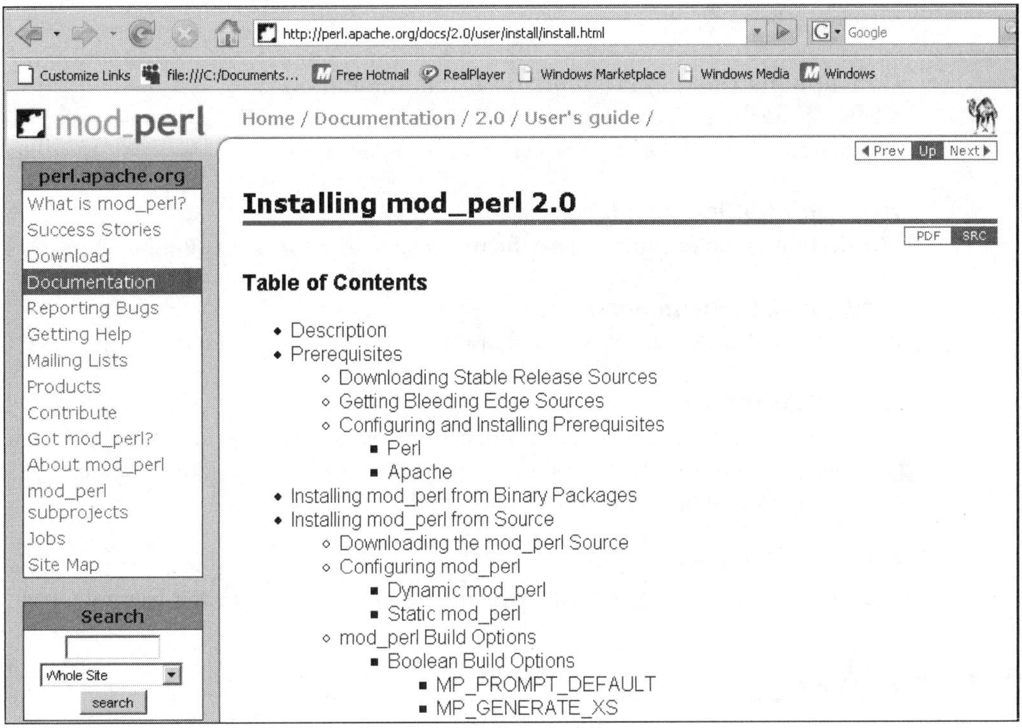

Figure D.7 Consult the official Apache site for downloads.

The following script was copied and modified from:
http://www.perl.com/pub/a/2002/03/22/modperl.html.
Check for the version of Linux/UNIX you are using.

EXAMPLE D.10

```
  % cd  /usr/src
%lwp-download http://www.apache.org/dist/httpd/binaries/httpd-2.0.55-
sparc-sun-solaris2.8.tar.gz
  % lwp-download http://perl.apache.org/dist/mod_perl-2.0-
current.tar.gz
  % tar -zvxf apache_1.3.20.tar.gz
  % tar -zvxf mod_perl-1.26.tar.gz
  % cd mod_perl-1.26
  % perl Makefile.PL APACHE_SRC=../apache_1.3.20/src \
    DO_HTTPD=1 USE_APACI=1 EVERYTHING=1
  % make && make test && make install
  % cd ../apache_2.0.55  (Check for the correct number here)
  % make install
```

***mod_perl* Documentation.** The *mod_perl* project features a lot of documentation, for both *mod_perl* 1.0 and 2.0. If there is anything you need to learn about *mod_perl*, you'll learn it here.

Conventions Used in the *mod_perl* Documentation
We use a number of conventions in this documentation, that are mostly easy to understand; if you're in doubt, look here for the explanation.

***mod_perl* 1.0 Documentation**
A collection of the documents specific to the *mod_perl* 1.0 generation.

***mod_perl* 2.0 Documentation**
A collection of the documents specific to the *mod_perl* 2.0 generation.

General Documentation
Here you can find documentation concerning *mod_perl* in general, but also not strictly *mod_perl* related information that is still very useful for working with *mod_perl*. Most of the information here applies to *mod_perl* 1.0 and 2.0.

Offsite Resources
mod_perl books, articles, presentations, and links to sites covering other relevant topics.

D.4 Resources

1. Bekman, Stas and Cholet, Eric. *Practical mod_perl*. O'Reilly and Associates, Inc.
2. Stein, Lincoln and MacEachern, Doug. *Writing Apache Modules with Perl and C*. O'Reilly and Associates, Inc.

Index

A

B

E

P

ALSO AVAILABLE FROM ELLIE QUIGLEY AND PRENTICE HALL

PHP and MySQL by Example

QUICKLY MASTER DYNAMIC, DATABASE-DRIVEN WEB DEVELOPMENT—NO EXPERIENCE NECESSARY!

Even if you're completely new to PHP, MySQL, and Web database development, this book will guide you through every step of building powerful, database-driven, dynamic Web sites. Direct from the world's top scripting instructor, Ellie Quigley, *PHP and MySQL by Example* illuminates every concept with tested code examples, screen shots showing program output, and clear, line-by-line explanations.

Classroom-tested in Ellie Quigley's Silicon Valley training courses and at Marko Gargenta's Marakana training company in San Francisco, this book takes you from the simplest PHP scripting and SQL querying techniques, all the way to dynamic, database-driven Web site construction with PHP and MySQL. From simple fill-in forms to program security and debugging, it's the only PHP/MySQL book you'll ever need!

ISBN-13: 9780131875081 • ISBN-10: 0131875086 • © 2007 • 912 pages

UNIX® Shells by Example, Fourth Edition

THE WORLD'S #1 SHELL PROGRAMMING BOOK—NOW FULLY UPDATED FOR LINUX AND MORE!

In *UNIX® Shells by Example, Fourth Edition*, Quigley has thoroughly updated her classic and delivers the information today's shell programmers need most—including comprehensive coverage of Linux shell programming with bash!

Drawing on twenty years' experience as a shell programming instructor, Quigley guides you through every facet of programming all leading UNIX/Linux shells: bourne, bash, korn, C, and tcsh. Quigley illuminates each concept with up-to-date, classroom-tested code examples designed to help you jump-start your own projects. She also systematically introduces awk, sed, and grep for both UNIX and GNU/Linux … making this the only shell programming book you'll ever need!

ISBN-13: 9780131475724 • ISBN-10: 013147572X • © 2005 • 1,200 pages

JavaScript by Example

THE DEFINITIVE TUTORIAL TO MASTER THE FULL POWER OF JAVASCRIPT

In *JavaScript by Example*, Ellie Quigley teaches JavaScript using the same proven approach that's made her the world's favorite scripting author and instructor. This book's unique and classroom-tested learning path contains hundreds of small, easy-to-understand examples that demonstrate the full range of JavaScript's power. One step at a time, Quigley guides new JavaScript programmers through every essential technique, from script setup to advanced DOM and CSS programming.

ISBN-13: 9780131401624 • ISBN-10: 0131401629 • © 2004 • 752 pages

Visit us online at www.informit.com for more information about these books and to read sample chapters.

PRENTICE HALL

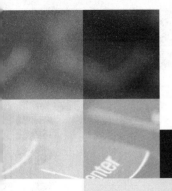

CD-ROM Warranty

Prentice Hall warrants the enclosed CD-ROM to be free of defects in materials and faulty workmanship under normal use for a period of ninety days after purchase (when purchased new). If a defect is discovered in the CD-ROM during this warranty period, a replacement CD-ROM can be obtained at no charge by sending the defective CD-ROM, postage prepaid, with proof of purchase to:

Disc Exchange
Prentice Hall
Pearson Technology Group
75 Arlington Street, Suite 300
Boston, MA 02116
Email: AWPro@aw.com

Prentice Hall makes no warranty or representation, either expressed or implied, with respect to this software, its quality, performance, merchantability, or fitness for a particular purpose. In no event will Prentice Hall, its distributors, or dealers be liable for direct, indirect, special, incidental, or consequential damages arising out of the use or inability to use the software. The exclusion of implied warranties is not permitted in some states. Therefore, the above exclusion may not apply to you. This warranty provides you with specific legal rights. There may be other rights that you may have that vary from state to state. The contents of this CD-ROM are intended for personal use only.

More information and updates are available at:
www.prenhallprofessional.com